FIELD SERVICE

DISEASES wounds and injuries (action to be (ed according to (lassification (on fly leaf)	Date of Admission		Date of Discharge			Date of Transfer				Number of days under treatment	Number or designation or ward in which treated	Religion	OBSERVATIONS Number and page of case book to be quoted for all cases recorded in it. In transfers the designation of the hospital or sick convoy, to which or from which transferred, must be noted here, and any other facts bearing on the man's destination.
	For original disease	By new disease supervening	To Duty	By new disease supervening	By Death	To		From					
						Sick Convoy	Other Hospitals	Sick Convoy	Other Hospitals				
al Instability			11·10·18						30·7·18	74	W·Cent	08	C.D. W.t Warring
ucholia			5·12·18						"	129	"	"	Home for dis. C.D.W.H. Warr
en. Pracox			4·12·18						"		"	"	C.D. 4.9 Manc
R Thigh			25·9·18						31·7·18	58	F11	R.C.	Home Jcy d. Hon 10 admis
Hand 2. (amp.)									1·8·18	45	V.D.	08	Stn. 52 alber tren
Fracture of finger 1st.			14·9·18						1·8·18	8	F12	"	Embarkation 9/150HOKa
mosis of Eye	3·8·18		8·8·18						2·8·18	58	Cent.	"	Tidworth M.H
ancer			28·9·18								"	"	Hom Jcy d Tim 10 admis
ncholia follow...			4·10·18								"	"	
onchitis			10·8·18						3·8·18	8	F4	"	Knit Sascombe trans on leave Home for disc
pned. in lung				4·10·18					30·7·18	24	F7	"	W.H Ashlin
w. arm						24·9·18	5·8·18			54	F7	08	M.E.H.Goshen
umatic fever			20·9·18						"	47	M.C	"	Furlo (C
as.			20·9·18						"	47	F.C	"	Furlo (C
sw. Back			25·9·18						"	52	F.B	"	Furlo (C.E
w Side L (Burns scar)						3·9·18			"	30	M.a	"	M.E.H.E'bour
used 2S.C.F R.7.						4·9·18			"	31	F.B	"	M.E.H.Ashton
sw L hip.						10·9·18			"	34	F.B	"	M.E.H.E'bou
w L foot R Thigh						7·1·19			"	156	F.B	"	M.G.H.Cold
w R Shoulder.						24·9·18			"	54	F.B	Pres.	M.E.N.Holdm
sw ear L.			10·9·18						"	34	M.a	"	Furlo (C.E
SW Ear R:			14·9·18						"	44	M.a	Bap.	Furlo (C
SW legs & arm (amp.)			16·9·18						"	43	M.a	08	Furlo (St
SW R Hand. (amp.)						30·8·18			"	26	A.B	"	SS.GH.Benn
sw Knee L (flesh)			30·8·18						"	26	F.A	Pres.	Furlo (St
SW foot R (flesh)			30·8·18						"	26	A.B	"	SS.GH.Oxfo
sw. arm R.						4·9·18			"	31	F.A	08	M.G.H.Ashto
SW arm L						15·10·18			"	74	M.a	R.C.	M.E.N.Wold
W L forearm (amp.)			31·8·18						"	24	F.B	08	# pending
SW Wrest						24·9·18			"	51	M.a	"	A.M.E.H.Wold
Jassed			20·9·18						"	47	M.C	"	Furlo
sw. arm L (flesh)						23·8·18			"	19	F.7	"	S.S.GH.huw
SW R Wrist			4·9·18						"	36	F.B	"	Furlo (C
CT Knee			25·9·18						"	52	A.B	"	Furlo
SW hand L			14·9·18						"	44	M.a	"	Furlo

FORGOTTEN LUNATICS OF THE GREAT WAR

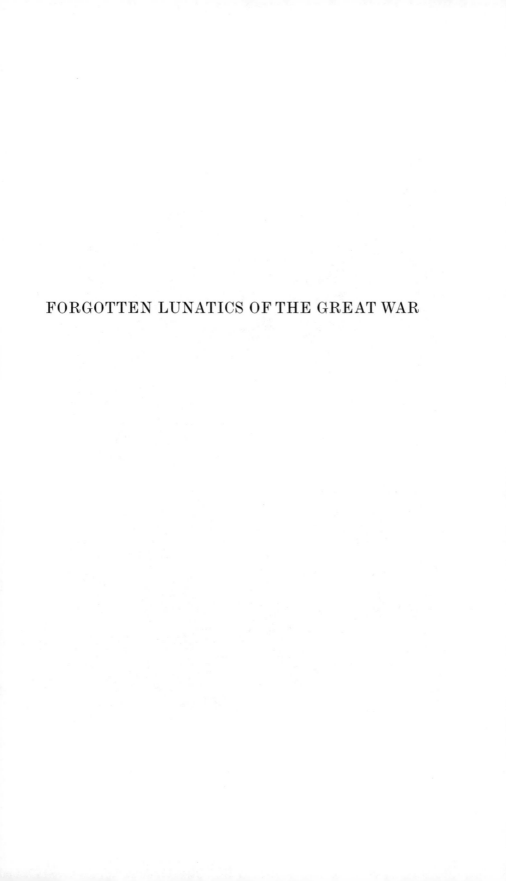

'The Old Manor Gang': Patients and Staff at the Old Manor Mental Hospital, Salisbury, probably in the early 1930s.

FORGOTTEN LUNATICS OF THE GREAT WAR

Peter Barham

Yale University Press
New Haven & London

Copyright © 2004 Peter Barham

Designed by Adam Freudenheim
Set by SNP Best-set Typesetter Ltd, Hong Kong
Printed in Great Britain by St Edmundsbury Press Ltd, Bury St Edmunds

Library of Congress Control Number 2004107441

A catalogue record for this book is available from the British Library

10 9 8 7 6 5 4 3 2 1

Frontispiece:
This rather raffish group of men, a few of them taking a break from their work, others looking
as though they are off to the races or about some shady business, is a rare example of a largely
impromptu gathering of patients and staff. Very likely, these are mostly war psychosis
pensioners, maintained by the Ministry of Pensions, of whom there were almost 300 at the Old
Manor at this time. The figure third from the left, with a time-piece dangling from his waistcoat
is probably an attendant, and the man on his left sporting a bow tie one of the ex-officer mental
patients.

Endpapers
A page from the Admissions and Discharge Register for Napsbury War Hospital with the entry
for Private Ivor Gurney, soldier, poet and musician. Following service on the Western Front,
Gurney was admitted to the Mental Department at Napsbury on 30 July 1918 with a diagnosis
of Dementia Praecox [TNA PRO: MH 106/1547]

To the memory of Roy Sydney Porter, historian,
'Genuine and Honourabled' friend to the forgotten
lunatics and to much else

Contents

List of Illustrations

I got quite used to carrying shellshocked patients in the ambulance. . . . Of course, these were the so-called milder cases; we didn't carry the dangerous ones. They always tried to keep that away from us and they came in a separate part of the train. But it happened one evening there were one too many of us nurses, so I didn't go with an ambulance and I was left on the platform. I noticed that some of our men from the column were still there, and then I noticed another sort of ambulance come into the station, not one of ours. It was completely closed up. I said to one of the men, 'What's this ambulance coming in? Haven't we done the train?' He said, 'No, Sister, this is from the asylum; it's for the hopeless mental cases'. I didn't look. They'd gone right off their heads. I didn't want to see them. There was nothing they could do and they were going to a special place. They were terrible.

Claire Elise Tisdall, Voluntary Aid Detachment (VAD) Ambulance Nurse, London District, interviewed in the late 1970s[1]

There are some men who 'funk' or dislike military service to such an extent that it sends them off their heads. It is a 'tall order' . . . for the State to take on the liability to support, possibly for life, a man who becomes a lunatic because he is a coward and fears to undertake the liability which falls upon him as an Englishman.

Civil Servant, Ministry of Pensions, March 1918[2]

Spurning the draft for the war on Troy, when Ulysses heard that the recruiting officers were coming, 'he feigned insanity, donned a felt cap and yoked a horse with an ox to his plough'.

Hyginus (fl 1st century CE), Fabulae[3]

It is more arduous to honour the memory of the nameless than that of the renowned. Historical construction is devoted to the memory of the nameless.

Walter Benjamin, from notes for the 'Theses on the Concept of History'[4]

Introduction

It is a truism that wars mutilate minds and bodies, but throughout the twentieth century the nature and 'reality' of war traumas (especially psychological traumas) have been the subject of heated controversy. Acrimonious standoffs between aggrieved ex-servicemen and the state in the prolonged afterlife of wars are the stuff of modern life, involving the competing claims of war pensions agencies, veterans' associations and divergent medical authorities.[1] This book is largely about the doings and beings, deeds and needs, toils and foils, of those ordinary soldiers of the Great War who experienced a prolonged mental crisis or breakdown during the action, or in anticipation of it, or sometimes after it, and their subsequent struggles, along with their families, to rebuild their lives and secure social justice – struggles that, in some cases, were protracted over more than half a century.

The day after he enlisted in February 1915, Private Walter Smith left home to report at the recruiting office but never arrived – his cap was found in a pond three days later and his body recovered the following day. Expecting to be employed as regimental tailor, Private Harry Barrows became very upset when ordered to go on parade, believing that he was surely destined for the front line, and hanged himself in a lavatory. Private William Padgett, who had been a stretcher-bearer at the Somme, and after that had been engaged in tunnelling, frequently under fire and wounded by shrapnel, was admitted to a military hospital suffering from melancholia, believing that his troubles were due to his sexual excesses. After two years in France, Private Major Jarvis could not be dissuaded from the belief that he was going to be shot for missing part of his kit and having vermin in his clothes. Sapper Alfred Jacka wept when he recounted how, weakened by asthma and the cold, he had lost control of himself in the field, for which he deservedly must be shot. Private Jim Irving, a cotton piecer from the West Riding, from a family all of whom were tuberculous, his sister just having died of the disease, had an epileptic fit whilst on guard at the end of April 1918 and had been having three fits a week ever since. Rifleman Walter Mitchell was brought back from the Citadel Military Hospital in Cairo in January 1919, morose and resistive, spitting out his medicine, masturbating, at times restless and singing, at others lying with his head covered and refusing to speak. In January 1920, Private Harold C was admitted to Whittingham Lunatic Asylum from the Pike Law Workhouse, where the Head Imbecile Attendant reported that he had been talking incoherently about his life in France, 'muttering something about new signposts being erected at Mons'. Private Donald Murray, who lost his left leg in the war, and then returned to live with his mother and to his former occupation as a clerk, was reported by his brother to have been neurotic ever since the war, going off the rails completely in 1923. Frederick Quinton, late Farrier Sergeant in the Royal Field Artillery, seemed to be doing quite well, until one day in June 1923 'his nerves appeared to be on the twitch and he could not keep still, constantly wandering from one place to another at all hours of the night'; and a former stretcher-bearer, Charles H, tried to establish a smallholding after the war but the responsibility weighed on him and, after burning the family furniture in the front garden, he was removed to the county mental hospital in January 1930 suffering from melancholia, 'principal aetiological factor: shell shock'.

Though these are all 'mad soldiers' of the Great War, it is obvious that the causes and circumstances of their mental crises are hugely divergent. Nevertheless, this was a historical moment in which solidarity with the whole community of serving soldiers counted for more than birth, merit or worth. 'No government is legitimate that does not show equal concern for the fate of all those citizens over whom it claims dominion and from whom it claims allegiance'. So writes the political philosopher Ronald Dworkin.[2] In 1917, the British government was obliged to pay reluctant heed to this fundamental egalitarian principle, if not for the citizenry in its entirety, then at least in relation to the mental suffering of all those citizens who had been enrolled in the imperial cause. Though the war produced emotional disturbance in bucketfuls, it also impacted on the social relations of lunacy, producing unanticipated opportunities and alternate outcomes for potential mad persons. Soldiers who might previously have been classified as lunatics were able to find other ways in which to mediate their predicaments; and some lunatics who might otherwise have remained in confinement took it upon themselves to find relief in becoming soldiers.

Wars are integral to the history of modern Britain and the question of whether the First World War was a major catalyst of social change has long exercised the historical imagination.[3] This book tends to the view expressed by Jose Harris, that many of the currents and counter-currents which were swept into prominence in the social sphere were already immanent in the life of society in the previous decades, but it is my purpose also to explore the lingering aftereffects of war, solaces and strategies as much as miseries and deprivations, in the lives of emotionally damaged ex-servicemen.[4] In the modern era, wars have entered more fully into the life of society, and war is not an episode distinct from civil life but woven into the fabric of modernity.

However, where some analysts have highlighted the militarization of social relations, the displacement of the civil by the military, and the co-option of humanitarian interventions to perfect the military enterprise, I shall show how civilian values and institutions have also penetrated more deeply into the life of war, forcing the closed fiefdoms of military institutions into a dialogue with the wider society, and producing compromises that may be inimical to military values.[5]

In the years leading up to the Great War, Britain appeared to be on the cusp of radical change. New-fangled ideas about citizens' rights were in the ascendant, some progress had been made in eroding what had been an exclusively property-based franchise, and there was a rising ground swell of resistance to the faltering pace of health and welfare reform. A system vitiated by poisonous divisions between the 'deserving' and the 'undeserving', between those who could afford to pay for private treatments and those forced to resort to demeaning statutory aid as paupers, was in small but still significant ways ceding to an emerging politics of social solidarity in which dependence was no longer 'the curse of one particular group'.[6] By the early twentieth century, in the wake of the strong public feeling that had been aroused by the scandalous deficiencies of medical care in the South African War, even servicemen were beginning to clamour for health care as a right, regarding it as a 'social wage' earned in the service of their country.[7]

If all this was indicative of a wider and stronger sense of entitlement among the citizenry, and of an emerging culture of social citizenship, there was one sphere in which the old hierarchies and divisions still very much prevailed – that most personal form of individual misfortune occasioned by emotional disturbance, psychological suffering and mental illness in all their varieties. When it came to ravaged minds, there was no semblance of equality, neither in professional attitudes nor in treatment regimes. For the great majority of the population in Britain in the early part of the twentieth century, to become the bearer of a mental illness diagnosis, and be removed to a lunatic asylum, was to be thrust into a position in life as ignominious as it was awesome. Lives were despoiled by the degradations of the system to which they were subjected, as much as by an originating disturbance. The barrier drawn in British society before the Great War between the community of citizens and the outcasts in lunatic asylums was every bit as severe and rigorous as that between citizens and slaves in the later Roman Empire.[8]

The years 1914–18, in which more than 5.7 million men passed through the British Army during the Great War, were to deliver a severe jolt to this disdainful class-based state of psychiatric mortmain, producing the conditions in which a disenfranchised constituency could start to exert a claim on the body politic and make some headway in remedying a basic injustice. The unquestionable patriotism of the volunteers of 1914 and 1915 did nothing to diminish the militant abhorrence of the majority of servicemen for the short-comings of the social order.[9] To borrow a phrase from R. H. Tawney, the 'horrors of war' were never permitted to eclipse the 'horrors of peace'.[10] Through the political lens of a coalition of classes in a citizens' army, indi-viduals became visible as citizens who had previously been quite invisible or regarded only in demeaning terms, and the welfare of the humblest citizen soldier commanded genuine attention in the public imagination.

Public feeling about the injustice that was being shown to servicemen suf-fering from 'nervous and mental shock' found expression in a broader sense of entitlement, embracing even the most insignificant ordinary ranker. The frontier between nature and justice was shifting a little, such that things that had looked like unchanging accident or destiny, inequalities that were just the result of fate, now looked like things that people could change and perhaps even had an obligation to change. Officers were given special consideration and psychological treatments, alleged rank-and-file soldiers and their families, even while ordinary servicemen were being trundled off to lunatic asylums. Though in the field there were 30 men to an officer, as many as one in six shell shock cases were officers. To ordinary soldiers, 'shell shock' had all the appearances of a privileged diagnosis and treatment system in which patients were regarded as recoverable, while they themselves were more likely to be written off as 'hopeless cases'. A supposedly 'progressive' military doctor such as W. H. Rivers was still operating within the consensus, enjoying his Freudian cake while upholding traditional class and gender values, subscribing to a hierarchical psychology in which a superior value was placed on officers over common soldiers, and psychiatric assessments were inextricably reflections of moral and social divisions.[11]

According to official figures, in 1937 there were around 35,000 war dis-ability pensions still in payment for ex-servicemen with mental disabilities. As many as as 10,300, around 30 per cent of the total, bore the label 'psychosis', and the vast majority of these, quite disproportionately so, were other rankers, ordinary soldiers rather than officers.[12] Although they form part of the con-stituency that is popularly known as the 'shell-shocked', little attention has been paid to them, for it is the neurasthenic officer whose profile has been most visible in the mental health historiography of the Great War. The irony is that, despite the enormous fascination with shell shock, the psychiatric history and aftermath of the Great War has been told only in a very partial way, leading the distinguished psychiatrist and anthropologist Arthur Kleinman to remark sardonically on 'Britain's fundamental divide between silent working-class soldiers . . . and upper-class officers afflicted with neurasthenia'.[13]

Yet the ordinary soldiers of the Great War suffering from 'nervous and mental shock' were not so much silent as silenced. Almost from the commencement of hostilities, the *démarche* of public policy, and especially the dynamics of the controverted territory of shell shock, were driven by public anxiety over the fate of the working-class soldier psychotic, or the citizen soldier in an acute mental health crisis. The war psychotic plays a central role from the start, and it is about him that much of the action pivots.[14] From the military angle, all this agitation over the fate of what were considered to be insane soldiers was either a secondary consideration or a nuisance, but from a civilian perspective nothing could have been more important. Even where it has not been told as a triumphalist narrative of enlightened Freudianism trouncing a misguided, organically-based psychiatry, the history of shell shock has generally been recounted as a narrative of military psychiatry. The civilian sphere has been cast either as a secondary domain into which goods have spilled over at a later date, the therapeutic successes in military hospitals providing a trigger for mental health reform, or as an irritating presence forever hovering on the fringes of the main action, malign public opinion interfering with issues that ought to have been left to the generals and their medical votaries.[15] I am going to argue, in contrast, that public opinion came to play a crucial role in the formation of policy over shell shock, and the mental health of Great War servicemen more generally, by promoting an agenda of citizens' rights.

The history of the forgotten lunatics of the Great War draws us not into a closed ward of pitiful souls or some freakish side-show, a tiresome diversion from the main arteries of historical development, but onto a busy concourse. It supplies a window not only on class relationships in Britain between the wars, an Orwellian landscape of Ministry of Pensions 'hardening' institutions, Poor Law mental wards and so forth, but also on turbulent currents in Europe and North America that are still bubbling today. Gathering pace since the last half of the nineteenth century, there has been a proliferation of discourses, embracing the state, corporations, the legislature and the medical profession, around the traumatic injuries to different categories of citizens – railway travellers, industrial workers, soldiers in action – allegedly caused by the seismic upheavals of technological modernity.[16] In one aspect, the controversies over the psychiatric veterans of the Great War look back to the conflicts over railway spine (that quaint period term for the mental as much as physical trauma arising from railway accidents), accident insurance and pensions legislation in the closing decades of the nineteenth century; in another they prefigure the grass-roots revolt among Vietnam veterans and their sympathizers that forced the psychiatric establishment to alter its language and categories, and propelled the landmark diagnosis of Post-Traumatic Stress Disorder (PTSD) onto the map of mental suffering.[17] 'Vietnam War veterans', writes Allan Young, 'are the first traumatic victims to demand collective recognition'.[18] That title more properly belongs with the 'mad soldiers' of the Great War, even though after the war their rebellion was defused, and war psychotics (or war psychosis claimants) were subjected to a process of creeping marginalization, like a fog descending.

Although this is not directly a book about shell shock, and does not address the whole gamut of conditions and debates that swarm around it, in another sense it cannot fail to be, since the very great majority, perhaps even all, of the subjects I write about in these pages, even though they were called by a variety of other names, associated themselves with the 'shell shock' label. Whether the term 'came first from the medical service or from the soldiers themselves', wrote the redoubtable A. G. Butler, 'will probably never be known – possibly medical officers adopted almost unconsciously a soldier's phrase'.[19] But what can be said with certainty is that, regardless of its origins, 'shell shock' very soon became not only a soldier's phrase, but a term that was adopted also by a wide band of sympathizers. In its radical usage, shell shock came to designate a psychological trauma in a contested terrain in which people who were experiencing mental distress or illness were trying to find new and more dignified bearings. When contemporaries remarked on the 'special place' to which 'hopeless' or bad cases were sent, 'place' was as much a moral category as it was a physical location.[20]

In piecing together the narratives of forgotten lunatics such as Albert Norris, kitchen porter, George Gomm, gentleman's hosier, and Albert Hardman, mortuary keeper, I am in large part engaged in an exercise in retrieval – to rescue them from the judgments, as often as not, of their contemporaries; or from the silence and anonymity of the bureaucratic ledgers and institutions in which they have been itemized and deposited.[21] That they have been treated with disdain or ignored is not just a matter of period prejudices; in certain respects the very same partialities and preferences are reflected in the judgments of some contemporary historians, for whom the 'poor, inarticulate, unlettered, shy' masses, the ordinary soldiers who fought and died silently in the Great War, or survived equally silently, are to be contrasted with the middle class, the 'great self-recording class', with its abundance of diaries and journals.[22]

There is a partial truth in this, of course, but it grossly underestimates the extent to which, in the aftermath of the war, formerly 'unlettered' ex-servicemen were drawn into recording their embittered experience at the hands of official agencies such as the war pensions authorities. Similarly, the survival of at least some of these testimonies is itself a reflection of how, by comparison with the pre-war state, these same agencies were obliged to assume a more concerted interest in the individual histories and fluctuating circumstances of a vast collectivity of working-class claimants.

Over the last few years I have crawled across the archival landscape, tracking down sites in which war psychotics might have left traces, from Exeter to Ipswich, and from Nelson, Lancashire, to Guernsey. It is, perhaps, not entirely accidental that some of the most revealing records I have come across are in a repository in a disused cotton mill in Lancashire that formerly belonged to the Ministry of Pensions.[23] Though it would be misleading to claim that it is feasible to reconstruct the histories of all these ex-servicemen, still a certain amount of fossicking in the archival undergrowth frequently yields scraps that, once juxtaposed, deliver startling insights into what was at stake for these individuals. Mental patients are, of course, notorious collectors of 'rubbish', finding meaning in items that have been jettisoned, and it may be that in this respect the social historian of the marginal and disenfranchised is also a madman of sorts.[24]

I was alerted to the existence of this population by a footnote from which it slowly dawned on me that here was a cultural mass grave, a 'pauper's pit' unrecognizable as a burial place because there were no signs of commemoration, waiting to be excavated. My aim in this book is to excavate the memory of this forgotten community, to communicate the extent and variety of the psychiatric fallout of the Great War, and to convey what it meant to lead a life as a war psychosis pensioner in England in the wake of the war. The shape of the book has evolved out of both the material, and my sense of obligation towards it. Along with a smaller cast, with whom I engage more intimately, we make at least the nodding acquaintance of a far greater number in this book. That is frequently as much as can be achieved in any case, for in many instances the biographical remains of these ex-servicemen are fragmentary and elusive, limited to the confines of a bureaucratic record, and several of the more rounded narratives have been pieced together from a multiplicity of sources. All the same, there are undoubtedly a lot of brief encounters in this text. 'Do we really have to meet the whole damn ward?' one might ask. Well, up to a point we must. As a historian (or at least my kind of historian) I proceed from a commitment to try to do justice to the community of memory as a whole. From this standpoint it would hardly suffice merely to foreground a small number of illustrative characters and exclude, or background, the rest. After all, the First World War inaugurated the 'era of the common soldier's name', in Thomas Laqueur's phrase; hence a forgotten community such as this can only achieve equality of remembrance through being named and recognized as individuals.[25]

Marginal figures, nonentities in official sights, these certainly are, but they also possess an affinity with an emerging counter-sensibility, truthful not to 'Big Words' but to the bodily and psychic inmost experiences of ordinary people. Ironically, even while these ex-servicemen were sojourning in the womb of war, the gestation was fitfully but steadily proceeding, shortly to erupt sprawling and squawking into the light, of the picaresque epic of Leopold Bloom, the Irish Jew, that rather special nobody, 'everyman or noman', outraged by the injustices of his time, who is the central character of James Joyce's *Ulysses*.[26] Though not intended exclusively as a history 'from below', the structure of this book approximates a kind of lunatic's progress, in which I pursue these ex-servicemen, many of them no less outraged by injustices than Leopold Bloom, on their faltering odysseys from the dismal fields of war into the institutions through which they journeyed, such as Napsbury War Hospital, Long Grove Lunatic Asylum, Fulham Road Workhouse, and Ministry of Pensions 'hardening' institutions. Undoubtedly this is a strange world, especially perhaps the labyrinth of war disability pensions. Needless to say, this book is not a primer on war pensions and I have tried to introduce just sufficient detail to clarify the matter in hand without becoming bogged down in the bureaucratic shifting sands. If it is sometimes a maze for the reader, perhaps it is of some comfort to remember that it was still more so for war disability pensioners and their families. Most importantly, the arena of war pensions was by no means trivial or secondary: for working-class men who had fought in the war it was perhaps in this period the single most important site on which the struggle for equality and for social justice was conducted, and that is why it inevitably figures so prominently in these narratives.

The study of war has begun to attract the interest of historians not merely for its harmful or catastrophic consequences but also for the experiments in social solidarity, a sudden and explosive intensification of social relationships, that it frequently forces into existence.[27] In this book I shall show that even if the populist triumphs of 1917–18 were in obvious respects short-lived, and Britain by the early 1920s was again a divided society in which governments looked with ill-favour upon the progeny of 'war socialism', still they were not snuffed out entirely. Notions of citizenship and of citzens' rights became more etched on popular consciousness, and the gains of the war period succeeded in seeding new developments, making their own mark on a politics of social solidarity that eventually was to issue in the European welfare state, repudiating the disdainful class- and race-based psychiatry that held its own until well into the twentieth century. If in part this is a dispiriting tale of faltering reforms and broken promises, testimony to the power of the interwar state in containing the challenges of mass democracy and redistributive socialism, it exposes also how, quite against the official grain, during and after the Great War a marginalized group became more skilled and defiant in laying claim to rights and justice, and in combating the discrimination against those diagnosed as mentally ill.[28] In this respect, some of the Great War mental health survivors I am writing about are the ancestors of the mental health system survivors of today, blazing a trail in which others would follow.[29]

In the official, not say military, mind, a certain ambivalence, embarrassment even, hangs over some of the ex-servicemen I am writing about, but they have, I believe, been unjustly neglected and sometimes disparaged. My aim is to restore them to our memory as honourable members of the community of serving citizens in the Great War, to be valued for themselves, regardless of whether they made good as soldiers. Rather than kit them out in a more 'correct' terminology, I have to a large extent followed the period vernacular in discussing them – 'insanes', 'soldier lunatics', 'service lunatics', the 'mentally afflicted', the 'mentally affected', the 'nerve-shaken', the 'nerve-strained', the 'nerve-shattered', and so forth – but I hope it will be obvious that my useage, as of diagnostic terms also, is mostly deeply ironic. No one can, I believe, undertake an excavation of this sort without being touched by it, and though I have tried to be even-handed in my assessments, the tone is unashamedly angry at points, not least in navigating the shoals of class feeling and morality, and the machinations of the Ministry of Pensions.

A striking and familiar feature of the imagery of many memorials of the Great War is a list of the names of people commemorated, and many churches and cathedrals hold Books of Remembrance which serve to solicit, as has been remarked, a 'public *naming* of the dead'.[30] Commendable though this is, the naming is rather selective and begs the question of the remembrance of those ex-servicemen who have effectively been buried anonymously in a cultural mass grave, all but excluded from the rolls of honour of 'the named' and the official sanctuary of remembrance. To have hidden the ex-servicemen I am writing about behind a cloak of anonymity would have implied that there was something discreditable or shameful about their histories. Hence I have taken the view that the naming of the nameless, and thus the restoration of their individualities, is a proper part of the work of historical reconstruction. Accordingly this is the procedure that I have followed, with the exception of some individuals where I have been bound by the confidentiality of medical records.*

The volume of material I have unearthed has led me finally to concentrate almost exclusively on the lives of ex-servicemen in England. It would have required a much longer, and different, book to have done justice to Scotland, Wales, Ireland and the dominions, into all of which the dispensations for war disability pensions, including the Service Patient scheme, reached to a greater or lesser extent, though I have provided some pointers in the notes. The club of war psychotics is mainly populated by ordinary soldiers, but it also turns out that there are rather more mad captains, barking brigadiers and other brass hats lurking in the psychiatric undergrowth than at first meets the eye. Though this is mostly a work of social rather than intellectual history, in Part III I do discuss the political and cultural currents that gave birth to the new psychology, and venture some comparisons between the national cultures of mental trauma in Germany and Britain during the Great War. I also touch on a bigger story of psychological theorizing in which psychosis comes to be reconfigured as the site, not of an aberration or of an enforced exile, but of our origins and our continuing habitat. This, one might claim, is the missing subject to complement the missing group that forms the main focus of the book.

* To obviate the needless, and patronizing, iteration of [sic], it is appropriate to note here that throughout the book all quotations from personal letters, diaries and so forth have been transliterated with original spelling and punctuation.

Prologue

THE HOSIER AND THE IMBECILE GO TO WAR

*It is estimated that when the war begins 14 millions of men will be engaged
in the conflict. Attack is possible by earth, water & air, & the destruction
attainable by modern war machines used by the armies is unthinkable & past
imagination. . . . Stupendous events come so thick & fast after one another that
it is impossible to realise to any extent their full import. One feels as if one
were dreaming. . . .*

Vera Brittain, 4 August, 1914[1]

*I am seeking to depict individuals, swimming desperately in collective currents,
attempting to keep their heads above stormy waters and to reach the other
shore. . . . There is little place for martyrs in this account, because it is not
particularly concerned with martyrs, or with persons in any way admirable or
exceptional. This is a chronicle of ordinariness, of privacy, representing as it
does an attempt, in revolutionary terms, to create a collective Diary of a
Nobody. . . . At least, whenever possible, I will allow them to witness for
themselves, in their own language. For the Revolution exists as much through
their narrow, unremarkable lives, or in their violent and bloody enterprises, as
in the lives of the great.*

Richard Cobb, 'La Vie en Marge: Living on the Fringe of the Revolution'
(1972)[2]

By a small quirk of fate, two former soldiers, Private George Major Gomm
of the 22nd Battalion Royal Fusiliers and Private Albert Francis Norris of the
3rd Battalion East Surrey Regiment, who had just recently been discharged
from the Army as no longer physically fit for war service, and unlikely to
become efficient soldiers, were both admitted to Long Grove Asylum near
Epsom in Surrey within a day of each other at the end of June 1916 to be
received into the fraternity of pauper lunatics.[3] Though they had a certain
amount in common, notably an encounter with mental institutions before the
war, they came from different stations, their life experiences shaped by divergent currents, in the moral and social topography of early twentieth-century
England.

The son of a master stationer, George had been privately educated until the age of fifteen and had enlisted in the Royal Fusiliers at Chelsea Town Hall on 11 January 1915, giving his age as twenty-one years, though he was actually five months short of his twenty-first birthday, and his occupation as gentleman's hosier at Shoolbreds, a well-known department store in the Tottenham Court Road.[4] Recruits to the old Regular Army had mainly been unskilled, semi-literate working-class youths, memorably apostrophized by the German Ambassador as 'the dregs of the population . . . morally degraded, idiots, undersized and pitiable beings', and the Army was still sometimes referred to as the dustbin of the nation.[5] In the forces that gathered under the sign of Lord Kitchener's New Armies, however, the respectable classes were vastly more visible in the ranks. Indeed, the service sector was disproportionately represented by comparison with men from industry, no doubt a product of a greater willingness to fight among the middle classes, but equally of a shift in the social base.[6] The late nineteenth and early twentieth centuries had seen the evolution of a richer and increasingly multi-faceted tapestry of middle classes, notably the expansion of the lower middle classes due to rising living standards and the proliferation of clerical, teaching and other tertiary occupations.[7] Contemporary surveys revealed that by comparison with, say, Leeds where seven out of ten men were 'hors de combat before they even shouldered a musket', in London, at least, George and his like were able to deliver a high proportion of healthy recruits. Prominent among them were shop assistants from West End stores who 'indulged in athletics', and clerks who were 'devotees of outdoor recreation' and defied slurs on the clerkly life by acknowledging a duty 'to live hygienic lives and to keep fit, knowing that if they had a breakdown they might lose their posts'.[8] Indeed, at Chelsea Town Hall in January 1915 George Gomm, if not exactly a stunning exemplar of England's 'farm of manhood', must certainly have acquitted himself as par for the course. His vital statistics – height 5 ft 6 inches, girth 34.5 inches, and weight not far short of 130 lbs – bore a striking resemblance to the profile of the average Grade I man – 'a combination of height 5 ft 6 inches, weight 130 lbs and chest girth 34 inches' – which the authorities were to extract from their extensive surveys of recruits at a later stage in the war, when the grading and calibration of human material had become a focus of anxious scrutiny.[9]

In the rush to the colours when George enlisted in 1915, there was a widespread assumption that a wholesome patriotic spirit was necessarily vested in a wholesome body, and that the volunteers were mostly all fit men. By the time the war had ended it was acknowledged that in reality there had been really very little to distinguish volunteers from conscripts. In 'the wave of enthusiasm which swept over the country in those early days when men were passed "fit" or "unfit" often after the most cursory examination by a single medical officer, a very large percentage of recruits were accepted for military service, in spite of physical disabilities'.[10] And so it must have been with George. We do not know exactly how rigorously he was medically examined, but when he enlisted the organized system for medical examination had not yet been established, and so he was certainly spared the ordeal of running the gauntlet of a medical board and appearing naked before the president.[11]

Moreover, any doubts that might have arisen as to his fitness would in any case have been dissipated by the knowledge that he had been a member of that vanguard of patriotic readiness, the Territorials, with whom he had served for a year, enlisting in the Queen's Westminster Rifles in 1913. A product of R. B. Haldane's ambitious plans for Army reform, the Territorials had been created as a sop to critics who, in the wake of the disasters of the Boer War, were baying about 'national inefficiency' and the parlous condition of the national stock. The Territorial Army was a means to demonstrate military preparedness and resolve without having to advance very far down the road towards the militarization of society, least of all to compromise the hallowed tradition of English voluntarism by invoking the threat of conscription. The Territorials enrolled a superior class of men than did the Regular Army, mostly upper working-class artisans and clerks aged between eighteen and twenty-four, who committed themselves for a four-year term. Some of them enlisted because they considered it their duty, others because they valued the associational loyalty and looked upon their unit as a club, spending about a fortnight under canvas every year, many of them joining rifle clubs to keep their marksmanship up to par.[12]

Yet there was still a strong current of amateurishness and make-believe to these earnest endeavours, and George Gomm could, perhaps, be taken as confirming the suspicions of national service hardliners that the Territorials would not be of much use when a war came. As it turned out, George's constitution was far more delicate than his well-nourished appearance might initially have suggested, for at the age of ten both his lungs had become infected by pneumonia, a potentially devastating malady in the early twentieth century, as psychologically unsettling as it was physically debilitating, which he was very lucky to have survived. Well might he have feared for his life, for he had a twin brother, Richard Moore Gomm, who had died from acute peritonitis just the previous year, six days of unrelenting suffering before exhaustion struck.[13] And then in 1913, in all likelihood during one of those fortnights under canvas with the Territorials, he was stricken by sunstroke, with symptoms of muscle cramps, nausea and vomiting, confusion and disorientation. Unpleasant certainly, but an episode that would have run its own course, except that in George's case it must have reawakened a memory of the anguish he had experienced when he thought he was dying from pneumonia. It appears to have precipitated an acute mental crisis, for at the end of September 1913 George, by order of Dr Gemmill, was admitted to the Male Insane Wards of St Pancras Workhouse from his lodgings in Gower Street in a 'restless and noisy condition', hearing imaginary voices and answering them. He spent most of the next week on the Insane Wards in seclusion, taking his food but sleeping very little, receiving a brief visit from his father and a mysterious Mr Dash on the Sunday afternoon, until he was removed to Hanwell Lunatic Asylum on Wednesday 1 October.[14]

The record of his stay there is sparse, but it may be remarked that he arrived at Hanwell on the cusp of a hygienic revolution at that establishment, for early in December 1913 the Lunacy Commissioners advised the asylum authorities of the 'necessity of supplying toilet paper for the use of patients'. Maintaining that pauper lunatics did not merit such cosseting, the asylum authorities stonewalled at such a preposterous proposal, but eventually conceded on learning that toilet paper was now being issued at all the other London asylums.[15] George was obliged to survive for a whole year in this institution, before being discharged home on trial at the end of September 1914.[16] Suitably convalesced, he returned to his station in the hosiery department at Shoolbreds on the Tottenham Court Road. Not for very long, alas, for just a few months later he was answering the call at the Chelsea Town Hall and legging it out to Flanders, swept along by the passions of the moment, and embarking on another display of manly virtues for which he was physically and emotionally singularly unsuited. Throughout the war, military and medical definitions of 'fitness' always remained sufficiently elastic as to accommodate an astonishing variety of human material. All the same, there is a greater likelihood that under the more nuanced regimens of the medical examining boards that evolved later in the war, where one member 'would take the chest, including of course the heart and the lungs, and the abdominal organs, inquire into his mental capacity, and ask him whether he is subject to fits and so forth', George's disability would have been detected, though probably not judged coarse enough to warrant rejection. In London at least, under the National Service Boards, he would very likely have been spared the firing-line, though not necessarily overseas service, and placed in Grade III, made up of roughly a third of men of military age in Britain who had been found 'incapable of undergoing more than a very moderate degree of physical exertion and could almost (in view of their age) be described with justice as physical wrecks'.[17]

But, physical wreck or not, when George enlisted the Army was simply a gigantic 'receiving machine' with limited capacity to discriminate. From what transpired later, it is obvious that George's feelings about what he was letting himself in for were highly conflicted, but we may surmise that he was bolstered by his father's patriotic ardour, and his desire to live up to the standards of manliness that his father extolled. For his part, George senior was either blind to his son's vulnerability or, more likely, was inclined to view it as a moral failing and to believe – and of course he would not have been alone in this – that the adventure of the battlefield might be the making of him. In actuality it was to prove his undoing. George was going to war carrying a double burden: not merely the expectations that attached to his own person, but also the hopes that had been extinguished in his brother and were now transferred to him. He was posted the same day he enlisted and for the next eleven months was on Home Service, mostly at Roffey Camp near Horsham in Sussex, and whilst there he again contracted double pneumonia, brought on by the unsettling (at least for him) conditions of military life. He was later to recount that he had had a 'nervous breakdown' at Roffey, as well he might, for he was pitched once more into a perilous condition, lasting perhaps several days, before which, in this pre-penicillin era, doctors were to a considerable extent helpless.[18] All of it was compounded in George's case by the unsettling memories it reawakened, and shame at the faltering of his manhood at this critical juncture.[19]

A year later, when quizzed by the medical authorities about a recent scar in his right arm pit, George at one moment said it was the result of a wound, at another of an operation for pneumonia, but the authorities concluded that it was most likely a surgical scar. Still, he was permitted only a very temporary sojourn in his sick bed, and was quite quickly considered to be ready to resume his duty as a soldier: on Christmas Eve 1915, George embarked with his battalion to join the British Expeditionary Force in France, spending the next three months in and around the front lines just to the east of Bethune in Picardy. On 2 March the Battalion left their billets at Barlin to move to reserve positions at Bois de Noulette, from where they relieved the 1st Royal Berks in front-line trenches, remaining in the front line for three days before being marched back to Bouvigny. Three days later they returned to the trenches, remaining in the front line for four days – '7 Other Ranks wounded' – and then proceeding to huts in Bois de Noulette, from where they moved to billets in Ourton, remaining in divisional rest for the next fortnight. After some further manoeuvres they returned to Ourton by route march and rail on 13

April, moving into trenches at Souchez on the 17th where they relieved the 2nd East Lancs.[20]

Not at this stage an especially eventful campaign, rather one characterized by moments of potential danger punctuated by long intervals of boredom and senseless routine, a nervous waiting game in which the constant changing of billets provided the most decisive form of relief. We do not have any information as to exactly what kind of action George saw in his three months in and out of the front-line trenches, whether he fired his rifle, or how often, or with what result, nor as to the effects on him of the sights of injured comrades and mutilated bodies, the sounds and smells that he experienced. However, the diary entry just a few weeks later of a young officer (a medical officer as it happens, not directly involved in the fighting, so perhaps more able to confide his uncertainties), shortly after commencing his tour of duty, conveys the sort of atmosphere that George would very likely also have ingested:

I've not yet got the hang of things. Am unsettled. Quiet start, then uproar at 7pm. . . . Such shows are planned and localized. I'm in the dark about them and about what one does in the event of an outburst just here; should be obvious but it is not. As far as I know, which is not saying much, there is nothing to hinder this bit of line from suddenly being involved in one of these astounding and inexplicable bursts of activity. It is this uncertainty and the suddenness of these shows that tries me. . . . The affair this evening was the worst I have seen. One moment the line was quiet. With no warning whatever, a section burst into sudden, virulent action. . . . Seen from here it was a picture of agony and sheer idiocy. The earth sprayed up in splashes of flame and smoke and soil. What looked like a man with no head – and probably was – leapt into the air. A trenchboard, spinning like a Catherine wheel, hurtled back over our line. Green, voluminous whorls of smoke unwound themselves in evil patterns, to be dashed aside by spurts from the ground or by coal-black air-bursts. . . . The noise is entirely outside my experience. I do not know how the Infantry stand its continuity, its repeated bouts of continuity that is to say, and still stay sane.[21]

Of one thing we can be certain – by the time he returned with his company to his billets in Ourton on April 13 1916, George was experiencing great difficulty in staying sane, and was already in a deeply traumatized state. At Bethune railway station at around 11.30 on the night of 14 April 1916, soon after the arrival of the leave train from Boulogne, Private Gomm was noticed by Corporal Leedham of the Military Railway Police to be wandering around the waiting hall. Apparently unable to venture any information about himself, he was brought before the officer in charge of transport arrangements who was able to extract from him only 'incoherent statements about "Divion", "heavy rain", "had a shock", and similar phrases'. Surmising that he was not drunk, and most likely at least temporarily deranged, an orderly took him to No. 33 Casualty Clearing Station, where he sat on the end of his bed in a dejected attitude, speaking to no one, answering the questions put to him by the Royal Army Medical Corps (RAMC) doctor only after long reflection, and stating that he thought he came to Bethune by train on 13 April, having had nothing to eat since then.[22]

In fact it is most improbable that George arrived at Bethune by train, and the most likely explanation for how he got there springs from his mention of 'Divion' which, puzzling though it may have been to the officer at Bethune Station, is the name of a village just three kilometres northeast of Ourton where George had been billetted. He would have had to pass through here in making his way to Bethune on foot, another 12 kilometres up the road. The record does not tell us whether he left his battalion shortly after reaching Ourton on the evening of the 13th, or the following morning, or whether he did indeed experience some kind of shock walking through the heavy rain. More likely, perhaps, the feelings that overwhelmed him as he trudged through Divion, having just taken the precipitate step of abandoning his company, were the culmination of a long season of anguish and uncertainty. In any case, it seems probable that he walked to Bethune and that, far from getting off a train, he was hanging about the station with a hankering to get on one. When Lt Gawe RAMC asked him what he wanted to do now, George as good as told him that he had had enough of this military business, saying that though he did not mind staying here for a day or two, after that he wanted to go home.

FROM 'FUNK' TO SHELL SHOCK

After training as a physician, Charles Samuel Myers had gone on to study psychology at Cambridge under W. H. R. Rivers, along with fellow student William McDougall, all of whom had been brought together in the renowned Torres Straits expedition of 1898.[23] Now he was already starting to make a reputation for himself as a mover and shaker in the controversial field of military psychiatry. He had started working in France as early as October 1914, and since March 1915 had been in post as Specialist in Nerve Shock, attached to a Casualty Clearing Station at St Omer, then the General Head-Quarters of the British Armies in France, where he was endeavouring to rally support for his novel position that there was a distinct category of nervous disorder that was neither 'funk' nor certifiable insanity. 'Many cases sent down as "mental"', Myers later wrote, 'owed their depressed or stuporose condition to temporary "nervous exhaustion" or to "shell shock"', which Myers regarded as essentially an emotional trauma in which, in the great majority of instances, the signs appeared to be 'traceable to psychical causes, especially, in the early cases, to the emotions of extreme and sudden horror and fright'. He was to experience persisting difficulty in getting his point of view understood and accepted by the military authorities, but by the early months of 1916 he had made significant headway with his success in returning to duty, with a negligible number of relapses, 31 per cent of the so-called 'mental' cases who had come his way in St Omer, who would otherwise have been sent home and lost to the Army through being disposed of as lunatics, and he had been promoted to Lieutenant Colonel.[24]

Though he was not its author, Myers had acquired some notoriety for having *authorized* the concept of shell shock in the professional literature, but already by 1916 this was a reputation that he was rather anxious to live down. In the experience of the military authorities, 'shell shock' was a thoroughly dubious innovation, by no means exclusively a therapeutic dynamo for mentally re-equipping soldiers to return to fight, or at least to some form of duty. On the contrary, it was fast becoming an ambiguous and porous domain, exploited by a diverse band of prospectors and travellers, an attractive exit ticket for 'dirty sneaks' and 'blameworthy weaklings' anxious to escape from the front line. As a means to limit the application of the label, and as a heuristic device to inhibit premature diagnostic closure, variants of the Not Yet Diagnosed (or NYD) label had started to make their appearance.[25]

Had George fallen into less discerning medico-military hands, he might very well been construed as a deserter, and dealt with accordingly, but significantly the suspicion of malingering was never raised in his case, not because the medical authorities whom he encountered were faint-hearted, but rather because George in his demeanour, and in his invocation of the rhetoric of 'shock' and 'nervous breakdown', seemed entirely convincing: he just *did* seem like a man who was in shock. Already bearing an NYD Mental label, on 16 April 1916 he was examined in St Omer by Lt Col. Myers, who obviously did not find anything especially remarkable about him, merely noting on a scrap of paper: '1276 Pte Gomm 22 R.Fus. is in a semi-stuporose condition as if recovering from a state of shock. I recommend that he be sent to No 8 Stationary for further observation'.[26] That was certainly validation of a sort, for not even a whiff of moral dubiety clung to him. Though it could still tilt either way, and there was plenty to play for, George had by no means been written off as a lost cause at this stage, either to the Army or to life, and Myers certainly seemed inclined towards a positive therapeutic result.

Charles Myers and his progressive colleagues in Flanders were busy trying to rescue 'shell shock' and 'temporary nervous exhaustion' from insanity, to expand the zone of the treatable and restrict the definition of the untreatable or incurable, and to demonstrate that many of the so-called 'mental' cases were due to temporary causes such as 'the strain of warfare, worry, insomnia etc., comparable to the temporary delirium of a fever or to alcoholic intoxication'.[27] At the same time, however, they could not afford to linger in waiting for cases to recover, and were under pressure to take decisive, if sometimes precipitate, action in separating the sheep from the goats, the temporary cases from the authentic 'mentals', those who could again be harnessed to the war machine from those who were intrinsically useless as soldiers. Myers was sceptical of the therapeutic potential of the Base hospital in the treatment of so-called 'mental' cases, believing that 'when they were in a Base hospital almost within sight of England, their chances of rapid recovery were very much diminished, since consciously or unconsciously they were influenced by the expectation of being sent home', but such were the pressures on facilities in the field that if a soldier did not recover very quickly there was no alternative but to send him home.[28]

If Charles Myers assessed that George was recovering from a state of shock, Lieutenant Montgomery, the Medical Officer in charge of the Mental Division at No 8 Stationary Hospital in Wimereux, one of four mental divisions in Base hospitals in France, seems to have had little clue how to assist in the recovery process, leaving George to grapple with his fears and uncertainties on his own. Not that George made it at all easy for Montgomery: he claimed not to know how long he had been in the Army or in France; asked his former occupation, he replied 'Tottenham Court Road' and started to whistle, and then broke off to say that he earned 2/6d a week; he confided that he heard voices saying 'God save the King on a night like this!' and that he shouted in answer to them; he muttered 'where was I between nine and half-past ten last night?'; he gave answers to questions that Montgomery found foolish or irrelevant, communicating mostly in fragmentary utterances: 'I had a nervous breakdown, remember smashing a window, getting hot, fresh air, how funny', followed by a burst of whistling, a pause, and then: 'Want to get back to England, that is all I think'; and he was impulsive, making rushes to get away and striking out when people passed him. Montgomery was struck by how frightened he seemed, believing that something was going to be done to him, and when he came to examine his pupils George exclaimed: 'God save me, don't you know Major Gomm!'[29] Though this is disconnected stuff, one can sense the connections lurking in the background and it is surely easy enough to intuit a narrative thread, but Montgomery seems to have been mostly a passive interlocutor, transcribing George's utterances rather than engaging with them.

George spent just four nights at No.8 Stationary Hospital, but long enough for Lt Montgomery to alter the diagnosis from NYD Mental to mania, and to convince him that since George was plainly psychotic he was a fit candidate for removal to D Block, Netley, near Southampton, part of the Royal Victoria Hospital, the regular unit for the treatment of mental disorder in the Army, and now the designated reception centre for cases of acute mental illness arising in the expeditionary forces. When George arrived there on 21 April on board the Hospital Ship *St George*, he was at once given a hot bath, and issued with a regulation blue hospital suit.[30] The next day he was examined by Captain Frederick Clindening RAMC, a paragon of soldierly and masculine rectitude with a lofty disdain for the emotional spillage that was leaking all around him, which he saw as a general incapacity to get control and play the game.[31] The Captain did not take to George at all, succeeding in getting a reply out of him only after much persuasion: 'Does not know where he was fighting. Will not obey an order. Has no manners. Walked away when being questioned. Is foolish and stupid. Cannot give an account of himself'. Clindening noted also that George worked in Shoolbreds where he 'jumps about behind the counter', a slightly camp insinuation, perhaps to indicate the questionable masculinity of a gentleman's hosier, though George may have been trying to share a joke with the humourless Clindening here, by way of conveying that his was really quite an *active* occupation – interestingly, in contemporary surveys shop assistants were classified as an 'indoor active', as opposed to an 'indoor sedentary', occupational group.[32] Clindening's strictures on George were in any case all par for the psychiatric course, since he typecast most of the soldiers who passed before him as 'foolish and stupid'. One might feel inclined to return the compliment, except that Clindening was no doubt sorely put upon by the drafts of distressed servicemen who descended on him in waves, as he clacked away on an old typewriter to fill out their details and complete their transfer arrangements, before they were moved on after a few days to the next station on their psychiatric pilgrimage.

On 2 May 1916 there were 24 admissions to the mental department of the County of Middlesex War Hospital at Napsbury, near St Albans, 21 of them from D Block Netley, George Gomm among them. Most were volunteers in their twenties and thirties who had served for a year or more, though there were seven or so who had only been in the army for a few months, and three regulars who had served for six years or more. When he was brought in,

George was quite considerably underweight for his age and build, just 8 stone 9 lbs, and his period of military training did not seem to have done much to improve him, for he was said to be 'poorly developed, muscles feeble and flabby'. The authorities at Napsbury made the routine inquiries of George's next of kin, advising his father that his son was under treatment for a nervous breakdown but that there was no cause for concern, and asking him for details of his family and medical history. George senior replied with candour, revealing that his son had been educated at a private school until 15 years of age; had had double pneumonia in 1904; sunstroke followed by a nervous breakdown in 1913 for which he had been treated partly at Hanwell Asylum and partly at home, followed by another bout of double pneumonia in 1915. He had never been intemperate in drink, had any fits or convulsions, seemed weak-minded in early childhood or at school, or threatened suicide, but (tellingly) his mother had had a nervous breakdown. To the question of whether he had ever been violent in any way George senior was silent. Whether he was aware of it or not, his revelations about the family history cannot have advanced his son's cause, and served only to assist the military authorities in casting him as a constitutional inadequate, for whom they did not need to assume any special responsibility nor make a focus of intensive therapeutic zeal.

Initially, like a fair number of other Napsbury admissions, he was entered in the register under neurasthenia, a provisional diagnosis that allowed for the possibility that he was not necessarily a certifiable lunatic and should be given a chance to recover. Though they acknowledged that while he was often restless or depressed and troubled, still there were days on which he was able to do useful work, the Napsbury authorities seem quite quickly to have given up on him, entering only the briefest of notes about him. On 12 June 1916, after just five weeks in the war hospital, George was brought before a medical board, where it was decided to discharge him from the army as 'being no longer physically fit for war service', and to send him to a lunatic asylum. In preparation for the transfer to Long Grove Asylum he was issued with a 'suit of plain clothes'. This was a modest concession to spare him the humiliation of the abrasive exchange of status that frequently befell a mad soldier discharged from the army under King's Regulations, who might find himself stripped of his uniform on arrival at the asylum, the trappings of his military persona handed over to the escort for return to his unit.[33]

THE CAREER IMBECILE

Albert Francis Norris was the product of a peculiarly Edwardian strain of intolerance towards individuals and social groups considered incapable of conducting themselves adequately as efficient citizens.[34] There are some instabilities in the official records over Albert's declared age, as indeed over other features of his biography, but it can be established that he was born on 7 February 1888 in Woodford, Essex, of Irish Catholic parentage, the son of Alice Norris, formerly Scorran, and Henry Norris, a signwriter. It seems that he first attracted official attention as a suspected mental case on 2 July 1912, when Relieving Officer Ernest Fields of the Wandsworth Poor Law Union was summoned to the Latchmere Road Police Station. On arrival, he found a man who struck him as strange in manner, declaring that he had been very wicked and dared not seek forgiveness, that life was not worth living and that he would be better out of it. As a front-line Poor Law operative, it fell to Fields to arrange for the assessment of suspected mental cases and to convey them to the workhouse infirmary or mental ward for observation. Albert was not entirely forthcoming, but Fields struggled to piece together his narrative and jotted in his notebook: 'Homeless 3 weeks. 11 Doddington Grove 1 week. Salesian Schools Battersea 6 years. Catholic Home Westminster Bridge Road 1 year. Homeless and destitute. No friends'. It turned out that Albert had been working as a porter at the Salesian School in Battersea for the previous six years, an establishment which had in truth served also as his family. It seems that he had either been orphaned or rejected by his kin, for he had lived for some years in a Catholic home, and we can at least surmise that a crisis had arisen in which Albert had fallen out with the Brothers and been ejected from his situation, followed by a few days in lodgings at 11 Doddington Grove, Battersea, and then, after his funds were exhausted, by destitution and nights in the workhouse.

In Albert's account, his brief sojourn in Doddington Grove was not intended to convey anything more than a reference to a fleeting encounter with a lodging house, but in the bureaucratic imagination of the Poor Law which Ernest Fields represented, it now became enshrined as Albert's 'last known place of residence', his final port of call in the civilized world, before disappearing into the void of homelessness. It was to join with other scraps of information that Albert divulged about his life – mention of a transitory encounter with a landlady or of a temporary occupation, for example – in being made to play roles well beyond their actual station and significance, such that a landlady who had no recollection of having met Albert at all found herself represented, several years after the supposed event, as his closest friend.

Albert's evident anguish was enough to decide Fields that he should be admitted that evening for observation to the Wandsworth Union Infirmary as an 'alleged mental'. The following day he had his first encounter with

Dr Frank Nixey, the assistant medical officer, who found him depressed, torpid and taciturn, but persuaded him to answer some questions in which he admitted that he had 'silly fits' in which he broke things up, as he had done in his situation at the Salesian School, and could not apply himself to work because his thoughts were dwelling on the future. In fact Albert had rather good reason to dwell on his future, for whilst Nixey did not probe any further into his unhappiness, his purpose being less therapeutic than administrative, Albert had already said enough to convince him that his apparent inability to control himself made him unfit to remain at large, and a proper subject for detention in a lunatic asylum. He was accordingly dispatched to Long Grove Asylum at Epsom on 12 July 1912, where he was entered in the asylum books as an imbecile, suffering from a congenital mental condition.[36] And there he might very well have remained indefinitely, for he combined in his person that paradoxical duality, in which asylum regimes especially delighted, of a type of uncertainty in himself, and his dealings with others, that amply justified his segregation as an inefficient, a blot on the drive to improve the national stock, coupled with a need for belonging, and an aptitude to please, that made him a most efficient and co-operative worker. In short, a boon to the asylum economy, had the circumstances of war not intervened and led him to choose a new object for his need for fraternity and belonging.

By the winter of 1915, the hungry war machine was penetrating ever more deeply into the recesses of Long Grove asylum, depleting its resources, luring away the choicest specimens to sate its appetite, and handing back its mutilated discards. By the middle of November, arrangements had been made for all single eligible men on the asylum staff to be attested for immediate enlistment, and the married men for the reserve, and the medical superintendent informed the committee that when all the single men had gone there would be only 58 permanent attendants left in the asylum. At this time war service still had the allure of an adventurous life, far preferable to the stuffy confines of a civilian occupation, and attendant George Riley was scarcely unusual in itching to kick over the traces, becoming decidedly surly towards his superiors when he was initially refused permission to enlist, leading the Medical Superintendent to threaten that he might have to deal with him summarily.[37] Quite a number of soldiers had already been deposited in the asylum from the war hospitals, and the authorities were plainly anxious to complete the formalities for their discharge from the army with unseemly haste. The assistant medical officer declared himself quite satisfied that the soldier patients had understood what was involved in signing the papers that had been sent to them for signature, a tell-tale sign that some mischief was afoot, because of course the standard line was that a lunatic was a lunatic, and his grasp of anything consequential, least of all an official communication, wholly unreliable.

We cannot discover how vocal Albert became in making known his own desire to be discharged the asylum, and to serve with the colours. From his subsequent actions, however, there can be no doubt that he must have been buoyed up by the patriotic stirrings amongst the attendants and some, at least, of the other inmates – and perhaps also by the ribald rumours circulating in the patient subculture that some of the female nurses had been spending their Christmas holidays living it up with soldiers, rather than in the sobriety of their own homes. When he got wind of this story, the Medical Superintendent summoned the alleged miscreants to his office, where Nurse Cook 'lied in a very bare-faced way to me'. It turned out that Nurses Clements and Cook had been baring more than their faces, spending the first night of their holiday with soldiers at the King's Head Hotel in Epsom, before decamping to apartments in Oxford. There is no record of how the decision was taken, but at the Committee meeting on 25 February 1916, after noting that Cow no. 504 still had a bad foot, and that there had been protests from the staff against the issue of frozen beef which several of them had found quite unpalatable, it was reported that Albert Francis Norris had been sent on trial into the care of the Mental After Care Association (or to give it its full title, the Mental After Care Association for Poor Persons Convalescent or Recovered from Institutions for the Insane).[38]

After four weeks of convalescence at one of the Association's homes in Southsea, for which they awarded him a grant of £7.17.9, it was reported that Albert was now 'convalesced' and had been found a situation as a kitchen porter at De Keyser's Royal Hotel at the eastern extremity of the Victoria Embankment.[39] Described in a guidebook shortly after the turn of the century as 'the particular resort of the continental visitor', where 'we may find a regular potpourri of highly respectable foreigners of different nationalities', by the time Albert arrived there it would most certainly have been vastly restricted in its clientele. Seen against the sordid backdrop of Long Grove Asylum, however, he must still have found it enormously alluring.[40] We do not know exactly how long Albert held his position there, but probably he had been there since the beginning of April, for by the time that the Association was reporting him as 'convalesced' Albert had enlisted in the army at Kingston-upon-Thames, giving as his address De Keyser's Hotel. Having been put through the routine medical, he had been passed fit for service, taking the oath, 'I swear by Almighty God that I Albert Francis Norris will be faithful and bear true allegiance to His Majesty King George the Fifth', and then been kitted out in uniform and posted to the 3rd Battalion East Surrey

Regiment on 4 May 1916. Hence, from being a career imbecile in a lunatic asylum, he now found himself, after an interlude as kitchen porter in a luxury hotel, embarked on the first stage of his military career as No. 19089 Private Norris.

Of course, we cannot assume that it was the intention, either of the Long Grove authorities or of the Mental After Care Association, that Albert should join the Army, or even that they believed he was fit to do so. However, they can scarcely have failed to have been mindful of the tentacles that were reaching out to him as he was being 'convalesced', and most likely assessed that he should be allowed to take his chances as best he could. His was certainly not an isolated case and, while at the Association's house at Southsea in preparation for his enlistment, he would have been able to talk tactics with other former inmates such as William Badger, who had been discharged from Banstead Asylum some weeks earlier and was also about to enlist. By this time, of course, the first Military Service Act, the so-called Bachelors' Bill, under which all male British subjects between the ages of 18 and 41 who were either unmarried or widowers without dependent children were called up to enlist, had been passed by Parliament, a momentous departure from the hallowed tradition of British military voluntarism.[41] Still, though conscription was now the order of the day, Albert's enlistment has about it a markedly voluntaristic character (for which securing his situation and the prestigious address it provided him were a necessary preliminary), and we may perhaps characterize him as a belated volunteer whose patriotic intentions were never in question, but who was unavoidably detained by other business in the intervening period.

As to his military career, it must be admitted that it was perhaps more exciting in the anticipation than in the enactment, for it lasted only 43 days and concluded with Albert's discharge from Dover Military Hospital, and from the army, on Friday 16 June 1916 as of good character but unlikely to become an efficient soldier. At this point an enlightened army liaison officer decided that Albert might benefit from another bout of convalescence with the Mental After Care Association, and Albert shortly found himself sat before Miss Vickers, Secretary of the Association, in her austere office at Church House, Westminster. But as its title rather implied, the Association only dealt with cases who were 'convalescent' or 'recovered', and who could be readily placed in a situation, and right now Albert, though he had by no means disgraced himself, was nonetheless downcast by his failure to make a good soldier of himself, and fearful of what was now to become of him. Having sized him up, and decided that he was no longer a promising candidate for their ministrations, Miss Vickers quickly bundled him off across town to spend the weekend at the Whitechapel Sailors' Home before bringing him before Dr Percy Smith, the Association's medical adviser, at St Thomas's Hospital on Tuesday 20 June.

Dr R. Percy Smith, known to his peers as 'R.P.', was already sixty-two when Albert encountered him, having succeeded Sir George Savage as medical superintendent of the Bethlem Hospital at the tender age of thirty-four, a post he held for 10 years before establishing himself in 1898 in private practice in Queen Anne Street, also lecturing in mental diseases at St Thomas's Hospital. An establishment figure with liberal leanings, he was a good old-fashioned paternalist, noted for his 'punctilious devotion to duty', who, according to his obituarist, 'saw and spoke with every patient every day' when he was at the Bethlem.[42] It is unlikely that he spoke to Albert for very long, but certainly long enough to concur with Miss Vickers that he was simply beyond the pale as far as the Association was concerned, an assessment which reflected as much on the utter want of provision outside the asylum system for persons of Albert's class in an acute mental health crisis, as on any limitation of the Association itself. Indeed, with its scant resources the Association was endeavouring to do what it could, for in 1916 it had received applications on behalf of 508 persons and had been able to find situations for 154 of them, so arguably Albert had been quite lucky first time round and had been given his chance.[43]

And here ended Albert's brief encounter with the rarefied world of Edwardian mental aftercare, for Miss Vickers now escorted him to the Wandsworth Union Infirmary, St John's Hill, Wandsworth, bearing a certificate stating that he was an 'alleged mental'. The next day he was once again brought before Dr Frank Nixey, still at his position, though now as Deputy Medical Superintendent, who contrived a set of 'facts' which he believed demonstrated that Albert was insane: 'He was in an asylum for 3 years being discharged last February. He has since been in the Army 43 days and various jobs been found for him which he admits he cannot keep. Also admits that he cannot "settle his mind"; that his temper makes him do foolish things, eg throwing one job up after another; that he cannot trust himself with anybody and at times suspects he has been robbed by people. States he cannot gain confidence in himself and does not feel safe at large'. This last – getting the patient to say that he did not possess much confidence in himself nor feel safe at large – was Nixey's favourite *coup de grâce*, and by the time Albert had confessed to this he was as good as on the bus back to Long Grove. And so it was that on Saturday 24 June 1916 he was received back into the sodality of asylumdom where, as far as the authorities were concerned, after these brief episodes of portering and soldiering, he resumed his rightful place as an imbecile (though a useful and pliable one, for he was quite quickly granted ground parole).

And for Albert this was, of course, also the day on which he was to make the acquaintance of George Major Gomm who was just settling in, having arrived from Napsbury War Hospital the previous day, and whose picaresque military career of one year and 161 days, some of it with the British Expeditionary Force in Flanders, must have seemed an eternity when weighed against the miserable proportions of his own 43 days. And it was on this day also that Mrs Pulley of 11 Doddington Grove, Battersea, was brought before Mr William Haggis, Chief Relieving Officer at the Wandsworth Union, having been summoned by letter, to find much to her surprise that her establishment had been cast by the Poor Law authorities, on the strength of Albert's testimony about where he had briefly lodged some four years previously, as Albert's 'last known place of residence'. But Mr Haggis, having staged many of these encounters before, was not in the least surprised to learn that Mrs Pulley was unable to supply any information about Albert Francis Norris, failed to recognize his name, and was positive that no person answering to that name had ever lived at 11 Doddington Grove nor, indeed, lest any loophole was still being left open, at any other address with her.

Part I

THE WAR MENTAL HOSPITAL

24 Sept.   Hilton is as big a fool as ever and spends most of his time in the estaminet.
6 Oct.   The shelling is very heavy ... I have not seen either Hilton or my groom this morning – they have been out here too long and their nerves have gone absolutely. It really is HELL.
13 Oct.   Hilton is hopeless as usual. I felt very rotten this morning, and asked him to make me some soup. It was awful stuff. He seemed to have mixed it with stable manure. . . . I lost my temper with him. He has now got the hump ... I am losing my nerve, it is no use pretending I am not.
22 Oct.   These Gothas are over again and I am getting so nervy. Hilton asked leave this afternoon ... He is not a coward, but his nerve has quite gone, and so, I'm afraid, is mine!
24 Oct.   Hilton is still missing ... He has been gone for two days. . . . Over they come again! Not one or two, but dozens of them!
25 Oct.   Hilton has been found but a wreck.
30 Oct.   No rations again today. Hilton, of course ... gassed slightly but imagines he is very bad.
14 Nov.   I have discovered why Hilton has been so strange lately. . . . His wife has gone off the rails, and has written saying that she wants to have nothing more to do with him.
28 Nov.   I was awakened at midnight and told that I was to get up at once as I was for England.
2 Dec.   This is a special hospital for shock and nerve cases ... a very luxurious establishment ... every officer has a room to himself, bathroom, closet etc and about three nurses to each. The food is exceptional ... fish, game etc galore.

[Captain H. J. C. Leland, letters to his wife on active service in France, 1917.[1] In December 1917 Capt. Leland was admitted to the Special Hospital for Officers at Palace Green, Kensington, the flagship of Lord Knutsford's exclusive war mental hospitals. The subsequent fate of his batman, the hapless Private Hilton, or of his groom, is unknown]

Chapter 1

THE NEW LUNACY PROTEST

VIRGINIA AND ALBERT

At roughly the same time, in May 1916, in a more opulent area of London than either Albert or George were likely to frequent, a young woman wrote to her sister about her anxieties in getting exemption from military service for her husband, and the pressure that her doctor, Dr Maurice Craig, was bringing to bear: 'Leonard went to Craig who said that he would give him a certificate of unfitness on his own account, as well as mine. He has written a very strong letter, saying that Leonard is highly nervous, suffers from permanent tremor, and would probably break down if in the army. Also that I am still in a very shaky state, and would very likely have had a bad mental breakdown if they took him. He thinks they ought to give Leonard complete exemption on these grounds, and strongly advises him not to put in anything about conscience, which annoys them. It is rather difficult to know what to do, as the Tribunals are so erratic . . .'. From behind the scenes she has learned that the War Office already has too many men, and 'will connive at any gentleman getting off; so the thing to do is to produce letters from Harley St doctors or the peerage'. This was obviously just the ticket, for the following month she writes to another correspondent: 'It is very difficult to collect the wrecks of life and describe them to you!. . . . Leonard has been completely exempted from serving the Country in any capacity. He went before the military doctors trembling like an aspen leaf, with certificates to say that he would tremble and has trembled and will never cease from trembling. It's a great mercy for us. But the whole of our world does nothing but talk about conscription and their chances of getting off; and they are all taken up with different societies and meetings and wire pulling . . . !'[1]

The writer is, of course, Virginia Woolf, and 'Leonard' is her husband, Leonard Woolf. It was not just physical distance or opulence that divided poor trembling Leonard from Albert and George, for they did not have anyone to pull any wires for them, either to exempt them from military service, or to lend them a hand if they got into difficulty. Nor in any case would they have received any sympathy from the Woolfs, for, as her biographer has remarked, Virginia Woolf's language for mental illness 'is often brutal and conventional, accepting apparently without irony the current official attitudes'.[2] That much is, perhaps, obvious and reflects the poisonous divisions of pre-war British society. Yet it is by no means the whole story for, even though Albert and George might have been surprised to learn of it, they and their kind had been the focus of a vigorous controversy that by the spring of 1916 had been unravelling for 18 months or more.

As Virginia Woolf's doctor, Maurice Craig helped her to go on believing in herself despite her nervous condition, and when the war came he protected her husband from adverse judgments about his weakness. Though George Gomm came from a more advantaged background than Albert, they were both marginal individuals, George because he was nervous and unmanly, at odds with the prevailing gender norms of his society, Albert because along with being nervous he was a denizen of the margins, a long-term inmate of a lunatic asylum. As a patrician physician ministering to the upper and upper middle classes, Craig confirmed and reproduced the basic hierarchy of Edwardian society. Yet that is not all that he was doing, for he was also in the vanguard of a liberal counter-current, promoting an approach to mental health care more in tune with the changing sensibilities and rising expectations of a democratizing society.[3] Ironically, it turns out to be Maurice Craig himself who during the war years was much taken up in meetings and wire-pulling on behalf of mentally disordered servicemen such as Albert and George, helping to moderate the official language about mental illness, to inculcate more tolerant attitudes, and to secure concessions from the authorities. Admittedly, the success of these reforms was only rather partial, and George appears to have missed out on them almost entirely, but, as we shall see, that reflects the tensions and contradictions in the wider society.

RISING ASPIRATIONS
Unquestionably, the introduction of the universal classroom in 1870, along with the financial and retailing revolutions of the 1880s, which together had sparked the growth of clerical and other service occupations, had led to an enormous proliferation of the lower middle class, and hence to a more open frontier with the upper working class, while the same period had seen also a massive expansion in the professions, such as the law, medicine and teaching.[4] Writing in 1909, C. F. G. Masterman believed that it was the middle class, feeling 'contempt for the classes below it, and envy of the classes above', which provided the key to the condition of England, but it was apparent to many contemporary observers that there were several middle classes, and that the boundaries between one gradation and the next were becoming more blurred and contestable.[5] Revealingly, social reformer Charles Booth, with his

colourful eight-layered taxonomy of shades of red, pink, purple, blue and yellow in which he attempted to codify the topography of poverty in London, admitted that 'the dividing lines between all these classes are indistinct', each possessing 'a fringe of those who ought to be placed within the next division above or below'.[6] The 'long dominion of the middle classes', averred the young Winston Churchill, was now over, and 'the people' were now at the helm; and there were fulsome proclamations and examinations of how Britain had become drastically polarized, albeit in rather different ways: the masses set against the classes; the nation sundered between workers and employers in the enmity between labour and capital; and the divide between those who were mired in poverty and those who were not.[7] Yet, in a period of burgeoning aspirations, the identities of 'the people' and 'the middle classes' were becoming more intricately intertwined than might at first glance be supposed, and not for nothing have the decades before the Great War been described as the era of the rise of 'respectability'.

With the Third Reform Act of 1885, the cause of political citizenship had been given significant (though, of course, still one-sided) momentum, and workers were increasingly affected by the ideal of a 'civil society', displaying a determination to secure for themselves, not least in contentious areas such as welfare and health provision, rights that gave unequivocal recognition both of their status as citizens and of what 'the people' properly deserved. Cross-class coalitions joined in a rhetoric of liberal populism clamouring for active citizenship and justice for ordinary people, the 'decent folk', and from the 1890s onwards there was an enhanced concern for the individual's public reputation, and a growing hostility towards a welfare system that demeaned citizens by forcing them to resort to statutory aid for paupers.[8] The Poor Law, T. H. Marshall famously remarked, 'treated the claims of the poor not as an integral part of the rights of citizens but as an alternative to them – as claims which could be met only if the claimants ceased to be citizens in any true sense of the term.'[9] The rise of respectability among the working classes had elevated expectations and standards, and by contrast, certainly, with the early Victorian period, a widely acknowledged stigma now clung to poor relief that 'expressed the deep feelings of a people who understood that those who accepted relief must cross the road that segregated the community of citizens from the outcast company of the destitute'.[10]

The Workmen's Compensation Act of 1897 had for the first time obliged employers to accept responsibility for accidents to their employees , and the 'New Liberalism' of the Edwardian period ushered in reforms that gave some expression to aspirations for welfare reform, notably the National Health Insurance Act of 1911 ('a stake in the country', Churchill called the new scheme, that would turn workers' heads from 'revolutionary socialism'), which provided a flat benefit in case of sickness, invalidity and unemployment to those working in selected industries.[11] Nevertheless, even though they were no longer forced to forfeit their voting rights as a consequence, those who fell outside the ambit of the Act had to turn just as before to the medical services of the Poor Law. Overall, there was widespread feeling that the social order was lagging behind the desires and aspirations of the people, and, contrary to the hopes that had been stimulated by liberal rhetoric, delivering only a very stunted form of citizenship. 'I assert with some confidence', R. H. Tawney noted in 1912, 'that there has rarely been a period when the existing social order was regarded with so much dissatisfaction by so many intelligent and respectable citizens as it is at the present day'.[12]

The citizen soldiers who went to war were a product of the culture of rising aspirations which these social mutations had generated.[13] Of course, the traditional working class was still in a majority in the other ranks, but it was the infusion of this social mix into the New Armies that wonderfully transformed the social status of the eponymous Tommy Atkins, as the private soldier in the British Army was popularly known. Contemporaries remarked on the variety of middle-class men who enlisted as privates ('barristers, solicitors, bank clerks, qualified engineers', as one recalled), and George Gomm typifies in many respects the altered social profile of the ordinary ranker in the Great War, the proliferation of clerkly types alongside the usual malnourished working-class recruits.[14] That a culture of militarism existed in Edwardian England is, of course, undeniable, but historians have recently highlighted powerful anti-militarist influences. In a democratizing society, military values, if not directly challenged, were at least tempered, and the strong imperial, and hence masculine and hierarchical, current in British political culture was counterbalanced by other forces running in an opposing direction.[15] Even though conscription had been recommended by three successive inquiries, it was still anathema across a wide spectrum of opinion, and the years leading up to the Great War had seen more concern with social reform than with consolidating a military presence.[16]

Reflecting on English attitudes towards soldiery as the next war was being fought, George Orwell remarked on the 'English hatred of war and militarism' which was rooted deep in history and 'strong in the lower-middle class as well as the working class'.[17] And these opposing currents were also reflected in the culture of the citizens' army, for the values and inspiration of British working men in arms remained, as John Bourne has remarked, 'obstinately civilian'.[18] From the vantage point of relatives, the serving soldier was always seen in his private civilian aspect, and there was 'much anxious solicitude as to the incapacitated' that refused to be subordinated to military values.[19] Stirred by patriotic fervour though most ordinary soldiers indubitably were, they never lost sight of the obligations they expected of the state in return for their patriotic services, nor did they leave behind their profound discontents with the existing social order and its failure to deliver adequate welfare reforms.

A DEGRADING DIVIDE

Though at times the screw was twisted more tightly on control of the margins, overall the political economy of medicine, as of welfare more widely, was becoming an increasingly contested arena. 'Productionist' medicine, to borrow John Pickstone's term, informed by collectivist notions of health in which norms of citizenship or fitness to live in society were determined by efficiency in the workforce or in the armed services, was being jostled by emerging forms of 'communitarian' medicine, in which the interests of the bosses and the generals were having to cede to demands for social solidarity and recognition of citizens' rights.[20] The treatment that was available to the very rich and the very poor in most spheres of medicine was vastly superior to what it had been only half a century before, yet even so 'for a majority of people in England and Wales, ranging from the "middling" sections of the middle class through to the unskilled working class, personal medicine was often either an object of stigma or an expensive and unaffordable luxury'.[21]

Amidst all the various objects of dissatisfaction, it was especially the mental health system which served as a symbol of people's discontent with the health and welfare system as a whole. The private sector was out of reach to most people, and in any case was viewed with suspicion, and for a wide spectrum of the population the only access to mental health care, especially for lengthy, in-patient treatment, was through the stigmatized and degrading pauper lunatic system. This was quite the most unreconstructed area of health care, epitomized by one eminent contemporary as 'a sort of early Victorian cul-de-sac of hopelessness and laissez faire'.[22] Even as in reality social classes were becoming more fluid and converging increasingly about the middle, what was on offer here was a divisive two-class system.

TERROR OF THE PHYSICIAN IN THE HIGHER SOCIAL GRADES

Maurice Craig reflects, in many respects, the contradictions of pre-war British society beating in one breast, liberal in one dimension, responding with the basic reflex of his class in another. In the recommendations for drug treatment set out in his highly acclaimed textbook published on the eve of the war, he delivers an eerie insight into a divisive, class-based medicine in which upper-

and lower-class bodies are embraced by the physician with opposing values. 'Hyoscin and hyoscyamin are drugs which are largely used by some authorities', he informs us, 'but they cannot be strongly recommended. They act by paralysing the nerve-endings in the muscles, and in this way they lessen restlessness in a maniacal patient'. Though their use is 'invaluable in some acute cases of excitement where the assistance at hand is insufficient to prevent violence on the part of the patient', unfortunately 'a somewhat extraordinary symptom, not uncommonly met with in patients who are taking hyoscin, is the terror they evince every time they see the physician who administers it to them'. Especially 'in persons belonging to the educated classes', hallucinations, usually of sight, 'are commonly met with in patients who are under the influence of these drugs'. Accordingly in acute cases, 'especially of persons of the higher social grades, these drugs should seldom, if ever, be employed'.

However, when it comes to chronic cases, particularly among 'patients belonging to the lower classes', the physician can ignore such scruples and 'the administration of a hypodermic dose of hyoscyamin is frequently most beneficial'.[23] In purporting to identify reactions to these types of drug, such as hallucinations and terror of the physician who administered them, that are specific to the educated sensibility, Craig conveniently overlooks the likelihood that these reactions are just as much present among working-class patients, with the crucial difference that in virtue of the cash nexus between doctor and upper-class patient, here they were a force to be taken note of. In the chronic and especially the lower-class cases, by contrast, the terror can conveniently be elided. Craig's description hints at a suppressed violence in the relationship between physician and working-class patient with which he actively, if unintentionally, colludes. The contrast between the classes derives not from the observation of 'real' variations in reactions to the drugs, but from a moral standpoint in which the reactions and scruples of one class of people are held to be significant and those of a second, and much larger, class can conveniently be ignored.

'TABLE D'HÔTE' WITH THE MEDICAL SUPERINTENDENT IN 1917

The fundamental divide in the asylum system between paupers and princes, with little in between, is grotesquely illustrated by advertisements for private asylums, pitched mostly at the upper or higher classes, with some concessions to the upper-middle. The keepers of these ostentatious establishments vied with each other over the range and refinement of the facilities that they were able to offer, even as the Great War was being prosecuted, and deranged servicemen from the battlefields were being ejected to pauper lunatic asylums.[24]

At Northwoods House, near Bristol, founded in 1833 'expressly for the treatment of the various forms of mental infirmity occurring in ladies and gentlemen of the upper and middle classes', the private gardens had been thrown open to the park with wide and extensive views of the surrounding country. Amusements of all kind were provided, such as horse and carriage exercise, concerts, golf, and a handsome and large billiards room, and suites of private apartments and separate attendants were available if required. Haydock Lodge in Lancashire made a special play of its exclusivity, telling how it was 'charmingly situated in a healthy and retired neighbourhood, standing in its own well-timbered park, with attached farm, garden, extensive vineries, conservatories etc'. Part of the house had 'recently been entirely reconstructed, forming a large Baronial Hall, with adjoining Billiards and Smoking Rooms, and Lavatories fitted with all the latest Sanitary improvements – the whole affording greatly improved accommodation for gentlemen'. There were private apartments and special attendants for those desirous of more privacy, daily prayers for the disconsolate, carriages for patients to take their leisure, and for those whose appetite was still unsated ' "Table d'Hôte", presided over by the Medical Superintendent, his Assistant and the Ladies' Companion' was also provided.

The registered hospitals, such as the Bethlem Royal and Holloway Sanatorium, near Virginia Water, 'a registered hospital for the cure and care of the insane and of nervous invalids of the upper and middle classes', catered to a somewhat wider constituency, but at most of these establishments the availability of care was heavily dependent on the anticipation of a prompt cure. The Bethlem was especially forthright in delineating criteria of admissibility, declaring that 'patients of the educated classes, in a presumably curable condition, are alone eligible for admission and may be received either FREE in necessitous cases or on payment of a fixed inclusive rate of two guineas a week'. It dwelt also on the categories of ineligibles, notably 'those who have been insane more than twelve months and are considered by the Medical Superintendent to be incurable'.

There was also a smattering of notices from county and borough asylums eager to attract private custom. However, there was some understandable uncertainty among the asylum authorities as to how to make their pitch; by comparison with the elaborate advertisements from the private asylums and the registered hospitals they were minimalist in style, short on words and on puff, with little attempt to embellish or conceal the humdrum reality of what was being offered. Inevitably, they were largely appealing not to the conceit of those who could afford to entertain a leisured image of themselves (even a flight of fancy that in entering a country house asylum they were going up a gear in the quality of their lifestyle), but to the pragmatism of those (there was a war going on, after all) whose imagination at the thought of embarking on the potentially ruinous business of the institutional treatment of an insane family member was already quite numbed, and whose resources for maintaining their self-respect in such a delicate matter were snagged between a rock and a hard place.

The County Asylum, Chester, offering accommodation for 100 private patients, promoted itself only as having 'excellent picturesque grounds'; the Corporation Mental Hospital in Portsmouth simply stated that 'accommodation is provided for ladies and gentlemen in two detached villas at a charge from £1 11s 6d upwards, including all necessaries except clothing'; the authorities at Lancaster had invented a pastoral hideaway, 'a home for private patients in a detached villa', called The Retreat, but they rather fumbled over its relation to the host establishment, stating that it was 'in connection with the County Asylum at Lancaster, but apart from the pauper department; terms from 25/- per week without extras'; Cumberland and Westmoreland Asylum was perhaps more adroit, and even though 'considerable' may not have been far enough, still it was further than most could afford: 'there are two villas for private patients beautifully situated in the grounds but at a considerable distance from the main asylum'.

Though the division between the pauper and the private lunatic may have reflected accurately enough the basic class division of early Victorian society, still it had long been recognized that the system sucked into its maw individuals from a wide range of positions on the class spectrum. As the Commissioners in Lunacy openly acknowledged, 'except among the opulent classes any protracted attack of insanity, from the heavy expenses which its treatment entails, and the fatal interruption it causes to everything like active industry, seldom fails to reduce its immediate victims, and generally also their families with them, to poverty, and ultimately to pauperism'.[25] An individual might start out in one of the more luxurious private establishments and then, if he failed to respond promptly to treatment and the bills continued to roll in, find himself downgraded by his relatives.

In the first part of the nineteenth century, the evolving asylum system had not uncommonly provided for a mixed economy of care. At Gloucester and Stafford, for example, asylums were created jointly by the county and a charitable body to accommodate private, charitable and pauper patients in a judicious moral configuration, with the private patients housed in the more stately central part of the asylum building, the charitable patients to the sides, and the pauper lunatics out of sight in the wings.[26] From the mid-century onwards, however, partly in reaction to the enormous pressure on county asylums to accommodate ever-increasing numbers of pauper lunatics, and also because institutions which were subject to visitation by local magistrates were disliked by the upper classes, some of whom even resorted to sending their insane relatives abroad in order to shun publicity, the two categories of private and pauper lunatics were assiduously separated and segregated in distinct institutions.[27]

Entranced by claims of emancipating as well as humanizing the mad, the mental health reforms of the early nineteenth century were supported by Chartists as much as by Tory traditionalists and aristocratic philanthropists, heralding a golden age of asylum building.[28] By the 1870s, however, there was scarcely a vestige of this pioneering enthusiasm in the stuporous condition of British asylums. According to the Commissioners in Lunacy, the recovery rate was no higher in the decade leading up to the Great War than it had been in the 1870s, and in 1914 the medical superintendent of one of the London asylums claimed that 'patients in asylums may be roughly divided into two distinct groups, namely those who have a prospect of recovery, forming about 10 per cent, and the hopeless chronic cases who make up the remaining 90 per cent'.[29] Admittedly, some public asylums did provide limited facilities for private patients, sometimes offering improved accommodation and superior meals, together with the privilege of permitting the lunatic to wear his or her private clothes, but this lean menu of personalized options made little or no difference to the treatment that was being offered, or to the chances of recovery, and were mostly merely a rather expensive licence to become a hopeless case wearing your own suit.[30]

The early twentieth-century British lunatic asylum may not have been exclusively a storehouse of incurables, but it was widely perceived as such, and this was no mere popular fancy, for that is just how it was depicted by authoritative voices in parliament as much as in psychiatry. Inflexibilities in the regulation of the poor and incapacitated were mirrored in the increasing inflexibility of psychiatric perceptions and judgments. Confronted by this 'motley crowd of persons of weak minds or low spirits', psychiatry spawned a condemnatory rhetoric masquerading as science.[31] The mental patient was confined not only physically, but equally bonded to a negative outlook in which mental illness was an expression of moral turpitude.[32]

THE NEW LUNACY PROTEST
The outbreak of the war, and the enlistment of a citizens' army, thus brought to a head animosities that had long been simmering. Lunatic asylums soon became more visible as the site for war hospitals, and the displacement of mental patients to make way for wounded soldiers was an accurate enough

image of their secondary social status, and a reminder of the fate that was likely to befall a serviceman who had the misfortune to become mentally ill. The military effort required co-operation and bonding, all citizens pulling together; the existing mental health provision reflected division: privileged arrangements for the minority who could afford them, a stigmatized system for the majority.

Even under the unpropitious circumstances of war, the families of titled lunatics whose routines had been disrupted were able to pull rank and secure assistance from high places. Sir John Molesworth Staples, who was alleged to be a homicidal maniac, had for several years been confined in a lunatic asylum in Belgium under the care of Frère Leonard and the Alexien Brothers. His brother, a certain R. Ponsonby Staples, took umbrage in the opening months of 1915, dispatching heated telegrams, when his efforts to have his brother removed from occupied Belgium to an asylum in the Netherlands were frustrated amidst allegations of unpaid laundry bills ('monstrous that Belgian priest's cupidity obstructs journey'). Amidst rather more pressing concerns, Sir Edward Grey, the Foreign Secretary, was obliged to intercede and affect an interest in Sir John's predicament. After some terse exchanges, the passage was cleared for his removal and the Foreign Office was finally informed in September 1915 that Sir John, who in actuality was not dangerous at all, taking no notice of anyone and talking perpetually to himself, and his retinue had arrived at the Meerenberg Asylum at Bloemendaal in the Netherlands. Here he was now installed as a First Class Lunatic, a designation that, in an era in which class distinctions prevailed in every sphere of life, was used quite without irony to mean a madman with means who could expect to enjoy a superior lifestyle for the duration of his sojourn as a lunatic.[33]

There had, of course, been a long history of rage against the errant ways of 'mad doctors', but the lunacy protests of the Victorian era had taken as their target the problem of wrongful confinement, concentrating almost exclusively on allegedly sane representatives of the upper classes who had mistakenly been detained in private lunatic asylums, and they did not have the public asylums and the vast majority of the population of the mentally ill within their sights at all.[34] However, the circumstances of the opening jousts of the Great War, in which it was reported that mentally distressed patriotic volunteers from the citizens' army were being dispatched to asylums, provided the seeding ground for a new form of lunacy protest that cast its net much wider to include the whole community of serving citizen soldiers.

This was the spark that provoked a vigorous and determined counter-reaction, fuelled by expectations and demands for social justice for servicemen, and in particular the right to health care, that were a product of a fitful but still palpable process of democratization in British society that had been under way in the decades leading up to the war.[35] A politics primarily concerned with the 'larceny of liberties', in Roy Porter's memorable phrase, was starting to be supplanted by a politics of equal dignity and recognition, and of positive rights.[36] It was not so much a question of the wrongful confinement of the sane, as of the wrongful confinement of the recoverable in categories and institutions dedicated to the 'incurable', a process which, at the very least, degraded their life-chances by association. And what was especially reprehensible was that those with limited means were vastly more likely to find themselves on the wrong side of this line.

At the outbreak of the war, little or no preparation had been made for a large influx of mental cases, the authorities blithely assuming that they could continue to dispose of the mentally unstable in the contemptuous manner to which they had been accustomed. At a very early stage, even before there had been a significant inflow of mental casualties from the theatres of war overseas, the military authorities discovered, much to their consternation, that they were going to have to overhaul their customary procedures for dealing with soldiers who were suspected of insanity. In the prevailing military culture, a soldier with nervous problems was either a lunatic destined for the madhouse or a malingerer. The lunatic asylum was a convenient sump for human rubbish. There was, of course, nothing peculiar about this attitude, since before the First World War soldiers were a highly stigmatized social group. If the Army was the dustbin of the nation, the lunatic asylum was perhaps its natural complement. The Army had a small unit for mental cases, a villa surrounded by tennis courts, in the grounds of the Royal Victoria Military Hospital at Netley, which catered for 125 men and a sprinkling of officers, mostly soldiers who had served at least ten years in the Regular Army. For many years now, the annual admission rate had averaged around 120.[37] The scale of the establishment testified to the ease with which the Army believed it could deal with the problem of mental disorder. All other cases were discharged under the King's Regulations and dispatched to public asylums, where they were made chargeable to the parish, just like any other pauper lunatic.[38]

Though the number of soldiers dispatched to public asylums by the end of 1914, some of them from D Block, Netley, others direct from their own units, was relatively slight, not more than 500 in all, it was sufficient to cause a public outcry.[39] It is certainly remarkable how early on in the development of the war these demands were made, and how strong the class alliance that had already developed around them. Even on a very generous interpretation, it would be difficult to make out a case for a significant proportion of these early psychiatric casualties as victims of war trauma, for many of them seemed to conform to the stereotype of the 'undeserving poor' or the 'residuum', and in that respect to typify the recruits to the old rather than the new Army. Yet it is noteworthy that in the popular opprobrium for the military recourse to the public asylum, the segregative intensity that had distinguished between the 'deserving' and 'undeserving' had to a large extent been dissipated.

Just as popular protesters in the years leading up to the war had mixed old and new approaches to poverty, insisting on their own virtue while attacking 'moral' explanations of unemployment, deploying not a rhetoric of class but one of citizenship, so by dint of their membership of the community of national struggle all citizen soldiers without discrimination were seen as meriting the responsibilities and obligations of the state.[40] The military authorities, much to their surprise and irritation, discovered that they were violating the principles and expectations of recruits to a citizens' army, and those of their friends and relatives, as to the standard of mental health care they should be receiving. But if this reflected a failure of imagination, and want of scruple in the military authorities, it also reflected the incapacity of many of the existing civil health institutions, rooted as they were in a class-divided society, to deliver the kind of social compact that a citizens' army – an alliance of forces from across the social spectrum – necessarily required.

Towards the end of 1914, debates in Parliament about the obligations of the state for the 'health of our soldiers' were becoming increasingly vociferous. By the spring of 1915, there were reiterated demands for soldiers who had become insane to be spared the fate of disposal as pauper lunatics, and instead be assisted by the Red Cross and made eligible for pensions as disabled soldiers.[41] Suspicions were by this time rife that 'men who have come back from the front and whose nerves have been seriously shattered, and whose mental balance has been temporarily upset' were being sloughed off, and deprived of the restorative enthusiasm that was available to other classes of disability.[42] The Under-Secretary of War admitted to the House that 'about seventeen' soldiers had been put into asylums by mistake, but it became apparent that a far greater number had been removed to asylums by design.[43] By no means were the mentally afflicted a minor category of disability:

There are a great many such. It is of very great importance that those cases should be dealt with at the earliest possible moment, not by means of asylum treatment or associating them with those who are insane – or indeed, treatment of any kind under the present lunacy administration – but that they should be treated as quite distinct cases; cases in which a period of rest may result in the restoration of their health; cases in which there may be the possibility of the best form of treatment in private homes or hospitals, distinct altogether from lunatic asylums.[44]

Analogies were drawn with the obligations of employers enshrined in the Workmen's Compensation Act under which an employer, having taken an individual into his employ, could no longer attribute the cause of an accident to the worker's unfitness for his occupation. Moreover, so it was argued, if an employer could plausibly venture some doubts about his own powers of judgment, this was not a credible maneouvre for the warfare state, since before being taken out of civil life into the army the recruit had to pass through a medical gatepost and be passed fit by medical experts. That, at any rate, was the contention.[45]

THE CREATION OF THE WAR MENTAL HOSPITALS

If there was a model to which not only members of Parliament but a much wider public were attracted, it was that of the hospitals founded by Lord Knutsford. Word had got out as early as the autumn of 1914 that Lord Knutsford, hospital reformer and philanthropist, was founding a series of hospitals for officers with nervous or mental problems to spare them the indignity of certification. The first of these was opened in January 1915 at Palace Green, Kensington, with space for 33 patients accommodated in separate rooms.[46] Lord Knutsford extolled its virtues:

> The house is quiet, 'detached', overlooking Kensington Palace, with a small garden of its own. It could not be better. . . . The Hospital is to be called 'The Special Hospital for Officers' as we are anxious not unnecessarily to emphasise to its inmates that they are suffering from shock or nervous breakdown. . . . It was opened yesterday and the Matron will be glad to show anyone over it is who is interested in this work, especially if they feel like subscribing, even an armchair.[47]

It is no exaggeration to say that, almost from their inception, the Knutsford Hospitals caught the public imagination, establishing a new benchmark for progressive mental health care, with an emphasis on smallness of scale and on individualized treatment, in which the number 30 was the cut-off beyond which a house became an impersonal institution. It would be fanciful to suppose that such a model could readily have been transposed across the social divide, but the lore of the Knutsford Hospitals was to enter into the critical demands of advocates of mentally disabled ex-servicemen over the next years. They were later to bait government to live up to their promises to the war disabled by establishing a network of large houses, capable of accommodating not more than 30 soldier mental patients, right across the country, a kind of Knutsford network of therapeutic communities for the rank and file. Put into a nutshell, the demand of the new lunacy protest was that the government should do a Knutsford for the soldiering masses. And, as we shall see later, if they were going to have the officer's treatment facilities, they might as well have a share in his diagnosis as well.

In the meantime, the concerns over the treatment of mentally disturbed servicemen were being placed squarely on the agenda in other quarters. The Select Committee which had been established under the chairmanship of Sir George Murray (and included W. H. Beveridge among its members) to report on the provision of employment for soldiers and sailors disabled in the war marked a firm break with the disdainful and negligent treatment of disabled servicemen by the Army in the past by underscoring the responsibilities of the state. Moreover, it insisted that the liability of the state could not adequately be discharged simply by awarding a pension, for it had a duty: '. . . to see that the disabled man shall be, as far as possible, restored to health, and that assistance shall be forthcoming to enable him to earn his living in the occupation best suited to his circumstances and physical condition'. And it is very striking that already in the early months of 1915, the Murray Committee delivered a strong recommendation for alternatives to the lunatic asylum for 'those who are mentally affected'. 'In many instances', they averred, 'confinement in a lunatic asylum might not be the most suitable means of promoting the recovery of the patient and would certainly prejudice him on his return to civil employment'. Though 'some of these men might, on a strict view of their mental condition at the moment, be certified as being fit cases for detention in a lunatic asylum', it is highly desirable that this drastic 'course should only be taken after a suitable interval has been allowed for recovery'.[48]

And very early on, the military authorities were obliged to capitulate. Aldren Turner, the principal psychiatric adviser to the Army Council, tellingly described how even before the end of 1914 it was thought 'desirable to provide an institution to which mental cases might be sent from D Block in order to obviate their transference to public asylums – a policy which was adopted in view of the special circumstances attending the cause of the disorders'.[49] The prototype war mental hospital was Moss Side at Maghull, near Liverpool, which had been built upon the villa pattern and hence was admirably suited to its new therapeutic and rehabilitative purpose, and was handed over to the military authorities by the Board of Control in December.[50] By this time, beds for wounded soldiers were at a premium, and towards the end of January

1915 the Board of Control, which presided over the administration of all the county and borough lunatic asylums in England and Wales, was approached by the Army Council with an urgent request for assistance in making available at least 50,000 additional beds. Thus was brought into being the Asylum War Hospitals Scheme, which had for its original object 'the securing of surgical and medical treatment of the most modern and efficacious character for a large number of the soldiers wounded or stricken with physical disease during the Great War'. Extraordinary though it may seem, there had orignally been no intention of making provision in the war hospitals for servicemen suffering from mental or nervous breakdown, but even as the scheme was being hatched this resolve was put under pressure, and in February 1915 the Board of Control started negotiations to take over parts of Wandsworth and Napsbury asylums for mental cases.[51]

This was just the beginning of an ever-widening net of specialized provision in which, as Stanford Read, the wartime commander of D Block Netley, described in a memoir published shortly after the war, selected civil lunatic asylums were one after another converted into War Mental Hospitals. In every case, all reference to lunacy or asylums was resolutely excised. In some instances the whole asylum was taken over, in others the facilities were shared with general medical and surgical cases. The War Mental Hospitals included: Napsbury (350 beds); Lord Derby's War Hospital, Warrington (1000 beds); Welsh Metropolitan War Hospital, Cardiff (450 beds); Dykebar War Hospital, Paisley (500 beds); Auxiliary War Hospital, Crookston (350 beds); Murthly War Hospital, Perthshire (380 beds); Northumberland War Hospital, Newcastle (100 beds); and Notts County War Hospital, Nottingham (540 beds). Irish mental cases were also provided for at the Belfast War Hospital (500 beds) and Dublin War Hospital (300 beds). By 1918 there were 4470 beds available in the British Isles for mental cases, roughly one-seventh of the total accommodation in the war hospital scheme assembled by the Board of Control.[52]

In the spring of 1915 the military authorities agreed that 'all cases of mental disorder shall be retained in a military hospital until after the War'.[53] Though there were some who still doubted whether alternatives to the lunacy system could reliably be provided under the auspices of the War Office, tending to see in military hospitals, particularly if they were located on former asylum premises, only lunacy doctors in military disguise, the government's announcements succeeded in quieting some of its critics. During the same period, the proposals for a Mental Treatment Bill, which would have permitted soldiers to receive treatment in civil asylums without recourse to certification, was withdrawn when it became apparent that the same object could be secured without the need for legislation. Though the authorities were to slide away from the commitment they had made almost as soon as it had been uttered, and were eventually to renege on it entirely, there can be no doubt that this was a watershed moment. The military authorities were now on the defensive. The asylum reflex was no longer available to them in the manner to which they had been accustomed. 'At an early stage it was thought to be *judicious and equitable*', Read wrote in a revealing turn of phrase, 'not to send the cases to ordinary civil asylums but to equip special War Mental Hospitals where all army psychotic cases should eventually be housed and treated'.[54]

Though neither Aldren Turner nor Stanford Read could quite bring themselves to say so, it was in fact public pressure to keep mentally disturbed servicemen out of the asylums that produced this spectrum of alternatives. Left to their own devices, there is every reason to suppose that the military authorities would continue to have dealt with army psychotic cases in the manner to which they had long been habituated. Much more was entailed here than the simple loss of a facility. The irony is that, in addition to organizing manpower to fight a war, the military authorities were being drawn into another agenda: they were having to compensate for the inadequacies of the existing civilian mental health system. Public opinion was demanding mental health facilities for soldiers commensurate with their status as citizens, a kind of Knutsford system for the other ranks, and the military authorities were obliged to provide them, even if there was no direct military advantage in doing so.

Chapter 2

'D WARD (IMBECILE)'

Netley Lunatic Asylum had opened in 1870, to all appearances a solid
suburban residence or, as Philip Hoare nicely styles it, 'an enlarged version of
an archdeacon's country villa', surrounded by tennis courts, set in the grounds
of the sprawling extravaganza that was the Royal Victoria Military Hospital
at Netley.[1] An extension had been built in 1908, accommodating a long communal ward, but it had not to any significant extent compromised the intimacy of the establishment which had only 124 beds, three of them for officers.
Known by the spare title of D Block, it had for some time been the exclusive
military treatment centre for cases of mental disorder, complementing the
Royal Naval Lunatic Asylum at Great Yarmouth, and was by and large a
placid backwater with little more than 100 admissions in the year before the
Great War.[2]

There has been some confusion about the role of D Block in the Great
War; it has been projected, along with the Neurological Section in the Royal
Victoria Hospital, which was formed early on in the war to treat more
promising cases, as being in the vanguard of a modernizing psychiatric
movement, providing new therapies for countless shell-shocked servicemen.[3]
Far from this being the case, it is not an exaggeration to say that, unlike
its therapeutic sister unit, D Block, as represented by the attitude of the
medical officers to their charges, remained strictly old Army, class-bound and
hierarchical, resolutely implanted in the era of funk and moral depravity,
disclaiming any affinity with the emerging paradigms of psychological
understanding, at least as they applied to the ordinary rank and file. Of the
12,320 overseas cases who passed through D Block between 1914 and 1919,
only 331 were officers, since most of the officers who came to Netley were
sent to the grand-sounding Welsh Hospital, actually a hutment in the grounds
of the main hospital, as Wilfred Owen, who was there in 1917, described in
a postcard to his mother.[4]

Though Stanford Read, the commander of D Block, had psychotherapeutic pretensions, they were not shared by the medical officers who interviewed
the vast majority of the thousands of servicemen passing through the unit,
and compiled the reports about them. In any case, D Block offered no

The palatial exterior of the Royal Victoria Military Hospital at Netley, viewed from Southampton Water. D Block, or the Military Lunatic Asylum, is nestled in the trees on the right, like a gamekeeper's cottage.

opportunity for the application of therapeutic skills, for the simple reason that it was not a therapeutic facility and made no claims to be. As the clearing station for all cases of psychosis returned to Britain from the expeditionary forces during the Great War, such were the numbers that passed through its doors, arriving in waves and moving on in batches, that the average stay was only five or six days. There was just time enough for the medical officers to interview the incoming patients, make decisions about them, and complete the arrangements for the next stage of their psychiatric journey, with no scope for more individual attention.

By contrast with the placidity of the pre-war years, pandemonium must have descended on this genteel establishment in 1914, yet in the annual reports of the Board of Control it was, revealingly, always represented as being considerably less than overflowing. Enormous though the throughput was during the war years – close to 4000 in 1918, for example – the admissions came in irregular rushes, periods of intense activity followed by days or even weeks of relative calm. By coincidence or design, the commissioners of the Board always contrived to conduct their visits during one of these periods of lull, when the establishment was well below capacity. When they called in October 1915, there were 71 inmates, of whom eight were foreign invalids and five

German prisoners of war, 'all of them, of course, having the same care and treatment as our own men'; in April 1916 there were 78 men and five officers in the house; incredibly, in 1918 there were only 39 patients under care; and in 1919 it was down to 21.

It is, perhaps, not entirely accidental that there do not appear to be any surviving photographs of D Block in operation during the Great War. One cannot fail to be struck by this contrast between the knowledge of the vast shipments of disturbed men, these crowds of suffering soldiers, and the image that the authorities contrived to present of a quiet country house with just a few residents at any one time, though of course with other beds always available in readiness lest any unexpected guests should decide to show up. The whole intent of the D Block regime was to see these renewed intakes, surges from overseas repeatedly bursting upon them, on their way as quickly as possible and not permit them to disturb unduly the tranquillity of the setting. The message to be conveyed was that after all nothing had really changed, the old guard was still in control. If there is a visual image to express this disconcerting reality, it is that of a composed and unruffled group portrait from which the throng of uninvited house guests, vulgar, emotional and overexcited, have all been skilfully airbrushed out.

Though it mistakes the name of the establishment, the reaction of Lance Corporal Ernest Morris's father, a former NCO with 30 years' service, on learning that his son had been received into the D Block fraternity, surely represents with poignant accuracy the meaning that it held within the military culture. This is the anguish of an old soldier schooled in the traditional outlook trying to reconcile his professional allegiance with his desire to salvage some self-respect for his son. He had been 'painfully surprised', he disclosed in a letter addressed to the commanding officer in January 1916, to find his son an 'inmate of D Ward (Imbecile) Netley Hospital'. Knowing from long experience that 'many men often adopt a subterfuge to get discharged from the Army', during his visit to the ward last Thursday he had questioned his son very closely 'to try and arrive at some solution concerning his present state of mind'. Finding that his mind was 'more or less a blank from the commencement of the New Year', he had concluded that his son had experienced 'a lapse of memory which will return after a rest' and came away 'thoroughly convinced that it is not in any way a plot on his part to get away from his duty in the firing line'.[5]

Not that the medical officers would have had such scruples. While there is no evidence that the inmates of D Block were in any way maltreated, it is also obvious that the human regard they received was at best perfunctory. It is as though the institution was bent upon putting over the message that the treatment they were being given was not what they deserved but a concession, an expression of weakness reluctantly conceded by the authorities, who left to themselves would have followed the traditional Army wisdom which held that if a man let his comrades down, he deserved to be shot, and if he was a 'looney' then 'so much the better'.[6] Though sometimes there is a narrative of origins, or of personal circumstances, that tries to shine through the unyielding clouds of Netley's authorities, these are largely narcissistic dispatches in which the army doctor fusses over the shortcomings in the serviceman's soldierly demeanour, and the lapses in the respect which he believes should have been shown to him ('will not obey an order', 'has no manners', 'walks away when being questioned' etc). In striking contrast with some of the records from hospitals in the field, or from war mental hospitals in Britain, there is rarely any expression of compassion, no effort to explore or comprehend the soldier's service experience (the hardships he had suffered or the fortitude he had shown), as though his admission to the psychiatric facility was by definition sufficient testimony of how lamentably he had failed as a soldier. These are not records of treatments so much as snapshots at this way-station by harassed, perplexed and sometimes angry observers. If there was one intent that linked together the disparate interventions of the D Block regime, it was perhaps that of putting these renegades back in their place (morally, socially and ideologically), reasserting the norms that had been transgressed, censoring them equally for saying too little, or giving inadequate answers, and for saying too much, for being too humble and self-deprecating, but also for displaying unwarranted self-confidence and self-satisfaction, and for being insufficiently mindful of the shamefulness of their current predicament.

Sapper Middleton, from Redruth in Cornwall, had recently been mining in the firing line with the Royal Engineers, and even before that had apparently already been very fidgety and nervous since having witnessed four men killed in the cookhouse in which he was working around Christmas. The medical officer who interviewed him at No. 1 Casualty Clearing Station in February 1916 reported: 'he answered my questions fairly well, but had no idea of his number, although he tried several shots. He slept a good deal but was constantly muttering in his sleep . . . he seems irrational in his statements. A patient in the next bed informed me that Middleton was in the trenches for the first time the other day when a shell exploded and killed some men beside him'. When Lt Col. Charles Myers examined him two days later he thought it probable that he was a case of shell shock, and later that week he requested that he be transferred to the Neurological Ward at the Royal Victoria Hospital Netley, with the diagnosis 'NYD Mental'. However, when Middleton reached D Block in readiness for his transfer to the Neurological Section, Capt.

Clindening did not dwell on the traumatic circumstances that might have caused Middleton's reaction, remarking instead on his ignorance and nervous demeanour ('he does not know what he is afraid of, he is extremely nervous and apprehensive'), concluding: 'He is dull, plaintive and stupid. Speech thick'. Middleton's diagnosis was eventually revised from neurasthenia to melancholia and after an interval he was sent to a lunatic asylum. Even though Charles Myers may have thought that he was a suitable candidate for a 'talking treatment', there was another influential strand of medical opinion which held that an uneducated Cornishman such as this ('speech thick') was scarcely worth bothering with, and fit only for the madhouse.

Though it had little to offer from a therapeutic perspective, D Block Netley did, of course, have a crucial administrative function in channelling the distressed serviceman towards the next station on his psychiatric odyssey. Perhaps its most significant function, however, was a largely symbolic one in delivering a denunciation of these military failures, in which the most practical credential was not so much a capacity to care or to understand as a rich line in psychiatric sneers and insults. The psychiatric outposts in the field had been too busy controlling the transgression, providing crisis management and exercising damage limitation, to bother with such ceremonial niceties. This was the last frontier before the serviceman vanished into a hinterland in which, though many of the institutions might be under military control, nevertheless they were more likely to be subject to the influence of civilian norms and concerns. So here was the opportunity to put on record the disgrace to the service that the serviceman had incurred in displaying such mental weakness, and to make an authoritative statement about him as a shameful individual.

There were some, such as Private William Rogers, who was sent to hospital a week after arriving in France in June 1915 saying that he had already felt weak before embarking, being unable to sleep for 'funny feelings', who were manifestly, despite their best endeavours, not up to the rigours of the campaign. The authorities were often quite vituperative about them, blaming the boys for their inadequacies, insinuating that they could have pulled themselves together with a little more effort, even that they were malingering. Stupidity, in its various guises, was the most obvious target – though rarely an innocent one, for stupidity was either held to possess its own cunning (perhaps as the mask worn by the malingerer), or else to be itself an expression of a kind of class cunning, a subversive tactic peculiar to the lower orders calculated to run rings around the establishment. Of course, when a medical officer at D Block Netley berated a serviceman for being a suspected malingerer this was largely rhetorical, for it was by then mostly too late to close the disciplinary door. Nevertheless it revealed how some medical officers looked upon their charges, considering them unworthy of their ministrations, and seemingly quite unwilling or incapable of recognizing the lessons about poverty, education and ill health that were palpable in the bodies and souls of the miserable individuals before them.[7]

Private Edward Gee had been in France for only three weeks, and spent most of that time in No. 8 General Hospital in Le Havre, where he had been admitted with a history of 'mental obtuseness as not likely to become an efficient soldier'. He was illiterate and had apparently never been to school, but told of how he had been a labourer, milking the cows, 24 in the herd, on a farm in Leicestershire, earning 24 shillings a week, though he could not recall how long he had worked for his last master. Though he denied drinking before leaving for France, he admitted that the scars on his head originated from a fight when he was drunk, and that he had enlisted in the army because he was out of work. Having scuppered whatever patriotic pretensions Gee may have possessed, Capt. Clindening concluded that his replies were 'quite unsatisfactory' and that he was probably a malingerer.

No more did the Captain take to Private Fred Peatfield, a colliery workman from Yorkshire who lived with his mother, and was admitted to D Block in January 1916 from the Mediterranean Expeditionary Force, having been transferred from a military hospital in Cairo: 'He wears a heavy dull stupid bloated appearance, he is intensely stupid, does not know how long he has been in hospital, will not answer questions or give any account of himself. Gazes about stupidly. . . . Knows where he is, knows that he is barmy, says that he does not know his drill and has never done any work since joining the army. Appears to be malingering'. The following month the Captain became acquainted with Private John Hurley, who had been removed from the trenches in February 1916 after a tour of duty that had lasted only two hours (though he had already been nine months in the army), and was then examined by an eye specialist who had concluded that he was obviously defective. Returned to England bearing the label of an 'idiot', he reported to the Captain that he had been sent to D Block because he was short-sighted and had an undescended testicle (which was true). 'He presents the type of low-class defective. He squints. His features are asymmetrical. Has a stammer in his speech. Says he cannot drill. . . . Says he went up the first night to fight and tumbled into the water. He is intensely dull and stupid. His attitude and manner are not convincing. Much of this is put on'.

Private Martin O'Brien, a baker from Stafford, told of how he had lost his reason through shellfire and being blown up by mines, and had 'got a shell shock in the trench' which had made him 'go a bit light-headed'. He had not been sleeping well since due to hearing the noises of shells and guns.

Admitting that he had quite often been drunk (and had five times been a prisoner for drink), he insisted, rather unconvincingly no doubt, that he had only taken to drink since joining the Army, to drown his sorrows. O'Brien was just the kind of case who riled the military authorities because they were torn between conflicting and inconclusive views of him as a malingerer and as a terminal lunatic, and were never quite able to rid themselves of the unmistakable sense that they were being made fools of. The doctor at the 8th General Hospital at Rouen confessed himself stumped: 'This patient has been in one day, he is very melancholic and I cannot make up my mind whether he is refusing to answer questions or whether he has loss of memory'. However, he inclined towards the conclusion that his condition was 'one of Dementia and nothing can be made out of him'. At Netley, as Capt. Clindening begrudgingly acknowledged, O'Brien was able to give quite a rational account of his experiences in the trenches. So overcome was he by dislike of the patient, however, that he was unable to settle for a more modest and qualified assessment that might have enabled him to make more out of him, instead sizing him up as a 'dement', with all the venomous intensity that he was able to invest in this attribution: 'He does not know the day, date, month or year. He does not know where he is, but knows he was sent here for being barmy'.

'Does not know this place', 'he has not asked where he is', 'does not know what this place is', 'knows he was sent here for being barmy', 'knows he is in a mental hospital': to 'know where one was', properly to 'know this place', was to acknowledge the nature and extent of the moral, social and existential pit into which the inmate had fallen and to which his own lapses had surely contributed. The inmate who railed against his fate, and tried to stand upon his dignity, could expect a stern rebuke. Armoury Staff Sergeant Ernest Dyer, a mason from Chelmsford, had been overseas for almost two years when he was taken to No. 11 General Hospital periodically shouting 'Madeleine', but declining to reveal who she was, spitting on the floor to rid himself of the poison that the Germans had put into him, and complaining that he could smell foul odours all around him. Though he admitted that he had been through an illness, when he arrived at D Block Dyer felt quite well and could not understand why he was being detained. Protesting that he had no business to be there, Major Read considered him truculent and disrespectful.

THE ROADS FROM D BLOCK
The roads from D Block forked in the direction of a number of war mental hospitals such as Lord Derby in Warrington, Dykebar in Paisley, Murthly in Perthshire, Napsbury at St Albans, and Maghull in Liverpool. Ernest Mantle

was one of those who took the Maghull fork, having gone out to France in October 1914, serving with the Royal Sussex Regiment. After being under shellfire in the trenches, on the morning of 27 January 1915 he had a 'fit' before losing consciousness for a time, spending the rest of the day just sitting around, unable to fire his rifle, feeling pains in his head, and reporting sick in the evening. Questioned about this episode at Netley ten days later, Mantle promptly answered that he thought it was due to shock because his mate's head was blown off by a shell close to where he had been standing. Private Groves, who was in the same company, reported that in late January Mantle had travelled on the same train as him, and had spent much of the journey wandering up and down the train in an excited state, staring out of the window and telling people that C and D companies were 'cut up' (according to Groves, they had suffered losses but were not 'cut up') and that he was in the thick of it.

The RAMC doctor at Rouen discovered that Mantle was also 'cut up' emotionally, his wife having left him and gone off with another man, and felt 'cut out' of the action, not having been with a woman for eighteen months, though when he was first married about six years ago he had enjoyed sexual relations ('indulged', as Lt Courtenay Wallis pruriently put it) three or four times a day. He wandered about the ward listlessly, or sat quiet all day without speaking, appearing insane to the orderly, but by the time he was brought over to Netley on 7 February 1915 on the Hospital Ship *Asturias* ('patient quite quiet while on board') his mental condition seemed relatively normal, even though it emerged at this stage that a brother had been an inmate of a madhouse.

After a few days at D Block he was transferred to Maghull, Dr Ronald Rows remarking nonchalantly on how he appeared to have been 'markedly impressed and somewhat upset by the death of some of his friends'. He shortly became more cheerful, even if he seemed unable to give a very clear account of the event which followed his 'so-called fit', and after a few weeks the medical authorities succeeded in readying him for a return to light duty, though still suffering from marked tremors of the facial muscles and hands. A serviceman was doubtless fortunate to be made the object of an active therapeutic programme such as this, even though it could scarcely escape the tension famously identified by Freud. Aimed not so much at the patient's recovery as at restoring his fitness for service, a form of treatment delivered by a physician under military command was inevitably confused by 'the insoluble conflict between the claims of humanity, which normally carry decisive weight for a physician, and the demands of a national war'.[8]

Chapter 3

THE NAPSBURY CAST

THE LUNATIC ASYLUM INTO A WAR MENTAL HOSPITAL
Meanwhile, at the County of Middlesex Lunatic Asylum at Napsbury, near St Alban's, an inkling had been received as early as February that the War Office intended to claim some of the accommodation in the asylum for conversion into a military hospital – for 'wounded soldiers' so it was hoped. But at a meeting towards the end of March 1915, along with a report on the recent escape of patient William Strange in a snowstorm, a circular letter from the Home Office about what to do in the event of bombardment (hang out a flag), and an estimate for two hair bins and a rack in the upholsterer's shop, Dr Rolleston, the medical superintendent, announced to the asylum management committee that he now had definite information that the military authorities wanted to take over the admissions hospital and two adjoining villas. Not, after all, for 'wounded soldiers', stretcher cases cared for by fetching young VAD nurses, but to provide around 350 beds for 'cases of nervous breakdown or those who may develop symptoms of insanity', no officers, alas, only ordinary soldiers. This was circumspect wording to deflect from alarms about a clientele of out-and-out soldier lunatics, partly to mollify the committee, drawn from local dignitaries with a weighting towards aldermen and justices, but more especially because the intention of this experiment was to provide an alternative to the regular institutions and categories of insanity. Here was to be a place where, under military rather than civil law, the Army Act in place of the Lunacy Acts, a soldier could live through a period of crisis, even a bout of madness, without being turned into a trade lunatic. In the letter that followed, the Board of Control attempted to draw the committee into this progressive therapeutic compact, expressing the hope that 'a considerable proportion of these cases will be cured without the necessity of their being certified under the Lunacy Acts, an attainment that will command general sympathy'.[1]

From this point on, preparations for the war hospital continued apace: mattresses, bolsters, bedsteads, blankets and counterpanes were ordered, along with two billiard tables; a high partition fence with heavy wrought-iron gate bolts was erected to separate the war hospital from the main asylum (so that the recovering soldiers might be spared any association with ordinary mental cases); Dr Rolleston was given a temporary commission as a major in the RAMC, and his assistant Dr O'Neill as a captain; and, after some initial hesitancy, the War Office agreed also to confer military rank on the male attendants who would serve as orderlies in the war hospital, persuaded that, as well as being conducive towards discipline, this would also tend to the 'happiness of the Attendants themselves, whose uniforms when they are off duty will show that they are doing good service for their country'.[2]

In the middle of May, after the recreation hall had been taken over as a dormitory by female patients who had moved out of the villas, and as two mares from the asylum farm were being put to Sir William Church's horse, and the committee were eagerly hiking the price of their surplus potatoes, the Napsbury War Hospital opened for business with two patients in residence and 40 more expected shortly. The pace obviously quickened, for early the next month there were 70, including one German officer. Any lingering illusion that it was to be a kind of genteel convalescent home for sensitive nerve cases was quickly dispelled. Already in July Dr Rolleston sounded a note of apprehension before the committee about the seriously disturbed soldiers, angry and distraught, volatile emotional reactions in solid physical frames, who were arriving from the theatres of war, calling attention 'to the acute nature of many of the cases', and telling of how a soldier patient had attempted to stab an orderly, doubtless leading some of the members to express quiet gratitude for the surrounding palisade.[3]

Still, by this time they had matters of more moment to occupy their attention. By the middle of June, the rising tide of broken and diseased bodies and minds was threatening to overwhelm all the facilities that had so far been made available in Britain, and the War Office had now made known its 'urgent desire' to have the rest of the asylum emptied of insane patients and be placed at its disposal as a war hospital for sick and wounded soldiers. The mental section would, of course, continue in existence, but would now form part of a much larger war hospital to accommodate, in addition to the mental cases, around 1350 soldier patients. The evacuation of the host population was to be a gargantuan task, for there were around 1500 inmates at this date and, over the next year, the bulk of them were to be evacuated and dispersed over no fewer than 18 institutions across the English asylum landscape.[4] These were anxious times for regular asylum inmates, as a young female patient wrote to her husband: 'it is in the paper they are suggesting taking over this Asylum for the wounded soldiers and they are sending the patient to other Asylums but I would rather go to the Workhouse of anywhere than another Asylum'.[5]

With the compliance of the War Office, 80 'harmless lunatic patients' were to be retained as a workers to ensure that the agricultural and horticultural economy of the asylum, the extensive gardens and the asylum farm, covering more than 420 acres, together with the bakehouse and the other workshops – shoemakers, tailors and upholstery – continued to operate smoothly. The military authorities made it a condition, however, that this lunatic labour force was to reside in a detached building in a distant part of the grounds, entirely segregated from the new war hospital. To prepare for the new arrivals, considerable changes had to be made to the structure: the existing Napsbury asylum railway siding was extended to allow hospital trains to run part of the way into the grounds, with the erection of a new landing platform; and to make way for the construction of an operating theatre, the mental section was relocated in the main asylum building. However, the Board of Control was at pains to stress, lest anyone suspect that its status was insidiously being diminished, that the new section had been formed from some of the best wards in the asylum and that the patients would continue to enjoy 'their full share of the amenities of the institution, including its beautiful grounds'.[6]

The former medical superintendent was now the officer commanding the whole establishment, and the running of the mental section was largely placed in the hands of four medical officers, hardly a huge complement for a 350-bed unit. The most recent appointment was that of Captain Hubert Norman from 1 February 1916 at a salary of £1 per day, with a furnished apartment, board, washing and attendance.[7] In the meantime, the Board of Control was anxious to convince a sceptical public that the location of war hospitals in lunatic asylums was wholly fortuitous, and bore no connection with the ignominy of the pauper lunatic system, of which the segregated space for the burial of pauper lunatics was perhaps the most affecting symbol. Accordingly an instruction was issued that soldiers who had the misfortune to die in asylums temporarily adapted as war hospitals should under no circumstances 'be buried in that part of a local cemetery which has been specially set apart for insane patients dying in the asylum'.[8]

GEORGE AND HIS PARTY

George Major Gomm had the misfortune to arrive on 2 May 1916 in the midst of all this upheaval with the preparations still under way, and he was to be moved on again before the new war hospital was really in full swing. There were 24 admissions to the mental section on that day, the majority of then in their twenties, though one was over forty, volunteers who, like George, had served for a year or more, together with six regulars. There were also eight soldiers who had been in the army less than 12 months, mostly 'mental deficients', such as Douglas Piddock, George Helmore, and William Wood-house. Eleven of the group were eventually discharged from the army and sent home; eight were removed to asylums and three to other war hospitals; and two were given furlough in preparation for return to duty. This represented a fairly typical snapshot of the Napsbury intake at this stage of the war, though George seems to have drawn the short straw in being given just seven weeks at Napsbury. Even by the standards of 1916 this was a raw deal, and on average his companions stayed five months, with one who stayed for ten (a neurasthenic who was eventually sent home), and one more than a year (a case of delusional insanity, finally dispatched to an asylum).[9]

Also in George's party was a company quartermaster sergeant who had gone off his head, CQMS Frank Duffern of the 1st Gloucesters, a former labourer from Cheltenham. He had already served five years with the colours before being sent out to France in April 1915. After being shocked by a shell, he had become forgetful, wandering off from his company and worrying about his accounts. As a result he had taken to drinking rum, which had made him still more anxious, and he now believed there was a plot against him involving the company money. The last time Duffern disappeared, the medical officer of the 1st Gloucesters recounted, 'he burnt his acquittance rolls and left the accounts in a company in a state of chaos'. He now requested that Duffern be 'committed to an institution as soon as possible', the sort of drastic solution to what was potentially no more than a temporary emotional crisis (and so it turned out in this case) that medical officers were prone to demand in the early part of the war especially, before more progressive voices had started to exert a significant influence on policy. Of course, Napsbury War Hospital was scarcely the 'committal' to an institution that was being asked for, but later in the war Duffern would very likely have been treated in the field, and returned to duty in a considerably briefer interval than the four months it took him to recover at Napsbury, though it may be doubted whether he would really have been fit again for the stress of front-line duty.

At this early stage of the war also, a few individuals fetched up at Napsbury not so much because their conditions necessarily warranted it, rather because 'supervision for lunacy' provided a flag of convenience under which to lift a soldier out of the action whom the authorities believed to be as much troubled as troublesome. Some of these cases might otherwise very likely have been punished as defaulters, and perhaps even executed if the situation had spiralled out of control, as could have happened with the crisis that blew up around Gunner Braines in January 1916.[10] This was a military culture in which there was still considerable resistance among the authorities to acknowledging the legitimacy of a psychological stress reaction. To the extent that a rudimentary resting place existed between the competent, functioning soldier and the lunatic destined for the madhouse, it was only tolerated on sufferance and, in a case such as this where the disciplinary stakes had already been raised, was scarcely negotiable. In his concern that he be dealt with justly, Braines's sympathetic commanding officer requested that he be placed 'under supervision for lunacy', not because he genuinely considered him to be mad, but because the consquences of not doing so were too awful to contemplate, and there was no other acceptable form of language or recourse available to him. Ironically, it was Braines himself who demonstrated considerably more perspicacity than any of his superiors and finally succeeded in putting the record straight.

A regular soldier with 10 years' service, who had rejoined on mobilization with an exemplary character, Braines had served with aplomb for a year and been mentioned in dispatches after Neuve Chapelle. Somewhere towards the end of October, however, 'he began to wear a rather wild look and behave so as to draw attention to himself from a disciplinary point of view'. One day, he wandered off into the country 'more or less half-dressed' and was away for the day 'apparently quite irresponsible for his actions'. For refusing to obey orders, he had already been sentenced by Field General Courts Martial to 18 months' hard labour, and he had now provoked his superiors to adopt still sterner measures against him, most recently by his absconding from his unit and attempting to board a train bound for Boulogne, declaring that he had 'trouble at home'. In the light of his service record, the officer commanding his battery with the Royal Field Artillery was at considerable pains, dispatching numerous closely written urgent notes in pencil on tracing paper from his position in the front line, to solicit a medical intervention to what was on the brink of becoming an unstoppable process of official retribution. 'I do not therefore think it likely', he averred, 'that he is purposely misbehaving or feigning lunacy in order to escape service. . . . I think it is only fair to this man to place him under supervision for lunacy, as the only course open for me, if he remains in my unit, is to treat him as sane and punish him for every offence he commits but for which, I feel, he is not mentally responsible'. Braines has, he continues, 'been treated with every consideration and the NCOs have nursed him more than is really good for discipline. I do not think he is malingering'.

At the end of January 1916 Braines was examined by Lt Col. Charles Myers. Knowing the score, Myers was willing to fall in with the request from Braines's commanding officer, assessing that he was not sane and required a period of 'prolonged observation' to 'arrive at a definite diagnosis of the nature of his insanity'. Capt. Plummer of the 26th Field Ambulance, by contrast, was less taken with such diagnostic dither, observing 'fine fibrillary tremors of the tongue and of the eyelids, and a marked increase in knee-jerks', concluding that Braines was on a terminal decline, for 'the physical signs, although slight, together with the complete alteration in his conduct and behaviours, are very strongly suggestive of an early stage of GPI'.

So what was up with Benjamin Braines? It turned out that he was extremely angry with the authorities. Despite his entreaties, he had not been granted leave for a long time, and he was distressed that he had been prevented from visiting his sister whose baby was ill and had subsequently died. He was also aggrieved that despite his exemplary service record he had been passed over for promotion. On admission to D Block he wisely gave a candid, but low-key, account of his protest, saying that he was very depressed, suffering from shell shock, had been continually in action and had got worried about his family at home. His self-diagnosis quickly won official acceptance, for from this point on there was no further mention of GPI or fibrillary tremors or the nature of his insanity. After only three months at Napsbury, where he sheltered under the diagnostic portmanteau of neurasthenia, he was discharged to furlough for return to duty. This was, of course, the first time in this saga that the term 'shell shock' had been evoked and, revealingly, it came not from the medical authorities but from the serving soldier himself, confirming that it was already, as very likely it had always been, part of the vernacular on the Western Front, evidence enough of a rather more progressive outlook than the majority of medical officers had been able to come up with.

'WHY AM I WHAT YOU SAY THAT I AM?'

Among George's party there was a significant minority, fairly typical of the Napsbury population at this stage of the war especially, whom if we are so minded we can legitimately typecast as 'mental deficients', for from a considered standpoint in military efficiency that is indubitably what they were. They might also be taken as exemplifying a hysterical reaction, except that my intention here is not to abandon the hysteric in a zone of his or her own, but to show how a hysterical reaction may throw light on a collective experience of the human subject in a particular place and time. An insight into what may have been at stake for some of the servicemen who took part in the Great War may be gleaned from the account of the subject whose life is bound to a traditional authority, and to a symbolic order (what Lacan terms the 'big Other'), that has been produced by the Slovenian philosopher and cultural theorist Slavoj Žižek in his lively explication of the theories of Jacques Lacan.

Žižek humorously illustrates the predicament of the subject with an example from Hitchcock's film *North by Northwest*, in which the CIA has invented a fictitious agent called George Kaplan to put the Russians off the track, reserving rooms for him in hotels, issuing travel tickets, and requesting him on the phone. The hapless Roger Thornhill, an American of no special distinction, happens to be in the hotel lounge as a clerk enters asking for Mr Kaplan, announcing that there is a phone call for him. Just at that moment Thornhill catches the clerk's eye, since by coincidence he had been intending to send a telegram to his mother, and the Russians who are lurking in the background mistake him for Kaplan and kidnap him, treating all his disclaimers and professions of innocence as further evidence of his guile. The subject, Žižek explains, is always attached to a meaning or label – a signifier in Žižek's terminology – which represents him for the authority figure. As a result he is loaded with a mandate which positions him in a symbolic network. However, the mandate is ultimately always arbitrary, and so, when asked to explain why he possesses it, and why he is occupying this place in the symbolic network, he is unable to account for it. Instead, his answer can only be the hysterical question: 'Why am I what I'm supposed to be, why have I this mandate? Why am I [George Kaplan] [George Major Gomm]?' or: 'Why am I what you [the big other] are saying that I am?'.[11]

Psychoanalytic reflection on such fraught questioning had been stimulated in the rich soil of female hysteria, for it is most of all the female hysteric who so stunningly exemplifies, non-plussed, submissive and resistant all at the same time, the predicament of the subject in the sway of the big other. For, in the last resort, what is hysteria, asks Žižek, if not an expression of the inability of the subject to fulfil the expectation that the other holds of her, 'to assume fully and without restraint the symbolic mandate?'.[12] We can see this dialectic at work in military social relations, most obviously in the subordination of ordinary soldiers to military discipline and the rigours of service on the war front, but equally in the perplexity and consternation of medico-military authorities. From each side, from the soldier to the authorities, or from the authorities to the recalcitrant soldier, there is an enigma about the other's desire, prompting questions which none of the parties can answer to their satisfaction, each suspecting the other of being guided by hidden motives or bending the truth: 'what does this person *really* want?'. Fantasies of conspiracies, or bogus theoretical constructions, fill out the void and, by delivering the semblance of a definite answer, serve to placate the anxiety or anger that has been stirred up in the subject.

There are countless experiences that exemplify this arbitrary dimension in which, even if the subject may willingly have embraced the signifier which represents him for the other, as by volunteering for the cause, still it becomes apparent quite soon that there has been a misunderstanding, and that the subject's idea of who he is, and of what he has let himself in for, is quite at odds with the mandate that has been foisted upon him by the authorities. Even if they were not sending telegrams to their mothers when the call came, many of them were going about their local business (often enough in proximity to their mothers) when suddenly, like Roger Thornhill, they found themselves projected quite outside their normal range, and forced to account for themselves as someone whom they never realized that they were. Fired by heroic scenarios of military adventure, the volunteers of 1914 and 1915 were quite unprepared for what they encountered, so it is hardly surprising that we should encounter individuals who give the impression that they find themselves on the wrong bus or train, the bearer of an unwanted or uninvited identity, or the victim of some misunderstanding or a breakdown in communication.

Young George Helmore, who was also in George Gomm's party, and had served for 10 months, was to learn at first hand why people later came to talk about the Great War as a runaway vehicle or a horse that was riding its rider. He had been out to Boulogne on a Sunday school outing before the War, and was quite unprepared for a turn of events in which his memory of a genial excursion was replaced by a helter-skelter journey that shook him up from head to toe. And perhaps that is why, after seeing shells burst at Ypres and on other fronts, he tried in his own way to apply the brakes on the misadventure of this runaway excursion bus, attending sick parade for no apparent reason, treating communications from his superiors with the utmost perplexity, remaining behind the transport lines when the battalion went into the trenches, and telling the doctor early in 1916 that it was still 1914 and surely time for him to go home.

And home was where Harry Batchelor, who before the war had been earning £1 a week as mate to a motor-engine driver, also intended to take himself. He had only been in France a week, and never gone further than the depot, when he told Capt. Tredell, who accosted him after he was found wandering on the *quai* near the leave boat in Le Havre, that he did not like France because it was too far away, and wanted to return to Southampton. Capt. Tredell inevitably pondered whether Harry was a fool or a malingerer, but Harry from his standpoint was conducting himself as though he had options, and was in some measure author of his own destiny, and could put himself back on the track from which he had been rudely diverted. John Cronin, thirty-seven years old, a farm labourer from the west of Ireland, claimed that he had enlisted in the Royal Irish Fusiliers in April 1915 on the supposition that he would remain in Ireland but instead, to his astonishment, within a few weeks he found himself on his way to Gallipoli, landing at Suvla Bay on 1 September, and spending nine weeks on the Peninsula, under fire in the trenches for a good part of it, once being knocked out by concussion when shrapnel shells fell close to him. It was a mystery to him why he had been sent out at all since he could neither drill nor shoot, a judgment about his capabilities from which the military authorities did not entirely dissent, though they were more inclined to pin the blame for his deficiencies on his moral character. After contracting dysentery, he lay for two weeks in a tent before being moved to a hospital ship, after which he did a stay of duty in Salonika and Serbia, before returning to Egypt, from where he was finally brought home in January 1916. By the time he reached Napsbury he had clearly had enough of these picaresque adventures, for he ate ravenously, talked mostly about food, and cried plaintively, announcing that he had never been away from home before and wanted to return to his mother.

Then there are cases that fully exemplify just that inability to comprehend and explain the mandate with which they have been loaded that Žižek instances, where the subject is alternately resistant, petrified and confused. One such was Arthur Archer, serving with the 3rd Hussars, whose stay at Napsbury overlapped with George, and who after 16 months in France as a twenty-three year old volunteer had written a number of letters to his mother from the front at the end of 1915 complaining of how 'neglected they all were'. After a spell in hospital with stomach trouble in January, he was given 10 days' leave at home, but tore up his uniform the day after he returned because 'he lost his temper at the thoughts [sic] of how he had been treated since he had been in the Army'. Promptly removed to the 1st London General Hospital, he sat about on the ward reiterating 'I don't understand!' thirty or forty times a day, becoming very agitated and destructive and having to be placed in the padded cell. At Napsbury early the next month he seemed at first to be more settled, but shortly he again became emotional, unable to control himself, bursting into tears and declaring that 'he was to be shot as in an action he could not stand it any longer and did not advance when he should have done so'.

By no means was it only the mad soldiers who were nearing the end of their tether. In a military hospital in France in November 1915, Private Arthur Arnold was very nervous, trembling a great deal, apparently in fear of something, for the only words he had uttered since admission were 'don't hurt me, Sir!' He was ravenously hungry all the time and kept pointing to his mouth. Ten days later he was no better, crawling about under the bed and playing with the springs. 'Persists in not knowing anything of himself. Will not answer questions or give an account of himself. Emotional. Says he does not know his country. He goes through a pantomimic action to show what work he did in civil life. Gait spastic and dragging'. Could Arnold be malingering, or was he suffering from dementia, or was there some other explanation? 'Major Meyers [sic] and the MO in charge thought it was a case of malingering but are now convinced it is a case of Dementia'. Arthur had apparently 'changed his attitudes and disposition several times', but he was not the only one to do so, and he was one of a whole class of servicemen who had confounded the ability of the attendant medics to comprehend what was going on with them and make an appropriate response. Traditional expectations of manliness and moral fibre were deflated by scores of unsettling displays in which a soldier burst into tears when questioned, or threw himself on the floor before the doctor, declaring that he wanted to do his duty by killing himself. Brought to account by their superiors, some medical officers found themselves behaving strangely like Arnold himself, unable to answer questions, their narratives in a state of deshabille. Often in the reports that were written about these servicemen at one of the stations of the cross on their procession from the battlefield to a military hospital in Blighty, we can sense the tension, the barely suppressed fury, the impotence of the authorities in the face of these scoffers, shakers and weepers: 'Very nervous, trembles and shakes when subjected to any excitement, he is morose and sullen. . . . Quite incapable of doing any military duty. . . . While he is not insane, he is useless as a soldier'.

MILITARY MISFITS

Though the authorities in the field determined that some of these soldiers were 'mentally deficient', mental deficiency was frequently simply a suitable flag of convenience under which to manage the equivocal patriotism of a group of servicemen, artisans and clerks, along with the unskilled, who, feeling the weight of the call, were impelled to the action and if discharged from the services would explore every avenue to find their way back in again. Yet when they arrived on the scene they invariably proved themselves very resistant to discipline, perplexed and uncomprehending at what was being asked of them, flouting the regulations at every turn, and behaving as though the situation in which they found themselves was not at all to their liking. Equivocation on this scale was, of course, by no means typical, but to a degree these reactions were merely an exaggeration of the outlook of the vast majority of ordinary rankers, volunteers as much as conscripts, in Britain's citizens' army, who would always remain citizens in uniform, unwilling to relinquish entirely their citizen selves and their prized individualities, or to become fully absorbed into the military machine; they might be deferential up to a point, but at a distance, drawing on a long tradition of mockery and ironic disdain for the pretensions of the governing class.[13]

Wilfred Francis, a tailor from Castle Cary, was considered to have 'gone wrong mentally', but there is a hint that he might also having been poking fun at the situation, offering perhaps a parody of artistocratic languor, for when questioned 'he gazed in a vacant way round the room, continually yawned, stretched himself, and saluted in a foolish manner'. Formerly a sea-faring man who had become a wanderer without fixed abode, Henry Brady had joined the Labour Battalion as a volunteer in 1915 and been employed digging trenches in France. Evidently, the regularity of his duties did not suit him, for in December the medical officer reported that Brady had several times 'unreasonably refused to obey orders, to fall in, go to work etc, giving foolish excuses that it was a wet day, that he didn't wish to go etc'. Robert Borland, a twenty-three year old clerk from Ealing, had enlisted around September 1914 and been evacuated from France in August 1915, only to return in a later draft just before Christmas, much to the chagrin of his superiors, who discovered that even after a long stint of Field Punishment No.1 he still remained indifferent to every role expectation that was laid before him, uri-nating on parade without falling out, continually refusing orders, reporting sick and saying nothing, and wandering about aimlessly, taking no interest in anything.

In the portrait gallery of the 'inefficient' soldier there were countless tragi-comic vignettes such as Pte Edgar Harper, a blacksmith from Camden Town, who was taken to hospital in Egypt from the Dardanelles with a record of being a bad drill, quite unable to slope arms, of having insulted a medical officer on being reprimanded for failing to wear boots, and of having shot at a major. At Napsbury in July 1916 he hotly denied that he ever shot at an officer, claiming that he would 'do himself in' rather than commit such a crime. Some cases seemed to enact a parody of the military recruitment system that even a dedicated scriptwriter could not have improved upon. Quartermaster Sergeant Ernest Webster was deemed to be 'hopelessly inefficient': 'He has no idea of office routine, cannot keep a correspondence register or even make out a ration indent or equipment indent correctly. He is nearly 47 years of age, short sighted, deaf, nervous and suffers from loss of memory. He is also utterly devoid of tact when dealing with subordinates'. His commanding officer could not recommend his demotion to a lower rank since he was quite unemployable in *any* grade.

There were some, of course, who should never have been embarked for the front line at all, and were quite worn out even before they started. It was obvious to Mrs Edwards that her son, who had been invalided from India in

1909 suffering from malaria, was not physically fit even for garrison duty when he enlisted again in November 1915, but a mother's entreaties were, of course, wholly nugatory and he was sent out regardless. When Edward Edwards reached Napsbury in the middle of June 1916, he was so exhausted after the journey from Netley that he could not stand without assistance, and was put to bed immediately and given brandy, his clothes saturated with urine. 'Unable to speak, mutters occasionally, eyes sunken, looked scared and was fidgety and resistive'. A month later the final note read: 'He has been slowly sinking from exhaustion for the past week, rallying from time to time, and died today'.

Then there were those who were brought down by just being in the military environment or on the margins of the action, like George Gazeley, a thirty-two year old boot repairer and early conscript who during the first few months of his service on home duty had several times reported sick with pains in his head. As the doctors apparently took no notice, he decided to take himself home without leave, for which he was court-martialled and sent to Wandsworth Prison for a month before being removed to hospital. At Napsbury, where the doctor ascertained that he had been considered delicate as a child, always shy and of a nervous temperament, remarking on his narrow head and facial appearance suggesting degeneracy, knee jerks normal but fingers tremulous when hands extended, he was depressed and miserable, making attempts to strangle himself and to push objects down his throat.

GENERAL PARALYTICS

That fellow I was with in the Ship last night, said Buck Mulligan, says you have g.p.i. He's up in Dottyville with Conolly Norman. General paralysis of the insane.

James Joyce, *Ulysses*[14]

Among all the transients who passed through the war hospital, undoubtedly the saddest were the GPI cases, or general paralytics as they were also known, whose genital afflictions had now gone to their heads. Under the stress of war, long-forgotten sybaritic misadventures were exacting their grim and relentless toll, for although it was discovered in 1917 that mosquitoes infected with malaria could cure General Paralysis of the Insane, malarial treatments were not widely available until some years after the war. In this era, once it became symptomatic the condition was invariably fatal, the patient not infrequently suffering a painful and protracted death.[15] Among its other functions, Napsbury also served as an administrative conduit for soldiers destined for county and borough lunatic asylums in order to die. The brief respite at Napsbury provided an interval in which not only to confirm the diagnosis, but in the later stages of the war also to put in place the arrangement whereby the soldier could be classified as a Service Patient, his maintenance paid for by the Ministry of Pensions, and thus spared the ignominy of a death as a pauper lunatic.

Having started to behave peculiarly while on leave, Private Arthur Smith was admitted from his home at the request of his wife and subsequently removed to Kent County Asylum. Though he had apparently 'denied venereal' to the authorities, it is hardly surprising that his wife refused to stand by him, for she disclosed that their last child was born soon after her husband was admitted to Woolwich Hospital for venereal disease nine years previously and had always been unhealthy, constantly breaking out into symptoms. A regular soldier from Abergavenny with a continuous service record of 24 years, including 17 months in the trenches without respite since November 1914, Sergeant George Lewis arrived at Netley in April 1916 with a diagnosis of confusional insanity. He claimed that he had been married a fortnight before to a Miss Frances Craven from Shrewsbury, to whom he now pencilled scores of tender notes: 'Please send half a dozen Players or Sweet Crop cigarettes, a little tobacco, 1 oz say, some matches, a couple of boxes, and a quarter of whisky or rum. Please write in return, love and kisses dear'. That his judgment was slightly adrift was perhaps indicated by his comparison of the mental ward at No. 2 General Hospital, Le Havre, to a palace. The diagnosis was amended to GPI at Napsbury when he had proved Wassermann positive, and he was removed to Monmouth Asylum two months later.[16]

The tale of Sgt Ernest Aubry Kemp's sufferings is not only a demonstration of how GPI could be precipitated by the stress of war service, but stands also as a tragic narrative of divine injustice in which youthful indiscretions were more than atoned for by the wounds he had suffered, and the heroic fortitude he had shown, on the battlefield. A former trade maltster from Great Yarmouth who had served in the regular army before the war, Kemp had been treated for syphilis by injections in 1906 and had been assured that he was cured. Re-enlisting from the reserve after war broke out, he went out to France in August 1914. After being wounded in the left buttock in September 1915, he was hospitalized for several weeks before returning to front-line duty. In September 1916 he was wounded again, this time on the scalp and top of his spine, and treated in England for three months before returning once more to front-line action in France. In October 1917 he was wounded in both hands but managed to carry on, until in February 1918 he was gassed and burned about his body, losing his powers of speech. After two months in hospital he was returned to his depot but was unable to function properly. In July he was admitted to Springfield Hospital, initially complaining only of neurasthenic symptoms – aches all over his body, inability to concentrate, very emotional and weeping frequently. In October, however, he started to project intriguing but grandiose schemes for the salvation of all lunatics:

> He states that he has millions of money and that he intends to make more millions by the sale of waste paper in hospitals. He states that on his discharge from the Army he intends to empty all the asylums in England by curing the inmates personally and that if he fails he is willing to be shot for it. He also intends to empty all the workhouses by his own acts. As he says these things he throws himself into a state of the utmost excitement, banging the table violently with his fists.

The diagnosis of GPI was confirmed at Napsbury in February 1919 and Sergeant Ernest Kemp was removed to Bexley Asylum as a Service Patient, his condition 'aggravated by service in the War', in all probability to die there.

'HUMILIATED AND INSULTED CHARACTERS'

All the tools of physical warfare can be understood as attempts to create in the enemy the broken mental state of a slave.

Jonathan Shay, *Achilles in Vietnam* (1994)[17]

Perhaps the most striking and disturbing feature of the Napsbury cast is a comprehensive and consuming sense of failure. Though there were no doubt some who, like Fred Peatfield, were apparently impervious to circumstance, always cheerful and laughing at everything, there cannot have been many of them. Most of these flouters and scoffers were also exceedingly timorous, and the other side of this seeming insouciance towards military life is an intense sensitivity and vulnerability produced by a culture of Great Expectations, in which recruits lived in constant fear of being reprimanded, punished or even shot for constantly falling pathetically short of the manly and valorous ideals that beckoned them onwards. These are people in a high state of vigilance, fear and tension, with depleted, or shattered, self-esteem. Frequently, delusory voices feed off negative self-images, and delusions of grandiosity compensate for the erosion of self-worth.

With all their frail hopes, these servicemen had been pitched into an alien environment in which there were constant threats to their lives and to the integrity of their personalities. The soldiers who went to war in 1914 and 1915 had been raised in a social 'atmosphere in which soldiering and games were equated, in which death was seen as unlikely, but where, if it happened, it could not fail to be glorious'.[18] As David Cannadine has remarked, they were in any case 'less intimately acquainted with death than any generation since the industrial revolution', and a soldier thus had more experience of death and dying – ghastly, brutal, prolonged and degrading – 'in a week at the front than he might reasonably have expected to have witnessed in a life-time'.[19] And sometimes the soldier was caught up, also, in a battle that was perhaps still more apocalyptic than the immediate onslaught, with tentacles stretching deep into the dispositional heritage and moral universe of Christian culture, in which persons of flesh, the body in harness to a fallen creation, were inevitably in bondage to sin and death.[20] It is difficult to conjecture at the disappointment, the narcissistic wounds, that must often have resulted, the person made to feel slighted or persecuted, 'got at' in various ways, the incessant noise and sense of threat, the lack of privacy, the enforced passivity of life in the front line, the sense of being violated or tampered with, compelled to ingest an atmosphere in which there was no escape from the tyrannical jurisdiction of a taskmaster who remained largely invisible. In his desperation, a soldier might try to compensate for his vulnerability and powerlessness by fleeing not only from his unit, but also from himself, as happened with poor Walter Barbour, who had somehow detached himself from his draft and was found wandering round the country looking for a medical officer because he was in great trouble, and was someone different every day, though mostly a general.

A common experience of being violated, or tampered with, or ravaged, could sometimes involve an appropriation of meaning, as though a crucial dimension of a person's identity had been lost or destroyed. Richard Moriarty, a Roman Catholic, was perhaps trying to convey something like this when he told the doctor that the experience which had finally sent him off his head was coming home and, going to a church, finding it empty. Sometimes it also possessed a definite erotic aspect in the emergence of untoward sexual feelings, stimulated by the experience of living in close proximity for weeks on end with other men. Private Albert Kogan demanded to know who was responsible for the 'dirty business' that was causing him to have violent erections all night long. Discovering that he was developing passionate urges to sodomize his comrades, Corporal John Franks, an analytical chemist from Birmingham, claimed that the doctor who had been treating him by suggestion at the 26th General Hospital at Étaples had stimulated forbidden desires in him, placing someone outside the window at night to detect if he was excited and baiting him to perform illicit acts. He was so disturbed by these experiences that in February 1916 he tried to kill himself by drinking laudanum from the medicine cupboard.[21]

This was a paranoid universe in which everyone was plotting or being plotted against; they were all at it or having it done to them, from the Field Marshal downwards, and a naive predisposition to trust others was soon eroded. William Buckland, a regular soldier who had served 13 years with the colours, including six in India, and had gone to France in November 1914, had become very depressed by the end of 1915, his resilience sapped, complaining that there was a weight on his head which was wearing him down, that he was unable to sleep, and that his comrades had turned against him and were now out to get him. Private Joseph Johnson, a scene painter from the Gray's Inn Road in London, 'had always behaved like an ordinary sane man' until roll call on 6 Feb 1916, when he started to provoke his comrades to bring about the end he feared by approaching Sergeant Simmons and asking him if he were under arrest. He accosted him again two days later, declaring that he knew the Sergeant was shortly going to Amiens to be a member of a Court Martial which was going to try him. At Napsbury he continued to maintain that his comrades were against him, and to march up and down all day as if on duty, as though he could get no release from the military machine.

For some recruits, all these insults and deprivations rekindled traumatic experiences in early life, as a result of which they were already prone to feelings of powerlessness, with expectations of repeated abuse, and to believe that they were worthless. As in a Dostoyevsky novel, the Napsbury cast are mostly a series of 'deeply humiliated and insulted characters' for whom 'as in a dance of death, humiliation without forgiveness calls the tune'. In regard to this experience of humiliation, of such intensity that it assumes almost a spiritual character, there is a profound need for forgiveness in order, as Julia Kristeva expresses it in her fine study of depression and melancholia, 'to give the depressed patient (that stranger withdrawn into his wound) a new start, and give him the possibility of a new encounter'.[22] Invaded by the omnipresence of death, exhausted by physical and emotional strains, the subject finds himself battling with symbolic collapse, unable to use language: 'As if overtaxed or destroyed by too powerful a breaker, our symbolic means find themselves hollowed out, nearly wiped out, paralysed'.[23] If in the nondepressive state, writes Kristeva, 'one has the ability to concatenate, depressive persons, in contrast, riveted to their pain, no longer concatenate and, consequently, neither act nor speak'.[24] By definition, the melancholic or depressive state involves a significant measure of psychomotor, affective and ideational retardation. Hence why some servicemen, mostly but by no means exclusively individuals of limited educational attainment and lowly occupational status, who looked to the authorities to be mental defectives, dements, or degenerates, were in reality largely depressed.

DELUSIONS OF UNWORTHINESS

The front line is thus a narrow zone of fear and death lying between two prisons. In this narrow zone two massive social organizations compete to enslave the soldier. . . . Terror, mortal dependency, barriers to escape – these are the characteristics of modern combat that mark it as a condition of captivity and enslavement as harsh as any political prison or labor camp.

Jonathan Shay, *Achilles in Vietnam*[25]

. . . and still it goes on, slaughter slaughter slaughter, with dicipline binding us together so that our indivuallity will not get an opening to go its own way, which in most of us, after seeing facts, would be back. Back home to the Rhine, and the Thames, and tell the people at home the truth that war is worse than murder.

Private Hiram Sturdy, diary.[26]

The conditions of life on the Western Front gave short shrift to any residual belief a man might have had that he was authoring the action of his own life, or that he had some control over his destiny, and demonstrated to him that at best he had a bit part in a fathomless and largely incomprehensible drama which, especially if he were exhausted and run down, easily defied classification and turned into an absurdist nightmare. Pte William Bellamy, a boot repairer from Middlesex, who had enlisted in 1914 and served in France since July 1915, and had frequently been under fire, was brought to No. 12 Casualty Clearing Station in July 1918 where, among other things, he reported that there was a farce on; someone was stealing his mind, he had been dogged and followed about in a wood in which notices seemed to refer to him; Sergeant Roberts who had been dead some time had spoken to him; he had attended a funeral which had seemed to him like a mock funeral and could even have been his own; and though he knew there was something going on, he couldn't get to the bottom of it.[27] He admitted to having been depressed and apprehensive for some while, and to being disappointed that he had been refused leave to come home and get married.

When he reached Dykebar War Hospital, near Paisley in Scotland, a few weeks later, he complained to the ward sister that he had been hearing voices telling him that he was going to be shot by someone. Shortly afterwards, when questioned by the doctor, he insisted that it was 'an idea only and that there is no one going to meddle with him'. We can readily imagine the interaction here, the sympathetic but still censorious doctor trying to prise out of the humiliated Bellamy an admission that the 'voices' were still at it; Bellamy, who knows the score psychiatrically speaking, quite sensibly denies it. But, of course, this adversarial encounter really misses the point, for it is not the presence or absence of the 'voice' that is crucial, but the miserable feeling that Bellamy has about himself that stimulates a punitive voice into being. He was hardly the epitome of the silent working-class soldier, though some might have preferred him that way, for 'if asked a question he will answer it, but wanders on from that to other matters and talks incessantly'. He was, rather, typical of the exhausted and humiliated soldier, worn out by the constant threats to his life and his sense of personal wellbeing, who was then rewarded by being told that he suffered from 'delusions of un-worthiness'.

Corporal James Batchelor, a thirty-seven year old professional soldier with 12 years' service, became very depressed and anxious in the summer of 1918, complaining to the medical officer 'of a feeling of something dreadful was going to happen to him'. Declaring he was 'quite sure that the officers of his Unit intend that he be shot', he expected Sir Douglas Haig to be present at the execution. He drew a map representing all the trenches in France on which he marked all the exits 'Gates of Death', and suggested that the only way out was suicide. After considerable hesitation, he then said 'he had masturbated since youth and thought that was the cause of his trouble'.[28] When he reached Netley he was 'unhappy, agitated, apprehensive, self-centred, unsociable and restless', as soon as he walked into the room asking Captain Forsyth for a chance, as he knew that he was soon going to be hanged. At Napsbury in October he again attributed all his troubles to early masturbation and still insisted that he was going to be shot, saying that his knowledge of his impending execution was confirmed when he saw a note on the table at the hospital in Étaples revealing that Sir Douglas Haig intended to be present. Batchelor was also styled as suffering from 'delusions of unworthiness' which, of course, mirrored his own sense of himself as the source of his own problems, but rather sidestepped surely pertinent questions as to how exaggerated expectations of manliness, together with repressive attitudes towards sexuality, might bring men to consider themselves as worthless human beings.

The experience of war service was doubtless prone to exacerbate and confirm a chronic sense of failure among men whose life experience had already led them to feel that they were something of a disappointment to those who had authority over them. When Major Renshaw examined Private Charles Abberley he reported that he was 'depressed and very childish in his manner', and for no reason had asked the orderly to cut his throat. He concluded that he was feeble-minded and perhaps an early case of dementia praecox. In actuality, however, had the Major troubled to read it properly, the case record described how 'last night the patient while in bed called the Ward Corporal over to him' and 'declared he was "being kept awake by his nerves"'; he said that 'he felt "funny and shaking with trying to take on – to make a soldier of myself"'; and 'asked the corporal to let him go to a quiet spot where he could take his own life'. The next day Abberley seemed quieter, and admitted he would 'enjoy being back at the farm' where his parents lived 'although he would have liked to make a good soldier'. The following day he was again disturbed and had to be placed under close observation, claiming he heard voices exhorting him, 'You daft bugger, cut your throat!'. He did not especially wish to die, he said, but had come round to the view that it was perhaps the best course when he 'can't make a good soldier'.

This was, after all, a culture in which an authoritative strand of opinion held that men who could not make efficient and brave soldiers deserved to be shot, and though some military authorities were more lenient than others, such attitudes formed part of the atmosphere which ordinary soldiers breathed. It would be naive to discount the effect that they must have had on impressionable youths such as Charles Abberley, and it is perhaps an ironic tribute to their masters that many of them should have internalized their lessons so well, and could scarcely be upbraided for having failed to attend in class. To a large extent, however, the responses of the doctors can only have confirmed Abberley's sense of his failings, for he was left to struggle along on his own with his fears whilst they proceeded to invoke constitutional explanations for his troubles, persuaded that 'a degree of congenital feeble-mindedness' was certainly present. Most reprobate were the patriotic failings he exhibited in his horticultural knowledge, and in his political opinions. Though he named eight English flowers, even after repeated promptings he neglected to name the rose; and to compound matters, he gave as 'the reason for Britain engaging in war the belief that she wanted more colonies'. From this time on, it is perhaps not altogether surprising that Charles Abberley became less and less approachable, and when he finally reached Napsbury a month later in August 1918 he had more or less ceased to communicate altogether.

And then there were those also who had to contend with news of a crisis that had blown up in the family that they were now quite powerless to influence and that was, perhaps, in any case a renewal of a long-standing pattern of ill-health in which individuals were either dying, or threatening to do away with themselves, amidst which even in more normal times it had been very difficult to maintain equanimity. When Private Walter Stevens, who was serving with the Army Veterinary Corps, was taken to hospital in Boulogne in June 1915 after laying 'about the stalls among the horses with his hands over his face, indifferent to his safety', and attempting to throw himself under a lorry, the medical officer noted: 'Family history bad. Uncle died in an asylum, sister suffers from hysteria, another sister attempted suicide by means of "spirits of salts", father died of tuberculosis'. A miner from South Wales, practically blind in one eye following a pit accident, Walter lay in bed with his 'hand over his face in an attitude suggesting mental agitation and depression', and 'in a voice broken with emotion' recounted that he had been worried for some weeks now by letters from his wife threatening to do away with herself.

Of at least a few of the Napsbury cast it could be said that they were lucky to be there, rather than to have suffered a lonely death by firing squad. In the opinion of Brigadier General Lowther, 'the execution of a man within their knowledge for an offence to which they are tempted has a most salutary effect on the bad and weak character'. After Private Oliver Hodgetts was executed in the vicinity of Pont Logy at 4.30 am on 4 June 1915 for deliberately absenting himself from his company with the 'sole motive of saving his own skin', having failed to 'pull himself together' when apprehended by his colonel, it was ordered that a notice describing his offence and the penalty that had been inflicted be read on parade to every squadron, battery, company and corresponding unit in the Division.[29] Though Private J. Bennett had been found guilty of running away during an attack, Brigadier General Rees asked that the sentence be commuted because 'the man was apparently too terrified to know what he was doing and therefore can hardly be described as deliberately avoiding the duty in question'. However, insisting that 'cowards of this sort' were a 'serious danger to the Army', and that the death penalty had 'been instituted to make such men fear running away more than they fear the enemy', the general commanding VIII Corps confirmed the sentence and Private John Bennett was executed by shooting at Poperinghe at 5.40 am on 28 August 1916.[30]

Several servicemen were executed after claiming that they had lost their way and had been walking round for several weeks trying to find their regiments; or that they had found themselves in situations in which, realizing that they had overstayed their time ('time lingered', as Private Atkinson put it, 'and I was gifted to temptation'), they had been afraid to return. Worries about their families also figured prominently in the defences of the court martialled. One night in July 1916 Private G. Lowton had refused to advance into No Man's Land, saying that he could not go as he had a wife and five children. The Brigade Commander recommended that his sentence be commuted on the grounds that his 'nerves and health' appeared to be 'below normal in consequence of shock', but the medical board were of opinion that he was 'in good health in every way'.[31] Private Bert McCubbin proffered a rather similar plea: 'I have a father somewhere in France leaving my mother at home with six brothers and sisters and always thinking if anything had to happen to us two what would become of them, which does not help me to get on a deal'.[32] Here also, senior commanders concurred in recommending that the sentence be commuted, but the commander of the First Army differed, maintaining that if clemency were to be shown to private soldiers who decline to face danger, 'all the qualities which we desire will become debased and degraded'. Privates Lowton and McCubbin were duly executed together at Lone Farm on 30 July 1916.

Quite a few of the Napsbury cast had got lost while in the field, becoming disconnected from their units, sometimes for days at a time, or, as with George Major Gomm, had apparently gone off deliberately. In some instances it is difficult to avoid the conclusion that the line which separated the soldier who was shot at dawn from the serviceman who was evacuated to a war mental hospital, the 'blameworthy weakling' from the 'weakling' who was given a ticket to Napsbury, was largely adventitious, reflecting local circumstances in the field, luck, and the sympathies of medical officers. All told, the Napsbury cast testify to the awesome moral power and efficacy of this disciplinary universe, for in so many of the inmates it had produced a state of mind in which they were fully persuaded that they *had* all run away and would shortly be arraigned for the offence.

Chapter 4

'GREETINGS FROM NAPSBURY'

DIVISIVE PSYCHOLOGIES

Much has been made of Britain's integral divide between mute working-class soldiers and agitated but still voluble upper-class officers, between the traumatic hysterias of the rank and file which had either removed or distorted their capacity for speech, and the anxiety neuroses or neurasthenias of the officer class which had done little to diminish an infinite capacity to verbalize their remorse-ridden conflicts.[1] Some respected cultural historians have, rather surprisingly perhaps, taken this distinction at face value, treating it not so much as a representation of how members of one class imagined or believed they differed from another class, but as a no doubt flawed yet still broadly truthful account of a real state of affairs. So, for example, Eric Leed maintains that the social distribution of symptoms in the war mirrored the pattern that had long been established in the peace: neurasthenia, 'a generalized anxiety syndrome that had been found primarily in private hospital rooms and exclusive sanitaria, was most common among officers', whereas the hysterical neuroses which predominated in the ranks were the very same disorders that had usually been 'found in public wards or outpatient clinics before the war'.[2]

Of course, just this polarity had been voiced by contemporary psychologists such as W. H. R. Rivers, who proposed a psychobiological schema in which the ordinary soldier is perceived as having regressed to a lower level in the evolutionary hierarchy whereby the interests of his combat group were sacrificed to his selfish survival instincts, whilst the officer functioned at a higher level on the evolutionary scale in which, however ravaged by a conflict between fear and duty, he sacrificed himself in the interests of the welfare of the collective.[3] John MacCurdy in his acclaimed monograph *War Neuroses*, published in 1918, argued that officers were especially prone to suffer from anxiety states in which they 'wished for death during the period of strain and fatigue preceding the final collapse', whilst ordinary soldiers were the chief victims of hysterical manifestations such as conversion hysteria, in which sufferers 'entertained the desire for disablement, for a "Blighty" wound or for some disabling illness'.[4] In Rivers's portrayal, while the officer was still laden by anxiety and depression even after he had been brought home from the field of combat, the ordinary ranker became 'relatively or positively happy' once his hysterical condition had secured him an exit ticket from the battle zone.[5]

'How utterly different Rivers's neurasthenic officer is from the common soldier', Allan Young has remarked in an incisive critique.[6] Indeed, and as Young goes on to argue, the polarity derives less from real differences in symptoms than from contrasting valuations of officers and common soldiers. To some discerning contemporary eyes, other rankers in mental distress frequently displayed the unmistakable signs of a neuropathic or psychopathic taint, many of them having 'a history of neurotic or psychotic stigmata' and an 'inborn or acquired disposition to emotivity', being 'almost as defective physically as they are mentally – under-sized, under-weight, narrow-chested, shuffle-gaited, slack jaws, with badly shaped heads, irregular features and vacant or restless expression'.[7] In her magisterial study of how doctors and patients tried to make sense of depression in the Victorian and Edwardian periods, Janet Oppenheim claims that 'the perspective of class background and bias always intervened between middle-class doctors and working-class patients, inevitably casting a very different light on the suffering of the affluent and the impoverished'.[8] Though the doctor might recognize signs of depression in the patient, describing how 'the face is drawn, showing signs of fatigue, while the emotional strain is exhibited by chronic frowning with considerable wrinkling of the forehead', their significance was diminished, or skewed, by the overriding judgment that standing before him was a morally and mentally weak character.[9]

In some military treatment units, feelings of unworthiness and low self-esteem in common soldiers were less likely to be seen as symptoms of a depressive condition for which treatment could be offered, than as a more or less accurate reflection of an inherent or constitutional inferiority. In this respect psychiatric diagnosis played second fiddle to a moral diagnosis. Even in a seemingly progressive professional idiom in which the traumatic hysterias were analyzed as an expression of the protest of the inferior, and mutism was seen as an outcome of repressed aggression, there was a highly functional, and largely unexamined, ambiguity around the meaning of 'inferiority' as between an existential predicament (the feelings of the depressed soldier), an objective class or status position (the 'oppressed'), and a moral judgment (the doctor's feelings about the depressed soldier and his class).[10]

So what may have carried over into the war from the peace was not so much the social distribution of symptoms as the predisposition to code working-class reality. It is not that the signs and symptoms common to the officer class were not in evidence in the other ranks, rather that they were submerged, disavowed and trivialized by the attitudes and interpretations that were imposed on them. Certainly, that is what the evidence from the Napsbury inmates very much indicates. Actually, many of them had wished for death; anxiety and depression still weighed heavily on large numbers of them; rather few were relaxed and happy; and the zeal they had shown in pursuit of their duties was no less excessive than that of Rivers's officers. Though the integral divide between the 'upper' and the 'lower' was, of course, reflected in certain basic structures and institutions, still the reality, as Arthur Kleinman has remarked, turns out to be 'more and more porous, fuzzy and complexly human'.[11]

THE NAPSBURY CULTURE

At Napsbury, however, the possibility of a more inclusive psychology starts to emerge. For what we witness there is a moderation of this divisive scheme of things, a muting of class antagonisms and prejudices, not a dramatic turnaround certainly, rather a fumbling, faltering, sometimes ambivalent, but nonetheless still significant movement towards a more egalitarian, and less opinionated, mental health culture; in this climate, psychological suffering in the ordinary soldier could be regarded as authentic, rather than as abnormal or evasive, and his dignity thus respected. The first thing that must strike us is the diversity of the psychological and social types who are gathered here: volunteers, regular soldiers and conscripts; a dentist, an engineer, a teacher or a stockbroker alongside a cotton piecer, a plumber, a miner or a stableman.

Of course, as we have seen, there were those present who had been brought down just by being in the military environment or on the margins of the action, and a few had been sent there simply as a means for the Army to rid itself of hopelessly inefficient soldiers. It is, no doubt, understandable that some of these simpletons and dreamers and malcontents should have been construed as mental defectives. However, it is quite misleading to define them only negatively by their military failings, for this is to concede overmuch to the rectitude of the general staff at the expense of acknowledging that these 'failures' also exemplify an alternative stance or vantage point within life, a competing sensibility one might say, in which, regardless of their limited articulacy and homespun horizons, they come over as possessing a certain kind of unalloyed integrity, hanging on to their own imaginings in defiance of the whizz-bangs in the Old Kent Road (to borrow from Siegfried Sassoon).[12] One does not mean to dispose of mental deficiency as a social problem to say that some of these simpletons and 'defectives' do seem to have a point.

Shakespeare, the American critic Harold Bloom has observed, 'always gets there before us, and always waits for us, somewhere up ahead'.[13] In obvious respects, some of the characters in the Napsbury cast resemble the poverty-stricken recruits, such as Francis Feeble, 'most forcible Feeble', 'a woman's tailor', whom Falstaff gathered to lead into battle against the French. Feeble and his associates are still up the road there ahead, waiting for us to join our own context up to theirs, and to help us to recognize, in answer to our uncertainties as to what these implausible soldiers are all doing on the battlefield, that they possess a significance that outshines their limitations.[14]

But the majority of the Napsbury inmates, increasingly so as the war dragged on, had been exhausted by long service and were, many of them, deeply humiliated and insulted characters, displaying an intense sensitivity and vulnerability. Far from being stifled, these voices were often described by the authorities as 'exceedingly loquacious', 'abundant, diffuse and expansive'. On occasions religion offered a cloak under which to parry with the authorities, as with Isadore Brooks, 'a peculiar looking undersized youth' from Stoke Newington, formerly a post boy at the Colonial Office, who had apparently experienced a spiritual awakening in the field in France. 'He is stuffed full of religious delusions – sees a "sign" in every trivial incident – the guttering of a candle, the fact that he goes on leave the day the Germans start an offensive – each incident is of startling religious portent'. Major Stanford Read, the Netley commander, was rattled by Isadore's insolent demeanour: 'He is self-satisfied and rather expansive. . . . Instead of *answering* many questions, he *asks* me some in return, as "what is war?", "what is a nation?", what do I mean by this and that.'

As we have seen, to assuage a querulous public opinion the military authorities had been obliged to compensate for the deficiencies of the existing public mental health system. Largely, perhaps, because, by comparison with some of the other war mental hospitals, there was on the whole no pressure here to return a significant proportion of the inmates to duty, Napsbury became the setting for an alternative social experiment in which we have the paradox of a domain under military control that has become the site for a form of carnival in which conventional norms have been suspended or relaxed.[15] The achievement of the mental department at Napsbury, and other comparable sites, was to bring into being the rudiments of a mental health counter-culture in which a serviceman could undergo a protracted period of emotional disturbance without being penalized or turned into a career lunatic. Napsbury was testimony of how it was possible to go over the top and come back, no mean achievement in a period when there was a tremendous anxiety about being seen to be on the rails, to be in control and to be behaving sanely. Inevitably, this state of things produced an insatiable hunger for reassurance that one's worst fears were not about to be confirmed, which only aggravated whatever insecurities may already have existed, fears of 'going mad' transforming the hearing of voices into a definitively terrifying experience, thus setting in motion a vicious circle of reaction and counter-reaction.[16]

At Napsbury it was also the *diagnostic* norms that were suspended. Many of the cases were classified as 'neurasthenia', which functioned in effect as a form of non-diagnosis, or *salle d'attente*, in which over a number of months, rarely more than nine, patients and staff could make up their minds as to which diagnostic train they were eventually going to clamber aboard.[17] When Sapper Gilbert Bowles reached Napsbury, he recounted to Capt. Hubert Norman, perhaps the most sympathetic of the medical officers in the mental department, how he had been in France from September 1916 through to February 1918, in the Somme, at Arras, Ypres, and Cambrai, under fire practically every day. He could not recall being sent down the line, or being in hospital in France, and before that he had to go back to the beginning of September 1917, when they were being heavily shelled, and two of his officers were killed, and he remembered helping to pick up the bodies. In the military hospital at Brighton he had been alternately depressed and disturbed by violent impulses, reporting a dream in which he escaped from the hospital after killing the doctor, several attendants and a policeman and then committing suicide, an expression perhaps of the indignant rage he felt at having been so much abused, or invaded, by destructive forces that he was powerless to influence.

The doctor at Brighton took him for a rather menacing oddity ('he is apathetic but has impulses to smash things . . . looks sullen and truculent, or smiles for nothing, probably Dementia Praecox') and it was only at Napsbury that he found in Capt. Hubert Norman an interlocutor who was able to receive his narrative, and revise the diagnosis to exhaustion psychosis. Gilbert revealed to Norman that he had been through a previous depressive episode in 1911, when he had felt life was not worth living after an attack of pneumonia which had precipitated severe pains in his head for four months. Norman also thought that he perhaps smiled unduly, but two months later he was smiling less and usefully employed.

HUBERT NORMAN'S HISTORIES
Here is one of those extraordinary histories which Hubert Norman managed to sketch so well in his rounded, almost feminine, hand.[18] Born in 1880, Private Jim McCarthy had enlisted in the Border Regiment in 1899, and been

in South Africa on garrison duty from 1903 to 1906 before serving in India, where he caught sunstroke soon after arriving and was unconscious for two days, and was then returned to England and discharged from the Army. He seems already to have had some mental trouble around this time because he recalled being sent to hospital under guard, but nonetheless he re-enlisted on 4 August 1914 and was posted to France almost immediately, finding himself in the firing line about five days later, seeing action at Poperinge and Zonnebeke, before being wounded in the right shoulder and leg at Ypres on 22 October, after which he was in hospital at Horton for two months and then discharged the Army on account of his nerves towards the end of December. About a fortnight later he re-enlisted in the Essex regiment, going out to France again in February 1915, where after a brief period in the firing line he was sent to the Dardanelles, holding out in the Pensinsula from 24 April 1915 until 8 January 1916 (by now he was a sergeant), with only seven days' rest at Mudros in all that time, until he contracted dysentery and was moved to Egypt and from there to Malta, where he had two operations for an abscess in his liver.

From a hospital in Blighty, he returned to duty at the depot until one night towards the end of 1916 he apparently left his guard, though he could remember nothing about going absent, and was found the next morning in a field. He was court-martialled and lost his stripes, and since then had been in various regiments, most recently the Labour Corps, doing 'odd jobs' but not 'regular duty', and a few weeks ago had become very depressed and was caught attempting to do away with himself. He was admitted to Napsbury on 18 April 1918 from a military hospital in Aylesbury with a diagnosis of melancholia; a small man, only 5 ft 3 inches, with brown hair, pale complexion and grey-blue eyes, dejected and apprehensive, looking very much as though he could be on course for an asylum. He confided to Hubert Norman that he had been affected by family tragedies, the death of his brother in Colney Hatch Asylum at the age of 25 and the suicide of his father in Jute Street, King's Cross, in 1897 when he was seventeen.

Being urged by Hubert Norman to tell his story, with its impressive recall of names and dates, the small currency of his military and medical history, the narrative of his existence spread across the map of imperial debacles, no doubt possessed its own therapeutic value, and by early June he was looking more cheerful and was occupied. We appreciate from this narrative how attractive military adventures, or misadventures,were to men with awkward temperaments and unhappy histories, a means to transcend doubt and uncertainty in a wider action, and just how easy it was to enlist and enlist again; but what comes through also in the telling is Jim Mc Carthy's resilience – here he still is depite everything – and it is obvious that in the engagement between doctor and patient that encouraged him to tell his tale, Captain Norman must have conveyed his respect for his achievement.

FINE LOOKS AND GOOD BREEDING

Still, the medical fraternity at Napsbury were sometimes prone to cultural arrogance, exhibiting an imperialist disdain for those from other ethnic backgrounds, particularly if they emanated from darkest Africa, treating an inability to understand English or a preference for another language as a moral failing. Pte William Hall was the son of missionaries who had been born in Nagasaki, and lived all his life in South Africa, and in his crisis he appears to have expressed himself in an African language in which, it may be surmised, he felt himself to be more at home emotionally. In the judgment of the medical officer, however, this was a definite self-abasement, in which Hall's body-language and sounds assumed the characteristics of a monkey. 'Patient is very negative in his response to any kind of request', reads one entry, 'he writhes and grimaces and adopts histrionic poses. He has spoken no English but much of the time is chattering in some other language'.

It counted for a good deal if the soldier was able to demonstrate some refinement or sophistication, to pass himself off as one of the educated classes, even if his occupational status was fairly lowly or if he was mostly self-educated. If the impression he made in this regard was strong enough, the blemishes of a former psychiatric record or of quirky ideas became more negotiable, or at least did not immediately upset the biographical apple cart. Pte Allan Smith from Guernsey, a single man who had been employed as a shipping clerk with the same firm for the past 25 years, had spent two periods of six months in asylums, first in 1910 and again in 1914, apparently suffering from mania, after which he had volunteered for war service. He had been up the line until a couple of months before his admission in 1918, when he had started to suffer from severe headaches, as happened to him periodically, as a result of which he had on one occasion struck one of his officers but later apologized, and because his weakness was known, so he claimed, he was not charged. Though he was possessed of some strange ideas, ascribing his headaches to a blow struck by a stranger in a street in London in 1910 whom he firmly believed was Doctor Crippen, and the lady with him Miss de Neve, and despite a family history of insanity on the paternal side, still he remained onside in the doctor's perception.[19] Because of his striking refinement and appearance of good breeding, he was excused the kind of rhetorical bludgeoning frequently administered to low-status individuals: 'He is exalted and talkative, a refined and well-bred man. He talks freely of his powers as a poet and a lover of music. I have seen some of his verses, doggerel but in a curious metre, not to be expected from an uneducated man'.

A clerk at Liberty's in Regent Street after leaving school, John Challenger had joined the regular army in 1913 because he had once been in the Boy's Brigade and felt that to be his vocation, but soon found himself in trouble with authority, confiding to Captain Hills at No. 58 Casualty Clearing Station that he had been awarded stripes, but subsequently degraded for striking the sergeant major. Though he claimed to be quite fond of some sergeant majors, he revealed that on a previous occasion before the war he had disliked the sergeant major so much that he had left the camp and gone home for three months. The clashing traits that he exhibited of old-fashioned deference, truculence and lack of self-consciousness confounded the medical authorities in the field, who suspected that he was a dementia praecox case. Though not yet certifiable, 'he is so erratic', Hills concluded, 'that he is unfitted for his duties'. At Napsbury, however, there was a rather different take on him, for though his 'manner perhaps of describing things is a little hyper-formal (old Army)' and he was by his own account 'rather unstable', still this was 'nothing particular' and he is 'rather a fine-looking boy'. 'Fine-looking' was, of course, code for good breeding and though it is, of course, conceivable that Challenger had 'recovered' from some acute condition, it is more likely that under the more relaxed conditions at Napsbury what had appeared in the field to be insubordination, or pathology, could now be recast as eccentricity, or as a rather vague instability, without any reproach to it.

SHELL SHOCK AT ARMENTIÈRES
Though 'shell shock' eventually came to possess its own publicists and legitimating theory as the rallying point for an alternative sensibility or ethos, from a military standpoint there was considerable ambivalence about authorizing a condition that seemed to let servicemen off the disciplinary hook, and sympathy was in the main limited and conditional, ringed by conventional reflexes, as the next two examples bring out. On 19 April 1916 Pte Charles Butterworth was able to give Capt. Hubert Norman at Napsbury an account of what happened after he was blown up by a shell at Armentières in December 1915. On the day of the explosion he was on sentry duty. He remembered the explosion but nothing subsequent to it until his speech returned in a hospital at Étaples two days later. He was then in a military hospital at Chatham, as he recalled, before being sent to a convalescent home where he was taken to a concert at the end of December at which he became very excited. He was able to speak when he went to bed but not when he woke up. At times he could 'form the words in his mind', at other times not.

He was not deaf but 'dull of hearing', and when he went home on leave he found that he could not hear unless shouted at and was quite unable to reply. From this time on Butterworth became mute, and we now pick up the story as it was told by others. From his home he was unaccountably returned to duty at Rugeley Camp, but five days after arriving there he still had not uttered a word and on 9 February, after causing a disturbance in his hut, he was removed to the camp hospital where towards the end of March the medical officer reported on his progress:

He has not spoken since admission to hospital, nor answered oral questions. For the first fortnight he took no notice of his surroundings. He lay in bed with a startled, distressed expression on his face. At times he stared into space, looking suspiciously around, and then suddenly ducked under the bedclothes, as if to hide himself or shut out some terrible sight. For some days he was very violent, struggled furiously with a guard of 6 men, and appeared to suffer from acute mania. After this phase he became quiet for about 10 days, was able to answer in writing simple written questions, but in a childish fashion. Then he again assumed a very dejected and anxious appearance and had a few epileptiform attacks. The last thing he wrote was 'I went to France. The Germans are coming. They will kill us'. He now is unable to reply to written questions and does not comprehend them; and his condition is becoming the same as when he was admitted to Hospital.

By the beginning of April the authorities at Rugeley concluded that Butterworth was probably heading for an asylum, and he was transferred to Napsbury bearing a diagnosis of confusional insanity caused by shell shock at Armentières, with the qualification that the disability had been caused by the 'effect of shell shock on an unstable nervous system'. On admission he was found to be dull and stuporose, apparently deaf and dumb, lying in bed staring vacantly, eyes wide open exposing the cornea, eyelids retracted. Then, during the night of 18 April, 'he woke up suddenly, became very excited and restless, and then shouted out that they must take cover from the shells which were coming over'. The excitement quickly passed over and the following morning he was able to hear readily, and to speak clearly and distinctly, and to give Capt. Norman the account of his experience set out above, telling him how the previous night he had dreamt that he was in the trenches and heard the shells with a noise as of gas ('a sizzing') in his ears.

Though it is, of course, the doctor who has written down this account, he is really only the *accoucheur* to a process that is set in motion and guided by the patient and, like ourselves as accidental bystanders, he also is made to feel that he is the privileged recipient of a disclosure, after weeks of silent protest, that the patient could after all have elected to deposit on another site. Though there is a lingering uncertainty as to whether the patient could have hastened the resolution if he had chosen to do so, or is merely the vehicle for a healing process that unfolds according to its own pace, this is nonetheless in an important sense an expression of patient power in which, after months of silence, the patient returns to the traumatic scene in his own time, and as a result recovers the power of speech.

Arguably, it was now both timely and safe for Butterworth to recover his faculties, since it cannot have been lost on him that if he delayed very much longer he would be certified, but equally he could now speak again reasonably confident in the knowledge that he would not be returned to duty. Whichever way we look at it, however, the doctor was relatively impotent in influencing the outcome, and perhaps in retaliation for the unacceptable lesson that he had the temerity to be teaching his medical keepers, even the moderate Capt. Norman resolved that Butterworth should be placed in an explanatory box that muted the significance of his crisis. Over the next couple of months a determined effort was made to establish a hereditary predisposition for his hysterical protest, and to elaborate a profile of malign influences that included his mother, who had apparently died as a 'lunatic' after being in an asylum for five years, his father, who was 'very excitable' and had given up working in town and taken up farming because of his nerves, a sister who confessed to becoming very depressed at times, and finally, to cap it all, a statement from the father that all his children were of a 'nervous disposition'.

This is not to say that Hubert Norman invariably struck a sceptical pose towards shell-shock cases, especially if the patient had a clean sheet ('no family history of nervous trouble') in his genetic as much as in his service record. Pte Y. H. Birchall of the 2nd Royal Sussex, a regular soldier with more than 12 years' service who had been through the South African war, fitted the bill perfectly. Here Norman cocks a snook at Major Ronald Rows and his team at Maghull Hospital, who had been rather grabbing the therapeutic limelight over the previous year or so, for their failure, spurred no doubt by their zeal in returning soldiers to duty as quickly as possible, to attend sufficiently to the medical needs of a distressed soldier.[20] Major Rows, Hubert Norman implies, was sometimes rather too eager to impress his superiors of his proficiency as a soldier, to the detriment of his duties as a doctor. Pte Birchall was thirty-five when he went out to France in May 1915, and Capt. Norman takes up his story: 'He saw much fighting and was under fire a good deal of the time. He was at Loos, Armentières, Lens. In September he was buried by a shell-explosion. This was on a Saturday morning and he remembered nothing until the following Tuesday. Then he was "in a shocking state": he could with difficulty see or walk, "green seemed to come before his eyes". He was emotional and wept'. After being shunted through a series of hospitals, Birchall was sent to Maghull in November where he remained until the day at the end of April 1916 when he left without leave to visit his mother who was ill in London, returning to the hospital four days later, whereupon Major Rows decided straightaway to return him to duty at his depot. When he arrived there, the commanding officer found him to be in a very depressed and nervous state, not having eaten for three days, and dispatched an anxious inquiry back to Maghull with the suggestion that Birchall was, perhaps, not 'mentally sound'.

A peevish rejoinder from Maghull stated that Birchall had improved considerably while in the hospital, and that his discharge was being considered, but that he had spoilt the therapeutic scenario by absenting himself without permission. Of his current distress it merely remarked: 'evidently the earlier condition of slight depression and inability to eat has returned. During his residence here he was not considered to be mentally unsound'. Rows reacted as if to reciprocate an act of individual defiance, but it seems that in reality Birchall's behaviour was more likely an expression of his distressed condition. And here the officers at the depot were rather more responsive than the so-called progressives at Maghull for, as Capt. Norman cuttingly noted, 'they saw he was ill and sent him to hospital'. Unfettered by expectations of remoulding active soldiers out of its distressed clientele (though, as with other dischargees, it is by no means unlikely that he may subsequently have re-enlisted), the therapeutic regime at Napsbury was conducive towards Birchall's recovery. After a month or so he was showing improvement – by early June there was only a very slight tremor of the hand – and he was sent home for discharge in early August.

Regardless of the qualms of the authorities, however, they could do little to stay the enthusiasm of servicemen themselves for these newfangled concepts, and one of the remarkable features of the Napsbury culture is the extent to which, quite unabashed, a soldier would elect to describe himself as having suffered from 'shell shock', not merely as the label for a condition, but as the index of a sensibility, even of what stereotypically can only register as a feminized sensibility, as when Pte Arthur Bowerman declared that he had shell shock, readily admitting that he had got upset and wanted to shoot his officer, quite unapologetic about himself as a nervous type who sometimes got excited and required to be held when he found himself under bombardment.[21]

By the beginning of 1916, even regular soldiers of the old Army were adopting the rhetoric of shell shock to describe their conditions. Pte Albert Plant, a steel-smelter from Shotton in North Wales, who had been in the Horse Artillery for eight years, and discharged after completing his time with a good character, had re-enlisted in the Gordon Highlanders on the outbreak of war, embarking for France on 19 August 1914 where he had been ever since without leave. He had been wounded in the arm, wrist and head, and recently had been in hospital after being buried on a number of occasions. His nerves had become frayed, and he had started to sleep badly and to imagine that the sergeants and men were calling him 'bastard' and other names, ganging up on him because he was a Welshman, even taking his letters and drugging his food, and he had arrived at D Block in May 1916 bearing the label of 'delusional insanity'.

On being asked to account for himself, he was by no means unusual in declaring that he had had shell shock but was now quite well thank you, for the idiom of shell shock was now well established among ordinary soldiers and their friends and relatives to convey a psychological condition that was serious in its intensity (even resembling 'madness' perhaps) but not at all dishonourable, and above all *temporary* and amenable to treatment. The suffering individual retained his links with the community of ordinary human beings rather than finding himself (as happened with the conventional currency of mental disorder) excluded from it. Predictably enough, Capt. Clindening at D Block had been less than captivated by Albert's account of his achievements and misfortunes, finding him boastful and unconvincing, but in fact Albert's own sense of what had happened to him, and of how he could now be helped, was quite percipient, for after four months at Napsbury he had become less irritable and complaining, and was working well, and he was discharged for return to military duty in August 1916.

RECOVERY

What counted most in the journey towards recovery was a willingness to engage in some kind of occupation, and after a decent interval all the weepers and shakers and melancholics were gently but forcibly cajoled into the gardens, fields, workshops or the kitchen, wherever they showed the most aptitude. The poet and musician Ivor Gurney was there in the summer of 1918, having been transferred from the Lord Derby War Hospital at Warrington, and he described how: 'We decouch ourselves at 6.15 or so; breakfast at 7.45 and get out on farmwork at 8.30 or thereabouts to hoe the patient mangel or collect the elusive spud; reap dock and thistle; the general care of management of all farm life weighs lightly, however, and we can see

NAPSBURY MILITARY HOSPITAL.   282.

A forbidding institution, perhaps, but set in congenial grounds.

trees and clouds, flowers and men as can the rest of outdoor people. A lucky life compared to Warrington's enclosed existence'.[22]

The most striking thing about the case histories for this period are the fluctuating assessments; presumptions about determinacy, and fixity of character and course, are all the time burst open. In October 1918 W. J. Mitchell is described as a 'big headed, miserable specimen ... dull & confused'; but by January he is said to be: 'bright, rational and open in his way of answering questions'. Strictures about constitutional inferiority, degeneracy and so forth, had at the very least to be moderated. Thirty-two year old Driver Alfred Butler was admitted from D Block Netley in April 1918 with a label of 'imbecility', but it turned out that he had just been brought home from Egypt after more than three and a half years of war service, having volunteered in August 1914 and served on the home front until August 1915, since when he had been engaged in watering the mules in foreign parts – in Salonika until May 1917, and in Egypt thereafter. According to the hospital report from Cairo, he had recently been under shellfire in the thick of the fighting which had made him nervous, headachy, 'exalted and noisy', culminating in two incidents in which he had threatened one man with a loaded rifle and hit another over the neck with a shovel, 'all on the slightest provocation'. The authorities in Egypt were insightful enough to recognize that Albert needed a change and complete rest, and that it was time for someone else to water the mules. After four months at Napsbury he was discharged home. Though he may have been a rather simple man, he had given good service with the expeditionary forces for three and a half years, and he did not therefore merit the epithet 'imbecile', delivered with the usual psychiatric venom.

In the later years, especially, the appraisals of the medical officers at Napsbury would have been unlikely for the most part to offend the families of their soldier patients, but in other military treatment units the perceptions of medical officers and relatives were frequently wildly at odds, deriving as they did from conflicting moral valuations. 'He is such a degenerate defective being', opined Dr Henry Yellowlees at the 26th General Hospital, in May 1918 after interviewing Pte Major Jarvis. 'Please write and tell me how Pte Jarvis who is suffering from shell shock is progressing', asked his brother on behalf of a whole bevy of solicitous siblings and in-laws. At Dykebar War Hospital, 'feeblemindedness' was the more moderate label offered, but by the time Major Jarvis reached Napsbury the gap between official and familial appraisals had narrowed still further, and strictures about degeneracy, defect, and feeblemindedness had faded from the picture entirely.

Here are some typical characters on the Napsbury stage. Driver Charles Hill, called up from the reserve at the start of the war, had served 12 months in France and was then admitted to hospital in England suffering from piles where he became very depressed, laden by feelings of self-contempt, guilt and unworthiness, convinced that the doctor had ordered him to be shot for failing in his duty, bursting into floods of tears whenever spoken to, and standing on the same spot for hours, quite unable to occupy himself. Private George Millard, a forty-year old dealer from Cambridge, had re-enlisted from the reserve at the start of the war and had served in France continuously without leave since October 1914; there he had been in four actions, most recently at Hooge, after which he had been admitted to hospital at the end of November 1915 with an incised wound of the throat, self-inflicted in a fit of passion when suffering from ague and cold because he felt he could no longer keep up with the younger men and sustain the efficiency of a good soldier. Sapper Alfred Jacka, looking very depressed and apprehensive, wept when he recounted how, weakened by asthmatic attacks and injury to his heel, he had lost control in France and found himself saying things about the Army that he did not intend for which he must deservedly be shot. 'I am not a German, I am not a spy', he intoned repeatedly to all around him. Private Richard Maddern, a thirty-seven year old quarryman from a village near Penzance in Cornwall, broke down and wept when being examined, saying that he could not get on in the army. Unable to contain himself like a man, he now feared that his mind was going and that he was becoming like his mother who had ended up in an asylum. Private Thomas Martel, who had served only eight months but had been in the firing line at Ypres, also wept when being questioned: 'Labours under profound depression of mind. Sits in one position with head bent between his shoulders and hands between his knees, a picture of infinite woe. Says he is deploring the fate of others who are so bad'.

There is not much to distinguish these individuals, but in fact Hill, Jacka and Millard were 'early' Napsbury (the class of 1916), and Maddern and Martel 'late', arriving in the spring of 1918, by which time, in answer to public concerns, the period that a soldier mental patient was permitted before being pronounced an 'incurable' had in many cases been expanded considerably. Four months or so later, Charles Hill was still standing on the same spot for hours, quite unable to occupy himself, and was removed to Warwick Asylum. However, after six months Thomas Martel had started to improve and no longer wept when questioned, and four months later he was discharged home. Like George Gomm, Arthur Archer had the misfortune to land at Napsbury early in the war, and since after three months his feelings of 'being generally persecuted since joining the Army' still persisted, he was hustled off to Long Grove Asylum in June 1916, just a few weeks in advance of George. James Arnold, who had persisted for so long 'in not knowing anything of himself', was conversing quite rationally by the spring of 1916, though still sullen and silent at times, and rather inclined to grumble, and was discharged as permanently unfit by the summer.

Private Martin O'Brien, who had so much incurred the odium of Capt. Clindening at D Block, arrived at Napsbury in an acutely disturbed state, unable to sleep for the noises like guns that constantly dinned in his ears, his memory for recent events so much diminished that he was unable to recall even what he had had for breakfast. Quite shortly, however, the scrupulous and fair-minded Capt. Hubert Norman quietly revised the military diagnosis of dementia to neurasthenia, and three months later O'Brien was cheerful and occupied, his memory much revived though still defective at points. By this time Norman had established that he had in fact been drinking freely for years and had had delirium tremens, or been bordering on it, on several occasions. By August 1918 Allan Smith, the soldier-poet from Guernsey, was very much improved, free from delusions, no longer ruminating on Doctor Crippen, amenable and usefully occupied. As for James Batchelor, Napsbury provided the conditions in which he was able to recover a more positive sense of himself, for by the end of the year it was reported that he was working well, his delusions of unworthiness had faded, and his mother was most anxious to have him home.

Yet there were limitations to Napsbury, for this was very much a take-it-or-leave-it therapeutic regime, permissive to a degree but robustly pragmatic, in which beyond the initial, and in some instances quite lengthy, interview with a medical officer, inmates were to a large extent expected to find their own way and cater for themselves emotionally speaking, pitching in with the collective life as best they could. Napsbury succeeded in providing the firm but benevolent conditions in which certainly a majority of inmates could make some headway on their own self-healing, enough at least to pull away from the shore of their own misery and despair into more buoyant waters. But it was far less successful with those who were stuck in the quagmire of their perplexities, and required some close engagement from a therapeutic interlocutor with a sympathetic grasp of what was at stake with them. Though they kept him nine months, it would have required a more intensive and prolonged therapeutic environment than Napsbury to provide the conditions in which Charles Abberley, for example, might have begun to recoup some sense of confidence and value in himself. As it was, he appeared to be a case of catatonic dementia praecox, quite unable to explain his thoughts, needs and wants, and he was removed to Staffordshire County Asylum in May 1919.

'Will probably improve rapidly under careful handling and supervision', the doctor at Northumberland War Hospital in Gosforth had remarked of twenty-three year old Alfred Hine in October 1918. 'Has a tendency to stand about in the ward but will sit down, if provided with a chair, and will study, apparently with interest, a pictorial paper handed to him. Can be induced to work to some extent'. At Napsbury, apparently, it did not occur to anyone to offer him a chair and try to engage him: 'he is dull, stands about, takes no interest in anything'. Hine had the bad luck to show up in the therapeutic domain right at the end of the war when there was pressure to scale down the business, and have everything done and dusted, the curables restored to the bosom of their families and the incurables packed off to asylums, an inauspicious moment for someone who was experiencing great difficulty in taking a stand in life. So in July 1919, the authorities made up his mind for him and dispatched him to Bucks County Asylum with a label of dementia praecox.

Undoubtedly Napsbury in some measure provided a soft alternative for a number of servicemen whom hardliners, if they could have had their way, would either have returned to military duty or dispatched to an asylum without further ado. There were, however, limits to the tolerance of the

Napsbury authorities in the relaxation of disciplinary standards, and there was a strict code of behaviour for soldier mental patients that to some extent belied the openness and informality of the regime. Taking advantage of the absence of physical restrictions, in April 1919 Sgt Jack Kendall left the hospital of his own accord and returned home, where, having changed into his civilian clothes, he promptly left again, ignoring the pleas of his relatives. In the middle of June he once more presented himself at Napsbury, claiming that he considered 'he had proved his sanity as he had been away for six weeks and earned his own living and shown himself quite well'. The Napsbury authorities did not dissent from Kendall's self-assessment, even if they did not grant him the plaudits he might have desired, for they pronounced him recovered and promptly returned him to his unit under escort!

There was not infrequently a testing of limits between soldier patients and the medical authorities. Sergeant Henry King was brought to Napsbury from his unit in High Wycombe at the end of 1918 with a label of 'mental instability' and a note from his medical officer reporting that he was fed up with the Army. 'He has a very assertive manner and openly states he won't wear khaki again. . . . In my opinion he is acting consciously to prevent being sent back to the Army'. No doubt at an earlier stage in the war he would have been returned to duty regardless, but at this point, with the ending of hostilities, there was to some degree a collapse of deference. Soldier patients and medical officers were both testing the waters, soldiers to determine how openly they could criticize the Army, doctors how much criticism or rhetorical flouting of military authority they could tolerate without being obliged either to affix a diagnostic label or to take disciplinary action. Three months after he was admitted, Sgt King was discharged without any psychiatric label attached to him or any disciplinary action taken, an ex-servicemen who by official consent was exactly what he took himself to be, no more no less, a man who was fed up with army life.

'GREETINGS FROM NAPSBURY'

In all 3515 servicemen passed through the mental division at Napsbury between 15 May 1915 and 25 July 1919.[23] Though all the inmates were considered certifiable when admitted, only a minority, never more than 30 per cent, quite a lot of them GPI cases, and diminishing over the years of the war, were dispatched to asylums, the majority being discharged from the army and sent home. Not too much should be made of this for, as we shall see, by no means all of those who were returned to civvy street were in a fit condition to stay the course for very long and, conversely, asylums turned out to discharge significantly more of the soldier lunatics who passed through their doors than the image of them as the final resting place of incurables might have predicted. All the same, the low proportion of asylum removals was certainly a barometer of therapeutic achievement of a kind, surely a testimony to the success of this experiment in promoting a more permissive approach to the relief of severe mental and emotional disturbance.

From its origin as a lunatic asylum, Napsbury was successively relabelled not just as a mental hospital, but as a general hospital which happened to have a mental department. There can be no doubt that it was a great boon for the soldier mental patients to find themselves nested in a generalist medical institution in which, apart from cases that were placed under restraint, there was a considerable amount of occupational and recreational – cricket, croquet and quoits – to-ing and fro-ing between groups of patients from different wards and classes of disability, together with relatively relaxed pass arrangements to permit soldier patients to venture outside the institution. [24] Though very probably there was some residual hesitation and uncertainty over the profile of the mental section, still there was no shame in dispatching a postcard to the loved ones back home with 'Greetings from Napsbury' (see page 88).

Coda

Albert Goes To War Again

Wouldn't mind being a waiter in a swell hotel. Tips, evening dress, halfnaked ladies. May I tempt you to a little more filleted lemon sole, miss Dubedat? Yes, do bedad.

James Joyce, Ulysses[1]

And what was now happening with Albert Norris, that indefatigable imbecile turned foot-soldier whose brief military adventure had so abruptly been terminated? There can be no doubt that he might have languished in Long Grove Asylum indefinitely had he not laid other plans.[2] During the second half of 1916, the news that reached the asylum was mostly of losses and stoppages and it became a conspicuously more deprived and cheerless environment: a number of attendants had been killed in action or died of their wounds, the entertainment budget in all the London County Council asylums for the winter months had been cut drastically, the cinematograph licence had been allowed to lapse, economies were even proposed in the consumption of tea, and Albert's companionship with his fellow soldier George Gomm came to an abrupt end in early September, when George was discharged from the asylum 'relieved', and taken home by his father.[3] The only bright spot was that the hospital band had now offered their services free of charge, and so the programme of patients' dances for the forthcoming season would not, after all, have to be cancelled.

But Albert plainly had his sights set on other dance-floors, for on a foggy evening two days after Christmas in 1916 he escaped. As the vexed Medical Superintendent reported to the Committee in January, he was found to be absent from the farmstead villa at dinner time, and was last seen by Attendant Routledge going for a walk round the grounds, and though 'the usual steps' had been taken, he had not been heard of since, although some of his clothing had been returned. In fact, it turns out that by the time the committee had got to learn of his escape, Albert was already employed again in his old situation at De Keyser's Royal Hotel, where it would appear that he must have given satisfaction, because he was shortly promoted from kitchen porter to waiter. That, at any rate, was how he was to describe his occupation in the future, and whether this was really a new station, or perhaps more likely the portering role with a service dimension added, need not concern us, but it does seem probable that Albert now had some form of direct contact with the clientele, and had managed to leap across the social chasm that separated a career imbecile in a public asylum from a waiter ('And how would you like your steak, Sir?') in a grand metropolitan hotel.

This was, in its way, an achievement, but plainly Albert never intended it to be more than a stepping-stone towards the next stage in his military career, for on 2 April 1917 Albert again enlisted at Kingston-upon-Thames, this time as No. 211451 Gunner Albert Norris in the Royal Field Artillery, based at Woolwich in South London. Alas, however, though his military character was 'good', it seems that learning to fire a rifle was perhaps not entirely his métier. Just three months later he was sent up to the military hospital in Woolwich with the statement that he appeared very depressed and absent-minded, and unable to give proper attention to training. 'At the present time he is more or less normal, being an interval between recurrent attacks of melancholia. During these latter, he is very depressed and morose and worries about trifles. Appetite is poor and he is persuaded to eat only with difficulty. Various thoughts, he states, came into his head to break things, although he never actually carries them out'. In July it was recommended that Gunner Albert Norris ('age: 30 years 11 months; height: 5 ft 9 inches; blue eyes; hair turning grey; trade: waiter'), suffering from recurrent melancholia, be discharged from the army 'in consequence of being no longer physically fit for war service', and that he be given out-patient treatment.

So Albert was now defined as having a psychological condition, with recognition of his emotional difficulties, rather than as a defective. The recommendation that he be given out-patient treatment was, of course, code for saying that his condition did not necessitate confinement in an asylum, and that he might instead benefit from a course of psychotherapy. It hardly needs saying that this was a world away from the contemptuous treatment that had repeatedly been meted out to him at the Wandsworth Poor Law Infirmary and by the medical authorities at the asylum. Even though Albert can scarcely be said to have succeeded as a soldier, his enlistment had at the very least provided the vehicle through which he was able to encounter a humane and respectful form of medical treatment that would otherwise have been inaccessible to him. Whatever other meanings his military career may have held for him, it seems that he had to go to war, and endeavour to succeed as a soldier, in order to be able to enjoy a reasonably congenial experience as a psychiatric patient.

Still, not for the first time in the history of health care, prescription out-paced delivery, and Albert never did manage to catch up with the psy-chotherapist who should have been assigned to him; he was discharged from the army, having served for 124 days, with a gratuity of £55. He again found himself alone and friendless in a lodging house in Gassiott Road, Tooting, with the inevitable consequence that before very long the tentacles of the Poor Law mental health system reached out to grasp him (and also to claim his landlady, a Mrs Freeman, as his nominated friend, a connection she hotly denied, 'we are utter strangers to Albert Francis Norris only being acquainted with him 8 days'). So he was re-united once more with Dr Frank Nixey, still at his post at the Wandsworth Union Infirmary, to whom he came over as depressed, nervous and fidgety, confessing with only a little prompting that he had escaped from Long Grove Asylum the previous December during a fog, that he lacked all confidence in himself and had been throwing up one job after another. And, inevitably, it was to Long Grove that he was once again removed.

Part II

JUSTICE FOR THE WAR PSYCHOTIC

– Are you talking about the new Jersualem? says the citizen.
– I'm talking about injustice, says Bloom.

James Joyce, Ulysses[1]

Chapter 5

'INSANE THROUGH FIGHTING FOR THEIR COUNTRY'

'British Beatitudes!.... Beer, beef, business, bibles, bulldogs, battleships, buggery and bishops'.

James Joyce, *Ulysses*[1]

THE 'REASONABLE INTERVAL' FOR RECOVERY

As the war dragged on, inevitably there were competing demands over beds, and the pretence that, apart from a few score obvious incurables, the great majority of 'soldiers rendered insane by the war', and still in need of treatment, could be held in temporary military hospitals until the end of the war could no longer be maintained. 'Cardiff keeping lunatics in military hospitals. Get rid of them', the newly appointed Secretary to the Ministry of Pensions interjected in his diary early in the spring of 1917.[2] As the *Lancet* promoted the treatment regimes in the new military mental hospitals, 'each patient is given a reasonable period of treatment with a view to recovery'.[3] Needless to say, with the war machine panting at its heels, 'a reasonable period' became a contested and elastic property, arguably more so in relation to mental problems than to other categories of disability, for reason was easily vexed and inclined to call 'time' precipitately, and so no wonder that many soldier mental patients and their families felt that a sword of Damocles was being held over them – 'recover or else'!

The War Office now announced that 'no definite time can be stated for which mental and neurasthenic patients are treated before being invalided as incurable', though 'generally speaking it may be said that patients are not invalided until there is no chance of recovery within a reasonable time'.[4] This was indeed a very general kind of speaking to befit a time that was far from reasonable, and the minister was now even unwilling to reveal what types of patients 'suffering from nervous balance or other form of mental disorder' were currently grouped by the military authorities as incurable, stating that it was 'difficult to be more precise' but that each case was carefully considered on its merits.[5]

The catchword here was 'incurability'. When the Under-Secretary for War reported that strict orders had been given that cases of mental disorder in serving soldiers were 'not to be treated as incurable, until it is absolutely certain that they are incurable', he thereby reinforced, lest anyone doubted it, the popular view of the asylum, and the Poor Law mental system as a whole, as degrading institutions for hopeless cases, to be avoided at all costs. 'Every chance', he went on, 'is given for the man to be cured', though 'if it is discovered that he is incurable, of course, he goes into an asylum'.[6] Of course. So sometimes 'incurability' is an administrative decision, a construction of the official mind, but sometimes it is a condition which is sadly discovered after every effort has been made to promote a more promising outcome, a fate whose pitiful diktat cannot be ignored. From an official standpoint there was obviously some advantage in blurring these distinctions, and playing one off against the other.

Thomas Salmon, an astute American observer of British medico-military psychiatric arrangements, did not mince his words in 1917 over the weasel justifications from official lips of the 'reasonable interval' that was extended to mentally distressed servicemen to get control of themselves before they were arraigned as incurables: 'This official attitude toward mental disease results in an average period of treatment far shorter than is required in even the most benign psychoses in civil life. It is evident that mental cases are insufficiently treated in military hospitals'. And he continued:

There is a strong tendency to adopt an entirely different attitude towards insane soldiers than the wonderfully generous one which the nation has adopted towards the wounded and those suffering from physical disease. In the latter, the Government readily admits its responsibility and makes liberal provisions for treatment, pension and industrial re-education, while in the former every effort is made to place the burden of responsibility and of support upon the patient or his relatives by magnifying alleged constitutional tendencies and minimizing the effects of military service.[7]

'It is a big question, both of policy and of finance', an official in the newly created Ministry of Pensions mused at the turn of the new year, 'whether it is desirable to extend the system of military hospitals for the special accommodation of lunatic soldiers'.[8] But in effect a decision on this big question had already been taken by the middle of 1916. Though the authorities were insistent that they were 'most anxious to safeguard nerve-shaken uncertifiable soldiers from any avoidable depression or suspicion associated with lunacy', where the depressive consequences could not be avoided they were now proposing some special arrangements. 'We have been very carefully considering the case of these unfortunate men', the Under-Secretary announced to the House in August. 'Where they are certified as lunatics, it is better for them and their relatives that they should go into the regular asylums, but we are trying to see that they shall have comforts and privileges and shall not in any way be graded with pauper lunatics or, indeed, even with ordinary lunatics. We shall try to get them special treatment if we can'.[9]

THE STATE AND THE DISABLED SERVICEMAN

Father Conmee crossed to Mountjoy square. He thought, but not for long, of soldiers and sailors, whose legs had been shot off by cannonballs, ending their days in some pauper ward, and of cardinal Wolsey's words: If I had served my God as I have served my king He would not have abandoned me in my old days.

James Joyce, *Ulysses*[10]

Talk of 'special treatment' raises the vexed question of war disability pensions, and of the state's obligations towards discharged servicemen. When the Great War broke out, war pensions, far from being a legal right, were a form of bounty granted by the Sovereign, the Royal Warrant providing the instrument by which the Sovereign indicated his pleasure that a pension should be bestowed. It had not always been so, for Elizabeth I, having been 'troubled whensover she takes the air by those miserable creatures', had inaugurated a halcyon interlude in which pensions were provided by statute, and could be claimed by right as a reward for service, without submitting to a physical examination or pleading poverty.[11] But by the late seventeenth century this generous form of entitlement had been eroded, and replaced by notions of pensionable disability in which to qualify for a pension the ex-serviceman's body came under scrutiny. Henceforth he was required to demonstrate that he was disabled, or impaired, in his capacity to work, sometimes having to display his wounds in court, and submit to the discipline of a treatment regime that fastened increasingly tight rules and regulations around the role of war disability pensioner, often obliging him to separate from his family.[12] John Evelyn recorded in his Diary in 1682 that the government of the newly founded Chelsea Hospital was to be 'in every respect as strict as in any religious convent'.[13] To this period we can date the origins of the war disability pensioner as a diminished character in relation to the state by comparison with the serving soldier, variously patronized and belittled, and always mistrusted.

Reviewing the fortunes of the war disability pensioner in the midst of the Great War, contemporaries were struck by the 'difference in outook between the Elizabethan statutory money pension paid to a man with liberty to spend it how he pleased, and the more modern idea of a pensioner subsisting on bounty and housed among a number of officials who were to govern his movements by the strictest discipline'.[14] Even as late as 1914, pensions took no account of family need, the Commissioners of the Chelsea Hospital maintaining that 'the pension is granted for the soldier himself, no matter what his domestic circumstances may be'.[15] The *Comrades Journal* represented a consensus of public opinion in maintaining that before the Great War 'the sailor-soldier, on conclusion of service, was not so much discharged as got rid of – cast aside like a sucked lemon', the 'fine freemasonry of the Services' degenerating 'into the rag-tag and bobtail freemasonry of the gutter and the workhouse'.[16] By no means were these merely polemical flourishes, Charles Booth, among others, having established in his researches on the lives and conditions of London's poor at the end of the previous century that 'among the saddest cases' swelling the populations of casual wards were discharged soldiers, army reserve men, 'some of them quite young men still, often under thirty, with good-conduct badges and good discharges' who, devoid of support and left to fend for themselves, 'gradually become more and more demoralized by the irregular life they lead'.[17]

Undoubtedly the creation of the New Armies had brought about a sea-change in what the British public were prepared to tolerate, and in the expectations they entertained of the state, and even if this contemporary account is somewhat roseate in its portrayal of state complaisance, still it conveys accurately enough the mood of the time:

> Swiftly on the outbreak of the Great War its grim potentialities gripped the imagination of the nation, and the old-time apathy of the State towards the disabled soldier was replaced by one of anxious solicitude. The change in attitude was but the reflex of a puissant nation's awakening to its responsibilities. Stirred to its depths – aglow with sympathy – the will of the people clamoured for some definite expression of the State's purpose regarding the future of the maimed in war.[18]

Until the formation of the Ministry of Pensions, there was no single department of state with responsibility for the discharged serviceman; instead there existed a fragmented infrastructure, involving a multiplicity of different agencies with piecemeal responsibilities. Though new warrants had been issued, 'no sort of codification had taken place, so that it was nearly impossible to ascertain even in the simplest case what a disabled man was entitled to'. The whole idea of 'aftercare' was largely a novel one, an official acknowledged, 'the State having been lamentably negligent of the men broken in war after discharge'.[19] By the beginning of 1916 this parlous state of affairs had impressed itself even upon the War Office, which traditionally had sought to insulate itself from such mundane concerns. 'I think pension matters are going to give more trouble than is realized', an official confided: 'somehow or other the matter has to be faced, and I am convinced that we shall not be allowed to put it off till the end of the War'.[20]

To plug the gaps in pensions administration, the quaintly named Statutory Committee had been created by the government the previous year to assist hard cases, and put some spine into arrangements for aftercare. It was forever short of funds, however, and imperfectly empowered to carry out the tasks that had been laid upon it, making it very evidently a stop-gap device by a government reluctant to demonstrate the resolve that the circumstances of this relentless war increasingly demanded. 'Petting the ex-soldier on the cheap is the note of all its activities', was the acid conclusion reached by Beatrice Webb, who as Mrs Sidney Webb had reluctantly been drafted onto the Committee by the Parliamentary Labour Party.[21] Its signal achievement was, perhaps, the setting up of some 300 Local War Pension Committees, covering the whole of the United Kingdom, which played a very active role during and after the war. The Committee did its own bit to restore the mentally afflicted to health, instructing Local Committees that 'careful medical analysis' had shown that, in many cases, 'the worst thing for a patient of this class is to be placed in an institution, and allowed to brood over his own ailments'. Instead, their efforts 'should be directed to finding employment for such cases, to giving them every encouragement and assistance, and to keeping always before them that they are curable and that in a short time they will be normal citizens'.[22] However, for the most part it was reduced to forming alliances with voluntary organizations, and to talk of creating 'auxiliary hospitals in borrowed houses', to put such solidity as it could into the arrangements for special groups of disabled servicemen.

'INSANE THROUGH FIGHTING FOR THEIR COUNTRY'

'I am not sure', the avuncular Cyril Jackson, who officiated at the Statutory Committee, informed the War Office, 'that I have very much sympathy with the idea that a man who is really a lunatic must be kept out of the lunatic asylum because he is a soldier, but evidently the matter wants thinking out'.[23] Quite evidently it did, and the agency which was to play the lead role in doing so was the Board of Control, which had been created just before the war to oversee the whole system of mental health care, partly as a replacement for the Commissioners in Lunacy of the Victorian period, who had never succeeded in shaking off the suspicions of libertarians, and partly to embody a more modernizing vision of administration rooted in the political currents that had been seeking to bring about reform of the Poor Law. In a supposedly modernizing context, the Board's authoritarian title was, of course, hugely ironic, itself indication enough of how it was squeezed between conflicting interests and visions of its objectives; but, in the current climate of strong public feeling about the fate of mentally disordered soldiers, it was anxious to live down the militaristic connotations in its profile, to be seen as seizing the popular initiative, projecting itself as attentive to individual rights and responsive to the concerns of the mentally disordered and their relatives.[24]

The Statutory Committee had experienced some difficulty in extracting from the War Office the figures of men discharged as lunatics from the Army. However it appears that up to the end of May 1916 there had been around 3000, though there were no statistics to indicate how these had been distributed in asylums and workhouses, and the War Office had not thought it profitable to put the effort into finding out.[25] This figure probably represents the most accurate quantification available of the overall number of servicemen who had been discharged directly into the public asylum system at this stage of the war, and considerably exceeds the total number of servicemen who had passed through D Block Netley by this point: around 2500, of whom not more than 1000 were sent to asylums. It must be concluded that at this stage of the war around two-thirds of the asylum admissions were from the Home Forces (and would have included Albert, for example), and had been dispatched there directly from their units or from military hospitals in Britain. Doubtless this tells a tale about the poor quality of many of the recruits, but it may also show that it was easier for commanding officers on the home front to dispose of 'mad' soldiers directly, without having to resort to the therapeutic rigmarole of permitting them a 'suitable interval' in which to recover.

As early as December 1915, there had, apparently, already been some inconclusive discussion about insane servicemen between the Board of Control and benighted pension officials from the Chelsea Hospital, who displayed their contempt both for soldier lunatics and for those misguided enough to believe that they merited special consideration. In June 1916, the Chelsea spokesman was still vexed that so much was being made of the 'stigma of pauperism', insisting that 'it would be a mistake to give too much attention to the so-called "pauper taint" 'since 'the patient was usually unconscious of it' and 'his friends generally recognized it as inevitable'. But this time round the Board of Control countered more robustly, aligning itself very deliberately with a wider current of popular feeling. 'There is . . . a strong feeling, shared by our Board', opined the chairman, Marriott Cooke, 'that the stigma is one to which men who have become insane through fighting for their Country ought not to be subject, and to avoid which, every effort should be made'.[26] The most remarkable thing about this statement, from the pen of a distinguished alienist and former asylum superintendent, is less the recognition of the stigma than the acknowledgement, for the psychiatric community of the time highly contentious, that there was indeed a constituency of men who had 'become insane through fighting for their country'.[27] The Board was now predicting that, in view of 'the present large armies, the numbers of soldiers who must be expected to become insane would be very considerable', and the immediate business was to remove epileptics, general paralytics and former asylum inmates who had found their way into the Services from the mental wards of military hospitals, to make way for 'fresh acute and curable cases'.[28] This may have been a stale and incurable bunch, but – as we shall see – even many of these were to be permitted (conditionally, at least, for the pensions bureaucracy always yearned to interpolate a qualification) to march into the future under the rhetorical banner of the insanity of war that was being hoist at this juncture.

If 'active service' had been injurious to these servicemen's mental health, just as damaging it would appear was a period of residence in a pauper lunatic asylum. The Board shared in 'the strong, widely prevalent feeling . . . that sailors and soldiers who have lost their mental balance while on active service in the course of the present War, should not be classed as paupers'. 'Provision for their health' demanded an alternative tack. If the Board of Control could not keep insane servicemen out of the asylum altogether, they could at least endeavour to keep them out of the asylum in its embodiment as a Poor Law institution. Having given the matter their 'anxious consideration', they came up with the proposal that insane servicemen should be placed in public asylums in a special category known as 'Service Patients', in which they would be classified as private patients and paid for out of a state pension, receive special privileges, such as a weekly allowance of 2/6d. for 'additional comforts', and wear a distinctive badge or even a uniform that marked them off from ordinary lunatics. If they had the misfortune to die in an asylum they would be spared the indignity of burial in an asylum cemetery or in a pauper's grave.[29] Overall, it was intended, in the populist rhetoric of the day, to attire them as 'honoured pensioners of the state rather than recipients of Poor Law relief'.

The Board of Control was able to take the lead with its proposals for the Service Patient scheme at this early stage largely because they were being hatched at a critical transitional phase in the creation of the institutional framework for the delivery and administration of war disability pensions. Actions in the field were already swamping existing facilities and resources with a far mightier tide of acute cases than could ever have been anticipated. After months of stonewalling, the War Office finally renounced all pretensions to be able to carry the burden of aftercare, not only for nervous and mental cases, but for other groups such as paraplegics, amputees, epileptics, and advanced consumptives. In the summer of 1916 Sir Alfred Keogh, the head of the Army Medical Services, let it be known that, in his personal opinion, the War Office would be wise to relinquish responsibility for the future of mentally and nervously affected soldiers to another agency.[30] Forced to retrench on earlier assertions it had made about the extended care that it could offer to disabled servicemen, the War Office was vacating a space in which it had now become politically feasible and expedient to create a unifying agency outside the military domain. However, though the Ministry of Pensions was already in existence as the Service Patient scheme was being negotiated, it still had to wait upon the demise of the Statutory Committee before it became fully fledged, and there was a critical interlude in which the Board of Control, in concert with the Statutory Committee, did much of the running.

Moreover, though it was quickly to create its own expertise around the whole subject, at this point at least the Ministry was a neophyte in everything that concerned lunatics and the whole domain of asylumdom, and was entirely dependent upon the Board of Control to serve as handmaiden and provide induction into the niceties of asylum culture. A pauper lunatic, Marriott Cooke instructed a Pensions official, is a 'person whose maintenance is wholly or partly chargeable to the rates of a Union, County or Borough', and a 'private patient' is simply 'a patient who is not a pauper'. Though the private patient had a distinct legal status under the 1890 Act, the relatives possessing a power over the person of the lunatic that was not available to the families of pauper lunatics, the institutional reality of private patienthood was highly protean, conveying a strong whiff of corporate mystification in which facilities or privileges that amounted to rather little were made to look more appealing to potential consumers. Some asylums did not accept private patients at all, others:

... while accepting them, provide no separate accommodation away from the pauper patients and merely grant them a few extra privileges, such as wearing their own clothes; again, others provide a separate ward in the main building for those private patients who are fairly controlled and able to appreciate special advantages, such as a diet somewhat superior to that supplied to the pauper patient; and lastly, other Visiting Committees provide separate accommodation for private patients in one or more detached blocks where the arrangements are of a higher order, and, in some instances, permit of a certain amount of classification, according to the patient's mental state.[31]

But if the Board appeared to be sailing confidently with the popular winds, and was being bolstered also by progressive medical opinion, there were other forces within the emerging Ministry of Pensions, and within the Treasury especially, that were intent upon scaling back and trivializing the Board's proposals and its displays of concern for the dignity of insane servicemen and their families. 'We presume', an official at the Ministry of Pensions mused, 'that the Asylum Authorities could generally judge whether a patient felt the pauper stigma'. In this unlikely event, perhaps 'it might be possible to raise a man out of the pauper class by inducing the Authorities to let him wear his own clothes or to let him have in cash or kind something above the cost of his maintenance.' Instead, he sneered, the Statutory Committee and the Board of Control had fallen for 'the popular view' and were now bent on devising a plan by which 'the lunatic soldier may enjoy a privileged position'.[32] The Treasury was already irked by the excessive liberality that was being shown towards disabled servicemen, even by the Chelsea Commissioners, and they were prepared to sanction the Service Patient scheme only on the strict understanding that care would be taken in all cases 'to secure the most favourable terms from Asylum authorities', spurning those institutions whose rates were especially high.[33]

SOLDIER, LUNATIC, PAUPER

Regardless of what the fiscal laggards may have wanted, however, the converging pressures from the War Office, which wanted the service mental patients moved out of the military hospitals, and from public opinion, which wanted them kept out of the pauper lunatic wards, to produce a publicly acceptable arrangement were mounting. 'I think we shall have a ruling at once as to insanity', Cyril Jackson announced in February 1917, 'as there is a good deal of pressing from various sources for these soldiers not to be counted as paupers'. In March, the Minister of Pensions confided that he was 'getting anxious in the face of the rising indignation at mentally disabled soldiers being treated as pauper lunatics'; around the middle of April, the War Office demanded to know what the Statutory Committee was doing to ensure that lunatic soldiers were not being put in pauper wards, and by the end of May, Cyril Jackson was becoming impatient with the Ministry of Pensions, complaining that a month had passed since he had written with 'certain definite questions as to the Lunatics' and was still awaiting a reply, warning that 'there are continually arising questions of individuals in Asylums on the pauper side and there is likely to be another explosion'.[34]

The 'pauper side' was certainly receiving quite an airing. In June 1917, it was revealed that 1216 men had been discharged from the Army for insanity and granted pensions, but the Royal Hospital at Chelsea was unable to say how many lunatic soldiers had been *refused* pensions, and claimed that to find out they would have had to sift through 240,000 sets of papers, an impracticable exercise in the circumstances.[35] In any event, it was obvious that there were quite enough of these refused claims to fuel the engines of suspicion, for over the previous months a whole string of cases alleging official miserliness towards mentally distressed soldiers and their families had been brought to light, as is revealed by the tale of three men of Leicester which had been reported in the press. Private Arthur Weavell, who had been serving with the 3rd Leicestershire Regiment, was admitted to the Borough Asylum at Leicester on 16 October 1914, direct from D Block Netley, not having been overseas in the current war, though he had previously served abroad. He had been refused a pension, and his wife and family were receiving out-door relief of 14/6d. weekly. Private Harry Sidwell, a gunner with the Royal Garrison Artillery, had been admitted to the same asylum in May 1915, only having done home service, and the Guardians of the Leicester Union had purloined the sum of £13.9.4 owing to him on his discharge as a contribution to his maintenance in the asylum. And Private Arthur Hughes, serving with the 10th Leicesters, was admitted to the asylum in November 1916, and though he was initially granted a pension of 4/8d. per week, the Royal Hospital Chelsea soon determined that his disability had neither been caused nor aggravated by his 'short military service'.[36]

Official decisions like these were, however, starting to be overturned as the result of an appeal either by family members to their MP, the action of a wider local constituency, or sometimes even by a member of the medical profession who had broken ranks with what appeared to be the military medical view. As the case of Private Allsop brings out, there was an emerging politics here involving dissension between military and civilian medical judgments. A married man with seven children who attested under the Derby scheme and joined from the reserve in August 1916, Allsop had been admitted to hospital in the following November for observation as to his mental condition, and discharged to duty a month later.[37] In January 1917, he was again admitted to hospital where he was given a diagnosis of idiocy ('congenital, obviously of deficient intellect and no use in the Army') and finally discharged the service, never having served abroad, and sent to an asylum in March 1917. The medical officer in the Military Hospital was of the opinon that he had 'always been simple minded', and as a result his claim for pension was rejected and he was fobbed off with a gratuity of £55. However, the medical superintendent of Mickleover Asylum where Allsop was finally dispatched begged to differ, believing that he had broken down under the stress of miltary service, and lent his support to an appeal that was being mounted by Allsop's family and other supporters in the locality. In another case, the Thrapston District War Pensions Committee was appealing against the rejection by the Chelsea Commissioners of a pension claim by Private Albert York, who was called up for service in March 1916, served at home for six months, and was then admitted to the mental department of a war hospital where he was given a diagnosis of dementia. In the opinion of the medical board, his condition bore no connection with military service but was probably due to masturbation and had most certainly been aggravated by Albert's lewd behaviour.[38]

These are both examples of 'gratuity men', servicemen who had either been refused pensions, often because they were believed not have seen any direct action, having served exclusively on the home front, or had been given a small gratuity in lieu of a pension. At this stage of the war gratuity thinking was the order of the day – fob off a large proportion of ex-servicemen (particularly if they were psychological cases) with a small grant; get them to realize that the gratuity was final and that their connection with the War Office and the Chelsea Hospital had been terminated and that the authorities now had done with their case; concoct a justifying theory which pooh-poohed the disability and placed most of the blame for the condition, and the onus for the remedy, on the man himself; and claim that this was an excellent scheme in which curative zeal and fiscal parsimony was harmoniously combined, the object being 'partly to lessen the pension charge but still more to cure the man'.[39] The High Priest of gratuity thinking was Sir John Collie who, as President of the Special Medical Board for Neurasthenia and Functional Nerve Disease, was charged with the responsibility for defending the ministerial ramparts against the oncoming pensions tide, going about his task with an imaginative relish that was forever imputing malign motives to those mentally distressed servicemen who had the misfortune to find themselves in his domain.

Above all, Sir John counselled suspicion and distrust. Though there were few malingerers to be met with (these had mostly been weeded out at an earlier stage), still 'gross exaggeration, both conscious and unconscious' was frequently encountered, and experience had taught him to be mistrustful of 'the value of alleged subjective symptoms' in the absence of physical corroboration. It was, he believed, 'unwise to place too much reliance upon a nervous manner, coarse tremor or marked stammering alone', for these were 'often induced or unconsciously exaggerated at the time of the examination'.[40] Thus when he 'thoroughly examined' Private A. A. King he found only that King was sleepless, jumpy and complained of 'battle dreams', 'all of which, be it noted, were subjective symptoms', and no evidence of disease, and awarded him a gratuity of £35. When a request was received from King's Local War Pensions Committee six months later asking that he be re-boarded because he was in distress, his funds exhausted, Sir John responded tetchily. Private King had been 'liberally dealt with', he insisted, the grant must have been spent foolishly, and if cases such as this were to be re-examined the 'object for which these gratuities are being granted will be effectually defeated'.[41]

George Barnes, the Labour MP who became the first Minister of Pensions, may all along have been a doughty champion of the disabled, urging as early as the winter of 1914 a minimum pension of £1 a week for disabled servicemen and for widows, but Privates Allsop and York were undoubtedly among the straggling contingent, estimated to number around 100,000, against whom Barnes inveighed early in March 1917: 'Hundreds of them have been passed into the Army who should never have been passed in – veritable weeds who ought never to have been there at all. . . . We shall assume some responsibility, and it will be measured by this. We shall put them back where we found them, and I think that is sufficient'.[42] For that maverick back-bencher, the Liberal MP James M. Hogge, the Member for East Edinburgh, the founder and leader until after the Armistice of the National Federation of Discharged Soldiers and Sailors, who had become a fierce advocate of the disenfranchised 100,000 'veritable weeds', this was far from sufficient, since in his opinion they were entitled to pensions 'by their physical conditions, financial need and service to the country'.[43]

Shortly after his appointment as Secretary to the Ministry of Pensions, Sir Matthew Nathan had already singled Hogge out as a potential subversive requiring a careful watch, pasting in his notebook a newspaper clipping reporting on a meeting in Edinburgh at which Hogge proposed a set of Pension Commandments for the Government: '1) Thou shalt overhaul the scale of pensions and fix a minimum below which no one will fall; 2) Thou shalt introduce greater elasticity into the scale and make the pension fit the man, not the man the pension; and 3) [underlined in red by Nathan] *Thou shalt shoulder the burden of every man accepted as medically fit if he is scrapped*'.[44] Hogge was already put out that he had been passed over as Minister of

Pensions, and his advocacy of the 'veritable weeds' did nothing to advance his ambitions, prompting Nathan later that year to warn Lloyd George against appointing him to the position.[45]

All the same, James Hogge was blazing a trail in which others were already following, for by the spring of 1917 the scene had shifted dramatically. The fiscal laggards were now being forced to concede considerable ground; traditionalists who had been holding the line on pensions for 'noble heroes' only were having to swallow their disappointment, and a more liberal interpretation of 'active service' was being promoted by officials who only a few months earlier would have denounced any such move. Historians have tended to suggest that mentally scarred servicemen received a raw deal at the hands of officialdom, maintaining that entitlement to a pension was subordinated to heroic values.[46] Of course, there is plentiful evidence in support of this interpretation. Even though the Board of Control was from the outset sympathetic to the claims of insane servicemen, at a conference in July 1916 they expressed the strong view that in making provision for pensions a distinction should be made 'between soldiers who became insane in this country without having been sent on active service and those who have broken down mentally abroad'.[47] It would be misleading to suggest that the viewpoint which Sir John Collie in particular epitomized was eclipsed entirely – indeed, as we shall see, this was far from the case, for in concert with other forces it was to live on, and largely to prevail, in the deliberations of the Ministry of Pensions throughout the interwar period. All the same, it is significant that the crucial decisions about the pension framework for mentally disabled servicemen were finally taken from a standpoint that, not to put too fine a point on it, was diametrically opposed to what Sir John Collie stood for.[48]

Chapter 6

JUSTICE FOR THE CITIZEN SOLDIER

One Macnamara who had served 2m[onths] appeared with his sister, but when I sat by the fire with him he would say nothing, I think out of his mind or barely sane. His sister said he wrote letters of interest for about a month, then one day came which made her know his mind was affected. . . . It was clear that the strain of the army was too much for him. It was agreed to grant his appeal.[1]

Sir Norman Moore, Ministry of Pensions Appeal Tribunal, 29 Jan 1918

CIVILIANS AT WAR

To what extent had those who later broke down been fit for service in the first place? Recruitment procedures were indisputably a shambles, and throughout the war military and medical definitions of fitness remained enormously elastic. Following a much-publicized fiasco in which the military authorities had deliberately been subverting the recommendations of civilian doctors, revised procedures under civil control were instituted by the National Service Board in 1917 to provide a 'human sorting machine for grouping men according to their degree of physical fitness' from 'one of the most valued assets of the State – a farm of manhood'.[2] Even now, however, only very cursory enquiries as to a man's mental condition were made, and there is abundant evidence that the unfit were still being passed as fit, with men being passed into Grade I or II who at best were fit for III or IV. All the same, the authorities were disarmingly candid about the quality of the fare that the great collective 'farm of manhood' was able to offer, commenting acidly not long after the Armistice that 'we may well be surprised that, with human material of such physique, it was possible to create the Armies which overthrew the Germans and proved invincible in every theatre of War'.[3]

We can, however, do no more than hazard a guess as to the proportion of the mentally afflicted who should never have been passed in the first place. Surgeon-General Bedford may have been shocked in June 1917 to stumble upon some of the 'specimens of humanity' which had been accepted into the

Army, 'men almost totally blind, deformed dwarfs of the poorest intellect, men with extreme oedema of both legs, almost unable to stand, cases of very severe and marked rheumatism, cases of marked paresis which rendered locomotion almost grotesque', and 'several cases of insanity which told their own tale at a glance'.[4] But those who were visibly and audibly barking on enlistment were in no sense typical of the psychiatric fallout of the war, nor were they drawn from the ranks of the 'veritable weeds' in large numbers, for many of them served for extended periods before breaking down. Though it is likely that at every stage of the war there were some who strove to cover up, and put a good face on, their disabilities at the examination, by no means could the destinies of the majority of recruits be read from the signs that were available to the recruitment board. As far as the boards were concerned, 'fitness' was a scarce and elusive commodity, and so a vague family resemblance would frequently have had to suffice. Moreover, in some instances, as with Albert Norris, like a marital couple who, unsuited though they may be, cannot quite bring themselves finally to give each other up, such was the need for manpower in the one partner and the lusty patriotic ardour of the other, producing its own unique synergy, that if the arrangement did not quite live up to expectations first time round, the breakdown or separation proved only temporary, leading the two parties after a brief interval to forget their disappointment at each other's failings, rekindle their romantic hopes in each other, and renew their embrace.

Thus, to a considerable extent, it would be a mistake to lay responsibility for the major psychiatric casualties of the war on the weaknesses and fallibilities of the recruitment system. 'Unfit' many of these recruits may have been, but it is not the kind of unfitness that could be readily measured and detected, or at least that could be accommodated within the calibrations of a recruitment procedure, for it could only have resulted in the conclusion that a very large proportion of the potential recruits which the 'farm of manhood' could muster were quite unsuited to the tasks that were being demanded of them, and quite unprepared, regardless of their resolve, for military life. A contemporary psychologist revealed in 1918 that the vast majority of cases of war neurosis he had studied were people who were 'well adapted to civil life but capable only to a limited degree of enduring the strain of modern warfare', since those qualities 'which may be the greatest assets to the civilian, and to the country in which he lives, may be just those characteristics which are most apt to jeopardize complete adaptation to trench warfare'. To make it incontestably plain that 'the ideal soldier must be more or less of a natural butcher, a man who can easily submit to the domination of intellectual inferiors', the examples he gives of these prized but disabling civilian qualities are 'independence of judgment, and a strong feeling of sympathy for those in pain'.[5]

'Men broke down in combat, in this war,' argues Samuel Hynes, discussing W. H. Rivers's study of shell shock, 'because their lives had not prepared them to face danger, because they were *civilians*'. And the lesson that he draws from Rivers is 'that *civilianness* itself, the experience of ordinary life in a civilized community, is a poor preparation for modern war and thus in an army composed of civilians there will be mental conflicts and breakdowns'. He notes, for example, how rarely acts of personal killing figure in war narratives, and comments: 'These civilian soldiers seem to hold back from confessing to the essential act that a soldier *must* perform but that a civilian must *not*'.[6] Though the spectre of death constantly hangs over the testimonies of the soldiers who became inmates of Napsbury War Hospital, it is noteworthy that the act of killing is mentioned hardly at all.

Of course, there were thousands who, even if in an important respect they always remained citizens in uniform, truly became soldiers, for a time at least, and it would be unjust to underestimate the staying power and resolve of many of those whose primary experience of life until now had been in 'clerical surroundings'. One such was Private Ernest Bacon, who wrote to his employer from a training camp in Wiltshire in March 1916 telling of how 'such sudden difference in life & surroundings . . . have naturally left me somewhat shaken. The men here are to say the least a very rough lot, not bad hearted but very foul mouthed. . . . I trust everything is in order at the office. . . . I must honestly say that I do wish I were back already. I could honestly say that my services would be of much more use in any civil capacity than in the Army so far as I can judge already'. However, when he wrote again in August under the cover of the British Expeditionary Force he was obviously 'well on the way' in more senses than one, still a civilian at heart but for the time being predominantly a soldier and learning to adapt to new surroundings: 'Will you kindly excuse roughly written note to say that I am well on the way. The home training has done me no harm, although I have felt rather done up at times. I may say I am at the "Base". The spirits of all here are bright and high. To bring one's self to pen and ink is rather a task after 5 months break from it, and not in clerical surroundings.' Five months later he went down with influenza and trench fever, but a few weeks into the new year he was back at the front line in the trenches.[7]

A failing as a soldier did not necessarily indicate a want of patriotic resolve, for those who remained perplexed, anguished citizens were often their own harshest critics in lambasting themselves for their ineffectual performance in the national cause, stymied as they frequently were by the distress they endured in being forcibly separated from their familiar surroundings, occupational as much as domestic. But if, in the circumstances, this was a matter of profound disappointment and regret for their friends and family, it was scarcely an object of reproach. Winifred Clark later recounted how when her husband Wilfred, twenty-nine years old at the time, was conscripted for army service from civil life in 1917, he became so hopelessly nervous, trembling and shaking, that he had to be brought home under escort, even before his uniform had been issued. After a period working on munitions to 'do his bit', he had been called up again, and served for two years with the RAMC without incident, venturing as far afield as Marseilles, but five years later he was unable to maintain his employment as a marble mason, so much agitated was he by the wrongs he had done, and the disgrace that he had brought on his family, that in March 1922 he had to be removed to Long Grove asylum.[8]

Out of the civilian experience of war on the Western Front more generally, there emerged a revaluation of military morality in which a value such as courage came to signify not so much a heroic and risky adventure as sheer staying power, stoic endurance, in the face of awful, awesome adversity. 'Civilianness', to use Hynes's term, became not only central to the experience of war itself, but central also to the wider social and cultural impact of the war, and to the deliberations and responses of official agencies to the casualties of war. On the Western Front in the summer of 1916 there was a revealing stand-off between opposing civilian and military values. On the night of 10 July 1916, a party from the 11th Battalion of the Border Regiment was ordered to take 200 yards of the enemy's front line trench and attack the support line, but even before the party set out men were reporting sick, saying that they could not 'go over', and such was the slow progress through the trenches, with some men taking wrong turnings, and the 'great lack of the offensive spirit in the party', that the attack had to be abandoned.

The Battalion medical officer, Lt Geoffrey Kirkwood, was unstinting in his defence of these reluctant foot soldiers. 'I must hereby testify', he stated, 'to their unfitness for such an operation as few, if any, are not suffering from some degree of shell shock'. At the enquiry that followed the aborted mission, he revealed that the attack a week earlier when the Battalion had 'lost all its officers, and more than half the men, had a most demoralising effect and the men had not recovered their mental equilibrium. . . . The few days rest at Contay sorting out deceased comrades' kits did not improve their mental state. . . . Digging out the dead in the trenches and carrying them down, as well as living in the atmosphere of decomposed bodies . . . exposure in open trenches under continuous shelling and <u>without</u> <u>sleep</u>.' Yet this was exactly the kind of sympathetic account of exhaustion and war weariness that was nicely calculated to rouse Kirkwood's military superiors to a state of apoplexy. 'The facts disclose a deplorable state of discipline and an entire absence of courage and of soldierly qualities', opined General Gough, 'and the conduct on the part of Lt Kirkwood shows him to be totally unfitted to hold a commission in the Army or to exercise any military responsibility. It is inconceivable how men who pledged themselves to fight and uphold the honour of the country could degrade themselves in such a manner, and show an utter want of manly spirit and courage, which at least is expected of every soldier and every Britisher.'[9]

Even if the point of view which Geoffrey Kirkwood represented was to a large extent trounced on the battlefront, the 'blimpocracy' was given its come-uppance at home in the later stages of the war when 'civilianness' sounded the keynote. The sway of traditional military values as the supreme tribunal, before which a serviceman who had failed to make a real soldier of himself was derided as an 'inferior individual', and his worth as a man put in question before God and his fellows, was at the very least arrested. Though it is certainly true that from the second half of the nineteenth century onwards the business of preparing for war had progressively penetrated into the wider society, coming to be seen as a normal and even as a desirable social activity, with military values and attitudes being carried over into the civilian sphere, still there remained in Britain a persisting hostility, among the working classes especially, towards the militarization of society.[10] The First World War produced in this regard a significant counterblast of 'civilianness', in which the citizenry succeeded not necessarily in thwarting, but certainly in restricting the dominion of militarized social relations over disadvantaged groups such as the psychiatric casualties of war.

DADDY WAS A LUNATIC

So where are they coming from exactly, these critical voices with their 'anxious solicitude as to the incapacitated', pressing for concessions from the 'blimpoc-racy' and for justice for those who had been mentally afflicted by their war service? Though it was by no means vocalized exclusively by women, most obviously this 'anxious solicitude' was the expression of a feminized stand-point on life; as Doris Kaufmann has remarked, women took the connection between war and mental illness for granted.[11] In no sense were these concerned voices 'innocent of public spiritedness', singing of 'private disgust and diffidence', and turning 'weakness' into a criterion of authenticity.[12] Still, by pressing the claims of other goods or values apart from the military life, a host of other actors within the civilian sphere was starting to assemble a formidable moral counterweight to the generals and military doctors. That they were in large measure successful in erecting such barricades of resistance to the incursions of military morality is not accidental, for they reflected a flourishing counter-current in Edwardian Britain, a contrasting vision of the political nation, more comprehensively egalitarian and pluralist, based around individuals as citizens, offset against the ruling imperialist, property-based, hierarchical and male-dominated establishment, with individuals pulled in alternate directions, towards uniformity and collective efficiency, but equally towards lifestyles that prized privacy and personal relationships and the cultivation of psychological individualism.[13]

A retired general practitioner who by his own admission wanted to 'do his bit' for national service, Montagu Lomax had secured a post as an assistant medical officer in one of England's largest county lunatic asylums. It is surely telling that in his searing exposé published soon after the war of the conditions that he discovered there, Lomax, 'that obscure and neglible person, a locum tenens', himself an instance in his temperament and position of a rather hesitant and uncertain form of manhood, delivers a feminized appreciation of the asylum scene as a bleak male-ridden domain from which the woman in a caring role is woefully missing. 'How often have I not wished', he writes, 'for a woman's co-operation when dealing with male cases, especially those "confusional" cases due to shell-shock in ex-soldiers, so many of whom are now drifting into our asylum wards'. He places towards the centre of his narrative as the exemplary service inmate a young soldier of twenty who was constantly visited in the asylum by his devoted sisters. 'The boy wanted mothering, not dragooning into obedience. With wise and gentle management he might soon have recovered; as it is, I fear to think what may have happened to him'.[14] Even if this affecting portrait of sisterly devotion to a dear brother, whose unalloyed innocence is so fanciful as to put Lomax's clinical judgment in question, is not wholly convincing, all the same it is well adapted to Lomax's polemical purposes, and succeeds admirably in persuading the reader that the asylum is an impersonal and degrading domain from which all decent and compassionate virtues have largely been extinguished.

And there is something else here as well. As Samuel Hynes remarks, the famous recruiting poster of the middle-class father with a little girl on his lap asking, 'Daddy, what did YOU do in the Great War?', would not have worked for previous wars because Daddy would simply not have been going to war.[15] In this war, by contrast, there was a vast recruitment of men like Daddy, a great swathe of middling sorts of people falling between the military and imperialist middle class at one extreme and the 'scum of the earth', who had long been the regular purveyors of material to the military machine, at the

Daddy, what did YOU do in the Great War ?

Daddy may well look pensive, not because he has anything to hide or be ashamed of, but because his is not an easy story to tell and very likely he is still at loggerheads with the Ministry of Pensions. He was not necessarily an officer during the war, and might well have passed through Napsbury War Hospital and Long Grove Asylum, and now be seated in an armchair at home in Wandsworth.

other. The problem with Hynes's narrative, however, is that his identification with the officer class leads him to transfigure Daddy and his associates into officers and temporary gentlemen, and so to retain a rather stereotyped and undifferentiated image of the ordinary soldier. Yet, in actuality, such middling sorts were assimilated into the other ranks as well, and for a complex of reasons not all of them were commissioned. Moreover, as we have already discussed, the aspirations of 'the people' were increasingly converging about the middle. The agitation over war disability pensions for psychiatric casualties was moved by an urgent desire to force an exit for ordinary soldiers who had become insane from the cul de sac of demeaning imagery, and to secure an official recognition that the soldier who had broken down was no less 'respectable', 'decent', and 'deserving' than Daddy. Daddy and his kind also comprised Montagu Lomax's primary readership, and so it is scarcely accidental that the young shell-shocked soldier in his narrative, 'well educated and well brought up', who had planned to follow in his father's career as a land surveyor had the war not intervened, and could as well have been an officer as an ordinary ranker, was explicitly drawn from just this constituency.[16] Among the various destinies that Daddy might have followed in the Great War, becoming an asylum inmate as a soldier lunatic was surely one of them.

THE MAKING OF THE WAR PSYCHOSIS PENSIONER

The long-suffering Cyril Jackson reported in a tone of some bewilderment on a meeting with Dr Hubert Bond of the Board of Control in which 'as a mental expert he said he believed it was impossible for any Medical Board to decide that a man's insanity had *not* been aggravated by service even supposing he had been previously in an Asylum and discharged'. The Board, Dr Bond had gone on to say, wanted to see an end to gratuities for insane servicemen and to press for acceptance of the general presumption that 'the fact that a man has passed the medical tests required for entry into either of the services ought, prima facie, to be sufficient to entitle him to be treated as a "Service Patient"'. The object of the Board of Control, Bond concluded, was that *all* men should be classed as Service Patients as 'otherwise injustice would be done'.[17]

How had things come to such a pretty pass? In the first place the liberalization of the pensions system had already, though certainly not as much as its critics would have liked, found expression in the new Royal Warrant, for 'in cases when there was any doubt as to whether a man's disability had been caused or aggravated by service or not, the benefit of the doubt was always to be given to the man and not to the State, as had been the tendency in the past'. As soon as the new Warrant became operative on 4 April 1917, the staff of the Ministry 'were immediately engaged on the great work of revising all the old awards' and of trying to make it 'as perfect and as workmanlike an instrument as possible for doing justice to the gallant men disabled in the war'. By the autumn there were nearly 900,000 cases on the books (including pensions and gratuities to disabled men, widows and dependants), and new awards were being made at the rate of about 14,000 a week.[18]

The scale of pensions had been raised all round, and the 'vicious principle' that earnings were to be taken into account in assessing pension had been abolished. A war disability pension was now based solely on an assessment of the serviceman's mental and physical condition as a pecuniary compensation for the hurt which had been inflicted on a percentage scale of increasing impairment: 20% for one testicle, 50% for both testicles, 100% for total blindness, loss of two or more limbs, lunacy and so forth.[19] Though a cachet still attached to a wound, the sway of the Royal Army Medical Corps over the military traditionalists had succeeded in enhancing the status of diseases, and for the other ranks there was now, at least in theory, a level playing field in which pensions for diseases attributable to war service had equality of status with wound pensions.[20] The rates for disabilities which had been aggravated by war service had also been raised to the same level as the rates for disabilities actually caused by service, a dramatic departure from traditional practice, for at the outbreak of war only diseases that were directly and wholly due to war service were eligible for any form of pension.[21]

By the summer of 1917, moreover, public support for the war could no longer be taken for granted. There had been a wave of industrial unrest, conscription was much resented, and Lloyd George's coalition ministry was concerned to allay fears about the militarization of society. Amidst allegations that the aims of the allies were 'Imperialistic and illiberal', politicians could no longer blithely assume that the working classes would continue to accept their leadership.[22] This was also the historical moment when, as Samuel Hynes has observed, there was a marked 'turn of language and rhetoric' in writing about the war at home and in the private prose of serving soldiers. H. G. Wells's Mr Britling found himself quite unable to finish his letter, and the idea of heroism, if not exactly rejected, had become more ambiguous and ironic.[23] 'The troops have settled down to war as slaves to their task', wrote a medical officer to his wife, capturing the ugliness that the war had imposed, 'it is a sad spectacle to see free citizens of a civilized empire thus degraded'.[24]

Not that all the forces of the left were gathered under the class alliances that pressed for generous war disability pensions for the mentally ill as for other disabled groups. Though Beatrice Webb found 'moral magnificence in the unsensational dutifulness unto death of millions now enlisting', expressing disdain for the misguided youths who had allowed themselves to be swept up into the conscientious objection movement, 'pasty-faced furtive boys' she called them, she did not find any magnificence in the work of the Statutory Committee. She was not interested 'in the pensioning of soldiers and their dependants', she declared rather peevishly, and 'except for the relation of the treatment of disabled soldiers to a reorganized medical service, all the details of the work bored' her.[25] Her position was hardly surprising, for she had been opposed to the Workmen's Compensation Act, and was in any case mistrustful of the lower orders, and it was no thanks to her that mentally damaged servicemen did eventually receive some immediate consideration from the state, for she would have readily sacrificed them on the altar of long-term collective health reform.[26]

SCALE OF PENSIONS THAT MAY BE GRANTED FOR SPECIFIC INJURIES.

Degree of disablement	Specific injury	Proportion corresponding to degree of disablement	Disablement Pensions						
			If not entitled to a Service Pension					Warrant or N.C. Officers entitled to Service Pensions	Private, &c. (Class V) irrespective of Service Pension to which entitled
			Warrant Officer, Class I	Warrant Officer, Class II, or N.C. Officer, Class I	N.C. Officer, Class II	N.C. Officer, Class III	N.C. Officer, Class IV		
		Per cent.	s. d.	s. d.	s. d.	s. d.	s. d.	s. d.	s. d.
1	Loss of two or more limbs Loss of an arm and an eye Loss of a leg and an eye Loss of both hands or of all fingers and thumbs Loss of both feet Loss of a hand and a foot Total loss of sight Total paralysis Lunacy Wounds, injuries or disease resulting in disabled man being permanently bedridden Wounds of or injuries to internal, thoracic or abdominal organs, involving total permanent disabling effects ... Wounds of or injuries to head or brain involving total permanent disabling effects, or Jacksonian epilepsy ... Very severe facial disfigurement Advanced cases of incurable disease	100	42 6	37 6	35 0	32 6	30 0	27 6	27 6
2	Amputation of right arm at shoulder joint	90	38 3	33 9	31 6	29 3	27 0	24 9	24 9
3	Amputation of leg at hip or : left arm at shoulder joint Severe facial disfigurement Total loss of speech	80	34 0	30 0	28 0	26 0	24 0	22 0	22 0
4	Short thigh amputation of leg or of right arm above or through elbow Total deafness	70	29 9	26 3	24 6	22 9	21 0	19 3	19 3
5	Amputation of leg above knee (other than 4) and through knee or of left arm above or through elbow, or of right arm below elbow	60	25 6	22 6	21 0	19 6	18 0	16 6	16 6
6	Amputation of leg below knee (including Symes' and Chopart's amputation) or of left arm below elbow Loss of vision of one eye	50	21 3	18 9	17 6	16 3	15 0	13 9	13 9
7	Loss of thumb or of four fingers of right hand	40	17 0	15 0	14 0	13 0	12 0	11 0	11 0
8	Loss of thumb or of four fingers of left hand, or of three fingers of right hand	30	12 9	11 3	10 6	9 9	9 0	8 3	8 3
9	Loss of two fingers of either hand	20	8 6	7 6	7 0	6 6	6 0	5 6	5 6

NOTE.—In the case of left-handed men, certified to be such, the compensation in respect of the left arm, hand, &c., will be the same as for a right arm, hand, &c.

Early in the second week of July 1917, when he was called to give evidence to the committee investigating the scandal over military recruitment in which the military medical authorities had been altering the criteria behind the scenes, passing as fit soldiers who had been certified unfit by civilian doctors, Surgeon-General Bedford antagonized civilian sensibilities still further by claiming that 'the civil practitioner all his life has been trained not to look farther than the individual himself, and he has never raised his eyes to the horizon of his country's needs'.[27] Surely, the chairman rejoined, 'the real difficulty was that the civilian doctor appreciated that heaps of men who could earn a living in civil life could not stand the Army with its routine'.[28] And on 13 July, just a few days after Bedford had appeared before the committee, the Board of Control met in conference with service and pensions representatives to thrash out an agreement over war disability pension entitlements for mentally ill servicemen that was to make enormous concessions to civilian sensibilities.

In its essential rudiments, this agreement would form the cornerstone of the pensions framework for servicemen of the Great War suffering from mental disorder that, contested though it assuredly was, remained in place, and informed the lives of a wide band of ex-servicemen and their relatives until the end of the twentieth century, when the last of the psychiatric war disability pensioners had finally died. Justice was the term that figured most prominently in this debate, setting the scene for a consensus in which a notion of common citizenship, or the community of serving citizens, was able to trump traditional military values as the operating standard.[29] A person's value was not made to hinge on his efficiency as a soldier; active service in the field or traumatizing conditions did not provide the benchmark, but rather army service as such; and it was not a requisite for entitlement to pension that a man should have had to show himself a bit of hero – it was enough that he had left his customary sphere and been received into the military enterprise.[30]

The shift of standpoint emerges most strongly in the memorandum prepared by two psychiatrists, Marriott Cooke and Hubert Bond, which was to play an integral role in formalizing the framework for war psychosis pensions. 'It must always be borne in mind', we are informed, that 'insanity as regards its origin is almost always a complex of two or more factors'. Even though one factor may appear to have been the principal cause of a mental breakdown, 'it is unsafe, if not impossible, to attempt to eliminate the relative proportion of influence of the several factors'. Pre-eminent causes of insanity are mental and physical stress, and whilst the stress of service may 'act beneficially on the majority of men . . . it has to be remembered, however, that a very large proportion of men, in at least the new Armies, had settled down in various civil occupations and had never anticipated either volunteering or being called on to serve in the Forces'. Furthermore, appearances of wellbeing even in those who have served only at home may be deceptive, for

it does not follow that those who have not been sent overseas, and who – as the result of open-air life, simple but regular food and systematic exercise – *look* in much improved health, have not been subjected to severe mental stress by reason of their entry into the Army and their many domestic anxieties both as to the present and as to the future. It is not improbable that those who have said least about their troubles have suffered the most.[31]

What starts as a rather unexceptional seminar paper on the causality of mental disorder shades into something much more provocative that identifies and brushes aside traditional stereotypes of military culture, such as the benefits of service, fortitude in the face of adversity, and so forth, that only a year earlier would scarcely have been negotiable, least of all by the Board of Control. And there is something else here as well: in this rather unadorned and hesitant prose, with its insistence on the difficulties of the whole enterprise, and its limpid refusal to call a spade a spade psychiatrically speaking, there emerges a model of psychiatric expertise that is perhaps best characterized as a form of psychiatric negative capability drastically at odds with the colourful and belligerent certitudes of conventional late Victorian and Edwardian psychiatry. And on closer scrutiny it is, perhaps, still more subversive than it first appears, for in its refusal to uphold conventional standards and assessments it effectively surrenders the ground, opening the door to a plethora of competing explanations of psychological woes.

In the personal notes that he made in preparation for the conference, Marriott Cooke said that the Board regarded themselves as 'the particular friends of the lunatics'. The line-up at the conference scarcely looked very promising in this respect – along with the delegates from the Board of Control there was the Parliamentary Secretary of the Ministry of Pensions, the President of the Royal College of Physicians, various representatives of the Army and Navy medical services, Lt Col. Sir John Collie, the Commander of D Block Netley, and a number of other civil servants.[32] This was hardly a hotbed of radicals, surely not the advocates that the soldier lunatics would have chosen to represent them had they been asked, but Marriott Cooke had doubtless read the political auguries correctly. Even if it went against the grain, as it surely must have for many of those present, the mandate under which they had been brought together was to deliver a workable framework to convince a sceptical public that the mentally scarred soldier or sailor was at last receiving justice.

The Board, Marriott Cooke averred, 'are quite unable to see how, short of the risk of grave injustice, [the individual's] service can ever be eliminated from the factors which have caused or aggravated the particular attack of insanity'. The urbane Maurice Craig, soon to be consulting neurologist to the Ministry of Pensions, was 'of the opinion that it was best to give pension in all cases. A breakdown before entry did not imply that a man must break down again, and if a man were accepted for service and then lost his mental balance, his breakdown must be due to the Service'. Dr Macpherson, representing the Scottish Board of Control, argued that no medical board could definitely say that a case of mental disorder was not caused by service; if it did, it was imposing a limitation on this category that did not exist as regards other categories of disability. There was evidently a mood of some fervour, for Dr Carswell drew attention 'to the evident feeling among those present that mental diseases must be regarded as due to service', and the Assistant Secretary at the Ministry of Pensions wrote to Marriott Cooke shortly after the meeting saying that 'the trend of opinion the other day was so strong on the impossibility of saying that the mental disease was not caused by service' that he was not sure the directive might not run: 'All cases of mental disease are to be considered at least aggravated by service'.[33] The excitement was perhaps too much for some, for in the record of the meeting in his notebook, Sir Matthew Nathan quite uncharacteristically misspelled Craig's name, perhaps as an unconscious rebuke for his preposterous proposal to expand the bounds of the pensionable constituency of the insane: 'Dr Craik [sic]: Even cases where mental affliction present at some date before enlistment should not be excluded from pension.'[34]

The overall message was that if the mentally damaged serviceman was to receive justice, then there needed at the very least to be some relaxation or moderation of conventional psychiatric postures. There thus came about a kind of psychiatric decommissioning, in which alienists and other mental experts handed in their weapons and relinquished their positions on the high ground of moral certainty; condemnatory voices were temporarily stilled, and replaced by a tone of hesitancy and respect in the face of the anguish that confronted them. Even the usual suspects of hereditary insanity such as general paralysis of the insane and dementia praecox were placed in a different and quite equivocal light. One may think of this as inaugurating an epiphanic moment in the history of madness in which, for a season, disorders such as dementia praecox were accorded an honourable place as war psychoses. The Great War psychotic is the product of a remoralization of lunacy. He is, one might say, the People's Lunatic rather than the alienist's. On this occasion, at least, the Board of Control could be said to have been doing the people's bidding.

Not surprisingly, curmudgeonly officials later denounced the sway of public feeling over the formation of policy on the psychiatric casualties of the war. 'Misguided public opinion had raised the psychoneuroses to the dignity of a new war disease', sneered the official medical historian of the war, and in our own time historians of a military persuasion have been no less irascible, berating public opinion for trespassing on the competence of generals and their medical votaries.[35] By no means was this exclusively a clash between medical and lay opinion, since official spokesmen frequently grizzled about the large numbers of doctors, general practitioners in civilian life as well as allegedly inexperienced medical officers, who had permitted their judgments to be influenced by the public mood. Yet, far from being a forcing house of fatuity, 'public opinion' at this historical moment was the concentrated expression of a prodigious diversity of the population united in promoting a popular agenda of civil rights and social justice. With a lineage in radical populism and a Gladstonian rhetoric of citizenship, a single-class communion of the 'masses' against the 'classes' embraced all serving citizen soldiers as 'our fellow-subjects, our fellow Christians, our own flesh and blood'.[36]

Edwardian society was torn by competing visions of the political nation; notions of common citizenship or of a comprehensive pluralist polity vied with traditional property-based conceptions, and many groups and individuals in public life were pulled simultaneously in both directions.[37] The exceptional circumstances of 1917 generated a concern with social justice for the *totality* of serving citizens that within the pensions culture produced a more inclusive understanding of 'due to service'. As a Pensions official explained: 'In times of peace when men were in the main "picked lives" and when the conditions of service were normal, there was a somewhat narrow interpretation. It is clear, however, that under the conditions of war with so many men . . . living a life so entirely different to that followed in peace time, a very wide and generous interpretation is necessary'.[38] Entitlement was to be based not on accomplishment in bearing arms, but simply on membership of the community of serving citizen soldiers. This is perhaps as close as we are likely to get in this period, and for some time after, to the embodiment of a common culture of rights-bearing equals.[39] Psychiatrists in particular were being forced to retreat and implicitly to accept that their traditional repertoires had mostly been in the service of less inclusive social visions.

John Macpherson, chairman of the Scottish Board of Control, aptly captured the resolve of the meeting: 'The fact is that there is a prejudice against insanity and a widespread superstition as to its moral causation which those of us who are more specially interested in the subject must do all we can to counteract'.[40] The superstition as to the moral causation of insanity was abundantly evident in the controversy over general paralysis of the insane. In April 1917, Cyril Jackson declared that 'these GPI cases are extremely difficult seeing that medical opinion apparently maintains that they cannot possibly be due to service', in fact they 'cannot even be aggravated in the ordinary sense by service'.[41] But in fact there was a significant strand of medical thinking which maintained the opposite. Progressive opinion triumphed at the conference in July 1917, Maurice Craig clinching the position that was adopted when he argued that: 'as the percentage of syphilitic persons who subsequently develop brain disease and insanity is small, it is clear that other factors must act as the determining causes . . . war service may supply these factors and therefore the condition must be regarded as attributable'.[42]

More than any other psychiatrist, it was Maurice Craig who lent his imprimatur to these machinations, and underwrote the medical authority of what was otherwise a rather contentious set of proposals, and so perhaps it is not surprising that at points he appeared to waver, telling Marriott Cooke in the aftermath of the discussion that it was 'a difficult matter to do justice to the man and the state', and attaching a note in which he qualified his earlier remarks about causality.[43] Temporarily, Craig had forgotten his commitment to the individual and was serving the state. But Marriott Cooke and the Board remained undeterred, and in the guidance they produced for medical boards they went as close as they reasonably could to saying that all cases of mental disability in servicemen should be eligible for pension.

A serviceman discharged on the grounds of certifiable insanity was to be regarded as pensionable unless definite evidence was forthcoming that he was 'the subject of insanity at the time of enlistment', or that before enlistment he had had more than one attack of certified insanity. Though the spectre of moral culpability, which had been so dominant in the conventional paradigm of mental illness, was not entirely excised, it was certainly minimized, and really only figured here in relation to those instances of alcohol abuse where a connection with stress of service could not be established. It quite deliberately also parted company with the paradigm of heroic trauma, in which there was an explicit connection between the mental condition and a traumatizing event, by stating that: 'The man's past history, the effect which military service, even at home, the change of environment, and the fear and anxiety caused by separation from his family, may have had on a man of neurotic temperament will also . . . be taken into consideration'.[44]

There was, of course, an ambiguity over 'neurotic temperament' since, after all, some might be considered constitutionally vulnerable and of poor stock; no doubt that nuance was intended, but it was certainly not all that was intended, and in this context the 'neurotic temperament' also prefigures a new and radically expanded understanding of normality, in which the neurotic is no longer the deviant or the isolate but everyman. Produced by interests that were sympathetic towards citizen soldiers, even to the plight of citizens who were reluctant and useless soldiers, the rubric dispensed with heroic pretensions, for it was not the battlefield which counted exclusively, but the military environment as such. By no means had every angle been considered at this stage, for the entire objective was to provide pensions for ex-servicemen who were certified as lunatics in asylums, and the question of the pensions status of the discharged war psychotic, or of the uncertified war psychotic in the community, had not even been recognized, but this was at least a start.

Of course this was not a great revolution in the mental health culture, sweeping away all the old prejudices. But by no means was it entirely trivial either. As Jose Harris has stated in one of the most insightful and helpful remarks for any student of this period: 'one reason why accounts of social life in this period vary so widely is the immense diversity of objective reality itself'. British society 'was not (despite the fashionable jargon of the Edwardian era) a coherent "organism", still less a "corporation", a "system" or a "machine"'. Harris is struck by the 'immensely varied, contradictory and fissiparous quality of many of the movements, values and institutions there encountered'.[45] As one might say, there were different shows in town. Of course they were not all equally significant, and what counted especially was how long they lasted. The War Psychosis Pensions show satisfies this criterion admirably. As we shall see, it ran and ran for another three-quarters of a century or so, becoming a rallying point for a significant counter-current, providing benefits for a great swathe of mentally distressed servicemen and providing the conditions in which, to some extent at least, the authoritarianism of traditional psychiatry ceded to styles of relations in which there was increased scope for negotiation and some element of client control. The narrative of the patient's illness was not to be entirely at the behest of the doctor's preconceptions.[46] And even if the show's managers were by no means its fondest admirers, and often administered it with gritted teeth, it is a tribute to the British polity that they were unable to close it down.

'IN A CATEGORY BY THEMSELVES'
Misquoting George Barnes's cruel jibe about 'veritable weeds' of the previous year, a pensions official warned that public opinion would demand an enquiry

'as soon as it wakes up to the fact that many of the pensions are not given to the disabled fighter but to what Mr Barnes, perhaps unfortunately, but quite truly, called "the unsuitable weeds"; the men on the outskirts of the war, given war pensions though they never felt war conditions'.[47] These were miserable specimens, he could not quite bring himself to say, who instead of playing up and playing the game were hiding from the field of play behind a woman's skirts. In waving the flag of traditional male heroism at this juncture, however, the pensions official had misjudged the popular mood which, having swung away from unquestioning support for the war, was starting to elicit a more elastic and subjective interpretation of what it meant to feel war conditions. From the summer of 1917 there were striking set pieces within the Ministry of Pensions in which military values were forced to yield before more sceptical political currents, for which the morality play of heroes and cowards was inadequate in the face of the immediate human dramas.

That implacable champion of the slighted and the marginal, James M. Hogge MP, had forwarded an appeal on behalf of a widow who had been refused pension and left destitute after her husband had been shot for desertion. The court martial, it was now proposed, had failed to appreciate that Private Harry Macdonald had earlier suffered from shell shock and might have 'wandered on the field owing to his recent illness'. The War Office, however, had stood quite unabashed by the judgment of the divisional commander in the field that Harry was 'a worthless soldier with no heart for fighting', opining that to give pension to the widow in such cases was 'really to put the coward on the same footing as the hero . . . who had died fighting to the last'. The Permanent Secretary at the Pensions, Sir Matthew Nathan, echoed the same sentiments, maintaining that military values could only be 'maintained by strong public reprobation of military vices', hence the state 'should not appear to diminish this reprobation by treating the widow of a man who deserts . . . in the same way as the widow of a man who by some glorious deed helps to win the war'.[48]

When John Hodge reviewed Macdonald's file shortly after he was appointed Minister of Pensions in August 1917 he could not disguise his consternation: 'I am seriously concerned over the case. . . . I don't think the Army authorities would from the lay point of view come well out of it. The record shows: (1) The man went through hell in the Dardanelles; (2) Wounded in the field; (3) Suffered from shell-shock; (4) Is given MD, a usual thing when the Dr hasn't time either for proper examination or thinks the man is seeking to evade duty. Being a shell-shock patient, is it surprising he wandered back to Étaples? I don't think so'. Though he has no compunction about 'pure cowardice', this is 'not a usual case of cowardice and desertion', and cases such as this are 'in a category by themselves'. At this point Nathan resolved to take his Minister in hand: 'Probably the decision arrived at in this case by those responsible for the discipline of our armies in France was a right one. Generally I think we shall have to accept such decisions and leave the poor women who suffer by them to charitable assistance. I scarcely think you would care to take the responsibility of saying that the Military Authorities have been wrong in any particular case and unless you do there is no power to grant the widow a pension'.[49] To Nathan's chagrin, however, the lay point of view got a result. Though the War Cabinet stopped short of questioning the military judgment, the following day it discounted the symbolism of the act by deciding in the wake of the publicity over the Macdonald case that the dependants of an executed man should after all receive a pension, a decision that occasioned embarrassment at the Pensions and 'seriously compromised the whole position of the Government' by opening the barn doors wide to other supplicants.[50]

'A CAP FLOATING ON A POND'

In the Boer War the military authorities had dealt with suicide cases on their merits, which was code for saying that it was generally regarded as a form of 'misconduct', and only in very exceptional circumstances were pensions awarded to dependants of the deceased. However, in the Great War, the Army Medical Department, having been jolted into upgrading its scientific credentials and modernizing its image, conceded that there was a sound medical basis to the verdict of 'temporary insanity' almost invariably recorded by the coroner in the civil court, and hence took the view (unless it could be proved that the man was not insane at the time he killed himself) that the 'insanity should be regarded as a disease contracted or commencing on active service'.

Yet the pensions authorities were rather less enamoured of the modernizing broom, believing that these dispensations went 'a little far' in letting in soldiers who might hardly have seen any service at all, and in the early part of the war they stalled over suicide cases, alleging 'misconduct' where they could make it stick, holding that pensions should only be awarded where it could be demonstrated that the serviceman had been under some 'condition of strain or shock beyond what he may experience from being called to the Army'. After he met with a road accident in which his hand was crushed, Pte Thomas Denning had become very depressed and shot himself, and even though the army medical authorities produced no evidence of impropriety and his character reference was 'good' (a 'more or less colourless grading' according to the Ministry), the Ministry gleefully produced a testimony from the unfortunate Denning's previous employer, a retired army officer, claiming that he had been drunk at the time of his death and had shot himself to avoid active foreign service.[51]

As a result of the authorities' obduracy, by the end of the war there was a long line of suitors at the offices of the appeals boards, each of them with a poignant and insatiable tale of loss that in many instances could only gesture – an army cap visible on the surface of a pond – at the inaccessible histories that lay behind them, and the turmoil and despair that had surely prompted these tragic deaths. Sapper Silas Sarjent enlisted in the Royal Engineers on 31 May 1915, committing suicide on 3 June after three days' service, there being nothing to account for the act, except for the observation that he had been used to a free and easy life, and had been drinking before his enlistment. Private Robert Ellender killed himself six months after joining up, allegedly because his wife had been misbehaving for a long time and he could not take it any more. Private Clifford Sparke shot himself one month after joining the army, leaving a letter stating that having been refused weekend leave to see his wife he had decided to go home regardless and was now afraid to return and face the consequences. Private Tommy Robinson killed himself after five days' service with the Royal Army Medical Corps, but he had no previous history of mental problems, nor was he in any kind of trouble with the military authorities, and nothing could be ascertained of what had driven him to his wits' end.

Married with three children, Private David Graven had gone to Winchester in a fruitless effort to look for work and then decided on 12 September 1914 to enlist in the army instead, killing himself five days later. The coroner in his summing up said that it was a very sad case and determined that Graven's mind had become unhinged through domestic troubles. Private Walter Smith of the Durham Light Infantry enlisted on 17 February 1915, left home the next day to go to the recruiting office but never arrived, and his cap was found in a pond three days later and his body recovered the following day. Though the coroner recorded a verdict of 'temporary insanity' in each case, the Ministry maintained that with one exception (Robert Ellender, though his widow was then barred from receiving a pension by her own 'misconduct' – adultery) they were all guilty of evading war service.[52]

These were the kind of cases that were being brought before the Entitlement Board, the Special Appeals Board which had been established in 1919 in answer to the demands of ex-servicemen's organizations to review pension rejections. By then, the families of some of these unfortunates had already found advocates in some sections of the press who were lobbying the authorities on behalf of the 'home man', whose spirits were easily broken if he was forcibly separated from the domestic hearth. 'He would write home', one widow recounted, 'and say that he could never eat the food given to him in the Army and would go for weeks at a time without proper food or sleep. His health at the time of death was shocking, when I saw him at the inquest he was a mere frame'.

The Pensions Editor of the *News of the World* was not alone in striving to remove the spectre of 'misconduct' from the 'home man' in his many variants, drawing the attention of the Minister to the case of a widow with four children, already in delicate health, who had been left destitute after her husband had jumped from a bridge into the River Ouse whilst under the influence of drink. Men of 'different shades, traits and dispositions' have been drafted into the army, he argued, and where some have adapted themselves readily, 'another man differently disposed and so devotedly attached to his home circle, wife and family, finds (no matter how willing he may be to do his duty in the service of the country) that his Military service requires his temporary severance from home ties, and not being possessed of sufficient will-power, the thought of such estrangement so works upon his mind that, in a moment of temporary insanity, he takes his own life'. He himself had an acquaintance, 'what one might term "a home man"', for whom the severance from the wife and family to whom he was devotedly attached was so severe that he committed suicide.[53]

Many of these appeals were successful, and even though the Board insisted in justification that it was merely confirming the usual method of giving careful consideration to each individual case in the light of the best available medical expertise, there was no doubt that the basis of entitlement had expanded considerably from the early days of the war. There was one case in particular that especially irked and perturbed the Ministry, giving them the message that some drastic overhaul of their moral operating assumptions was well overdue. A tailor who had already lost one brother in the war, and with three others in hospital, Private Harry Barrows's service with the colours lasted all of six days at the end of September 1917. Expecting to be employed as regimental tailor, Harry had apparently become very upset, hanging himself in a lavatory when he was ordered to go on parade, believing this to be a prelude to service in the front line, even though it was explained to him that 'it was the duty of everyman in khaki to know how to salute and hold himself properly'. The Ministry did not mince its words in its decision: 'Six days service and shirked Military Duty. No pension.' And 'no pension' meant just that, not even the 15/- given to widows under all circumstances. Harry had always been a good father and husband, Mrs Barrows testified in her appeal. He had worked for 16 years at Colman's & Oldland, tailors, at the corner of Moor Street, and it was wrong to attribute his death to misconduct, since the thought of being separated from his home and large family had so unnerved him that even his patriotic ardour could not restore his balance. The Entitlement Board obviously found this touching profile of private and local attachments convincing, for, accepting that Pte Harry Barrows had been 'driven out of his mind by being called up to do parades which he did not expect', and that there was no moral impropriety in his failure to 'hold himself properly', Mrs Barrows was awarded her pension.[54]

Rankle as it inevitably did against their moral instincts, Pensions' officials tacitly disparaged the so-called medical expertise that could deliver such aberrant judgments. Still, the Ministry was bound to uphold them, and not only that but also to make the best case for them to the Treasury. It was under these circumstances that Maurice Craig was once again brought in to help draw up a suicide formula with the accent on 'strain of service' or 'war strain', and the kind of legitimating rhetoric that would provide convincing advocacy on behalf of Barrows and his fellows. According to George Mosse, shell shock became a metaphor for unmanly behaviour, and the shell-shocked soldier 'bore not only the burden of his sickness', he also took on the image of an outsider to normal society as an incomplete man.[55] Such atavistic reactions abounded, of course, but they did not necessarily always prevail in a cultural scene that was rather more contradictory and diversified than Mosse acknowledges, for, particularly in the later stages of the war, there was an emerging current in which militaristic standards of manly superiority were seen as rarified or out of touch with contemporary circumstances. The so-called 'incomplete man' became more defiant, with his own backers and supporting expertise, patriotic up to a point, but unapologetic in prizing privacy and domesticity as the source of his own 'completion'.

So it was that in the modernizing perspective set out in a revealing letter from the Ministry to the Treasury in November 1920 'everyman' in uniform much more closely resembled Harry Barrows, with all his uncertainties about how to hold himself, than the upright soldier of old. Abhorrence for the soldierly life is just a fact to be reckoned with, one kind of predisposition among others, rather than a trigger for moral opprobrium:

In judging the question of attributability or aggravation the Minister is advised by mental experts that he cannot insist . . . on proof of exceptional mental and physical strain such as would be involved by long spells of duty in front line trenches or constant exposure at a base to enemy air-attacks. In their view a much broader view must be taken. It must be remembered that under the Military Service Acts vast numbers of men were enrolled in the Army to whom a soldier's life was absolutely abhorrent, and that many of these were civilians in middle age, on whom any drastic change of environment and routine must necessarily have had a profound nervous effect. In such circumstances ordinary military service of even a few days might well of itself produce an unbalanced mental condition.[56]

Yet for the Treasury these were still cowards by another name, and they were reluctant to relinquish the talisman of 'improper conduct', asserting that they could accept the medical argument so long as there was no question of awarding pensions in cases where 'the suicide was directly or indirectly prompted by the desire to evade any form of military duty'. The Pensions authorities were thus cast (and not for the last time) in the ironic position of having to explain to the benighted that in embracing the perspective of the mental experts they would have to dump some of their moral baggage, since the 'insane impulse' which had brought about the suicide *necessarily* took the form of a desire to terminate a state of affairs which had become intolerable. After a little more jousting the Treasury eventually conceded, the Pensions insisting that the question of whether the insanity had been caused by 'war strain' was 'purely a medical one', an assertion of 'doctor knows best' providing the forceful rhetorical closure that shut the door on old certitudes, and opened the window onto a whole brave new realm of explanatory possibilities.[57]

Coda

Albert Gets a War Psychosis Pension

Dispiriting though it surely was to find himself escorted once more up the asylum drive in September 1917, Albert Norris was not so easily abashed. The experience of his second enlistment had left him with a strong sense of unfinished business, and a heightened feeling of determination that came out of the realization that the window of opportunity which the war presented might very soon close. Long Grove Asylum was no less of a hole than on the last occasion he was there, but this time round at least there was a bigger crowd of soldier patients to choose from. Before very long he found a kindred spirit in Henry Hollis, a married man from Lewisham, about the same age as him and also a Roman Catholic, who even though he had been admitted from a military hospital, and classified as a Service Patient by the Ministry of Pensions in recognition that his condition was due to war service, had been branded a 'moral imbecile' by the Long Grove authorities. Having been sent out on trial in October, and then brought back to the asylum at the end of the month, Henry had his own reasons to feel aggrieved with his situation. And at 6.10pm on 10 January 1918, a couple of weeks after the anniversary of Albert's previous escape, Albert and Henry chose their moment in presenting to recently engaged temporary attendant Reynolds slips of paper on which was written 'Please pass this patient out to the Male Hospital, signed Attendant Cobb', and the hapless Reynolds having fallen for this ruse they both made a break for it.[1]

The medical superintendent occupied himself in taking 'the usual steps' but in the meantime Albert, probably after putting up with Henry and his family for a week or so, on 29 January 1918 presented himself for examination by the National Service Medical Board at Camberwell in South London. Observing that his physical development was good, the Board noted that he had 'defective teeth upper jaw' and had 'suffered from melancholia at times', but placed him as fit for service in Grade III.[2] There was nothing here to indicate that Albert was an escaped lunatic or had spent several years in an asylum. So was this an omission that reflected once more the incompetence of recruitment procedures, the unfit still being passed as fit, lunatics slipping through the net and finding their way into the army, even under the revamped system which had now put recruitment under civilian medical control?[3] Arguably not, in as much that to identify Albert as an intermittent melancholic rather than a full-time lunatic was on all fours with the recognition that he needed out-patient treatment rather than full-time detention. In this hour of the nation's extreme need, military and medical structures were reaching out to meet him, cognisant of his limitations but equally of his aptitudes, and if there was a failing it was that the system was not always in place (as with the availability of out-patient treatment) to provide the support that was needed.

In any event, Albert now found himself setting out on the third stage of his military career as No. 274029 Pte Albert Norris in the Labour Corps, serving at home for the first month. Then on 3 March 1918, in what he must surely have experienced as a vindication of his determination over the past two years, he found himself embarked with the expeditionary force, doing duty in a variety of postings in France and Belgium over the next two months or so, where he exhibited rather more talent with a spade than he had with a rifle until, predictably enough, in the middle of May he experienced a relapse. From No 8 Stationary Hospital in Boulogne, he was dispatched to Murthly War Hospital in Perthshire, via the inevitable D Block Netley, where they turned him round in three days, arriving in Murthly on 30 May in a very confused state and remaining under treatment there for almost six months. The discharge board considered that he had been suffering from delusional insanity, aggravated by service during the present war, and though they found him quite unfit for further service (three enlistments were surely enough) they remarked that 'he answers intelligently though he looks rather worried', in itself a poignant assessment against the background of the designation 'imbecile' under which he had languished in an asylum for several years. Pte Albert Norris was finally discharged from the army on 19 November 1918, having served for 295 days, by far his longest enlistment, and been received into the glorious company of war psychotics, with a temporary war disability pension of 5/6d. a week for 26 weeks, and entitled to wear a silver badge.

The war visited the margins in a double action, exacerbating the deprivation of institutions such as lunatic asylums, pushing their inmates deeper into the margins, or not infrequently beyond them into the afterlife, but also expanding the frontiers of active citizenship and beckoning existing marginals to apply for membership.[4] It thus provided the conditions under which Albert and his kind stood a rather better chance than before of being able to escape from the periphery, and establish at least a toehold in society. In Albert's trajectory through different medical sites, we can recognize the shifting historical dynamics in the political economy of medicine in the first part of the twentieth century that John Pickstone has recently analyzed.[5] From a minimalist medical regime, expressly concerned with administering care and protection to an outcast community of lunatic paupers, Albert eventually progressed to a medical setting that was certainly productionist in intent, but also possessed a strong communitarian dimension, in that he continued to receive a respectful form of treatment as a citizen even when it was obvious that he was unable to return to the fight as a soldier.

Building on a climate of pre-war welfare reform in which workers had been able to secure some 'positive' freedoms in maintaining rights as citizens even when they were sick, army medical services represented a model not simply of the productionist state, but also of an emerging civic compact, in which hospitals and clinics were to become institutions from which all classes could benefit. Albert's repeated defiant vaults from his exile in an asylum into the community of serving citizens are a figure for the contested dynamics of a society in which the health and welfare *ancien régime* was still very much alive even as a new one was struggling to emerge.

Part III

'REVOLTING' PSYCHOLOGY

Is it known that psycho-analysts (some have been given commissions) are at their pernicious work in the lunacy wards of our great war hospitals?
'Decency', 4 January, British Medical Journal (1917)[1]

Chapter 7

HOW THE WEAK PROGRESS

'WEAK AND DEGENERATE PERSONALITIES'

Writing amidst the social and political upheavals that followed in the wake
of the Great War, one of the leading authorities in psychological medicine
offered his mordant reflections on the psychological posturing that had been
precipitated by four years of fighting, telling of how the 'endless physical exertion and hardship', the strain of a succession of shocking experiences with no
prospect of a definitive outcome, had produced 'a general war-weariness and
the ever-growing desire to return from the toils and dangers of battle' and
'increasingly a morbid mental change, or *combat neurosis*, which above all
afflicted less stable, emotionally excitable, nervous and infirm personalities'.
This illness, he continued, was 'the exact parallel to the accident neurosis (that
is, the reluctance of weak-willed persons to return to work after suffering an
injury) familiar to us from peacetime and which has been spawned by pension
legislation'. Under the pressure to expand the net of recruitment, 'more and
more incompetent, mentally deficient, infirm and morally inferior persons had
to be drawn into service' and 'after a short time many ended up in the lazarets,
were carted from one place to the next, frittered their time away, and succeeded in disrupting the physician's work with their bothersome dissatisfaction'. The flight into an hysterical attack is, he claimed, 'generally the last
escape for those personalities who are underdeveloped and ill-suited to ward
off the dangers of day-to-day life, especially children and adolescents, women,
as well as excitable, unstable and weak-willed individuals. In the case of the
mature and emotionally well-anchored male, these antiquated defence mech-
anisms against overwhelming external pressures no longer have a role to
play'.[1]

This is the formidable Emil Kraepelin, fervent acolyte of that paragon of
emotionally well-anchored manhood, the 'Iron Chancellor' Bismarck, endeavouring to expunge not merely the bitterness of defeat on the battlefield but also
the drubbing that professional elites had received in the November Revolution, in which soldier councils had burst into the mental hospitals demanding
the release of fellow servicemen mistakenly confined as lunatics, and psychiatrists and neurologists had maintained weapons in readiness in their consulting

rooms for fear that they might be attacked by frustrated war pension claimants, or patients incensed by the treatment that had been meted out to them in military hospitals.[2] Rebounding from the stutterers, shakers, shockers and weepers swarming about him, Kraepelin retorted with a salvo of insults from the rich repertoire of turn-of-the-century psychiatric contumely – unstable, weak-willed, nervous, infirm, emotionally excitable, mentally deficient, incompetent, morally inferior – to account for the 'morbid mental change' that had produced such a shameful dissolution of manly virtues. In the imaginings of many German psychiatrists, the psychiatric fallout from the war was spreading across the social and political landscape, heralding, in the words of one observer, not so much a revolution of the proletariat as of the psychopaths.[3] The vanguard of mass movements, according to Kraepelin, is notable for the 'active involvement of the Jewish race' (attributable to the 'frequency of psychopathic disposition in Jews', their 'harping criticism' and 'rhetorical and theatrical abilities'), alongside individuals with hysterical traits, dreamers, poets, manic-depressive busybodies, professional swindlers, and pimps.[4]

Kraepelin was the prime exponent of a doctrine which held that mental illness inevitably resulted in a progressive decline. With the goal of 'cutting nature at the joints', and so identifying natural disease entities, his professional mission was to chart an ecology of losers.[5] The identification of a whole class of incurables, far from blighting scientific hopes, was hailed as a significant milestone on the path of psychiatric progress, and for quite some years before the war, Kraepelin's voraciously expanding nosology had been receiving widespread adulation in the United States especially, and in England also 'was rapidly taking possession of the minds and imaginations of the younger men'. At a meeting at the Royal Medico-Psychological Association in London in 1909, the members concluded that in his identification of the dementia praecox patient (the precursor of what was later to be known as schizophrenia), Kraepelin had 'given a meaning to the incoherent mutterings, the gait, attitude, conduct of even a terminal dement, all these features having acquired a significance which previously they had entirely lacked'. As a result, the alienist was now able to recognize that he was witnessing 'the quiet collapse of jerry-built brains under the strain of their own weight'.[6]

Kraepelin epitomized the asylum culture of turn-of-the-century Europe, where lunatic asylums had become storehouses of those considered unfit for life in society, and alienists were engaged in the corporate mission of imparting to the suffering inmates the news that their membership of the ordinary human community had been permanently suspended. 'Psychiatric discourse', Andrew Scull has acidly remarked, 'now exhibited a barely disguised contempt for the mad, those "tainted persons" whom it sequestered on society's behalf'.[7] In a textbook published on the very eve of the Great War, Charles Mercier revealed that insanity did not occur in 'people who are of sound mental constitution. It does not, like smallpox and malaria, attack indifferently the weak and the strong. It occurs chiefly in those whose mental constitution is originally defective, and whose defect is manifested in a lack of the power of self-control and of forgoing immediate indulgence'.[8]

ANXIETIES OVER MODERNITY

In his forebodings and judgments, Emil Kraepelin embodied a standpoint in life both as man and as scientist, and a perspective on the turbulent currents of his time, that transcended his national context. Querulous professional opinion in a number of countries was united in believing that the misguided beliefs and fantasies of persons of weak will were being dignified into a worldview, and making inroads into the cultural mainstream, under names such as 'neurasthenia', which for Kraepelin exposed not the exacting conditions of modern life so much as psychic deficiencies in certain population groups, an outcrop in the spreading ecology of psychological weakness and psychic degeneracy.[9] Jeremiads against 'weak and degenerate personalities' (or more accurately against 'weakness' however it might manifest itself) had been much in vogue since around the turn of the century. For Henry Maudsley, writing in 1867, the weak and degenerate posed no special threat because they appeared bound to extinction as 'the waste thrown up by the silent but strong current of progress', nature having decreed that the 'weakest must suffer and some of them break down into madness'. Two decades or so later, however, in reaction against the strengthening political muscle of the working classes, they were being envisaged as tumescent and ominous counter-currents to the forces of progress that, far from fading, were multiplying and becoming more obstreperous.[10] The ascendancy of the common man was undermining the national stock, since democracy had succeeded only in further enfeebling the will of the weak-minded individual by situating him in a 'bustling mechanism' through which he became involved in 'mutual interaction', 'essentially steered by the experiences jostling him from all sides'.[11]

Anxieties over the direction of modernity had already been exacerbated in European countries in the decades leading up to the outbreak of the Great War by the patently double-edged consequences of advances in the industrialization of space and time. In many respects, the lived experience of modernity had become synonymous with 'shockery' as a succession of frissons and bumps for which the railway train was deservedly the most striking icon, combining as it did the thrills of speed and the scintillas of the buffet car with the horrific spills of blasted bodies and buffeted psyches.[12] Much more than a recurring event, the railway accident had become the site for a bitterly controverted category of illness known as *railway spine*, in which the concept of trauma had leapfrogged from its habitat in the injured body to become the sign for a form of personal suffering that was located in the victim's inner world or psyche. Scrambled in the railway accident were more than bodies and bones, more even than the psyches of those directly affected, for what took the impact also were cherished cultural beliefs (not least those that men entertained about themselves) about the inviolability of the robust male to emotional hurt. As Ralph Harrington has remarked, within the conventions of the time 'to suggest that an active, unemotional businessman was vulnerable to hysteria . . . was to undermine not merely a medical but a moral model of what it mean to be a civilized human being'.[13]

The railway accident victim was the first of a series of traumatic types to foment a clash not just between somatic and psychogenic explanations, but between competing constructions of the psyche. Railway spine became the pace-setter for a rising compensations culture, in Europe as in the United States, to which corporations and state departments quickly reacted by hiring doctors to produce disease categories, such as *Unfallsneurose* or accident neurosis, also known as 'Kraepelin's syndrome', which spurned the claims of sufferers by shifting the spotlight from the traumatic event to the alleged inadequacies, exaggerations and greed of the victims. Indeed, in the portrayals of Kraepelin and other psychiatric sages, the so-called traumatizing events were effaced entirely as a causal force, their place taken by the liberalities of a misguided pensions legislation. The allure of a pension was more than sufficient, so these experts opined, to account for the rash of self-seeking, hysterical and neurotic syndromes among the psychologically weak-minded.[14]

THE PSYCHIATRIC WAR CASUALTY IN BRITAIN AND IN GERMANY

In Britain, as elsewhere, the stirrings of democracy and the expansion of the polity were accompanied by outbursts of intolerance towards social groups considered incapable of contributing to the efficient functioning of the social machine. A new demon appeared at the end of the nineteenth century in the rise to prominence of the 'mental defective' as the collective name for a number of familiar characters, such as the idiot and the imbecile, together with a group of 'high-grade' defectives who were now accorded the novel soubriquet of the 'feeble-minded'. In answer to pleas from educators and philanthropists for the permanent segregation of defectives, bodies such as the Metropolitan Asylums Board erected specialist asylums for the imbecile poor in which as many inmates were crammed into as small a space as possible, day rooms doubling as dormitories, just one partition down the middle, 40 beds in each section, with scarce room to pass between them.[15] Audacious historians such as Mathew Thomson have recently got us to see that the invention of the feeble-minded, and equally of the problem of mental deficiency in general, were offsprings of the project of creating and sustaining democratic subjects, with the 'mental defective' serving to mark the frontier, in the eyes of liberals as much as conservatives, between the responsible citizen and the naturally irresponsible.[16]

The Great War may indeed, as Daniel Pick claims, have 'provided a heightened sense of the theoretical and political failure of pre-existing conventions and models', but the voices of Kraepelinian orthodoxy were by no means silenced.[17] In Britain as in Germany the *topos* of weakness was still prominent – expressed as a distaste for anything that smacked of a humanitarian grovelling before the rising tide of the weak and the decrepit – in many of the interpretations of the psychiatric casualties of the war that were in currency. 'The first thing that was predicted of this War', professed one observer, 'was that human nerves, especially civilized nerves, could never stand the strain. Our sensitive neurasthenic nervous systems, keyed up and pampered by the abnormal conditions of everyday life, would break down under the shock of its horrors'. So, in actuality, what has been 'the net result of continuous war upon the nerves of soldiers'? 'Astonishingly little, on the whole', for there has been no genuine emotional trauma to speak of. Though when a soldier is 'blown up and knocked down' it seems as if 'the very breath were going to be blown out of your body, and your head split and your hair torn by the vicious blast and whizz of the shells', still 'after twenty or thirty minutes of gasping and reeling, you gradually adjust yourself, realize that it is not going to kill you after all, or even do you any serious damage'. As to shell shock, it is simply 'the revelation of the measure of nervous unfitness and mental unbalance admitted into an army', a large share of it 'merely ordinary insanity occurring in wartime and having its delusions coloured by the fears of the battlefield'. In 1919 already the writer had the foreknowledge that there was a 'great body of lasting or permanent shell-shocks, who linger on for months or even years to try the souls and defy the healing skill . . . of doctors and specialists'; many of these hopeless case are 'almost as defective physically as they are mentally – under-sized, under-weight, narrow-chested, shuffle-gaited, slack jaws, with badly shaped heads, irregular features and vacant or restless expression'. Take 'fifty or more of them together and the impression of what the mental experts term "constitutional inferiority" is unmistakable, and this is confirmed by hundreds of actual measurements – height, weight, chest-girth, muscular-power – taken in the larger special hospitals for their care'.[18]

Opinions of this type were conspicuous in debate and in the medical literature in Britain, and never faded from the scene entirely, making a resurgence in the 1920s. Yet during the war itself they were not permitted to define or delimit the responses to the psychiatric casualties of the war, and, as we have seen, at decisive moments they were sidelined or overturned. Herein lies the signal contrast with Germany. Though there were obvious continuities between the reactions to mental disturbance in combat troops in the various belligerent countries, in important respects differences of national context proved to be determining.[19] In Germany the die had already been cast by pre-war alarms over the explosion in the population of the mentally ill, a four-fold increase in the asylum population of urbanizing Prussia in the three decades leading up to the First World War, for instance, when the population as a whole had increased by less than 50 percent, raising concerns about the psychic effects of urban life and prompting psychiatrists to revise their mission statements to prioritize the promotion and control of national health and fitness.[20] Though there were progressive psychiatric institutions which had attracted international admiration, where pioneers such as Hermann Simon had perfected the method of 'active therapy' a few years before the Great War, these therapeutic growths were vulnerable and pitifully inadequate in what were perceived as the overwhelming circumstances of an ever-expanding population of psychiatric misfits.[21]

Furthermore, medical professionals in Germany had traditionally thought of themselves as state representatives, whose task it was to encourage, and where necessary exhort, their patients to acknowledge their duty towards the collective interest and display their patriotic zeal. It is, then, not altogether surprising to learn that with the outbreak of hostilities, fuelled by fears of national decline and the pressing needs of the national community, German psychiatrists and neurologists largely reacted by subordinating the interests of soldier patients to those of the state, disparaging compassionate responses towards the suffering individual that discounted the welfare of the collective. As Paul Lerner has shown, most German doctors concluded quite early on that the so-called war neuroses were for the most part not causally connected with the circumstances of the war at all, but were essentially psychological reactions in terrified and weak-willed individuals unwilling or unable to place the national interest above their selfish desires. The military context proved all-enveloping, and hostile encounters between physicians and soldier patients were portrayed in militaristic terms in which the patient had become an enemy in the doctor's sights. In their reports the medical authorities skilfully side-stepped the events of the war itself by placing the blame for symptoms on wish complexes, notably the desire for a pension, which had resulted in the simulation of illness in an individual who by his constitution was already pre-disposed to psychological weakness.[22]

In the civilian domain away from the military hospitals, over 140,000 asylum inmates in Germany died during the war period from sickness and disease, their resistance weakened by the starvation diets to which they had been subjected in the interest of wartime economies. At Berlin-Buch Asylum, for instance, the calorific value of the diet fell from 2695 in 1914 to 1987 in January 1918.[23] 'It could almost seem as if we have witnessed a change in the concept of humanity', eerily proclaimed the psychiatrist Karl Bonhoeffer, 'we were forced by the terrible exigencies of war to ascribe a different value to the life of the individual than was the case before'.[24] Significantly, Kraepelin detected a grim justice in the mortality statistics, believing that the 'iron fist of war' had managed to stem the degenerate tide and for the time being ease 'the economic burden posed by incurable patients'. He urged against the release of compassionate impulses to such adversities, maintaining that 'humanitarian efforts to support the weak and to help the suffering, sickly and the decrepit serve to counteract significantly a systematic rearing of the fit: they load the shoulders of the able-bodied (on whom our hopes for the future rest) with ever greater burdens'.[25]

Not that the unfortunate inmates of English lunatic asylums during the war were touched by the springs of communal solidarity. The annual death rate in English asylums climbed to over 20 per cent in 1918 from a pre-war average of between 10 and 11 per cent, and in 1917 and 1918 around 17,000 inmates died, their deaths very probably caused in many cases by drastic reductions in diet to save money, not as high a death rate as in Germany admittedly, but still shocking: casualties of the war without any memorial, as John Crammer has poignantly observed.[26] Yet as it turned out – and significantly the keynote was set early on, long before the outcome of the war was determined – offi-cialdom on the British side was driven to take up a position towards psy-chiatric casualties that diverged hugely from the German one. On the German side, as we have seen, the war succeeded only in strengthening the hands of the diehards, and in exacerbating pre-existing hostilities between doctors and psychiatric patients, resulting in the disavowal by the majority of psychiatric opinion of any causal connection between war service and emotional distress. Far from asserting a new direction, this was business as usual with a vengeance. On the British side, by contrast, though the military authorities attempted to take action to stem the tide and tighten controls, and psychiatric old-timers rumbled their disapproval, there was no such collective dissocia-tion from the meaning of the outburst of madness provoked by the experi-ence of war service. Even though there were pockets of resistance, and governmental concessions were frequently succeeded by administrative chaos, the establishment eventually hoisted the white flag right across the whole terrain of mental health, from the common or garden anxiety neurosis to the wild woods of mania, dementia praecox, and general paralysis of the insane, conceding that these were all pensionable disabilities which may have been either caused or aggravated by war service.

What could account for such a sudden and marked divergence between two nations that after all, as we have already seen, were to a large extent congruent in their professional psychiatric cultures – Germany leading and the British psychiatrists following gamely after? There is, of course, the old canard that it was the epidemic of shell shock in the British, French, German, Italian and American armies which sounded the death knell for materialist psychiatry, and ushered Freud and his company onto the pitch laden with their kitbags of psychological explanations.[27] There are two things wrong with this account. One is that the line between the German and British responses to emotional distress in their respective armies was already drawn well before the epidemic of shell shock became visible; the other is that far from eschewing, or being trounced by, psychological explanations, the German psychiatric fraternity drew upon them with relish. Among other considerations, the litigious history of railway spine and pensions neurosis in the late nineteenth century should make us wary of conjuring the believer in psychogenic causes as a white knight. Furthermore, on the British scene it is far from obvious that psychological explanations as such won out over materialist accounts, or were recognized as having done so. If there is a fault line, therefore, it is unlikely to be this.

As Doris Kaufmann recounts, at an early stage in the prosecution of the war the German Supreme Army Command decided to hand over responsibility for the interpretation and solution of the problem of mentally ill soldiers to the psychiatric community.[28] One could not make a comparable statement about the British case, not least because there was no unified 'psychiatric community' under military control, any more than there was professional unanimity in civilian life. Nor were the military medical authorities able to hold sway over, and insulate themselves from, the rude foot soldiers of public opinion and the institutions of democratic society. There were no soldiers' councils storming the British mental hospitals, nor was there some kind of palace revolution in the citadels of psychiatry. Yet even so there was a widespread cultural commotion, involving an alliance between progressive mental health professionals and the advocates of ex-servicemen, in which the citizen soldier with severe mental health problems gained a place in the imagination of the citizenry. Together they brought about a deal that Kraepelin would surely have taken as evincing exactly those concessions to the forces of psychological degeneracy and weakness that he was excoriating in Germany.

There is, as we already seen, a background to these developments in the contradictory currents in social and political life that abounded in the closing decades of the nineteenth century and the opening years of the new one. Simultaneously demotic and hieratic, militarism, the cultivation of imperialist visions, and the pursuit of administrative rationality, jostled alongside 'progressivist', egalitarian and feminist counter-currents. Largely in response to the growing political power of the working classes and the emergence of a more educated and discerning population, the lines of social class had become progressively blurred, and governments had been prodded into adopting more fulsome styles of welfare, doing more than just provide care and protection 'at the margins', and into taking faltering steps towards a politics of equal dignity or 'positive' rights, 'civic' along with 'liberal' freedoms, as in the introduction of old age pensions and national health insurance in Britain.[29] The right of the governing class to impose a social order in which a rich and educated minority lived individuated lives, while the lower orders were subordinated to collectivist norms of efficiency, was being challenged by an emerging consumer consciousness prizing the rights of private individuals to possess a subjectivity and biography that was uniquely theirs, and to make demands of the state to help them maintain a sense of dignity and self-respect.[30]

Neither in Britain nor in many other parts of Europe was the overall climate militarist. In the years leading up to the Great War, militarist wings in European politics had been clipped by the stirrings of democratization, and on the eve of war many socialist parties campaigning on anti-militarist programmes proved to be in the ascendant.[31] It is, perhaps, a paradox of modernity that whilst industrialization had undoubtedly led to the increased penetration and expansion of the military into civilian life, at the same time the potential scope for militarization in democratizing societies was limited by the dependency of the military on the co-operation of the citizenry, and the reciprocal penetration of civilian norms into erstwhile closed military fiefdoms. Most striking, perhaps, was the 'complex revolution in the moral consideration afforded the wounded and the dead on the field of battle' in which the accent was increasingly on the *equality* of bodies, and on extending the 'decencies of nurture and memorial beyond the aristocratic elite to the common man, the new masters of the age'.[32]

THE GREAT WAR AND BONDS OF MUTUAL DEPENDENCY

When the Great War erupted onto the British scene, it exacerbated these currents, conflictingly in part but also prompting alliances, accommodations and pragmatic adjustments. The voracious and insatiable war machine, daily renewing its unprecedented claims on the vulnerable human frame, was pitted against the implacable demands of an anxious and informed public. Supportive though it was of the national struggle at the outset, public opinion was never less than vociferous in reminding the state of its obligations towards those who were putting themselves at risk on its behalf. John Keegan has written movingly of how the comradeship which 'flourished in the earthwork cities of the Western and Eastern Fronts, bound strangers into the closest brotherhood . . . and bonds of mutual dependency'.[33] These conditions engendered a reciprocal attentiveness to human needs that formed a stark contrast with the inequalities in the home society. Here a young medical officer, not long qualified, based at a field ambulance station in the cellars of a chateau at Contalmaison, not far from Albert in the Somme, describes a recurring subterranean experience of congestion in which intense overcrowding, and the press of bodies on each other, rather than being an index of poverty, marking a division between stations in society, now drew all ranks and classes into its belly:

> Throughout my stay at Contalmaison the flow of work in our cellars was uncertain; times of slackness alternating with times of great stress, when the place filled with scores upon scores of reeking, bleeding men. These times of great stress were not isolated incidents, to be dealt with, cleaned up, then forgotten, like a railway accident. They recurred regularly. They went on and on and on. Stretchers blocked the cellar floors, the passages, the battered shelter that remained above ground and the approaches outside. Often we worked for hours and hours on end without respite: at the crude dressing-tables, at men grounded on stretchers, at men squatting or sitting. It was emphatically not sheer muddle but the congestion beggars description. Our working space was limited. We got in each other's way. There was a constant movement of bearers shuffling and staggering with stretchers, negotiating the cellar stairs, seeking a way in or out and a bare space whereon to deposit their burdens. . . . Sometimes a man on a stretcher would vomit explosively, spewing over himself and his neighbours. I have seen mounted troops brought in with liquid faeces oozing from the unlaced legs of their breeches. Occasionally a man would gasp and die as he lay on his stretcher. All this was routine; and the waiting crowd looked on perforce. It looked on unconcerned. No one spoke much during these seemingly endless periods of congestion . . . we got on with our work with no needless words.[34]

Human frailty under these desperate circumstances engendered strong feelings about the rights of all men, without discrimination, to be clothed in a thick and psychologically perspicuous conception of need.[35] Not long arrived at the Front, Wilfred Owen wrote to his mother in January 1917 railing against some sentimental and perverse images that had recently been published of the searing reality which he now encountered. 'They want to call No Man's Land "England" because we keep supremacy there. . . . No Man's Land under snow is like the face of the moon, chaotic, crater-ridden, uninhabitable, awful, the abode of madness. To call it "England" . . . .'[36] Indeed, but then one might also be led, as of course Owen was himself, to fix a critical eye on the divisive and divided image of England itself that was visible looking down the long telescope from France. And this is exactly what innovating psychological observers at home were doing in turning their sights onto the warts and blemishes of the prevailing psychiatric establishment and the wider mental health culture. Steeped in the emotions of citizen soldiers returning from the dismal fields of war, these emerging theories were to find in human frailty and weakness – the weakness that made men behave uncommonly like women – the key not to the isolation of an aberrant sub-species, but to an understanding of what is at stake in human lives.[37]

Chapter 8

PSYCHOSIS AND LIFE

Fear of madness leads to a flight to an extreme of sanity which is a false step in civilisation; it means a flight to the logical and the conscious and the easily planned, and a loss of contact with individual integrity, and the hidden depths of the personality of each person.

D. W. Winnicott (1949)[1]

SHELL SHOCK AND MENTAL HEALTH IN BRITAIN

The currents running in social and political life before the war were, of course, reflected also in ideas. Out of the biological awakening of the mid-nineteenth century, a subversive principle had emerged, an affiliate in the scientific domain of the nascent solidarities in the social, which played on a fascination with connectivity, and with destabilizing traditional demarcations, leading Charles Darwin to conclude that the multitude of life-forms past and present were all interconnected. 'We are all netted together', he jotted in his notebook in 1838.[2] That was exactly the kind of inspiration that had urged the anatomist G. Elliot Smith and the psychologist T. H. Pear, two dedicated members of Ronald Rows's team at Maghull Military Hospital, to produce *Shell-Shock and Its Lessons*, a small volume that was quickly to achieve iconic status in the new psychological landscape that emerged out of the war, and which by 1917 was already into its second edition.

Charles Myers and his progressive confederates in Flanders had been busy trying to rescue neurosis from insanity, but in Britain during and after the war there was a radical lobby which was pushing the frontiers still further by questioning the fundamental axioms on which mental stability rested. Smith and Pear were in the vanguard of a group of observers who were starting to fashion psychological theories that were more inclusive than the divisive and condemnatory rhetoric of psychiatric orthodoxy, entertaining a vision of an indeterminate mental health culture in which differences among categories and conditions, not least those between insanity and the psychoneuroses, became progressively blurred and negotiable. And here, also, as we shall see, is a bigger story of psychological theorizing, much energized by the Great War, in which psychosis is reconfigured not as the site of an exile but as the site of our origins and of our continued residence.

Among the military authorities the phenomenon of shell shock was not surprisingly the cause of enormous consternation, but in this small gem of a book, far from provoking reproach, it is transfigured into a lance to conduct 'the painful probing of the public wound, the British attitude towards mental disorder', made up of a 'shifting and unstable blend of apathy, superstition, helpless ignorance and fear', a long phase of denial succeeded by an abrupt, dramatic and most often terminal exodus. In defining shell shock, Elliot Smith and Tom Pear cast the dragnet very wide to include 'all those mental effects of war experience which are sufficient to incapacitate a man from the performance of his military duties'. Shell shock became less the marker for a specific condition, or set of conditions, than for a wide-arching perspective affirming the emotional origins of mental disturbances. 'It is not in the intellectual but in the *emotional* sphere', they write, 'that we must look for terms to describe these conditions'.[3]

The problems of shell shock were not in the least unprecedented, but simply the eruption under circumstances that inevitably threw them into prominence of regular problems of 'nervous breakdown' that were entirely familiar to those who had been willing and able to recognize them, but which for the most part had been hidden, ignored or traduced in workaday British society. The lack of preparedness and foresight, and most of all the utter lack of psychological sophistication in the authorities, that contributed to the crises on the battlefront to a large extent simply mirrored the perverse cultural routines of the homefront. 'Shell shock' was embraced by progressive thinkers and practitioners such as Elliot Smith and Tom Pears in reaction against an apparatus of contempt for ordinary mental distress that was still being hardened, not in the wild swamps of misguided popular belief, but in the front parlour of professional psychiatric opinion, according to formulae prepared by dedicated medical scientists. Currents that had received only a very limited airing before the war now had the ear of popular opinion, as the authors had evidently hoped, presaging the eventual emergence of a mental health culture in which emotional conflict and disturbance could be admitted, not as aberrations taking place on the fringe, or in damaged or degenerate frames, but as the stuff of how human beings constitute themselves.

Though there were more qualifications in the text than some of its critics were willing to acknowledge, still it delivered an unequivocal fillip to the movement for the recognition of the psyche as the essential hinge in human functioning. Old stagers of the psychiatric establishment complained that they were being foisted into a seditious and disconcerting psychological call to arms. 'Most noticeable', opined Lt Col. Sir Robert Armstong-Jones, Medical Superintendent of Claybury Asylum, a pillar of the psychiatric establishment who took particular exception when distressed servicemen had the affront to weep copiously in his presence, 'is the changed relationship here accepted between the mind and the body . . . we now have the view put forward that there exists a reciprocal causal relation between the two'. He could scarcely find himself 'in agreement with authors who adopted so wholeheartedly the exclusively emotional origin of shell-shock as against the physical origin' and who were insistent that the news about the psychic suffering of servicemen carried lessons for the mental health system as a whole.[4] The impudence of a critical perspective in which shell shock, far from keeping to itself, was made to yoke together the sundered parts of the mental health culture, even snaffling insanity, stuck in his craw, especially when the question was asked: 'What percentage of the inmates need ever have entered the asylum? . . . this question cannot be publicly asked too often. . . . It is conclusively proved by the experience of other countries that a large proportion of the patients might have been cured without being sent into an asylum'.[5]

Already before the Great War progressive opinion was admitting the serious social stigma of the asylum, insisting on 'the necessity for teaching the medical profession and the public that many mental disorders are absolutely recoverable, that good hospital and scientific treatment save man, that the mere economy of our monster institutions represents a sham economy paid for by the patients and their families, and that psychiatry must extend beyond the asylums'.[6] For anyone lower on the scale than the privileged echelons of the upper-middle, upper and titled classes, the institutions and categories of 'lunacy' provided the only option for being a mentally ill person, the exclusive monopoly carrier – there was no other way to go, the alternative was to stay at home and not to travel. The asylum was the crucial determinant in how sufferers came to ponder what was at stake for them in being mentally ill, and to measure the gap that now separated them irrevocably from ordinary mortals. Of course, this inevitably impacted on experiences such as hearing voices, of which people became more fearful in anticipation of the consequences. 'Lunacy' and the 'lunatic asylum' were not, therefore, simply receptacles for 'natural kinds', for the very existence of an environment structured along these lines impacted powerfully on the kinds themselves, not infrequently hastening the end – the descent into an apparently incommunicable psychosis – that was most feared.[7]

Just before the war broke out, news was spreading of therapeutic developments, primarily in the United States, but ironically also in Germany as in other continental nations, that were hugely more promising than anything on offer in public asylums in Britain. The Swiss-born psychiatrist Adolf Meyer had addressed an international congress in London in August 1913 with news of the innovations he was promoting in the Phipps Psychiatric Clinic at the Johns Hopkins Medical School in Baltimore, which had just opened under his direction. Meyer was following in the path of the great Eugen Bleuler, director of the Burghölzli Hospital near Zurich, who since 1890 had been trying to bring psychological understanding to mental patients with severe conditions such as dementia praecox, which he was later to rename as schizophrenia. In sharp contrast to Kraepelin, for whom psychological suffering hardly constituted an invitation to dialogue, Bleuler's approach was steeped in a commitment to achieving therapeutic rapport with the patient.[8] Meyer took this therapeutic dynamism a stage further by locating it within a genetic-dynamic or developmental theory of reaction types, according to which mental health and illness were not dichotomous conditions but constituted a gradient, along which individuals moved depending on their inherited propensities and the stresses to which they were subjected.[9] Though Meyer claimed that the funding levels of the Clinic were modest, it was able to boast an impressive ratio of 10 physicians to every 90 patients, a revelation which staggered British psychiatrists, not least because it had apparently been judged worthwhile to make such a significant investment in patients who would most likely have been regarded as hopeless cases in their own institutions.[10] Even though the comparison was not entirely fair to the British mental health system, since the Clinic was largely financed from philanthropic sources, and was by no means representative of American state psychiatric institutions, the Phipps Clinic quickly established itself (along with the Boston Psychopathic Hospital which had opened in 1912) as a benchmark of progressive mental health care.

The wholehearted engagement with emotional reality was potentially a subversive undertaking in itself, in as much as it exposed a common ground into which all servicemen were thrown, regardless of station or rank, and opened windows into the subjectivities of ordinary soldiers. However, to reach a position where he could grasp what was really at stake in an individual life, the practitioner had to be willing to stare down his own prejudices and to jettison naive sympathy as a guide. 'For unless the sympathiser has a true appreciation of the patient's condition, and can look at things from his point of view, he cannot really feel *with* the sufferer. The latter may arouse in the would-be sympathiser tender emotions and sympathetic "pain" but unless the sympathiser has the insight, the pain, to put it crudely, is not likely to be "in the same place" as that of the patient'.[11]

It was of 'vital importance, in dealing with cases of illness due primarily to specific anxieties and mental conflicts', to discover 'the *real* nature and causes of these anxieties and conflicts'. Having discarded the traumatic literalism of the so-called commotional theory, the reality that counted here was the subjectivity of the suffering individual, which was not bound by the topography of the external world or by the divide between war and peacetime lives. Indeed, the 'worries of civil life' might weigh as heavily as 'the terrifying experiences of warfare', as when 'emotional disturbances in children, due to the cruelty of drunken parents, a rankling sense of injustice', or 'the appalling conditions created in some of these homes by nervous and irritable parents' proved to be 'the real trauma which the "shock" has served to re-awaken'. Though slurs had been made against them (by military medical officers mostly), 'in the military hospitals there have been hundreds of patients suffering from psychoneuroses, who are demonstrably neither women nor neuropaths'.[12]

Many of these men, Elliot Smith and Tom Pear remarked, 'have suffered intensely', concealing their emotional troubles for as long as possible, 'until endurance is intolerable', echoing almost exactly the sentiments of Ernst Beyer (a war neurotic himself, as it turned out, who had been treated in a psychiatric ward in Danzig), one of the few German doctors to defend shell-shocked soldiers from the assumption that they were inferior and cowardly individuals, and instead to insist that they were 'exceptionally sensitive people whose psyches cannot simply be disregarded, but rather must be taken into account in all cases'. 'I want to reach the point', Beyer continued, 'where we do not try to ascertain whether a shell exploded near a patient or whether a man was buried or was grazed or hit squarely by a shot, but instead where we ask how the man has suffered subjectively'.[13] Smith and Pear had more or less reached that point themselves when they asserted that 'the war has shown us one indisputable fact, that a psychoneurosis may be produced in almost anyone if only his environment be made "difficult" enough for him'.[14]

Of course, there were those who, even though the world of the war did not at all correspond to the old paradigm, were desperately trying to continue to judge it by the old 'objective' standards. It turned out, however, that the emotional landscape in which protagonists were moving was one in which 'subjectivity' had come into its own, and had to be given its measure. This new kind of 'reality' could not be reduced, or relegated, to the 'back' (or nocturnal) space of dreams and pathology. Memories and emotions intruded into the organization of space and time, with the result that it was radically disrupted. Trivial though the subject's personal anguish might be by comparison with events in the public domain, the experiencing subject was the centre of his own world, not merely a pawn in someone else's – his subjectivity *was* his world, and the 'war business' might sit very uncomfortably in it. What did the war mean to George? What did George mean to the war? The answer to the first question has usually been ignored in favour of a critical riposte to the second. Traditionally, of course, 'inner worlds' were supposed to adapt to 'public events', but here perhaps the lesson was that public events were obliged to concede to subjective realities and acknowledge their own integrity and facticity. Public events rubbed against private worlds, lives were framed by emotional topographies in which special places, times and significances were always hovering on the fringes, cropping up unexpectedly, producing networks of association and interconnection every bit as complex and intricate as the dense layerings and interweavings of the topography of the trenches, full of prohibitions, traps, gullies, blanks, fractures (elusive fragments of memory) and wholly unexpected conjunctions (wild leaps across space and time).

PSYCHOSIS AS THE ACTION OF LIFE

This was also the 'reality' that had excited Millais Culpin, who was to join Elliot Smith and Tom Pear and their colleagues at Maghull in 1917. Culpin was to sketch fruitful lines of development that would be enlarged upon by a younger generation of theorists in the postwar period, maintaining that the distinction between neurosis and psychosis was mostly social rather than scientific, and reconfiguring psychoneurosis on the ground of psychosis. Born in 1874, he was a rugged individualist in temperament as much as in physique who had spent his late teens and early adulthood in the Australian outback, where his father, a general practitioner, had removed his family in an attempt to escape the London fogs. He later returned to train in medicine at the London Hospital and, finding himself attracted to surgery for its relative certainty and robust good sense, he then practised as a surgeon for some years, supposing that he had found his métier.

His experience in the Great War was to change all this, not because of any dissatisfaction with surgery as such, but because so many servicemen were brought before him bearing diagnoses of physical conditions the existence of which he was unable to verify. Enlisting in the RAMC on the outbreak of war, he served as a surgical specialist until the end of 1917, first in Portsmouth and then in France, treating the fallout from Passchendaele and the Somme. Ironically, though, he discovered early on that the expertise he was now developing was that of a kind of negative surgical capability. The occasions on which he actually got to practise surgery were rapidly decreasing in proportion to his growing awareness that the body which was often presented to him was a psychosomatic entity with complaints, including abdominal symptoms and deformities of the foot, that were largely psychically driven.

These emotional forces could not, of course, be identified by the naked eye, but instead required the use of other senses, and the development of a sensibility quite at odds with everything for which his medical training had prepared him. 'Within my own sphere as a surgeon, whether in France or in England', he later recalled, 'scarcely a day passed without providing at least one example of hysterical symptoms masquerading under a false diagnosis'. Not infrequently, 'hysterical contractures were subjected to surgical treatment proper to organic diseases, but provocative of ill-results when employed upon men who were themselves producing the deformity'. After reaching his own diagnosis and finding that his scalpel would not be needed, 'I would take the man into a side room where, with an opening "This is man to man", I told him, as best I could, my opinion as a surgeon and invited his'.[15]

It was his experience on the furrowed path from the front line that revealed to Millais Culpin how we are netted together psychologically. 'I saw the shell-shockers who were sent down from the firing line to be shipped straight to Blighty', he later recounted, 'I had not learnt how to spell psychology, but I could see that here was something the man himself was doing'.[16] Resolving to kick over the traces of his mechanistic medical training, he abjured surgery for psychotherapy and the new psychology. After the war he became variously a neurological consultant to the Ministry of Pensions, Lecturer in Psychoneurosis at London Hospital Medical College, Professor of Medical and Industrial Psychology at the London School of Hygiene and Tropical Medicine, and President of the British Psychological Society.

In the warm glow of hindsight there is the undeniable excitement of a medical scientist caught in the act of migrating from one paradigm or model to another, from the diseased body on the operating table awaiting the ministrations of objective medicine, to an apprehension of how somatic functioning has been diverted by the artful psyche.[17] In the immediacy of the situation in the field, however, there was a sense of helplessness that only someone with Culpin's personal strengths, impelled by a defiant reaching after truth, could afford to acknowledge. He experienced a crisis of his surgical manhood in which, unable to wield his instrument, he was reduced to acknowledging his uncertainty not only to his putative patient but also before his irate colleagues. Early on in the war, he identified on his ward two cases of hysterical deformities of the foot. Each of these men 'had spent months in a hospital where, with his fictitious disease, he fitted into the scheme of things; his being invalided with that disease would have fitted too, and no one would have worried, not even the hysteric himself, if the disability had remained for the rest of his days'. It was soon impressed upon Culpin that 'life would have been smoother for me if I had not interfered with a false diagnosis that made the road, wherever it led, so easy for all. I did not realize that my interference posed a problem no one cared to face, though my own helplessness when called upon to treat these two men should have warned me'.[18]

It hardly needs saying that when the surgeon found himself stripped of his expertise, the patient might very quickly have been exposed as a malingerer in retaliation. Culpin was obviously no pushover, and not averse to unmasking those who appeared to be using the cover of disability to their advantage. Overall, however, his experience of these psychological casualties led him to reflect not on their moral defects but on the emotional complexities in being human, and what he grew to recognize as the power of the unconscious over the body. Whilst he could see that 'here was something the man himself was doing', he could also see that the man was stirred by an action which he could only very partially recognize, if at all.

Theories of the aftereffects of concussion, 'separated synapses, dissociated cerebral centres, punctiform haemorrhages, gas-poisoning from high explosives' and so on were soon discarded as so many fantasies that were 'no nearer to reality than was the explosion of thunder as the voice of an angry god'. The shell-shock cases served instead to establish for Culpin and other observers that these 'minor psychoses', as he was later to term them, taking 'psychosis' as a generic term to designate action in which the psyche takes part, 'had their origins in mental processes of which the sufferer was unaware'. These experiences opened for him, as it did for others, a perspective not so much on human aberration as on a dimension of human life for which quite new intellectual and therapeutic resources were needed. He resolved not to 'put upon the material sciences more than they could carry' and, though forced to admit 'the existence of problems before which our education has left us powerless', he eventually came to appreciate the opportunity for creating a therapeutic method out of his own powerlessness by inviting the patient himself to become the instrument in his own cure.

News of his psychological awakening having reached the authorities, in November 1917 he was invited by Col. Aldren Turner, consultant neurologist to the War Office, formally to abandon surgery and for the time being to dedicate himself to working with psychiatric casualties of the war. 'Armed with scepticism but impelled by curiosity', he was dispatched to Maghull for some training where: 'I soon knew that Captain Bernard Hart, Professor Pear, and Major Rows had something to teach me. I had read a brilliant article by Charles Mercier ridiculing Freud's theory of the unconscious, and not a word on the other side. That theory, honestly and impartially set forth, among others, now gave the key to many of my perplexities'.[19] As a result 'a new world opened up, when under the influence of the Maghull teaching, I began to treat shell-shocked men by the apparently simple plan of getting them to talk of their experiences'.[20]

From early on he was a provocative contributor to the burgeoning literature on war neurosis. Already in January 1915, he published a paper in the *British Medical Journal* asserting that most of the 30 cases of trench foot, a fungal infection produced by prolonged exposure to cold and damp conditions, quickly becoming gangrenous if not treated, which he and a colleague had studied, proved to be hysterical.[21] Yet, ironically, at the very same time, a maverick as ever, he was busied in criticizing and dismantling the whole idea of a war *neurosis*. The term 'neurosis' attributed, so Culpin believed, a misplaced concreteness to what should properly be understood in a psychological dimension, the tyranny of the word hindering recognition that 'the symptoms are determined by an emotional state'. He recalled how, as a medical student, if a puzzling patient appeared the word got about that 'Dr Dash says it's functional'. But what could this mean? '"Functional nervous disorder" left us with a vague impression that something was happening in the man's nervous system which produced symptoms that no fellow could be expected to understand', carrying the supposition 'that there is really something wrong with the nerves concerned and that if our knowledge were complete we should be able to recognise the something and treat it according to the rules of a materialist philosophy'. As he later realized, 'this supposition of a pathological anatomy', a truth about the diseased body that only awaited discovery, was 'a form of metaphysics'.[22]

Culpin concluded that the dissension over shell shock in the Great War in all essential respects reproduced the controversy over railway spine in the previous century, for which the mental explanation had also been bitterly contested until 'finally two surgeons, Herbert Page and Furneaux Jordan, brought the pathological theories to the tribunes of the scientific canons' and 'established the view that the symptoms were the reactions of the man as a whole and had no relation to any lesion of the nervous system'.[23] Alas, 'this history of abandoned fiction had been forgotten when the Great War began', and 'the same mental attitude that had – not to put too fine a point on it – made a mess of "railway spine" now evolved a pathology of shell-shock whose only relation to science lay in the use of anatomical and pathological terms'. Events were to show, however, that 'shell-shock was a reaction of the individual to the terrors and dangers of warfare and that to put it in the category of physical injuries was a disastrous mistake' and only resulted in a wrong handling of the situation.[24]

Culpin had also another, and equally significant, objection to the term neurosis. It set up a divide which he believed to be quite artificial from supposedly more serious conditions that were grouped under the heading of psychosis. Provocatively, he chose to reconfigure neurosis as a minor psychosis, asserting that 'neurosis is action in which the neuron takes part', whereas 'psychosis is action in which the psyche takes part'. In Culpin's portrayal, the nervous patient is now reconfigured as a psychotic. Though the term psychosis was typically applied to disturbances that ended in certification, the distinction from neurosis was social rather than scientific, and there was no justification in pathology for the supposition that they constituted discrete clinical states: 'Both conditions are at present usefully studied only as alterations in the reactions of the patient as a personal entity; they are both psychoses, though the second case shows a more fundamental change than the first'. To the objection that his proposal may frighten the public, who 'now draw such a sharp line between "mental disease" and "nervousness"', he rejoins that 'a trend of modern psychiatry is to educate the public towards the removal of the stigma that attaches to mental disease and the present terminology is a pandering to the conception of a stigma'.[25]

A rather similar line is taken by Stanford Read, the former commander of D Block Netley, writing in the early 1920s, who gives a sympathetic portrait of the psychotic patient, believing that there is a tendency 'for medical men prematurely to recommend commitment to an institution'. The mental processes which are provocative of the psychoses are, he claims, 'in no way different from those met with in so-called normal functioning' and 'it is by no means easy to say where the dividing line shall be drawn between the minor and the major psychoses'. Nor, contrary to superficial appearances, is the psychotic completely cut off from his fellow human beings, for though the connections may be faulty, or the wires twisted, the psychotic is still in the communications business: 'If we regard mental symptoms, not as indicative of diseases, but more as evidence of an individual's defence against it, as a striving towards cure, we can surmise that, if the reactions of a minor psychosis fail in this object, further and more desperate attempts may result in major psychotic symptoms wherein the patient may find some compensation'. Psychotic patients 'are so often needlessly shut away where society will not be offended by their presence', yet 'with kindly and proper supervision there is no reason why many a major psychotic should not have liberty. . . . Much of the anti-social behaviour shown by such patients is only the result of a want of understanding and a mishandling on the part of those responsible for their care. When we have, as in America, a well-trained and organised social service, segregation will become less necessary'. Read looks towards a time where society may be brought to look upon mental disease 'with a kindlier and saner eye, as is the case in the town of Gheel in Belgium, where over a thousand psychotic and certificated patients live with families and, with perfect liberty, mingle with the inhabitants'.[26]

Maurice Craig nicely captures the pace of shifts in psychiatric opinion in this period. In the 1912 edition of his widely acclaimed textbook, he had quoted approvingly Henry Maudsley's definition of insanity as meaning essentially 'such a want of harmony between the individual and his social medium, by reason of some defect or fault of mind in him, as prevents him from living and working among his kind in the social organization. Completely out of tune there, he is a social discord of which nothing can be made'.[27] However, in the 1926 edition we learn that ' "Insanity" is a separate conception with no real meaning in scientific medicine; it is a legal classification applied to persons certifiable under the Lunacy Act'.[28] As to the latter, Craig was equally forthcoming in his evidence to the Royal Commission in the same year that 'certification has nothing to do with medicine, I may say. It is an embarrassment . . . of the relationship of patient to physician. Therefore it is never sought so far as the medical people are concerned. It is an obligation placed upon the medical persons by the State'.[29] Not that everyone was swept along by the excitement of the new psychological landscape. The distinguished social psychiatrist J. R. Lord, a leading light in the budding mental hygiene movement, reproved the clinical psychiatrist for having been 'too long obsessed with imperception, illusion, hallucination, delusion, confusion, amnesia etc and largely blind to the basic significance of morbid impulses, strivings, motives, desires, cravings, feelings, affections, anxieties, emotions and passions, of which they are merely reflections'.[30] By contrast, Hubert Norman, who had treated the soldier inmates at Napsbury War Hospital with such sensitivity, was still sitting comfortably in the old paradigm and did not share in this psychic universe at all. 'The Great War', he expostulated, 'demonstrated to all but the pessimistic bewailers of human deterioration how essentially stable the nervous system is'.[31]

In one of his first works, written in the late 1930s, the child psychiatrist and psychoanalyst John Bowlby also dwelt on the similarities and indeterminacies between neurosis and psychosis, arguing that it was impossible to draw any line between the two. Some neuroses were more severe than some psychoses, with patients passing easily from one condition to the other: 'The schools which hold that there is an abyss separating psycho-neurosis from psychosis or one psycho-neurosis from another fail wholly to take the time element into consideration. . . . Few people remain the same throughout their lives whilst many show at successive periods an unstable personality, symptoms of psycho-neurosis and of psychosis. It is therefore absurd to conceive of a patient in terms of any one condition. He must be thought of as *an indi-*

vidual of certain potentialities, a unity of which the particular traits and symptoms shown at any one moment are but fleeting expressions'.[32] Tellingly, he invokes Aubrey Lewis, a rising star in the inter-war British psychiatric firmament, in a rejection of one-sided explanations that echoes very directly the memorandum of 1917 that did so much to advance the fortunes of psychiatric war disability claimants. 'Every illness', Lewis writes, 'is the product of two factors – of environment working on the organism: whether the constitutional factor is the predominant and determining influence, or the environmental one, is never a question of kind, never a question to be dealt with as an "either/or" problem; there will be a great number of possible combinations according to the individual inherited endowment and training, and the particular constellation of environmental forces'.[33]

FROM BISMARCK TO HUMPTY DUMPTY

Dr Dixon: (Reads a bill of health) Professor Bloom is a finished example of the new womanly man.

James Joyce, *Ulysses*[34]

Millais Culpin and others drew the lines of this new psychological landscape in broad brush, but it was left to a younger man, born in 1896 and more exactly a contemporary of the servicemen who saw action in the Great War, who had himself served as surgeon-probationer on a destroyer in the last part of the war before he had even qualified in medicine, to chart the contours of what he termed 'the histology of the psyche'. 'Only yesterday I saw a man suffering from shell shock put under Hypnosis by the man who looks after mental diseases at Bart's. This man could never do Psychoanalysis because it needs patience and sympathy and other properties which he does not possess'.[35]

This was the young Donald Winnicott writing to his sister Violet from his digs in Paddington in November 1919. The mental expert at Bart's to whom he referred was the very same Sir Robert Armstrong-Jones, that standard-bearer of the psychiatric old guard, who had protested against the suggestion that shell shock bore any lessons for mental health culture. Like others of his generation, Winnicott turned to psychoanalysis in the hope that it was the fork in the road that might lead him to psychiatry, not 'as a blind therapy' but instead 'as a complex but interesting concern for the human being who finds life difficult and whose problems we can feel to be represented in ourselves'.[36] Elliott Smith and Tom Pear had alluded to 'difficult' environments, but it was Winnicott who was to fashion an attitude to life around the

consciously chosen ordinary (and for that reason also in a specialized psychiatric context quite provocative) word 'difficult'.

'The fact is that life itself is difficult', he later wrote; 'if an insane person is
studied in sufficient detail the course of the illness becomes intelligible as an
expression of the difficulties inherent in life' or of inherent problems of individual development.[37] Winnicott very much exemplifies the new type of manliness to which Alison Light draws attention when she describes how in a
'quest for a bearable masculinity which could make what had previously
seemed even effeminate preferable to the bulldog virtues of 1914', the post-
war world 'needed to give way to a more modest, sometimes agonised sense
of English manliness'.[38] In 1923, the same year in which he took up an
appointment at the Paddington Green Children's Hospital, Winnicott came
into psychoanalysis through having personal difficulties of his own, and found
in it not simply a therapeutic method but also the theoretical support for
his reflections on emotional development ('normally difficult and commonly
incomplete') and on the vicissitudes of psychic growth.[39]

The psyche is forged 'out of the material of the imaginative elaboration of
body functioning', having as its most important duty the binding together of
past experiences, potentialities, and the present moment awareness, and
expectancy for the future. Thus the self comes into existence'.[40] Right from
the start, Winnicott was contributing to a reconfiguration of the topography
of psychological weakness in which human beings were no less robust for
being vulnerable, and the quality and intensity of emotional disturbance was
no different in Paddington from what it might be in Picardy:

> Sometimes there is a history of onset following some event that was so excit-
> ing or so productive of anxiety that the child could not deal with it, the idea
> behind the event producing feelings that child found intolerable. Such an
> event might be too sudden and unexpected, as when a sudden gale blows
> open the window, and the door bangs, and all is in confusion; or too, great
> fear or rage may be evoked by some event such as unwanted sexual enlight-
> enment, the sight of the parents in bed together, or witnessing a quarrel
> between adults, the birth of a baby brother or sister, the sight of a man with
> a paralysed leg, or of someone's false teeth etc.[41]

In the psychological forcing grounds of Flanders and Picardy, men were
exposed to conditions in which they were jolted into recalling, reliving, and
repulsing the intensity of infantile feelings which normality depended on
forgetting. And, inevitably, these feelings were often psychotic, for 'the study

of psychosis is the same as the study of the very early psychological history of the developing individual'.[42]

Though he may only have addressed the question directly in passing, the emotional fallout from the war forms the backdrop to Winnicott's personal and professional development. One might say that he became a genealogist of shell shock, for whom the breaking shells are not so much artillery shells as the egg shells of emergent and contested identities. 'In psychology', he wrote, 'it must be said that the infant falls to pieces unless held together, and physical care is psychological care at these stages'.[43] Furthermore, 'it must be remembered that the *early stages are never truly abandoned*, so that in a study of the individual of whatever age all the primitive as well as the later types of environmental requirements will be found'.[44] For Winnicott, Humpty Dumpty provides the surest touchstone or reference point, much in the way that Bismarck did for Emil Kraepelin. 'It is useful to think of the nursery rhyme of Humpty Dumpty', he wrote, 'and the reasons for its universal appeal. Evidently there is a general feeling, not available to consciousness, that integration is a precarious state. The nursery rhyme perhaps appeals because it acknowledges personal integration as an achievement'.[45] There could scarcely be a more ironic contrast to Kraepelin's notion of the 'mature and emotionally well-anchored male'.

In Winnicott's thought there are frequent echoes of what Millais Culpin had been arguing, and while they pursued rather different career trajectories their paths did cross, most notably at a conference on 'Neurosis in the Child' in 1936, where they combined in debunking and excoriating the notion of the 'neurotic child'. Winnicott believed that there was really nothing to distinguish between the normal and the neurotic child, whereas 'the popular use of the word "neurosis" expressed the fallacy that neurotic symptoms were in themselves abnormal'. For his part, Culpin detested the word 'neurosis', the currency of which marked 'one of the dark ages in medicine' (still worse was the word 'neurotic'), preferring the term 'benign psychosis', which he thought was not very different in children and adults.[46]

Spurred and emboldened by the faltering confidence of the erstwhile male elite, D. W. Winnicott had rebelled, along with others of his generation, against the insensitivity and divisiveness of the inherited canon, not merely as a psychological guide, but also as the standard by which to judge those of a lower social class. Beating a retreat from blimpishness and its moral confines, they were seizing the ground on which to acknowledge the pains, griefs, hopes and expectations of others, to solicit their story-telling urges, regardless of disability, class or gender.[47] It is as if Winnicott had posed the question: 'suppose we treat the shell-shocked not as inferiors or as oddities but as everyman, and try to remake our understanding of ourselves in their image, where would that take us?'. And where it does, indeed, take us is precisely into the kind of subversive psychological landscape that we discover in his writing, in which maleness is an option or variant in what is essentially a radically feminized ecology.

In the negotiation and maintenance of emotional anchorage, the harbour master is invariably a woman; the boat of personal identity is always bobbing on the waters of the mother's psychic needs, or floating in the wake of a woman's emotional interior; the child lives on in the adult ('it must be remembered that the *early stages are never truly abandoned*'); depression is not an aberration but to be valued as part of the fabric of life ('the capacity to become depressed, to have a reactive depression, to mourn loss, is something that is not inborn, nor is it an illness; it comes as an achievement of healthy emotional growth'); normality is indistinguishable from psychological suffering ('the fact is that life itself is difficult, and psychology concerns itself with the inherent problems of individual development . . . probably the greatest suffering in the human world is the suffering of normal or healthy or mature persons . . . this is not generally recognised'); and sanity atrophies if it is unable to freshen its parts through acknowledging a kinship with madness.[48]

In certain respects we are, of course, running ahead of ourselves with these ideas. Even though they emerged out of the cultural upheaval produced by the Great War, in the inter-war period at least they were to a large extent having to sail against the wind, criss-crossed by other currents that were mostly resistant to the clarion calls of democratizing psychologies. It was to be some time before what Kraepelin took for weakness would be codified in a definition of moral progress as 'an increase in our ability to see more and more differences among people as morally irrelevant'.[49] Yet, as we shall see in the rest of this book, in other ways they are extraordinarily germane. If we attend to the experiences of ex-servicemen in the aftermath of the war, it is as though in many instances these clinicians, many of whom were after all their contemporaries, had got to them before us and based their theories on just these individuals.

Part IV

HOMECOMINGS

And did the Countenance Divine
Shine forth upon our clouded hills?
And was Jesualem builded here
Among these dark Satanic mills?

Bring me my bow of burning gold:
Bring me my arrows of desire:
Bring me my spear: O clouds, unfold!
Bring me my chariot of fire.

I will not cease from mental fight,
Nor shall my sword sleep in my hand,
Till we have built Jerusalem,
In England's green and pleasant land

William Blake[1]

Chapter 9

FAMILY FORTUNES

'WILL YOU HAVE HIM HOME?'

There were a variety of ways in which a family might come to learn that their husband, son or brother was suffering from a 'mental' problem of some kind; from an official source obviously, but also from rumours that were circulating and the communications of other soldiers. Invariably, relatives were pitched into an emotive terrain in which they fumbled for clarification and reassurance in a tangle of words and images that were alternately obscure and rife with foreboding, anxiously scrutinizing every scrap of news that came their way for the portents that it contained. When they learned in May 1918 that he was an inmate of the Lord Derby Hospital at Warrington, Ivor Gurney's family feared the worst, because they had just heard from a friend, Miss Emily Hunt, that her nephew, who was a sergeant not far from where Gurney had been stationed, had written to his mother telling her that Ivor had 'gone out of his mind'. At the request of Gurney's younger sister, Dorothy, a mutual friend wrote 'to the Administrar at Warrington asking if Ivor had really gone out of his mind. He received a very satisfactory reply stating that it was expected he would soon be convalescent', and that 'Ivor's complaint was merely "nervous breakdown"'.

This was obviously reassuring, though there was still some lingering uncertainty over the seriousness of his condition and the type of institution into which he had been put. Gurney had told them in a letter that 'they keep them a long time at this Hospital', from which Dorothy supposed that he will 'still be under the Doctor for some time'. He had also mentioned a 'jolly Irishman who tells wonderful tales, but who, poor chap, has lost his memory', all of which made it 'appear to be a mental hospital' and implicitly to confirm their worst forebodings. But, still, he had been writing poetry and asking for music, from which Dorothy was eager to convince herself that he 'has only had a temporary breakdown owing to his trying to work at music and poetry as well as signalling examinations'. Then the next month there was news that he had written to other friends 'telling them that his complaint is "Nervous Breakdown from Deferred Shell-Shock". That is just about what it is and is rather relieving'. But this was shortly followed by news of Gurney's suicide threat which was not at all relieving, and just about let the elusive complaint slip back into the ocean of uncertainty.[1]

Some wives or mothers, though naturally alarmed by the tidings from the military authorities, were quietly confident that the person they had known, even if he was currently absent, was not entirely lost, and might be brought back to them by the restorative powers of the home environment. Private Henry Ashdown was no stranger to military service, having first enlisted in the Army in 1895 when he was under age, until his mother had entreated the authorities to release him. Latterly he had worked as a school caretaker before re-enlisting in answer to Lord Kitchener's appeal, serving in France since November 1914, where he had been occupied mainly in the transport section with pack mules. He had been 'knocked off his feet a few times with shell bursts', but had never received 'wounds or gas enough to go off duty', though he was in a mine explosion at Givenchy in 1915, and a bad shell attack at Combles at Christmas 1916. By January 1918, however, he was exhausted and was evacuated home with various physical and mental complaints. When he reached Napsbury in August, he could hear voices calling on stretcher bearers to 'form fours' and he was convinced that he had done something very wicked and was to be sent back to France to be executed, and would never see his wife again. Though Mrs Ashdown must have been shocked by the condition in which she found him, she was far from disheartened, giving a robust answer to the inquiry from the War Hospital about her knowledge of his health: 'I have known him since he was a telegraph boy and have always known him to be perfect as regards his mental health and in every way and I can safely say that it is only the long service and strain of the present war, and I feel sure that as soon as he got home and a little stronger he would be quite alright'.[2]

From the Lord Derby War Hospital, along with the routine inquiry about the history of nervous trouble in the family ('including uncles and aunts'), the named relative was also asked: 'should he not be fit to return to duty and have to be invalided from the Army at some future date would you be willing to receive him at your address?' There was a delicate ambiguity in posing the question like this, for under the guise of a simple inquiry about whether the wife or parents would be willing to receive their loved one back in the home (and, under the circumstances, who would hold the door fast?), there was the more insidious question of their readiness to assume the responsibility for the care of a potentially rather disabled and disturbed family member. Needless to say this was a rather risky strategy, and the Lord Derby seems to have been unusual in attaching this principled question to their routine inquiry form. Some might have been lulled by the persuasive rhetoric of homecoming into quashing any doubts that might have arisen about taking on hard cases, but for others the question allowed them latitude to reflect that their loved ones were perhaps not so loved after all, or only rather conditionally loved, and hence to reconsider their positions. In her reply to the authorities, Mrs Bartram, the wife of a clerk serving in the Labour Corps, starts by furbishing a myth of pre-war psychological innocence:

> In reference to my husband, there is no 'nervous' or 'mental' trouble in any way connected with his family and he has never been like it before and never had fits or touched spirits and very seldom beer and was very moderate and clean in his morals. He had no worries or troubles in any way, and always wrote to me most cheerful and I always used to write to him cheerful. The only thing that grieved him was because we were parted, we were always devoted to each other and I cannot understand it at all, why he is like he is at present.

Most cheerful she may have been, but she is rather less cheerful at the prospect of her husband returning home in a diminished state:

> I could not have him home unless he was well and could go to work as I am not strong enough myself to work and keep him. He was earning good money before joining the Army. I have every hope that he will recover. He was a perfect husband and everybody who knew him speaks well of him. If there is anything else you wish to know I shall be most pleased to answer. . . .

There is, then, a dark underside to this tale of unalloyed innocence: if Mr Bartram cannot be returned to the domestic economy in the unsullied condition in which he is fondly remembered, then Mrs Bartram is not at all sure that she wants him back. She may in any case have suspected that her husband had not always been quite so 'moderate and clean in his morals' as he maintained, for it turned out that he had contracted syphilis ten years previously, before his marriage most likely, and was now a suspected GPI case, having become very exalted and grandiose, eccentric in his actions, and unclean in his personal habits. In this instance, the War Hospital authorities took the hint and packed him off to Claybury Asylum.[3]

FITFUL REUNIONS
Like the evocatively-named Sapper Othello Crabtree, a cotton-mill hand from Todmorden in Lancashire, who was brought home 'wounded gas' in August

1917, admitted to the Welsh Metropolitan War Hospital in Cardiff and then transferred a little over a year later, now bearing a diagnosis of melancholia, to Storthes Hall, the West Riding Lunatic Asylum near Huddersfield, to take up residence as a Service Patient, quite a number of servicemen were dispatched directly to asylums from the war mental hospitals.[4] Overall, however, the war hospital authorities were most reluctant to become involved in the business of institutionalizing discharged soldiers, wherever possible leaving it up to the relatives to petition the relevant civil authorities.

From the military angle there were obvious advantages in returning as many servicemen as possible to their homes, not least because in the early part of the war the authorities had been so much berated for dispatching them to asylums. Certainly there were some relatives who importuned the authorities to discharge their sons and husbands from the war mental hospitals, or on occasions even took matters into their own hands. William Heath, a twenty-eight year old former clerk, had experienced a nervous breakdown in Salonika and had been passed through a chain of war hospitals from Malta to Dykebar in Scotland before reaching Springfield War Hospital in February 1919. The ardent desire of his younger sisters to restore him to the bosom of his family induced them to smuggle him out in July and take him to the family home at Sittingbourne. From here he was shortly reunited with his wife, who inevitably became the rather uncertain beneficiary – William was morose and depressed, imagining that everybody looked down on him and took him for a coward, frequently giving way to ungovernable temper – of this sisterly bravado.[5]

All the same, there are strong indications that at different stages of the war when there was pressure to release beds, either to make way for fresh cases from the front, or – as in the early months of 1919 – in response to growing clamour from the civil authorities for the closure of the war hospitals. To this end, the natural desire of relatives for the return of their menfolk was played on to advantage, with some soldiers discharged in a dicey mental condition to say the least. Many women – for inevitably it was mostly they who bore the brunt of the responsibility – cannot have known what they were letting themselves in for when they found themselves witnessing the unnerving spectacle of their distressed kinsman brought to the family home under military escort and left there, signalling the abrupt termination not only of his military career but also of whatever care arrangements might so far have been in place. George Munson's younger daughter Eileen was conceived around Christmas 1916, the last time he was home on leave before embarking for Mesopotamia. The first time that Eileen set eyes on her father was in the spring of 1919 when George, a former clerk, was brought to the family home off Tooting Broadway in south London under escort from Notts War Hospital

This series of images of homecoming, with titles such as 'A Knock that Mother Will Know', 'The Meeting' and 'Telling the Story', was produced for propaganda purposes, largely to reassure relatives. The homecomings of mentally distressed servicemen invariably punctured this sentimental idyll, for these reunions were far from harmonious, the stories frequently painful and confused, or simply impossible to tell.

(where he had apparently spent most of his stay in the padded room), the culmination of a circuitous route from Mesopotamia. George spent just a couple of weeks at home before his wife Beatrice was forced to petition for his removal, telling of how he had repeatedly been making wild threats to thrash her, to murder the doctor at the war hospital and to drown himself.[6]

Nathan Levy's homecoming was even more curtailed. A former gentleman's tailor, Nathan was discharged from Murthly War Hospital, Perth, and brought to his sister's home in Rotherhithe by two orderlies on Sunday 5 January 1919. Only four days later he was admitted into the Parish Street Institution, and from there removed to Colney Hatch Asylum, on the entreaty of his brother-in-law, also a serving soldier. Since Nathan had arrived home, he reported, he had behaved very strangely, continually murmuring to himself and looking in the glass, treating everyone with suspicion and walking about the house all night long: 'He is beyond our control and I would like him placed under proper care as I am due back tonight at Cornwall and I don't think it is safe for my wife and children to be left alone in the house with him'.[7]

Formerly a clerk in the traffic department of the London County Council, George Henry Lawrence had served with the colours for four years 71 days, including 15 months with the Territorials before the war and 18 months in France as a gunner with the Royal Field Artillery. Discharged on 6 August 1917 as medically unfit for further war service with a disability pension of 28/– weekly for six months, he returned home to his pensioner parents and younger sister Ellen in Streatham, South London. We do not know what happened exactly, but it may reasonably be inferred that George was already in a highly disturbed state when he reached his front door. One might wonder at the cavalier decision to eject from the military treatment environment a vulnerable and distressed young man who was so obviously quite unprepared to make his next move. Not least in reuniting with his family who must have been equally unprepared, and quite out of their depth, in finding themselves face to face and alone with a George Lawrence who was so abruptly and incomprehensibly removed from the son and brother they had formerly known.

On 11 September 1917, doubtless as the culmination of a dismal process that had been unwinding for the past four weeks, in which among other things George had burnt his pension papers and his identification card, George's father summoned the police to the house. PC Sullivan found George 'sitting in a chair and when spoken to he refused to reply and seemed lost and strange in his manner', but afterwards 'he got up and began throwing his arms about'. Not altogether surprisingly, he 'became excited and resistive' when he realised what was afoot, and was hustled off in a police car, the neighbouring curtains in Fernthorpe Road all twitching in unison, to the Wandsworth Union Infirmary on St John's Hill to be interviewed by Dr Frank Nixey: 'He is depressed and silent, for the most part refuses to utter a word or take any food. He frequently sits in an attitude as if listening intently and believes that someone is after him to do him harm. No conversation can be held with him and he requires constant supervision'.

George was so obviously a case for certification that a period of further observation in the Infirmary was considered superfluous, and a Reception Order was signed the same day by a Justice of the Peace: 'I, William Rines, having called to my assistance E. W. Nixey of Wandsworth Union Infirmary, St John's Hill, in the County of London, a duly qualified Medical Practitioner, and being satisfied that George Henry Lawrence, a soldier, formerly clerk, of Wandsworth Union Infirmary is in such circumstances as to require relief for his proper care and maintenance and that the said George Henry Lawrence is a person of unsound mind and is a proper person to be taken charge of and detained, hereby direct you to receive the said George Henry Lawrence as a patient into your asylum'. So there it was, former Gunner Lawrence was now a certified lunatic, and that day he was admitted to Long Grove Asylum in Epsom, bodily condition on admission clean and good, apart from blisters on both feet.[8]

Two days after George Lawrence was received into Long Grove, Rifleman Albert Styles, a year older than him, height 5ft 4 inches, fair complexion, light brown hair, blue eyes, scar on his left buttock, gunshot wound to his face, left arm amputated below the elbow, made his way to his parents' home in Tooting Bec, only a mile or so away from where George had recently so hurriedly departed. A former golf professional and valet, Albert had served with the 13th Battalion of the Rifle Brigade in France for almost two years and been discharged from Queen Mary's Hospital, Roehampton (military character 'fair', character awarded in accordance with King's Regulations 'honest and willing'), where he had been fitted up with a stump and with a disability pension of 27/6d. for nine weeks, after that reducing to 13/9d. He had enlisted in the Rifle Brigade in September 1914 from the Cooden Beach Golf Club in Bexhill, Sussex, where he had been in the employ of Lord Delaware for two years, mostly sleeping on the premises at the club. Before that he had been a valet at the Constitutional Club in St James's, Piccadilly, for three years, and previous to that in a situation at Portland Place as under-valet for about six months, travelling to Scotland with his master, Sir Somebody Somebody.

This, at any rate, was the story of titled and unspotted ('no blood relation on either side have been to asylum') connections that his dejected father related to William Haggis ten days later, for the Albert Styles who had returned home was anything but the accommodating servant, refusing to see anybody, sitting for hours 'in a vacant sort of manner', imagining that everyone around was a German, barricading himself in his bedroom, and not taking his food. After ten days' observation in the Wandsworth Infirmary, Albert also found himself bundled along the trail to Long Grove where, tragically, he was not destined to survive much beyond the Armistice, falling a victim to the implacable scourge of asylum dysentery, and dying in January 1919.[9]

It was quite a typical pattern this, peremptory discharge from the Army or some military treatment facility, followed by an unsettled and unsettling interlude at home, or with relatives, of varying durations, extremely curtailed in some cases, quite prolonged in others, but in each instance sharing a lack of restitution that would in all probability at some point spill over into crisis. Regardless of the abundance of kindness and sympathy that might very well have been shown, it was very difficult if not impossible to achieve a satisfactory form of emotional settlement. Indeed, what was most unsettling was precisely the tension, or gap, between the settled terms of existence that were now on offer in the domestic environment and the expansive emotional horizons of feeling and memory to which the former soldier found himself exposed. The tension was exacerbated inevitably by the constraints of a buttoned-up and psychologically relatively unsophisticated culture, typically culminating in an outburst or display that proved to be the last straw for family and friends. If he was lucky, the ex-serviceman might be routed back into the military mental health treatment system, or some hopeful alternative, but most often he had to take his chances in the regular asylum system.

These homecomings were mostly fitful reunions precipitated by the stress of war service, but on occasions we also catch glimpses of military careers that had never properly left home or got under way at all, in which the episode of war service was rather obviously a brief diversion from, or an alternative outlet for, a life that was already in serious emotional trouble. By coincidence, George Wayland Bellringer, a forty-one year old draughtsman, was experiencing a personal crisis, precipitated allegedly by marital circumstances, on the outbreak of the war, and as an inmate of Croydon Mental Hospital from September 1914 to 14 October 1915 his patriotic leanings were inevitably stymied. But within a fortnight of his discharge he endeavoured to make up for lost time by enlisting in the 28th Middlesex Regiment, not, it must be admitted, with great success, for as early as February 1916 he was a patient in Tooting Military Hospital, apparently not having travelled very far in the interim. A month later, having separated from his wife, he was discharged home to his ageing mother, and soon became aggressive towards her, culminating in his removal to Cane Hill Asylum, at which point his brief blossoming as a soldier looked to be no more than an interlude in an unfolding career as a mental patient.[10]

FAMILY HARDSHIP
Of course, it quite often happened that the soldier who was removed to an asylum had been the family breadwinner. Now a Service Patient, before the war Tom Challiner had supported his brother and four sisters, the whole family having been orphaned. Numerous examples of such hardship were brought to the attention of the Ministry of Pensions by Local War Pension Committees, but the Ministry dragged its feet because concessions to the

dependants of service lunatics were perceived as the thin end of a thick welfare wedge. 'Assistance in the case of the man in an asylum', opined a fastidious official, 'is likely to be the prelude to assistance in many other directions'.[11] In mid-June 1919, John G was removed to Colney Hatch Asylum 'suffering from unsoundness of mind due to war strain', his illness caused by 'a great shock he received in France at Cambrai when an ammunition dump close to his wagon line was blown up and for two or three days after he said he was not right in his mind'. John's departure was a severe blow to the family, for his mother was a widow and in poor health. Before the war he had been the main support to the family, earning between 40 and 50 shillings a week as a silver smelter, supplemented by his younger sister's wage of 10 to 15 shillings as a blouse hand. They were both 'piece workers', hence their earnings were subject to fluctuations and no doubt the actual household income was often rather less than this. But in John's absence it was very difficult for his sister to maintain the home. The rent had been increased from 8/6 d. to 12/-a week, and though in a good week she was able to earn up to 20/-, frequently there were days when she was laid off and was obliged to turn for help to her married sister.[12]

A few families had already been afflicted by the death of the mother even before the father became a mental casualty of the war. William Flynn may have had the misfortune to be made an asylum inmate, but nevertheless he was reckoned to be in rude health. Revealingly, however, he was described by the clerk to the Bethnal Green Guardians as deceased and his children as orphans:

Six orphan children FLYNN, adopted by the Guardians, and now maintained at the Swinton Schools, Manchester, children of the late William George Flynn, no. 18466 Essex Regiment, 34/- per week being received from the Pension Authorities, the children being sent to Manchester under an arrangement made by my Board. . . . The children are Ellen (aged 12), Elizabeth (aged 7), Dorothy (aged 4.5), Emma (aged 8), Kathleen (aged 11) and William (aged 10).

With increasing attention from the press, the Ministry of Pensions was compelled to adopt a more proactive stance in such cases, and a few months later it was reported that the Minister was 'very desirous of getting away from the care of the Bethnal Green Guardians the six children of William George Flynn'. The clerk had not entirely erred in describing William as dead, for the Ministry had been given the legal opinion that the motherless children of ex-servicemen who had become insane due to war service should be treated

John G, formerly a driver with the Royal Field Artillery, shortly after he was admitted to Colney Hatch Lunatic Asylum in June 1919. He had endured a gruelling war. Enlisting in September 1914, he had gone out to France in April 1915, was in the thick of the action at Cambrai in 1917, wounded in the head in March 1918, and finally discharged in January 1919. Before the war he had been the mainstay of the household, and his absence was a grievous loss to his family.

in just the same way as those of a serviceman who died as a result of the war. However, it eventually occurred to an astute official that, notwithstanding the dismal therapeutic record of the asylum system, the dead might conceivably awaken and reproach the Ministry for the provision that had been meted out to their children during their demise.[13]

'NEVER A LUNATIC UNTIL HE JOINED THE ARMY'

Women were in any case more inclined than men to take the connection between war and mental illness for granted, and in the answers they gave to the authorities it was obviously not in their strategic interests to leave any chink uncovered for an official doubting Thomas. For the most part, relatives were quite unabashed about the circumstances that had left their kin insane. Typically, there were variations on what Clara Shambrook said about her husband John: 'His present condition of health is I am certain brought on by his army service'. Fred, one wife confided, 'was never a lunatic until he joined the Army'. 'Probably shell shock', remarked another, 'my husband has been serving in France for eighteen months with the Howitzers and I should think that is the cause of his terrible condition – giving his life for his country'.

Relatives did not, however, invariably identify with heroic images like these, ironic though many of them were, nor did they all hanker after a war disability pension for their distressed kinfolk.[14] It is plain from the records that there was an unquantifiable, but conspicuous, minority who patently did not. Particularly in the early part of the war, when heroic expectations of a more traditional kind were still riding high, and before the jousting over war disability pensions had got underway, some families could not disguise their disappointment over the failings of their wimpish kin. Hopes were not infrequently dashed that war service might have transformed a wayward and burdensome son and brother into a manly patriot, or that God in his mercy might have provided a honourable pretext on which to dispatch him into the afterlife. John Butler's patriotic excursion to 'the East' (he knew that he was in Salonika, but the country was simply 'the East') was a welcome relief from what had in all likelihood been a long-standing domestic problem, and the news that he had been made to do an abrupt about turn ('an imbecile . . . unfit for any service in this command') and return west came as a bitter disappointment. His sister asked the authorities not to discharge him 'unless he is quite fit mentally and able to look after himself and earn his own living, as there is only my father (65 yrs) and myself (26 yrs) at home and we are not able to look after him'. Needless to say, the military authorities were quite unwilling to become the custodian of a family problem and John was sent back home a few weeks later.[15]

Another beneficiary of a bracing familial outlook was Private Billy Kirkham, who joined the Army in June 1915 and, though already a bag of nerves when he came home on leave in September, shortly afterwards was sent out to join the Mediterranean Expeditionary Force in Gallipoli, getting as far as Lemnos before contracting dysentery soon after disembarking. Repatriated in February 1916, he became very depressed, saying that he had suffered all his life and had had enough of it, leaving a note of story-book pathos before attempting to strangle himself: 'Dear wife and sisters, Please bury me with mother and father. Fondest love to you all, and God bless you, from your broken hearted husband and brother, Billy'. His sister was quite unsparing in her opinion that war service was just the sort of adventure holiday that might have brought Billy to his senses and made the kind of man of him which his marriage had, apparently, failed to do:

My father was strange a little before he died and my older sister is funny at times and is attended by Dr Billings and my brother Pte W. H. Kirkham as been under the Dr twice with Nervous Debility 3 years since, he was living with me then and was 4 months bad and the Dr told me to keep the upper hand of him or he was afraid he would have to go to an Asylum. He advised him to get married he thought it might set him up but he seems to get worse. He was on furlough in Sept and was bad then with his nerves. When well is of a cheerfull nature. Dr Billings Church Street Blackpool as been his Dr all his life, so if you care to write to him shall be pleased. He as been a great responsibility to me for years ever since mother died, he lived with me 10 years before he was married and I was proud when they passed him for a soldier thinking the change would do him good.[16]

There was no need for the authorities to ponder how to reject an application for a war disability pension from Billy Kirkham, since his sister had done their work for them. However, it was generally fathers of the old school who were most resolute in checking their sympathies for their distraught sons. Since being demobilized, Reginald Sandy, son of a solicitor's clerk from Balham, had been studying hard in a draughtsman's office. Just before Christmas 1922 he had become melancholic and reserved, according to his father neglecting the young lady with whom he had been dancing regularly, and was taken into the Wandsworth Infirmary in a state of considerable anguish. Making laboured efforts to think in answer to questions, he merely jerked out phrases such as 'where's a nurse?' and 'there's no harm in love!'.

Though the relieving officer had scribbled '?case for SP class' in the margin, tellingly Samuel Sandy, very much a superior sort of clerk it would appear, made no mention of war service as having any bearing on his son's case. He merely stated that if he could afford to make his son a private class case he would shoulder the burden himself (there was some doubt, he admitted, as to whether he could do so immediately because of an imminent property purchase). Most likely, he perceived his son's existential pinings and uncertainties as an exhibition of weakness, a failure to live up to the expected standards of manliness, epitomized in his inability to maintain the badinage with his young lady, and could not bring himself to enter a claim for his son as suffering from a legitimate war-related disability.[17]

Ironically, it seems that George Major Gomm may also have been of this company. When we last heard of George he had been discharged 'relieved' from Long Grove Asylum by his father in September 1916 and returned to his family home in Hammersmith. There is no record of what transpired in the interim, but on 8 December 1919 George Gomm was admitted to the Fulham Infirmary in St Dunstan's Road from his home in Agate Road, Hamersmith, and removed to Long Grove Asylum a week later.[18] At this point he was a beneficiary of a shift in the moral topography of mental health care that had already taken place since the war, for when the Fulham Infirmary was reconstituted in May 1919 after the closure of Fulham Military Hospital, the Guardians resolved that in future the 'mental ward' of the Workhouse would now form part of the Infirmary, and just a few weeks before George was admitted had engaged Oscar Eagles, Thomas Hudson and Fred Hedges as Attendants on Male Lunatics.[19]

Revealingly, however, when he was admitted to Long Grove for the commencement of what was to prove to be a lengthy sojourn, George was never classified as a Service Patient nor made an accredited war disability pensioner. In the asylum register there is no reference to his military service, his condition simply attributed to 'insane heredity'.[20] There is no reason in principle why he should have been excluded from the war pensions slate, since he had had only one admission to an asylum before the war. The most likely explanation is that he did not find an advocate in his father. George Gomm senior, we may surmise, shared the prejudices and values of his time, and most probably encouraged the frail and nervous George to join the Territorials, and later volunteer for war service, even though he had already exhibited quite serious mental health problems, no doubt because George senior believed that the military life might prove to be the making of his son.

He can scarcely be blamed for this, for after all there was psychiatric wisdom on hand which concurred with this outlook, maintaining that war service 'with its strenuous open-air life, regular hours, abundance of food, constant healthy mental activity, limited access to alcohol, and ample time for sleep during training', far from pushing types like George over the edge, might actually prove a prophylactic and provide 'ideal conditions for combating their mental instability' and render 'many of them capable of even withstanding "shell shock"'.[21] It is probable that George senior was ashamed of his son, believing him to be unmanly, a disappointment to the honour of his family and his country, and had at an early stage already set his face against seeking official recognition for him as a psychiatric casualty of war. Far from being disconcerted by the indifference of the authorities, or by the psychiatric slur on his son's heredity, he could not fail to agree with them, for after all the boy took after his poor mother who had herself had a nervous breakdown, very likely in the wake of the death of George's twin brother Richard.

In this regard, George Gomm epitomizes the vulnerability of so many of the psychiatric casualties of the Great War whose histories we are examining. Though significant concessions had been extracted from the authorities, in any one instance so much would depend – not merely in getting a positive result from the pensions system, but even in the identification of the disability – on the calibre and tenacity of the ex-serviceman's friends and advocates. In principle, George's class position might have given him the edge over someone more disadvantaged, but without a genuine ally he had no hand left to play.

Chapter 10

OFFICIALDOM AND THE PENSIONER

THE WELCOME FROM THE ASYLUMS
In the summer of 1916 the Board of Control had canvassed support for the Service Patient scheme from all 97 County and Borough Asylums in England and Wales. The majority were broadly supportive, though there were some who adopted a very negative view of the soldier mental patients themselves, considering them unworthy of the privileges and considerations that it was intended to bestow upon them. Many of these latter institutions, however, recognized that the political currents were against them and, having aired their grievances, lent the scheme their begrudging support. Heavily dominated by magistrates, justices of the peace and other local dignitaries, asylum committees were mostly eager to position themselves in the main currents of popular feeling, anxious not to be portrayed locally as backwoodsmen, even if this entailed some implicit acknowledgement of the deficiencies in their own institutions.

There was, however, a vociferous minority which delivered a severe rebuff to the proposals, declaring that public asylums were unsuitable places in which to 'maintain soldiers and sailors discharged on account of mental disorder brought on by service in the war'. Public opinion, protested the Birmingham Asylums Committee, would 'severely criticize and condemn the course proposed' and the measures entertained would 'in no way improve the patient's position'. 'Large houses capable of accommodating not more than thirty patients should be taken in various parts of the country', they urged, the words 'asylum' and 'mental hospital' not to be associated with them, and the whole scheme to be managed by the pensions authorities, with no involvement from asylum committees or poor law guardians. A number of other counties, such as Cornwall, followed suit, also believing that 'large houses should be established in various parts of the country', and there were other variants on these segregative recommendations, some highlighting a therapeutic benefit alongside the moral and political justification, maintaining that 'a greater percentage of recoveries would be secured' on this basis.[1] Some months later, when the Board of Control was still dragging its heels, the Lancashire Asylums Board went on record as representing 'the whole of Lancashire' in striking 'the strongest protest against a soldier or sailor who has lost his reason through wounds or stress of service in either Force being subjected to the indignity of being sent to an Asylum through the Poor Law procedure and his name entered in a pauper list'.[2]

What was at stake in the advocacy of a entirely separate care system for the soldier mental patients? In an obvious respect they can be seen as divisive, recreating traditional distinctions between the 'deserving' and the 'undeserving', and these resonances are certainly not absent. Indeed, they were lighted upon by some asylum authorities in complaining about 'the invidious selection of any particular class of persons for preferential treatment', believing that it would only 'further emphasize the stigma attached to the inmates of County Asylums'. Consider, they asked, the 'case of a widow who loses her three sons in the war and becomes insane from the subsequent shock, why should this woman be classed as a pauper lunatic any more than a proposed service patient?'. The same considerations applied also to munition workers and 'others deserving well of their country when overwork in its service has occasioned a breakdown'.[3]

There is, however, another slant to these segregative demands, especially to the advocacy of a nation-wide network of 'large houses'. Here the insane citizen soldier became the stalking-horse for a modernizing current urging the root-and-branch reform of the mental health system so as to provide standards of care to which the citizenry as a whole might aspire. In the immediate aftermath of the war, Alderman J. Taggart, speaking as 'the father of the Lancashire Asylums Board', extolled the achievement of the Lord Derby War Hospital in the erstwhile Winwick Asylum as pointing the way for the future. 'You have passed through your hands some hundreds of soldiers who were suffering from mental trouble, and you have now a thousand men occupying beds in the west wards who are suffering from mental trouble, but not one of these, I am proud to say, has either been branded as insane, or been touched in any way by the Poor Law'.[4]

Hardly surprisingly, the Board of Control was incensed by all these calls for a separate system, deeming them wildly impractical and founded upon a complete misapprehension of the extent and urgency of the problems with which the authorities had to deal. The majority of asylum committees gave the proposals their fair consideration, but it would be a mistake to exaggerate their enthusiasm for these special arrangements for service mental patients. They had only a limited claim on their attention, not least because there were so many other pressing issues of corporate deprivation and individual decrepitude to deal with among their own more immediate circle. How to provide food for hungry mouths, and what action to take in respect of

GREETINGS FROM

DINING HALL

MAIN KITCHEN

MAIN ENTRANCE

NAPSBURY

F.2. WARD.

EAST GATE.

1. The novelty of this card is that it is so obviously a product of a topsy-turvy society at war. Once the carnival of the war hospital had ended, and the institution had reverted to its regular role as a lunatic asylum, there were no more 'Greetings from Napsbury'.

Ward F 4. The County of Middlesex War Hospital. Napsbury.

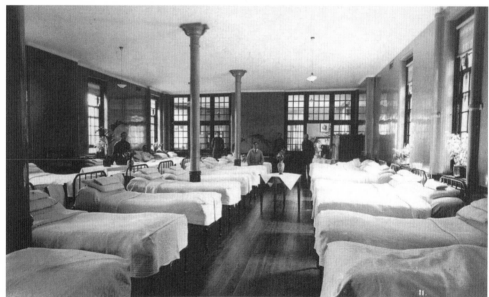

Ward M 5. The County of Middlesex War Hospital. Napsbury.

2 and 3. A war hospital this may have been, but the numbering of the wards is still that of the regular lunatic asylum (F for female wards, and M for male). Even on a general ward for wound cases (F4), the patients and nurses are made to hover in the background. M5 is very likely one of the mental wards – the beds are more closely spaced since it was by and large only used at night – and here the patients have been excluded from the frame altogether, with the exception of one patient in bed in the far corner, and possibly the short man standing back centre wearing overalls. The uniformed figures at the back are asylum attendants rigged out as honorary members of the RAMC for the duration of the war.

4. The svelte figure of Sir Maurice Craig. Indubitably a member of the
establishment, but a doughty champion of the psychologically damaged
common soldier nonetheless.

5. Pte Ivor Bertie Gurney in 1915. A soldier in uniform but still 'a dirty civilian'. As if to subordinate his military identity to his civilian or artistic self, Gurney wrote 'Bartholomew' on the mount of the photograph, the nickname by which he was known at the Royal College of Music, a play on Bertie, pronounced 'Bartie'.

6. A convalescent ex-serviceman on crutches posing with nurses. Scenes like this were commonplace during the Great War, since rank-and-file soldiers as much as officers were eager to be portrayed as individuals, cheerfully greeting their destinies. However, photographs of leavetakings from war mental hospitals are notable for their absence. Not least, there were rarely any female props in these places to add some glamour to the photo-opportunity.

7. A few war psychosis pensioners may well have been among this company. But they would have been carefully selected from those who could be relied upon to obey the injunction to 'sit down on the parliamentary side of your arse for Christ' sake'.

WOUNDED SOLDIERS FROM MINISTRY OF PENSIONS HOSPITALS ENTERTAINED TO TEA ON THE TERRACE OF THE HOUSE OF COMMONS JULY. 25 TH. 1933.

FIG. 31.

FIG. 32.

FIG. 33.

8. Three stages in the recovery from shell shock. The erect bearing of the serviceman at stage three was trumpeted by Dr F.W. Mott in his study *War Neuroses and Shell-Shock* (1919) as a 'most extraordinary recovery'. We may consider, however, that the patient seems rather less discomfited when he started out.

INSTRUCTION IN RUG MAKING
AT THE SIR FREDERICK MILNER HOME.

THE POULTRY FARM AT THE SIR FREDERICK MILNER
HOME.

9 and 10. Occupational activities at the Sir Frederick Milner Home for 'nerve-stricken' ex-servicemen. Here is the New Womanly Man in action, busied in decidedly unmanly activities such as rug making, basketwork and poultry farming. All this is quite authentic, but the aura of feminized respectability, conferred by wearing a suit and tie under every conceivable circumstance, is surely contrived – a foil to deflect potential donors to this charitable cause, the Ex-Services Welfare Society, from dwelling on unseemly emotion among the recovering 'nerve-stricken'. At least the apprentice poultry farmers can manage a smile and look at the camera!

11. C.R.W. Nevinson, *A Group of Soldiers*. Nevinson worked for a short period as an orderly on a mental ward in a military hospital and produced an image of a shell-shocked soldier with drooling lip that tended towards cliché, caricature even. The paradox is that in *A Group of Soldiers* Nevinson is much more successful in conveying an image of physical fatigue and emotional suffering exactly because he is *not* trying to make a point of portraying a mental case.

asylum staff invalided out of the army who were now fit only for limited service, these were the dominant preoccupations in the last part of 1916. Could working patients be induced to work harder during the week if they were given luncheon on Sundays as well as on weekdays? This was the kind of question asylum committees liked to ponder in ensuring the smooth functioning of the asylum economy. The war had already been quite disruptive enough, and to that extent the Service Patient scheme, with its quirky privileges and concessions, was an intrusion.

And what of the medical superintendents within this groundswell? Though it is true that alienists were more likely to be counted among the sceptics and critics – and there were certainly some who reacted to displays of sympathy for their soldier mental patients as though they were risible misconstructions of morally depraved individuals whose tribulations bore no conceivable connection with the trials of war service – by no means was this was the inevitable reaction. In any case, in the early stages of the war especially, it did require a rather capacious psychiatric imagination to accommodate the typical service mental patient under the banner of the gallant soldier. Some asylum officials remonstrated against the spirit of a moral reassessment in which the unprepossessing character with whom they had long been acquainted had now been transformed into a patriotic veteran, returning lists of ex-servicemen in their asylums with appended comments such as: 'Arthur Page: undoubtedly a malingerer; Claude Wheeler: was a patient here prior to the War and should never have been enlisted; Basil Lewis Blunn: patient had been in this asylum for many years prior to the war; Horace Vivian Tremlett: this man is apparently suffering from General Paralysis; Mathew Mousley: patient's attack may possibly be due to strain of Army Training'. The aptly named Dr Hamilton Grills, medical superintendent of Chester Asylum, could identify only one case in all of the previous year's admissions where he was confident that military service was the cause of the breakdown. The medical superintendents of the London County Council asylums asserted that many of the soldiers and sailors who had been sent to asylums were 'alcoholics, criminals, epileptics and general paralytics' who had been 'found to be useless for the defence of the country'.[5] Dr Knowles Stansfield from Bexley, one of the LCC asylums, was vehemently opposed to the scheme, claiming that of the 61 soldier patients who had been admitted to Bexley, only five had served abroad, 12 were suffering from General Paralysis of the Insane and of the remainder 20 had had one or more previous attacks of insanity. So far as the patients at Bexley were concerned, 'the proposals of the Board of Control are uncalled-for' and it would be 'extravagant and unjust, and from every point of view ill-advised, to make such a distinction between soldier patients and hundreds of patients who are far more genuinely the victims of the battle of everyday life'.[6]

Many asylum superintendents undeniably felt that their reputations had taken a pummelling over the war years, and that they had been put in the shade by upstarts from the Royal Army Medical Corps trumpeting their therapeutic successes. The introduction of the Service Patient scheme gave them an opportunity to reassert themselves, either by carping at this new current or by mobilizing it to their advantage. Jason Gemmel, who presided over Whittingham Asylum in Lancashire, with over 2800 inmates the largest in the land, and who was already much disliked by the Board of Control for his obstreperous plain speaking, derided the Service Patient scheme as a sham, patriotic leanings fusing with a healthy northern contempt for metropolitan hypocrisy. Maintain all the insane servicemen in military hospitals until some months after the war had ended, he demanded, and thus save them 'from the taint, or at least documentary evidence, of insanity which but for the extraordinary vicissitudes through which they had passed, would probably never have occurred'. Additionally: 'There is another point concerning which there should be no dubiety. That is that all insane soldiers and sailors should be accepted as Service Patients irrespective of former attacks of insanity, a history of heredity or mental deficiency, or any form of insanity due to syphilis contracted years before the War. The Country has made use of them in its defence and ought not to discriminate in order to avoid its responsibilities. . . . If all are not included in the scheme of Service Patients there is bound to be further agitation'.[7]

Dr W. F. Menzies, medical superintendent of the Third Staffordshire County Asylum at Cheddleton, maintained that only those with previous 'alienistic experience' were able to 'weigh the value of the various causes of insanity and are alone able to tell which patients should, and which should not be, with advantage to themselves, classified as Service Patients'. Sympathy and respect for the patriotism of some of his patients combined with familiar moral condemnation of others to produce a view of Service Patient status as a selective therapeutic instrument, to be applied with advantage to the deserving in helping them 'towards recovery and towards becoming a useful member of society'. Six soldier lunatics in his asylum had so far been classified as Service Patients, of whom four were 'so deluded and even dangerously homicidal that they are utterly unfit to derive any benefit from the classification'. Against this another patient, Harry Shaw, who would have been 'speedily cured by classification', had in the meantime been discharged 'after a tedious recovery'. And a second case, Thomas Woolley, was not eligible because he had never served abroad, though he was 'the most perfect instance of functional hemiplegia and aphasia which one ever gets after real shellshock', in his case a 'mimetic affection from seeing shellshocked cases in Hospital'. The moral superiority of overseas over home service did not, he insisted, bear critical examination:

> For example, John Frost, a ne'er-do-well, moral defective, with ... many convictions for minor crimes, has never lived so well in his life, although he is utterly undeserving and would never have been included in the Army except under a system of compulsory service. On the other hand men like Jack Heraty, Thomas Woolley, William Allen and Henshall Gater voluntarily enlisted from patriotic motives, although on account of age or other like reasons for which they were not responsible, they did not serve abroad. And yet the way in which these two classes of men faced the national crisis was utterly different.

As it happened, by the time that Menzies was taking up the cudgels for Jack Heraty and his like, the tide was already turning in their favour, and towards the end of 1917 No. 64535 Gunner Henshall Gater, late Royal Garrison Artillery, married with six children, was granted a pension for mental breakdown aggravated by military service in the war in place of the gratuity of £80 he had previously been given.[8]

STARVATION RATIONS BUT BURIAL WITH HONOURS

In late November 1918, a notice was distributed to the medical superintendents of all the London asylums, among them Hanwell, informing them that the Headquarters of Eastern Command was prepared to arrange for the services of firing parties and bearers, with a gun carriage, to attend the funerals of Service Patients. There would be no charge, and a request by telephone – Gerrard 63, extension 35 – was all that was required.[9] Yet this gentlemanly, bespoke arrangement contrasted sharply with the living conditions in many asylums, which appeared rather nicely calculated to ensure that there would be frequent calls upon the services of military firing parties and bearers.

At the behest of some friends of inmates, Lt Col. Frederick Mott made arrangements to inspect the Service Patients at Hanwell Asylum in February 1919 and found there 71 soldier patients, some of them still in uniform, 40 of whom had served overseas. 'Each man was asked whether he was satisfied with the treatment. All said they had no cause to complain of the treatment but several complained of an insufficiency of food and one man persistently reiterated that they were starved'.

Mott discovered that the soldier patients received the same diet as the other patients. 'The only privilege I could find that these soldiers had was that some wore their uniform. Otherwise they mingled with, and were treated as, civilian patients with no privileges'. He found the food unappetizing, 'especially the 2 oz of oatmeal as porridge with $^1/_2$ oz of treacle four days a week for tea', and insufficient. Roughly 2200 calories, well short of the minimum calorific value of 3145 prescribed by the Army Council for patients in military hospitals, and of the daily allowance of 3380 calories received by patients at the Maudsley Neurological Clearing Hospital where Mott was himself based. Moreover, the Army Council had also recommended that neurasthenic patients should have an extra meat allowance and 'as these soldier patients at Hanwell were suffering from a nervous affection', Mott believed that 'they too required consideration as regards increase of meat ration'.

However, that was not how the medical authorities at Hanwell (or indeed the other London asylums) saw the matter. They insisted that the Hanwell dietary allowance was entirely adequate 'for *chronic* cases, such as most of the Service Patients are', at the same time acknowledging that other considerations might have to be weighed 'if the Service Patients are to be regarded from the philanthropic point of view as men who have rendered service to their country'.[10] The much-lauded preferential treatment of the Service Patient was exposed as a sham, but the revelation had the merit of highlighting the moral economy of these degrading regimes. Not least the status of chronic mental patients as worthless individuals who had apparently never rendered any kind of service to their community, and the disturbing facility with which these ex-servicemen, not long returned from the battlefronts, some of them still in uniform, were assimilated into their ranks.

THE PENSIONS AND THE TREASURY

Right from its inception, the Ministry of Pensions was prone to a rather paranoid sense of itself as a beleaguered fortress of objectivity and incredulity amidst a great tide of misguided sympathy. In the cause of debunking spurious claims, delegitimating the military lunatic whenever possible and reassimilating him to traditional moral norms, the Ministry's mistrust was by no means restricted to ex-servicemen and their families. It extended also to members of the medical profession not under their control, leading officials to propose that one of the Ministry's own medical officers should wherever possible sit on a medical board as 'a safeguard against the acceptance of impossible cases'. Medical superintendents of asylums were not infrequently castigated for being unduly gullible in submitting claims for men in asylums who were listed in records available to the Ministry as 'deserters', or in maintaining that an ex-serviceman's lunacy was attributable to or aggravated by service, taking on trust 'claims to wounds and much service at the Front, particularly by neurasthenic and shellshock types, which prove on enquiry to be without foundation'.[11]

The Ministry of Pensions has generally been viewed in a rather niggardly light by historians, with good reason for the most part, but it needs to be recognized that in securing allocations for war pensions the Ministry had in each instance to fight its corner with the Treasury, a very powerful force during and after the war.[12] Though there was considerable internal dissension over the concessions that had been made to the psychiatric casualties of the war, still it is largely due to the unabated zeal of the Ministry of Pensions that a discourse about war psychosis in its multiple forms entered into the fine capillaries of the state bureaucracy in the interwar period – from the procedures of the Insane Group, and its subdivisions such as the Insane Index Section, through to lengthy interchanges with other state agencies. Officials were obliged to acquaint themselves with the finer points of psychiatric conditions such as dementia praecox, no longer as objects of moral opprobrium, but as facets of a progressive medical discourse legitimating entitlement to a war disability pension.

From the outset, the Treasury looked askance at liberal pension provision for lunatics, sneering at the ineptitude of the Board of Control when it acknowledged difficulty in dividing cases of insanity into those which had been caused by the war and those which had not. Initially, the Treasury was only prepared to countenance the Service Patient scheme on very limited terms, insisting that payments be made to the wife or dependants just sufficient to place them 'in the same position financially as if the soldier were dead'. The Treasury view was that service lunatics were by definition 'hopeless cases', or socially dead, and it became obvious from information collated by Ministry officials in 1917 that by comparison to other disabled groups the Service Patient and his relatives were receiving a very raw deal, the maintenance of a service lunatic costing 'less than any other form of treatment with the possible exception of epilepsy in certain Epileptic Colonies'.[13]

As an inducement to persuade the war disabled to leave their families and enter treatment, it was agreed that only seven shillings a week maintenance would be deducted from their pensions, and the balance paid in full to their families. The Treasury was eventually persuaded to extend this liberal dispensation to other categories of 'incurables' so long as treatment in an institution could 'reasonably be held to be beneficial', but drew the line at service lunatics. A civil servant showed just how iniquitous their situation was by comparing the treatment received by a paraplegic in a specialized home with the maintenance of a service lunatic in an asylum. Though each man was entitled to a similar pension, there the resemblance ended, for the total cost of maintenance in the asylum was charged against the lunatic's pension, but only seven shillings against the paraplegic's. 'As a result the wife of a lunatic (late private) with 4 children was likely to receive 33/9d. per week, compared with the 54/3d. received by the family of a paraplegic'.[14] Paying the wife of a service lunatic the widow's rate of pension placed her at a disadvantage, Pensions officials insisted, though their choice of words rather belied the sincerity of their advocacy for these lost causes. Periodically, the wife of a service lunatic 'feels compelled to visit her husband thus incurring considerable travelling expenses' and she was in any case barred from re-marrying.[15]

As a Ministry official confided, disgruntled relatives were not in short supply: 'complaining of food and other treatment meted out to Service Patients, insisting that they are no better than Pauper Patients except in name, and denying that the Service Patient has all the rights and privileges of the Private Patient. . . . In one case recently a Service Patient was removed by request to a private asylum, in another the classification was cancelled by request, in another the offer to classify was refused because the father (a doctor) preferred his son to be treated otherwise, and could the relatives afford it the requests to de-classify would doubtless increase'.[16] Even Pensions officials themselves acknowledged misgivings. 'What are we getting', asked one, 'except a change in terminology and in uniform?'.[17] 'Service Patients are on precisely the same footing as Private Patients', asserted the Minister, for they are not 'associated with Pauper Patients any more than are Private Patients'. But this only went to show just how slippery the asylum floor was, for in most asylums private and pauper patients mingled with each other constantly and were only distinguishable by their clothing.[18] In asylum records it is by no means unusual to learn that families of middling means removed their sons from the public asylum system at their own expense. For example, Percival T, the son of an outfitter from Barnstaple, had been gassed in France and was removed to Wonford House, a private asylum in Exeter, in the spring of 1919 believing that the 'past war is all a myth' and becoming 'exceedingly violent if thwarted in any way'. But in this and like instances, if the case dragged on the family may have been obliged at a later date to bite on the Pensions bullet and return to the public asylum system, their means exhausted.[19]

Complaints about discrimination against the wives of service lunatics were voiced from a variety of quarters, from the Parliamentary War Pensions Bureau to the News of the World, and in December 1919 the Ministy of Pensions announced that the distinction had been removed, and that the wife of a Service Patient was now on a level footing with the wives of other men in hospitals.[20] Still, the Treasury continued to discriminate against service lunatics and their families on other fronts, resisting proposals to alleviate the hardship of the parents of Service Patients by bringing their cases more into line with those of single men under treatment for a disability other than insanity.[21] Powerful advocacy by relatives and local war pensions committees on behalf of 1000-odd servicemen in asylums whose claims for pension had been rejected resulted in the recognition by the Treasury in the summer of 1917 of an anomalous group of 'non-pensionable' or 'non-attributable' service lunatics. The Board of Control remonstrated that it was scarcely good policy both to give this group special consideration and to say in the same breath that it was of only a temporary character, but the Treasury was willing to make concessions to the 'non-pensionables' only on condition that the arrangement did not extend beyond the period of the war and 12 months afterwards.[22]

This was a small victory for those with advocates willing, or able, to speak up for them, which did at least win them some time, but undoubtedly there were many others who were not so lucky. The Board of Control successfully took issue with the principle of refusing Service Patient status to servicemen who had suffered a mental breakdown perhaps three or four years before joining the Army, pointing out that such an 'unlimited condition would never be imposed in the case of a man suffering from physical disease, such as bronchitis or kidney mischief'. Even so, previous asylum history was sometimes a bar to entitlement, as was evidence of serious negligence or misconduct.[23] Despite the entreaties of Maurice Craig and others, a disability pension was by no means automatically granted to all servicemen who had the misfortune to end up in an asylum, and it was widely acknowledged that there was a submerged and unquantified group of Great War servicemen in asylums between the wars who received no official recognition.[24] In 1918, less than 150 servicemen admitted to asylums were rejected for classification as Service Patients, 'due either to a previous Asylum history making the case non-attributable or to proof of misconduct causing the lunacy', but these were halcyon days, for by the mid 1920s more than 60 per cent of claimants were being rejected.[25]

NEGOTIATING WITH THE PENSIONS

Significant concessions had been won for ex-servicemen considered to be certifiable and now under treatment in asylums. However, those discharged from war hospitals, and now trying to renegotiate their war pension entitlements from a base in their own homes, laying claim to the continuing effects of their impairments, to the disadvantage which they had suffered, or to a recurrence or worsening of their conditions, found themselves in a much more tenuous position. The pension supplicant and his advocates were frequently hard pressed to establish the legitimacy of their claims, and of their renewed sufferings, against a seemingly implacable bureaucracy much inclined to insist that the disability had passed away, or had already been compensated for, or bore no conceivable connection with the trials of war service. Though the small war pension for delusional insanity awarded to Albert Norris was renewed for a period, and increased to 8/- a week, the medical board soon determined that aggravation had 'passed away', and that there were no grounds for further award, and with no one to plead for him Albert's brief sojourn as an Imperial War Disability Pensioner ended in April 1920.[26]

Especially in the last part of the war, and for a time afterwards, there was considerable hardship and uncertainty among the dependants of servicemen, quite frequently widowed mothers as much as young wives, forcing them to pick up a pen as importuning letter-writer and supplicant to an unknown bureaucracy. Despite this unaccustomed role, they often managed in an earthy and unadorned style to pack a punch and get down to the bare bones. Poor Mrs R, whose son William was in Mickleover Lunatic Asylum in 1918 'through his wounds and shock', had a rude awakening in store because the Pensions were retaining a large portion of his pension to pay for his upkeep in the asylum. After the war some small leftovers (7/6d. or so) very likely did trickle down to supplement her old age pension, and whatever other savings she might have had, but scarcely enough to make her feel that she had been obliged, to the extent that she was asking: 'I am sending 7/- nearly every week in things but I don't know how to afford it, so I should like to know where the 27/6d. a week is going. I am sorry to say that my son as been in Mickleover at Derby 3 or 4 months through his wounds and shock. So will you kindly oblige and see into the matter for me and oblige his mother'.[27]

After James Barraclough was discharged from a war mental hospital, the pension that was intended to support him in his convalescence fizzled and faltered. Along with innumerable others, his father found himself pitted against the surly and unyielding bureaucracy of the Ministry of Pensions at a time when he and his family were already at a low ebb in trying to find their bearings, and a pointer to a hopeful direction, in the unfamiliar topography of insanity and its outposts. Frank Barraclough wrote feelingly to the Pensions as to imply that the balances that now concerned him (he was a bank cashier by profession) were not exclusively fiscal. 'It is now two months', he complained to the Ministry in July 1918, 'since my son's pension expired and I am hopelessly in the dark as to the future – also as to the past and the present – in the absence of certificates without which the balances of pension, overdue, cannot be drawn and an arrangement made for renewal'. He wrote again in August when his unrequited need (it seems that he missed his lunch) had yielded only a couple of brusque postcards and an inconsequential encounter:

Am I ever likely to hear anything further from your Dept about my boy's pension? The pension expired on 12 May – I heard nothing. I waited a month – heard nothing. Then I wrote – a post-card came along. I asked for an appointment and apparently my case was bisected – one Branch replied and I kept the appointment which was so inconclusive that I just as well may have had a bit of lunch and stayed away. However, I learned something and in consequence wrote to the other Branch – result another post-card addressed not to me but to my son! . . . I have hitherto shunned all other sources and dealt solely, officially – must I be compelled to consult someone, or are you really prepared to act? Surely one has anxiety enough without this additional callous delay.[28]

Thomas Snowden expressed himself equally forcefully in presenting his credentials to the appeals tribunal:

I do not think I am being compensated sufficiently for the disatvantage [sic] that I am placed in, through being an inmate of a mental institution. I find it is a detrement [sic] to me and it may be for years to come of obtaining any position of trust which position I held for many years during my career in the service. I have tried work in ship repair yards but find there is too much noise for me. I may also state that I have been rejected for appointment as postman by the Medical Officer.

Born in 1879, Snowden was a former agricultural labourer who had enlisted in the Royal Navy in 1896, rising to become a Petty Officer. In June 1919 he had been admitted to the Royal Naval Hospital in Plymouth with a history of behaving in his own home as a 'dangerous lunatic'. Awarded a 100% disability pension for insanity for the four months that he was an inmate, on his discharge the pension was reduced to 30%, and a few months later to 20%.

A Pensions official gave a thumbnail sketch of how Thomas came across at the tribunal: 'Man states: unable to scale rigging; suffers much from depression; nervous in traffic; prefers being alone; quiet in mind; gets on well at home; sleeps fairly; dreams sometimes disturb him'. Of course, being able to scale the rigging is hardly an essential requirement on civvy street, but for Thomas it was, perhaps, a figure for the failings of his manhood at this juncture, not least the disadvantage of an identity as a former mental patient. However, here was an example of how the official understanding of the compensation that a war disability pension was intended to provide frequently clashed with that of the pensioner. The state was quite indifferent to the disadvantage that Thomas had suffered through becoming an inmate of a mental institution and the bearer of a psychiatric identity, restricting its consideration to a medicalized assessment of functional incapacity and 'effective disablement'. Anticipating that his residual disabilities were mostly temporary, and that he would soon be scaling the rigging of everyday life again, Thomas Snowden's application for increased compensation was rejected.[29]

William Bray and his family also had a hard time in getting the ear of the Pensions. A former piecer in a cotton mill in Oldham, Lancashire, William Bray had enlisted in the Navy and seen service afloat until he was invalided from Plymouth Hospital in November with 'functional disease of the brain'. His condition was defined as 'not cured', but his capacity for 'earning a full livelihood in the general labour market' had apparently only been lessened by 10 per cent and he was awarded a pension of 6d. a day, or 3/6d. a week, for six months, subsequently renewed for another five months. At this point, even though he had in the meantime been hospitalized again for four months, he was given a gratuity of £19.7.0. in final compensation for his disablement, now defined as neurasthenia.

In the spring of 1918, William complained to the Ministry about the stoppage of his pension, demanding a re-survey, alleging that he was in bad health and 'cannot work regular', but the Pensions ignored his request. Three years later his mother dispatched a forceful letter declaring that she had already written several times but had never had a satisfactory answer, receiving in reply a curt note stating that as far as the Pensions were concerned the extent of William's disablement was insufficient to qualify him for a war disability pension. Though he had been able to hold down a job for a time, earning 30/- a week as a piecer with a spinning company, a crisis was obviously looming, and in the summer of 1921 he was removed to the mental ward of the Oldham Union on the recommendation of his general practitioner. Having attended him since 1914, Dr Monteith was in a position to vouch for the decline of his health: 'then (pre-war) good, now exceedingly bad, mentally and physically'. In early September he was discharged not much improved to his home in Boardman Street, where his parents were becoming increasingly distraught at his plight. Now it was his father's turn to do a bit of plain speaking to the Pensions: 'Please will you look into my son's case as he is unfit for work through war service. . . . I want paying from the time he was discharged in 1916 and immediately as I cannot afford to keep him'. Three weeks later the cycle repeated itself, and after a fortnight on the Oldham Mental Ward William was again discharged. The strain on the household was now palpable:

> I think he is not being treated fair it is practically through his bouts [illnesses] that his mother is now an invalede the anxiety and toiling with him she is now no use for household duties. He ought to have proper treatment in some convalessent home but I can't afford it myself he has cost me enough already a long time years in fact sorry to say if I am writing too much.

William's war service had apparently stimulated a taste for the orient which Oldham could scarcely satisfy, and he imagined that he was now in regular communication with the voice of a Turkish woman he had met in Salonika. By November Mr and Mrs Bray could take no more of these oriental babblings, and after William was bundled off to Whittingham Asylum his father mustered all his rhetorical resources in issuing an ultimatum to the Pensions: 'I wish to say you are long-winded in notifying me the result of my son's claim to pension. Will you please answer this letter to the best of your ability. . . . If you don't answer soon this letter I shall write to the War Secretary and also give all my papers into the hands of the best solicitor in Oldham'. Finally stirred into action by an incensed rank-and-file complainant, the Pensions now delivered William Bray a full war disability pension for dementia praecox for as long as he remained in the asylum.[31]

Like William Bray, George Collins had also been awarded a gratuity in final compensation for his disability. A miner from Nottinghamshire, Collins had served with the Portsmouth Battalion in the Royal Marines Light Infantry, and found himself fighting alongside Anzac troops in the ill-starred and hastily-improvized plan to wrest control of the Dardanelle Straits by landing ground troops on the Gallipoli Peninsula. The War Diary of the Royal Marines Brigade for 13 and 14 July 1915 leaves little to the imagination as to the scale and degree of the physical and mental attrition on the Peninsula:

> Casualties very heavy. Colonel Eveleigh, RMLI, commanding Nelson, killed. Nelson reported only 4 officers and 120 men left. . . . Portsmouth Battn Colonel Luard killed. All officers killed or wounded except Temporary Captain Gowney (wounded on next day, leaving Transport Officer and Quartermaster only in Battn). . . . All trenches in very bad state, rotting bodies in heaps everywhere and men obliged to wear respirators, even then vomiting very bad and much sickness.

Col. Clark later testified that 'most of the men of the Portsmouth Battalion RMLI were at that time totally unfit to be in the front line owing to dysentery, gastric troubles and continuous wear and tear'; and Lt Col. Weller submitted that:

> sheer physical weakness from dysentery was at the root of everything. . . . Further, men who had been up all night in the front line could get no sleep by day owing to the plague of flies which swarmed over everyone and everything. . . . The only thing for the men to do by day (if they were strong enough to walk to the sea) was to bathe. Even here, if too many bathed at once they were shelled and the numbers of dead mules that were always floating near the shore made bathing very unpleasant.[32]

George was able to give only a fragmentary account of his experiences in Gallipoli in 1915, but he recalled a bayonet charge followed by hand-to-hand fighting directly they landed; being dug into a position which was continually shelled over a number of months where he was partly buried several times; and another charge where he lay close to Turkish lines for two days, before managing to get back to his own trenches at night. He became more and more shaky, and later learned that he had been carried away unconscious on a stretcher after a shell-burst and returned to England in November 1915 in a disoriented state ('he did not know people or places'), and admitted to the Royal Naval Hospital in Great Yarmouth as as a dangerous lunatic.[33] By the following summer he had apparently recovered, and after his married sister had written to the Hospital saying that there was 'a good home awaiting him' where he would be well cared for, he was discharged by the Fleet Surgeon on 30 August 1916 ('he was not victualled here for today'). His earning incapacity was assessed at one tenth, and he was granted a pension of 4/8d. a week for eight months, after which the Pensions decided that it would be expeditious to remove him from the pensions slate entirely by dealing with him under the scale for minor injuries, and giving him a gratuity of £44, not before deducting the payments that already been made to him.

But from the outset it was obvious that the Pensions were being unduly sanguine about his prospects, and that George was suffering from rather more than the residual effects of a minor injury. His sister later gave her version of events:

> I Nellie Mansbridge sister of George Collins had charge of my brother when he was discharge from the navy. He was brought home by an attendant from Royal Naval Hospital Gt Yarmouth and was in my charge 4 months. He

worked at Welbeck Colliery on light work on the pit top averaging about 3 days a week owing to illness. He was allways very bad with his head and depressed and very peculiar at times in fact I was afraid he would have to be taken away. To my knowledge he was as fit as any young man liveing before the War.

One of George's former workmates, who had been with George on the pitbank until they were both dismissed when the pit was reduced to one shift, reported that he 'was a good worker although he was very ill and repeatedly had to rest and kept putting his hands to his head'. And George's general practitioner corroborated these accounts: 'I have attended George Collins since his discharge from the Army in 1916. He first complained to me that he was suffering from after effects of shell shock in October 1916. and I found on examination that knee jerks were exaggerated, very irritable, general feeling of malaise. Formed the following opinion as to his general health: – "He is still very excitable and is quite unable to perform his full work as a coal-miner" '. Early in 1920 George initiated what was to prove an extremely protracted correspondence, requesting a re-survey:

a very good job we have only one child, thank the Lord, and I can tell you Sir we have had our share of trouble since I left the Royal Marines. . . . Since I was discharged 30th day of August 1916 I have had a lot of illness and was at home from work last year for nearly 6 months with typhoid fever and I can tell, Sir, we have had a very hard struggle in life.

In reply, the Pensions raised the stakes by advising that him that when he was last medically examined 'it was stated that no disability existed from the shell shock for which you were invalided', and that his case could not be reconsidered unless it could be shown that he was still suffering from shell shock. Though they conceded that he had a legitimate call upon treatment provision by taking him into a Pensions hospital for three months in 1923, still the Ministry was adamant that the disability of shell shock for which he was now claiming compensation was 'part of the insanity which has already been considered by the Ministry', and for which he had been granted a final gratuity in 1917. His treatment was apparently to little avail, for two weeks after he came home he was complaining that his head was 'now most terrible, I can't sleep nor do anything for these terrible pains in my head . . . when these pains come in my head I see all I went through at the Dardanelles and the pains are just the same as the guns going off'. Even so, the Ministry stonewalled his repeated pleas ('I have filled two lots of forms in and never had a Medical

Board') for a reconsideration of his entitlement, ignoring the seasonal invocation of his domestic privations ('all the money I have coming in is 11/- Loydd George money to keep me, my wife and 2 children with. . . . God above knows how we are living this Christmas' [sic]) and telling him that his right of appeal against the finality of the award had in any event now lapsed.

Sometimes a claim for a war disability pension could be wonderfully assisted if the claimant was able to mobilize advocates in his local community. Robert Dent, a miner from Newbiggin-on-Sea in Northumberland, had seen action at the Somme, following which he had been hospitalized for five days for shell shock before being returned to duty, and had subsequently been awarded a pension for trench foot. After the war he recommenced his occupation as a hewer at the local pit, but following a period of emotional disturbance he was admitted to Morpeth Mental Hospital in the summer of 1924. Though a claim was shortly lodged alleging that he was experiencing a recurrence of the shell shock from which he had suffered in 1916, the Ministry of Pensions refused to classify him as a Service Patient, maintaining that there was 'no evidence to connect the shell-shock with his present disability, which is of purely constitutional origin and unconnected with war service'. Hannah Dent testified that when her husband came home from the War she had found him queer in manner, and he had become worse since ('he was strong and healthy before enlistment . . . since discharge he became a total wreck'), and Dent's panel doctor also supplied a narrative linking his current crisis to his war service. However, it was the advocacy of the Reverend Fogg, the vicar of Newbiggin-on-Sea, hinting strongly that there was likely to be a local rebellion if the Ministry did not back down, which clinched the position, producing a change of heart in the Ministry that vindicated the popular perception of Robert Dent in his locality as a victim of shell shock:

> From my own observation, from the talks I have had with the local people, and from the local doctor's evidence I am convinced that we have a MOST CLEAR CASE. By Dent's conduct and ravings, we have sufficient evidence that he is suffering from shell shock. Local opinion is very strong. Mrs Dent is appealing against the Board. May I appeal to you, Sir, on behalf of people who are suffering acutely as the direct result of the War? I take this course because I feel the case is a genuine one. Since my own War Service I have tried to help the ex-service man, never did I feel that I had a clearer case.[35]

ROUGH JUSTICE

The Pensions were specially resistant to two categories of people – the mad and the Irish.[36] In his dealings with the authorities, Michael Cunningham had the double misfortune of having to account for a two-year stint in an asylum before the war, always an awkward adjunct to a cv, and of being an Irish Catholic from Belfast. Cunningham's war service straddled the entire period of the war, and he could plausibly lay claim to a personal narrative of patriotic pluck in which, despite episodes of nervous collapse, he managed to get back on his feet and re-enter the fray. Even so, the authorities constructed a counter-narrative in which Cunningham's hallmark – expressed in the image of him as 'a rabid Sinn Feiner' – was not so much patriotism as political and psychological instability, and even his tenacity in re-enlisting in the army was seen to reflect his unhinged condition. After he had been discharged following an air raid in which a bomb exploded close to where he was standing, the Chelsea Commissioners informed Cunningham's wife that the 'unfortunate disability' from which her husband, 'the discharged Soldier named in the margin', suffered was 'in no way attributable to his recent military service'.

In the margin was where the pension authorities wanted to leave him, but Cunningham was to re-enlist in the services twice more. At the end of 1917 the authorities were persuaded to award him a gratuity of £70, converted to a 30% pension after the gratuity scheme was abolished, though the Ministry simultaneously demanded repayment of part of the gratuity. However, they shifted their ground after they received a report revealing that Cunningham was a 'rabid Sinn Feiner', peremptorily reducing his pension to 20%, the start of a concerted drive to edge him off the war disability slate by tapering his pension to the point of extinction. Although Cunningham found allies in the Belfast War Pensions Committee, the Ministry ignored their entreaties, renewing their demands for the repayment of the gratuity, at the same time producing a medical adviser to challenge Cunningham's traumatic narrative ('he has a story of a shock from bomb explosion in October 1915 but I can find no confirmation of the alleged incident'), and to claim that his war service had no bearing on his condition since instability was his normal mental state: '... the fact of his two years in a Lunatic Asylum ... he cannot have been much real use for a good many years. ... The case appears to be one of Dementia in a minor degree growing slowly worse with advancing age'.

If they intended to goad him into a truculent reaction they succeeded admirably by instructing him to to direct his communications to the Pensions representative at the Grand Central Hotel in Belfast:

This establishment is not I am sorry to say the Place where men of my Religious and Political beliefs may apply for justice although Religion during 1914 was not mentioned in Belfast Sir. ... My position to refund the whole of part of this amount is I am quite sure already knowing to you.

You must be aware that all Catholics (ex-servicemen included) has been deprived of the right to work and earn a living in this city of cowards, bigots and some knaves. Therefore I am not in a position nor am I at all willing to consent to any further deductions being made from my Pension until an impartial inquiry into this grievance has been made.

Even for a mad Irishman, however, as for many other claimants in their dealings with officialdom in the immediate post-war years, a form of rough justice was eventually done. In November 1923 Michael Cunningham's case was taken to an appeal tribunal which, having reviewed the evidence, concluded (in a decision no less grounded in medical expertise than the position adopted by the Ministry) that his condition had indeed been aggravated by his war service, and awarded him a 60% pension for life. 'The decision of the Tribunal', averred an astonished Pensions official, 'is amazing but the man is to be congratulated'.[37]

Chapter 11

'A VERY PUBLIC MADNESS'

THE WORKHOUSE AND THE MADHOUSE

At the beginning of the twentieth century the institutions of the Poor Law were still the only source of state aid, not merely for the impoverished but for those without the means to afford private medicine.[1] With roots in the sixteenth century, welfare in the form of 'poor' laws, minimalist in provision as much as intentionally stigmatizing, treating recipients not as citizens but as peculiar objects of welfare, was encountering mounting hostility and repugnance. Since the late nineteenth century, modernizing Poor Law administrators had endeavoured to create specialized institutions catering to particular categories of need. Groups like the elderly were now accorded rights and privileges, no longer merely part of the 'impotent poor', and 'alleged lunatics' received treatment in a specialized 'mental' or observation ward in the workhouse infirmary or the workhouse itself.[2] The Poor Law is in a 'constant process of evolution and development', maintained the Association of Poor Law Unions in 1918, and Infirmaries 'are rapidly assuming a position with the General Public as Municipal Institutions in the same way as Public Libraries and Parks are regarded'. The Association was lending its support to a new regime of public assistance under which the Workhouse Infirmary would be restyled as 'The Local Infirmary', and the term 'Local Patient' would replace 'Pauper Lunatic' or 'Pauper Patient'.[3] Of course, this consumer-friendly localism was largely a ploy by which the Poor Law authorities were endeavouring to keep pace with the reconstructionist mood of the times while maintaining a grip on power. But even if these modernizing pretensions, and the place they occupied in the affections of the public, were exaggerated, still – as we shall see – for ordinary people in a mental health crisis there was some substance to them.

There can be no denying that ex-servicemen and their families were frequently humiliated by their association with the Poor Law system. There are frequent references to individuals' alarms and anxieties at having been stripped of markers of personal identity and social status, such as personal clothing, spectacles and medals, which had disappeared into some inaccessible corner of the bureaucratic system. A disconcerting experience in itself, but doubly so in that the implied message was that the system did not consider that they were the type of people who would have need of such items in the future, or who possessed the sorts of biographies and histories that a medal might legitimately adorn. John Willcox, who had served in the Boer War and other campaigns, was a rather typical recruit to the old Regular Army for whom soldiery had provided a reprieve from destitution and who had no life outside the Army ('you see', his sister wrote, 'he has practilly [sic] done hardly any work, most of his time has been in the Army'). After John was removed to Long Grove via the Infirmary from a Ministry of Pensions hospital in Tooting, his sister wrote to the Wandsworth Union in some desperation having lost track of her brother's personal belongings. 'If they are at Wandsworth would you kindly let me know if I can have them. Also his medal that he says is with them, so that in the event of him coming out of the Mental Hospital I shall be able to take his clothes to him'. Though John's civilian identity might for the present be in storage, his sister was obviously determined to keep it warm for him.[4]

Occasionally it was a wife who gave voice to what many people must have felt, but rarely expressed directly, in their dealings with Poor Law officials. Emmie Krivan had already been mortified to learn that in the course of removal from the Wandsworth Infirmary to Colney Hatch Asylum, her husband, a former tailor who had served for two and a half years in the Middlesex Labour Battalion, had been stripped of his personal belongings, including his pince-nez. Sadly, it turned out that Anthony Krivan was suffering from GPI, dying in the asylum within a few weeks of his admission. A month later his widow received a package from the Wandsworth Union containing her husband's belongings, together with a note informing her that 5/11d. had been removed from the balance of his cash as a maintenance charge for the night he had spent in the Infirmary. This was a degradation too far, and she did not mince her words in her communication to the relieving officer:

> If I might mention, this is scandalous, knowing he was an ex-soldier and sent to you from Military Neurological Hospital Tooting. . . . I think it degrading enough, and I feel it very much, that he was sent to the Union, he was no poor man on joining the Army. I own 5/11 is but a small sum, but I can make good use of it since I am deprived of my Husband and have two children to support, secondly it is the principal [sic] that I claim this money, therefore I give you opportunity of forwarding that sum to me before putting the matter in other authorities to deal with.[5]

Government spokesmen were frequently in the position of appearing to claim that was there was a kind of dedicated admission track for ex-servicemen to asylums that circumvented the Poor Law system. Regardless of the rhetorical detours that might be made around it, however, the Poor Law Unions and their institutions were far too closely woven into the fabric of British society in the early twentieth century for it to be feasible to circumvent them entirely. A spokesman for the medical superintendents of all the London County Council asylums divulged that, as a rule, ex-servicemen were admitted 'from the Workhouse as pauper patients, and may not be classified as Service Patients for several weeks, or even months, afterwards'.[6] When it came to earthing the ex-serviceman's narrative in the communities of his birth and residence, and to establishing the parish in which he had a settlement, appeal was invariably made to the Union, which as often as not functioned also as a registrar of births, marriages and deaths. At a local level, only the Unions had the bureaucratic means to corroborate the claims to entitlement that were being made.

The next of kin would be sent a notice to attend at the Guardians' Office to be interviewed by the settlement officer, bringing with them 'any of the books named opposite that you may have in your possession – marriage certificate; certificate of death of husband or wife; birth certificates of all children; all rent books; all receipts of rates and taxes; parchments showing dates of enlistment and discharge from the Army'. In September 1918, Private George Masters was being readied for a transfer from the Welsh Metropolitan War Hospital to an asylum where he was to be classified as a Service Patient. The Hospital advised the Whitechapel Union that in order to complete the order of admission they needed to determine whether Masters had a settlement in the parish of Whitechapel. His mother and wife were accordingly interviewed by the settlement officer to corroborate the information given, confirming that he had resided in the hamlet of Mile End Old Town since his birth at Tollot Street on 6 Sept 1885.[7]

The guidance that the Boards of Guardians received from the Local Government Board on how 'soldiers and sailors disabled by mental disorder' were to be dealt with was quite unequivocal: unless circumstances dictated otherwise, the ex-serviceman should be removed 'directly to the Asylum without any intervening period of maintenance in the wards of the Poor Law Institution'.[8] In reality, however, not only was this quite impracticable, but it is far from obvious that it would have been in the ex-serviceman's interest to cut the mental ward out of the action in this way, for the result would undoubtedly have been a quite considerable increase in the overall numbers of ex-servicemen who ended up being certified in asylums. The irony is that, in its anxiety to fend off public opprobrium, the Local Government Board was actively undermining the role of just that institution which was making quite a creditable job of keeping ex-servicemen out of pauper lunatic asylums. Far from being simply the stepping stone to a madhouse, the initiating chamber in a prolonged ritual of degradation, the mental ward not infrequently played a more positive role in defusing a crisis than it has been given credit for. Even if it was hardly a therapeutic showpiece, in some places at least it marked a break from the minimalist and undifferentiated care of the destitute 'at the margins'.

BEEF TEA AND BROMIDE

At least half of the cases admitted to the male mental ward, or observation ward as it was more commonly known, in the Fulham Road Workhouse in the City of Westminister between 1917 and 1923 were ex-servicemen.[9] Perhaps significantly more, but it is impossible to say because the only information available comes from what the inmate himself chose to say, or papers he was carrying on him revealed, or in some instances from a relative. Less than half of these ex-service admissions were dispatched to an asylum, and though a few were transferred to alternative treatment facilities, the majority were discharged after a stay lasting generally just a few days, and inevitably no longer than the statutory maximum of 14 days. During this time the inmate was usually put on a regimen of eggs, milk pudding and beef tea and, depending on the case, was administered liberal doses of bromide or paraldehyde, apart from which there was little else in the medicine chest.[10] Though it lacked therapeutic pretensions, the observation ward did provide a protective environment of a kind (not infrequently with a little help from the padded room) that permitted, if not exactly a crisis resolution, at least an abatement of a kind.[11]

An ex-serviceman could evidently expect a fair hearing from Dr Sandiland, the medical officer here. James Murphy, a former window cleaner, had been sent in by the doctor at Brixton Prison in February 1918 'as insane & needing asylum care and treatment'.[12] His sister had given a very bad account of him, claiming that he had been discharged from the Dublin Fusiliers for misconduct after firing a rifle through the roof of his tent when mad drunk, and that he had subsequently been sheltering absentees and trying to hinder recruiting. Still, even though the auguries did not favour Murphy, Dr Sandiland was admirably empirical, judging him not by repute but on his experience, and finding him to be 'quiet and well behaved and quite coherent in every way', and unable to detect any sign of insanity, he discharged him. Quite frequently, the ward had a real function in defusing a crisis, as it did for George Clayton, a twenty-six year old boot repairer, who was brought in by the police in September 1919 apparently suffering from loss of memory. 'When seen by me,

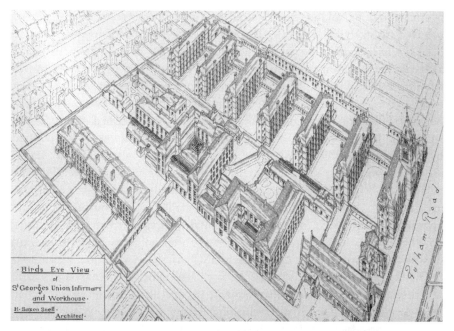

The forbidding stacks of the St George's Union Infirmary and Workhouse (subsequently the City of Westminster Union Infirmary and Workhouse), on the Fulham Road. On census day in 1901 there were upward of 1500 paupers in residence here.

he would not speak but commenced to grind his teeth and clench his hands. He had a wild ferocious look and appears to me likely to become suddenly violent. He is therefore sent here for observation as I consider it unsafe to admit him into a ward in charge of a single nurse'. The following day he was quite vacant, unable to speak, staring strangely in front of him. Two days later, however, when his wife visited, he started to recover and it emerged that he had been blown up at Loos in 1915, captured and taken prisoner, and had been subject to 'fits' ever since. The following day he confided to the doctor that he did not feel safe about himself – anything might happen, he might injure his wife or children. However, being able to communicate his fears to a sympathetic interlocutor doubtless helped him, temporarily at least, to feel safer about himself, for three days later he was said to have made 'steady improvement' and to be 'quiet and rational'.

For the small minority who were brought in from their own homes by the relieving officer in response to a domestic crisis, admission to the observation ward was generally a prelude to certification in an asylum. Frederick Bull, postman and ex-soldier, had 'locked his wife in her room and generally behaved strangely', and Charles Davies, labourer and woodchopper, who had been discharged from Napsbury War Hospital two months previously, had allegedly been beating his wife about. Most of these servicemen were drawn from the ranks of the skilled and unskilled working classes, or from the lower middle class, but there were a few individuals of a higher station who had perhaps fallen on hard times, or whose kin had spurned them. Victor Montague James Ponsford, a twenty-five year old accountant, was admitted by the relieving officer in November 1920 in an acutely maniacal state, claiming to hear his mother's voice, from his parental home in Lupus Street, Pimlico, adjacent to Belgravia; though not the smartest address, certainly not a poor area by any means. He had a scar from a bullet wound on his thigh and appeared to have been in a military hospital for mental treatment. He must have been in a troublesome condition because after only four days on the ward he was dispatched to Long Grove Asylum. Charles Green, a cook, was admitted by the relieving officer as suffering from shell shock in January 1923 from a genteel address in Montpelier Square, mostly likely at the behest of an anxious employer, for his distinguishing infirmity was that he appeared to ignore the presence of the person speaking to him. Though his reply when it finally arrived was rational enough, he took several minutes to answer a question, thus rather destabilizing the culinary preparations. In the event, however, after ten days on the observation ward he had speeded up his reaction time, and having shown himself able to deliver a reasonably prompt dialogic return was permitted to resume his position in the kitchen.

A few of these ex-soldiers were simply out of funds. Ernest Farmer had been invalided out of the army in the spring of 1917 with a weekly pension of 29/- for shell shock which had apparently been terminated some months later. 'Is apparently penniless at present & underfed & has been badgering at War Office, Lord Roberts Disabled Soldiers Fund etc'. Ten days later, on a regime of egg and milk pudding, he was noted to be improving, answering brightly and coherently. Quite a number were treatment failures from the military hospitals, or had at the very least been discharged prematurely. William Dorgan, discharged from a Ministry of Pensions Neurasthenia Hospital five weeks previously, jumped into the Thames and was rescued by the police. Frederick Cannell, a former engineer who had received in-patient treatment for nervous trouble at the Maudsley and at Ewell, and still had occasional twitchings of the left side of his face and arm, was brought in by the police from a Ministry of Pensions out-patient clinic declaring that he had killed his wife with a hammer. When he was admitted he denied the tale, however, saying that he had a wife and six kiddies now living but was subject to 'bad turns' when he did not know what he said or did. Frank Ayres, a fish porter from Stepney, was also brought in by the police from a Ministry of Pensions clinic where the medical officer had found him to be completely disorientated and suffering from delusions. In point of fact his worries did not seem to be at all delusory, for he had been blown up in 1917, and been in various hospitals since, and now was understandably rather concerned about his prospects, stating that he had not been able to sleep lately as he been very worried about earning enough money to keep his children. He was put on paraldehyde for several days before being transferred to the Ministy of Pensions mental hospital at Ewell in Surrey, though it may be doubted whether a combination of sedation and work discipline would have assisted Frank to fill the hole in his life. It was not so much work skills or discipline that he lacked, as work opportunities in an increasingly lean economic climate.

'NO MORE PALACE FOR ME!'

Arrah, sit down on the parliamentary side of your arse for Christ' sake and don't be making a public exhibition of yourself. Jesus, there's always some bloody clown or other kicking up a bloody murder about bloody nothing. Gob, it'd turn the porter sour in your guts, so it would.

James Joyce, *Ulysses*[13]

By far the largest group of inmates at Fulham Road, however, were individuals who had come to the attention of the police by acting strangely, or sometimes by causing a disturbance, in a public place. Montague Bridge was brought in by the police in November 1920 after behaving strangely in an ABC tea shop, talking incessantly about naval and military matters. Robert Torrington, a railway clerk, who had been discharged as 'nervous breakdown' from the army two years earlier, was found by the police in Villiers Street in December 1919, shouting, singing and waving his arms about. Frank Abrams, a butcher who had been wounded in the thigh during the war, went to Downing Street in October 1920 and made a scene, throwing down his crutches and declaring that he could stop the coal strike if he could only speak to the Prime Minister, which was quite enough to convince the medical officer at Brixton Prison that he was in the early stages of insanity. And Peter O'Leary, a schoolteacher who had been treated for shell shock at Netley, was admitted by police after assaulting a priest in Westminster Cathedral from whom he had been soliciting information about the Grand Archangel Michael.

By no means is this public dimension incidental, for it transpires that the great majority of the inmates were variously enthused, or invaded, by the political fervours of the moment, and quite beyond their direct experience in uniform were demonstrably stirred and affected by the war. And even if they were no longer combatants, still they were being chased by the Germans, or the Germans were interfering with their shaving brush, or they had a message to give to the King or some other important personage. William Hawkins, a milkman, drove in a cab to the Admiralty where he announced that God had sent him and he was going to take command of the fleet and 'smash' Lenin and Trotsky. William Fletcher, a former house porter, had been in the West Riding Asylum from 1910 until he escaped in 1916 and joined the East Yorkshire Regiment, serving for two years and 49 days until his discharge in July 1918. One day at the end of April 1919 he wandered into the Westminster Hospital, announcing that he had just foiled an attempt by the Germans to blow up the Houses of Parliament. James Hegarty went to Bow Street Police Station asking for protection, believing that he was being persecuted by Sinn Feiners and that 'a certain person named Aston Stagg MP for Kerry was following him and trying to assassinate him'. And Joseph Morrison, who had been wounded on the Somme and had since had a lot of domestic trouble which had driven him to drink, also presented himself at Bow Street to announce the theft of plans for the design of submarines which he claimed he was shortly due to discuss with the renowned Irish lawyer and politician Sir Edward Carson.

These individuals were many of them living public lives in the double sense of conducting their lives, and making themselves conspicuous, in public places, and also of feeling that public events had entered into their inmost being and had, in some special sense, replaced what one might have called their private concerns. John Davies, a former messenger, was very noisy and boisterous on the ward, haranguing large crowds at the top of his voice, and on waking up at night at once started to address a meeting. The collapse of private worlds into public identities was strikingly evinced by William Selby, a former solicitor's clerk, who in the Strand Palace Hotel, and later on the observation ward, insisted on calling all the people whom he addressed by the name of public figures, thus the police inspector as 'Granville Barker' and one of the attendants as 'Hindenburg'.

In a study of William Blake and his times, Jacob Bronowski made the astute comment that: 'Each kind of madness is a distortion of privacy, at its boundary with the social world'.[14] Under the strain of the world, he went on to remark, the privacy of the mad may explode outward, resulting in a redefinition or appropriation of the public domain in terms of the individual's private concerns, as when Lewis Wall, a former naval officer, walked into a police station at nine in the morning having been walking all night, his clothes dripping wet, and ordered bed and breakfast. Alternatively, privacy may collapse inward and be overwhelmed by, and made subordinate to, the social world. Of course, this is more likely to happen at some historical moments than others. Unquestionably, the time of the First World War was just such a moment of enormous emotional intensity, producing a sense of unity and belonging – of affinities between spheres – that disrupted, and sometimes imploded, the barriers between private and public domains, stimulating wild conjectures and conjunctions in the imaginings of marginal men. In September 1918 ex-soldier John Frost was insisting to everybody prepared to listen to him that he *was* Lloyd George and that everybody else was his 'affinity', harping all the time on the word 'affinity' (12.20pm 'continually talking, arguing and using strong language'; 8pm 'still talking').

Under these emotive circumstances an individual might feel himself in his inmost being to be a member of the national family, the body politic, as personified most directly in the person of the King, and hence to consider the royal family as his kin, or else to discover that he had an intimate connection, previously quite unknown to him, with a titled family. So, for instance, Thomas Byrne, an accountant who had twice been 'buried' in France, had several times visited 12 Grosvenor Square over a two months' period and informed the residents that he was the son of a major, that the property belonged to him, and that his name was now Prince Obelinski. And so it is not entirely surprising to encounter individuals who may previously have felt themselves to be quite marginal, but have now experienced an awakening or calling in which they imagine themselves to be the recipient of a special piece of knowledge or revelation that has been vouchsafed to them, and which it is their patriotic duty to entrust to the head of the family. George Batty, a clerk, went to Buckingham Palace in April 1917 insisting that he could stop the war by seeing the King but would not reveal any details; Walter Rayson claimed to have a vision from God telling him to go to the King and warn him of the imminent annihilation of England by aeroplanes; Ernest Welch, a footman from Aberdare, who had been treated for 'mental trouble' whilst in the army, called at the Palace to see his mother and father, the King and Queen, claiming they were his only relatives in London; Arthur French, a waiter, had written to Buckingham Palace on several occasions to say that he was coming to sign the King's books, and finally presented himself in July 1919; Benjamin Tomkins called at the Palace several times to see His Majesty about some money that he believed was due to him; Charles Smith arrived at the Palace to see the King, claiming that he had a wireless message and was being followed by armed men; Jacob Michaels was discovered trying to get into the Palace to apprise the King of the injury to the morals of the people caused by a lot of 'psychology' going about which was hindering all good works; William James Sinfield, who had been in Netley suffering from exhaustion psychosis, was found outside Buckingam Palace in November 1923 tampering with the gates, claiming that the King was his father and that he considered the Palace his home; and Charles Meggy called several times at Marlborough House to see Queen Alexandra, whom he said was his mother.[15]

Some of these characters were clearly seeking approval, some form of repair to their self-esteem, or some reprieve from the anguished uncertainty in which they found themselves. Samuel Roskofsky, a Jewish confectioner, was found by police in May 1923 crossing and recrossing the street, claiming that he was attempting to reach the Queen to collect the Victoria Cross for his war service. George Yeasoudas, a ship's fireman, called at the Palace to be baptized by the King, saying that he 'had enough of the Devil'. As late as 1924, Thomas Lewis, a labourer from Bethnal Green, was still haunted by his failings on the battlefield, believing that he was going to be shot. He arrived at the Palace bearing a letter for the King telling of how he was being driven from pillar to post, imploring the monarch to 'lift this barrier' off him and give him a chance in life.

By no means were these entrants hustled off to the asylum for, up to a point, admission to the observation ward allowed for a cooling-off period in which they could collect themselves, retreat once more into the safety of their own privacy, and acknowledge that their biographies and identities bore no connection with the domains into which they had intruded.[16] It was, perhaps, forgiveable to proclaim oneself King on Thursday so long as one abdicated no later than the following Monday. 'No more Palace for me', Benjamin Tomkins wisely declared the morning after his last aberration. Two days after his visit to the Palace, footman Welch said he could not understand how he had behaved so foolishly and was taken home by his brother-in-law. Following his escapade in Downing Street, Frank Abrams became quiet and well behaved, and his brother was allowed to take him home three days later. And by the end of the week, Thomas Byrne had scaled down his original conviction that he was Prince Obelinski to a lingering belief (based, so he claimed, on indications in newspapers and enquiries at the Polish Legation) that he was in some way connected with the Obelinski family, and was discharged to the care of his sister Helen. John Davies came perilously close to the line by constantly addressing a crowd, but he managed to stay on the right side of it: 'Highly plausible and talks a good deal of nonsense and is distinctly eccentric but not quite certifiable and is distinctly good natured and of a happy disposition and apparently quite harmless'. Though Robert Torrington became violent after being brought in by the police from Villiers Street, attacking an attendant, and had to be put in a padded room, a week later he was 'quite coherent and rational' and was discharged home to his mother 'fully recovered'. An asylum escapee who had applied at the War Office for enlistment only to be exposed by the medical board at Whitehall, Charles Creagh had been brought to Fulham Road by the police. It was doubtless intended that he be should returned to his station as a lunatic, but finding his conduct exemplary Dr Sandiland sent him home to his mother instead.[17]

But others were not so lucky. The type who most assuredly was on a hiding to nothing was the individual who appeared to be trying to get above his station or to stand upon claims to his high-ranking social connections. Thus George Needham was quickly carted off to Hanwell when he started yelling and shouting, thinking that he was a 'brass hat' and calling for his orderly. William McKee also moved his delusions up a gear, still insisting that he was the King, but now promising also to make the medical officer a Prince and the attendant the Master of Horse. When he was admitted, Ernest Turner began calling out 'all right Admiral' to some imaginary person, and sitting up in bed in a listening attitude, but the next day he became very noisy and unmanageable, declaring that he *was* Admiral Turner, frequently making for the door to 'hear the music'. And George Elhams, even after repeated doses of paraldehyde, still stood upon his claim to be the King's nephew, forever pestering the attendants to be allowed to set out for the Palace. As to John Frost, aka Lloyd George, five days later he was still spotting 'affinities' and talking incessantly, and was removed to Long Grove. Though Charles Meggy was discharged home to his wife, six weeks later he was back again, claiming that he had directions from God to go to Marlborough House, and this time he was given a ticket for the asylum. After five days on the ward, George Baker, who had suffered from 'nervous debility' in the army, was still very restless, bragging that he was 'too intelligent' to do any work, that Lloyd George wanted to see him, and that he 'would get satisfaction' at the Cenotaph, all of which – the last threat especially – was quite enough to secure him a ride to Cane Hill Lunatic Asylum.

And William Sinfield, alas, remained in a profound state of melancholy, feeling that he had been exiled from paternal love and support. First relief attendant's report: 'nothing much can be obtained from him, as he has been asleep ever since admission, except waking up for his meals'; 2nd relief attendant's report: 'At tea-time he answered rationally, said he had wandered from home "more than once", and attributed his doing so to shell shock'. The following day, 1st relief attendant: 'strange in manner, appears lost and confused, says the King is his father and that he ought to be at the Palace'; 2nd: 'continues strange, had his head bent on his breast for hours, was unwilling to answer anybody'.[18] From then on there was little change in him, and shortly he was removed to Claybury Asylum.

Chapter 12

DEMOBBED TO THE ASYLUM

LUNATIC CHELSEA PENSIONERS

Right from the outset, the real worry for the Ministry of Pensions was over the public relations dimension of the Service Patient scheme. The very idea of the service mental patient proclaimed an association between the lunatic ex-serviceman and the public sphere; and there was the additional fact of acute public interest in his welfare. The uncertainties over how to deal with this dimension are evident in the debates about how the Service Patient should be dressed. Originally the Board of Control proposed to clothe patients who had become insane on account of war service in a military-style uniform, taking their lead from the uniform worn by a small number of regular soldiers from a former campaign who were inmates of Bethnal House, a private asylum in East London. The Board embarked upon an anxious correspondence with Bethnal House, asking whether the uniform was supplied in stock sizes or whether the tailoring firm measured each man, and Private Reynolds, one of the soldier inmates, was brought before the Board to display his uniform.[1]

Envisaged here was a contingent of lunatic Chelsea Pensioners, that elite corps of uniformed elderly and invalid veterans, in which the ex-serviceman would have been made to conform to a certain image that bore the mark of his heroism and his nation's tribute, but equally of the soldier's gratitude for the beneficence that had been shown him. However, it was quickly borne in upon the Board that this rather quaint little script belonged to a former era, experience of the treatment of mental cases in the current war revealing that, for the most part, soldier mental patients did not want to wear military attire, were disinclined to display gratitude for the considerations shown them, and that 'anything that tends prominently to remind a patient of his connection with the Army and with War service may have a deterrent effect on his recovery'.[2]

The Chester County Asylum was by no means alone in warning that a distinctive uniform, far from conferring the honour that was intended, 'would become in the public mind the badge for mad soldiers,' with Claybury believing that it 'would certainly stamp the patient as a "lunatic" soldier or sailor when out walking', thus forcing upon the Board of Control a belated

Queen Elizabeth II gets three cheers from the old soldiers of the Royal Hospital, Chelsea, on the occasion of her Golden Jubilee. The Chelsea Pensioners had long been reliable loyal subjects, but the Ministry of Pensions knew that it could never count on the Service Patients to cheer lustily for the reigning monarch.

recognition of the treacherous shoals into which they were sailing in fostering an association between the soldier and the madman.[3] The impersonation of Napoleon or of General So-and-So had, of course, long been part of the dramatic stock-in-trade of the madhouse, but there is nothing about soldiery or the military life as such that is put in question here, for these routines are part and parcel of the repertoire of the madman himself who in the next hour or day may elect to become someone else. For soldier lunatics to have worn officially sanctioned military-style uniforms, however, it is soldiery itself that would have been put in question, or forced to bear a face that undermined the confidence the public were supposed to have in it, as though it had ventured into the darkness and returned no longer quite itself.

Wounds have, of course, always been accepted as an inevitable by-product of war, sometimes even as tokens of heroism. However, even though shell shock may have been assimilated into this schema to some degree as a wound or trauma that was produced by extreme circumstances, it is doubtful how far shell shock was ever envisaged as a badge of honour. It has tended to figure more in ironic portrayals of heroic remembrance, precisely by insisting on the contrast between the traditional representation of the soldier and the reality that was delivered by the current war. The Service Patients could not readily be turned into ceremonial objects before the public gaze like the Chelsea Pensioners. In the decades after Waterloo, for example, the Chelsea Pensioner had lived a largely ceremonial existence, and people of rank would visit the Royal Chelsea Hospital to see the pensioners at work and at prayer.[4] However, the Chelsea Pensioners were a carefully selected group of loyal veterans; the Service Patients, by contrast, were a highly heterogeneous group, many of whom had a reputation for flouting and parodying military discipline, being known to salute repeatedly in an exaggerated and foolish fashion. The Ministry was therefore fearful of the public relations disaster that might ensue if the Service Patients were to form part of the community of remembrance at the Cenotaph.

THE MISSING DEMOB SUIT

Instead of the proposed uniform, it was decided, instead, that the Service Patients should be clothed in lounge suits, the Ministry providing a special allowance for this purpose. This was, however, merely the prelude to repeated disputes over responsibility for the Service Patient's clothes. After John Peters was discharged as a Service Patient from the Lancaster Asylum at the end of 1918, he wrote to the Clerk of the Asylum to point out that it was the 'usual method' when a soldier was discharged from the army to be fitted up with a pair of boots, a pair of drawers, a waistcoat, two flannel shirts and two pairs of socks, with the addition of an overcoat if it was winter, but that in his case he had been sent out without the drawers. Peters was obviously quite angry about the matter, requesting that the official let him know as soon as possible 'so that in case you won't provide the above I shall know exactly what to do, I am only asking for what I am entitled to'. The medical superintendent at Lancaster Asylum stood by his former patient, pressing the Ministry of Pensions to fund the cost of a full kit of clothing such as soldiers were provided with on leaving the army. The Ministry attempted to pass the buck to the War Office, who answered that Mr John Peters, late No. 2879, Private, Lancashire Fusiliers, was not entitled to any further issue of clothing from army stores, since on transfer from a military hospital in Brighton to the Lancaster County Asylum he had been in possession of: 1 pair boots, 2 flannel shirts, 2 pair socks, 2 pair drawers, 1 pair braces, 1 small kit complete (brushes etc), and 1 waistcoat.

So he may have been, but the medical superintendent had a different slant on the fortunes of John Peters's kit, for to his certain knowledge Peters was admitted to the asylum not from a military hospital but from the Salford Union on 24 March 1916. Of course, the War Office was bound to report that the ex-soldier was transferred directly to the asylum, bypassing the Poor

Law authorities, because that is what was supposed to have happened. But it very evidently did not, and there were clearly plenty of opportunities along the way for a pair of drawers to go missing. With so many agencies involved with an 'interest' in John Peters's kit, and in being more or less economical with the truth about it, bickering with each other, and producing competing fictions about how he was being cared for, it is not difficult to understand why he should have felt angry and without redress, for after all this offical to-ing and fro-ing John Peters was still without his drawers.[5]

By no means was the Service Patient invariably issued with a demob suit on his discharge from the army to assist him on his passage into 'civvy street', for not infrequently the soldier patient was admitted to the asylum in khaki, which was then removed and returned to his unit by the escort, and if the asylum gave him one of the custom-made suits for Service Patients it generally tried to maintain on his discharge that it was their property. In any case, exclaimed one asylum superintendent, what need did Service Patients have of a demob suit, since most of them were chronic incurables? It was surely pointless to mothball the Service Patient's private identity indefinitely on the off-chance that he might one day want to bring it out of wraps and go for a walk in it. Instead of hanging his demob suit in the cupboard, why not allow the Service Patient to wear it in the asylum, with the onus on the asylum authorities to provide a replacement in the unlikely event that the patient recovered? This proposal endeared itself to the Board of Control for, even though the Ministry was already paying a grant to asylums for the purchase of special clothing for Service Patients, here was a fine way of economizing that would enable them to divert those funds to other purposes. And thus was 'civvy street' deflected into the asylum corridor.

The ambiguities in this arrangement lent it wonderfully to abuse at the expense of the patient, who regularly found himself in a tug-of-war, one agency vying with another in claims over his clothes, and forever in search of his missing demob suit. If he was not a soldier anymore, he could scarcely be considered a citizen. All this acting out over the Service Patient's clothes was hugely expressive of how the authorities actually felt about him, proclaiming him an honoured citizen in one breath, but then behind the scenes behaving as though they owned him and had a claim over his body, manipulating and stripping him as though he had no person which he could call his own, and was now a 'thing' to be played with, infantilized, moralized, and then discarded at will.

A ONE-COACH FUNERAL FOR THE SERVICE PATIENT
Instructions were issued by the Ministry of Pensions in August 1918 for the burial arrangements of Service Patients dying in asylums whose bodies were

not removed by their families for interment. The arrangements should be special but not elaborate; a contract should be made with a local undertaker to supply coffin, shroud, hearse and bearers, and to conduct the funeral; burial should take place not in the asylum cemetery but in the local churchyard or cemetery, and not in ground which may have been set apart for the burial of pauper lunatics from the asylum.[6] Inevitably the Ministry stinted over charges, and official parsimony over funeral expenses was a regular source of vexation, not merely for asylum administrators but also for those families of Service Patients which made their own arrangements and sought reimbursement from the Ministry.

Service Patients were also protected from the depradations of the Anatomy Acts. In the early 1920s, when there was a scarcity of bodies for the anatomy departments of medical schools, sinister-looking officials from the Ministry of Health began to descend on asylums in search of unclaimed bodies. By this time, however, even asylum superintendents were starting to recoil at the indignities inflicted on their friendless pauper patients, remarking that bodies unclaimed at death were on occasions claimed months or even years after, and that 'patients without friends would get to know how they were to be disposed of, and some might regard it with great horror'.[7]

A circular announced that, should the relatives wish to make private arrangements, a grant of £7.10.0. might be reclaimed from the Ministry, though for all funerals of Service Patients 'it should be noted that only one mourning coach may be provided, and this *only where necessary and usual*'.[8] Curiously, the Ministry failed to provide any guidance on how the *necessity* of mourning any particular death was to be calibrated. A council labourer from Exeter with a wife and five children, another son having died of consumption, John R was said by his wife to have been 'cheerful and good in every way' when in health. A former corporal in the South Staffs Regiment who had joined the army in 1914 and served at Madras, Secunderabad and Bombay, he was admitted to Digby Mental Hospital (the former City of Exeter Asylum) in the spring of 1922 from the workhouse infirmary, where he was diagnosed as suffering from GPI ('cause: syphilis; contributory: war stress, malaria'). After a painful and protracted decline, much of the time so restless that he was only safe in the padded room, he finally died in January 1924.

His widow requested a private funeral, the body to be brought home from the asylum, with two carriages for mourners, in breach of Ministry guidelines. Mr Bidgood, the undertaker, took the unusual step of attaching a note to his invoice for £10, 'to be a help to the family as this has been a very distressing case', explaining that 'owing to condition of Body' the polished elm coffin, lined with white swansdown, sidesheets, wadding and pillows, had been 'made

4 inches deeper than usual'. To no avail, alas, for no amount of protestation about the manner or circumstances of his dying was able to persuade the Ministry of Pensions that a service lunatic merited more than a one-coach funeral.[9]

'WE LIVE LIKE LITTLE PIGS ABOUT THIRTY IN A LARGE ROOM'

The Service Patients had all become denizens of asylumdom, distributed in 90-odd county and borough asylums right across the land [for the list see Appendix I].[10] Here are two examples that give an insight into what it meant to be an asylum inmate. A twenty-six year old porter and ex-soldier, Harry S attempted suicide after landing himself in trouble for stealing a watch to impress a girl whom he hoped to marry, and ended up in the City of Exeter Asylum. Shortly after Christmas in 1921, he wrote to his married sister in London to try to explain his situation to his family. It is, perhaps, fitting to reflect on the irony that the reason why we are able to read it is that it was never posted – intercepted by the hospital censor, it slumbered in a pristine condition in its envelope for the rest of the century, not, we may intuit, because it was too 'mad', but rather because it was altogether too convincing. In the light of the almost insuperable difficulty of negotiating a credible identity from a base as a certified mental patient in a lunatic asylum, Harry gives it his best shot. Since Alice and her family were deprived of the opportunity to 'understand a bit of it', it perhaps falls to the historian to try and make up for lost time:

Dear Alice and all,
Just a few lines to you, to let you know, you will surprised of the new address. Well I got so bad at Epsom, with my ways, and fits, they transferred me to the above address but I am getting on alright now or rather improving a bit. I got transferred about 2nd of November but I suppose I will be here for a long period, but never mind, I will have to put up with it, as the saying is. I hope that all at home is getting on A.1. I hope that Flo is still at her job and doing well, i suppose that she will soon be engaged, as she heard from her soldier boy or has she got another boy, but I wish her the best of luck. How is george and wife and baby is getting on as I hope he wont be like me end his days in an Asylum like me and that it is no benefit in being in a place like I am in. I am very sorry I have not written to you before this, as I have been very bad, being in a padded room, and only having bread & milk for meals and nearly starved. I suppose there is not much work in London, just I hope that George is still at work. I hope that you will write to me knowing that

you have an insane boy amongst the family owing to the dam war. I give my best love to all and I hope they enjoyed the Xmas alright. While I was at Epsom I got engaged to a girl down in Devon when I was on leave, but I suppose that has put the cap on it for I have not heard of her since I have been here. Sory I cant say no more, so must close, giving my best wishes to Liz, & George, and I hope they are alright and keeping well. Hoping to hear from you soon, so Goodbye from your loving Brother, Harry. Sorry I cant write any better as my nerves are very bad but I am doing my best so that you can understand a bit of it. x x x x. [sic][12]

Occasionally we catch a glimpse of the anguish and loneliness of an ex-serviceman abandoned as a 'hopeless case' in a mental institution. An errand boy before the war, and now just twenty-one years old, Colin T had been admitted to the City of Exeter Asylum by the police after smashing the plate glass at Wheaton's shop, and given a diagnosis of dementia praecox. 'Yes I did do it', he confessed to the officer, 'I'll tell Wheatons about staying at home whilst I was out in the trenches'. 'He is emotional & weeps easily', we learn, and spends much of the day writing 'most foolish letters' in which 'he claims kindred with titled people and fails to realise his position', most recently stating that Dr Snodgrass, the city treasurer, was his uncle. And at night he is often noisy in his sleep, 'shouting words of command & drill'. What are these 'most foolish letters' for which the medical superintendent repeatedly berates him? 'Dear Grandma', he writes in a note addressed to Her Ladyship at the Bishop's Palace:

Should drop you a line to kindly inform you that am not improveing my health seem to remain the same as what enter this Hospital seem to make miserable with the trains passing to and fro cant enjoy myself much only a game of billiards evenings we live like little pigs about thirty in a large room. I never expect to get well taking in one another breath. Been here nearly two years three months and seen the Committee nine times. . . . Why they should seem so hard on me done no harm whatever to them seem such a terrible thing. Good have such splendid weather now summer coming on like plenty of sea-side. Would you kindly oblige for applying for me [sic].

This is not entirely 'foolish' surely, and yields a poignant insight of a kind into Colin's desperate situation and his invention of imaginary connections to help him reach across the chasm that separates him from ordinary life. Consider also this to another correspondent, where he conveys the lack of proper medical care, his blighted hopes and deteriorating health, and his frustrated attempts to make himself understood before the asylum committee:

> Just a few lines to kindly oblige by getting me out of this Asylum has one of the patients is worst than a Sergt Major bullying any one it enough to brake my heart. Have been before the committee eight times. Having been on Active Service four years and four months should like to know if I am entitle to liberty. . . . Could you kindly get me out as soon possible my stumps of teeth are rotten and I am afraid am septic poisoning slightly in the stomach, yours truly, an Exonian, CT[12]

RESPITE AT THE ASYLUM

Contrary to official assurances that the asylum was the exclusive redoubt of the incurable, and that the ex-serviceman who was in the least responsive to treatment was in no danger of being sent to such a place, it was by no means the case that if the ex-serviceman did take the road to asylum, it was necessarily on a one-way ticket. After all, even government figures showed that of the total number of ex-servicemen who had 'passed the border' into the asylums, exactly a third had been discharged.[13] The indications were that the asylum did after all perform some other functions, or, just as likely, that some of those who had been branded as hopeless cases with such complacency turned out to have something going for them after all. The smaller rural asylums were, perhaps, more suited than others to providing a respite function, as with St Audry's, the Suffolk County Asylum, whose customer-base of agricultural and provincial town trades was amply displayed in the regular occupations of the inmates – horse-hair worker, silk weaver, carter, hay dealer, wheelwright, draper's assistant, grocer's assistant, white smith, farm bailiff, block and spar maker, gardener, and gamekeeper, along with innumerable labourers and farm workers. And it is from such backgrounds that a number of ex-servicemen were admitted, during and after the war, who had returned from their service changed men, and become impossible to manage in the home.

George C, a grocer's assistant from Sudbury, was depressed and entirely wanting in initiative, and was said by his father to resent advice and show a vicious manner when spoken to; Arthur T, a gardener, had been on active service for three and a half years and had suffered from shell shock, and now sat about idle and listless most of the day; Bertie W, a shoemaker, had also seen service abroad and now had the War and the Kaiser on his mind, and recently he had turned the kitchen table on his mother and threatened to 'do for her'; Albert B, who had joined the army in October 1916 after three rejections, was admitted in June 1917 suffering from melancholia, silent and self-absorbed, refusing food, iterating 'I am messed up altogether'; George B, a deckhand in the RNR and a fisherman before the war, was admitted in April 1918 suffering from melancholia, labouring under the delusion that people on board ship looked at him as if he were to blame if anything went wrong; and William L, a former farm labourer who had contracted malaria and been struck on the head by a mule while on service abroad, harboured persecutory ideas, keeping knives in bed with him, according to his wife.

Within four months George C was more cheerful and sociable, reading newspapers and working on the farm; Arthur had asked 'if he may go out to work until he is thought fit to be sent home' and was put to work in the garden; though still 'done for' and 'messed up', Albert B had become less depressed, doing small jobs about the ward, and three months later announced one day that he too would like to work in the garden; Bertie was more cheerful and had started work in the bootmaker's shop; a month after he was admitted, George B was in better spirits, playing games and reading, eager for outdoor employment, and telling the doctor that he had been subjected to great nervous stress whilst on patrol at sea night and day two months ago, but that the rest since admission had done him good; though he was still reticent and evasive, persecuted by some invisible agency, William L managed to continue working on the asylum farm. For most of these men, the asylum provided the structure and companionship that enabled them to pick up the threads of civilian life in just a few months, and even though William L never properly emerged from his crisis, he managed to retain a foothold in ordinary existence. Significantly, none of these individuals appear to have been spurned, or neglected, by their families and friends, and several of them were visited regularly, Arthur by his brother-in-law and two sisters, Bertie by his sister and mother, William L receiving a whole stream of visitors during the two years or so that he was an inmate: his father, step-father, wife, mother, daughter who came down from Norfolk, sister and several friends.[14]

JEWISH SOLDIER LUNATICS

In the asylums that served the urban heartlands especially, we not infrequently come across members of ethnic minorities, such as the Jewish community, who had served the Empire in the Great War. Interestingly, there are a number of individuals here who, even though they appear to be heading for chronic destinies in a lunatic asylum, succeed in turning themselves round, drawing on the inside track of their own affiliations or their spiritual resources, to the amazement of their medical keepers. Morris D, a fish salesman who had served in Egypt, was admitted to Colney Hatch with a diagnosis of dementia praecox, giving 'Hebrew' as his religion, and music halls and watching boxing as his recreations. A fortnight previously he had started to talk foolishly, becoming rough, throwing the bedclothes away, putting his food under the table, shaking his head and praying a great deal more than normal, and now 'he is restless and noisy, shouts to imaginary people, cries for no apparent cause and prays', and is also 'spiteful towards the attendants'. Three months later, however, he was 'quite well', answering questions 'smartly and clearly', and explained 'his silence one month ago as being due to feeling out of sorts as a result of constipation'.[15]

Abraham B, a former cloth-cutter who had served in the Royal Fusiliers, had been in Claybury for a month before his transfer to Colney Hatch in October 1919 bearing a report which said that he was 'dull morose and depressed' and 'upset by a feeling of inefficiency as he states he will not be able to follow his previous occupation in civil life & would rather go back to his Battalion. He has no desire for exercise or recreation. Says he feels rotten inside and all over him. . . . He looks always sad and dejected and takes no interest in life'. At Colney Hatch, having admitted that he had 'recently heard the voices of nurses and of patients at Netley Hospital and other institutions', he was given a diagnosis of dementia praecox, and said to be 'dull, slow and weakminded . . . very tardy in his reaction to questions'. A month later, however, there was 'slight improvement' and he was 'more civil, more amenable to discipline', and by the following spring he had 'made considerable progress', taking interest in 'the games and amusements of the ward' and 'working well in the tailor's shop', and in July 1920 he was discharged from trial as recovered.[16]

Another Jewish patient, Abraham F, a cabinet-maker and ex-soldier, presented a 'miserable and dejected appearance' when he was admitted in July 1920, lying 'curled up in bed all day, taking no notice or interest in anything', and refusing to speak – but four months later he was working well, more sociable and much less depressed.[17] Nathan L, a tailor and ex-soldier who had already had a spell as a Service Patient at the end of the war, was apprehended by PC Beales after behaving strangely at Notting Hill Gate, holding up the traffic, only partially dressed, and unable to give a coherent account of himself. After treatment in a padded room, he still made 'many foolish statements such as that there is nothing absurd in wandering about the streets half-naked', that he has been 'covered with lice since the year 1917', and that he was 'anxious that the world should acknowledge his divinity'. However, though the authorities considered that he had 'no mental insight', he soon became 'cheerful and amenable', making known his desire to resume his occupation as a tailor, and after an 18-month stay he was discharged.[18]

There are, however, also strong indications, as the records of Napsbury War Hospital also hinted, that under some circumstances members of ethnic minorities received a very raw deal indeed at the hands of both the military and civil medical authorities.[19] Take the case of Samuel L, for example. A twenty-eight year old Jewish cap-maker, born and educated in Russia, now living in Whitechapel but speaking no English, Samuel had been conscripted into the 366th Reserve Employment Company, and not long into his service in March 1918 had been imprisoned for a day for some relatively minor breach of the regulations. Though normally of a quiet and restrained temperament, Samuel's anxiety about joining the Army was now compounded by a situation in which he did not understand what was happening or what was expected of him. As a result, intensely frustrated by his inability to communicate his needs and concerns to those in charge, he became violent and hysterical for four hours, so the record relates, culminating in his admission to the Maudsley Hospital. Far from alleviating the situation, however, the transfer served only to escalate the crisis, for there was no interpreter available and before very long Samuel was being handed his credentials as a hopeless case ('refuses to speak', 'disorientated', 'stupid looking') in preparation for his removal to Colney Hatch Asylum. Here he languished for two years under much the same cloud of suspicion and reproach before his family succeeded in negotiating his discharge.[20] Sporadic openings for respite there assuredly were, but there are plentiful examples that the asylum system was still famously capable of living up to its reputation as a manufactory of hopeless cases.

Coda

A DISAPPOINTED HOMECOMING

'AN IDEALISM THAT COULD NOT BE CONTENT WITH REALITIES'

'Shall I.B.G. always be defective nerves and nothing else?', the poet and musician Ivor Gurney questioned in March 1918.[1] He did not contest his neurasthenia, which had long been a playful, anxious and not infrequently ironic accompanist in his repertoire of self-descriptions, but he was determined to make it work for him, to put whatever spin on it he felt appropriate, and to assert a presence in poetry and song that was palpably something else, and never just the outcrop of a diagnosis or a bag of nerves. Consider, for example, the shifting semantics of 'neurasthenia' in his letters written during his war service; they display a conflict in Gurney himself between the idea of neurasthenia as a weakness for which the rigours and discipline of army service may provide the cure ('we should all lapse into neurasthenia were we not driven'), and as a creative capability that he wants to embrace.[2] Determined to overcome his 'weakness', he has learned the 'knack of kicking myself into doing things' and acquired a 'name for being extremely cool under shell-fire', discovering that ironically 'neurasthenia leads one to a strange praise', as he puts it in a typically Gurneyesque turn of phrase.[3]

At the same time, the Army's use of language jars on his sensibility and the military life exacts its toll ('the callousness to certain things such a life must develop'), inducing a tension with another distinct sense of neurasthenia as the delicate plant of the creative capability that he wishes to foster, a sensitivity in which doubt and creativity are intertwined and artistic potential may wither at the vine ('either I am a great musician or a chronic neurasthenic').[4] He hopes that army life may strengthen him, make him less prone to chronic neurasthenia, but there is a risk that in doing so it may stifle or snuff out his creative capability: 'to be neurasthenic – to wonder what my capabilities are . . . to suffer all this in the thought-vacuum in which the Army lives, moves and has its being, is a hard thing.'[5] Neurasthenia in this connection is also a synonym for Gurney's irredeemable and incurable civilianness, which no amount of military drilling can extinguish, a sense of value that he holds on to through thick and thin. 'I'm not a soldier', he tells the sergeant major, 'I'm a *dirty civilian*'.[6]

His ambivalence is accentuated after he is sent home to hospital in England, and reaches a point where he starts to rebel against the military 'cure' for neurasthenia. Is his current weakness something that he should overcome to get him back to the Army to fight the good fight; or is the Army a false value that is taking him away from where his neurasthenia should be leading him? Though at one instant he declares that the state of his mind 'is a sickness caused by real circumstances now, not by imaginary', there is an uncertainty in him as to whether this is a positive development. The 'real' may be a false god (a product of the failure of someone else's imagination), whereas 'imagining' may produce a visionary creativity.[7] In an elegiac reflection on his friend Will Harvey, who at the time was 'missing on patrol, presumed killed', Gurney observes that he was 'full of unsatisfied longings – a doctor would have called it neurasthenia, but that term covers many things, and in him it meant partly an idealism that could not be contented with realities'.[8] No more was Gurney himself contented with realities, and he extols just this sense of neurasthenia at the decisive moment (or 'break') when he hears Beethoven talking to him: 'What would the doctors say to *that*? A Ticket certainly, for insanity. No, it is the beginning of a new life, a new vision'.[9]

'TO BE RELEASED TO THE CHANCES OF COMMON LIFE'
The 'new life' largely failed to materialize, however, and Gurney was far from enchanted by the post-war scene. When he again seemed to be heading for the brink in September 1922, his brother Ronald bundled him off to Barnwood House, a classy private asylum on the outskirts of Gloucester, in a flurry of justices and certificates, explaining to him that while he was not yet insane he soon would have been. Although he appreciated the kindness of the attendants, many of whom were ex-service, Gurney did not take to Barnwood at all, chafing at the confines of what he quickly saw was a regular private madhouse. 'I am treated as a lunatic, led about by an attendant . . . walk in a small compound', he lamented, 'anything rather than to remain here'.[10] And then came this in a letter to his confidante Marion Scott:

Yesterday Ronald came but he doubted that the talk of my pain was more than electrical delusion. . . . After the War, what hopes there were! To earn a living and write praise of England! Surely the ordinary desirings of a mind seeking fulfilment, after the manner of seekers after Truth, lovers of mankind and the pleasures and joys God-sent. . . . These words mean what they say. To have mercy, to release me from here, for the pain of Barnwood House is great. St Albans was nothing to it. . . . A soldier and an artist asks to be released to the chances of common life – to work or to be allowed to die.

... The negation of God is here. ... I have written to Knapsbury ... I am up, but not moving about. Sitting still, and being agitated. Have mercy and rescue I pray.[11]

To be released 'to the chances of common life' – Gurney's plea echoes exactly those of the advocates of ex-servicemen in the aftermath of the war. But, of course, in actuality there was an asymmetry between the investment in the repair of battle-scarred soldiers on the front line, and the faint-hearted gestures towards resettlement on the home front, and Gurney is a witness to the frailty of those hopes.[12] Gurney epitomized the hope for an England in which, regardless of his 'neurasthenia', or perhaps even especially because of it, he could be a vital contributor to the life of the community. With his bundle of hopes, Gurney was himself doing battle with conventional pieties of psychological weakness as a defect to be eradicated or held up to ridicule, and instead holding up his personal vulnerability as a rallying point for an alternative stance on life, a window through which others could climb. Like Jay Gatsby of West Egg, Long Island, Ivor Gurney possessed an 'extraordinary gift for hope, a romantic readiness', a capacity for wonder and the 'colossal vitality' of an illusion that went 'beyond everything'.[13] Writing from Flanders some years earlier, very likely in the knowledge of the Russian Revolution, he had taunted the 'Prussians of England':

Our silly dreams of peace you put aside
And Brotherhood of man, for you will see
An armed Mistress, braggart of the tide
Her children slaves, under your mastery.
We'll have a word there too, and forge a knife,
Will cut the cancer threatens England's life.[14]

From the summer of 1918 he cherished a fond memory of Napsbury War Hospital, near St Albans, exactly for the spirit of hope it exemplified, its openness and receptivity to the common life, working in the fields or looking out on 'a glorious great sky ... with blue and white, steelgrey and black vivid upon it, and any amount of green to show it off', and now in desperation he wrote to Knapsbury, as Napsbury had become in his imagination.[15] But of course the Knapsbury (or Knapsfield, as he also called it) of his remembrance, part of the wartime K family, along with khaki and knapsack and Knutsford, where the Lunacy Acts were suspended, and he had been able to work in the fields just like the rest of outdoor people, was no more: there was just plain old Napsbury, a regular asylum along with all the others. The negation of

God was the extinction of hope, the hope that was always on the lookout for connections and ligatures, the hope that there could be another mode of meaning behind the obvious, and that others might recognize his pain as more than 'electrical delusion'. It is, instead, the world drained of meaning, material without being real, Napsbury in place of Knapsbury, dominated by types like his brother Ronald and his mother who, believing that there was something the matter with him, deprived his talk of its capacity to signify and connect, with the additional irony that he was a captive now in a bespoke private asylum, so remote from the 'chances of common life'.

The flip side of his enormous capacity for hope was an equally capacious sense of disappoinment and betrayal. 'After-War so surely hurt', he was to write.[16] Or this:

One asked little, but how has the time betrayed
Us, who looked trusting to years that war's pain had paid
The all night watching, fear endured, pain denied.[17]

In 'Strange Hells', he evoked the 'strange Hells within the minds war made':

Where are They now on State-doles, or showing shop-patterns
Or walking town to town sore in borrowed tatterns
Or begged. Some civic routine one never learns.
The heart burns – but has to keep out of face how heart burns.[18]

His editors and biographers have drawn attention to his strong conviction that he deserved to be rewarded for the sacrifices he had made, indeed that he was owed something for his war service. Writes George Walter: 'Being Gurney, this is not a simple matter of material recompense for his wartime military service; rather it is part of that elaborate network of beliefs clustered around ideas of beauty, creativity, suffering and recognition which permeate so much of his later work'.[19] The title of his poem 'Strange Service' is a metaphor for the disturbing experience of service in the Great War, the disturbance, in part, to customary meanings or associations of 'service'. The serviceman has been asked to do 'dreadful service', and in the official designation of psychiatric war casualties as 'Service Patients' we can surely hear an ironic echo of 'strange service'.[20]

A profound source of grievance was his belief that his right to a full pension for his 'strange service' had been rebuffed. According to one of his biographers, Gurney was not granted a full pension in October 1918 because his condition was considered to be 'aggravated but not caused by' the war. Even if Gurney himself believed this, as he may well have done, it is a misconception, arising from a misunderstanding of how the war disability pension system worked.[21] Since 1917, an 'aggravated condition' was, as far as the scale of the award was concerned, on a level footing with a condition directly caused by the war, for what counted in determining the award was the level or degree of disability. Gurney was awarded only 12/- a week, or a 30% disability pension, not because there was a question about his entitlement, or because the shadow of a hereditary condition had got between him and his just deserts, but simply because at that time he seemed to some extent to be a going concern to the doctors who examined him, and not disabled enough to justify a larger or full award.[22] The niceties of these bureaucratic calibrations could only have irritated Gurney, a displacement of his conviction that it was simply the fact of his service, without any scruple, that ought to weigh with the authorities. Indeed, in the narrative of post-war experience that he later wrote in the asylum, he evidently found the horse-trading with the pension authorities over his psychiatric credentials especially demeaning:

Thanked my aunt for her kindness sincerely every night – worked as hard as possible under circumstances. It was a life to admire. Before God a good one. I needed money to support me in taking a post. Why betrayed is not known. I had made application for full pension of 25/- instead of 12/- because I wished to write with it – believing my work in music and verse to be good. It had been promised for *this* reason; but I gave in application the reason 'after-shell-shock', which was false, but it seemed best to believe that the pension was to be given, and the reason not then important. But considering my courage and hard work it was dreadful to be so broken. The torments were bad; the courage deserved a reward.[23]

It had been 'promised' because Gurney believed it was his due or just reward in the context of the pledges that had been made to ex-servicemen in the immediate aftermath of the war. Principled character that he was, *that* was the reason he clung to. From such a singular standpoint any other reason that might be admitted was necessarily false, regardless of any legitimacy it might possess in its own right. For Ivor Gurney, to have to demonstrate his entitlement, and invoke 'after-shell-shock', smacked too much of special pleading and an unbecoming grovelling before the authorities.

'. . . THE REALLY, REALLY TRULY LINE'
Composed in the City of London Mental Hospital at Dartford, *First Time In* is an extraordinary poem, based on Gurney's experience with the 2/5th

Gloucesters who first went into the front-line trenches on 29 May 1916, about the initiation of a group of young soldiers into life as it is lived in the line. In itself it is an accomplished evocation of the experience of a serviceman on the Western Front, but it takes on a special resonance in the light of our knowledge of the circumstances of its creation. It becomes a figure also for our own unnerving initiation into the line where Gurney is stationed at present, listening to his recollection of his war experiences, and being instructed on life in the combat zone, from a position in a lunatic asylum:

We entered, took stranger-view
Of life as lived in the Line, the Line of war and Daily
Papers, dispatches, brave-soldier talks, the really, really
Truly Line; and these the heroes of story.

Never were quieter folk in teaparty history.
Never in "Cranford", Trollope even. And as it were, home
Closed around us. They told us lore, how and when did come
Minnie-werfers and grenades from over there east;
The pleasant and unpleasant habits of the beast
That crafted and tore Europe. What Line mending was
When guns centred and dugouts rocked in a haze
And hearing was – (wires cut) – All necessary
Common sense workmanlike cautions of salutary
Wisdom – the mechanic day-lore of modern war-making,
Calm thought discovered in mind and body-shaking.
The whole craft and business of bad occasion.[24]

Through his clarity and assurance in speaking to us, Gurney forces us to surrender any lingering beliefs we may still hold that there is a hard-and-fast line, or a categorical distinction, to be drawn between the type of people who live in asylums and those who reside on the outside. Instead we come to recognize that in 'the really, really Truly Line' where there is tremendous contention between psychic forces, still the psychotic has not lost his connection with ordinary humanity or his capacity for human contact ('the Line of war and Daily Papers'), and the inmates do not conform to the stereotype of the madhouse or the mad hatter's teaparty ('Never were quieter folk in teaparty history'). If much of the time Gurney's universe was put under electrical control, and he lived in expectation of persecution, with electrical tricks frequently played upon him, the creation of a poem such as this is a demonstration of how he was able to establish a zone of relative tranquillity in himself ('Calm thought discovered in mind and body-shaking'), to exercise a form of self-care, even of 'Line mending', perhaps, after the wires had been cut. He marvels, respectfully and ironically, at 'The whole craft and business of bad occasion', whilst we marvel also at how he goes about the business of crafting his poems, his war experience recollected and distilled, while living in the line of the lunatic asylum, surely a 'bad occasion' par excellence. As he put it himself in a letter from Dartford: 'The pain of a twelve hour day in a ward is great. A twelve hour day and eating too much. . . . Imprisonment would be better, though I have nothing worse than misdemeanours since the war to reproach myself with. . . . A twelve hour day, small exercise and a crowded ward do not make for happiness'.[25]

Part V

HARD TIMES

Watching this man go to the colliery to draw his compensation, I was struck by the profound differences that are still made by status. Here was a man who had been half blinded in one of the most useful of all jobs and was drawing a pension to which he had a perfect right, if anybody has a right to anything. Yet he could not, so to speak, demand this pension – he could not, for instance, draw it when and how he wanted it. He had to go to the colliery once a week at a time named by the company, and when he got there he was kept waiting about for hours in the cold wind. For all I know he was also expected to touch his cap and show gratitude to whomever paid him; at any rate he had to waste an afternoon and spend sixpence in bus fares. It is very different for a member of the bourgeoisie, even such a down-at-heel member as I am. Even when I am on the verge of starvation I have certain rights attaching to my bourgeois status.

George Orwell, *The Road to Wigan Pier* (1937)[1]

'ANY MAN IN ANY STREET'

TOMMY ATKINS HAS MENTAL HEALTH PROBLEMS

In the aftermath of the war the furore over the disposal of ex-servicemen in lunatic asylums showed no signs of abating, continuing well into the 1920s, more intermittently thereafter, finding outlets not only in the national but also in the medical press. The announcement of the Service Patient scheme did little to assuage the public mood, or to persuade the community of serving citizens that they were receiving social justice, for public misgivings were inflamed by reports that the government had been economical with the truth in describing the special arrangements for Service Patients in asylums. The existing lunatic asylums will 'continue to cast a stigma of pauperism', wrote one correspondent shortly after the Service Patient scheme was announced, and 'the nation will not be satisfied until . . . special institutional treatment and care is provided'. 'This will give trouble', interjected the Pensions Secretary wearily in the margin.[1]

Official figures showed that almost 12,000 former servicemen whose disorders were accepted as having either been caused, or aggravated, by service had 'passed the border' and been certified in the asylum system.[2] Following the Armistice there were renewed demands for segregated facilities for ex-servicemen with mental disabilities, among them the extravagant proposal that had been aired previously to establish large houses across the country, capable of accommodating not more than 30 patients, a kind of Knutsford network of therapeutic communities for the masses.[3] A committee of inquiry also reported that 'the number of men in whom neurasthenia in some form has first displayed itself after discharge from the service has proved to be beyond the expectation of the best judges'.[4] The psychiatric aftermath of the Great War was becoming increasingly visible. Plainly, Tommy Atkins had mental health problems. And Tommy Atkins, insisted a contemporary recording his experiences as an orderly in a war hospital, was not a mere type: he is simply 'the man in the street – *any* man in *any* street', or the man on the proverbial Clapham Omnibus.[5]

In Parliament, the flamboyant Captain Charles Loseby, during his brief parliamentary career, was a staunch advocate of ex-servicemen in asylums, repeatedly triggering heated exchanges with Major Tryon, the aptly named Minister of Pensions. The treatment allowance on which many disabled ex-servicemen and their dependants relied, maintained Loseby, was only given on condition that they entered asylums, 'with the result that in many cases they are rendered permanently insane'. And he invited 'my hon and gallant friend' to 'render his practical sympathy to a vigorous movement that is on foot to redeem these unfortunate men from the positive torture of lunatic asylums'. The Minister must realize that 'some of these institutions are places of positive horror, and that in some cases a man would not receive fair play or anything approaching fair play'.[6] A deputation from the National Federation of Discharged & Demobilised Soldiers and Sailors called on the Prime Minister demanding the creation of a country-wide network of special mental institutions for ex-servicemen. Even more moderate voices joined the fray, an editorial in *The Lancet* opining that while 'the removal of all certified ex-service men from public asylums would no doubt entail some expense', nonetheless 'the removal of the stigma of the asylum from sailors and soldiers broken in the war would make an appeal to universal sympathy'.[7]

MAURICE CRAIG HOLDS THE LINE ·

From the outset there had been dissenting voices within the Ministry over the concessions for disability pensions for war psychoses. They surfaced again in the autumn of 1919 when Knowles Stansfield, a medical superintendent of the old school who did not mince his words, and who had let his distaste for the Service Patient scheme be known as soon as it was first broached, wrote a letter to *The Times* alleging that the great majority of ex-servicemen suffering from mental disorders were disturbed before the event. 'The misguided statements of members of the House of Commons and of others in the public Press', he intoned, 'based upon the erroneous assumption that every man who joined the Forces was mentally sound, created an infinite amount of trouble for the Services, and the pension authorities are now reaping the fruits. . . . Of the very large number of soldiers suffering from mental disorder who have come under my personal observation, it was only in a very small percentage that I could satisfy myself that the mental disorder was the outcome of the actual stress of service'.[8]

Plainly, this was the tune that the malcontents had been waiting to hear, for it was quickly reported to the Director General of Medical Services that Dr Stansfield's experience as regards 'the connection between insanity and service is very much that of the medical staff here'. The 'lunacy formula' which had been drawn up in 1917 'at the instance of some of the greatest authorities on lunacy' had from the outset presented difficulties, not least because the

Ministry had been put on the defensive. At this juncture the wise counsel of Maurice Craig was once again sought, and it is remarkable that at this pivotal moment in the aftermath of the war, with the fortunes of the military caste whom Knowles Stansfield represented still at a low ebb, that Craig was resolute in holding the line on the liberal dispensations that had emerged from the wartime consensus, robustly confident that he had the majority of public and medical opinion behind him. Eager for an opportunity to buck the trend, Pensions officials had requested permission to circulate the letter to medical boards, but Craig considered that this would be most unwise. For his authority he reached back to the conference of July 1917, which 'was very emphatic in its view that any mental disorder arising in a person engaged in miltary service must be regarded as certainly aggravated by, if not attributable to, that service'. Dr Stansfield's conclusions, he averred, 'certainly would not be generally accepted by the majority of either medical or lay persons'.[9]

PUTTING TOMMY ATKINS IN HIS PLACE

However, the authorities balked at all the proposals for segregated facilities, and practicability was by no means the only consideration, for at issue also was the visibility of Tommy Atkins's mental health profile. Assigned to special units, the mad soldiers could have become inhabitants of a kind of modern Bedlam for, as Roy Porter has described, in the early modern period Bethlem Hospital became the model of madness itself, and as 'Bedlam' it came to represent lunacy to the nation. Significantly, Bedlam had been thrown into the limelight largely because of its public role in harbouring all sorts of political madmen, notably patients committed by the War Office; understandably, the establishment was rather disinclined to recreate this spectacle in early twentieth-century Britain.[10] Rattled by the drubbing that cherished military values were receiving at the hands of progressive mental experts, there were many who believed that the authorities had already made far too many concessions to civilian sensibilities. By 1920 the military establishment was anxious to distance itself from the psychiatric spillage of the war, to minimize its cultural significance, and to reinstate in the public mind a more traditional moral vision. It was time to put Tommy Atkins in his place, and for the War Office to represent shell shock to the nation.

It is against this background that we need to understand the report produced in 1922 by the War Office Commission of Enquiry into 'Shell-Shock', under the chairmanship of Lord Southborough, which has come to assume almost an iconic status in the literature; indeed, much of the historiography of shell shock continues to pivot around it.[11] Ironically, that reputation perhaps goes to show just how well it managed to discharge its mission, for it is an extraordinarily ambiguous cultural document which both exemplifies the power of shell shock as a cultural metaphor, and tries to play down its significance and resonance. In a speech in April 1920, Lord Southborough had posed the kind of questions about ex-servicemen whose mental health had been damaged by the war that any intelligent and compassionate layman might have posed: 'Are there not now a very large number of men doing nothing but drawing their pensions, whose health and condition might be greatly improved by an organization designed to find them a little work as a beginning?'. And as to a number of 'sad cases of a severe, mental type where hope of the restoration of the mind has been practically abandoned', he wonders whether they are 'to be permanently kept in homes' and if the treatment there is of 'the most suitable kind'.[12]

This was just the kind of probing of the mental health culture that had been advocated by Elliot Smith and Tom Pear as long ago as 1916, but the following month Lord Southborough was invited by the War Office to chair the committee that was intended to 'investigate the whole question of shell shock', and the resulting report epitomizes a much narrower perspective on the mental health terrain than the questions he had started out with. Indeed, in all important respects it tries to restore an older moral vision, in which there are sharp distinctions between the neuroses and insanity, a nervous breakdown is viewed as a disgrace, and the asylum is made the locus of hopeless cases and of a condemnatory attitude towards mental disorder. 'The man who has been in any asylum', averred an eminent alienist before the committee, 'is a damaged article'.[13] Some of those very same progressive mental experts who had contributed to the wartime liberal reforms, notably Maurice Craig, also took part in the work of the committee, alongside more traditional figures. There is nothing peculiar about that, for these were fairly typical representatives of the early twentieth-century liberal elite, pulled in two directions simultaneously, towards a more pluralist society on the one hand, tolerant of individual differences, but equally, like all the middle classes, fearful of socialism, and hence supportive of the military establishment.

Though there have been some excellent discussions of the report, historians have failed to contextualize it adequately. To put it rather starkly, one of its main objectives is to rein in, and marginalize, the mental health profile of the ordinary soldier, in particular the concessions to public feeling that had been made through the creation of the Service Patient scheme and the legitimation of the status of Imperial War Disability Pensioner for war psychotics. And it achieves this in the time-honoured English fashion by pretending that the group that is to be isolated does not exist. Though ex-servicemen in asylums are mentioned in passing, there is no mention here of the Service

Patient scheme, or of the basis on which the Ministry of Pensions accepted liability for several thousand cases. Nor, just as remarkably, is there any reference to the medical authority that underpinned these decisions, not least because it is impossible to tell this story, to provide the narrative for it, without making admissions that undermine the traditional position. However, in a series of articles which he wrote for *The Times*, Lord Southborough is rather more revealing about the discussions that went on in committee. He describes how the shell shock statistics were augmented by: 'The large number of cases . . . of mental disorder. . . . These numerous cases were classified under "shell-shock" – an imperfect diagnosis. Dismissing these cases as of definite origin, the Committee found themselves confronted with. . . .', and he then moves on to other matters.[14]

'Dismissing these cases as of *definite* origin . . .'. Of course, that was the exact reverse of what the 'mental experts', some of the 'greatest authorities on lunacy', had concluded only a few years earlier, and of what Maurice Craig, appealing to the majority of medical opinion, had proclaimed in his riposte to Knowles Stansfield as recently as 1919. Through the vehicle of the Southborough Committee, the military establishment was getting its own back on the civilian lobbies to which it had been forced to make a long string of concessions since 1914, and seeking to reoccupy some of the lost ground. Here was an opportunity to undo some of the mischief by which traditional psychiatric lore had been sidelined and once again, as Sir Frederick Mott, himself a member of the Committee, counselled, 'to place each case under its proper caption'.[15]

'At the beginning of the war', wrote the psychiatrist D. K. Henderson in 1918, 'no one had any realisation of what an important problem the care and treatment of our nervous and mental cases was going to be . . . the sooner we, as a nation, come to realise that it is of the utmost importance to tackle this problem of nervous and mental disease occurring in the Army, the better it will be for the Army, for the State, and for our national peace and security'.[16] The visibility of the mentally distraught in the armed services had become an issue for the authorities; partly, obviously enough, for what it reflected of inefficiencies and inadequacies in recruitment procedures, and for the burden and consequent expense it placed on the medical services, but also for the impact it was having upon the public. If the ranks of the mentally distraught continued to swell, confidence in the war effort was likely to be sapped. More worrying still was a tendency for members of the public to over-identify with these casualties and consider them, not as misfits, but as integral members of the community of serving citizens enjoying special rights and considerations. Hence why, in the Report, the 'general sentiment of the public' during the war was much derided, and the use of the term 'shell shock' lambasted as a sentimental flight from unpleasant truths about vice, moral cowardice, and mental inadequacy. The term came as a great relief, averred the Committee, 'to the relatives of a soldier who had broken down mentally, or who by reason of an inherently timorous disposition could not face the military life, or whose natural tendencies had led to his getting into trouble'. Indeed, 'it may be said that to the public mind any condition which arose during the war and which gave rise to the assumption of irresponsibility of conduct by the individual concerned was to be ascribed to "shell-shock"'.[17]

A few witnesses, such as W. H. Rivers, entered a more nuanced understanding of stress and mental trauma, heaping ridicule on an official culture in which the habitual advice to soldiers on 'seeing their friends at their sides with their heads blown off and things of that sort' was to 'put it out of your mind old fellow, and do not think about it . . . imagine that you are in your garden at home'.[18] But as the War Office now represented shell shock to the nation, the lesson of the war was that only the inferior break down. 'The general consensus of opinion', they averred, summoning German medico-military authorities in support of their conclusion, 'was to the effect that with the exception of the temporary recoverable cases of psychoses and epilepsy, the stress and strain of war acted only as an exciting, revealing or exaggerating cause'.[19] Wrote the prominent German psychiatrist Robert Gaupp: 'The psychiatric analysis of the individual cases points to a psychopathic basis in most of the war psycho-neuroses and psychoses'.[20] The only genuine war neuroses or psychoses were those which recovered quickly. Though Stanford Read, the former commander of D Block, wrote sensitively about psychotics in the 1920s, telling of how they were frequently put away unnecessarily, he struck a very servile pose before his former military paymasters, drawling about how ex-servicemen had 'drifted' into asylums after the war.[21] This was arrant nonsense, for while a man might drift into a saloon bar, people did not drift into lunatic asylums – they were put there against their will.

The old dichotomies were reinstated, among them a regression to a two-class model in which the citizen soldier is displaced by the neurasthenic officer, and other rankers with mental health problems are pictured as belonging to the classic residuum: putting Tommy Atkins in his place meant returning him to the back streets – to the East End, as it were, in the traditional urban demonology, rather than the up-and-coming areas of Lavender Hill, Battersea, or Wandsworth. The Report delivers in slightly more veiled form the sentiments of that scurrilous brand of psycho-political doggerel to be found in the writings of the likes of Woods Hutchinson and Lord Moran. 'Take fifty or more' of these 'lasting or permanent shell shocks' together and 'the impression of what the mental experts term "constitutional inferiority" is unmistakable'; they have 'limped into war half-men'.[22] The ordinary citizen soldiers are silenced, and hence there is invented what Arthur Kleinman characterizes as 'Britain's fundamental divide between silent working-class soldiers . . . and upper-class officers afflicted with neurasthenia'.[23]

SHELL SHOCK AND THE ASYLUM

It was repeatedly stated by government spokesmen that cases of shell shock were not sent to asylums, a destiny reserved for only the hopeless and incurable mental cases, and this is the position that was re-affirmed in the report of the Southborough Committee. So what really happened? The record is quite unequivocal: even as the Committee was in session in 1920, shell-shock cases were being admitted to county asylums in droves, the great majority of them from workhouse infirmaries or other Poor Law institutions, confirming once again that here also the reality diverged very sharply from the official position. Of course, it can be claimed with some justification that in many instances the 'shell shock' label was applied by the patient himself or his relatives, and was not necessarily an official diagnosis. But even the resources of official disingenuity could not disguise the fact that the recognition bestowed by the Ministry of Pensions on the great majority of these cases as authentic war disabilities wonderfully confirmed just those causal connections between emotional distress and the experience of war service that ex-servicemen and their relatives were insisting upon in embracing the rhetoric of shell shock.

Questioned about the applications of psychotherapy in institutions for the insane, Sir John Collie, President of the Special Medical Board for Neurasthenia and Functional Nerve Disease, and subsequently for a brief period Director General of Medical Services at the Ministry of Pensions, gave a characterful display of the animus in the military medical establishment towards those who believed that shell shock had breached the boundary between the neuroses and insanity:

There is no connection between neurasthenics and lunatics. . . . If a supposed shell shock case commits suicide, or is interned in a lunatic asylum, it means a wrong diagnosis has been made. . . . What the authorities do in asylums for the treatment of their people one has very limited knowledge of, but I am sure psychotherapeuty [sic] would be useless to minister to diseased minds. In the insane man there is a distinct organic change in the brain tissue, while in neurasthenia there are purely functional passing conditions in which persuasion, discussion and analysis does have a wonderful effect.[24]

Mathew Thomson has proposed that the diagnosis of shell shock be interpreted as a sign of patient power as much as medical control, and the co-option of the term by relatives and others is equally an indication of a shift in power relations.[25] The argument of many ex-servicemen and their families was the reverse of John Collie's, for they believed that they were being denied not only the officer's treatment facilities, but also his diagnosis. Ordinary soldiers were being put into asylums, and given other labels, who as officers would have been ticketed as shell shock or neurasthenic, and treated in a specialized facility such as one of Lord Knutsford's hospitals. In appropriating the idiom of shell shock, they were trying to convey an attitude towards mental illness in which 'psychotherapeuty' was far from 'useless to minister to diseased minds' and the suffering individual was not irrevocably beyond the reach of ordinary understanding.

According to the benighted Collie, these aspirations were an expression of lay ignorance, but for an authoritative steer that these consumers were ahead of the game in keeping the lines between 'neurasthenics' and 'lunatics' open, take this from Maurice Craig writing in 1922: 'The question of the treatment of insanity is daily increasing in importance, for knowledge of functional mental disorders is rapidly advancing and what was considered by medical men five and twenty years ago to be a psychosis is now regarded as a psycho-neurosis and as recoverable in a short time provided suitable treatment is forthcoming'.[26] By the end of the war, shell shock and its variants were cropping up in every corner of the mental health system, sometimes replacing but often nestling alongside a more conventional causal vocabulary, their usage determined by a number of sources, including patients themselves, their relatives, Poor Law officials (notably relieving officers) and medical practitioners. Examples of diagnoses from an asylum admissions register for 1917–18 include: 'shell shock'; 'war service'; 'worry over the war'; 'cruelty whilst a POW in Germany'; 'nervous breakdown: congenital and service during the present war'; 'army troubles'; 'shell-shock and love affair'; and, finally, that traditional character, the wanking warrior – 'war stress and masturbation'.

'NEW SIGNPOSTS AT MONS'
Here are some examples from the intake of ex-servicemen into Whittingham Asylum, the largest in the country, in 1919 and 1920. The disabilities of this group are of some interest, since a large proportion of them were cotton-operatives; this occupational group was specially singled out in an inquiry commissioned by Sir Auckland Geddes, as Minister of National Service, into the state of the nation's manhood as stripping poorly, and displaying a col-

lective nakedness that was decidely unglamorous. Cotton-operatives (weavers and spinners), the inquiry revealed, made a disproportionate contribution to ranks of Grades III and IV, men who were physical wrecks or senile before they reached forty. Of 290 cotton-operatives examined by the Stockport Board in April 1918, as many as 169 (58.2%) fell in Grades III and IV, while the national average for Great Britain was 24.4%. Comparing them to colliers, the report described how:

> The differences . . . are evident in the waiting-room, and become very strik-ing in the examination hall. The colliers as a class are well developed and muscular, and strip much better than the cotton operatives. So evident are the differences in physique between these two classes of men that one is forced to the conclusion that they represent the effects of their respective occupations and conditions of life, and that in the case of the cotton-operatives work in the moist and overheated atmosphere of the mills, when extended over long periods of time, has a profound effect upon their health and physique . . . one cannot doubt that we have here a remarkable and arresting illustration of the effect of our industrial system upon the health and physique of one class of workers.[27]

From the few shards of information that exist about these unhappy lives, we have the impression that the great trouble for many of these men was that they could not be the way they imagined other men to be.[28] John K, a drawer-in and ex-soldier from Lostock Hall near Preston, was admitted from the Ribchester Institution in the Preston Union in December 1919. Cause: 'the War'; suicidal: 'yes, threatens'; dangerous to others: 'yes, strikes'. 'He is depressed and has delusions, for example he fancies he has committed some offence whilst in the Army, and has a fear of being arrested'. James W, single, a labourer and a Wesleyan, was admitted from the Chorley Union in July 1919; cause: 'shell shock'; suicidal: 'yes, he was taken out of the canal on May 21st, having jumped in'. Scribbled on the reception order in pencil was the remark: 'dementia praecox, not hopeful'. Clarence G was admitted from the Preston Union in February 1920, having previously been in military hospitals, including Maghull, following service in Egypt and France where he had been wounded three times. Cause: 'shell shock'. The doctor at Ribchester Institu-tion stated: 'he is depressed and melancholic and takes a dismal view of his ailments'. Nelson S, aged twenty-one, single, a wool comber and former private in the Notts & Derby Regiment, was admitted from Burnley Union Workhouse in November 1920, where the Male Officer recorded: 'NS has fits of weeping about 4 times per diem. He cannot be got to remain in one place but wanders about appearing lost. He does not seem to comprehend what is said to him'. Cause: 'war service'.

William W, a weaver and former private in the Lancashire Fusiliers, was admitted from Blackburn Union, in December 1919. Cause: 'shell shock'. His wife Mary Jane told the Relieving Officer: 'He is always complaining of shooting pains in the head. He sometimes sits staring vacantly for hours, and at times has not spoken to her for several days, then suddenly gets up, goes out and gets drunk'. Harry P, a roller polisher in the iron trade and former private in the Welsh Regiment, was admitted from Ashton-under-Lyne Union in December 1919. Cause: 'war service'. According to his sister, 'he is very melancholic, sits all day by the fireside quiet and seldom speaks. His great trouble is that he cannot be like other men. He has attempted suicide by cutting his throat with a razor'. Richard H, a cotton twirler, was admitted from the Clitheroe Union in March 1920, having been in the Maudsley Hospital, Denmark Hill, the previous year. Cause: 'shell shock'. 'Patient is morose in manner and at intervals bursts into tears'. His wife Jennie reported that 'he was invalided from the Army suffering from shell shock on July 19th 1919, and that last night he threatened and attempted to strangle her'.

Harold C, a labourer at a print works, was admitted from the Accrington District in the Haslingden Union in January 1920. The Head Imbecile Attendant at the Pike Law Workhouse reported that 'he talked incoherently about his life in France' and that he had 'found him in bed lying on his face, muttering something about new signposts being erected at Mons'. And George B, a married weaver from Burnley who had served as a private in the Royal Army Medical Corps, was admitted to Whittingham from Burnley Workhouse as early as November 1916 where he had been very depressed, with frequent fits of crying, saying that he was tired of life. According to the superintendent of male mental wards he was suffering from 'delusions', which seem to have been exhortations, voices exclaiming 'Germans!' and 'Get out of bed!', routine occurrences in George B's military environment, by which he still found himself emotionally barraged.

The great majority of these ex-soldiers were drawn from the ranks of the skilled or unskilled working class but, interestingly, there was one gentleman among this intake who appears to have degraded himself in the perception of his family by casting off the decorum and self-restraint expected of a man of his station. Franklin H, gentleman and ex-mill manager, who had served from November 1914 to December 1917, was brought to the Asylum on 19 July 1919 after being examined by a Justice of the Peace and two doctors at Clitheroe Police Station. 'Somewhat wild and excitable in appearance and extremely talkative', his manner was 'restless with intervals of nervous exhaustion'. Cause: 'war service'. No doubt he had been emotionally troubled for some while, but a crisis had obviously been looming, since he had started to make himself conspicuous in the neighbourhood. Mr James Ramsbottom, solicitor, reported that on two occasions in the past week the alleged lunatic 'had suddenly rushed up his front garden at 10.30pm and shouting at the top of his voice had called by name several people in the neighbourhood and used very bad language'. His wife confided to the doctor that his language and personal behaviour were 'most disgusting and immoral', all of which constituted 'an entire change from his conduct previous to his return from France in December 1917'.

Each of these shell-shocked soldiers was made a war disability pensioner, and classified as a Service Patient, and their dependants granted allowances. Alongside these distressed men there were also female residents of the Asylum who had been affected by the war, for instance Jemima P, a cotton weaver and a Wesleyan, who had attempted to hang herself because of 'trouble over her son in the Army', though women like Jemima received no official recognition of how the war had blighted their lives. Many of these entrants were still there several years later, but three of the shell-shock cases – John K, James W (who had been ticketed 'dementia praecox, not hopeful'), and Clarence G – recovered within a year or so of being admitted, as did Jemima P.

THE ASYLUM DOCTOR AND THE SOLDIER MENTAL PATIENT

It is noteworthy that the Southborough Committee not only ignored the existence of the Service Patient scheme, but also overlooked the participation of squads of doctors and pensions officials in maintaining it, and in providing expert confirmation – a considerable labour this – of precisely those categories and judgments that the Committee was bent upon repudiating. In the case of an ex-serviceman whose insanity had arisen after discharge from the Army or Navy, the Ministry of Pensions was heavily reliant on the assessment of the medical superintendent of the asylum, who was required to supply details of the ex-serviceman's condition and history, and his opinion as to whether the disability had been caused or aggravated by his service in the Great War. To assist him, he was given a copy of the formula which had been drawn up at the decisive conference in July 1917.

A small sample of 16 cases which were reviewed in the first months of 1920 by Dr J. Marnan, medical superintendent of Horton Road Asylum in Gloucester, gives a fair idea of the labour that was constantly involved in completing these assessments and, more especially, of the sympathy that, in this instance certainly, the alienist brought to his task. Such sympathy was by no means universal, but it was more widespread than the rather negative image that has prevailed of asylum superintendents in this period might have led one to expect, and it proved to be considerably more tenacious over the next years than the Ministry of Pensions would have liked. According to Dr Marnan, of the 16 cases, 13 had probably been aggravated by war service, one was not attributable, one was doubtful, and one had been caused by domestic worry. At least six of these men had had lengthy and arduous army careers, Gunner Archibald A having served in India and Gallipoli, for example; Pte Watson W and two others in Egypt; and the rest in France. The record is embellished by small details that help to individuate these biographies: 'his mother states that he has been getting strange since his hand was injured by boiling tar while working with the Labour Corps two years ago'; 'worry over pension and double hernia sustained while working in trenches abroad'; 'his daughter died in February 1919 and he was unable to get leave – wife states that he began to get strange then'. The effects of the sun in Egypt and Mesopotamia were also identified by three of the group as having contributed to their distress ('states that the heat in Egypt made him feel very ill').[29]

Only two of the group could be characterized as military failures: Pte Oliver W, who had become ill six months after joining up and then spent most of his time in hospitals until his discharge, and Pte Willie P, who was passed into the Army C3 in August 1918 and according to his wife was much upset by army life, and who also spent most of his time in hospital until he was discharged unfit in February 1919. Nevertheless Dr Marnan concluded that both of these individuals belonged in the 'aggravated' category, 'worry over joining the army' having exacerbated Oliver W's melancholia. A sad case was that of Pte Fred B, whom the doctor was constrained from rating as a casualty of the war, but whose distress was a product of the domestic hiatus caused by war service. While he was at war his wife had flouted uxorial conventions by twice giving birth to a baby of which he was not the father, the second in March 1919, since when Fred had apparently declined into delusional insanity.

Though a record of previous asylum admissions, or a doubtful family history, could certainly be made to count against an individual, this was not invariably so. In the relatives' usage, shell shock is often the figure for a less condemnatory approach to mental disorder or for an alternative moral aetiology, but sometimes doctors also shared in this. In March 1918, Thomas M, a company sergeant major, was admitted to an asylum as a Service Patient, and the doctor noted on the case sheet: 'married 1896', and then: 'bigamous married 1916 (shell shock)'.[30] Are those Thomas's words – did he say 'I was so shell shocked when I first met Nellie' or words to that effect; or is this the doctor's construction on what Thomas told him? We cannot be sure, and in the end it does not matter, because the term is evidently part of a shared vocabulary between doctor and patient.

Despite his patient's questionable upbringing ('mother was a drunkard') and history of successive asylum admissions in 1905, 1909 and 1910, the doctor was unstinting in his applause for Pte William A's gallant service record. 'He enlisted in August 1914, was all through the Dardanelles campaign, then in Mesopotamia, and was invalided home in March 1918 with shell shock'. There is an accord here between doctor and patient in which the doctor readily corroborates William's own account. The emotional crisis is attributed directly to the circumstances of the battlefield and the doctor does not attempt, as he could so easily have done, to assimilate it to William's psychiatric biography. Classified as a Service Patient on the doctor's recommendation in April 1920, he was shortly afterwards discharged recovered. There is, however, a twist to this tale, for William had to be re-admitted two years later. At this point, jibbing at the asylum doctor's connivance with the narrative of war disability, the Ministry of Pensions invoked their own medical adviser to determine that William's condition was not after all connected with his war service but was, instead, the reawakening of the original condition that had brought him into the asylum before the war.[31]

Though sympathy was not in short supply, there are other instances where ex-servicemen had to battle against the mind-sets of traditional medical superintendents. Inward-turning attitudes, as in a privatized display of feeling through letter-writing, might be held unbecoming in a working man. William F, a tin miner fron Cornwall, had joined the army in September 1914, serving in India, Egypt and France, until he was sent to base for 'nerves' in 1918. After leaving the army and recovering at home, he had returned to work at the tin mines but the noise of explosions had disturbed him, and he had then taken on surface work at another mine until it had been forced to close down. He had been receiving in-patient treatment at a Ministry of Pensions hospital until he was transferred to the City of Exeter Asylum after admitting to hearing voices saying 'the doctors could do him no good and he had no hope of getting work for about 6 months', a pretty fair assessment of his social circumstances and the impotence of medicine to improve them, it might be thought. Though he was 'quiet and tractable' on admission, settling down to work on the asylum farm, the medical superintendent considered him 'very self-centred', writing 'daily letters to his wife'. However, after a few weeks he was discharged, no more hopeful of finding employment, perhaps, but for the moment presenting a more appreciative face to the doctors. 'I arrived home with my wife quite safe on Friday last & am keeping quite well', he wrote to the medical superintendent, 'thanking you for your kind treatment whilst under your care'.[32]

'ANY MAN IN ANY STREET'

After 1918 there began to appear something that had never existed in England before: people of indeterminate social class.

George Orwell, *England Your England* (1941)[33]

In the *Life And Labour of The People in London*, the magnificent survey conducted by social reformer and statistician Charles Booth at the very end of the nineteenth century, Wandsworth was, with one exception, by far the largest sanitary district in London. Made up of five sub-districts, Clapham, Putney, Streatham, Tooting and Wandsworth, it combined with Battersea to form the largest Poor Law Union in the fiefdom administered by the erstwhile London County Council, encompassing a wide area bounded by Clapham and Battersea to the east, Balham and Tooting to the south, and the more prosperous Putney to the west, with a population just after the Great War of around 496,000. The construction of the railways, and the opening up of stations in rings around central London, had been the catalyst to the transformation of open fields into housing estates, such as Shaftesbury Park, 'a social fortress of the respectable working class'.[34] Though every class was represented from 'yellow' to 'black', it showed up as pre-eminently 'pink' and 'red' on Booth's topographical map, predominantly long streets of two- and three-storey terraced houses, mostly constructed in the last quarter of the nineteenth century, a mixed area composed of 'working class comfort', together with the lower middle class of small tradesmen, comfortable artisans, clerks and other city workers, alongside pockets of the well-to-do, middle-class families keeping one or two servants.[35]

'The generations from Victoria's Jubilee to the affluent 1960s', Roy Porter writes in his social history of London, 'were to witness a remarkable breaking down of traditional barriers, an equalizing process, and a new mobility both physical and social'. By the time of the First World War the trends that Booth had observed had strengthened, for though there was plenty to be concerned about, grinding poverty was on a downward curve; there were visible signs of public improvement, and Wandsworth had in many respects come to epitomize the emerging London of the new century, the steady erosion of the 'outcast London' of the Victorian era, and its replacement by a 'solid improving self-respecting and often patriotic working class'.[36]

Drawing upon reception orders, and what were known as Pauper Lunatic Examination Books, in which William Haggis, the General Relieving Officer,

Wilna Road, Wandsworth, two or three years before the outbreak of the
Great War. The children are posing for R. J. Johns, a noted period photographer
of South London scenes.

and his staff took down details from the relatives of the 'alleged lunatic', in
most cases his wife, I have identified a group of 120 ex-servicemen who were
brought into the Wandsworth Infirmary, on St John's Hill, for observation
during the period 1918–25.[37] Within 14 days most of them were transferred
to lunatic asylums, though by no means were they all destined for long-term
careers as mental patients. 'A very large proportion of the soldiers who manifested psychic disturbances', ventured one authority in the early 1920s, 'were
really potential psychopaths before they entered upon military service'.[38] As
we have seen, this was precisely the diminished and demeaning profile of
Tommy Atkins and his mental health problems that springs from the pages
of the report of the Southborough Committee, in which deprivation and
depravity form the moral and constitutional backdrop to the typical sufferer.
But what do we discover if we try to filter this imagery through the grid of a
locality such as Wandsworth in the immediate aftermath of the Great War?

There are three striking features to the war service profile of this group of
ex-servicemen. First, as many as 108 of the group had served overseas; second,
60 per cent had served for three years or more, and only 10 for less than 12
months; and third, 70 were volunteers, who had enlisted in 1914 and 1915,

Wandsworth Infirmary, photographed by R. J. Johns c.1912. 'Workhouse'
proclaims the sign. Even though, in actuality, Wandsworth Workhouse had been
moved to another site, the association had not been annulled, and incoming
patients were left in no doubt that they were stepping through the portal of
a Poor Law institution.

and the rest conscripts. As the culmination of a process that included the families' histories collected by the Poor Law relieving officer, the advocacy of relatives, the clinical assessments by the medical superintendents of the asylums,
and the scrutiny of medical and service records, the Ministry of Pensions was
eventually persuaded to recognize all these cases as war psychoses, either
caused or aggravated by service, and to classify them as Service Patients for
the time that they were in asylums. The examples that follow are intended to
reflect the social, occupational and ethnic diversity of this group, spanning a
wide spectrum.[39]

A large proportion of them were married, either before the war or in marriages contracted shortly after it. Though for some the war inevitably delayed
or interrupted the raising of a family, others increased their progeny undeterred by the grim business overseas, and the prospect of death or disablement, in procreative salvos that produced a steady counterblast to the
decimations of war. In the great majority of cases, therefore, the emotional
traumas of these returning servicemen were not borne alone but, for better
and worse, spilled into the shared reality of family life involving two or more

generations. Joseph Harbour had married in November 1914 and alongside war service had managed to father four children before being removed to Long Grove in the summer of 1920; Edward Connington had six children born between 1912 and 1922, and was admitted to Cane Hill in 1923; when Fred Quinton was taken to Banstead in 1924, his wife Louisa stated that she had six children under sixteen at home, a son of eighteen who was in the army, and a seventeen-year old who had been working with his father; Frederick and Frances Hill had two boys, one born before the war and one just after; Frank and Annie Nicholson had a daughter conceived just before Frank went to war in March 1915; and Rupert Softley, married soon after his discharge in 1917, was admitted to Colney Hatch Asylum in September 1920 following the birth of his second child.

Despite their inner perturbations, these were in most respects markedly stable lives, and many of the people concerned had been at their present residence a long time. Frank Paull, a postman, had been living in Stanley Street, Battersea, for 15 years; Ethel and William Turner had lived at the same address in Wandsworth for 13 years; George Stephens, also a postman, and his wife had been at their current address for 18 years; Margaret and Joseph Wilkins had moved to 76, Malva Road on the day they were married in September 1914, coincidentally only two doors away from Robert Fletcher's family at number 78; before the War, Alfred Land had lived with his mother at 45, Malva Road, and after his marriage took up residence at number 64. Of course, there were exceptions. William Stewart had been drafted into the Labour Corps as a C3 man in the spring of 1916, and after he found employment as a clerk with the Ministry of Pensions in 1918 he and his wife were forever on the move, moving from one set of furnished rooms to another, maintaining a kind of shabby itinerant gentility, very likely propelled onward by William's inner directives as much as by force of circumstance, the cycle only broken by William's crisis and admission to the Infirmary.

Clerks and various professional trades, including a schoolteacher, a jeweller, an accountant, a draughtsman, a stockbroker and a music-hall artist, formed a sizeable minority. Frederick Hill, a thirty-eight year old insurance agent, had enlisted as a private in the Machine Gun Corps, been wounded twice and promoted to corporal and finally to staff sergeant instructor. His wife Francis reported that he had never received a pension on his discharge, just £42, which had long ago been spent. Fred had announced about a month ago, she said, that he felt queer and that the use of his legs were going, but he had seemed all right until he came home from business about seven one evening in April 1923 saying that his mind had gone. According to the doctor who saw him later that evening: 'He is acutely depressed, can give no reply to questions, makes no effort to think, says despairingly that he cannot, buries his face in his hands and sobs convulsively. No attempts to comfort him are of avail.' On admission to Long Grove Asylum a few days later he was found to be moderately nourished and in fair general health, but with defective teeth and a tendency to flat feet. Alfred Beebee, most recently employed as a clerk, had been manager to a musical instrument dealer when he married Florence in 1919, having enlisted in the East Surrey Regiment in August 1914 and subsequently discharged from the service as permanently unfit in January 1916. Florence reported that until 1920 he had been receiving an army disability pension of 5/6d. per week, reduced from 27/6d., and in October 1923 he was brought to the Infirmary in an emaciated condition, looking morose and depressed. 'He lacks any interest in the environment and for the most part refuses to reply to questions, though apprehending what is said to him. Can speak in a faint whisper to say he cannot talk'. According to Florence, though the doctor had now given him a sleeping draught, he had had no natural sleep for about three weeks and had seldom spoken for the past fortnight, but this week he had become worse, losing his capacity for speech altogether.

Donald Murray enlisted in January 1916, lost his left leg in the war, and after demobilization in 1918 returned to live with his mother and to his occupation as a clerk. His brother reported that he had been neurotic ever since the war but had been markedly strange for the past 18 months, gradually going off the rails, until one day in November 1923 he had handed in his shirt and some books at the doctor's house to 'prove the efficacy of material things provided by others', declaring that he was disturbed by the present chaos in the world and believed that revolution was the only cure all round. Having served with the Cycle Corps since 1914, Donald Laing was already bad with 'nerves' when he left the army about a year after the Armistice, so his father reported, though he soon got married and found employment as a commercial artist. However, at the time of the election just before Christmas 1923, his mother noticed that he seemed rather strange and was 'ramping on about politics'. In January he became increasingly unsettled, claiming that his employer and workmates did not take him seriously and were calling him a 'mutt'. Suspecting that he was being followed, one night he even made his wife and baby walk about Wimbledon Common in the pouring rain in order to elude his pursuers.

Though there was a fair sprinkling of ordinary labourers in this group of ex-servicemen, tradesmen and artisans from the upper or skilled working class formed the great majority: a vulcanizer, a gardener, a taxi driver, a boot repairer, a plumber, an upholsterer, a messenger, a tram driver, a hall porter, a fitter's mate, a waiter, a postman, a carman, a greengrocer and sundry others. Born in 1894, William Pembury was called up from the reserve in August 1914 into the York and Lancaster Regiment, serving throughout the war until his discharge on 9 March 1919 without an army pension of any kind, resuming his duty as a postman exactly a month later. He was twice admitted to the Infirmary in August 1923, and Mrs Rose Pembury (signing herself 'Pembery') said he seemed fine after he was first discharged until one night he again became strange and could not sleep, complaining of pains in the head and a 'thick feeling across the forehead', saying he could see stars sparkling in front of him, and continually getting in and out of bed and wandering about the house. In the Infirmary he seemed nervous and apprehensive, 'prevaricating in answer to questions, continually and furtively disappearing into the lavatory for no reason'. Rose submitted to William Haggis the particulars he had asked 'in reference to my Husbond Mr W. J. Pembery admitided in Hospital . . . refering to his Regemental No and Regement'. She had two small children and her mother-in-law living with her at home in the Wandsworth Road. 'I am receiving £2.5.0. per week from the Post Office as my husband's pay which will be reduced later to half. I have no other means. Rent is 10/- per week. I have no insurance'. No one else in the family had been 'afflicted mentally' and she felt sure that William's 'present state is caused through his army service'.

Frederick Quinton, late farrier sergeant in the Royal Field Artillery, had had a distinguished military career, enlisting in the Royal Artillery in 1898 at the age of 19, where he was posted as a gunner and then as a shoeing smith, serving for 12 years, including the South African War, for which he was awarded the Queen's South Africa Medal. He re-enlisted in August 1914, serving continuously until his discharge in 1918, after which he found employment as a smith and farrier in charge of sick horses. In May 1918 he was given a disability pension of 32/- for four weeks, then reduced to 6/6d. for 48 weeks. After being discharged from St John's Infirmary where he had been admitted for observation as an 'alleged mental' in April 1920, he attended the neurological hospital in Tooting as an out-patient. Showing signs of deterioration, he was admitted to the Ministry of Pensions hospital at Ewell where, as his wife Louisa reported, he remained 'for about five months as a mental case'. He seemed to be doing quite well until, one day in June 1923, 'his nerves appeared to be on the twitch and he could not keep still, constantly wandering from one place to another at all hours of the night'. Discharged recovered from Long Grove after six months, a year later he again became restless, quite unable to settle himself to anything, according to Louisa, and was soon back in the Infirmary, alternately whistling, singing and weeping.

Occasionally we catch a glimpse of the solitary struggle of a man with his inner demons. Edward Connington, a former motor driver, had enlisted in November 1914 and been wounded in France, completing his service in the rank of sergeant with an exemplary character reference ('an efficient and capable NCO with good control of men') and a gratuity of £19. He had seen action also in Egypt and Salonica, where he had contracted malaria, from which he had suffered periodically ever since, and which may have had a bearing on his subsequent mental state. Brought to the Infirmary in June 1923, he confided to Dr Nixey that this was 'the third attack of a condition which makes him feel he must end it all for his wife and six children unless he gets out of the house and far away. This makes him clear off suddenly to avoid if possible the strong impulse to do them in. He exhibits a considerable degree of depression in consequence'. His wife Florence recounted that in December 1921 he had wandered away for a week before giving himself up to the police in Coventry, and in October of last year he had tramped to Birmingham and back.

There was also a small number of immigrants and foreign nationals who had fought in the Great War and either settled in Wandsworth or found their way there in the aftermath of the war. Andrez Zemel, apparently without any friends or relations, appears to have come to England just before the Great War and to have suffered shock when the ship he was returning on from Egypt was torpedoed. From Guildford Military Hospital he was dispatched to a Jewish shelter in East London, where he was discovered by the Russian Society and befriended by a Miss Alexandra Boudayevski, who put him up at her home in Streatham for a month. Finding him troublesome, often depressed and crying, imagining that he was a German and shortly to be hanged, she eventually took him to the Infirmary, where 'he was told he was mentally ill' and removed to Colney Hatch Asylum. Francois Stanislaus Besingère, a gardener and ex-soldier, an 'Alsation, naturalized now into an Englishman', had lived in England since 1910 or so, together with his 'reputed wife' Marie, and served with the Rifle Brigade in France and Italy. Since the war he had been acutely nervous, but in the spring of 1924 he became worse, depressed and brooding, worrying about all sorts of things associated with his naturalization, alleging he was 'in our army for no good', and inclined to 'talk for hours giving details of terrors, plots and animosities, and an extraordinary list of rooms and lodging places in the past few years, right up to recent days'. A Russian who came to England as an adolescent with his family around the turn of the century and settled on Balham Hill, Alexander Leon had served with the Surrey Yeomanry from August 1914 through to July 1919, and since the war had always been unsettled, unable to maintain his employment as an oil and petrol salesman. Recently he had become worse, confused and disorientated, incapable of sustaining a regular conversation, and much addicted to masturbation.

It should not go unremarked, lastly, that there was a small minority of ex-servicemen who passed through the Wandsworth Infirmary on their route to an asylum, whose mental disorder appears never to have been recognized by the Ministry of Pensions. One of these was Walter Rackstraw, a carman from Ram Square, who had served in the Royal Field Artillery from January 1916 through to February 1919 when he was discharged without a pension. In the late afternoon of 8 September 1923, Walter met with an accident in Wandsworth High Street when his van crashed into a bus and, although not thrown himself, his horses were injured. Maud Rackstraw, his wife, reported that the next day he started painting the house in a peculiar fashion, using all sorts of colours, often bursting into tears. After a week in the Infirmary he seemed more settled, but a day or so later complained of feeling ill and loss of energy, unable to finish the simplest task, with frequent fits of depression, seemingly always on the verge of weeping. One might have expected that at this point a connection with Walter's war service would at least have been explored, some memory of what he had witnessed in those years, perhaps the brutal carnage of horses behind the front lines, having been rekindled by the accident, but the record is completely silent on the question. And Walter Rackstraw died in Long Grove Mental Hospital 10 years later, never having received any official recognition of a link between his disability and his military service in the Great War.

What strikes us about many of these cases is their indeterminacy: they do not sit comfortably within the conventional psychological and social dichotomies, nor can they readily be configured in the moral universe of constitutional weakness and degeneracy. If they are not obviously heroes, neither are they 'quivering creatures', 'misshapen creatures from the towns', who were 'cowards before they were soldiers': instead, they inhabit the blurred, grey contestable area where the majority of lives are conducted.[39] The terrain that they inhabit is not that of 'insanity' as traditional psychiatrists understood it, rather it is the indeterminate psychological landscape to which psychological observers such as Maurice Craig, Millais Culpin and D. W. Winnicott sought to give expression after the war. In the main, these are solid and respectable citizens who inhabit a social landscape in which the frontier between the upper working class and the lower middle class has become more open and traversable; and to that extent they represent a model of the citizen soldier that is not the possession of any particular class group, but instead offers itself as a potential focus for cross-class alliances. If they are not all of them like Daddy in the recruiting poster, some of them are; and Daddy was living if not in their street, then in a neighbouring one; he was attending the same infirmary and was a patient in the same mental hospital: all told, a member of the same company, as he had been during the war, and now again after it. On these various counts – moral, psychological and social – one might then claim that the Wandsworth citizen soldier is more than himself: he is everyman, a fitting representation of '*any* man in *any* street'.

Chapter 14

LUNATIC OFFICERS

My fellow patients are 160 more or less dotty officers. A great many of them are degenerate looking. A few are genuine cases of shell shock. One committed suicide three weeks ago. The bad ones are sent to another place.
Siegfried Sassoon to Lady Ottoline Morell, 30 July 1917[1]

To us the lunatic officer is by no means the new and rare species he seems to be to you. We have a settled procedure for dealing with him.
Civil Servant, Ministry of Pensions, 1919[2]

THE INVISIBLE POPULATION OF MAD OFFICERS

At first glance there are remarkably few lunatic officers, just 300 or so, in private mental institutions and registered hospitals between the wars, a much lower proportion than one would expect. This statistic is misleading, however, because the Ministry of Pensions dealt only with officers suffering from mental disability who were 'in more or less needy circumstances', and who had mostly been treated in Lord Knutsford's Hospitals, such as Palace Green and Latchmere House at Ham Common, before being certified as 'hopeless cases', straitened by their jackets as much as in their pockets. Of course, temporary officers – those 'temporary gentlemen' from a wide band of the social spectrum who were such a specialty of the Great War – were perhaps more likely to find themselves in straitened circumstances than the regulars, qualifying only for war disability pensions, and not for service pensions, but the middle classes were struggling under the burden of heavy taxation in the aftermath of the war, and some families could not bear the expense of prolonged treatment and maintenance costs.[3]

The Ministry acknowledged in 1918 that the lunatic officer with family responsibilities whose disability was determined neither to have been caused nor aggravated by his war service was very badly off under existing regulations unless he had private means. In such a case there was no alternative but to dispatch him to a public asylum where the Ministry had powers to accord him the privileges of a Service Patient, but was not in a position to do anything for his wife or dependent relatives. Ironically, officers in this position were worse off than 'non-attributable' other rankers, partly because their numbers were so small, and no doubt also because these were shameful conditions for which there was no organized lobby. In 1922 there seem to have been a score or so ex-officers in county or borough asylums, though some of them were in transit towards more salubrious establishments, but occasionally we fall upon what is obviously a tragic case.[4] Lieutenant William Harvey, a marine engineer before the war, had served as an engineer in the Royal Navy from 1914 to 1919, returning to his brother's home in Putney in 1923, his mental state deteriorating rapidly, resulting in his removal to the Wandsworth Infirmary ('patient has no means'), and thence to Long Grove where he was confirmed as suffering from GPI. 'Petulant, impulsive and obstinate. Unduly amused at noticing a button off my coat. Frequently repeats "I'm a clever engineer" after being asked what branch of engineering he is in'. His brother, Gordon, believed that he must have contracted the disease in the Pacific sometime in 1914 or 1915, but an appeal to the House of Lords for his entry into a naval asylum on account of his brain syphilis was rejected on the grounds that it was neither attributable to nor aggravated by service.[5]

At the behest of the War Office, the Ministry started to take an interest in insane officers around the middle of 1917, proposing to send certifiable cases to mental institutions at a rate of £2.2.0. weekly, though in exceptional cases, where constant attendance was required, they were prepared to pay a weekly charge of £3.3.0. For these fees, opined a Pensions official, 'we ought to get something very definite in the way of separate bedrooms'. In all cases, a charge of 4/6d. per day, calculated to be the normal cost of messing, was deducted from the officer's full pension.[6] The negotiations over these arrangements were mainly with the registered hospitals, voluntary or charitable foundations, of which there were 13 or so, notably the Holloway Sanatorium at Virginia Water, St Andrew's Hospital in Northampton, the Retreat at York and Bethlem Royal in London. There were also anomalies such as Scalebor Park in Yorkshire which, controlled by the West Riding County Council, and hence ranked as a county asylum, had nonetheless been designed and maintained solely for the treatment of private patients, accommodating around 150 inmates in the gentlemen's division.[7]

Needless to say, the responses of these establishments to the overtures being made to them were less than enthusiastic and not infrequently prickly. Their misgivings were partly fiscal, for two guineas was not a great deal, and some of them were quite explicit in the view that they were being asked to plunder their charitable funds in the support of deserving cases who should be properly funded by the state. But such misgivings were as much administrative, for it was not lost on these institutions that they were being asked to take charge of failures from the military treatment system, and they had understandable cause for anxiety about the debris of the trenches that might be coming their way. Hence why in most instances the willingness to accept a number of officer cases was hedged about with restrictions – owing to the shortage of male staff, 'it will be quite impossible, as we are situated at present, to admit dangerous patients'; 'in the "Chronic" department of this Institution were are quite full, a circumstance which . . . limits us to the kind of case which we could admit'; 'the committee reserve the right' to request that any patient who becomes particularly 'troublesome or obnoxious' be removed to some other institution, or 'to discharge any patient whose state or habits render him unfit for treatment and association with the other patients in the Hospital'. Furthermore, if it was expected that men of the officer class would all be allocated private bedrooms and sitting rooms, they were to be disappointed, for single bedrooms were by no means the norm and often reserved for those acute patients who were considered to need it, rather than for a wider class of patients who happened to desire it. At Manchester Royal Lunatic Hospital in Cheadle, for example, it was proposed to distribute the lunatic officers in the different galleries; and at the Holloway Sanatorium, 'as dormitory accommodation only will be provided, it is obvious that patients cannot be admitted under this arrangement who are noisy, excited, of faulty or destructive habits, who require any special nursing or attention, or who are suffering from General Paralysis of the Insane'. In brief, only very well-regulated and straitened officer lunatics indeed.[8]

Most of these officers were of the lower ranks, maintly lieutenants and second lieutenants, but there were quite a few captains and majors, a couple of lieutenant colonels, and a brigadier general (from a private address near Dublin) along with a score or so nurses. Additionally, there were a small number of officers drawing disability pensions from the Ministry who were residing with doctors or in so-called 'borderline' homes, or sometimes in their own homes; these were hard cases who were being kept out of the asylum system, such as a lieutenant colonel living with a Dr Underhill at Maidenhead, and a second lieutenant who was living at home but was seen periodically by Dr Maurice Craig; for such arrangements the Ministry was prepared to pay a charge of £4.4.0. weekly. Though they must have been in need of the funds, not all these borderline cases were willing recipients of the attentions of the Ministry: Captain Fletcher, 'will not have communication with Ministry'; Captain Dainty, 'unable to get him to accept treatment'.[9]

However, this group is only visible at all because it was being supported out of public funds, and is really only the tip of a submerged population of lunatic officers, the size of which is quite unknown. In the network of private mental hospitals across the land there was a mixed economy of officers who were supported partly by the Ministry and partly by private means, but equally a probably much larger population who were funded wholly out of their own means and hence did not figure in the official returns at all. The Ministry was quite explicit that it had no wish to interfere with the arrangements for well-to-do officers, confirming that 'it would be left entirely to the friends of those officers who are well-off and become insane to make, as at present, suitable and complete arrangements for their treatment concomitant with their social station and financial position'.[10]

At Barnwood House in Gloucester, for example, there were scarcely any inmates towards whose maintenance the Ministry contributed, but there were invariably several melancholic majors in the house and at least one general.[11] Just occasionally, on a drowsy afternoon in an archive, one may stumble across a record in which a window is opened briefly onto a room, perhaps in an annexe on the South Coast belonging to a high-standing private madhouse, and momentarily one may catch sight of them, some of the brass hats from the Great War, in one corner sits Brigadier . . . and there by the window General . . . and, gesticulating wildly, over in the far corner . . . can it be no . . . no surely not . . . but yes it is. . . . Alas, dear reader, the bonds of confidentiality do not permit me to divulge their identities!

CAPTAIN HAWS TAKES THE HARDEST PATH
Dr Street, medical superintendent of the Haydock Lodge Asylum in Lancashire, a vintage private madhouse, told Capt. George Haws's father plainly that his son was a lunatic. That was all par for the course in those days, to call a spade a spade, psychiatrically speaking, but the wily doctor was also making a pitch for the prolongation of his services and letting it be known that in his opinion Capt. Haws, a medical student before the war, who had been shell-shocked at Gallipoli and dealt a cruel blow even before he had seen action when his battalion was involved in a railway accident at Gretna in Scotland, in which many of his fellow soldiers were decapitated or burned alive, was now certifiable, and likely to remain that way, a 'hopeless case' or one of nature's 'incurables', for whom permanent residence in a private asylum of standing was the most likely horizon.[12] The Captain had in any case not much benefited from his stay at Haydock Lodge with its baronial pretensions, for which the Ministry of Pensions had been footing the bill, and now,

incensed, his father removed him from the asylum, resolved as he put it 'to take the hardest path' and assist his son to make his own way outside the asylum system.

However, struggling under the burden of heavy taxation, his father could only afford to maintain his son in the short term, and if the Captain intended to retain his claim to a disability pension he had no alternative but to fall in with the bureaucratic requirements that the Ministry of Pensions imposed on him. In 1919 the Ministry labelled his pensionable disability as dementia praecox and neurasthenia (an unlikely combination, but not an unprecedented one in this period). For the Captain this was tantamount to an exile, an unwarranted re-routing of his existence to some lonely outpost beyond the pale of ordinary comprehension. Though he never succeeded in completing his medical studies, he made masterful use of his insider's knowledge, acquiring a reputation for turning up at the medical boards that periodically probed and pronounced on his life and circumstances (as many as 19 by 1923), eccentric in appearance, bearded and whiskered, armed with a textbook and ready to refute the diagnosis.

By 1923, however, having found a wife and set himself up in a rented cottage in the country, he was extolling the virtues of self-sufficiency, working his two-acre garden, growing fruit and vegetables and keeping fowls to supply his needs. Though the strain of the interminable examinations by the pension authorities was taking its toll, he now felt more confident in writing to them in fulsome terms, urging them to make this assessment the final one. He reminded them of the ordeal that had commenced in Gallipoli, starting with nerve exhaustion, 'then the exhausting month of observation, never being without an orderly or another observer, being shut in a cabin at the beginning of the voyage, with heavy bars across the windows, and a couple of orderlies outside the door at first to see I did not leave the cabin, although I had not been told to stay there, with the result that I decided I was a mental case and answered as such'; and 'during the long years since the gradual growth of the idea of lunacy . . . like a slow growing cancer, until I am at last, I believe, a certified lunatic (I hope I am wrong but believe this is true) and as liable to incarceration in some oubliette as a known criminal is to arrest'. It may be doubted whether the Pensions learned anything from this communication about the anguish of a person with a mental illness diagnosis in maintaining a foothold in ordinary life, but they eventually took the hint, finalized the Captain's pension at 100% for paranoia (delusional psychosis), a conclusion that was as reassuring in one dimension as it was unsettling in another, and left him alone to cultivate his garden.[13]

SPECIAL CONSIDERATIONS FOR THE LUNATIC OFFICER

Officers were frequently in receipt of special considerations and favours from the Ministry of Pensions that were denied to ordinary rankers, especially if they had importuning relatives of some station. Captain C. B. Collenette had enlisted as an ordinary ranker in September 1914, been commissioned in March 1915, promoted to captain in August 1917, and awarded the Military Cross in January 1918. His mental health started to decline quite soon after the war – possibly affected by a severe war wound to his arm – and he was admitted to the Old Manor Mental Hospital in Salisbury in the early 1920s from Hendon Workhouse following an incident that had brought him to the attention of the police. A few years later, following vociferous complaints from the Captain's mother that he had been struck by an attendant on a number of occasions, and was not getting enough individual attention, the Ministry agreed to sanction an additional charge for the services of a special attendant to accompany the Captain on his walks in the grounds and otherwise attend to his needs. Medical officers from the Ministry were in any case more kindly disposed to men of their own rank and station, and to entreaties from relatives of the genteel classes, but there may also have been an element of damage limitation in this concession, for some of these relations were in a strong position to stir up trouble if disposed to do so.

Unlike the families of ordinary Service Patients, the relatives of officers were invariably treated with civility if they called at the Ministry personally, the Captain's nephew requesting an interview in the early 1930s with Dr Prideaux to discuss his uncle's future welfare, saying that he had visited him recently and, 'greatly pleased at the wonderful improvement he has made lately', was anxious to support the Captain in his endeavour to get the certificate cancelled and be set at liberty. From the standpoint of the Ministry this was an instance of the 'dangerous relative', a potential loose cannon who, persuaded by the normality of the patient, taking a madman's word for his bond, concludes that he is wrongly confined. What the Captain specially communicated to his nephew that so impressed him as to his normality we do not know, but a letter to the Ministry a year or so later leaves no doubt about the Captain's feelings: 'This institution here is in serious disorder – riot; and the men are crying out against injustice. Please arrange for my immediate transfer. . . . It is impossible for me to stay here any longer'. Instead of the brusque rejoinder that would have been the lot of the ordinary soldier's nephew, Dr Prideaux did not hesitate to accommodate him, though no doubt endeavouring to persuade him of the error of his ways ('bad case, understand your feelings, but everything possible is being done . . .').[14]

An institution such as the Old Manor undoubtedly provided for quite a relaxed life style, and sometimes a measure of assocation with the regular life of the community, even for officers who had been certified. A local tailor would regularly call at the hospital to measure up the officers for suits. One officer sang in the local operatic society; another became a warden at the local church; a third went on an excursion to Lourdes with a nurse, at the port on his return declaring himself for a lunatic in answer to the customs officer's routine inquiry; a fourth went on a fishing and shooting holiday to Ireland, also accompanied by a nurse; and there was also the apocryphal tale of a Captain S who had a key made to the outside door that led directly from the hospital garden into the street and, having bought himself a bicycle, spent most of his days playing golf.[15]

The experience of Lieutenant James Barraclough as a war psychosis pensioner poignantly evinces the special attentions that officers were held to merit. Born in Grimsby in 1896, Barraclough was briefly a civil servant before enlisting as a ranker in August 1914, receiving a commission in the Dragoon Guards in November, and was subsequently 'in the Irish rebellion and under fire in the trenches in France'. In January 1917 he reported sick and was admitted, via the inevitable Netley, to the officers' mental hospital at Latchmere House, Ham Common, in a restless and emotional condition with the delusion of being poisoned, and a diagnosis at this stage of confusional insanity. He remained there until November when he was discharged at his father's request with the apparent intention, after a period of recuperation in the country, of going to the Argentine. Though in the meantime the War Office had determined that his military career was at an end, and that he was now to become a 'non-effective' officer, the process was handled with customary dignity and discretion ('To relinquish temporary commission on account of ill-health contracted on active service. To be granted the honorary rank of 2nd Lieutenant. Submit to the King'). The 'non-effective' by no means inevitably transmuted into the 'ineffectual', and it is striking that already at this point, with the outcome of course still quite uncertain, the Lieutenant's disability was unquestioningly attributed to his war experience.

His convalescence stalled, however, and the Argentine was soon abandoned, and in May 1922 he was sent to live in the private house of a Dr Ellis in Ware. Residing in a doctor's own house was 'a very favourite mode of treament for the more wealthy classes', as Maurice Craig remarked just before the Great War.[16] Lending itself to exploitation by the unscrupulous, it equally held out the hope of a wholly conscientious encounter that really might turn the corner for the afflicted person. And for an interval, certainly, Dr Ellis appears to have succeeded in nudging his patient along the path to rural self-sufficiency of a kind (a much-promoted salve for the nerve-stricken ex-serviceman in those years). In July 1923 the Lieutenant was removed from his care and sent on three months' trial to a pedigree poultry farm in Hertfordshire, accompanied by an attendant paid for by the Ministry. But chicken farming was not his vocation, and over the next few months the Ministry apparently concluded that, regardless of whether he settled inside or outside an institution, Lieutenant James Barraclough suffered from a severe war-related disability justifying the award of a permanent pension at the highest rate, with no further requirement to reaffirm his credentials before periodic medical boards.

In February 1925 his father received the letter that must have dispelled the family's uncertainty, as much as it must have drained the cup of hope. His son, the Pensions authorities informed him, had been granted retired pay at the rate of £210 per year for life in respect of his disability, assessed as being 100%, which was now named as Dementia Praecox and is 'regarded by the Ministry as attributable to his military service during the Great War'. In moving along the spectrum from confusional insanity, through acute mania, to dementia praecox, the medical advisers to the Ministry had, of course, ratcheted up the severity of the condition. But if there was a window of opportunity here to escape liability, claiming that the pensioner's misfortune was after all, contrary to initial appearances, to be accounted for by some deficit in his constitution, they did not take it, and the Lieutenant was accordingly installed in the pantheon of fully accredited war psychotics.

A year later, as if perhaps to avail himself of full membership of the club into which he had been elected, he again took up residence at Latchmere House, remaining there for the next five years, in keeping with his station submitting an invoice to the War Office from the Wilkinson Sword Company for the renovation of his cavalry sword and the supply of a brown scabbard. In the spring of 1931 he returned once more to his parents' home in London where, with the exception of a brief interlude, he remained until 1944. However he was by no means insensible to wider political currents, for in August 1936 he was said to have been upset by accounts of the Spanish Civil War. From time to time he upbraided the Ministry for their oversight in respect of some dimension of his entitlement, complaining that an item in *The Times* had exposed how he had been cut out of an increase in pension rates, or annexing another part of his body to his traumatic narrative, maintaining that his imminent need for dental treatment was caused by an old gunshot wound to his mouth. The Ministry was consistently forebearing in its responses ('may it be borne in mind, please, that the officer is very seriously affected mentally, and indeed is probably certifiable') though it drew the line over the dental treatment, averring that 'exhaustive search of your service records during the Great War does not reveal any evidence that you sustained a gunshot wound [in the] mouth'.

In the mid 1940s, however, with both Lt Barraclough's parents now deceased, and a brother who was entirely uninterested in him, the Officer's Friend – the officers' welfare officer at the Ministry of Pensions – made arrangements for his admission to Camberwell House, a private mental hospital in South London with a small coterie of officer war pensioners, as a voluntary boarder. As it happened, the medical superintendent here was Dr Hubert Norman, late of Napsbury War Hospital, and a few months into his stay the Lieutenant dispatched a rather despairing line to the Officer's Friend:

> I have just returned here and am being very badly treated by the junior staff and the Medical Superintendent. Dr Norman has taken their side and sent me to a lunatic ward. Capt. Roberts and Capt. Priestley of the 1st King's Dragoon Guards have left and I consider that as my liberty has been confiscated I should terminate my contract here. Please act at once. . . .

The Ministry was at once prompted to write directly to Dr Norman in terms that evinced a degree of personal concern for the officer's feelings and wellbeing that would have been inconceivable in the case of an ordinary ranker: 'the officer seems unhappy, and we feel that some action is necessary. . . . We should be more than grateful if you would be kind enough to see the officer yourself and go into his trouble so as to, at any rate, give him the idea that we have his welfare deeply at heart'. In the event Hubert Norman succeeded in calming the situation, reassuring the Ministry that the Lieutenant was now more settled and no longer agitating to leave, but if his discontent had lingered there is no doubt that the Ministry would have stood by him and, acknowledging that he had options, found him an alternative situation.

In the next years, the medical advisers from the Ministry on their annual inspections of the war pensioners invariably remarked on the Lieutenant's personal habits: 'masturbates in French letters and leaves them in bed' (January 1946); 'getting full of somatic symptoms which he will talk about for hours . . . still wears a sheath every night & wraps himself up in all sorts of garments at night to keep the "interference" off' (January 1947). Such proclivities did not diminish the estimation in which he was held, however, for later that year, largely prompted by the post-war climate of 'reconstruction', the Officer's Friend once again acted as the Lieutenant's advocate, making out a sympathetic case for him as an individual who with the right support could be helped to reside outside a mental institution:

> It would appear that he is now anxious to be considered for a Supplementary Allowance on the grounds of unemployability. . . . I would be very grateful if you would give the case your sympathetic and careful consideration as possibly it would be a good thing if the officer could, at some time or other, leave Camberwell House, as it does not seem fair or right that this officer should spend the rest of his days in a place of this description. I am quite certain that if he had somebody sympathetic who could look after him, he would be quite all right outside.

One could, of course, generalize these recommendations as to what was 'fair' and 'right' to large numbers of other psychiatric war disability pensioners, but the fact that they are invoked so selectively in relation to a small cast of officers throws into relief the warped mentality of the Pensions bureaucracy. Even in the Lieutenant's case it turned out to be wishful thinking, it must be said, for he spent the rest of his days in a mental institution, dying in 1979.[17]

AN OFFICER MANQUÉ

In certain respects Ivor Gurney is an exemplary figure in the body of psychiatric casualties of the Great War precisely because he was *not* an officer, allying himself insistently with the community of suffering of the ordinary rankers, such that one may justifiably see him as a spokesman for the 'oddballs', those with a 'talent' that ran against the grain or were 'out of sorts' with the general direction of things. There has, however, been some reticence about locating him within these bearings, and even in permitting Gurney so to locate himself. The irony is that Gurney, who took such pride in being an ordinary foot soldier, was treated by his friends as a kind of officer manqué, one of those temporary officers who turned out to be an equally temporary gentleman in post-war Britain, reproaching the authorities, and whoever was prepared to listen, for what he felt to be his diminished status. In striking such a posture, however, they succeeded only in spiting their own face, and also Gurney's, for they were not in a position to provide for him along the lines of a real gentleman, being forced to accommodate him in a public institution.

When Ivor Gurney was in crisis in 1922, his friends, most of them professional people, were anxious to 'get the Pensions people to accept liability for his condition as arising from shell-shock, and, if possible, to get him a total disability pension for life'. A few days later, F. W. Harvey was able to reassure Marion Scott, Gurney's long-standing friend and confidante, that the Pensions authorities had been swung round: 'I was never really afraid of it, but of course it is necessary on top of illness to prove that it is a result of the war, and the shell-shock explanation has now been accepted by the Ministry'. Accepted it may have been, though of course the Ministry would not have put it quite like that, but Gurney's friends were still mistrustful of the Pensions people, as they rather patronisingly called them, believing them to be actuated largely by fiscal parsimony and 'only too glad to get out of their responsibility on any pretext'. A little later, another of Gurney's friends, William Kerr, a tax inspector and also a minor poet, wrote to Marion Scott that Gurney was 'to go at once to a Pensions hospital at Ewell'. Gurney's general practitioner, Dr Terry, would make it clear to the medical superintendent at Ewell:

a) that Ivor is an exceptional person and of great talent; b) that he must on no account whatever have him certified a lunatic without consulting his friends. . . . It is possible that the Supt. at Ewell will take an interest in Ivor and he will be asked to furnish Dr Terry with periodical personal reports on Ivor. If he is a decent sort of man, of course he will. If however, he seems inclined to take up the point of view that Ivor is just an ordinary patient and that he won't be interfered with (of all these arrogant high priests of medicine, I gather Superintendents of these places are the most arrogant) we shall have to bring pressure to bear on that Supt. . . . I daresay you in town could get in touch with Sir Maurice Craig, who is almost a Pope among them. So you see that we can really – once the Pensions people are committed – get Ivor transferred anywhere – with a little tact and pushing.[18]

In the event it was not to Ewell that Gurney was taken but to Barnwood House. His brother Ronald was shrewd enough to appreciate that Barnwood was a wrong turning, and quite without hope for his brother. It was not a working man's asylum at all, but mostly the haunt of leisured or retired individuals and, whatever else it had to offer, occupational zeal was not one of its strengths, all of which was anathema to Gurney, for whom the opportunity to keep working counted above all else. The officer class was quite conspicuous in the dayrooms and lounges and Gurney had for company a melancholic major general and a deluded major from the Indian Army, along with a smattering of professional and trades folk, a minister, a couple of drapers, an itinerant teacher, a surgeon, a draughtsman and a few individuals of private means.

The medical authorities at Barnwood quickly concluded that he was incurable. The 'police station business is perhaps gone too deep for cure', remarked an assistant medical officer of Gurney's complaint about the persecution he was being subjected to. Arthur Townshend, the medical supremo, though genuinely fond of Gurney ('he is such an extremely nice fellow and it is a most pathetic case'), conveyed a deep and dispiriting sense of medical impotence in the face of such an intractable case, displaying more confidence in the arrangements for hiring a motor car than in anything directly connected with his profession. Trying to be helpful, a Pensions official in Gloucester pointed out that there were other private asylums, such as Fisherton House in Salisbury, soon to be re-named the Old Manor and to accommodate a large contingent of war disability pensioners, both officers and other rankers, where Gurney could 'receive equally good treatment at a very much smaller cost than at Barnwood House'. However at this stage Gurney's friends were too obsessed with finding him a situation that befitted an 'exceptional person' to be able to give a fair hearing to a proposal that implicitly asked them to lower their sights.[19]

For the most part treating him as a recherché sensibility, Gurney's friends never acknowledged any link or identification with the collectivity of psychiatric war casualties. Their disdain for 'the Pensions people' had the result that they were largely ill-informed about the provision that the state was actually making for the rank-and-file war disabled, never trusting the Pensions authorities sufficiently to allow them to be helpful, accepting their ministrations only very reluctantly. Much of their shot-calling, not least the proposed appeal to Sir Maurice Craig as the champion of individual exceptionalism, was simply the bravado of the middling middle classes, resentful at being forced into a dependence on the Ministry, frustrated at their inability to more than nibble at the luxury amenities of private health care.

An exception here was Gurney's mother, Florence Gurney, who has generally been rather disparaged, by members of her own family as much as by the metropolitan literati with whom Gurney kept company. There is no doubt that she was a truculent and moody woman, but her letters from the late 1920s after Gurney had been admitted to the City of London Asylum reveal the anguish of a mother as a helpless spectator to her son's misery and isolation, who found the scene at Dartford deeply repugnant and was angered by the treatment that had been meted out not only to Gurney but to other psychiatric war returnees. 'Such waves of anguish keep going over me', she wrote in August 1927, 'I wish I could do something to make him better or that we could get him to a smaller place tis like a lot of cattle there he says it is hell poor old boy'. Unusually among Gurney's friends and acquaintances, she identified with working people and hence readily associated her son with the community of psychiatric war pensioners: 'they talk about these War patients having a place to themselves I think that would be as it should they will never have their names on the roll of honour but I dont think that they ought to be crowded up like a lot of cattle but be treated honourably their whole life is ruined'.[20]

Since liability for him as a war disability pensioner had already been accepted, Gurney could have been classified as a Service Patient (of whom there was already a group at Dartford), receiving the privileges of a private patient, paid for by the Ministry, with an additional grant for his clothing as well as pocket money for his personal needs. It is difficult to understand why his friends did not pursue this course. There would certainly have been no disadvantage to Gurney in terms of the care that he was getting, for he did not receive any special privileges from the Dartford authorities that would not have been the lot of the Service Patients in the hospital.[21] There might well have been benefits, not least in drawing on the know-how and moral support of the Ex-Services Welfare Society, which was actively representing the interests of ex-servicemen in mental hospitals and had already established a cottage scheme in the grounds of the City of London Mental Hospital in the 1920s.[22] Not least, Ivor Gurney himself might have identified with this company, even if his friends did not, and found in it a salve of sorts. However, indifferent or oblivious towards these currents, his friends opted to classify him as an ordinary private patient, with the result that the onus of financial responsibility for his maintenance fell on Marion Scott.

That, certainly, was where the hospital administration were content to leave it, fixing the charges at their own discretion. They could not deal with the Ministry themselves over the payment of Gurney's pension, they advised Marion Scott, she must take it upon herself to do so, a brazen untruth since they were already in touch with the Ministry on a regular basis in securing payments for the Service Patients in the hospital. As the years drew on, the funds that had been donated by friends were depleted and it fell upon Marion Scott, herself a woman of limited means with other claims on her resources, to make up the shortfall.[23] Finally, 'Ivor Gurney died intestate . . . on the 26th December 1937 and without adequate assets even to pay his funeral expenses let alone debts'.[24] But the irony of this sad tale is that Gurney's fate was by no means foreordained by the constraints of the time, or the miserliness of the Ministry of Pensions.[25] Instead, his pauperization was a product of a proud and well-intentioned, but ultimately myopic, effort to support this distraught genius with only limited recourse to the state, as though to ensure that he conformed to the type of the lonely suffering artist, spurned by the society which he had yearned to serve. If the mad officer and his class were to be envied, perhaps the least enviable were the financially straitened determined regardless to continue living by their lights.[26]

'HARDENING'

There had been no real shift of power and in 1919 we went back to 'normal'
with startling speed

George Orwell, letter to *Partisan Review* (1942)[1]

THE LAST GASP OF THE POPULIST PROTEST

The 1920s were to bring a reassertion of traditional psychiatric realism and familiar moral norms as a counterweight to the erosion of psychiatric deference that had been stimulated by hopeful tidings about new treatments, and to the unabated protests over the failure of medical authorities to persevere with hard cases. All the same, as late as 1922 some life was still left in the populist protest of the war years, a furore breaking out over the decision to demote to the pauper class several hundred 'non-attributable' Service Patients for whom responsibility had been accepted on a temporary basis. Local authorities published the names of 'noble heroes' who were being ignominiously degraded, such as Alfred George Cole, Ronald Chevalier, William Moore, Ronald Stewart, George Whitmore, and Horace Frank Cox from Banstead Mental Hospital.[2]

In a matter of weeks the government had 'shipped a great deal of water over this storm of the lunatic ex-service men' and even the Minister of Pensions was forced to concede that the official projection of the 'non-attributables' as made up of stay-at-home misfits and malcontents, who were to a man disturbed before the event, would not do. 'In the case of insanity it was practically impossible to say whether the insanity was or was not due to service', an official admitted, so the 'original decision as regards the insanity of certain ex-service men, now estimated to number 800, as non-attributable to service could not really be justified'. 'For my part', confided a civil servant from the Treasury in a rare display of compassion for the mentally ill, 'I think that the benefit of the doubt ought to be given to all ex-service men upon whom this most forlorn of all misfortunes has fallen'.[3]

To allay public concerns the Ministry of Pensions set about reviewing the histories of all the 'non-attributables', eventually concluding that a mistake had been made in around 150 or so cases. The Treasury had previously complained about being kept in the dark over uncertainties and ambiguities of interpretation in the assessment of war disabilities, and it certainly got what it was asking for in a lively correspondence in which the Ministry sought to renegotiate the status of these 'non-attributables'. In view of the 'very definite medical opinion' he has now received, the Minister believes that 'an injustice has been done to men who, by reason of their condition, were not in a position to defend their own claims'.[4] Remarkably, in a number of instances the Pensions authorities invoked dementia praecox as a war psychosis, maintaining that the cause of the pensioner's condition had been wrongly ascribed to a congenital mental defect 'owing to a failure to recognise the true diagnosis, Dementia Praecox'.

Among these was J. H. V. Osborne, late Painter Second Class, No. 224455 Royal Navy, who had been invalided in July 1916 with 'delusions'. His 'delusions' were accepted as aggravated by service, but in June 1918 a resurvey board reported that Osborne, while not very strong mentally, seemed normal, his delusions having faded, and the board decided that aggravation had 'passed away'. When they recurred two years later, resulting in his admission to an asylum with a diagnosis of delusional insanity, it was concluded that because he had been quite 'normal' in the interim his current condition should be construed as a new disorder unconnected to his military service. However, the reconsideration of the case by the 'specially qualified mental experts at Headquarters' revealed that Osborne was after all a case of dementia praecox, a disability in which 'there are frequently long remissions when the sufferers seem well', but the recurrence of symptoms is inevitable: 'It cannot, therefore, logically be held that aggravation had passed away because the man was stated to have been "almost normal" during a remission'.[5]

There were certainly precedents for this sort of aetiological manoeuvring in the capacious repertoire of psychological medicine, but in view of the outlook which prevailed among the majority of British alienists it was certainly a rather innovative interpretation of dementia praecox. Moreover, it reflected a deliberate shift in policy, for in May 1922 an instruction was issued by the Director General of Medical Services that 'in future, cases of Dementia Praecox should not necessarily be regarded as only aggravated by service, but from the point of view of entitlement each case should be considered on its merits'.[6] In other words, direct causality was no longer ruled out, and dementia praecox had been promoted from a second- to a first-class war psychosis. In the skirmishes with the Treasury over the regrading of the 'non-attributables', it was forefronted as a chronic, reactive condition that, unlike congenital conditions, could be directly attributed to war service and, unlike an acute reactive condition such as delusional insanity, persisted even when it appeared to be in abeyance.

Another 'non-attributable' whose status was revised was Sam Goldstein, who had orginally been refused a war disability pension, and given a diagnosis of moral insanity, on the grounds that his condition was hereditary, and aggravated by his misconduct – masturbation. On review, however, the medical specialists concluded that Goldstein's masturbation was merely a symptom of a disability which was in reality wholly attributable to war service, and that he should all along have been classed as a Service Patient. The Treasury was rather reluctant to let this and like cases through, but it eventually acquiesced: 'the dog is at the moment sleeping and the main thing is not to wake him as there are further concessions to which we may be driven (fresh cases, responsibility for dependants, other disabilities etc)'.[7]

Though the review of the 'non-attributables' was initiated when the Conservatives were in power, it fell to a Labour administration to produce a settlement. Soon after Labour took office in 1924, there were heightened expectations that F. O. Roberts at the Ministry of Pensions and Philip Snowden at the Treasury would quickly redress the wrongs of their predecessors:

Dear Comrade, I am instructed by a mass meeting of the Bow and Bromley Labour Party to express their congratulations and hearty thanks to yourself and the Ministry of Pensions for your action in transferring the 760 ex-service men in Mental Asylums from the charge of the Poor-Law Authorities to the Ministry of Pensions ... the Party hope this is the first step by the new Government in securing the establishment of the Principle 'Fit for Service, Fit for Pension'.

Celebration was premature, however, for from the outset Roberts was cagey, informing a delegation led by George Lansbury MP and his son Edgar Lansbury, chairman of the Poplar Board of Guardians, that 'there were involved skeins discovered when they entered the doors of the Ministry and some of them remained to be disentangled'. And soon afterwards there was a climbdown by the Labour government, invoking medical science as the impartial arbiter, declaring that, after the most careful consideration, the claims of 600 or so of the 'non-attributables' to be recognized as war-related disabilities had been rejected. The small number of reassessments that had been conceded were obviously token and arbitrary, but they had the merit of lending a scientific veneer to what would otherwise have been a shameful political decision, and overall the medical findings had the effect of making the political settlement that eventually emerged, meagre though it was, seem generous. As an alternative to relegation to the pauper lunatic class, it was agreed that the rump of the 'non-attributables' would be admitted to a new class in the asylums, under the ludicrous title of the 'Ex-Service' class, to be paid for by the government as a national charge from an Exchequer grant. Here they would receive just enough to lift them beyond the ambit of the Poor Law, permitted funeral expenses but otherwise no frills, not even the weekly 2/6d. pocket money that the accredited Service Patients received, and most definitely – and on this the Labour and all subsequent administrations were adamant – no more allowances for their dependants.[8] And if this was the last gasp of the populist protest that had invigorated the People's Lunatic in 1917, it was also the last ride for dementia praecox as a first-class war psychosis, for after these ritual skirmishes with the Treasury never again did the Ministry of Pensions send this feisty aetiological specimen into action.

THE REALISTS SPEAK OUT

The realists were also much rankled by the new climate of public relations that had even affected the naming of psychiatric disabilities. Indisputably, the Great War marked a turning point in forcing official agencies to take account of the sensitivities of a much broader spectrum of the population over how they were defined and described. Ernest Morris, a former window cleaner from Oxford, who had served with the Royal Garrison Artillery in France from May 1917 to January 1919, found that he was afraid of heights and unable to resume his occupation. After delivering a 'very indefinite hedging story of his life in the Army', confirming their suspicions that he was an evasive and unreliable character, he had been labelled a 'moral imbecile' by the medical board. Eventually, after receiving a strongly-worded letter from the Oxford War Pensions Committee, which had tried without success to place Marsh on a training course in poultry farming, only to discover that no centre would accept an applicant bearing such a label, the Ministry acknowledged that the designation of 'moral imbecility' might be rather a handicap in social life. It was proposed instead that 'the disease should be termed "feeblemindedness"', not much of an adjustment, perhaps, but just sufficient to open the door to further training.[9]

Pressure on the Ministry to recast its language, and implicitly its moral assumptions, did not abate. In the early 1920s it was obliged to issue an instruction, *Description of Disability in Mental Cases*, announcing that 'in order to avoid the use of the terms Insanity, Idiocy, Imbecility etc in notifying the pensioner of his disability' it had been decided that alternative terms for the various mental disorders would in future be used. Typically, the

Ministry insisted that these new terms were 'medically more correct', so as to give the impression that policy directives were steered by medical progress rather than anything so mundane as a client rebellion, though some of these redesignations – 'constitutional psychopathic inferiority' in place of 'imbecility' or 'moron', for example – could scarcely be considered progressive.[10] This was really only the start of a long and faltering process in the revaluation and reform of the language of mental health that was to unravel over the course of the century, encountering frequent cuffs and rebuffs along the way. Experience with Great War cases, it was stated in 1940, had shown the 'inadvisability of using such terms as "imbecility", "congenital mental deficiency" and "feeblemindedness" in notifications or correspondence with claimants', but the fact that it was still found necessary to repeat this message as late as 1940 is sufficient indication of how ingrained prejudices in this sphere still were.

However, for those still steeped in the moral certitudes of a generation that was used to calling a spade a spade psychiatrically speaking, without any beating about the bush, to use the period idiom, all this renaming occurred 'for no underlying scientific reason', and was a flight from reality, or a denial of unpleasant truths, 'done for the sake of the public'.[11] Sir Frederick Mott evinced this attitude when he complained that in recent times the label neurasthenia had been 'employed to cloak ignorance, to help deception and to aid fraud', to avoid certifying people as insane and 'thus satisfy the scruples and susceptibilities of friends'.[12] Lord Macmillan, chairman of the Royal Commission on Lunacy and Mental Disorder from 1924–6, also struck a pose of realism towards scruples over the stigma of mental illness:

One would like to analyse what the stigma really is. The stigma means this, that the person has, owing to his misfortune, or his fault sometimes, ceased for a time to be a normal, rational human being. No amount of beating around the bush, or calling things by different names, no amount even of humane treatment will obliterate the fact that in a person's life there has been an episode, a pathological episode, if you please, which to some extent will place him apart from others. Is not that almost inevitable?[13]

Another unpleasant truth denied by cranks and dreamers was that the majority of psychiatric war veterans were hopeless cases. 'During the war it was wisely instituted', Frederick Mott averred in a speech that wonderfully confirmed the image of the asylum as a dustbin of incurables, 'that no soldier should be sent to an asylum until it was found out that he was incurable, and in that way a great many received early treatment and were saved from going to an asylum. I can conceive of nothing more dreadful than for a man to be taken to an asylum feeling he will never get out of it'.[14] Complained a psychiatrist addressing a meeting of the Royal Medico-Psychological Association in 1920: 'One is ever confronted with discontent on the part of relatives with regard to the presence of Service Patients in mental hospitals' and over 'the failure to adopt certain methods of treatment to which prominence has lately been given by the Press'. Though the public 'is disposed to regard the Service Patient as one who is curable and ought to be cured', in actuality the Service Patients were mostly chronic incurables, for 'a very large proportion of the soldiers who manifested psychic disturbances were really potential psychopaths before they entered upon military service'. Once in it, 'they involved trouble, anxiety and cost; now that the war is over they are burdens to the community, and unfortunately likely to continue as such'.[15]

Under the banner of 'early treatment', medicine had succeeded in expanding the universe of the 'saved', but the wartime experience did little or nothing to puncture the dominion of a cosmology of the 'damned' in official ideology. Shortly after the war, legislation was being considered that would have barred an individual who at some point in his or her life had been certified in an asylum from receiving treatment as a voluntary patient in proposed new clinics for the treatment of incipient insanity. 'The stigma of insanity which attached to his previous detention under certificate', so it was alleged, 'would follow him and would taint the institution or home in which he might be received, to the detriment of the other voluntary boarders there'. In reaching this moot conclusion, the Minister of Health had been influenced by the 'admirable results' achieved in the military hospitals 'for the treatment of cases of shell-shock and nervous disorders occasioned by war service', which 'were due in large measure to the vigorous avoidance of all suggestions of the "mad-house"'.[16]

'The word "hopeless" should never be pronounced', urged an article in the popular newspaper *John Bull*, much read by servicemen, in October 1918. It is worth quoting at some length, for what it discloses of the strengths and limitations of contemporary protests on behalf of rank-and-file servicemen with severe mental health problems. For it turns out that this admirable sentiment is less a statement of principle than a recommendation for a progressive treatment regime for 'mentally-wounded heroes' who deserve something better than 'natural' or 'congenital' lunatics. The belief that they can be restored to 'complete mental health', along with the obeisance to the restoration of 'useful citizens', rather gives the game away. If the restoration is incomplete, and the citizens who emerge less than useful, they may after all be candidates for the closed ambulance for 'hopeless cases', the 'incurables', which Nurse Claire Tisdall had witnessed at the railway station:

Suppose that only after the most careful observation and treatment, and when doubt is out of the question, a soldier is sent to an asylum as insane. Is that, even then, the way to treat our mentally-wounded heroes? Is it right that they should ever go to an Asylum? ... When they are declared insane, is our duty done, and may we then callously dump them with the congenital lunatic? ... Even if we are heartless, this is a foolish policy. With an obscure disease, produced by an extraordinary set of circumstances, the word 'hopeless' should never be pronounced. If the more desperate cases are kept in Homes, altogether apart from natural lunatics, they may well recover in the end, and useful citizens be restored to the service of the State. We go further – and in this case we pretend to know as much as any expert whose vision has been distorted by gazing constantly on the really mad. We maintain that in almost every instance shell-shock patients admitted to hospital might be restored to complete mental health. Oh, what a burden on the conscience of the authorities ... if all possible means are not taken to prove us right – or wrong![17]

All the same, this was just the kind of pie-in-the-sky idealism that was calculated to raise innumerable hackles. For the realists 'incurability' was a fate or destiny which the unfortunate mental patient, despite the best ministrations of modern medicine, had inevitably disclosed, and besides which all restorative hopes and communitarian embraces – as a citizen or fellow human being – could only fall silent. To build villa residences about the asylum estate where inmates could live more private and domesticated lives would 'waste a great deal of land and money with no good result', scoffed one medical superintendent, 'for the idea that some of these patients would recover under the new conditions, or would not have become chronic under other conditions, is fallacious and based upon the imagination of cranks and dreamers ... and not upon facts which are well known to those of us who have spent the greater part of our time in this world living amongst cases of mental disease'.[18]

HEBB THE HARDENER

In the 1920s the Ministry of Pensions became increasingly vexed by the proliferation across the social landscape of a class of what it termed 'post-war Inefficients', the Inefficients joining the Insanes and other rejects in the nominalization of adjectives of which this period was very fond, a hangover from the utilitarian calculating universe of Gradgrind in previous hard times. Before the Great War, Beatrice Webb had advanced, quite without irony, 'a great social drainage scheme' to provide for the institutional segregation of various categories of inefficients.[19] The ideology of 'national efficiency', and the movement it had inspired, was famously extolled by H. G. Wells, himself one of the company of Co-Efficients, in his utopian tract *Anticipations*, published in 1901, in which he endorsed eugenicist proposals for the 'sterilisation of failures' so as to 'check the procreation of base and servile types' and of 'fear-driven and cowardly souls'.[20] Needless to say, during the war years such ideology had lost a great deal of impetus, its acrimonious edge blunted, and had been partially transformed into a more reformative consensual politics.

Between the wars, however, the spirit of Webbism and the cult of the Efficients found a fitting successor in Hebbism, and the castigation of the 'post-war Inefficients'. These last were a motley brotherhood of chronic neurasthenics, 'harmless lunatics' (including 'special cases of mild dementia praecox who are free from dangerous or vicious propensities'), intermittent epileptics, mental defectives and mental deteriorates, all of them psychiatric casualties of war who had been awarded disability pensions of one kind or another, but 'were precluded on account of their disablements from competing with their fellows in the labour market and so providing for the maintenance of themselves and their families'. Allegedly there were around 4000 mentally defective ex-servicemen scattered about the country who had been able to maintain themselves before the war, but who now, 'owing to the additional strain put upon them by their War service and the ousting them from their grooves and their existence as automatons', had become incapable of adapting to post-war conditions.[21]

All these diverse bands of inefficients were the province of the redoubtable John Hebb, at that time an assistant director in the medical department of the Ministry, but later to become Director General of Medical Services, notable both for the animus he bore against the fashion for psychotherapy that had come out of the war and his taste for segregative solutions for social misfits. And it was in this latter domain that Hebb was to distinguish himself by promoting a methodology of institutional 'hardening', as a manly alternative to the softer and floppier influences that had been prevailing. In Hebb's 'hardening' universe, with an exclusively male staff and the inmates performing the domestic chores, there was no place for 'special psychological treatments' or 'intensive psychotherapy'. Rather, 'improvement in the condition of the disability is looked for from the discipline, supervision and occupations to which the men will be put'.[22]

Though they had been given legal advice that they could not hold against their will in Ministry institutions 'war disabled ex-service men . . . of unsound mind with a view to their ultimate cure', officials endeavoured to retain inmates within their moral compact by impressing upon them that all future pension and treatment privileges (there was, of course, no mention of rights) would be withdrawn if they walked out. 'The institution could not be worked as a hotel', the Hardener chortled, for if a 'case discharged itself with the acquiescence of friends', then 'any aggravation should be washed out'. That is to say, what had previously been classed as a disability attributable to war service would no longer be so considered, as patent a demonstration as one could find that diagnostic assessments were driven by moral and disciplinary rather than medical criteria.

Though it was to thrive in more charmed circles in post-war Britain, within the Ministry of Pensions the initial burst of enthusiasm for psychotherapy ebbed away quite quickly when officials discovered that it was stimulating an indolent attitude towards the pleasure of treatment for its own sake, at the expense of seeking gainful employment. As early as 1921 many of the out-patient clinics which had mushroomed towards the end of the war had either been closed, or were operating with greatly reduced staffs. Out-patient treatment had in any case become unpopular with the Ministry because they were unable to exert sufficient controls, pensioners frequently succumbing to the softer influences of the home environment. Hebb endeavoured to curb the interventions of medicine, instructing that men who were working 'should be disturbed as little as possible by recommendations of treatment either in-patient or out-patient'. As to 'these men who go for hardening', he sneered, they 'should not require anything more than the occasional attention of the general practitioner'.[23]

Like most experiments in the Pensions universe, this one was driven by conflicting currents, with any one doctrine or point of view always liable to trip over its double opining the opposite. One body of opinion worried about how to get pensioners to stay in institutions, another about how to induce them to leave; 'hardening' institutions were equally envisaged as colonies for chronic incurables who if left in the community would 'impair the social machine', and as pioneering experiments in community care in which rehabilitative zeal could turn the psychiatric casualties of war into effective citizens. 'They know that they could never keep a job, and their knowledge is a constant deterrent to recovery', asserted one authority, but under 'sympathetic guidance, free of all responsibility and with assurance of their future welfare' these men may again be turned into economic units. The colony, he concluded, was the passport to a 'care-free life', the 'surest sedative calculated to put them on the high road to that recovery they had almost ceased to hope for'. The sting in this patronizing nonsense is in the phrase 'free of all responsibility', for it was envisaged that, 'freed' from their friends and families, these unfortunates could be loaded into institutions and colonies where they would be 'free' to produce economically but no longer to reproduce. Though colonies themselves were hardly ever realized in the form in which they had been imagined, the colony ethos helped to legitimate centres such as Saltash in Cornwall, a former convalescent centre, which was re-opened by the Ministry in 1923 as a prototype 'hardening' institution with accommodation for up to 500 patients.[24]

The Ministry had for some time acknowledged that there were indeed many Service Patients who could be de-certified if suitable alternatives to the asylum could be found. At present, however, they were 'almost hopelessly handicapped on arrival home' in large part because 'it is known that they have come straight from an asylum'. So how does the Ministry propose to remedy this state of affairs? Why, by admitting the Service Patient to a 'hardening' centre for a period before he returned home 'with a view to his restoration to the ordinary conditions of civil life being graduated and adjusted to the requirements of his condition'.[25] It is unclear how these graduated preparatory measures were intended to address the prejudice that the former Service Patient was likely to encounter in his locality, unless 'hardening' was taken to mean the development of a thick skin. In any case this was typical of the Ministry's approach to a social problem – having acknowledged that it was a *social* problem, to beat a hasty retreat from the insight and convert it into an individual problem.

When Saltash opened, 492 patients were drafted there from their own homes, from regular asylums, and other Ministry of Pensions hospitals right across the country. After a few months' operation the medical superintendent advised that 'that within a measurable period 22 (4.5%) of the cases will, by treatment in Saltash, be sufficiently improved to become effective citizens', but as to the great majority he was 'not yet able to express any very confident opinion'. Not a very flattering picture, but rather more promising than the reality, for as it turned out by the end of the year there had been 109 discharges of which 53 had taken their own discharge against medical advice, 27 had been dismissed for flagrant misconduct, and just 14 had improved sufficiently to undertake employment. Predictably, the Pensions heaped most of the blame onto the unpromising material, but it is obvious that the bulk of inmates resented the institution, not least the forcible separation from friends and kin.[26]

In the following years the Ministry still maintained that a large proportion of inmates had been enabled 'to lead a contented and quasi-normal life', but an inquiry into Saltash-type 'hardening' regimes concluded that the typical psychiatric war disability pensioner was far from contented:

We were impressed by the number of men who complained that the very name of their disability was sufficient to shut the doors of employment against them, many employers being averse to taking on a neurasthenic for any form of work. The Neurasthenic thus carries with him a definite stigma of unemployability as pronounced as the man with facial disfigurement.[27]

Economic conditions so aggravated the strain under which men with war neurosis were living, another group of clinicians advised Hebb, that it was 'difficult, if not impossible, to say where the one cause ends and the other begins and therefore to attempt even approximately any definition of the limits of our responsibility'.[28] This is not what the Ministry wanted to hear, for it only exacerbated the sense of indeterminacy and relentless expansion that already hung about the domain of war neurosis, a quagmire of uncertainty in which a 'genuine' war disability was compounded by other influences, the battlefields of war now succeeded by the battlefields of social life, war neurosis by 'economic neurasthenia'.[29] 'Economic relapses' should be made ineligible for treatment, it was proposed, enabling the Ministry to check a large proportion of admissions to their hospitals and to scale down their operations.

But how was the line between the 'genuine' and the 'economic' to be drawn? 'Neurasthenia is not really a medical disease at all', the Ministry's medical advisers cleverly argued, 'but a social and economic reaction, the extent of which can only be determined by probing into the man's mode of life.'[30] Predictably enough, once the Pensions scalpel began to probe pensioners' social circumstances, it was concluded that many 'such persons would have felt the effects of such stress, and would have had considerable difficulty in re-adaptation, even if they had had no war experience'. Sympathy for the ostracized and disadvantaged was replaced by scepticism and mistrust, for it was now found that 'the statement made by the pensioner that he lost his employment on account of his disablement is very unreliable'.[31]

The predicament of the war psychotic is in many ways similar to that of the neurasthenic or war neurotic in the official landscape of post-war 'inefficients', muted sympathy mixed in with censure and recrimination for his failings. It was admitted in 1924 that 'discharged lunatics undoubtedly have difficulty in obtaining employment', for a scrutiny of 100 cases had shown that more than 70 were without employment. Moreover, even if he was awarded the highest pension rate, and many were not, the family income exceeded only by a few shillings the income received by his wife and dependants while he was in the asylum, a state of affairs that could only 'tempt a wife to prefer to have her husband re-certified and sent back to the Asylum'.[32] Ironically, however, as the bearers of a diagnosis that was a recognized medical currency, those who had been through the asylum system were sometimes at an advantage in the war pensions stakes. Medical reductionism did at least pay them the compliment of authorizing the legitimacy of a condition that was unaffected by fluctuations in its surroundings. 'Neurasthenia', by contrast, had become the name for a contested domain of war suffering in which 'medical' and 'social' factors were inextricably interwoven, and in which the Pensions authorities were relentlessly engaged in discounting the degree and legitimacy of the suffering. By deflating medical pretensions over neurasthenia, and exposing the welter of social forces that amassed around it, the Pensions authorities to a large extent succeeded in dissolving it into a social field. In consequence, the war neurosis pensioner was made acutely conscious of the unbearable lightness of his war disability.[33]

CARRY ON SALUTING!
John Hebb presided over generic 'hardening' regimes for a motley constituency of 'inefficients', but there was also a dedicated hardening institution especially for Service Patients. By the summer of 1923 the Ministry of Pensions had concluded an agreement to take over part of Storthes Hall Asylum in the West Riding of Yorkshire for 'the special treatment of Insane Ex-Service Men'. Additional hutted accommodation was to be erected in the grounds and and the regular inmates were to be transferred to neighbouring asylums in a scenario reminiscent of wartime military incursions into the civilian health domain.[34] Storthes Hall, or the Ministry of Pensions Mental Hospital at Kirkburton, to give it its full title, represented an attempt to recreate the therapeutic enthusiasm of the war years in the mental health sphere and, in answer to popular demand, finally to deliver some of those specialized facilities for the treatment and rehabilitation of ordinary soldiers who had become psychiatric casualties of the Great War.[35]

But even though it boasted a mansion and extensive grounds, complete with tennis courts, cricket pitch and bowling ground, the Ministry of Pensions Hospital at Storthes Hall, with a capacity of around 350 beds, was scarcely an example of the 'large house capable of accommodating not more than 30 patients' which had long been clamoured for, nor did it exactly avoid 'all suggestions of the "mad-house"'. Indeed, it was rather obviously just a regular mental hospital, not necessarily an inauspicious setting surely, since the mental department at the Napsbury War Hospital had succeeded admirably in transcending the limitations of its location, but this was 1924, not 1917 or 1918, and there lay the rub.

Under the class alliances that lasted as the war was being fought, there had been a popular swing towards the People's Lunatic, as distinct from the malign establishment's creation, but the climate of opinion changed rapidly, hastened not least by middle-class fears and anxieties over working-class disaffection and the spectre of socialism. During the Great War there had been a change of attitudes as 'ordinary people no longer saw their society hierarchically nor their place within it deferentially', and the 'obsequious states of mind on which hierarchy had depended' were undermined. By the early 1920s, however, the middle classes had regained their confidence and poise.[36] The class stereotypes of all those who fell outside the norms of patriotism, respectability and efficiency, which to a large extent had been muted during the war years, were now rekindled in their full vigour, heralding an extended period of heightened class antagonisms.

The concessions and reforms which the extraordinary circumstances of the war years had produced, while scarcely a bonanza, are perhaps best understood as signs of a premature awakening, hastily aborted, of a social democratic definition of democracy which was not to return until after the next war. This short-lived vision was to be rudely replaced, as Ross McKibbin has powerfully argued, by a definition of democracy that was mostly individualistic and spearheaded by a modernizing middle class.[37] The dispensations and arrangements for war psychosis pensioners were not dismantled, but the legitimating rhetoric to a large extent fizzled away, to be covered over and replaced by other stratagems and concerns, and there was no more talk of ex-servicemen who had become insane through fighting for their country.

Between the wars the Conservative Party to a large extent manufactured 'the public' as a club in its own image, installing its own bouncers at the door, and making membership exclusive to the 'constitutional classes'. Ostracized from this moral and political consensus were the manual working class, the unemployed, all those who could or would not work, or were truculent and lacking in deference about the work place, and who in the hostile images and stereotypes that prevailed were largely projected as being the authors of their own misfortunes.[38] These currents are as much in evidence in psychiatric wards, in the transactions between doctors and patients, as they are in the factory between bosses and workers. The Ministry of Pensions largely conducted its business within the same polarities, on the side of the virtuous, hard-working patriotic public against the ranks of sundry malcontents, inefficients, malingerers and exaggerators for whom a war disability pension had become a preferred lifestyle. In the mental hospitals, Service Patients were frequently censured for lacking deference, showing 'a mixture of hostility and apology' towards the doctor, and ridiculed for trying to rise above their stations, failing to realize the degradation of their true positions, as with William Henry Hitchcock, a boot finisher, 'self-centred with many petty complaints', who did a little ward work, but 'since being classed as a Service Patient has put on airs'.[39]

It might, of course, be claimed that the problem lay in part with the 'unpromising material', in the jargon, that was sent to an institution like Storthes Hall, but the question of 'promise' is inseparably interwoven with the prevailing images and circumstances of a period. In answer to Macmillan's lordly conceit, exhibiting the arrogance of a class taking its own point of view for reality, a progressive psychiatrist tried to reconfigure stigma in the life experience of ordinary working people, proposing that the working person's spade produced a different reality. 'The practical point of view of the poorer classes', he retorted, 'is that at present if a person has been certified he is unemployable'.[40] In the rather unpromising conditions which obtained in the 1920s and 1930s, in which the long-term mentally ill in public asylums were to a large extent moralized in the same rhetoric as the unemployed, the currency of promise was at a discount. Correspondingly, for members of the 'unpromising' classes it required a huge, not so say delusory, stretch of the imagination, or a capacious store of inner resources, to feel promise in themselves and to sustain a faith in an alternate outcome to the chronic and marginal destinies that appeared to be their lot.

When Arthur A was brought back home from Netley at the end of the war, his sister Emily Jane later recounted, 'he broke windows in the bedroom, pulled curtains down, washed clean socks in a chamber [pot], blackened his face with soot' and was altogether 'raving mad, counting his fingers and doing all sorts of tricks', burning his thumb when he put his hand in the kitchen fire. At Colney Hatch Asylum he became more cheerful, getting on well with the other inmates, and graduating over a couple of years from being 'a very foolish and irrational patient' to being granted cricket-pitch parole, permitted 'to go out to the field for exercises', behaving well and working in the upholstery shop; yet overall he was still held to be 'to be without much initative and ambition' and to lack 'a great realisation of his own deficiences'.[41]

Arthur was in many respects quite typical of the Storthes Hall recruits, for a certain ambivalence and equivocation hung over their dispatch there, reflected also in the character of the regime itself, in which rehabilitative zeal was combined with schooling in a greater awareness of inmates' own deficiencies. Not that this was an especially well-considered strategy, for most of the recruits were all too conscious of their alleged shortcomings and failings, and already existed in a state of chronic uncertainty as to where they stood with their Maker, their fathers, their bosses, their commanding officers. . . with authority in general.[42] How had they acquitted themselves in the war, what was their place in the scheme of things, why did they feel so unwanted etc? Some of them had developed 'delusions of unworthiness', such as Charlie G, who according to his mother had been constantly groaning since he had returned home from Netley with an orderly, declaring that he was a wicked man and ought to be blown to hell, and William F, who was sometimes so downcast over his prospects that he was prone to be neglectful, especially at meals, putting his porridge into his tea. Others discovered that body parts had gone missing, Walter G stating that his 'stomach had gone' and that he had 'no back passage', and Horace T, a former clerk from Liverpool, reporting that he had lost his brains, his head was empty and he had no proper feelings left; or complained of a great mystery which they were unable to fathom, William T telling that he was getting closer to the bottom of a big problem which still eluded him because he had learned that imagination was high treason. And then there was Charles C, who had broken down absolutely during the war, accusing himself of being a traitor to his country and of 'swinging the lead', declaring that he was not worthy to live, he was the outcast of the earth, crippled before he was born, denying that he had a name and demanding a complete examination to settle the mystery of his birth, as late as 1931 still worrying about 'origins' and 'being', asserting that he had not yet been 'enlightened' about the earth.

Inevitably, there were those also who were uncertain over their standing with the Ministry of Pensions or some other government agency, such as poor Frank W, who was forever writing letters and repeating strings of reference numbers bearing on the progress of his case in numerous ministries with such rapidity that his speech amounted to gibberish. 'Brusque and inclined to be dictatorial in conversation, stating it is high time his discharge was effected according to the conditions made known to the War Office, the Ministry of Health and the Board of Control. . . . Has given up work as he considers he has done enough to warrant discharge'. When last we hear of him, on the eve of his removal to another asylum on the next instalment of his chronic destiny, he poignantly declared that his case was now cleared up, and all his reference numbers at last in order, a conclusion with which the doctor felt strangely unable to concur. To compensate for their placelessness and uncertainty some found consolation in masturbation, others in developing 'fantastic' delusions, anything to relieve the burden of their marginality, and to indicate that they might after all count for something in the scheme of things, for which inevitably they were scorned all the more by the Pensions medical fraternity for being so silly or fatuous (a favourite term in the lexicon of psychiatric dismissal) as to suppose that there was anything in the least bit special about them, or that they held any title to encroach on the fireside from the outer darkness.

The Storthes Hall inmates who won approval from the Pensions authorities were the pliable deferential types like John K, 'well conducted and well behaved, works devotedly in the bootshop, and pursues the milder forms of amusement in the evenings', and William P, who 'industriously pursues his efforts at drawing', both of whom were discharged to a Ministry of Pensions Convalescent Hospital, and sundry others who provided compliant labour under a soubriquet such as 'useful in coal squad when in good humour'. The Daily Report Book provided a record of inmate diligence, listing the patients who had attended divine service; or been employed in one of the workshops – with the shoemaker, the tailor, or the upholsterer, in the stores or the kitchen, on the wards or in the gardens; or unemployed, because they were sick, too low-spirited, too excited, or simply unwilling; or taking exercise, in the airing courts, on the asylum estate, or (for a small minority) beyond it. The type who rubbed the authorities up the wrong way, by contrast, was the soldier mental patient who 'nurses a sense of grievance', and fails to take heed 'when the errors of his conduct are pointed out to him'. Instead, he so forgets himself as to become 'a source of great disquietude and discontent, utterly regardless of all rules and regulations, impertinent and insulting', persisting, like Harry F, in writing letters with more than a hint of menace taking the form 'Sir, I had an interview with you the other day but I did not like the way you treat me':

I stated to you how I had my parole taken from me for nothing at all and I should like it back at the same price, if you please, and I want you to con-sider it over within the next few days what you intend doing about it, as there are other patients practically do and say what they like and are allowed to carry on with it. If I make the slightest mistake, you have no mercy for me and you have not got a more straighter patient in the hospital than I am.

Harry managed to force the issue in more senses than one, for in April 1929 he escaped from a dormitory at Storthes Hall in company with another patient by forcing the metal guard from the window, making his way to the home of his brother in Hull, who at once wrote to the hospital to say that Harry had arrived and that he was prepared to accept responsibility for him. The author-ities could in any case have done little to oppose the outcome, but they begrudgingly acknowledged that though Harry was 'facile' with a 'furtive demeanour', still he had improved under treatment and was able to 'keep himself under control and occupy himself industriously' if there was 'any immediate privilege and benefit to be derived from it'.

However, the excitation around John W, a former farm labourer from Sheffield who had been sent to Kirkburton from Wakefield Asylum, where he had been a patient since 1917 after serving his country overseas for a number of years, was more tempestuous. The authorities took against him from the outset and there was no common ground on which a therapeutic rapport of any kind could have got started. 'Is of low grade of intelligence: presents in his ears and shape of head marked stigmata of degeneration'. 'He is a high grade imbecile', it was iterated three years later:

> From the history he gives, without any exhibition of shame or excuse, he has never done any good. He tells me when in the service he was always in the guard-room for desertion. 'Too much work in soldiering'. His attitude towards work, as he expresses it, is that it is degrading & something to be avoided.

His immediate relations were equally tarred by moral censure as loafers and scroungers affecting mental disability, for it was alleged that his brother was 'at home with "shell shock" doing nothing', and that his father also 'does nothing' and 'appears unable to work'. In this, as in many other cases, so bent were the authorities upon institutional treatment, considering that they alone knew best what was in the patient's interests, that they did not scruple at riding rough-shod over emotional sentiments and ties if they judged that the family was not a suitable ally in the treatment process.

The provisions of the Service Patient scheme had, however, given the family new powers. Given that John had been an in-patient since 1917 it is, perhaps, understandable that by 1931 he and his family might have felt that their reunion had been somewhat delayed, and they had deferred to the authorities for long enough, and so decided to take matters into their own hands. Having taken him out for the day, his mother sent a telegram to say that she was taking him home for good. After 'being warned by police', John was brought back to the hospital 'with great difficulty' by two orderlies. Nonetheless, his mother persisted with her resolve, as was her right, and her son was discharged to her care against medical advice early the following month. This was a bold move in a society in which, even if psychiatric patients had at points been able to wrest power from doctors, and to negotiate alternative settlements, the culture of medical deference was still solid, and medical superintendents were capable of striking terror into the hearts of the relatives of Service Patients who were unaware of, or lacked confidence in, their rights.

Albert T, the youngest of 14 children, who had served in the army for three years, two of them in India, was now moralized by the good doctor as 'a chronic masturbator': 'feeble minded, curses freely, masturbates openly, no sense of shame'. His mother had asked to take him home on leave for the weekend, but her request had been misinterpreted as a call for his discharge, leaving her to worry that she was guilty of flouting the doctor's authority:

> Do not think sir that I am thinking for one moment that my son is yet in a fit state to be discharged from the hospital my whole hopes confidences are entirely intrusted to you as a great Mental Specialist to know far better than I do when he is in a fit state to be discharged I am only to pleased to see him improving so well under your care ... if I have made myself misunderstood to you I enclose to you my sincere appology.

All this grovelling achieved its immediate aim, but Albert's hopes and confidence were by no means entrusted in the 'great Mental Specialist'. Periodically, the medical superintendent was to be made the recipient of further communications purporting to be from Albert T's mother, in actuality forged by Albert himself, requesting that he be allowed out on leave, to which for the most part he acquiesced. Some time later, a few weeks after he had ecaped from the asylum, Albert cheekily sent a friend to collect his belongings with an accompanying note plainly in the same hand: 'ı Trulby hat   ı pair of pants   ı grey bag and brown one   the bags are at ward 2   ı army discharge paper   ı silver badge ı new tie   will you kindly let mrs Fitzgerald have these articles for me and oblige   Albert T' [sic].[43]

The atmosphere at Storthes Hall was most strikingly exemplified by two ex-soldiers who to a large extent functioned like automata that had been programmed to reproduce their routines, even though the parade grounds and battle-fronts had long been vacated. A former colliery labourer who had been 'gassed at the War', William S had given himself up to the police as 'the wanted man', his wife telling of how he had regularly been standing in the middle of the kitchen floor at attention or doing drill for three hours without moving from the one spot. For his part, James M behaved in 'a very silly fashion, running up and down, dropping on all fours, sitting down and rising up repeatedly, making numerous gestures and adopting curious attitudes'. He rarely spoke except to 'verbigerate' a few phrases such as 'good morning' and 'I'm very well, yes I'm very well, yes', yet perhaps the most striking thing about him is that he was 'constantly saluting', not as an occasional performance, but repeatedly, hour by hour, day by day, for years.

At war hospitals such as Napsbury, Craiglockhart and Maghull, the circumstances of the war provided the conditions for more relaxed and egalitarian treatment regimes that were not entirely subjugated by traditional military values. However, the irony is that having taken its mandate from the War Office, the Ministry of Pensions was never able in the interwar period to transcend its enthusiasm for, and subservience on, a house style of military social relations in which the war psychosis pensioner was always made to feel like a failed soldier, and his failure as a soldier inevitably made the measure of his failure as a citizen and as a man. The military model of therapeutic progress, which continued to provide the standard for the Ministry of Pensions, is adroitly conveyed by Frederick Mott in his depiction of the three stages in the recovery of a shell-shock case in which the soldier is, first, slumped rigidly in a chair; then, held upright between a nurse and an attendant; and, finally, stands by himself in an erect position, 'holding himself like a man' (see plate 8).[44]

The truth of it is that Storthes Hall was a kind of failed Craiglockhart or Maghull, deserted by the circumstances of national crisis and unity that had lent such urgency and purpose to those earlier therapeutic endeavours. Now there was no battle-front to which to attempt to return these men, just the battle of everyday life, and who could get excited about that? The lead actors were also missing – no Dr Rows or Dr Rivers to be found here. Hence what we find at Storthes Hall are frustrated doctors and patients confronting each other, the Pensions medical personnel hankering after a military road show whose moment had long past. The ex-service mental patients were always judged by their relation to soldiery and could never be forgiven, or released, from their failings as soldiers, nor granted permission to remake themselves in an alternative image. James M was but one of a kind, for there were other mad saluters – however, at some point the saluting had to stop. In 1931 the Storthes Hall show was wound up, the hutted recreation hall was dismantled, the asylum was handed back to its regular managers, and the rump of the ex-service inmates was dispatched to institutions such as the Old Manor in Salisbury, in which the Ministry had taken over a wing, and the Royal Naval Hospital in Great Yarmouth, in order to continue their chronic destinies. And a few – including James M – were returned to the asylums whence they came.[45]

Chapter 16

THE SERVICE PATIENTS BETWEEN THE WARS

TAKING CARE OF THEIR 'PRIVATES'

Quietly [Bloom] read, restraining himself, the first column and, yielding but resisting, began the second. . . . He read on, seated calm above his own rising smell. . . . He tore away half the prize story sharply and wiped himself with it. Then he girded up his trousers, braced and buttoned himself. He pulled back the jerky shaky door of the jakes and came forth from the gloom into the air.

James Joyce, *Ulysses*.[1]

There were 150 or so Service Patients at Whittingham Asylum in the 1920s, distributed throughout all the male wards, 'enjoying the privileges of their class' and attired in 'distinctive clothing', khaki suits made on the lounge pattern, along with 'soft shirts, collars and ties', though a few who refused to wear khaki had been issued with blue serge suits. They were regularly visited by medical officers from the Ministry of Pensions, and the visits had an important role in exposing the institution to outside scrutiny, for they frequently drew attention to defects in the regime as a whole. To that extent, the Service Patient became a vehicle for a concern with the dignity and individuality of the mental patient that assisted the Board of Control in promoting the norms to which the mental health system needed to level up. The asylum authorities at Whittingham maintained a rather insensible view of their charges, and in the 1920s they were involved in frequent altercations with the Board over the privacy and dignity of the mental patient's body, the Board urging reforms that had regard to the mental patient as a person of sensibility likely to be offended by degrading forms of communality, such as the sharing of towels and toothbrushes.

When the Board objected that only a few of the patients had nightshirts, the Lancashire Committee failed to grasp that a nightshirt was a distinctive garment, not a day shirt on overtime duty, declaring that it was in any event not customary for the working class in Lancashire to change their shirts at night. In their experience, the Board rejoined, the fashion for nightshirts was spreading among the working class, and 'besides advocating it as a sanitary measure, it is a provision which is much appreciated when the night-shirts are of full length so as to be warm and comfortable in bed'. The Commissioners also remonstrated over the number of toilets without dwarf doors in the sanitary annexes, asking the authorities to imagine 'how very objectionable it is to a person using a closet to find himself (still more so, herself) fully exposed to the gaze of another patient passing by. To a patient for the first time in an institution, it must savour of a shock and indignity, the infliction of which it would be very hard to justify in the minds of the public'.[2]

The intense preoccupation with the Service Patient's suit by the inspectorate from the Ministry of Pensions, even in the mid 1930s still emphasizing that they were clad 'in civilian clothing of good quality', bordered on the perverse, as though the neatness of their attire could compensate for the neglect of their health, or provide for the dignity of patients, in what was acknowledged to be a deprived and disgusting environment. The Ministry would only pay for dentures for Service Patients if one of their own medical officers, rather than the medical officer of the asylum, had been able to examine the patient before the teeth were extracted, indication enough that they were intent upon assessing rather more than the state of the patient's mouth. Riled though they frequently were by these stipulations, asylum doctors were in consequence insidiously drawn into proffering character assessments of reliable inmate workers whose longevity might be boosted by the provision of dentures, at the expense of perhaps more needy patients whose life prospects were less valued.

At Whittingham in the early 1920s, there were hardly any drinking mugs supplied to patients at dinner; there were scarcely any overcoats available for male patients; none of the inmates were shaved (though the medical superintendent said he was making arrangements to have some of the patients shaved); there were no nail brushes on any of the wards; it was unusual to catch sight of a toothbrush; and there were no dental services (though the question of a dentist for all the asylums in the county was 'under consideration' by the Lancashire Asylums Board). Mr P, who had been an asylum inmate during this period, described how, despite frequent epidemics of gastroenteritis, there was only one toilet in a ward for 45 people: 'You can understand the position if a dozen men were rushing at one time'. Though some roller towels were provided, 'patients get up in the middle of the night and use them for purposes for which they are not meant'. Nominally, toilet paper was kept in the scullery, but since no other writing paper was available it was mostly commandeered by patients for writing notes. 'There is no privacy. As a matter of fact, I felt that very keenly myself'.[3] The inmates were frequently made to strip in the open dormitory on a bleak cold day, all the

One of the main entrances to Whittingham Lunatic Asylum, where the Medical Superintendent had his offices, c.1910. This postcard was probably one of a 'limited edition' for use by the asylum authorities. The doctor may have been sending his compliments, but for the Service Patients and other inmates on the back wards in the 1920s there was rather little to write home about.

windows thrown open, and then wait their turn for a bath. At Hanwell in 1925 there were only seven gramophones for 47 wards.[4]

As a reflection of an increasing concern with privacy and self-respect, it is noteworthy that in the periodic reports which the Ministry of Pensions circulated to interested parties such as ex-servicemen's associations, mention was frequently made of the Ministry's success in 'securing such refinements as private underclothing' for Service Patients in asylums. In sending out assurances about the homely condition of his 'privates', the Ministry was able to convey the message that, regardless of the torments that were assailing him, or the indignities that he might be suffering, nonetheless the ex-serviceman in a public asylum remained in charge where it really counted and, in that very English phrase, was still king of his own castle.[5] Of course, these bulletins were targeted at a respectable audience of concerned outsiders, secure in the privacy of their own castles (their underpants as much as their homes), for to those on the inside track who were knowledgeable about the operation of a regular lunatic asylum, the supposition that the impersonal laundry system could have been attuned to such personalized requirements was quite preposterous.

DOWN AT THE MANOR

The Service Patients arrived at the Old Manor Hospital in Salisbury in two waves in the spring and summer of 1923, a total of 174 in that year, mostly from asylums in the west of England, a few from Birmingham and the Midlands, and a sprinkling from London and East Anglia. Between times there were sporadic admissions, but the next wave only came in the summer of 1931 with 115 admissions from Storthes Hall.[6] The largest private licensed house in the land, with a licence to receive 672 mental patients, including 542 pauper or criminal lunatics, Fisherton House Lunatic Asylum had been functioning for almost a century, surviving on, alongside its pauper intake, a staple diet of clerics, some them quite high-ranking, in varying states of psychological dilapidation.[7] After the Great War it found itself financially straitened, however, and having already resolved to curtail the pauper side of the business, and to rebrand itself as the Old Manor, the contract with the Ministry of Pensions was a welcome boost to its coffers. Though it was promoted by the Ministry for its own public relations purposes as an establishment for promising cases, where they would be given individualized attention and specialized treatments, in reality the vast majority came there on a one-way ticket, with just a handful of discharges, largely to Ministry of Pensions hospitals, and a small number of escapees.

The new arrivals came laden with their own emotional histories, contorted life narratives many of them, as though some of these former servicemen had assumed a position or rhythm between 1914 and 1918 from which they had never been able to extricate themselves. James C's wife reported that he had not slept since he had returned home from the front in 1915, and had told the Sister at the military hospital that he had no wish to live and 'that it was no use trying to patch him up'; John B, a former painter, was said to have developed 'peculiar gestures' and was 'constantly doing military movements with only his shirt on'; Herbert B was continually haunted by memories from Rouen; Henry B had been strange ever since he came out of the Army according to his wife, burning photographs and papers, throwing out all the things in the sitting room and putting funny pictures in the window; William K was mostly silent, complaining of pains in his head, and if addressed he frequently began to cry; Esau K, suffering from melancholia, took a considerable time to reply to questions, rarely taking the initiative in conversations, yet 'will shake hands with one dozens of times within the course of five or ten minutes without giving any reason for doing so'; and Albert L 'imagined that people were drilling in the yard and that airships were around him all night', frequently muttering to himself 'Oh dear, Oh dear!', still believing in the late 1920s that his life at the hospital was mixed up in some business regulated by Army headquarters. Frank B, a former printer's assistant, was stated to be 'very demonstrative', 'saluting the doctor frequently in the course of a few minutes', and even in the mid-1930s he was 'constantly saluting people' and writing long letters signing himself 'A Genuine and Honourabled Disabled Discharged Soldier':

Gentlemen – Sir I am writing a letter has stated concerning my self. I have been the army six years continous service and been right through the thick of war front line every time. I have been in many engagements indeed. . . . My complaint and disability (Honourabled War Service). . . . I have a very good army character. A steady trustworthy deserving man was wounded in ACTION and a very good civilian character. . . . I sincerely wished I was in the army now. I should loved to be in the 20th Hussars.[8]

Such insults to the soul could not be supported indefinitely, and mercifully, perhaps, the bearers of these narratives mostly died before the start of the next war, though the 'honourabled' Frank survived until 1951, 'a useful worker who has limited parole', his saluting urges by then somewhat abated. One of the few to be discharged was George B, a former private in the labour corps, who had previously been in a war hospital at Cardiff, where he had 'resented being under "lock and key"', stating that it would 'eventually drive him mad'. In the casebook there is a photograph of George in his uniform, looking rather uneasy, standing in a sitting room, with a bookcase in the background. When he arrived at the Old Manor he was given to 'talking on religious matters to a great extent', and it was 'difficult to rouse rational interests in him', but the following year he was 'working well in the tailor's shop' and 'conversing normally'. Though in January 1925 he became 'very emotional on hearing yesterday of the death of his mother', the medical superintendent was pleased to report that he had shortly 'regained control over himself', and later that year he was discharged on trial to the Ministry of Pensions 'hardening' centre at Saltash in Cornwall.[9]

Underneath a rather unpromising exterior, George F, a former commercial clerk who had served with the expeditionary forces, turned out to be quite a savvy operator. When he was admitted in October 1923 from Brookwood Mental Hospital in Surrey, he mostly sat all day with a book on his knees which he never appeared to read, his head bowed down over it, to all appearances mute and semi-stuporose, never altering his position, until one day in

June 1928 he surprised the medical superintendent by calling out to him and talking garrulously but incoherently for ten minutes or more (alas, the doctor gave no indication of what he was talking about). He continued to converse sporadically for the next three months or so, until in October he again became mute, his head once more 'bent over a book which he does not read'. From this point on, however, he opened a new line of communication, routinely handing the doctor a large collection of rubbish at the end of each day, until one evening in June 1930, when the attendants were diverted looking for another patient, he scaled the wall in the cricket field and escaped, never to be recaptured.[10]

However, the majority of Service Patients who came to the Old Manor were there for the long haul. In the late 1950s there were 130 or so still in residence, such as George B, born 1894, ex-soldier, admitted in 1923 from Herrison Asylum, brown eyes, grey hair, vacant expression, thin features, rarely speaks, smokes a pipe; John T, born 1888, admitted in 1923 from Winson Green Asylum, Birmingham, polisher & ex-soldier, brown eyes, dark hair going grey, no teeth, medium build, cap generally well down over his eyes and wearing all sorts of knick-knacks; and Colin C, born 1884, admitted 1923 from Worcester Co. Asylum, ex-soldier, next of kin nephew, a major in Woking, erect posture, grey hair, looks melancholy, quiet and inoffensive, enjoys patients' social club.[11] Though these are just a few shavings from chronic destinies, in most instances pretty much the sum of their biographical remains, it would be a mistake to suppose that the Old Manor was a neglectful or pitiable environment.

In fact, the opposite was the case, and within all the limitations of the interwar mental hospital landscape in England, the Old Manor was undoubtedly a superior institution in which to pursue an involuntary career as a Great War psychiatric war disability pensioner, even for an ordinary ranker without any private funds to draw upon. Not, it must be admitted, because it was especially up to date as a hospital, at the cutting edge of some new outcrop of therapeutic zeal – in that respect it probably lagged behind the field – but because it was comfortable and pleasant as a home to live in, providing more privacy than residents would have enjoyed in a regular mental institution, a more varied menu of amenities, and a relatively relaxed parole regime. Though the periodic clinical assessments by the doctors were generally rather more jaundiced, in the perception of the nursing staff the Service Patients were to a large extent a contingent of the shell shocked. In the opinion of one former nurse who started working at the Old Manor in 1937, 90 per cent of the Service Patients were shell-shock cases ('they were in the trenches for years') and the other 10 per cent were 'gas related'. 'The experience they went through in the trenches in those days must have been awful', claimed another nurse of the same generation, 'they were given no option or they'd be shot'.[12]

Even if this heroic imagery is rather idealized in relation to probably quite a significant proportion of the ex-service inmates, still it had the inestimable advantage of helping to stimulate and sustain a benign therapeutic environment for what might otherwise have been seen as rather unpromising cases. In 1923, when the Service Patients first arrived, a cinema projector for silent films was installed in the ballroom, and to accommodate the arrivals from Storthes Hall in 1931, a new wing was built, with a day room and a billiards room on the ground floor, and individual cubicles, rather than the standard dormitory, above. There were diverse workshops, including one that made pewter boxes and mugs as a speciality, together with opportunities for work on the land and in the gardens; also provided were numerous sporting activities, cricket, hockey, football, badminton, and even tennis and croquet, these latter mainly for the officer types, along with a regular programme of entertainments and excursions.

Of course, in a mixed-economy mental hospital in this period those from a higher class, and with means of their own, had the upper hand. Alongside the Service Patients, there were 20 or so permanent Great War officer patients (majors, captains and lieutenants), many of whom were accommodated in individual rooms in Bemerton Lodge, a mid-Victorian villa built in the Italianate style. In keeping with this lifestyle, at Christmas time they reputedly also received gifts such as gloves, scarves, pyjamas and wallets from ex-service associations, where the other ranks were merely given cigarettes.[13] There was no formal obligation to do so, yet even the nurses addressed the officers by their ranks, and officer patients were quick to light on any breach of such courtesies. Though the arrangement was quite 'unofficial' as far as the hospital was concerned, some of the other ranks were employed by the officers as batmen, to make their beds and clean their rooms.[14] The hospital also had two motor cars, which were at the disposal of those who could afford it to make excursions into the countryside, as was Hume Towers, a convalescent and holiday home with adjoining villas in Bournemouth, which had been acquired by the hospital. When the medical officer from the Ministry of Pensions made his annual inspection, he set up his table in the ballroom where the Service Patients were gathered as a group, waiting their turn to exchange a few words with him, but it was only the officers who were granted private interviews later that day.

All the same, the other ranks were by no means excluded from the remembrance networks nor from the parties that travelled to London in response to invitations extended by the 'Not Forgotten' Association to take part in the annual garden party at Buckingham Palace, or the Christmas party in the Royal Mews, or who visited the Royal Tournament at Earls Court. However, the Service Patients tended to feel more relaxed at these latter events than at the Palace garden party, a retired nurse recollecting how the group he was accompanying, too shy to ask directions to the toilets, relieved themselves in the royal rose bushes. Similarly, efforts were made by the Old Manor to maintain the bonds between service inmates and their regimental associations. Frank R was able to go on holiday because he was the beneficiary of a residual estate managed by the Official Solicitor, to which application could be made on his behalf by the hospital authorities, but he was in a small minority and, as late as the 1950s and 1960s, regimental associations would still sometimes pay for a holiday for a Service Patient and the expenses of a nurse to accompany him.[15]

ALTERNATIVES TO THE ASYLUM

In August 1917, Sir Frederick Milner and others, representing an association of recuperative hostels, fastened on the limitation of the homes being established by the Ministry of Pensions for the 're-education and training of patients who as a result of shell-shock think they cannot speak, hear, see or walk'. There was another class of patients, they maintained, who were 'in danger, after discharge, of drifting into asylums, or who have already been committed to asylums for insufficient reasons'. The Pensions Minister had consistently failed to distinguish between those soldiers who were 'genuinely certifiable' and the

uncertifiable, who are not dangerous or unfit to be at large, but who simply for convenience' sake are committed to asylums because no alternative place has been provided. . . . Our disabled cannot now be treated in the manner which proved convenient in bygone days before every citizen was compelled into the Army. It is upon the Pensions Ministry that the task of their re-establishment devolves and on that Ministry will fall the credit or disgrace. . . . There is nothing which the public regard with greater or more natural dread than the possibility of being shut up in an asylum; and if at the end of the war many hundreds of our brave defenders should be found relegated in needless and heartless fashion to such a position, there is nothing that will stir up greater bitterness.[16]

'Certification', these advocates of alternatives to the asylum were arguing, was frequently just a convenient trope under which to banish the psychiatric casualties of war from society and place them in the control of alienists as incurable cases. A former Conservative MP who had been forced to give up his seat because of his increasing deafness, Sir Frederick Milner became the pre-eminent champion of the war disabled early on in the war, founding the first recuperative hostel for shell-shock victims at Hampstead, together with hostels for deaf soldiers and sailors, and latterly, through his association with the Ex-Services Welfare Society, founded in 1919, becoming an implacable opponent of the government's handling of mentally afflicted ex-servicemen.[17] If Milner was sometimes indiscriminate in his judgments and mawkish in tone, still he possessed a keen instinct for the underdog, and the cause to which he lent his name was robustly polemical in attacking flagrant social injustices.

From its inception, the mission of the Society was to promote alternatives to the asylum for ex-servicemen through recuperative homes and hostels, and the creation of aftercare regimes along the lines of those already pioneered in the United States and some other European countries. In the Society's apologetics, the certified lunatic was not a natural object, the inevitable culmination of a process to be borne with resignation, but the adventitious product of a misdirected politics. The mission of the Society was to offer 'hope and healing' to 'unfortunate Ex-Service Men labelled as insane or on the borderland'. 'It is a poor return, indeed', they constantly iterated, 'for all that such a man has undergone . . . to label him "Lunatic" and leave him to his fate'.[18] It was exactly their unrelenting refusal to concede the 'necessity' of the establishment's actions in the warehousing of incurables that attracted governmental ire. 'The whole suggestion of Milner's letter', fulminated the Minister of Pensions over one of Sir Frederick's gothic pen portraits of psychiatric neglect, 'is that the 6000 ex-service men who are in lunatic asylums are there quite unnecessarily and also that they are put to unnecessary suffering . . . this suggestion is baseless and mischievous'.[19] There was, moreover, absolutely no need for charity or voluntary initiative for the mentally afflicted of the Great War, since the state was addressing every conceivable aspect of their needs. 'Far from its being necessary to appeal to private charity . . . there has been an organized effort of medical skill backed by ample and generous financial provision', and the Minister is 'definitely of opinion that no contributions for this object are required from private generosity'.[20]

There was a heated standoff at the Ministry in which Colonel George Stanley, the Parliamentary Secretary, remonstrated at the Society's demands for homes for ex-servicemen as alternatives to the asylum: 'What else could be done? Do you mean to say every county should set up a home? . . . We really cannot work together so long as this sort of thing is being said'. The Ministry, insisted the Colonel, was bestowing every consideration upon lunatic ex-servicemen: 'They are private patients and are treated exactly the same as I should be if I went off my head . . . exactly the same as any private individual who happened to go off his head would be treated'. It fell to Sir Lisle Webb, the Director General of Medical Services, to give the lie to these specious claims: 'In the case of officers we pay up to 6 guineas a week. Officers are sent to the sort of place – probably some private home or certified nursing home – to which you and I, if we unfortunately had mental disease, would go. . . . They are most comfortable homes'. No doubt they were, so long as 'you and I' were not mistaken for one of 'them' and dispatched to an asylum.

In his riposte, Everett Howard, the general secretary of the Society throughout the interwar period, reflected the shifts in social relationships to which the experience of the war had lent impetus. Not a refined man in the traditional mould, his was the outlook of those returning from the battlefields who were no longer prepared to accept the 'old settlement':

> I do maintain this, that the country could have shown its gratitude by putting these men into proper places. . . . I am looking purely from the ex-serviceman's point of view and I am speaking of the Tommy. . . . I know hundreds of men in my regiment, men who never reached commissioned rank, men of education and good circumstances, men of good social position – what happened to these men? They are in ordinary asylums living under pauper conditions. Is it fair to that type of man?[21]

When the Sir Frederick Milner Home at Beckenham in Kent was opened in September 1924, it was reported in *The Times* that the home had a 'situation amid peaceful and picturesque surroundings calculated to have a beneficial influence in promoting the curative work for those suffering from the strain of war'. The residents 'will be drawn from all classes and will be cared for free of charge'; they will be given 'special medical treatment and individual attention', and bedrooms have been provided 'to meet the comfort and requirements of individual patients'.[22] This was just the kind of provision for ex-servicemen 'from all classes' treated as 'private individuals' that did seem convincing. Insist though they might 'that a direct and personal interest is taken by the Ministry in each of its pensioners in Mental Hospitals and that a paternal watch is kept over all the conditions appertaining to their welfare and treatment', the Pensions could never shake off the suspicion that it was caring for war pensioners as secondary objects of welfare rather than as deserving citizens.[23] The 'home' that is being figured here is, of course, not only a therapeutic home but also an idealized picture of the nation. Through an alliance between Tory paternalists and liberal modernizers, one-nation conservatives and medical holists, the Ex-Services Welfare Society was able to offer a symbolic vehicle for healing the divisions and shattered nerves in the national home.[24]

Images of 'respectability' prevailed in its publicity, largely because the Society was anxious to reassure its supporters that 'nerve-wracked' ex-servicemen who had emerged from asylums were really just colourless sorts of people who could safely be invited to tea or to the garden fete. During the Depression they were variously portrayed in the Society's literature as taking to their beds, succumbing smilingly and uncomplainingly to medical ministrations ('doctor knows best'), or feeding the hens (always wearing suits and ties), or engaged in purposeful activities like rug-making. Passive images of a domesticated and compliant masculinity helped to distract donors to the society's cause from apprehensions about clients as potential agitators.

In its appeals the Society was certainly given to exaggeration, presenting an absurdly sentimentalized portrait of mentally damaged ex-servicemen. '6000 Known Warriors and 21 Ex-Service Women Nurses in Lunatic Asylums', ran the strapline for the Armistice Day appeal in November 1923.[25] It went on: 'They gave more than life. When the call came they were clean-limbed, clear-brained men. In their country's service they sacrificed that without which life is but a husk of aimlessness . . . burdensome. War broke their reason. They were brought home. And because they had nothing, having given all, their Country put them away in pauper asylums'.[26] But if sometimes overdrawn, the Society's polemics had the merit of lampooning the hollowness of 'modernizing' rhetoric which maintained that the asylums were now on a sound medical footing and that the ex-service inmates were all 'as happy as they can be owing to their affliction and . . . receiving the greatest kindness and consideration'.[27] 'My Society has always strenuously contended', the general secretary apprised the Ministry in 1923, 'that it can give better treatment to all ex-service mental cases than that which is provided in lunatic asylums'.[28] This was a lofty claim, but it was not entirely unconvincing. What made the Society threatening was that it was always searching for, and claiming to detect, signs of life among a group who were regarded by the Ministry as socially dead. With their talk of 'hope and healing', the Society's activists refused to accept closure, forever prodding the corpse of the hopeless case, and envisaging their clients as potentially knowable people with whom one might have a conversation. This put the shivers up the Ministry, who were always fearful of permitting contact with ex-servicemen in asylums lest the dead might indeed turn out to have awakened.

Emboldened by her contact with the Society, Mrs Helena Laurie of St John's Wood, whose son, Robert, was a Service Patient at Hanwell Asylum, had the

The Armistice Appeal from the Ex-Services Welfare Society in 1924.

temerity to call upon Dr Daniel, the medical superintendent, to inform him that in her opinion Robert, having 'made good progress in a steady way', was 'now sufficiently well enough to be transferred to a quiet home'. Robert Laurie had served more than two and a half years in France with the 1st Battalion Royal Berkshire Regiment, been promoted to corporal and discharged from the army with a medical category of A1. Mrs Laurie emphatically believed that with a 'change of scene, quietude, and away from the stifling atmosphere of the worst cases of lunacy', his 'broken nerves would surely be recuperated'. Writing to the Society after this encounter, Dr Daniel pulled no punches in snubbing Mrs Laurie's optimism: 'Robert Alexander Laurie is suffering from Dementia Praecox. He is dull, slow and foolish, lacks interest in himself and is untidy and slovenly in his habits. He does no work and cannot apply himself to any work. . . . He takes no interest in current events and rarely if ever reads the Daily Paper. He is quite unimproved and unfit to be discharged. I can give you no other advice except that he should remain in a mental hospital'.[29]

Though in an obvious way the Society was absorbed into the antagonistic ideological currents of the 1920s and 1930s, it was also energized by a flux ignited by the experience of the war and its immediate aftermath that was greatly more populist, enjoining solidarity with the disadvantaged ex-servicemen in asylums against an untrustworthy establishment. This more radical strand was inevitably tempered over the years, but it was never extinguished entirely, and the Society was always willing to pick up the cudgels on behalf of individual ex-servicemen who found themselves in difficulties, or to take up the cause of the several thousand ex-servicemen in mental hospitals whose claims had been rejected by the authorities. In the mid-1920s it was giving around 3000 interviews a year, by 1930 as many as 8500. The Society and its officers possessed a self-confidence, quite lacking in the Ministry, which largely came from the conviction that mentally disabled ex-servicemen were on their side. It might justly be claimed that the Society combined in an awkward but productive tension a more orthodox reformist or meliorist form of philanthropy with a long tradition of grass-roots activism 'grounded in experience of damage inflicted by care-givers and custodians', in which mad persons and their supporters had protested 'their negative designation in the eyes of society'.[30] The strength of the Society was that it was capable of assuming different voices, sometimes protesting on behalf of a broader middle-class constituency, sometimes on behalf of 'the men' or the other rankers, as a totality against an uncaring and cheese-paring establishment.

The Society's repeated pronouncements that it could offer better treatment in the Society's homes than in the public asylums were, many suspected, born of bravado rather than sound judgment. However, in notable respects they were vindicated by the reports of Dr Edward Mapother, medical superintendent of the Maudsley Hospital, who since 1925 had served as honorary medical consultant to the Society and was to remain closely associated with it until his untimely death in 1940, on the industrial workshops which had been established in Leatherhead, Surrey. These are, Mapother wrote in 1928, a 'triumphant success', progress in these patients having gone further than he had observed anywhere else, which he ascribed largely to the 'self-respect derived from self-support' and 'the novel sense of security'. Among them were 'cases representing minor degrees of schizophrenic reaction who had already under stress exhibited all the manifestations of severe Dementia Praecox . . . but who are at present interested, alert and useful'.

The following year he has come to appreciate that it is a misnomer to refer to the residents and workers as 'patients', since 'here the men are rightly encouraged to regard themselves as not suffering from current disability'. In 1932, he remarks again that 'the most striking achievement is to be seen in the case of certain patients whose previous symptoms had unmistakably been those constituting the initial phase of the disease shown by the majority of degraded patients in a mental hospital. Several such patients were among the happiest and most effective workers, and also among those in whom apart from history it would have been difficult to detect any abnormality'. Ironically, he goes on to say, these improvements may present difficulties for those who are only receiving temporary pensions and are thus liable to appear before Boards for review, and 'it may be extremely difficult to get justice done'.[31] Dr Mapother forebore to disclose whether the residents and workers were now reading the daily papers, but, all told, his remarks could be taken as encouragement that hopeful travellers like Mrs Helena Laurie were by no means guilty of wishful thinking.

'MUSTN'T EXCITE THE LUNATICS!'

It must, though, be admitted that the Ministry of Pensions did not take at all kindly, not merely to hopeful travellers, but to displays of interest in the welfare of Service Patients in asylums of any nature. In ways that were, perhaps, not fully obvious to those who supported it at the time, the creation of the Service Patient scheme was provocative, seeming to legitimate the idea that conditions of modern warfare could drive men insane. From this point of view, the Service Patient was a kind of anti-hero, a moral object lesson in the horrors of modernity, and while the founding declarations of the Board of Control did not, of course, make such connections explicit, it did not rule them out either. Hence, perhaps, why in the inter-war period the Ministry was very anxious about the management of public opinion, fearful of any resurgence of the populist protest that had so influenced policy in the aftermath of the war.

The memory of these transgressions would take a long time to fade. 'I need not remind you', the Accountant General muttered darkly in 1947, 'that this Service Patient business was one of our main headaches after the 1914 war'.[32] As far as the Ministry was concerned, not simply had the patients to be put away, but the meanings and resonances that might have developed around them, and turned them into collective symbols, also had to be put out of reach. Even in the late 1950s it was admitted that 'our first reactions are to be cautious in correspondence about mental cases'.[33] Right from the beginning, the Ministry treated as potentially seditious requests from local war pension committees or ex-servicemen's associations to visit groups of Service Patients in asylums. When the Secretary of the Stepney & Poplar branch of the British Legion requested permission to interview the Service Patients at Claybury, the Ministry tried to fob him off by allowing him to visit one particular patient, a Mr Wood. The Secretary wrote back:

I believe you have misunderstood my letter. I am no more interested in Mr Wood than the others. I am interested in the whole of the ex-service cases in the institution. I do not wish to be bound down to one case, but as I have heard from several sources the treatment to these fellows, I thought you, as direct representative of the Ministry, could get for me this permission. I have several times been to Claybury to enquire into the cases of individuals, but on each occasion I have been bound down to Mr Wood.[34]

Even when the overtures were encouraging, the Ministry would not be drawn. In 1925, a Mr Pennington from Durham was so impressed by the treatment of the Service Patients at Storthes Hall that he proposed to take a delegation down there, so that their appreciation of the Ministry's care of these war-disabled pensioners could be put on record. Fearful, perhaps, that Mr Pennington was being disingenuous, or that his comrades might prove more discerning, the Ministry puzzled over how he had managed to ferret his way into Storthes Hall in the first place, informing him brusquely that 'the Minister is medically advised that visits by other than friends or relations of Service Patients are likely to excite them and thus be detrimental to their treatment'.[35] The potential power of the Service Patient's testimony in the imagination of the Pensions authorities was boundless. 'We, of course, know', asserted Hebb the Hardener in 1930, 'that the ex-soldier is a perfect masterpiece in making a plausible story, and the veracity of these can only be judged fairly and critically by those who have been through the same experience. This is one of the reasons why the evidence of a casual visitor concerning what is taking place in a hospital, derived from a patient, proves of little or no value'.[36]

As far as the Ministry was concerned, the service lunatics no longer figured in a national narrative, and neither they nor their representatives were invited to participate in the remembrance ceremonies at the Cenotaph. From being portrayed as soldiers of the Great War who had broken down in the course of their service, they had become mental patients who happened to have had careers as soldiers at some point, and questionable ones at that. On the occasion of the Coronation in 1937, it was announced that at the request of the King 'a personal message was to be addressed by name to every ex-service officer, nurse and man of the Great War' who was still being treated in hospital for 'wounds or disease due to war service'. 'All those who fought for his father, King George the Fifth, and their country in the Great War', the King assured his war-disabled subjects, were 'always in his remembrance'.[37] The Ministry was not moved by this royal directive, however, hastily intervening to prevent the Service Patients from being included in the community of remembrance through this ritual of personalized naming, demurring that it 'would be likely to provoke jealousies and friction, and would be inadvisable in the interests of the patients themselves'.[38]

NO CREDIT FOR THE HOPELESS CASE

As late as 1937, relatives of Great War pensioners, some of them solid middle-class citizens, were still at loggerheads with the Ministry. Until rudely disabused by the Ministry, many of them had been living for quite some years in the fond belief, supported by a widely shared sense of what justice must surely have delivered, that the war pensioners in asylums were indeed receiving pensions. 'This is a most unfortunate case', confided an official: 'The pensioner's father, Mr Alfred Gostelow, who has written to Sir John Jarvis MP, appears to be a man much respected in Guildford, and in addition was a member of the War Pensions Committee during the war and later. Although he undoubtedly feels that he has a serious grievance against the Ministry, you will note that his letters to Sir John Jarvis are moderately worded'.

The case, he goes on to say, had an unhappy start because Mr Gostelow's son's condition was first rejected by the Ministry in December 1918 'on the ground that it was "mainly hereditary" and not due to or aggravated by service'. His father then went to great pains to redress the slur on the family honour, and to prove there was no history of insanity in his family, with the result that the Ministry finally backed down and accepted liability. Even so, the original grievance still rankled, and salt had now been added to the wound through the mistaken impression conveyed to him that, after the deduction of maintenance charges from his son's pension, who was still a Service Patient in an asylum, a balance was accumulating to his credit.

Mr Gostelow had now been brusquely advised that there was no balance in his son's favour at all. As it turned out, in the eyes of the Ministry 'hopeless cases' did not deserve any credit. Even though the honorific of Imperial War Disability Pensioner had been bestowed on him, the reality was that as an asylum inmate he had forfeited his pension, and in lieu the Ministry had undertaken to pay for the costs of his treatment, including maintenance, 'additional comforts' and pocket money. That, in sum, was the chastening enlightenment that Mr Gostelow now received from the Ministry. Only if his son were discharged recovered, they went on to say, would an additional grant be made, and until that moment arrived 'no amount can be deemed as standing or accruing to your son's credit'.[39]

This is now the final sting in the tail, for it insinuates the notion of a slumbering pension, with a shadow balance to its credit currently shrouded in darkness, that would resuscitate itself if the pensioner recovered, in which event he would retrospectively be considered to have been receiving a pension all along. Only if the pensioner had realistic prospects of becoming once more an 'efficient economic unit' was he entitled to a past as a fully-fledged war disability pensioner, in which he could, to a degree, be said to 'own' his pension. Behind the mystifying rhetoric, the reality of it is that war pensions are not so much rights as privileges, to be removed or toyed with on a bureaucratic whim. As for those unfortunates sojourning indefinitely in asylums whose progress towards economic efficiency has miserably stalled – in the sight of officials, these are truly 'human wrecks', to be maintained at the state cost, but strictly on sufferance.

The war psychosis pensioner was in one aspect a 'positive' creation, but he was hedged about with regulations which frequently changed, and was treated with enormous ambivalence, sometimes downright suspicion. Though the prevailing social ideology placed a high value on economic self-sufficiency, if the pensioner was a single man there were severe restrictions on his capacity to save for the future, as though the right to possess a vision of a possible future that he might wish to save for had itself been removed from him, and he was to a large extent pauperized. The dispensations for Service Patients included weekly pocket money of up to 2/6d., but the Pensions were vexed to receive reports that the special ward at Claybury Asylum, which had been allocated to Service Patients, had become a gambler's den, patients gambling among themselves with the money that had been granted to them by the Ministry in its benificence, some of them accumulating large sums of money. In other institutions, so the Ministry learned, Service Patients were saving their pocket money, slowly building up balances to their credit. Accordingly, a directive was quickly issued forbidding any system of 'pooling' grants or saving for special purchases, instructing that pocket money was to be spent exclusively on the weekly consumption of 'small comforts' such as cigarettes.[40]

These considerations embraced also the pensioner's family, whose avarice knew no bounds in the official imagination, and whose interest in the pension was much more likely to be attributed to greed than to any legitimate sense of entitlement deriving from the bonds of kinship. The Ministry was fearful that too many powers might accrue to the role of war pensioner, and so what they gave with one hand, they were inclined to take away with the other. The war psychosis pensioner, one might say, was straddled between two welfare paradigms, a traditional one (albeit a bit reformed) based on the Poor Law and refurbished in the Mental Deficiency Act of 1913, and an emergent embryonic one, less individualist, more socio-democratic and based around social rights, looking forward to something like T. H. Marshall's universe of social citizenship in which 'the basic equality of membership' had finally been 'enriched with new substance' by joining civil and political rights with rights to welfare and health care resources.[41]

'VOLUNTARY LUNATICS'

As reforms became visible in the mental health landscape, the Ministry of Pensions was always lagging behind the field, upbraided for being out of step. With the Mental Treatment Act of 1930, the words 'asylum', 'pauper, and 'lunatic' were officially abolished, and replaced by 'mental hospital',' rate-aided person' and 'person of unsound mind', and an ex-serviceman classified as a Service Patient was no longer by definition a certified case. But in the late 1930s the Ministry was rebuked by its legal adviser for entertaining a notion of 'voluntary lunatics', and regarding all Service Patients as though they were by definition lunatics.[42] Around the same time, the Ex-Services Welfare Society proposed to acquire a property by the seaside as a holiday home for Service Patients from mental hospitals who 'in the opinion of the Medical Superintendent would benefit from a change of surroundings, climate and conditions'. However, Pensions officials were unable to rouse themselves from their Poor Law mentality, declaring that they could find no place for such a wild proposal in their scheme of things, since when the 1890 Lunacy Act was created 'it was never envisaged that a pauper patient would require to go on leave for purposes of their health'.[43]

Apprised that the National Health Service (NHS) Act of 1946 entailed 'the complete severance of the Mental Health Service from the Poor Law', nevertheless the Ministry still hankered after the *ancien régime*. The Service Patient was now a potential beneficiary of brave new policy innovations such as Unemployability Supplement, but the Ministry was anxious to keep pensioners and their relatives in the dark about their entitlements. Asked whether the 'Are you Sure?' leaflet had been brought to the notice of pensioners in mental hospitals, the Pensions replied that it was 'deemed undesirable to send a leaflet to a pensioner in a mental hospital' and that leaflets were only sent to pensioners who were 'compos mentis'. Moreover, they were not sent to next of kin either, since they might have 'raised requests for benefits . . . which it had not been deemed appropriate to consider in such cases'.[44]

In 1949, news was received of a minor rebellion by the Service Patients at Warlingham Park Hospital in Surrey who contended that since hospital treatment was now free to all citizens at the point of delivery, the Ministry had no right to deduct maintenance charges from their Pensions.[45] There were similar murmurings of discontent from other quarters. Alfred August Bennett had been a Service Patient in a mental hospital from 1921 until his death in 1953.

After he died his son was appalled to discover that only around £12 remained from his father's pension, the bulk of it having been plundered over the years to pay for his treatment and maintenance. Moreover, the Ministry would connive only at a small grant towards funeral expenses. Mr Bennett made his feelings known to the *Sunday Pictorial*: 'On the face of it there seems to be something radically wrong for the personal funds of a man totally disabled in the service of his country, and condemned to a living death, being used to keep him'. In these and similar cases the Pensions maintained in slightly more circumspect language that the very idea of 'personal funds' or of a 'personal pension' was illusory, the war pensioner being the property of the state. 'Pension is intended to help towards current maintenance and it is not unreasonable to provide for a pensioner's maintenance from his pension . . . the pensioner is clothed and maintained at the expense of the state'.[46]

Even on the eve of the Mental Health Act of 1959, the Ministry was still moving in the universe of certified lunatics and the 1890 Lunacy Act, observing with some astonishment that in the future the patient 'will not be retained as a hospital in-patient when he has reached the stage where he could return home if he has a reasonably good home to go'. In itself this is an unexceptional statement, but it is remarkable for what it discloses of the suppositions on which officials had been operating, not least the axiomatic assumption that the mental patient was incapable of managing his own affairs, a belief that as they openly admitted had still prevailed 'for administrative reasons' long after the Mental Treatment Act of 1930.[47] Since the pauper lunatic was proclaimed to have become extinct in 1958, it was no longer considered necessary to provide the dwindling population of Service Patients with lounge suits, since 'the clothing now provided under the NHS for mental patients generally is of good quality and should meet all their reasonable requirements'.[48]

The Service Patients themselves begged to differ, however, for by the early 1960s there were rumblings indicating that they were far from happy with the clothing issued to them, and wanted to buy their own. At the war pensioners' wing at the Old Manor Hospital, on occasions regimental associations stepped into the breach to pay for a 'civvy' suit for a Great War pensioner who wanted one, in place of the ill-fitting hospital suit of worsted grey trousers and jacket.[49] As a result of these discontents, the issue which had been put to sleep in the 1920s as to whether Service Patients should be allowed to accumulate savings was again revisited, this time round, in a changing culture in which even mental patients were starting to be regarded as consumers with tastes, and sensitivities as to how they were perceived by others, with rather more success.

Sir Hubert Bond: 'The word "trauma" has been used by someone this afternoon, I believe?'
Lord Horder: 'I should have called the man to order. I am sensitive to the word. I did not hear it to-day. . . .'

Horder Committee, 3 July 1939[50]

It is not possible to convince the man in the street or a great part of the medical profession that the war was not responsible for every attack of insanity which had its onset during war service.

Ministry of Pensions Memorandum, 1939[51]

Even within the ranks of army medicine there was a sizeable shift in this period away from traditional military values, and it is, surely, rather remarkable to hear from the lips of the army medical services in 1931 an admission that there is a consensus of opinion that 'there is something in a normal Army life which is conducive to mental trouble'.[52] Yet, of course, ideas that appear progressive in one sphere, may be destabilizing in another, and by the time that preparations were being made for the next war, all the talk about justice and fair play for the lunatic, and the revaluation of mental troubles in military contexts, had ceded to a harsher and more familiar perspective in which mental disorders were to be accounted for by the 'constitutional factor'.

That the war psychosis pensioner should have been the object of so much defensive skirmishing is scarcely surprising when we consider the costs involved. As early as 1923 it was apparent to the Treasury that service lunatics comprised more than 50 per cent of the cases for whom 'permanent provision would have to be made by the State in some form or another'. Though the psychotic disability group was relatively small, economically it was not insignificant, since even in the early 1930s it comprised just over 10 per cent of disabled ex-servicemen in all categories with the most severe disabilities. Throughout the interwar period the psychotic or 'insane' cases absorbed a disproportionate share of the budget for psychiatric war disability pensioners and their families, as much as 60 per cent of the overall treatment budget in 1924, and just under 50 per cent in the later 1930s (see Appendix II, 'The Burden of Costs').

By the late 1920s the 'constitutional factor' had already begun to play a strategic role in disengaging the connection between war service and disability. The Ministry had circulated a list of some of the pathological classes that it was now presumed to influence, including psychopathic inferiors, psychopaths, and individuals with psychotic personalities of various types, such as the 'shut-in type, the manic depressive and the paranoid'. The 'constitutional factor' was strategically useful, not merely as a buffer between the originating war experience and the current condition of the former serviceman, but also as an instrument in deflecting or blunting the relevance of social experiences, such as, for example, unemployment during a period of economic blight, that might otherwise have tended to bolster the ex-serviceman's case for disability pension. Persons 'who are constitutionally predisposed to neuroses are peculiarly susceptible to economic pressure, domestic discord and dissatisfactions of all kinds'. Under 'post-war conditions of civil life . . . when anxiety has been widespread and economic pressure universal, such persons would . . . have had considerable difficulty in re-adaptation, even if they had had no war experience'.[53]

The constitutionalist argument served two interests rather well – if mentally disordered servicemen were all disturbed before the event, then there was clearly no need to give them pensions; and from the fact they were all inherently off-balance, it followed that they had no lessons to teach the rest of society about the conditions of modern warfare, and could conveniently be excised from the mainstream cultural narrative. The idea that modern warfare could drive people insane was a serious threat to morale and put the whole frame of military/social relations into question. In the creation of the category of the Service Patient, and the liberal provisions for pensions for ex-servicemen disabled by mental disability, the establishment had tacitly owned up to a causal connection between its own machinations and the miseries suffered by quite a proportion of its subjects. Arguably, this was the kind of collective self-awareness that had to be sharply disavowed in order to mobilize for the next war. Certainly, by the end of 1939, in a number of influential committees, the historical record had been readjusted, and the provisions arising out of the Great War made for Service Patients, proclaimed as a source of pride by government departments for over two decades, were evidently judged a mistake and an embarrassment, and we may perhaps find in this a clue as to why the history of the Great War service lunatics has all but been expunged from the official record. Genuine traumatic reactions, it was now alleged, recover quickly and are of temporary duration; those that linger on, and become chronic, are evidence of inherent instabilities. Cupidity strikes the keynote in these debates: the greedy war pensioner, vitiated by constitutional defects, is ungrateful for the help that the state is giving him; the individual stands to gain something by a traumatic neurosis, and it is the lure of the gain which drives the production of the traumatic neurosis itself.

Interestingly, one of the few establishment figures to utter heresies in the company of the 'constitutionalists' was Edward Mapother, who for many years already had been strongly supportive of the rehabilitative efforts of the Ex-Services Welfare Society. In the summer of 1939, in what turned out to be the final months of his life, almost alone against the assembled ranks of Sir Farquhar Buzzard and Lord Horder (Physicians-in-Ordinary to the King), Sir Adair Hore (now the Permanent Secretary at the Ministry of Pensions), and other luminaries, he mounted a claim for a subtler understanding of the neuroses and psychoses of war. Not only did he question the dominance of the constitutional factor, he also disposed of the idea that genuine shock reactions were by their nature only temporary: 'I think people may suffer from neurotic and psychotic disabilities which are, as far as is ascertainable, entirely the result of the war and that they may be left with permanent disability from them'. During the War there were many cases 'in whose past you could trace nothing to label them as constitutional neurotics, unless you start with the theory that everyone who becomes a neurotic has a constitutional basis', but then 'you are arguing in a circle'. And in answer to Farquhar Buzzard's disdainful suggestion that chronic neurasthenics were all in it for the money, he delivered a retort not entirely unfamiliar in the history of psychiatry: 'Excuse me, I dispute the facts! You get these cases in people who have never drawn pension'.[54]

'Less than 10% of the psychoses for which entitlement to pension has been granted', the Ministry now alleged, 'can really be said to have a war basis', dismantling at one fell swoop all the subtle calibrations that had been made over two decades and more, by countless medical practitioners and mental specialists, of the variable impact of war service on ex-servicemen.[55] This was a kick in the teeth not only for thousands of war pensioners but also for a great part of medical opinion. What about the line that had so carefully been determined between the 'attributables' and the 'non-attributables', for example, and the innumerable decisions over entitlement that had been considered by appeal tribunals? Where did this now leave Captains Haws and Collenette, Lieutenant Barraclough, Privates Hill, Beebee, Laing, Murray, Pembury, Quinton, and all the others we have considered from Wandsworth and elsewhere? Were these just frauds and impostors, with no title to be included on the war pensions roster, on all fours with George Major Gomm, who had never received any official recognition for the mental scars he had received as a result of his war service?

This was, of course, just the message that had been trumpeted by Knowles Stansfield, that old-fashioned knight errant of psychiatric realism, in his letter to *The Times* in 1919, which had so much warmed the cockles of Pensions hearts until they were quickly doused by Maurice Craig. As it happened, this was to a large extent the last hurrah of the monocled Col. Stansfield, for so irksome did he find the changes of the post-war years, never succeeding in reconciling himself to them, that he soon retired from his post as medical superintendent of Bexley Asylum, which he had held for 23 years, and retired to San Remo.[56] Ironically, he died in 1939, just too soon to receive the news of the deliberations that were, rather strikingly, the counterpart of the conference in July 1917 which, taking its cue from the equalizing demands for social justice for the community of serving citizens, had peremptorily dismantled the fixtures and fittings of the hierarchical moral armoury of psychiatry. If the conclave which had met under the extraordinary circumstances of 1917 had, in its way, been 'excessive' in proclaiming that entitlement could scarcely be refused to anyone, the gathering of 1939 was no less 'excessive' in determining that the majority of stress reactions were the product of deficient constitutions. Not for nothing did Edward Mapother remark to a colleague in September 1939 that the medical establishment was now siding with the Germans in concluding that there was no such thing as war neurosis or psychosis.[57]

The psychiatric history of the next war is beyond the scope of this discussion, but if the aspirations of the establishment were now to draw a line under the equivocations and concessions made by 'the greatest authorities on lunacy' in 1917 that had repercussed down the intervening years, and to return to a tidier epistemological universe in which categories were clearly demarcated, all bearing their proper labels, they were to be disappointed. In the judgments of the appeal tribunals that were convened in the late 1940s we can once again hear echoes of the hesitant but thoughtful psychiatric voices of the Great War. 'It is quite impossible for us to disentangle', a tribunal averred: 'how much of this serviceman's disorder may have been attributable to one factor rather than to another ... it is impossible for us to say on the evidence that this disease, namely Schizophrenia, from which he was suffering, was not due to his war service. . . . We therefore make the recommendation to the Minister that the applicant's disability . . . is attributable to war service'. And to the belief of the Ministry that their assumptive universe could rest comfortably on the cornerstone of 'inherent predisposition', Mr Justice Denning had this to say: 'The fact that a man has an inherent predisposition to a disease does not mean when an event happens which precipitates it, that it is not attributable to war service'.[58]

Coda

Connie and Alex

The Ministry of Pensions frequently liked to present itself as the Service Patient's truest friend, the stalwart and steadfast buddy who stood by him while those who should have been true to him were either defiling the marital bed, or had long ago abandoned him. Of course, it is not difficult to find examples that conform to this stereotype of neglect, such as Francis S, a Service Patient at Digby Mental Hospital in Exeter, who told the authorities in 1929 that he was anxious to see his relatives since he had not been visited for seven years or so, and had received no word from them. The affection was scarcely mutual, since by the mid-1930s they still had not called on him or even dropped him a seasonal line.[1]

Though the public mood was diverted by the austerities of the twenties and thirties, and in significant measure placated by 'modernizing' promises – 'the up-to-date mental hospital' was a phrase now frequently on official lips – still a concern for the fortunes and wellbeing of ex-servicemen in asylums, even if it dimmed, certainly did not languish. It was kept alive by specialist organizations such as the Ex-Services Welfare Society, as well as the ex-services juggernaut of the British Legion. At Whittingham between the wars, for example, the Red Cross unfailingly remembered the Service Patients by sending them presents at Christmas such as cigarettes, cakes, and gramophone records.[2] There are reports also of how regimental associations maintained links with ex-servicemen in asylums, visiting them from time to time, or taking them on outings, though it is uncertain how widespread these were.

Moreover, in actuality there was a constant flow of visitors from the relatives of asylum inmates, and a determination in numerous instances to maintain a bond of a kind despite the bleak economic and ideological clime. Private Alexander G had come back from the war with a 'frightened, terrified, suspicious expression', and for the rest of his days he was invaded by inner demons, still in the late 1930s beating the wall with his boots to fend off his persecutors. From the Edmonton Infirmary he was transferred first to Napsbury, and thence as a Service Patient to the Ministry of Pensions wing at the Old Manor, where he remained through to his death. Despite his handicaps, his capacity to sustain a form of rapport with those with whom he had always been close never deserted him. Throughout the years there was a regular correspondence between successive members of his family and the hospital; first his older brother, Arthur, and then on his brother's death his younger sister, Connie, inquiring after Alex's health, remitting small sums from his provident society, and periodically arranging to visit him and take him out for a few hours.

Arthur advised Dr Martin, the medical superintendent, in February 1927 that another brother had died, and asked if he could come to the hospital to inform Alex personally. If, as sometimes happened, brother and sister were obliged to alter an arrangement, they unfailingly sent a telegram to the hospital: 'regret not able to see brother today please inform him'. Not that their sensitivity towards their brother, and their effort to maintain a sense of his individuality that transcended his situation as a mental patient, was entirely reciprocated by the medical superintendent. Dr Martin invariably delivered a downbeat assessment of what he considered to be a regular chronic case. 'I regret to say there is no real improvement to report in Mr G's condition', ran a typical message, 'he is still solitary in his habits, and at times noisy owing to the imaginary voices which trouble him', furthermore 'he does not employ himself'.

Nor did the medical superintendent seem inclined to reflect on the disparity between the ability to communicate, and to sustain the emotional bonds of a relationship, that Alexander G displayed on his outings with his siblings, and the indifferent and uncommunicative figure portrayed in the hospital case book. 'Wanders aimlessly', reads a typical entry, 'is silent & self-absorbed & unoccupied . . . at times walks about Day Room putting his head under the table and shouting out "You dirty dogs!"'. In the militaristic period idiom that was equally audible in the mental hospital culture, it was remarked in a mitigating spirit that he 'pulls himself together when the doctor addresses him'.

In 1938 Connie complimented the doctor on the improvement she had observed in her brother, expressing gratitude for his care and kind attention, but Dr Martin was consistently disparaging, merely reiterating that he was noisy and still troubled by voices. When Alexander G died in 1944 towards the end of what was officially termed the 'New War', Connie travelled down from London for the funeral on a wet November day. In her remembrance he was still not only a cherished brother but an ex-serviceman who had done honourable service for his country in the Great War, late private in the North Staffordshire Regiment. In the clinical record, however, the memory of Alexander G's military career had by this time long been eroded, and he was just that impersonal and anonymous object, 'a depressed and hallucinated patient in Ward 17'.[3]

PART VI

MAD ACTIVISTS OF THE GREAT WAR

Mad persons may be mad, but they are not stupid. Inevitably, we would recognise and act upon the discrepancy between being promised that we were the same as everyone else and being treated as burdensome, dangerous, inferior aliens. By the mid-1970s there were substantial numbers of people (including the author) who had been brought up in a civil-rights climate, lived for years being thought of as psychotically ill, been enabled to live with their distress predominantly within the community, yet had been excluded from the anticipated respect and dignities. We had too little to lose not to act. Unlike fellow-psychotics of a previous era, we were living in the community. We could really taste the discrepancy and do something about it.

Peter Campbell, veteran mad activist, poet and trainer (1996)[1]

Chapter 17

INDEPENDENT LIVES

THE WAR PSYCHOTIC IN THE COMMUNITY

Despite the best efforts of ex-servicemen's associations, amidst the austerities of the early 1920s the public profile of the Service Patients rapidly diminished. The wartime class alliances had, in any case, long since abated, and, as Ross McKibbin has reminded us, it is easy to be forgetful of the degree of class antagonism that existed in England in the wake of the Great War.[1] Readers of the *Morning Post* were persuaded that the majority of Service Patients in asylums were by now lost causes who did not merit additional favours from the public purse. Though there was an emerging discourse about bringing the mentally afflicted back into society in the interwar period, the terms of welcome were highly conditional. In the prevailing doctrine, only the 'socially efficient', and those who could be buttoned into a very restricted conception of 'normality', merited the return to full citizenship and the 'chances of common life'.[2]

To borrow from John Pickstone's typology once more, communitarian trends were tempered by productionist requirements.[3] Reconstruction, stated a contemporary text, is all about 'the maintenance of national efficiency, the production of efficient military or economic units'. Now that the 'importance of helping the man who has been maimed in the defence of his country to get back to the social life of the community, and to become once more a productive unit', has been realized, the aftercare of the disabled soldier constitutes a 'most important piece of social reconstruction'. And what of those in whom 'this principle finds no sphere for fruitful application', and who fail to become efficient economic units? The writer has an answer: these are 'human wrecks', 'shadowed lives that do but await the "Great Release"'.[4]

Writing in the mid-1920s, the distinguished social psychiatrist J. R. Lord nicely exemplifies how communitarian enthusiasms could comfortably consort with productionist strictures. We must, he urges, soften the attitude of the 'group mind' towards the 'mentally afflicted person' and 'find for him a place *within* the community during his necessary segregation as we do those sick in body, and not one outside of it, or on the fringe of it, estranged from the world as though he were a pariah or outlaw' and, finally, 'at his recovery to welcome him back to full citizenship, and to find him suitable work so that he may live and thrive – which is the birthright of all men'. Making allowances for the male gender privilege, all of this has a very contemporary shine to it, until we read on and appreciate that the 'full citizens' he has in mind are but a minority of the asylum population, around 30 per cent by his calculation. 'One wholesome function of the Lunacy and Mental Deficiency Acts', he goes on to say, 'is the segregation from the public of those who, by reason of mental disorder or defect, impair the social machine by their inefficiency as citizens, and that the more thoroughly this is done the better for the home and for the nation'. 'The proper place for such a person', he concludes, 'is undoubtedly a mental institution'.[5]

Fortunately for the mentally disabled ex-servicemen we have been discussing, there were other currents in social life. As Jose Harris has described, if in this period 'there were many aspects of modern urban and industrial life pressing individuals into an apparently more uniform and more communal mould', the very same pressures also 'generated the opposite process – the proliferation of an infinite variety of tastes, styles, functions, habits and beliefs, and an accentuated emphasis on private life and personal relationships'.[6] On the war pensions hustings, as we saw earlier, the advocates of the 'home man', or the serviceman whose primary allegiance was to his family, were able to trim the sails of traditional military moralists. The 1920s and 30s, Alison Light has also argued recently, saw 'a move away from formerly heroic and officially masculine public rhetorics of national destiny . . . to an Englishness at once less imperial and more inward-looking, more domestic and more private'.[7]

These trends provide useful guidance in exploring the destinies of war psychosis pensioners in this period, for it turns out that quite a large group of around 5000 ex-servicemen, many of them bearing diagnoses of dementia praecox, manic-depressive psychosis, and delusional insanity, managed to escape the fate of permanent incarceration, and to live largely community-based lives, maintaining if you will the Napsbury tradition of the certifiable leading uncertified lives. Though, of course, they were not to know that when they set out on their journeys as war pensioners, many of those whose narratives we shall explore were in for the long haul, another half century or more in several cases, some of them surviving into their eighties and nineties, the last one that I have been able to identify dying in 1991.

In that respect they are not wholly representative, for the mortality rate among Great War disability pensioners was in any case high compared with the general population, and may well have been still higher among the mentally disabled, and there was a downward curve in the population of psychiatric war pensioners towards the late 1930s.[8] All the same, in looking at those who survived the longest, and journeyed through different political, social, and welfare eras, we can learn more about what was crucially at stake for the individual: inwardly in terms of his subjectivity, locally in terms of the man in his local world, and externally in relation to official agencies, in being the long-term bearer of an identity as a shell-shock victim or a Great War psychiatric disability pensioner, a sub-category of that portentous species, the Imperial War Disability Pensioner.

Whose narrative is this exactly? By no means is it a medical narrative, but it would at the same time be misleading to say that it is always that of the war pensioner rather than of the doctor, because there may not always be sufficient material there for us to be able to say confidently that this is the pensioner's story. Sometimes it is the historian's narrative which, originating in a concern for what was happening to these war pensioners, tries both to expose the contested dynamics around them and, without bringing undue closure to these accounts, to identify the opportunities and constraints that embraced them. The historiography of the 'silent working-class soldier' has obscured much of what were actually very noisy encounters. Even though to some extent the Blimp class got its own back on liberal modernizers and social justice enthusiasts, the psychiatric aftermath of the war was far from petering out. In an important sense the action was just warming up, with countless personal troubles waiting to break beneath the skin of social life, followed by the long struggle for sufferers and their families to secure justice.

The category of the community-based war psychotic was never envisaged, or planned for, and did not consort at all comfortably with any of the models that the Ministry of Pensions entertained. Though there were some moderating voices, the Ministry took the view that you were either mad and locked up in an asylum, or fit and ready to report for duty at your workplace outside it. The occupation of this zone was to a large extent a consumer-led initiative, which started to emerge in the immediate aftermath of the war and never ceased to be intensely controverted. Various pressures combined to force the Pensions to revise its original expectations: war psychotics were discharged from mental hospitals as 'recovered' but turned out to have long-term disabilities; numerous families insisted on managing in their own homes the care of pensioners who would otherwise have become long-term residents of institutions; and some war pensioners were resolute about making a go of it in the community, even though they would manifestly never become 'efficient economic units'. Finally, there were those, as the Pensions was begrudgingly brought to acknowledge, who though plainly certifiable by the Pensions lights, had against the grain become personally and socially viable with the financial support that a war disability pension was able to provide.

There was frequently no resting place, in that, having won one contest or challenge, the psychiatric war pensioner soon found himself having to face another. But by no means is this a negative story entirely. Though it would be a mistake to exaggerate the profligacy of the war pension scheme, nonetheless war disability pensions did provide a basis on which individuals and families could live independently who might otherwise have been forced to resort to institutional care.[9] Communitarian gains, one might claim, provided the platform on which consumerist opportunities and alternative life-options could in some limited, but still significant, measure be made available. Inevitably some were more vocal than others, and in many instances kin were their most assertive allies and advocates, but we may justly think of this group as the contemporary equivalent of the mad activists of today, rebelling against the limited and demeaning destinies – destitution or a career as a lunatic – which the society of their day had contrived for people with severe mental health problems.

In a social climate that increasingly prized domesticity and private life, a sizeable number of psychiatric war pensioners were able to forge a viable alternative to the 'independence' of the efficient economic unit extolled by official doctrine on the one hand, or to the social death of a mental institution on the other. But the irony of this, as we shall see, is that what might be counted as relative successes were won in the teeth of consistent opposition and intrigue from the Ministry of Pensions itself. The paradox of the Ministry is that it was in business both to honour and maintain the connection between war and disability, and to repudiate and deny it wherever possible, and it was consistently taking two steps forward to a more egalitarian form of social welfare, grounded in a commitment to social justice, and two steps backward to paternalistic and class-bound ideologies and practices.

WRESTING HIS OWN FUTURE

In the 1920s and 30s the Ministry promoted institutional treatment as the preferred form of intervention, admitting mentally disabled pensioners to Ministry hospitals for 'hardening' or socialization into work roles, largely because they had more control over ex-servicemen under these conditions. Separation from families was integral to these regimes because domestic life and influences were perceived as being soft, and subversive of the discipline that such regimes were intended to inculcate. This was 'social reconstruction' at work – a form of *community* care that endeavoured to retain the pensioner as an efficient economic unit as an alternative to banishing him to an asylum.[10] The disclosure that he had all along been a beneficiary of community care would have come as a surprise to William P, since he had been languishing 16 long years in Ministry institutions, mostly on the other side of the country from his home and family, and had quite missed out on seeing his daughters grow up.

Born in 1892, William P had served in China with the South Wales Borderers and been in the fighting at Tientsin. Just two months after returning to England he had been sent to the Dardanelles in time for the landing, where he was wounded and contracted dysentery, his health breaking down generally. At the end of 1915 he was admitted to Maghull where he lay motionless all day, melancholic and lethargic, making no reply to questions, complaining of sounds in his ears like the buzzing of bees, though the authorities managed to elicit from him that in Egypt he had gone with women a good deal, and sometimes been insubordinate. Though he had emerged from his stupor, and returned home to his wife and family in a valley town in South Wales, he seems to have lacked confidence, not least because the economic conditions did not favour him. From about 1918 onwards he had been a permanent inmate of Ministry of Pensions hospitals, latterly at Orpington in Essex, and was now considered to be suffering from dementia praecox, a 'DP' in the medical shorthand.

The medical reports from the 1920s and early 1930s were consistently bleak: 'No complaints, always "alright". Disinterested. Bored at being asked how he is, fidgety and wants to leave the room. Never volunteers a remark, always distant and inaccessible' (21 February 1927); 'Very fidgety and ill at ease on interview. Never volunteers a remark. No friends. Very inaccessible. Subdued. Merely picking up paper now. Deteriorating slowly' (1 August 1928); 'Man appears resigned to the idea of remaining in hospital. It is extremely unlikely that his present state could have been maintained outside – freedom from all care and worry, regular routine of occupation, good food, occasional interviews have kept him in a stationary state' (15 April 1933). William, however, was rather less inclined to give praise for his institutional good fortune, or to feel himself relieved of care, experiencing certain constraints on his freedom, together with a load of worry about what was going to become of him. Understandably, his family in Wales had also started to voice their concerns, and enlisted the support of their MP. Now put on the defensive, the Ministry medical staff became increasingly rebarbative. 'Pensioner agitating for discharge, cannot say why, no outlook, no plans whatsoever', the doctor curtly commented. 'This man is considered to be a DP, stationary while in hospital. Automaton, incapable of independent life. It is thought that maintenance of his present relatively satisfactory mental state is dependent on retention in hospital and that discharge would be highly experimental' (15 September 1933).

Then, suddenly, 16 months later, there is a divergent appraisal: 'This man has woken up to an extraordinary extent of late, to the surprise of the staff who have known him over a number of years. He has become talkative and the general appearance of DP has, at least temporarily, vanished. His two daughters are waitresses in the Conservative Club, St James Street, and the man now asks for his discharge to keep his wife company. I have known him for ten years and for his present state there has been no counterpart'. William may indeed have woken up, though perhaps he had never been quite as stupefied as the doctor supposed, more likely depressed and befuddled by his circumstances. Unfortunately, however, it is not possible to identify an analogous awakening in the doctor, who continued to ruminate on his deficiencies, and William must have found himself increasingly trapped, not only in an institutional hole, but in a malign administrative and medical mentality with not even a peephole of hope, into which he could only sink deeper.

Learning that it was intended shortly to transfer him to another Ministry hospital, the present one being due for closure, he believed (probably quite correctly) that his fortunes were likely to deteriorate still further, and that in an important respect his life – in the sense of a person having any kind of life to look forward to – was now on the line. 'Entered consulting room and went on his knees in a praying attitude, saying he did not wish to go to Cosham and desired to go home. He has sufficient insight to know that he is not right mentally and he believes that this transfer to Cosham will mean a stepping stone to asylum. His negativism in this respect has reached a climax and there is no dissuading him' (11 May 1935). There *was* no dissuading him either, for the next day, assisted by his wife, he broke with this disciplinary regime and left for home, no mean achievement in the teeth of official threats, the doctor issuing denunciations even as he was walking through the gates: 'discharged against medical advice, his action is part of his negativism and he is not mentally responsible'.

With their 'negativistic' bile, the Pensions medical authorities lacked the insight to see that William was treading the path of hope, for the following month they were still pressing him to return to his station as an in-patient. But William was holding fast, and buoyed-up by his rediscovery of the domestic hearth, he wrote a moving reply, wholly devoid of rancour, that nicely turns the hospital's phraseology on its head and makes William his own occupational therapist:

The thoughts of further inpatient treatment is an horror to me. . . . I've desided in my best interest that home treatment will benefit me greatly. I feel much happier and more contented here. My Wife is a real Pall to me. She love to have me home and the feelings of being home to me is unde-scribable after sixteen years of inpatient treatment . . . I thank the Medical Advisers and Hospital Staff for there kindness on my behalf. At present, I'm doing occupational treatment in the garden and Wood Work. My Wife fully keep me occupied. Hours pass like minutes.

There were similar protestations of conjugal bliss from Mrs P herself ('after 16 years in hospital I just love to have him home and sir I do all in my power to make him happy') but understandably she was initially also rather ambiva-lent about the homecoming, more especially in a period when apprehensions gathered like storm clouds about someone who was not strictly 'normal'. Still, there are no signs that either of them seriously wavered over the course on which they had now embarked. Over the next three months they would have needed every ounce of their resolve, for the Ministry did everything in its power to undermine their position, proposing at one stage to penalize William for his peremptory refusal of treatment by cutting his pension in half, and sending an inquiry officer, a kind of sleuth in the Ministry's employ, to spy on them in their home town and dig up some incriminating evidence:

The enquiries were carried out without reference to the pensioner and his wife, although I managed to observe both of them from a shop opposite their house. Mrs P came to the door and looked up and down the street several times as if she were expecting someone. I noticed she was nicely dressed and had no hat on. She appeared to be rather young, very clean and I assume she had finished her housework for the day. I also observed the pensioner moving about in the front bedroom upstairs and, as far as I could see, he was either painting or doing some form of decoration. Of course, I could not see him clearly. The bed clothes were folded neatly on a chair in the window of the room.

And who could the fresh and bonnetless Mrs P have been waiting for in the street? For her lover, of course, as the malicious Mrs Evans who ran the grocery shop over the way (no doubt the very vantage point from which the Pensions sleuth was observing the suspects) was eager to insinuate. Though she had heard that Mr P was 'mental', she had not observed anything out of the ordinary herself but: 'She told me that, if the man was mental, she would not be surprised, as it would be due to his wife. She said that during the time he was in hospital his wife carried on with several men.... She said the woman is "fly" ... Mrs E is about 60 years of age and in my opinion is not a woman who would make random statements'.

Still, the inquiry officer was bound to reveal that his efforts to encourage the townspeople to make out that William was 'mental' had been in vain, for when he called on someone who had known William even before the war, 'this person told me she was surprised he was mental in any way as when she knew him he had always appeared quite normal with the exception of being a little irritable at times. She attributed this entirely to the effects of the war and told me that his people were quite normal and that in her opinion perhaps the man was run down'. Moreover, William's social circumstances were far from propitious, as the officer's report laid bare: 'Even if the man wanted work, he would find great difficulty in obtaining same locally as nearly all the men are unemployed or working 2 days a week only. At the time of my visit to the Employment Exchange yesterday, they were getting ready for the signing on of 2 collieries which have closed down. This will apparently bring all the local collieries to a stand-still, for how long I do not know ... the Area is definitely very depressed'.

Even so, there were officials at the Ministry who did not find this assessment as compelling as it might appear, or saw in it only what they wanted to see, for though the doctor at the Pensions hospital had considered William not be mentally responsible, it was now proposed (on the logic that if he was not a lunatic in a madhouse then he was very likely a skiver) that 'there is a definite deliberative element in this man's mental condition and that the symptoms are to some extent within his control'. In the event, gently prodded along by the intervention of the local MP, a superior form of medical wisdom did prevail. Summoned to appear before another medical board, William, 'a tall muscular man, apparently well cared for' became 'timid and frightened', with his oft-repeated 'I'm happier at home' exhibiting his fear of being sent back to hospital. Concluding that there was, perhaps, after all some merit in helping him to lead his own independent life, the authorities awarded him a 100% war disability pension for dementia praecox.[11]

MAD AT THE PENSIONS: 'LEAVE SEVERELY ALONE'

Another pensioner who was seriously intent upon leading his own life was Walter P. Wounded in action in France in April 1917, he had broken down after he was invalided back to England, eventually recovering from an acute attack of manic-depressive psychosis and being awarded a small pension for paranoia in 1920. 'A startled-looking man with somewhat prominent eyes, he is at the time of examination moderately cheerful and answers questions without evasions or hostility'. The details of his history at the hands of the Ministry of Pensions in the intervening years are rather obscure, and little more is known than that he was an inmate of the Ministry hospital in Ewell for a time in the early 1920s, and after that a Service Patient in one of the LCC asylums for a couple of years, before returning to his home town in Devon, but by the mid-1930s Walter P was far from cheerful, and had become enormously hostile towards the Ministry.

The following account by a medical officer from the Ministry who called upon him at his isolated country cottage, with the intention of conducting a medical board to review his pension, reveals in dramatic fashion the intensity of this adversarial relationship. We can only guess at the humiliation and powerlessness that Walter P must have experienced in his dealings with the Pensions bureaucracy, but he had obviously concluded that his only recourse in wresting a future for himself was through domesticity and an intensely private existence. Perhaps the most extraordinary feature of this account, much abbreviated here, is that, even though he acknowledges that the strength of Walter P's feeling is quite specific to the Ministry, and that he was very likely perfectly sane in his ordinary social relations, only becoming a 'dangerous lunatic' when confronted with a representative of the Ministry, never at any point does the medical officer reflect on what could have brought an ex-serviceman like this to feel so angry about the pensions bureaucracy:

A domiciliary visit was paid to this pensioner on 4/10/37 at approx 4.30pm. His cottage is completely isolated and is approached by a very steep unmade cart track.... The cottage door was open and I received no answer to repeated knocks. On looking around I saw a man in an adjoining allotment who was coming towards the cottage, having heard me knocking. He turned out to be the pensioner and stated he was expecting me.... A rather tall spare man of athletic appearance and physique. Clean in his person but untidily dressed in a pair of old and much soiled grey flannel slacks and dirty white shirt open in front. Expression rather wild and eyes 'shifty'.... His greeting was somewhat reserved and he displayed an air of suppressed excitement...I sat down on a chair at the table and the pensioner took up a position standing in the middle of the room between me and the door.... On producing his documents for the purpose of proceeding with the Medical Board the pensioner showed immediate signs of excitement, asking 'What is this all about?', 'Who are you?' etc. I spoke to him quietly and he appeared to quieten down, stating that I was a gentleman and very different to the Ministry officials he had met in the past.... However shortly he again became excited and accused me of being sent there to do him down and that I was probably there to get him locked up in an asylum and that he would see me dead first – he would listen to no reasoning or reassurances to the contrary – he was now in a highly excited state and quite incoherent in his speech. He alleged continuous persecution by the Ministry of Pensions and others. . . . He then began to rave about wars and the people who made wars and accused me of being one of these and it would be better for all concerned if I was dead. . . . Wishing him good day I left the garden and proceeded to climb the steep approach track. He followed me out of the garden calling me a coward and many other filthy names – he continued to shout at me until I had reached the top of the hill. . . . I am of the opinion that I was extremely fortunate to escape from this interview without serious bodily injury. . . . He is obviously insane and certifiable but if left severely alone appears to live quite peacefully with his wife and child. . . . His delusions of persecution are such that he is liable to become a dangerous lunatic if approached by a stranger and especially by anybody connected with the Ministry of Pensions. I would suggest that this pensioner be left severely alone in the future and if possible a Final Award be made at the 100% rate. He is obviously quite incapable of any employment or of mixing with his fellows and there is no prospect of any material improvement taking place.[12]

And leave him severely alone is just what they did.

'IT WOULD APPEAR THAT THE MAN IS ABLE TO WORK'
There were others, however, who encountered numerous obstacles in trying to lead their lives on their own terms. Straddled between the stark alternatives of a hopeless case or a sprightly citizen, it was frequently very difficult for pensioners to lay legitimate claim to a middle ground in which they were in equal measure viable, in one or more areas of their lives at least, and disabled in another. In the estimation of the Pensions any one of these attributions tended to annul the another. Pronounced 'recovered' in 1923, Andrew H received a rather unwelcome communication: 'I am directed by the Minister of Pensions to inform you that. . . . it is certified that you are not now suffering from the disability, Manic Depressive Psychosis, for which you were pensioned and in these circumstances it is regretted that the pension awarded to you will cease'. The pensioner's emotional difficulties had not abated in the least, but since he made 'no complaints at the last examination' his mental condition has been pronounced sound and his disability pension terminated. It then took Andrew and his family the best part of 45 years to get it reinstated. Only in 1968, following strong representations from the Huddersfield and District War Pensions

Committee, did the Ministry confide that having 'carefully considered all the evidence' their senior doctors had now concluded that Mr H's present mental disorder was after all attributable to his war service.[13]

This is an extreme example and typically the Ministry would abruptly reduce the pension at the first sign that the pensioner was again fit for work. Robert Dent was a miner from Northumberland whose claim to a pension was vindicated following the advocacy of the vicar and other local activists. Discharged recovered from Morpeth Mental Hospital in November 1924, he resumed his occupation as a hewer at the local pit, with the inevitable result that his pension was cut. However, Dent was obviously still far from well, complaining of being kept awake by a hissing noise in his right ear, and very easily becoming agitated. By his own account he went 'off the deep end' in the summer of 1927, appearing at the pithead and threatening the lives of the miners who were due to descend the pit. In his ordinary social relations, the indications are that he was both respected and liked in his local community, living mostly a fresh-air life, playing golf, and sometimes going to the pictures, though he admitted to being upset by war films. Yet in the opinion of all who knew him, including his panel doctor, in everything that concerned his occupational identity he was a lost cause, having acquired the reputation of a madman. His inability to find employment reflected not so much an innate disability as the negative reactions, hostility even, of local employers. The North Northumberland War Pensions Committee rallied round him, putting pressure on the Ministry, eventually succeeding in raising his pension to a 60% rate after maintaining that the knowledge of his condition in the locality, lucid for periods, at others acting like a madman, would prevent him from supporting himself in the future.[14]

Not that local advocacy was always effective in securing a positive result from the Pensions. Following a period in a mental hospital, Samuel Dampier had been awarded a war disability pension at the 30% rate, and in 1933 he remonstrated with the Ministry:

For fifteen years I have been quite unable to follow an occupation. . . . Since leaving HM service I have existed mainly by trying various ways of earning a livelihood such as taxi driving, selling ice cream, greengrocery, window cleaning, gardening, housework etc, all of which I have had to give up in time owing to 'my nerves'. For instance, I would think I had 'won through' and then reaction would occur, making concentration and will power an effort, and life generally seem absolutely hopeless. Believe me, sir, I have tried very hard to overcome the various peculiar emotions, and as soon as I feel I've really 'won through', back I go again, as bad as ever.

In confirmation of his zeal the good citizens of his town supplied him with a testimonial: 'We the undersigned have at various intervals during the last twelve years employed Samuel D at gardening,window cleaning etc. At times he has been strange and eccentric and our toleration of it has been entirely due to the fact that we knew of his discharge from the RN to have been from nueresthania. In our judgment he is quite incapable, physically and mentally, of following any regular employment'. None of this was sufficient to persuade the Ministry, however, who – perhaps fearing that he might have to be certified and that they would be asked to assume a major responsibility for him – determined that his 'present unfortunate condition' was unconnected with the war disability for which he had already been pensioned, and was instead caused by the natural progress of a disability which predated the Great War.[15]

The Pensions authorities were advised by his panel doctor that William Matthews, a fisherman and former deckhand in the RNR, from Brixham in Devon, was 'frequently the victim of melancholia and generally not possessed of sufficient mental stability to enable him to earn a living'. However, the doctor also revealed that, with his encouragement, William had 'undertaken a light job with his boat in the summer, mainly to occupy his mind', and that 'in this way he is able to earn about £2 a week for three months in the year, out of which he has to take the cost of upkeep'. William had been admitted to a mental hospital as a Service Patient on two or three occasions in the 1920s, but he had managed for the most part to make a go of it on the outside, supported by his two spinster sisters with whom he lived. He had been awarded a pension at the 70% rate, but inevitably notice of such seasonal odd-jobbing triggered suspicions in the official mind. Either William was slacking (the fact that he could do a bit showed that he was capable of doing more), or he was doing more on the sly and exaggerating his disability.

The Ministry dispatched the usual sleuth to Brixham, but his report did nothing to confirm their suspicions about William: 'does a little interrupted fishing but thinking of selling his boat, feeling unequal to carrying on this employment; complains he feels miserable – life not worth living at times; headaches now and again; sleeps poorly; always on the worry; finds it difficult to initiate a conversation'. But no more did it lead the Ministry to conclude that William had a serious mental health problem which interfered with his occupational capacity: 'It is difficult to see that he is disabled to such a high degree as 70%. . . . It would appear that the man is able to work and does so, in two of the somewhat limited number of occupations available in a fishing town like Brixham'. In this instance, however, the bid to erode or terminate a war disability pension for a community-based pensioner was stalled. A more sympathetic medical counsel eventually prevailed with the argument that if the

This is customer relations Ministry of Pensions style. After months of waiting, former seaman William Matthews receives a personal notice telling him that he has a disability called 'constitutional psychopathic inferiority' which is entirely 'due to service'. Absurd, but not untypical. Such flagrant contradictions reflected the muddle in the Ministry of Pensions, straddled between rival outlooks and between the new century and the last.

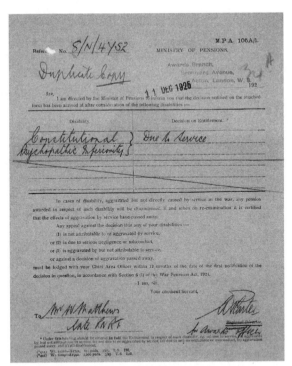

pattern of William's existence was looked at in the round, it was very much what it had been since coming out of the asylum in 1926, i.e., up and down, so for a time he might appear more capable than he was overall.[14]

'NEVER SO HAPPY AS WHEN EMPLOYED ON SOMETHING'

Another pensioner who had difficulty in shaking off the suspicion that he was feckless and failing to pull his weight was Robert R. After recovering from shell shock in 1917, he was not up to resuming his pre-war occupation as a cloth finisher, and even after completing a training in carpentry with the Ministry of Labour was unable to hold a job for very long, suffering from disturbed sleep, headaches, irritability and inability to tolerate noise, with the result that the Ministry of Pensions, vexed by his lack of progress, induced him to enter one of their own hospitals to be taught some work discipline.

However, Robert R did not take to the regime at all, and in September 1928 he was accused of 'fostering a mild rebellion' in the Ministry hospital when he attempted to obstruct a medical officer and nursing staff from removing a troublesome patient, and 'incited other patients to do likewise', using 'threatening language'. Dismissed for 'insubordination', he was certified first at Banstead and then at Prestwich Mental Hospital, escaping after seven months, and later maintaining that it was 'an absolute hell and fifty years behind the times'. Unable to find employment, he was again persuaded to enter a Ministry hospital but with the same unsatisfactory result as on previous occasions, though in this instance his exit was less dramatic. In answer to routine inquiries over the next few years about the nature and extent of his disability he was direct and to the point: 'What is your present illness?' 'Psychosis. Words falling into one another. Headaches. Losing control for no reason'. A medical report of 1935 also disclosed that, though he had tried working as joiner for a fortnight, he could not do it, becoming 'muddled in his words when talking to people'.

This was not enough to allay the suspicions of Ministry officials, however, who, considering that their investment in his training had not paid off, pondered reducing his pension. Ironically, however, the social inquiry report from the Ministry rather took the wind out of their sails, tacitly also taking a snub at their own 'hardening' regimes. It revealed that if Robert R was not very successful in competing on the open market, he revelled in his domesticity and did not at all conform to the image officialdom held of him. These were all precarious existences we have been discussing, the more so because a spectre of blame hung about their failings. Robert R illustrates the path followed by quite a number of these protagonists, fashioning a life that was more inward-looking and private, yet still productive, even if not as an 'efficient economic unit' on the lines extolled by official agencies. During the time he had lived at home since his last bout of 'hardening' in 1931, the report disclosed, his condition was considered to have improved:

He is not so excitable and he stutters rarely. . . . He spends a considerable amount of time on an allotment he rents. He cycles a little . . . does part of the housework when his wife is out at work, goes for walks with his children and visits the cinema with his wife and children. He is considered to be very far from a lazy man and is never so happy as when employed on something.[17]

Chapter 18

WAR PSYCHOSIS PENTATHLONS

There were some who were truly in it for the long haul, plying their war disability wares before disbelieving or sceptical state agencies across several decades – running interminable heats in war psychosis pentathlons, as I have come to think of them. If in obvious respects these are exceptional cases, at the same time it is they who can most deeply instruct us, at the most basic material and emotional level, in what was involved in being a mad activist in interwar Britain. Among the most tragic figures were distressed individuals whose personalities and circumstances to a large extent forced them to brazen out on their own the trials of being a mentally damaged ex-serviceman, leading them into repeated altercations with the pensions authorities to which there was never any real resolution, and from which they invariably emerged disheartened, but always ready to re-enter the lists on another day. Though the Ministry of Pensions frequently extolled itself as representing 'a new and larger view of the State's obligations towards those injured and killed in a national war', with the best of will it is all but impossible to detect any trace of this 'larger view' among these innumerable petty manoeuvres, in which the state pares away at the self-esteem of the ex-serviceman, using its powers to cherry-pick medical assessments that are to its liking, produced by doctors who have swallowed the Pensions shilling, and shelve the rest.[1]

Ever since the Service Patient scheme was first mooted, the Pensions had been inclined to view it as a cemetery of hopeless cases, a memorial to the state's benificence in honouring its obligations towards the war disabled, in which the normative resident, thin, haggard and stooping, with a sluggish tempo, would nevertheless 'in the ordinary way, and given his time' prove himself to be 'most accommodating, ready to lend a hand at any odd job', 'quiet and reserved, expressing no decided views on anything . . . quite resigned and submissive'.[2] As we have discovered, the middle ground between the stupor of the hopeless case and the cheery and efficient citizen presenting himself punctually at his workplace was, for the Pensions, to a considerable extent an unknown and uncharted territory, viewed with much foreboding.

That this was a representative cast on life in this period among sections of the middle and the higher classes is brought out in the following reported exchange between Lord Macmillan and an asylum inmate. 'I said, "Would you like to leave this place?; she said, "Yes, I would". I asked, "Why?" and she said, "I would like to go into service and make a little money for myself". I said, "Suppose now I got you out tomorrow, where would you go?" Her face fell absolutely: she said, "I do not know, where would you send me?" I said, "If you start life again as a citizen you will have to make your way in the world". A complete blank supervened. What is one to do with that class of case, because it would be cruelty to send that class of case into an unsheltered world?'[3] But where after all does the 'cruelty' reside here? This 'harmless lunatic' is represented as emitting a 'complete blankness' but the blankness is not in her, nor is it an expression of her incompetence; it is rather the non-place, the existential and material condition of social exclusion, in which she and her class are maintained. And this was exactly the hinterland in which Albert Hardman and George Collins, both of them holding decided views about everything, anything but resigned and submissive, had perforce set up their psychiatric war disability stalls after the Great War.

'HOPING YOU'LL SHAKE THINGS UP'

As a sick bay attendant in the Royal Navy, it fell to Albert Hardman to look after mental cases. Even though his ship had been involved in a collision at the Battle of Jutland in May 1916, he had given 'complete satisfaction' until, one day in May 1918, after a night shift in which he had been looking after an insane officer with GPI, he apparently experienced a severe crisis himself. Invalided from the service with a temporary disability pension for anxiety neurosis, he at once enlisted as a ship's steward, very likely to prove to himself that he could still function effectively at sea, but after eight months he was forced to abandon the nautical life. For about seven years he then held another position in caring for the mentally damaged as an attendant with the Metropolitan Asylums Board, before starting a new situation as a mortuary keeper. It appears that in the late 1920s his reponsibilities began to weigh heavily on him and he found himself heading for an emotional crisis. As a habitué of the forlorn and forbidding institutional universe that accommodated both the truly dead, and those lost or damaged souls who were truly believed to be as good as dead, Albert can have had no illusions about the death of hope and of self-esteem that was the likely consequence of being certified in a mental institution. Hence he was much aggrieved in the autumn of 1928 to find himself (in his own words) 'certified insane upon sanction of Ministry of Pensions doctor and taken to Colney Hatch', where he remained for two years classed as a Service Patient.

Undoubtedly Albert must always have had a rebarbative temperament, and in the immediate aftermath of the war was already inclined to speak plainly to officialdom ('hoping you'll shake things up'), and to be unsparing about his personal relations (describing his wife as a 'deaf virago'). However, by the time he had been deposited back at his home in 1930 from a Ministry of Pensions rehabilitation hospital, he was a deeply angry man, believing that having 'taken me on two occasions from my work and against my wish', the Pensions should be taking a rather more proactive role in assisting him to challenge the negative context within which he was now obliged to live as a discharged lunatic with a diagnosis recently upgraded to delusional psychosis. 'Surely I am entitled to something better than a bare existence? . . . I will be quite satisfied if you can fix me up with a job'. To which the Pensions retorted that it had, of course, no responsibility for the loss of his employment, nor was it in a position to find work for him. Some weeks later Albert had only been able to find work as a kitchen porter and had still not had an answer to his request for a review of his pension:

When am I going to hear something about my award from the Board – after being in a mad house? If you really want me to gain publicity, and show how you are messing men about, I will do so. The Medical Officer asked me to enter hospital. I am working for 30/- a week after being deprived of a £7 a week job and being certified insane. He asked me to try and carry on outside of Ministry of Pensions hospitals. I promised I would so. I have a wife and two children to keep. I have been ground down. . . . When are you going to wake up – this is the thanks I get for trying to carry on outside. . . . If you wish me to enter the Workhouse say so. I gained this job such as it is by lies, when they find out I am an ex-lunatic they will discharge me.

Other letters follow in quick succession: 'Isn't it about time I heard something, it is 4 weeks since I had a Board. When are you going to buck up? If you mess me about any longer I am quite content to return to Colney Hatch. It is far better there than starving, which you are forcing me to to do. How would you care to exist upon a £1 a week after being deprived of employment? In Colney Hatch I got good food and an easy time although society deprived me of work and liberty'. And a week later:

I hope that you will give immediate attention to my case. . . . If something is not done immediately I shall take drastic measures as I am disgusted with it all. Why not play the game? It seems that I've played it and lost. BE HUMAN! . . . I am *disgusted*. Why the Hell fire didn't you let me stay in

Colney Hatch instead of liberating me to starvation and poverty? I am quite prepared to take the short cut out. It seems that you are forcing me to do so. . . . If I don't hear something this week, then you will. Remember you are messing around with a desperate customer who is trying to play the game and KEEP OUT OF HOSPITALS.

An appeal to his MP in the summer of 1930 eventually succeeded in jolting the Ministry into giving rather more sympathetic consideration to Albert's situation, and to his determination to recover his lost status and dignity, awarding him a 100% war disability pension for life. He is 'very unstable and liable to break down at any time with any economic strain or stress', the referee for the Pensions reported. 'Has just started a job as a kitchen porter and is anxious to carry on and keep it. . . . I think he should be given this chance, as he is happier having a job to go to and something to occupy his mind. Has a grievance against the authority who put him in mental hospital'. Still, it was not much of a chance that Albert was being given, since he was in fact working as pantryman in a large restaurant from 8am until midnight, and after six months the stress of the job (not least the loss of sleep which had led to a state of depression in which, as Albert later reported, he sometimes 'punched' himself on the jaw to pull himself together) caught up with him and he was admitted to a Ministry of Pensions hospital in April 1931.

Complain though he did that Albert was 'full of the "dirty way" in which he had been treated', the medical superintendent here had little more to offer than to entertain the hope that 'the thought of re-certification may induce the patient to conform to institutional routine'. After ten days Albert concluded that the establishment could do nothing for him. The limitations of the Ministry of Pensions hospital were a reflection also of the limited options that were available in the wider society to a vulnerable person like Albert from a background that, while not wholly disadvantaged, carried no special weight. By and large there was a stark choice between plunging into the occupational thick of it (assuming, of course, that there was a job to be found) and getting out of it altogether. Still unable to find employment, Albert did odd jobs at home but, frustrated by his lack of fulfilment, he became increasingly edgy, and prone to lose his temper. On the petition of his wife in April 1931 he was taken into Brentwood Mental Hospital as a Service Patient, where he was described as a 'man of deficient emotional control and little moral sensibility' and diagnosed as a 'moral defective subject to attacks of sub-acute mania', 'a degenerate type with stigmata'.

Prior to his release some months later it was admitted that he had 'made a real effort to conform to Hospital life', together with 'many protestations of his intention to endeavour to conduct himself better at home in the future'. Predictably enough, however, the cycle of domestic discontent soon repeated itself, a rather matter-of-fact report from the Ministry telling of how of how Albert 'apparently had trouble at home and hit the wife', as he 'could not stand her nagging him', with the result that events again took a turn for the worse when his doctor appeared at the house one day to certify him, with a person he presumed was a magistrate, Albert managing in the nick of time to escape over the back fence.

In 1936 he was living in Liverpool, having decamped there, as he described, in his determination to stay out of mental hospitals and fashion an alternative to an existence as a career lunatic. Stirred by the political currents of the late 1930s, Albert was initially hopeful of getting back into the swing. When the navy spurned the offer of his services, he registered with the Royal Merchant Navy Reserve, badgering the Pensions to allow him to commute 1/- of his pension to buy some kit ('I *shall* go to sea, I am determined about that'), and spicing his entreaty with some topical bravado: 'If you don't assist me to commute the magnificent sum of 1/- then I'll join the Blackshirts and let the public know all about how I have been served. . . . Sincerely hoping that you have more sense than the bumptious non-efficient, short sighted fools who seem to make their own government at the Ministry of Pensions administrative department'. Though he never went to sea, he succeeded, 'after being idle for years owing to war disability', in finding a position of sorts. However, even though he gave satisfaction in his employment, he was dismissed when a superintendent of police chanced to recognize him as the man he had put into Colney Hatch Asylum some years earlier: '*I have lost all my positions owing to my disablement,*' he remonstrated with the Ministry, 'I have been treated worse than an ex-convict or murderer – they are given a chance to make good – I get no chance whatever, seems I am to be persecuted all my life this way. . . . I consider that this is the last straw'.

And so in a sense it proved, for in the last years of his life Albert became increasingly isolated, living alone in a caravan with a dog for company, still taunting the Pensions for their perfidy ('hoping you are all happy at Blackpool but it seems you need some Croton Oil to wake you up'), but terrified of being put away in a madhouse for good. Equally desperate to receive treatment, he mailed a stream of terse messages that, whilst they left no doubt about the depth of his anguish, were not well calculated to rouse official solicitude and, apart from arranging a session with a neurologist, the Ministry did not come up with anything: 'I need attention immediately but no local practitioners, these only scrape through with an MB and know nothing and take the easiest way out by placing a man in a mad house . . . I'm nearly round the bend but believe I can pull out, some paraldehyde would do the trick, I'm sure ... I'd be grateful for an early reply'.

In the early 1950s he was still writing to the Pensions, sometimes as much as 15 pages, retracing his entire history ('Dear sir, I will give my service firstly ...'), asking that his pension be commuted to enable him to buy a cottage and start a garden, and putting a lurid spin on the narrative of his incarceration ('upon occasions I spent weeks in padded cells and was kicked into insensibility by attendants, and starved'). Much of this was at variance, certainly, with his previous accounts, where it was not so much the conditions at Colney Hatch that riled him as the loss of his liberty, but still emblematic of a keen and infrangible experience of disappointment and betrayal that had been the ground bass of his existence, certainly from the time of his first post-war crisis in the mid 1920s, when the psychiatric treatment system into which he was steered by the Pensions, far from mollifying his self-doubts, seemed only to aggravate and confirm them. In 1953 the Pensions tried to point him towards the disablement settlement officer at the Ministry of Labour and National Service, but by then it was too late for Albert to be joining hands with the new-fangled agencies in the post-war social landscape, and he died a lonely death of coronary thrombosis in his caravan on a farm in Hertfordshire in August 1956.[4]

'JUSTICE FOR MY DISABLEMENT'
Indisputably Albert Hardman had a serious mental health problem, but still he is able to teach us about the experience of being a mad person in inter-war Britain ('I'm 100% Colney Hatch and Brentwood' as he put it), and of his protracted struggle to stay in the swim and get a foothold in social life. Albert's goal was to secure justice, and to establish an identity and position in society that was not indelibly marked by being the bearer of a mental illness diagnosis, or by his brush with the institutions and categories of psychiatry.[5] George Collins is equally determined to secure justice for the damage that been done to his life-chances by his experience as a serviceman in the Great War but, as we shall see, he falls foul of an augmenting current in the war pensions system that was resolved to disavow protestations of authentic psychological trauma by invoking the 'constitutional factor' at every opportune moment as a strategic device to disengage the connection between war service and psychiatric disability.

When we last left George Collins, a former miner from Nottinghamshire, the Pensions were still stonewalling his plea for a reconsideration of his entitlement to a war disability pension, claiming that he had been fully compensated with the award of a gratuity in 1917. However, in 1925 the

Pensions relented and allowed him to be examined by a special board which delivered exactly the result that they did not want, reporting a permanent deterioration in his condition which had at the very least been aggravated by his war service in Gallipoli. Yet if George could be truculent, the Pensions could certainly prove themselves his match, and for the rest of that year they stalled over his application, still holding to their original line.

Having failed to find work at another colliery, George in his mounting frustration assailed the Pensions with a constant stream of letters demanding that he be notified of the outcome of the Board. These, even if they evince a rather naive faith in the moral sentiments of a beleaguered state bureaucracy, now intent upon identifying any conceivable loophole that the legal or medical imagination could concoct to reduce or repudiate its liabilities, graphically communicate the heightened expectations and disappointments of the disabled ex-serviceman in the aftermath of the war – the enduring effects of his war experience; his diminished prospects; his impoverished circumstances and accumulating debts; his good moral character; his belief in his right to compensation for the suffering he has endured and to a life that is something more than mere existence; and, above all, the injustice he feels:

> My burden is great. I never knew what illness was previous to war. Since my discharge I have never been free from nerve trouble especially my head I have terrible pains and noises in my head and fall dissy. I have never been able to earn a lively hood when I was at work I never made more than three days work from my nerves been so bad. I have not been able to work since 1923 and on no pension has made it much harder for us. Been on no pension since 1917 . . . all we have is 29/- to keep five of us and coal and light and house rent. So you can imagine how we are existing. Dear Sir, I hope you will kindly oblige me by return of post.

And again:

> I only want concession adequately for my terrible sufferings and my losses with not being able to follow my accustomed calling as a miner and having lost good jobs of work through my disability due to War Service . . . I gave my services in 1914 and didn't want to be fetched up and served my King and Country well and I want justice for my disablement . . . I was a picture of a man when I went out to the Dardanelles and I came back a mental wreck.

Though he was eventually notified that 'after careful consideration of your case' a special grant had been awarded him of 12 shillings a week, the

Pensions did not cease to vilify him, asserting that that 'like many others of this class, though unable to maintain himself, he has added a family to his other responsibilities', and that 'even if his pension was raised he would not be likely to "make good" at present'. A few years later, however, shortly after George Tryon was returned as Minister of Pensions in the National Government of 1931, the Ministry was jolted into reviewing his file following a renewed salvo of letter writing in which Collins enjoined his MP to take up his case. As a result of this intervention, in 1934 he was again brought before a medical board which reached the startling conclusion that but for his military service George Collins:

> ... might have gone through life without any mental breakdown. The conditions and strains of service in Gallipoli were very severe from the point of view of shell fire, general discomfort, living conditions etc. The record of the Hospital in 1915 shows that the breakdown was a severe one, and followed the recent period under shell fire. It was these reasons which guided the Board in forming the opinion that the aggravation was severe and that the present condition was due to the persistence of that aggravation.

The board recommended assessment of disability at 60%; they found that George's condition was much more unstable than at the time of the previous board; that he would be useless for any occupation in the labour market owing to his emotional state; and that he would probably at some stage become a certifiable case. Not perhaps in its conclusions, but certainly in its overall tenor, this was very much in the spirit of what George had himself been arguing all these years about the impact of the Great War on his life. 'Might have gone through life without any mental breakdown': how were the officials at the Ministry of Pensions, with their insistence that there was a 'marked constitutional element to his condition', to reconcile themselves to that? Simply by using the prerogative of their position to ignore the board's recommendations, apprising George's MP on behalf of the minister that they were 'medically advised' that his condition was mostly constitutional and that 'no grounds are seen upon which it can be certified that the effects of Mr Collins's Great War service, which terminated more than eighteen years ago, are operating to bring about any present need for treatment'. It is difficult to imagine a more forceful demonstration than this of how one of the ironic functions, and by no means a subsidiary one, of the Ministry of Pensions, that monument to the enduring presence of the past in the minds and bodies of ex-servicemen of the Great War, was to repudiate and deny the connection between war service and disability, turning the war into history and severing its link with the present.

From this point on George Collins became a kind of sad caricature of the importuning supplicant, petitioning the state for its mercy, still in 1948 presenting the ritual calling card of 'one who went over the top on many occasions at Gallipoli Campaign with bayonet and would again for my dear King and Empire', and might now be said to have gone over the top once too often. As it turned out, he had had quite a good war, managing to secure a position as a gateman at a factory for about five years, but with the influx of returning servicemen into the labour market his 'mental history' again became a liability and soon after the war he was again unemployed. As in 1934, a medical board in the early 1950s found that deterioration in his condition was 'for the most part wholly due to War Service'. However, the Pensions authorities resorted to their familiar wiles, producing another medical adviser to bury the news and confirm their own assessment. For the remainder of Collins's life until his death in 1967 they rejected his entreaties, toying with him mercilessly, latterly diagnosing him as an 'hysterical psychopath', insisting that it was his constitution rather than the war which had the upper hand.[6]

'NOT AN ACQUISITION TO THE CLUB'

Inadequate though protagonists such as Albert Hardman and George Collins obviously seem, we have in large part been recounting a narrative of structurally produced inadequacy involving a protracted and, frequently vicious, dynamic between the distressed ex-serviceman and the pensions bureaucracy. These escalating and unrequited struggles, exacerbated by the heightened class antagonisms of the period, reflected in part the determination of the Ministry of Pensions to hold the line, but equally the social vacuum in which these disabled veterans were trying to survive, leading them to entertain expectations, and make demands, of the Ministry that it inevitably could not satisfy. The trajectories of both Hardman and Collins were clearly calculated only to maximize their frustrations, so it is perhaps apposite to introduce an example which demonstrates that a war psychosis pentathlon could sometimes produce an alternate outcome.

After being shell-shocked at Albert, Henry Morris had been badly served by the Ministry in his endeavours to get himself back into work, and in the early 1920s he had been shuffled off to the Ministry of Pensions wing at the Old Manor Hospital in Salisbury where he very much looked to be heading for a chronic destiny. Fortunately for Henry, however, in 1926 he was one of the more promising Service Patients selected to enjoy the privileges of the Ministry's 'hardening' centre at Saltash in Cornwall which, even if it pathetically failed to live up to its stentorian promise, had the inestimable value of raising his horizon beyond the confines of a mental institution. With spring in the air, Henry was set upon enjoying himself in the Cornish lanes, asking in April if he could be allowed to join a cycling club in the neighbourhood. This quickly earned him a rebuke from the Ministry doctors. 'He would certainly not be an acquisition to the club', they advised, 'and the view expressed to him today is that it is not very fitting that a man requiring hospital treatment should be running about the countryside cycling with other people who are earning their livelihood during the week'.[7] This is disingenuous talk, of course, for the fact of it was that, in the eyes of the Pensions, Henry, a working-class mental patient, was trying to climb above his station and affecting to be one of the middle classes. Nor was his weakness for cycling clubs his only peccadillo, for he had also taken the initiative to enrol on a Spanish-language course at the YMCA which, far from winning approval from his psychiatric keepers, attracted the mordant snub that he now 'likes to think of himself as one of the educated "classes"'.

Still, Henry was not easily deterred, for in the 1930s he emigrated for a time to British Guiana where he struck up a romantic attachment with a Portuguese woman whom he subsequently married, returning to England in 1940. However, amidst a florid outbreak of the manic-depressive psychosis that he had experienced in the past, he soon fell into poverty and was forced once more to lay his war disability credentials before the door of the Ministry of Pensions. Predictably, the Ministry produced one of their own medical specialists to whistle the familiar tune that he was 'a poor type of man with little power of resistance about him'. However, he was again fortunate in finding a zealous advocate in the British Legion to demonstrate convincingly that his poverty had driven him to make several attempts to work, even when he had been quite unfit to do so. In the next years, though his life did not cease to be a narrative of hardship, it was also spared the unremitting frustration before the Pensions bureaucracy that befell Albert Hardman and George Collins. To some degree it was also leavened by contentment, and by some small coups, as when Henry succeeded in obtaining an educational allowance for his daughter from the Ministry.

MEDICINE, MISCHIEF AND MARGARINE

The variations in the scale of the awards that war psychosis pensioners were given is quite extraordinary. Contrary to what officials sometimes alleged, there was no inconsistency in the fact that an ex-serviceman who was given a 100% award turned out to be in regular employment. It did not necessarily imply that his disability has ceased to be 'effective' in the Ministry's terms, for the full pension rate was also given to other categories of disability, such as the blind, some of whom by re-training had found full-time employment. All the same, the variations between pensioners in the scale and timing of awards, the fact that some got 100% awards and others considerably smaller assessments, and that some awards were made final at a relatively early stage and others only after a titanic struggle, was by no means a direct reflection of medical 'realities', not least for the reason that the medical assessments themselves were deeply controverted.

Far from being an innocent bystander to the politics of war disability pensions, medicine was at every turn an accomplice to whatever mischief was being perpetrated, though not necessarily a willing one. The Ministry of Pensions always strove to put a plausible medical face on whatever decision it chose to make, but the factors that affected outcomes were frequently entirely local and adventitious—the advocacy of friends, the personality of the pensioner or the whims of a medical officer. Sometimes outcomes reflected a wider political concern that had nothing directly to do with medicine or the integrity of the case under consideration. In a political climate that was becoming increasingly inclined to look askance at the ease with which psychiatric war pensions had been awarded to Great War servicemen, John Clinton, formerly a corporal in the Royal Army Medical Corps, was refused classification as a Service Patient when he was admitted to the Grangetown Mental Hospital in Dublin early in 1940 for a recurrence of his manic-depressive psychosis. He had been received into the same institution as a Service Patient on nine previous occasions, and there had been no change in his circumstances, but the medical adviser to the Ministry now took it upon himself to assert that all the previous classifications had been a mistake. Unwilling to become the fall guy for such chicanery, the Irish authorities protested loudly. Recognizing that in the circumstances of renewed national crisis a quarrel with an Irish hospital was rather unwise, the British authorities quietly backed down, and John Clinton was reinstated as an Imperial War Disability Pensioner.[8]

The war psychosis pensioners we have encountered reflect in many ways the diverse, and not infrequently indeterminate, social composition of the other ranks in the Great War. Even though George Collins and Albert Hardman, say, would scarcely have been eligible applicants for Daddy's club, the membership of others may have been more negotiable. And in just these disparities – of class and station, obviously, but therefore also in associated body language and codes of behaviour – we may find another clue as to why certain individuals were dealt with more serenely by the Pensions authorities, where others achieved at best a very rough form of justice.

The illness career of Lance Corporal Alfred B, a postman from a town on the south coast before the war, who had served as an operating theatre attendant in the RAMC, started in 1917 when he was given a diagnosis of confusional insanity, later amended to manic-depressive psychosis, complaining that he saw frogs coming out of his mouth at times and that his head was in a vice, suspicious of his neighbours and quarrelling with everyone. Her husband had never known a day's illness in his life, pleaded his wife, revealing at the same time that two of his brothers had been inmates of the Hampshire County Asylum for a considerable period, the elder brother having been invalided from the Royal Marines in 1905 and detained in the asylum until Christmas 1915. It is a reflection of the inconsistencies, and sudden surprises, that the war pensions culture could spring that these glaring abnormalities in his family stock were not held against him, as of course they were in many other cases, and there was never any question about the attributability of his condition to his war service. Not that he was in any sense a compliant or domesticated war pensioner, discharging himself in 1920 from the Ministry of Pensions hospital at Ewell against medical advice and giving as his reasons:

I could not eat the food – margarine on a very thick slice of bread is not palatable. I went there for rest and treatment but was locked in a room. There was no rest – someone was trying to play the piano and the gramophone was in use. This made me very irritable and I was in the wrong every day. I want to do some work and Ewell Neurological Hospital is alright for those who do not want to work, so I ran away, having previously told the authorities of my intentions to do so.[9]

In the usual run of things this was just the kind of defiance, and expression of personal caprice, that the Pensions authorities would have found quite unpalatable, but in this instance they appear to have taken it in their stride, steering him into out-patient treatment for a time before concluding in 1924 that he was 'totally unfit to carry on an remunerative occupation' and awarding him a permanent 100% war disability pension for manic-depressive psychosis. This was normally the sort of conclusion about incurability that the Ministry reserved for 'hopeless cases' in asylums. As we have seen, they were for the most part extremely reluctant to make final awards at this level at such an early date to war psychosis pensioners in the community, holding out for as long as possible against the prospect that they might at least improve, if not recover, always on the *qui vive* for a justification to pare the current award still further before making it final.

So why the capitulation in this case? Of course, we can only speculate, but the likelihood is that Alfred B, even though he appears not to have been educated beyond the secondary level, conveyed an 'educated' or 'respectable' demeanour that put him a cut above the average psychiatric war pensioner. In his fortunes with the Ministry, however, as much as in his antipathy for margarine and thickly-sliced bread, he was scarcely typical of his comrades in arms, regarded as wearisome journeymen, most of them, on their prolonged and stuttering odysseys, barnacled with the encrusted deposits of countless small frustrations and disappointments.

Chapter 19

CARING: FAMILIES AND DOCTORS

'A GOOD WOMAN'

Always see a fellow's weak point in his wife. Still there's destiny in it, falling in love. Have their own secrets between them. Chaps that would go to the dogs if some woman didn't take them in hand.

James Joyce, *Ulysses*[1]

Why did some people manage to take the route of relative independence in a domestic setting, rather than complete dependence in an asylum? The answer almost invariably is a good woman, typically a wife, but also a mother, a sister, or a sister-in-law. Though there was clearly an element of dependence, and almost certainly also of strife, in every case, such that one can reasonably say that the narrative of these relationships was certainly marked, if not defined, by the experience of the war, they covered a very wide spectrum indeed. Towards one end were a cluster of women who were carers above all else, looking after a husband or a son who, though not bedridden, was incapable of looking after himself beyond certain rudimentary essentials, and whose social interactions had to be constantly monitored, and at the other a number of individuals for whom bouts of dependency, or low-key caring requirements, might jostle alongside other occupational roles. Needless to say, there were variations in which an individual might move to a different position on the spectrum, perhaps temporarily if a crisis blew up, or more permanently if the worsening of a condition interacted with the natural decline of the ageing process.

To a large extent we can, of course, only speculate as to the toll which these disabilities took upon a relationship. William H, who had been a driver in the Royal Field Artillery, was for five years an inmate of Middlewood Asylum suffering from delusional insanity, initially as a pauper lunatic because the Ministry of Pensions refused to recognize his condition as a war-related disability, until the decision was overturned by an appeals tribunal in 1923. Mrs H had been married to W since 1913, and in 1926 she decided to bring him home, recounting at the time of his death in 1970 at the age of seventy-six how she had 'fetched him out of a mental hospital over forty-four years since'. She had known him, she went on to say, 'from when he was sixteen years old. He was always well before he went to war. Since then I have had years and years of looking after a mentally sick man. He was like a child but also frightening at times . . . I only had one year of normal married life before he joined up and then it was a life of misery and always having to watch him'.

For Mrs H the history of her marriage was indissolubly interwoven with the effects of the Great War, and when her husband died she mourned especially the loss of the man who had never really returned to her in 1918. However, the Ministry was wholly insensible to this heartfelt narrative of sacrifice and devotion, rejecting her application for a war widow's pension on the grounds that the cause of her husband's death was unconnected with his war disability, perhaps as a belated revenge for the rough handling the department had received at the appeals tribunal almost half a century earlier, and only backing down following an impassioned plea from the chairman of the Sheffield War Pensions Committee, a retired colonel.[2]

By 1936 Mrs P could tolerate her husband's abusive behaviour no longer. At her instigation he was admitted to Mapperley Mental Hospital, where he remained until his death in 1966 at the age of eighty-one. A former steel worker, James P joined the army in 1915 and suffered shrapnel wounds to both legs at Ypres in July 1917, the injury to the left leg being so severe that it was necessary to amputate the next day. His mental disturbance started shortly after he was wounded, and though his marriage had been satisfactory before the war, from then on it was marred by frequent and sometimes violent quarrels. After he died the Ministry brought in a doctor to 'confirm fully the propriety of full rejection' of the widow's claim for a war pension on the grounds that her husband's life, far from being curtailed by his war disability, had been 'considerably further prolonged in this gentle atmosphere with expert medical supervision'.

Still, on this occasion without undue fuss the Ministry eventually accepted the opinion of another medical officer, reflecting also the more holistic understanding of traumatic injury which was become more widely accepted in the 1960s, that Mr P's wounds 'were of such severity that they had a profound effect on the man's whole physical and mental make-up and on his power to resist disease'. It was thus acknowledged that the totality of Mr P's biography in its physical, psychological and relational dimensions, embracing also the history of his marriage, through its successive mutations, had been profoundly affected by the trauma that had befallen him in 1917. Regardless of the duration of his physical existence, his life had in crucial respects been diminished and curtailed by his war disabilities.[3]

Whatever they may have felt privately, for the most part these carers carried out their duties uncomplainingly, only giving up, and then sometimes only temporarily, if the situation had become intolerable and a woman felt that her own safety, or that of a child, was threatened. During this period there was for some wives, perhaps, a measure of satisfaction and pride in being seen, in a local community or among a wider network of kin, to soldier on across the years as carer for a husband who had been damaged in the national struggle and to refuse to give up on him, and confine him to the warehouse of hopeless cases, as she could so easily have done. Of course, at a time when traditional family values were vying with a more emancipated consciousness, some women would at the least have felt deeply ambivalent about treading this path. Even so, for those who had already tied the knot, divorce was not an option even if the husband turned out to be an 'incurable lunatic'. Divorce may have been a fact of life in England after the Great War, but it was still regarded very much in Victorian terms. Though as early as 1912 a Royal Commission had recommended extending the grounds for divorce, putting husbands and wives on an equal footing, war had stymied such progressive aspirations.[4] The insanities of the Great War must frequently have introduced a new strain of unhappiness into the institution of marriage, but not until 1937 did 'incurable insanity' provide legally recognized grounds for divorce in Britain, with equal rights for both partners.[5]

Even if some of the wives of war disability pensioners now divorced their husbands, they did not necessarily do so in a hurry. Mrs H married shortly after the war, supported her husband Charles through innumerable crises, and stood by him for 20 and more years after he became a permanent resident of a mental hospital as a Service Patient in 1930, only divorcing him in the early 1950s. It is remarkable, also, how many of these marriages were contracted after the war and the future husband had been discharged from a military mental hospital, or even from a regular asylum. An identity as a shell-shock veteran, or a psychiatric war disability pensioner, was obviously not altogether a barrier to a successful courtship, even though it must have been apparent from an early stage that this was unlikely to be a regular marriage. Of course, despite the privations and uncertainties, sometimes the idea of caring for one of these agonized individuals may have had its own positive attraction, holding out the prospect of an alternative and softer model of manliness, a more egalitarian marriage perhaps, so different from the norm.

FATHER GOES TO THE ASYLUM
What did it mean to have a Service Patient, a war psychosis veteran of the Great War, for a father? One of those who married after the war was Gunner

Charles A from Croydon in Surrey, the ninth of 13 children, who had served in France with the Royal Field Artillery. Though he survived the war, 'he was broken psychologically and was invalided-out around 1917 as shell-shocked'. For about 16 years he struggled to maintain several occupations, his wife and daughter, and his sanity, until he gave up the fight and was hospitalized in the early 1930s. Apart from a brief interlude after the Second World War, he remained a resident of a mental hospital through to his death in 1961. Finessed though it inevitably is through the values of a generation for whom shell shock has become a commonplace trope, and the generosity of spirit of a woman in her maturity anxious to preserve a fond remembrance of her father, his daughter recalled several decades later how she grew up 'with a distinct hatred of war, particularly *that* war, for the terrible conditions which the men had to endure, the enormous number killed, the half-life for the maimed and deranged suffered thereafter.' Poignantly she describes how, 'I never really *knew* my father: my main recollection is of a shuffling, round-shouldered old man wearing a perpetual frown and wringing his hands'.[6]

John H still remembers the day, he must have been about five, when his father, Charles H, was removed to the asylum. His Uncle Frank had come round and John sat on his shoulder and watched as a Black Maria arrived with two policemen to take his father away. He recalls, as does his brother Maurice, his mother sitting by the fireside and weeping. She had signed the form and, remorseful though she later was, she was afraid that he might do something violent. John has never spoken about this before, having bottled it up for 70 years. Even as children, the boys realized their father was not well. John has vivid memories of his father's 'troubles', chopping all the furniture up into little pieces and putting them on the fire until there was nothing left. Mother used to say that when he had a bad turn, he *had* a bad turn. He was somehow preoccupied with fire, at one stage believing that his wife was communicating with someone else through smoke signals. He never hit anyone in the family, it was just *things* he went for, but he seemed unpredictable, as though he could easily lose control.[7]

Charles H had volunteered for the army, falsifying his age, when he was seventeen and served three years in France, some of it in the Machine Gun Corps and with the South Wales Borderers, and also as a stretcher-bearer, though the details of his war service are rather vague since he never spoke about it. The boys were all so young when he was committed, and when they visited him in the asylum it was the last thing they wanted to talk about, just family matters. Not that mother knew much either, dad kept it all

Private Charles Arthur H
in uniform, c.1916.

to himself, never volunteering anything, though she always said that he took badly because of his experiences in the trenches. 'Gassed', said John, followed by some kind of breakdown, because he had heard mention of 'relapses'.

Father and mother had already got to know each other at grammar school when they were fifteen or sixteen, though there was nothing between them until after the war. Mother was training to be a teacher but had to give it up when her mother died in the influenza epidemic of 1919. Father had done an apprenticeship as an engineer, but he came from a rural background and after the war decided to go into farming, establishing a smallholding with some help from the family, mainly buying calves and pigs and fattening them for market. During the 1920s it was a real struggle to make a go of a smallholding and bring up a large family – five boys and one girl, though one son died of meningitis when he was two – on about 30 shillings a week, not a huge sum even though wages were very depressed at that time. It was obvious to all of

Charles H and his future wife when they were still
pupils at grammar school, c. 1912.

them that dad had been broken by the war and the strain of surviving
after it – mother had always said this, for, after all, dad had been a volunteer;
moreover she had known him before the war, so she knew what he was made
of, and that there was no history of insanity in the family.

Charles H was removed to Horton Road Asylum in Gloucester on 25
January 1930 and entered in the hospital register as a farmer, aged thirty-one,
suffering from melancholia, 'principal aetiological factor: shell shock'.[8] At this
time he did not have a disability pension of any kind and his wife had a lot
of difficulty in securing one, enlisting the secretary of the local branch of the
British Legion, and the local MP, Captain Derrick Gunston, to fight the case
for her. 'Shell shock' was what the British Legion stated on their claim. Mother
wasn't the kind of woman who would sit around doing nothing, Maurice
recalled, after all she was a teacher really even if she had had to throw up the
chance of teaching, and she wasn't afraid to tackle anybody if she thought
they could help. She always seemed to know the right person to go to, Roy

remarked. Capt. Gunston was in any case already an acquaintance because he lived in the village and had been used to buy dressed chickens from them.

Mother was ashamed at having to 'beg' for their pension, John believes, though as far as she was concerned there was no shame in what had happened to her husband, and she always rallied to his defence. After all, it was all down to the war wasn't it? Maurice still feels angry with the military authorities – they did not want to know about soldiers once they were out of the army and took no responsibility for what had been done to people during the Great War. His anger increased through his own service experience in the next war when he was brought to realise that the authorities didn't give a f – unless they were really put under pressure to do something. There is, he feels, a strong class dimension to this – it was alright if you were an officer, they would look after you then, but not if you were just an ordinary soldier.

Though it was certainly very late in the day to be initiating a fresh claim for a war disability pension, it was successful and Charles H was made a Service Patient.[9] When the pension eventually came through (£2.11.6. a week, Maurice remembers the amount well because he used to collect it from the post office), mother bought a bicycle from a catalogue so she could visit father at the asylum, cycling 20 miles each way in a day, sometimes returning quite late at night, the kids quite scared because they had been left alone in the dark. Sometimes she went by train, but the warrant from the Ministry of Pensions would only pay for a limited number of trips, even though it did allow her to take one or two of the children with her. Many of the staff at Horton Road had served in the war and so were sympathetic – John recalls that the porter wore a British Legion badge. Mother got on well with the medical superintendent, perhaps because dad was ex-service, and they would go to the asylum and sit in the front hall on long benches, the commissionaire sitting behind his desk nearby, a special consideration because children were not really allowed in the establishment at all. When dad was brought down he was always neatly dressed in a suit and tie, taciturn and quietly spoken, reluctant to discuss his 'troubles', eager only for news about his family.

The 1930s were a dark time, a pit in the memory, when dad never came out of the asylum at all, and he was often put in the padded cell because he had been fighting with other inmates (a message would come through to say that they could not visit because he was unwell). During this period there were, in any case, fine gradations of class feeling in Britain and though Maurice insists that dad did not go out looking for a fight, he was very proud and sensitive and because of his war troubles easily felt slighted. In the mid-1930s the family moved to a council flat, and mother found a friend in the woman next door whose husband had left her with young kids to bring up on her own. Visits to the asylum were made easier because they knew that father was there because of what had happened to him during the war. However, George was put out when a school friend of his age brazenly told him that in his parents' opinion his father's condition had started *before* his war experience. Still, the attendants seemed to respect him a bit more than the others because he was an ex-serviceman, and also because of his upbringing, not an educated man exactly, but he had gone through grammar school and passed his examinations, and compared to the majority of people in that place, a lot of them really bad cases from poor backgrounds, he was *cosmopolitan*. His family background was very good, his father was a surveyor, and he always had decent clothes. Only twice did Maurice goes as far as the wards, and that was when dad was physically ill. He was scared of going up there because though father had long periods of lucidity, perfectly normal when he was well, he was put on a ward with some very menacing mad people who were quite out of it all the time.

Eventually father became more settled, working a lot in the hospital vegetable gardens, and in the 1940s he was allowed out on leave to stay with Uncle Frank and later with his sons for a week or so at a time. By this time, Maurice felt, his father was improving, the periods of lucidity were becoming longer, the lapses into confusion shorter, and hopes were raised that release from certificate might be on the cards when in 1954 tragedy struck. Gashed on the head after he was thrown from the side-car of a motorcycle when it swerved to avoid a dog, the hospital where he was taken neglected to give him a tetanus injection. Shortly after he returned to the asylum he developed lockjaw, dying a week later, the Horton Road authorities blithely assuming that he had been given the injection but never bothering to check, a wholly avoidable death. Their mother had stood by their father during these years, still visiting him, though not so frequently in the 1940s, finally divorcing him at the beginning of the 1950s, and surviving herself until 1986, her children joined in compassion for the sorrow of her life.

CARED FOR AT HOME

The Ministry of Pensions contrived to reject Llewellyn Dyer's claim for a war disability pension with a spurious medical testimony that he was a 'congenital idiot', but the appeals board quickly pointed out that this was scarcely plausible since he had been employed as a railway clerk before the war, and as a third-class writer in the navy during it, requiring 'moderate intelligence at least'. Getting the Ministry to accept liability, and to proffer a more dignified label under which to accommodate their son, was only part of the problem for his parents, however, for it must have been obvious to them, and all who came in contact with him soon after he was disgorged from an asylum at the end of the war, that this young man had been severely damaged and was most unlikely ever to be able to manage on his own, let alone earn his living. The parents were faced with a stark choice: either to trundle their son back up the asylum drive, and hence accept the pitiful fate that routinely befell hopeless cases, or to take it upon themselves to care for him at home. Though we do not know what specially moved them in one direction rather than another, the record shows that having made the commitment they clung to it, even though their resources were obviously limited, caring for Llewellyn with a dignity that would not otherwise have been accorded him.

A medical report from 1928 described how Llewellyn was 'not working beyond doing a little cleaning up about the house at times', only answering questions in a monotone when pressed, though he did show some interest in cricket. Though he had for some time been receiving a 100% pension, even at this late stage the Ministry was still reluctant to make it permanent ('he may get better'), finally capitulating a couple of years later. Mrs Dyer died in 1933, and one may conjecture that the burden of care contributed to her early death. In 1951 Llewellyn was described by Derby Welfare Department as 'a full Disability Case of 40/- per week awarded for shell shock sustained during the First World War' (though the formal diagnosis was still dementia praecox and so it remained). He was still living with his father at this time, who was then eighty-one and was receiving only an old age pension of 30/- plus a supplementary allowance of 13/6d. In the post-war climate of civic beneficence, Llewellyn was entitled to apply for Unemployability Supplement and in the answers he gave lurks the yawning chasm that separates his present existence from his life before 1914: 'When did you cease to work for salary or wages? "1914"; What and where was your occupation then? "Clerk, Midland Railway Derby"'.[10]

William C, from a country town in Devon, who had worked as a decorator before the war, was considered by the recruiting officer to be in the veritable pink of health when he attested with his brother Henry in February 1915. 'I have examined the above-named recruit and find that he does not present any of the causes of rejection specified in the Regulations. He can see at the required distance with either eye; his heart and lungs are healthy; he has the free use of his joints and limbs; he does not suffer from hernia; and declares that he is not subject to fits of any description'. This was just the ticket to set him on the road to the East, serving in Mesopotamia before being wounded slightly at Secunderabad, in India. He was then stricken by paratyphoid, and suffered three bouts of malaria, before becoming psychotic in the summer of 1918, seeing visions and declaiming irrationally, after which he was invalided home.

At the Dykebar War Hospital they put the cause of his condition down to stress of campaign and malarial infection, but in the City of Exeter Asylum William found himself in an unreformed psychiatric environment where the authorities invoked a string of contributory factors such as congenital defect, adolescence, and masturbation, all much emphasised in the case-notes ('demented and hallucinated – a masturbator', 'grins and nods foolishly'), giving the impression that it was above all William's defective moral character that was the cause of his downfall on the battlefield. Initially he was granted a 100% pension for dementia praecox attributable to war service, but the local pensions officials produced a medical expert to argue that 'this man was in trouble early in service and presumably was always mentally unstable and should be considered aggravated and not attributable', a wildly disingenuous claim since William had served for more than four and a half years, most of them in extreme climactic conditions, and was only in trouble towards the end after a long episode of fever.

The Ministry refused to relent, however, and in 1922 William ('the appellant') was brought before a tribunal, accompanied by two brothers, to justify his claim for a war psychosis pension for dementia praecox. 'I was a printer's mate pre-enlistment . . . I joined the 4th Devons in 1915 and got on fairly well. . . . I was rather deaf, but not as deaf as I am now. I did the usual training before going to India.' At this point, the record continues, 'the appellant became confused and began to talk about Spiritualism and was not asked any further questions'. His brother Henry then picked up the thread, stating that he had been with William in Mesopotamia in 1916: 'I was with him for 6 months. . . . We had a very bad time and he was perfectly well. . . . When we separated in Bombay my brother was as normal as I am now.' In the wake of the Great War there was a significant revival of spiritualism in England, and talk of communing with the dead may very likely have inclined the plain men of the panel to conclude that there were innate peculiarities in this family history, for the Ministry got its way in this instance and William's disability was downgraded from attributable to aggravated.[11]

Though this gave Ministry officials an additional weapon (they could now always try to claim that the effects of aggravation had passed away), in the event it was something of a Pyrrhic victory. William's father, a tailor and out-fitter from a country town in Devon, who from the outset had been mistrustful of official intentions towards his son, had in the spring of 1921 taken William out of the asylum 'relieved' ('stated to chatter to imaginary persons but not to give trouble') so that he could be cared for at home by his family. The Ministry would have been wary of challenging the continuation of a 100% disability pension in such a case, involving a large, closely-bonded and obviously respectable family, for fear of the local ructions that would have resulted had they tried to do so. And from this time onwards William was cared by his family, his sister-in-law acting as the main carer for a long time until, presumably, a next generation took over.

It was going to be a very long haul indeed. In 1952 we learn of how when spoken to William 'answers without any meaning and talks of the moon and points to his mouth', and cannot be left alone in the house. 'Spends whole day in bed, makes no effort to get up. Has to have his meals brought to him, then messes it about and rolls it up into balls and then puts them in the bed. Rarely uses a knife and fork. He goes to have a bath and shaves himself but rarely washes'. Though the family means appear to have declined over the years, William's sister-in-law was not awarded a constant attendance allowance until the early 1950s, and while the doctor considered that William was well cared for, and not in need of in-patient treatment, he noted that the living conditions were 'fair only, country cottage, plain bare room, in bedroom chair and small wardrobe'. In 1965 William seemed 'well looked after and happy', though it was obvious that caring for him was no less demanding: 'He continues to be noisy and destructive, is restless at night and sometimes gets up and moves the furniture about the room. He tends to tear his clothes, (especially handkerchiefs from which he strips the hems)'. In the reports over the following years there was little change, William spending most of the day in bed, wandering about the room at night and shifting the furniture.[12]

Among those families who had abandoned their Service Patient relatives to institutions, very likely often with a heavy heart but concluding that there was no alternative, there are sometimes glimpses of an unexpected change of tack some decades later, during the Second World War especially; this was in part perhaps because their circumstances had changed, some now having reached retirement age and so with more time on their hands to play a caring role, but no doubt in part also because the new war had rekindled memories in families of the sacrifices their kin had made in the Great War. For instance Walter H, who had been admitted to Whittingham Asylum in the spring of 1920 from the Lord Derby War Hospital suffering from morbid delusions of unworthiness, chiefly of a persecutory nature, was discharged into the care of his uncle in Preston in October 1942; and Richard W, who had also been admitted to Whittingham in 1920 from the Ribchester Poor Law Institution, was taken home by his brother in August 1941.[13]

'THE NEW DOCTOR'

And then from the 1950s onwards something else happened, for there appeared the doctor with a new kind of sensibility who noticed things that had either not been noticed before or certainly never remarked upon. Doctors were now being encouraged to examine their own emotional and moral reactions to difficult patients, and to become more alert to what Winnicott called the 'psychological basis of unwellness' and to dimensions of their patients' lives that might previously have escaped them.[14] In the interwar period it is rather unlikely that we would have stumbled upon the following account, in which a doctor acknowledges quite candidly that the death of his patient was hastened by a failed relationship whereby both doctor and patient had been incapacitated and unable to help each other, the patient to convey his symptoms, the doctor to understand and interpret them. Of course, resistance to examination had previously been remarked upon quite frequently, but generally in a context in which the patient was blamed or belittled, and there was far less recognition by the doctor that what was accessible to him was the outcome of a relationship to which he had himself contributed.[15]

Charles A's melancholia started in June 1917 as the culmination of the stress of a long campaign in which he had been buried and wounded. Though he managed to do light work in the 1920s and 1930s, and for the most part to stay out of asylums, he never really recovered and was given a final award of 70% for manic-depressive psychosis in 1930. At different points along the way doctors had noted how resistant he was to examination ('frightened of examination & suspicious', April 1945; 'difficult to examine and resents questioning', December 1952), and his wife also reported that Charles was frightened of what the doctors might do to him, reluctant to admit even to her that he had a pain lest she send for the doctor. But it was left to his family doctor to explain how this history of unsatisfactory medical encounters had contributed to his death:

I last attended the deceased on the 20th Nov 1967 at his home. I ascertained after considerable time and much questioning of himself and his widow that he was suffering from severe abdominal pain. I did advise hospitalization for next day. It was late in the day. . . . There is no doubt in my mind that he had the greatest difficulty in describing his symptoms and for me to interpret them. . . . This difficult state of mind was present on the date of the last attendance and was always present on every other occasion that I attended him. It was always difficult for him to explain what was wrong, apart from a positive visible structural condition. . . . His death in my opinion was unexpected, untimely and was accelerated by his mental instability.[16]

Though some of Charles A's fears may have been irrational, he was also representative of a generation who carried with them disturbing memories from the earliest years of insensitive and sometimes humilating encounters with doctors, and who may at a certain point along the way have withdrawn into themselves and pretty much abandoned their efforts to communicate. That was certainly the conclusion which Manfred Bleuler reached in his study of prevailing psychiatric attitudes towards patients with psychotic conditions in the first part of the twentieth century: 'The patient and those who were healthy had ceased to understand one another. The patient gives up, in abject resignation or total embitterment, any effort to make himself understood. He either no longer says anything or says nothing intelligible. In so doing the naive observer declares, out of hand, that the patient has lost his reasoning powers'.[17]

A case such as Charles A's inevitably poses the question of just how much of what was transmitted by doctors, especially in the interwar period, as expert testimony of their patients' pathologies, was in reality vitiated by the doctor's prejudices, and his failure to provide the conditions in which the patient could begin to talk to the doctor, and the doctor start to listen. Just these questions are raised by the cases of Walter B and Herbert J, whose inner worlds, and long histories of emotional suffering, only really became visible when doctors remarked upon them in the 1960s. Born in 1899, Walter B was admitted to the Lord Derby War Hospital in October 1919, suffering from exhaustion psychosis, having served with the Royal Irish Rifles, but the diagnosis was later changed to feeblemindedness, then to that period diagnostic oddity 'constitutional psychopathic inferiority', and finally he was awarded a disability pension for amentia (or severe mental deficiency). Walter was obviously discontented with these mutations, and far from oblivious to them, because on a self-report he gave as the definition of his disability 'SHELL SHOCK' in capitals and then in brackets in small letters: '? feeblemindedness'. An asylum inmate on and off throughout the 1920s, he was probably quite lucky not to get stuck there for life, and what undoubtedly saved him was that he succeeded in finding a wife soon after his discharge from the Lord Derby. 'His mental state does not permit of his making any statement of his complaints', the authorities observed when they awarded his final pension, and 'it was also difficult to obtain information from the wife who is quite simple'.

That neither Walter nor his wife seemed inclined to make much of a statement does not seem altogether surprising in the light of the humiliating labels that had been attached to him. For its part the Ministry of Pensions had obviously resolved to style him a dement, award him a pension of sorts and forget about him as an undeserving case who would not benefit from any form of psychotherapeutic help. In the early 1960s, however, graphic reports on his emotional state start to appear in the records which confirm that when he declared that he was suffering from shell shock Walter was telling a truth about himself that the authorities had either dismissed or were unwilling to notice: 'he sits at the table with his head bent low and supported by both hands. He appears apathetic and not to be listening and will not reply to questions. Between periods of intense depression he is very restless'. And a later report tells of how 'during the night he has bad dreams and shouts or screams'.[18]

Rather similar to Walter B is Herbert J, who had enlisted on 9 August 1914, even though he was under age, serving as a gunner in the Royal Garrison Artillery. After being wounded in the head, he had finally been invalided out of the service with a diagnosis of 'feeblemindedness' as a perfunctory label both to explain away and dismiss his emotional suffering. When Pensions officials learned in 1922 that he was in full-time work they pestered the medical board to reduce its assessment, but the board refused, saying that when they examined him 'he showed every sign of being on the verge of a severe psychosis'. Like Walter B, Herbert's saving grace was that he had married in 1920, and it was his wife who became his exclusive carer after he was forced to give up work in the mid 1920s. Through the Bristol Local War Pensions Committee she applied for constant attendance allowance as early as 1923, but it was to take another 40 years before her application was successful. It was really only with the new kind of medical sensitivity that emerged in the 1960s that the nature and degree of Herbert's psychological suffering, in which he was still ravaged by dreams of the front line, came to light: 'Inability to sleep owing to bad dreams & in consequence is afraid to try and get to sleep. Dreams are mostly of the German breakthrough in March 1918 when he was wounded in the head. Describes his experiences clearly and rationally'. And then a few years later: 'Fit but frightened-looking man. Seen in bed because he had the "Horrors" last night – nightmares in which he relives his frightening war experiences. . . . He has not been out of the house for the past year – is frightened to go out'.[19]

It is noteworthy, even in the records of war pensioners in asylums, how rarely from about the mid-1920s onwards the war is remarked upon, as though even the mentally disturbed had decided to leave their memories of the war behind and to go about their daily business as mental patients, only uttering the sorts of preoccupations and complaints that mental patients were supposed to utter. Now, while we should not conclude from cases like those of Herbert J and Walter B that all the war disability pensioners had to a man been reliving through all these decades the German breakthrough of 1918, or some other assault, it certainly seems likely that the impact and continuity of the trauma of war experience was consistently under-reported, as though a cultural censor had been at work which either expunged war-related communications from the record, or collapsed them into pre-existing psychiatric conditions. No doubt some pensioners woke up belatedly to the recall of memories which had lain hidden for years, but it seems also likely that doctors, in caring for these patients and their families down the years, woke up belatedly to an awareness of the long fuse of traumatized memory that was still burning in many of these former servicemen of the Great War.

Chapter 20

FUTURES

It turns out that William P's resolve, with the active support of his wife, for he could not have done it alone, not to permit himself to be broken by the Ministry of Pensions doctor, and to discharge himself from the hospital against medical advice, was quite the most significant action he took in his life. More than 50 years later he was still living in his home town in Wales, and drawing his war disability pension, dying in 1987 at the age of ninety-five. William C died in that year too, also aged ninety-five, at the same address in a country town in Devon to which he had moved in 1921, almost 70 years since visions had erupted in his psyche in Mesopotamia in 1918, having been cared for by his family for almost 66 years. William Matthews, the former fisherman from Brixton, who aside from periods in a mental hospital had been living with his two spinster sisters since the Great War, got married in 1949. He also became the beneficiary of Unemployability Supplement, one of the innovations in the post-Second World War policy environment, filling in the application form himself and recording that he had ceased to work for salary or wages in about 1929, describing himself as formerly a 'small boat oner fishing Brixham', and dying in 1966 aged seventy-eight, his wife outliving him. Thomas Snowden, who after the Great War had been unable to scale the rigging in everyday life, also married for the second time after the Second World War, his first wife having died a few years earlier. His 30% award for insanity had never been increased but he managed to secure an allowance for his new bride ('the above named Great War disablement pensioner has been granted an allowance of 3/- weekly in respect of his wife') and died in 1963 at the age of eighty-four, his occupation given as retired doorkeeper at the Post Office.

Walter P, who had threatened to give the Pensions doctor a basting when he called upon him at his remote cottage in 1937, wrote to the Pensions in the 1950s in a fine hand inquiring about pension allowances for his two sons, one of whom was going on to do an apprenticeship in horticulture, the other in engineering, and when he died in 1990 aged ninety-three he was still receiving a 100% award for manic-depressive psychosis and gunshot wound right arm. Robert Dent, the former miner from Northumberland, had one further admission to hospital in the 1930s, following a report from the British Legion that he had been rough in the house and writing letters about cabbage growing to unknown people, his general practitioner Dr James Angus recording that he was still suffering from 'effects of shell shock/ manic-depressive psychosis'. At the time of his death in 1968 at the age of seventy-five he was still living with his wife in Newbiggin. Robert R, who had given so much trouble in Ministry of Pensions hospitals, but delighted in his domestic life, and was 'never so happy as when employed on something', was reported to be still working as a case maker in the 1950s. He married for the second time at the age of seventy-seven in 1972, dying in 1980, all this time in receipt of a 100% war disability pension for psychosis. And former Lance Corporal Alfred B, who spurned the margarine and was awarded a 100% war disability pension for manic-depressive psychosis as early as 1924, appears to have survived, and perhaps even thrived, outside institutions, bringing up a family, and dying in a nursing home on the south coast in 1989 at the age of ninety-nine.

And what of George Major Gomm and Albert Francis Norris, the gentleman's hosier and the former career imbecile turned hotel waiter? Nothing is recorded of how George fared at Long Grove Mental Hospital between the wars, but we do know that in the early 1940s he was made a voluntary patient, and that in May 1947 he was discharged as 'recovered', reflecting in part perhaps an improvement in his condition but more likely also a change in attitudes, together with rather more buoyant conditions in the labour market. It appears that on leaving the mental institution where he had resided for almost 28 years, George found himself a position as a ward assistant at the Royal Hospital and Home for Incurables in Putney, where it is poignant to reflect that he may very well have been been engaged in the care of other veterans of the Great War. Sadly, this new chapter in his life was soon curtailed for, never having been in robust health, he died of heart disease at Hammersmith Hospital two years later at the age of fifty-five. As to Albert Norris, it seems that he lead a wayfaring life between the wars, working as a general labourer and living in lodging houses and casual wards, his last known address the West End Institution in Southampton, dying in Park Prewett Hospital in Hampshire in November 1948 at the age of sixty. His existence was, perhaps, an improvement on what appeared to be his destiny as a career imbecile in 1916, but it was surely also a testimony to the failure of the intervening decades to deliver on the promises of the war years.

Former soldier John G, who had been wounded at Cambrai in 1918, died in Friern Psychiatric Hospital, where he had been admitted in October 1920 when it was still Colney Hatch Lunatic Asylum, in December 1987 at the age of ninety-two. For the last decades of his life he bore a diagnosis of schizophrenia, one of the last survivors of the legion of service lunatics, having lived

Ex-Serviceman John G at Colney Hatch Mental Hospital in the early 1930s.
Though his years in the institution have inevitably taken their toll, still he
possesses a dignity and bearing, and could be taken for a teacher, a scoutmaster
or an impecunious left-wing intellectual.

through almost seven decades in the fluctuations of psychiatric torpor and
enthusiasm, and the equivocal benevolence of war pensions administrations.
That there is, unfortunately, very little of interest to report about his institutional existence is by no means a reflection on John, and entirely a product
of the dismissive and routinized codes in which the lives of chronic mental
patients were inscribed, even in a supposedly progressive establishment such
as Friern. A small aperture on his life would momentarily open every month,
or more likely every second month, typically permitting a glimpse of some
failing in his conduct or some excess in his emotional state, but never a sense
of him in the round and of what might have been at stake for him.[1] Certainly,
he was not always entirely contented with his lot, for on 10 September 1935
he 'impulsively threw a gutta percha chamber [pot] at the Medical Superintendent who was visiting the ward at 5.30pm', for which he was secluded
until 7pm, but this failed to dampen his spirits, for less than a month later he
repeated the offence.

But we are, at least, on surer ground in acknowledging some facets of
the revolution in welfare and health care that John and other mental health
survivors of the Great War lived through. The agitation over service lunatics
had taken as its standard the rights to social justice to which servicemen
were entitled as members of the community of citizens in arms, but these
equalizing demands were for the most part targeted exclusively at serving

citizen soldiers, and did not bring any immediate gains for the mental health care of the citizenry as a whole. Yet the clamour over Service Patients undoubtedly bolstered the impetus towards mental health reform for, as G. K. Chesterton and others remarked shortly after the war, the treatment meted out to mentally distressed ex-servicemen had 'opened the eyes of the public to the fact that the life of patients in asylums is often one of prolonged misery'.[2]

Though we should certainly be wary of exaggerating the pace and scale of change, nevertheless diverse influences coming out of the Great War combined with a 'modernizing' spirit that was abroad in the interwar years slowly to infiltrate even the quintessentially sealed and secretive environments of mental hospitals. No longer could they retreat as heretofore into the citadels of their own solipsism as the guardians of the unwanted. Instead, they were induced to become more venturesome and outward-looking in proclaiming themselves as settings in which citizens in need were not necessarily off-limits. George H, one of the original 'non-attributables' who had been reclassed as an 'ex-Service Patient' in 1924, had for 37 years been an inmate of Digby Mental Hospital, the former City of Exeter Lunatic Asylum. Over the decades he had mutated in the institution's estimation from being 'a nasty and weakminded imbecile with delusions' to an accommodating and appreciated member of the company of chronic mental patients. When he finally died in 1954, his son wrote to the hospital authorities to express his gratitude for the sensitivity shown to him during the course of his father's final illness.[3]

In the early 1970s the War Pensions Agency (the successor to the Ministry of Pensions, now disbanded) inquired whether John G was fit to join the new wave of 'capable' psychiatric pensioners with their own bank accounts who could attend to their financial affairs with minimal assistance from the hospital authorities. Though it was a little late in the day (he was then almost eighty) to be turning John on to a bank account, in itself the proposal marked a decisive and scarcely imaginable shift from the niggardly paternalistic culture of the 'Insane Group', the name of the administrative section in the Ministry of Pensions which dealt with service lunatics, in which John had started his long career as a Service Patient.[4] William R had been admitted to the Mickleover Lunatic Asylum in April 1918, and died in an institution named the Pastures Hospital in 1964, spending the last five years of his life in a villa in the grounds called 'The Woodlands'.[5] It turned out that this was the original establishment re-branded under a new name, heralding a revolution in mental health care that was eventually to culminate in the closure of almost all of the 90-odd county and borough lunatic asylums in which the Service Patients had been dispersed after the Great War.[6] At the time of John G's death in 1987, the mental hospital in which he had long been a resident was almost as ready to expire as he was, and if he had survived just a few years longer he might very well have found himself re-settled in a supported residence in the community, as part of Friern's ambitious and carefully controlled closure programme.

Coda

The Captain's Valedictory Letter

Captain G. W. Haws suffers from the mental illness schizophrenia and is considered to be incapable of managing himself or his affairs in a normal, rational manner. He tends to be asocial and withdrawn in his habits. . . . Periodically, however, he becomes excited and talkative and he will then freely express many abnormal ideas that he is being ill treated and persecuted.

Dr Benjamin Chester, Report to the Trustee Officer of the
Standard Bank of South Africa (1963)

The above-named officer has written a long, rambling letter amounting to 15 sheets of closely written handwriting (both sides of the paper) and we feel that there would be no point in forwarding a copy. . . . It is not clear in his letter what periods of time he is talking about as he refers right back to the 1914–18 War.

F. Tomkins, for Controller, Ministry of Pensions (1963).

Captain George Haws again offered his services to the War Office at the start of the new war, but after that we lose sight of him for a long period until, in the early 1960s, he surfaces unexpectedly in a long letter addressed to the Controller of the Ministry of Pensions from a nursing home in South Africa where, it turns out, he had been living since being certified insane in 1943. He had booked a passage from Liverpool to Canada after war was declared, but direct sailings were cancelled and once more he found himself re-routed under the impress of war through France, Switzerland and the Italian lines to South Africa, where some 20 years later, he was still waiting for a ship to Canada. For many years, he recounts, he had not really minded the long delay to his onward passage but matters are now very different due to the changed conditions at the nursing home, for there is talk that it is going to close down and be allowed to die out. Although a new patient does arrive occasionally, replacements of the aged and infirm patients are no longer taking place as they pass away, and overall the patients are being allowed to dwindle away in numbers, deliberately, as part of the gradual closing down, though this of course is only conjecture.

Personally, the Captain lives in a 'rondavel', a one-roomed building, about the size of an infantry officer's bell tent, in one corner of the ample grounds, having his meals sent over and only going across to the main building for baths and other necessities, such as to be seen by Dr Chester, his regular medical attendant who took over the practice when Dr Felix du Toit died some years ago, or to see the draper from the local suburb of Bramley who supplies his clothing. Now in his seventies and seriously disabled by arteriosclerosis, the brunt of it is that the Captain would like to escape the clutches of the nursing home and get the Ministry of Pensions to agree to a private arrangement with a nurse to whom he has become attached, as he is now completely incapable of doing anything for himself as regards providing for his needs, buying clothing or doing any other shopping. Indeed, his movements are limited to the necessary journeys about the place, over to the main building to visit the Duty Room, to leave lists with Matron for fresh supplies or for the chemist, or to to the office to leave the monthly list of requirements such as tobacco and matches with the book-keeper. Some time ago he has had to give up going to the WC, some 50 yards away, instead using his bed-chamber, which he empties morning and evening, for Dr Du Toit told him that the only thing to do about his cramped muscles was to lie down until they relaxed, which sometimes takes months.

He has had great difficulty in dressing as regards his jacket, and at this time, which must have been towards the end of the war, he was wearing his military tunic, lightweight khaki, for clothing was scarce, but with the Royal Scots buttons off, because it was obvious that he would never need his uniform again, so he had them mounted on cardboard and sent to various museums, replacing them with ordinary buttons. But when pulling his jacket on he could not give the wriggle and twist to his shoulders and body, and just shrug it on, as one normally does, as it caught behind somewhere about the shoulder blades, and had to be slowly dragged up over his back, with the result that the collar and upper part of the light coat, worn as an unbuttoned lounge jacket and not as a buttoned up military tunic, invariably became folded in underneath, without his being aware of it for some time. The crisis was reached some five or six years ago when he was wearing a lumber-jacket, as he had to go over to the Duty Room (the 'Diens Karmer' in Afrikaans) and ask the night nurse to help him on with it.

His diet is nothing special as it is all just restrictions, weak tea (the colour of an amber traffic light) without milk, and a jug of hot water to water it down, but he can manage undercut of beef, or mutton, or pork as chops and such like, and in the winter when things will keep he opens a 12oz tin of bully-beef which also, like undercut, is cut across the grain, and so is in short length fibres. Fortunately he can manage pastry, such as jam tart or boiled suet puddings with syrup (taking syrup honey instead of sugar with his porridge), pancakes and such like, but he is not allowed chocolate, not that he ate much, just a few small squares, about two to a slice of toast, with his buttered toast at bed-time, these small squares, less than one inch by half an inch being broken off a quarter lb slab of plain Albany chocolate, as a variation of toast and cheese. At one time his face muscles were so rigidly cramped that he had difficulty in moving his jaws to masticate, even having to break up a plain Maric biscuit, allowing each piece to slowly dissolve in his mouth. He could not manage meat, just eating the potatoes and gravy and pudding, nor could he eat a banana, a soft edible, as he could not work his jaws laterally but only up and down and could only do this same movement with his tongue and not curl it over, and lick round the teeth, as one normally does. And it must have been around this time also that his speech muscles were affected, making his speech slow and difficult, and even now it is much worse in the winter time when the cold affects him, making him annoyingly slow, with almost a halting speech these days, though when he made an effort, quite unexpectedly, he suprised himself by a bellow instead of normal conversation across the ward.

The problems were really worst with his nether parts for he had trouble with his trousers as he could only move his forearms and wrists, his shoulders being locked, so that when leaving the WC he could often could only get one leg of the braces at the back done before his cramped muscles became too fatigued to work and he had to leave things like this, with only one button holding, and attend to the other brace and button an hour or so later when his arm muscles had relaxed. Another trouble that he had in the bath was that his legs were so tightly closed that it was as if they were tied together at the ankles and, pulling himself erect by the taps, he had to turn round, moving one foot at a time, in several movements, and balance by moving the left leg, for he always turned to the left in this bath. And the clenching of his legs had a queer effect for the muscular contractions pulled his scrotum back permanently, so that his testicles were jammed, and crushed between his legs, especially during the night when asleep, though by the end of the summer things improved.

He apologizes, finally, for the length of this letter but it is, so he claims, his first communication since the 1914–19 War period and so the description of his diseases and aged infirmity and incapacity has of necessity been rather lengthy. Yet if the letter itself is long, the act of creating it must have been exceedingly protracted, for it has been years since he could sit at a table to eat or write, or was able to do his occupational therapy, such as the weaving of scarves. Instead he has to write propped up in bed, holding the writing pad or such in front of him on a small board in his left hand, as he is doing now, or sitting up at the door of his rondavel, in a folding canvas armchair, and he is in no doubt that after completing this communication he will be laid up exhausted for a few days.

Of course, this is a valetudinarian, and perhaps valedictory, narrative, and the progressive and incurable illnesses which the Captain records are a figure for the mental disturbance that has dogged the last 50 years or so of his life, just as the re-routing that culminated in his protracted sojourn in South Africa is a figure for a life that has variously been derailed and derouted. Despite everything, the Captain is still, so to say, master of his own rondavel, painting a Grand Tour of his situation, weaving between a smaller and a larger canvas, from his physical circumstances to the démarches of history as they have impacted on his suburb, at once tender and ironic, in which rancour and suspicion have given way to *souci de soi* and concern for others. The deprivations notwithstanding, nonetheless there are sensual pleasures, the Maric biscuits and the small squares of Albany chocolate.[1]

Hysteria, it has been said, is in our time no longer a question of the wandering womb but of the wandering story, the narrative of the displaced and powerless struggling to find a foothold on the glacial slopes of official indifference.[2] From an official angle, nothing could be more ridiculous than that the Captain should address such a voluminous and intimate communication to the Controller at the Ministry of Pensions, but what such a reaction inevitably overlooks is the weight of the luggage that many of these survivors of the Great War are still carrying. Tomkins (for the Controller) may have found it strange that as late as the 1960s the Captain should have returned in his memory to the 1914–18 War, but the Captain and others could surely be forgiven for wondering how the Pensions could have become so forgetful of the circumstances of its own origin and of its own function as a memorial to the enduring presence of the past in the minds and bodies of war disability pensioners.

Still haunted by the failings that he may have displayed at Cape Helles on the Gallipoli Peninsula almost half a century earlier, which had led people in the vicinity to comment unfavourably upon him, Captain George Haws was leading the contingent of footsore, but still spirited, mad activists into a new offensive. He was voicing the determination of psychiatric survivors of the Great War to secure a proper recognition from the establishment that had sent them into the fray, of the baggage they were still carrying so many years down the trail. The weight of their narratives should receive its proper measure, and they should be permitted to place their own imprint on the body of the Ministry of Pensions, thus ensuring that their personal histories were securely lodged in the collective memory.

REMEMBERING THE FORGOTTEN LUNATICS

Ay, now I remember, Nosey Flynn said, putting his hand in his pocket to scratch his groin.

James Joyce, Ulysses[1]

. . . touching their still ears with words, still hearts of their each his remembered lives.

James Joyce, Ulysses[2]

Disposal of property of deceased Service Patient, Harry Gardener, to his father: 6 5-Franc notes; 2 Frs. 50c cash; documents; overcoat, trousers, waistcoat, jacket, cap, drawers, undershirt, cardigan, shirt, collar, 2 prs hose, braces, boots, 1 kit bag, 4 handkerchiefs.

Private Harry Gardener, died Colney Hatch Lunatic Asylum, 3 May 1922.[3]

'It is the burden of those who care for the suffering', argues moral philosopher Stanley Hauerwas, 'to know how to teach the suffering that they are not thereby excluded from the human community. In this sense, medicine's primary role is to bind the suffering and the non-suffering into the same community.'[4] This is a provocative requirement to lay upon mental health care at any point in the modern period, and it is not without ambiguity, but it possesses a special resonance in the extraordinary circumstances of the First World War in which the interests of the generals and the politicians were in critical respects trumped by demands for a system of care expressive of social solidarity. Though notions of common citizenship had prospered as an audible leitmotiv in the political culture, something more than an aggregate of scattered imaginings, it was only in the unique circumstances of the Great War that the equality of being of all serving citizen soldiers came to possess the weight and substance that was sufficient to displace, for the time being at least, the hegemony of fusty class- and gender-bound partialities and discriminations. It is perhaps one of the ironies of the Great War that it is able to return answers to Stanley Hauerwas's testing stipulation that, if they are sometimes equivocal and faltering, are in many respects compelling and moving, and succeed in breaking new ground, or reclaiming ground that had been lost, and laying some authentic claim to the title of a solidarity among strangers.[5]

Restricted and discriminatory norms of 'efficiency' clashed with an expanding sense of community and with new developments in psychology. Even if this did not exactly herald the dawn of a psychological demos, the wartime alliances forcing concessions which in certain respects were ahead of their time, a nod towards an emerging agenda of human and social rights that was still shackled by the ball and chain of the *ancien* health and welfare *régime*, still they were hustled into the future with the gathering momentum of democratization. With the Representation of the People Act of 1918, the British electorate tripled in size, extending the franchise to virtually the whole of the adult population (though women under thirty were still left in the cold), inevitably provoking alarms among the rearguard that the 'irresponsible' would now be permitted to infiltrate the electorate, leading to demands that anyone who had been an inmate of a lunatic asylum, or a Poor Law institution, during the qualifying period should be disqualified. Significantly, however, these proposals were quickly quashed when it became apparent that they would have had the effect of disenfranchizing all shell-shocked soldiers who had recovered. Not only that, they would also have discriminated against the poor, for it was alleged that it was not unknown for aristocrats to be fetched out of private madhouses to attend critical parliamentary votes. This debate demonstrated, claims Mathew Thomson, that 'it was no longer considered acceptable for the franchise to discriminate according to economic or class status'.[6]

The Great War proved to be a historical moment at which the message started to seep through that there was something seriously awry with a science of psychiatry that had not put its moral relations in order by prizing equality and a willingness to show solidarity with its patients.[7] In promoting the Service Patient scheme, and in widening the scope of what counted as a psychiatric war disability, it was the achievement of progressive voices in the mental health lobby, notably that of Maurice Craig, to take a stand on the side of ordinary soldiers of all classes experiencing a mental health crisis or suffering from a mental disorder.[8] Though they later recovered some of the ground, the military establishment lost possession to a considerable extent of the meanings and determinations of the psychologically traumatized ex-serviceman. This was a new episode in a uniquely modern form of politics, the ramifications of which still haunt us today, which had begun with the controversies around railway spine in the nineteenth century.[9]

It was in this sense, perhaps, that war became an instrument of radicalization, as midwife to the 'gestation of a new social ideal', as a top civil servant put it, hardening the resolve of those who hankered after change, and breaching small windows of opportunity in the stockades of reaction.[10] Progressive forces did not, of course, sweep all before them, but even if much was obstructed and repulsed, still the achievements of this historical moment helped to fuel a counter-current, to provide the inspiration for other movements as for individual lives, and to become a seminal cultural resource that could be returned to and drawn upon. In their preoccupation with intimacy of scale – large houses to accommodate no more than 30 patients – the therapeutic visions of this period look forward and backwards at the same time, backwards to the moral therapy movement of the early decades of the nineteenth century, and to the asylum as it was envisaged by crusading reformers before the hordes of paupers bore down upon it in the second half of the century, but forward also to the therapeutic communities of the Second World War. There is a poignant sense in this period of the missing therapeutic community, a hole in the heart of the wider society, whose moment has not yet arrived.[11]

In the absence of an official policy or programme of community care in the interwar period, to a large extent it fell to ex-servicemen and their families to manufacture alternatives to the chronic destinies that would otherwise have greeted them. But war disability pensions brought a potent innovation into the political economy of psychotic lives. Though it was originally envisaged that they would play second string to reconstruction, eventually war disability pensions became a survival kit in the barren environment of mass unemployment, itself a product of the disruptions of war. My purpose has not been to extol them as a good in themselves, but to examine how at a particular historical moment they came to play a strategic role in improving life chances, and remedying basic injustices, for a disadvantaged constituency. Along with all its negative effects, writes Arthur Marwick, the Great War 'did provide the working man everywhere with a unique possibility, which would not have come about otherwise, of bettering his lot'.[12] And we can perhaps at the very least say of psychiatric war disability pensions that they helped to mitigate the circumstances of those whose lot would otherwise very likely have deteriorated. Tellingly, in the late 1920s, when 'fair starts' were a scarce commodity, Millais Culpin admonished those who maintained that pensions liberality was fuelling a compensations culture: 'If everyone, after appropriate treatment and a fair start in life again, had known that he would receive no pension, many of them them would be in a better state now than they are; but great injustice would have been done to perhaps a greater number'.[13]

In our contemporary culture, Kirby Farrell has argued, 'trauma is both a clinical syndrome and a trope, something like the Renaissance figure of the world as a stage: a strategic fiction that a complex, stressful, society is using to account for a world that seems threateningly out of control'. People not only suffer trauma, 'they use it, and the idea of it, for all sorts of ends, good and ill. The trope can be ideologically manipulated, reinforced, and exploited'.[14] By comparison with the other options on offer, the status of a psychiatric war disability pensioner was rather compelling, and through the honorific of a shell-shock identity it became a little easier to negotiate social life as an ex-serviceman even with a long-term mental disability.[15] A vast spectrum of emotional and psychological trauma cases came to be anointed and transfigured as war disabilities. Among them was Rifleman Victor William Breeze, who had enlisted in the 21st City of London Regiment towards the end of February 1915 at the age of twenty-seven, serving on the home front until 26 April, a total of 62 days, when he was discharged the service, 'military character indifferent', 'inattention on morning parade and neglect of duty', 'feebleminded', 'does not understand an order' and 'frequently incapable of arming himself correctly'.[16] Four years later, when former Rifleman Breeze was admitted to Long Grove Asylum suffering from mania, his claim for a war disability pension was successful and he was elected into the fraternity of Service Patients. At either end of the spectrum, admittedly, there are individuals who seem obviously to fit the part of familiar characters, the 'hero' or the 'malingerer', the 'authentic' and the 'counterfeit', but the vast majority of service lives were spread about the middle, in the blurred and contestable area where there are no clear answers, and who is to say that Victor Breeze does not belong here as well?[17]

The ex-servicemen who figure in these pages were most of them experiencing uncontainable forms of personal suffering in which they were reduced to a state of helplessness, their defences overhelmed, deprived of what is essential to life and frequently pitched into a condition of melancholy. Were not many of these cases, it may be asked, examples of what today would be termed post-traumatic stress disorder or PTSD? Though there are limitations to the records, if we were so inclined we could certainly construe a fair proportion of them as that, but in so doing we would miss the point that critics such as Kirby Farrell and Allan Young are trying to impress upon us in arguing that post-traumatic stress disorder is not so much a truth that has been discovered, as an invention or strategic fiction.[18] In the house of trauma, as Robert Young wisely remarks, there are many mansions, and in discussing trauma we are always 'slip-sliding around from the language of bodily impacts to that of events and enduring – perhaps incapacitating – forms of distress in the inner world'.[19] The real lesson that sensitive contemporary observers such as D. W. Winnicott took from the histories and experiences of emotionally traumatized ex-servicemen was not about the pre-eminence of a specific syndrome, or chain of causality, as much as an understanding of the emotional suffering of ordinary people and of what was truly at stake in their lives considered as emotional beings.

Over the war years the agitation of public opinion succeeded in binding them into the community. Yet with the passage of years these bonds have been undone or distorted. With the appearance after the war of a spate of memoirs in which was manufactured the myth of the heroic volunteer, the Service Patient all but vanishes, along with the conscript, a victim of the post-war myth of participation, trumped by the shell-shocked officer.[20] In all this there was an unwitting complicity between an establishment anxious to reduce the burden of war pensions and guard against a repetition of such profligacy; a psychiatric profession for whom by the late 1920s and 1930s the surviving war pensioners in asylums held us as much interest as the rubbish awaiting collection; and a public still haunted by heroic hankerings, who found comfort in the myth of shell shock as a means of bridging the gap between heroic and domestic values without having to relinquish either.[21]

The war psychotics and the psychiatric disability pensioners of the Great War have become strangers to us, oddities, but this is a consequence less of how they became in themselves than of what has been done to them through the distorting lens of officialdom. Also, it must be acknowledged, through the preferences and distortions of historians, for in the historical afterlife they figure most commonly in the ritual procession of cripples and the disabled to illustrate a thesis such as the pity of war, before being hastened back to the barracks of oblivion.[22] Yet what ought to strike us most of all about this cast is just how *ordinary* they are. Undeniably, the most fitting visual icon of the forgotten lunatics, in itself and also for the storm of protest it evoked, is the portrayal by the artist C. R. W. Nevinson, during his controversial career as an official war artist, of four Tommies standing at rest entitled 'A Group of Soldiers' (see plate 11).

This picture depicts 'the type of man . . . not worthy of the British Army', bristled Major Lee, the censor at General Headquarters, in November 1917, subsequently referring to it as 'the Group of Brutes', and another critic denounced it as representing 'a gang of loutish cretins'.[23] Intoned the War Office: 'the Germans will seize upon the picture as evidence of British degeneration'.[24] In his defence Nevinson said that he had tried accurately to represent 'the British working man in khaki', and that all these four men were *portraits*: 'men I chose quite haphazard from the Tubes as they came from France on leave'.[25] He had, he said, tried to express the 'loathsomeness' of the enlisted man's life in the trenches: 'the men were so unutterably wretched, their misery was so intense, that the result of it was mad laughter'.[26] Any one of these physically and emotionally exhausted soldiers, with all their intense fragility and ravenous hopes, might be among the company assembled in these pages. Like Harry Gardener, for instance, who died in May 1922, remnants of the wages of war still mouldering in his pocket, enough even by postwar prices to buy a posy for his sweetheart and stand a round of drinks at an estaminet. It is exactly the gritty ambiguity and indeterminacy of these portraits that is socially and psychologically apposite, and that is just what the censors and traditionalists recoiled against. If these are 'degenerates', then degeneracy lived in '*any* man in *any* street'.

NAMING THE NAMELESS

– Who is he if it's a fair question, Mrs Breen asked. Is he dotty?
– His name is Cashel Boyle O'Connor Fitzmaurice Tisdall Farrell, Mr Bloom said, smiling.

James Joyce, *Ulysses*[27]

Finally, in renewing these bonds we must recognise that the forgotten lunatics can only achieve equality of remembrance through being named.[28] In reading these names, or reciting them out loud, we can savour the rich and varied tapestry of the nation that went to war between 1914 and 1918, the knotted skeins of its collective manhood and the tang of parental yearnings, the imaginary cordite of their lineage, that propelled these volunteers and conscripts on life's journey: Ethelbert William Arnold, Harold Baff, Winder Barker, Abraham Baruck, William Bendall Beard, Alfred Beardwell, Montague Bettle, Arthur Bircumshaw, Victor William Breeze, Arthur James Bloodworth, Harry Brighouse, Claude Loraine Brown, Walter Buckle, Albert Edward Bunker, George Cadwallader, Harry Cant, William Wood Cant, George Henry Cardy, Maurice Chasty, Arthur Kent Childs, Sergius Choat, George Leonard Cockle, Sam Conerlensky, Othello Crabtree, Alfred Crack, John Crisp, George Croton, John Crummey, Ernest Cullabine, Hubert Cumberbatch, Majuba Victor Dale, Barnet Daniels, Joseph Dempsey, William Dignum, Levi Dixon, George Dobbie, John Joseph Duddle, Benjamin Ely, William Entwhistle, John Fritz Francisco Eugenius, Frederick Felton, Samuel Fenn, Sidney Youlden Fewings, Walter Fright, Charles Claud Gallop, Ernest Lawrence Garner,

Henshall Gater, James Alexander Gauge, Frederick Edwin Gilkes, George Major Gomm, Ernest Ashton Goymer, Percy Grimbly, Arthur Grimes, Walter Grimshaw, Percy Gritzhandler, Benjamin Grumwell, Esau Gully, Ivor Bertie Gurney, Herbert Hancy, John Willis Harker, William Heap, Ernest Hopcroft, Victor Ellison Horner, Horace Horlick, Charles Arthur Hudson, John Moses Jones, Frank Jowett, Walter Kemp, Frederick Kettle, John Kitchen, Percy Studwell Langham, Leonard Seth Lewis, Percy William Liddle, Horace Lines, Railton Longrigg, Harding Maisden Lugg, Chalmers Manners, Ernest Mantle, Fred Mixer, James Clement Mole, James Edward Mellody, Arthur Mendle-sohn, Frank Messenger, Barron Wells Morter, Harry Mountain, John Philip Mumme, Herbert Mutimer, William Stanislaus McKenna, Harold Nightin-gale, Albert Francis Norris, Cyril Nudds, Henry Ormerod, Arthur Willie Painter, Richard Palfrey, Harry Plotkin, Walter William Portlock, Sidney Ernest Raison, Ernest Reddy, Maurice Charles Ridley, William Rimmer, George Rippingale, Solomon Scoble, Henry Bence Scudamore, Cornelius Scully, Percy Self, James Semaine, John James Shambrook, Thomas Sharrocks, George Shimeld, Arthur Noel Sidebottom, Cyril Siggers, Albert Sinkinson, John Ewart Slaven, Albert Sly, Frederick Slammers Southgate, Joseph Willoughby Stathers, William Spiby, Leonard Street, Alfred James Steggell, George Stollery, Herbert Lawrence Sudds, Samuel Tapsfield, William Tasker, John Thom, William Tickle, Percy Tong, Albert Treadaway, Horace Harold Treasure, Samuel Welham, John Wharf, Booth Widdop, Arthur Window, Albert Workman, Bernard Coppock Wright. . . .

Appendix I

THE MAP OF SERVICE LUNACY

DISTRIBUTION OF SERVICE PATIENTS IN LUNATIC ASYLUMS IN ENGLAND AND WALES, 1 January 1922 [from *Parliamentary Debates*, Vol. CXLX, 30 March 1922, cols. 1502–1504]

Name of Asylum	No. of Service Patients
County Asylums	
Beds, Herts and Hunts	29
Berks	46
Brecon	26
Bucks	40
Cambridge	20
Carmarthen	22
Chester: Chester	79
Parkside	61
Cornwall	40
Cumberland	35
Denbigh	59
Derby Co.	33
Dorset	28
Durham	104
Essex: Brentwood	82
Severalls	53
Glamorgan	99
Gloucester	44
Hants: Knowle	57
Park Prewett	3
Kent: Barming Heath	75
Chartham	37
Lancaster: Lancaster	107
Rainhill	204
Prestwich	292
Whittingham	134
Winwick	–
Lincoln: Bracebridge	41
Kesteven	14
London: Banstead	150
Bexley	85
Cane Hill	110
Claybury	172

continued

Colney Hatch	85
Hanwell	98
Horton	–
Long Grove	165
Middlesex: Wandsworth	82
Napsbury	50
Monmouth	41
Norfolk	53
Northampton	47
Northumberland	29
Nottingham Co.	25
Salop	34
Somerset: Wells	17
Cotford	31
Staffs: Stafford	53
Burntwood	67
Cheddleton	54
Suffolk	37
Surrey: Brookwood	28
Netherne	75
Surrey: East	49
West	21
Warwick	54
Wight, Isle of	8
Wilts	33
Worcester: Powick	41
Barnsley H.	20
York, North Riding	13
York, West Riding: Wakefield	135
Wadsley	35
Menston	127
Storthes Hall	72
York, East Riding	14

Borough & City Asylums

Birmingham: Winson Green	54
Rubery Hill	72
Brighton	27
Bristol	36
Canterbury	6
Cardiff	45
Croydon	19
Derby	23
Exeter	14
Gateshead	18
Hull	32
Ipswich	13
Leicester	39
London, City of	18
Middlesbrough	42
Newcastle-upon-Tyne	43

Name of Asylum	No. of Service Patients
Newport	12
Norwich	28
Nottingham	47
Plymouth	37
Portsmouth	43
Sunderland	37
West Ham	61
York	21
TOTAL	**4985**

Asylums with 100+ Service Patients

Prestwich	292
Rainhill	204
Claybury	172
Long Grove	165
Banstead	150
Wakefield	135
Whittingham	134
Menston	127
Cane Hill	110
Lancaster	107
Durham	104

This is a snapshot taken on 1 January 1922 listing the numbers of Service Patients in 67 county and 24 borough and city asylums. As will be seen, the asylums with the largest intake are mostly in London or the North. It is worth remarking on the concentration in the Lancashire asylums, partly because this area was a major recruiting ground for the services, but also because there were several asylums here with enormous capacity (Whittingham was the largest in the land, with around 2300 inmates), so overall these figures reflect the densities and distributions on the map of asylumdom as much as any other influence. There were no Service Patients in Winwick or Horton at this time because until recently these had been war hospitals. Similarly, in some instances the population in an asylum may be an artefact of the disruptions of the war, as with Park Prewett in Hampshire which had been the No 4 Canadian Military Hospital in the later stages of the war, and had only opened as a regular asylum in 1921, whereas in others (the eight Service Patients in the asylum on the Isle of Wight, for example) it more accurately reflects the local demography.

Not too much should be made of the total figure of service inmates, since quite a sizeable number had already been discharged or died (especially the GPI cases), and the average total was to increase significantly over the next years with the influx of new admissions. In 1922 there were 873 Service Patients in the London County Councils asylums, rising to 907 in 1925, and still in 1934 there was a population of around 750 [LCC, *London Statistics*, Vols 28, 30 & 38]. Of course, these figures merely reflect official decisions in the classification of ex-servicemen as Service Patients, and take no account of service inmates whose classification was still pending, or in whom it had been refused.

Appendix II

THE BURDEN OF COSTS

Relative to the overall expenditure on treatment and pensions for psychiatric war pensioners and their families, the psychotic or 'insane' cases were absorbing a disproportionate share of the budget throughout the interwar period. Though the psychotic disability group was relatively small, economically it was significant, for in the early 1930s it comprised just over 10 per cent of ex-servicemen with the most severe disabilities. 'In general, tuberculosis, organic diseases of the heart and psychoses stand out as the conditions with the most continuous and severe degrees of disablement.... In the aftermath of the war as judged by the award of pension, it is the diseases of lungs and heart and brain which remain the most conspicuous items in the sum of the State's aggregate liability, whilst the wounds... have relatively healed'. [T. J. Mitchell and G. M. Smith, *Medical Services: Casualties and Medical Statistics of the Great War*, p. 350]

CAUSES OF DISABILITY AMONG BRITISH FIRST WORLD WAR PENSIONERS

Disability	Number of cases	% of all disabilities
1. Wounds and amputations	324,722	38.0
2. Tuberculosis	65,370	7.6
3. Respiratory diseases	55,383	6.5
4. Organic diseases of the heart	31,502	3.7
5. Functional diseases of the heart	44,855	5.2
6. Neurasthenia	58,402	6.8
7. Malaria	44,749	5.2
8. Rheumatism	33,908	4.0
9. Ear diseases	23,772	2.7
10. Psychoses	13,030	1.5
11. Dysentery	8,025	0.9
12. Nephritis	15,837	1.8
13. Other causes	135,933	15.9
All disabilities	855,488	100.0
of which	80,000	died of war-related conditions or diseases
	229,034	remained seriously disabled

SOURCE: T. J. Mitchell and G. M. Smith, *Medical Services: Casualties and Medical Statistics of the Great War* (1931), p. 349.

Service Lunatics as a Burden
Already in 1923 it was apparent to the Treasury that lunatics comprised more than 50 per cent of the cases for whom 'permanent provision would have to be made by the State in some form or another'. The other 5000 or so were made up of chronic heart and bronchitis cases, cases of serious disfigurement and a small number of neurasthenics. [TNA: PRO T 161/222/S.22685]

Approximate Costs in 1924 of Treatment and Allowances of Lunatic and Mental Ex-Service Patients Whose Disability is Attributable or Aggravated by Service in the Great War. It can be seen from this table that the Service Patient category was absorbing more than 60 per cent of the overall treatment budget for Great War psychiatric cases. [NB: these figures do not include pensions for psychotic pensioners outside hospital or for neurasthenic pensioners not receiving treatment.]

Nos.	Category	Maintenance	Family Allowances
	Service Patients	£	£
5859	County or Borough Mental Hospitals	364,500	204,000
450	Ministry Special Hospitals (Old Manor & Storthes Hall)	51,000	
	Non Certified Cases		
800	Special Neurological Hospitals (Ewell & Saltash)	104,500	22,000
750	Ordinary Neurological Hospitals	109,000	20,600
c.3500	Out-patients at Ministry Neurological Clinics	50,000	60,000
	TOTAL	679,000	306,600
	GRAND TOTAL	985,600	

[TNA: PRO PIN 15/2499]

Numbers under Treatment for Psychosis and Neurasthenia. Note how quickly provision for out-patient treatment declined.

	Psychosis	Neurasthenia	
	IN	IN	OUT
1921	6271	2951	6975
1924	6300	1550	c.3500
1927	6458	1373	541
1930	6195	867	218
1936	5689	364	40

[TNA: PRO PIN 15/2401]

Numbers of Pensions in Payment for Psychosis and Neurasthenia.

	Neurasthenia	Psychosis
1927	32,970	12,200
1929	32,570	12,100
1930	32,440	12,000
1936	30,220	10,900

[TNA: PRO PIN 15/2401]

The Decline in the Service Patient Population 1933–1950. 'The 1914 War cases should cease to be a problem in a few years' (Ministry of Pensions 1951).

Year:	1933	1940	1948	1949	1950
Nos in mental hosps:	5994	5285	4036	3914	3760
No of deaths in year:	139	186	143	157	128

[TNA: PRO PIN 15/4082]

Combined Treatment and Pension Costs in November 1937 for Psychiatric War Pensioners (Other Ranks only). The War Psychotics (5500 Service Patients in mental hospitals and 4800 pensioners living outside hospital) account for around 47 per cent of the total budget.

Insane Cases	£
5500 Service Patients. Family allowances per annum:	180,000
Maintenance costs:	400,000
4800 pensioners @ average of 32/– weekly	280,000
SUB-TOTAL	860,000

Neurasthenic Cases	
25,521 pensioners @ average of 14/– weekly	950,000
GRAND TOTAL	1,810,000

[TNA: PRO PIN 15/3144]

Cost of Great War Pensions in the Context of Government Expenditure (in £ millions). Allowing for administrative costs, psychiatric disabilities accounted for about 5% of the total expenditure on war pensions in 1937. Not a vast sum in the overall context, or in proportion to other disabilities, and it may be argued that the imbalance between psychosis and neurasthenia reflects less the excessive burden of war psychotics than the parsimonious expenditure on neurasthenic pensioners. The sharp rise in defence spending in 1937 was a signal that pressure on war pensions budgets was likely to become more acute.

	Total Government Spending	National Debt	Social Services*	Defence	War Pensions
1920	1592.1	324.8	411.8	519.7	104.7
1924	1027.0	305.4	365.0	130.9	70.3
1928	1094.7	305.1	434.3	125.1	57.5
1932	1138.0	281.2	511.1	110.4	47.5
1937	1303.5	209.4	554.7	254.7	40.5

* social services inc. social assistance and assurance, health, education, housing etc [A. T. Peacock and J. Wiseman, *The Growth of Public Expenditure in the United Kingdom*, pp. 164–5, 168–9, 184–5]

Notes

Abbreviations

BL	Bodleian Library, Oxford, Dept. of Western Manuscripts
DRO	Devon Record Office
ESWS	Ex-Services Welfare Society
GA	Ivor Gurney Archive, Gloucester Library
GRO	Gloucester Record Office
IWM	Imperial War Museum
LCC	London County Council
LMA	London Metropolitan Archives
LRO	Lancashire Record Office
Nelson	Benefits Agency Filestore, Department of Social Security, Nelson, Lancs
Parl.Deb.	Hansard Parliamentary Debates, House of Commons
RAMC:	Royal Army Medical Corps
RNSMB:	*Report Upon The Physical Examination of Men of Military Age by National Service Medical Boards from November 1st 1917–October 31st 1918*, Parliamentary Papers 1919, XXVI, Cmd. 504
SFRO	Suffolk Record Office
SRO	Surrey Record Office
TNA: PRO	The National Archives of the UK: Public Record Office
WL	Archives and Manuscripts, Wellcome Trust Library for the History and Understanding of Medicine
WRO	Wiltshire Record Office
WYAS	West Yorkshire Archive Service

Epigraphs

1. Quoted in Lyn Macdonald, *The Roses of No Man's Land*, pp. 215–16.
2. TNA: PRO PIN 15/864.
3. Gaius Julius Hyginus, *Fabulae*, XCV. I am grateful to my cousin, George Tsagrinos, for his help in identifying this source. Translation adapted from an excellent website on the Trojan War: www.calliope.free-online.co.uk
4. These lines, reproduced in four languages, are inscribed on Walter Benjamin's memorial at Port Bou where he is buried. Momme Brodersen, *Walter Benjamin*, p. 262.

Introduction

1. See Mark Micale and Paul Lerner eds., *Traumatic Pasts*. 'What would be so very wrong', asks a leader in a British national newspaper in May 2003, echoing almost verbatim the sentiments of ex-servicemen and their advocates during the First World War, 'with the Government allowing a little leeway towards those who have been prepared to fight for their country?' (*The Independent*, 6 May 2003).
2. Ronald Dworkin, *Sovereign Virtue*, p. 1.

3. See, inter alia, Arthur Marwick, *The Deluge*; idem, *War and Social Change in the Twentieth Century*.
4. Jose Harris, *Private Lives, Public Spirit: Britain 1870–1914*, pp. 251–52.
5. See Roger Cooter and Steve Sturdy, 'Of War, Medicine and Modernity', and Bernard Taithe, 'The Red Cross Flag in the Franco-Prussian War'.
6. Peter Baldwin, *The Politics of Social Solidarity*, p. 31. John Macnicol has drawn attention to the 'endowment of the marginalized' by socialists such as the Independent Labour Party in the 1890s, who commandeered the term 'endowment' in language that 'stressed rights, justice and the claims of citizenship' to 'imply that the working class should enjoy the same automatic "citizenship" right to support from the state in times of need that the wealthy enjoyed through family legacies' (*The Politics of Retirement in Britain 1878–1948*, pp. 138–39).
7. Mark Harrison, 'Medicine and the Management of Modern Warfare: an Introduction', p. 4.
8. Peter Brown, *Poverty and Leadership in the Later Roman Empire*, pp. 61–63; Brent D. Shaw, 'Loving the Poor', *New York Review of Books*, November 21, 2002, pp. 42–45.
9. As Niall Ferguson argues, the popular enthusiasm for the war has been exaggerated. Many men enlisted because of the rise in unemployment sparked by the economic crisis that the war had unleashed. Trades union membership doubled in Britain during the war and in 1918 the Labour Party increased its share of the vote from less than 8 per cent to nearly 24 per cent (*The Pity of War*, pp. 444, 273–74).
10. Quoted in J. M. Winter, *Socialism and the Challenge of War*, pp. 154–55.
11. See chapter 4.
12. TNA: PRO PIN 15/3144.
13. Arthur Kleinman, *Writing at the Margin*, p. 249.
14. In the historiography, the war psychotic has tended either to play a minor part or, in the account of one distinguished historian, misinterpreting a chart, to show up at the ball only very late. Eric Leed claims that 'more pensions for psychotic illnesses were granted by the British government in 1929 than had been granted in the four years immediately after the war' (*No Man's Land*, p. 189). However, the gradient to which he refers is for final, i.e. permanent, pensions for psychotic illnesses, not for temporary pensions, which had been granted in abundance in the postwar years. As we shall see, the Ministry of Pensions delayed making an award final in the hope that the pensioner would recover, and the pension could thus be curtailed or terminated, but by the late 1920s they could hold out no longer.
15. Martin Stone, 'Shellshock and the Psychologists'; Ben Shephard, *A War of Nerves*, p. 28.
16. See Mark Micale and Paul Lerner eds, *Traumatic Pasts*.
17. W. J. Scott *The Politics of Readjustment: Vietnam Veterans since the War*; Ben Shephard, *A War of Nerves*, pp. 355–68.
18. Allan Young, *The Harmony of Illusions*, p. 142.
19. A. G. Butler, 'Moral and Mental Disorders in the War of 1914–18', p. 99; Ben Shephard, 'Shell-Shock', p. 33.
20. 'The bad ones are sent to another place', remarked Siegfried Sassoon about his fellow patients, 'dotty officers' all of them, many of them 'degenerate looking', in the military hospital at Craiglockhart (*Diaries 1915–18*, p. 183).
21. Even if this work makes some claim to originality in charting an area of the mental health landscape of the Great War that has been obscured or neglected, I am hugely conscious of travelling in the wake of the labours of others but for whom I could not even have set out on this exploration. It was a revealing footnote in Martin Stone, 'Shellshock and the Psychologists', pp. 266–67, n. 16; some striking passages in Philip Bean, *Compulsory Admissions to Mental Hospitals*, pp. 40–41; and a suggestive paragraph in John Crammer, *Asylum History*, p. 77, that started the hare of this topic running in the first place. Allan Young's insightful inquiry, *The Harmony of Illusions*, into the historicity of post-traumatic stress

disorder (PTSD) as a product glued together under necessitous circumstances out of a congeries of cultural resources, has influenced my thinking about the invention of the war psychotic in the last years of the war. Mathew Thomson's spotlight on mental deficiency ('Status, Manpower and Mental Fitness: Mental Deficiency in the First World War') has already shown what can be achieved in breaking ranks from a narrow concentration on shell shock. His ironic appraisal of the hospitality shown towards mental defectives, the feebleminded, idiots and their cognates in Britain between the wars, *The Problem of Mental Deficiency*, has also been of inestimable value in reflecting on the fortunes of mental health survivors. Though it makes brief sorties into other parts of the map, for the most part this discussion is confined within its own bailiwick, and I make no pretensions to cover the ground of Ben Shephard's masterly treatise, *A War of Nerves*, on the whole subject of shell shock and its varieties, albeit more closely allied to military history and psychiatry than my own perspective. Similarly, though I have cavilled at a tendency to pillory the mental health profile of the ordinary ranker in the historiography, Peter Leese's work has already made amends for this to a considerable extent in delivering a sense of the military diagnostic and treatment culture as much more sprawling and diversified than could be trimmed into a neat synoptic model. His much-cited PhD thesis of 1989 has now been published as *Shell Shock: Traumatic Neurosis and the British Soldiers of the First World War*.

22. Samuel Hynes, *The Soldiers' Tale*, p. 32. For a splendid counterblast to such assumptions about the 'inarticulate masses' see Jonathan Rose, *The Intellectual Life of the British Working Classes*.

23. On primary sources for the First World War generally see Ian F. W. Beckett, *The First World War: The Essential Guide to Sources in the UK National Archives*. The sources I have drawn upon are all identified individually in the notes but, broadly, those I have found most rewarding for the mental health history of the Great War and its aftermath are: various series in the Public Record Office, esp. PIN 15 & PIN 67 (Ministry of Pensions files), PIN 26 (a 2% sample of individual war disability pension files), and MH 106 (records of war hospitals etc); Boards of Guardians records of Poor Law infirmaries etc; records of individual mental hospitals in various county record offices; and files of war pensioners who survived into the 1960s and beyond in the former Ministry of Pensions filestore, now the Benefits Agency Filestore, administered by the Dept of Social Security, in Nelson, Lancs. Now that all the claimants are dead, the future of the records I consulted at Nelson is uncertain. It now seems likely, however, that they will after all be preserved.

24. There is, after all, a certain parallel between the lunatic asylum and the state archive: both are repositories of 'discarded stuff'; both derive from the power of the state in assembling dispersed objects on a single site; and at the same time both question authority 'by holding warring discourses in a promiscuous and mutually contaminating contiguity' (Gonzalez Echevarria, quoted in Harriet Bradley, 'The Seduction of the Archive: Voices Lost and Found', p. 111).

25. Thomas Laqueur, 'Memory and Naming in the Great War', p. 152.

26. *Ulysses* was composed, in flight from the inroads of war, in Trieste, Zurich and Paris, between 1914 and 1921.

27. See Bernard Taithe, *Defeated Flesh: Medicine, Welfare and Warfare in the Making of Modern France*. The argument that wartime conditions provided a propitious soil for innovation in social policy was famously advanced by Richard Titmuss ('War and Social Policy' in his *Essays on 'The Welfare State'*).

28. John Macnicol has given a masterful account, complementary in certain respects to what I am assaying here, of the emergence of old age pensions in the early 20th century as 'the centrepiece of a redistributive socialism that had to be resisted by the state at all costs' (*The Politics of Retirement in Britain*, pp. 6–7).

29. Liz Sayce, *From Psychiatric Patient to Citizen*; Peter Barham and Marian Barnes, 'The Citizen Mental Patient'; and Peter Campbell, 'The service/user survivor movement'. The demands of disability rights movements that the experiences of the disabled, including their histories,

be treated as part of the mainstream of society has resulted in an upsurge of curiosity about the historical experience of people with disabilities both in the academy and among a wider public. There is now mushrooming interest in the history of disabled veterans from a variety of wars and conflicts, and of the mutations in the relationships forged by modern states with disabled ex-servicemen. See especially David Gerber ed., *Disabled Veterans in History*. See also the Disability History Museum, a vast digital collection of documents and images relating to disability history in the United States (www.disabilitymuseum.org).

30. Adrian Gregory, *The Silence of Memory* (Oxford, 1994) p. 23; see also, Alex King, *Memorials of the Great War in Britain* (Oxford, 1998) pp. 184–87.

Prologue: The Hosier and the Imbecile Go to War

1. Vera Brittain, *Chronicle of Youth: Great War Diary 1913–17*, pp. 85, 87.
2. Richard Cobb, *Reactions to the French Revolution*, pp. 130–31.
3. Long Grove Asylum was built between 1903–7 as the Tenth London County Council asylum on plans prepared by the noted asylum architect G. T. Hine (Jeremy Taylor, *Hospital and Asylum Architecture*, p. 152).
4. My account of George Major Gomm is largely drawn from his medical records at Napsbury War Hospital at TNA: PRO MH 106/2221 and his service records at PRO WO 264/1375. His Napsbury file also contains his medical records from his active service in France. James Shoolbred & Co, silk mercers and drapers, were already established at 151–58 Tottenham Court Rd, on the east side at the corner with Grafton Street, at the turn of the century, and the firm also had other shops in the same street (*Kelly's Post Office London Directory*, 1900 & 1915).
5. Count Metternich, the German ambassador, quoted in Niall Ferguson, *The Pity of War*, p. 102. On the pre-war army and its reputation see John Bourne, 'The British working man in arms'; D. Gill and G. Dallas, *The Unknown Army*; and Leslie Hall ' "War always brings it on" '.
6. On recruitment to the new armies see Ian Beckett, 'The Nation in Arms, 1914–18'; Clive Hughes, 'The New Armies'; and J. M. Winter *The Great War*, esp. chapter 2.
7. For shifts in the class fabric in Britain in this period see especially: Jose Harris, *Private Lives, Public Spirit*; David Cannadine, *Class in Britain*; and Ross McKibbin, *Classes and Cultures*. In the late nineteenth and early twentieth century, writes Cannadine, 'there was a noticeable proliferation of the "lower middle class": that army of clerks and office workers, who were neither factory labourers nor factory owners, but who merged into the working class beneath and the prosperous middle class above. . . . In terms of income, expenditure, occupation, and way of life this was a huge swathe of British society to encompass within the misleadingly homogenised "middle class" ' (*Class in Britain*, p. 117). See also Geoffrey Crossick, *The Lower Middle Class in Britain 1870–1914*. For a comparative observation on 'the remarkable diversity of the metropolitan "middle classes" ' in all the belligerent countries in the Great War see Jon Lawrence, 'Material Pressures on the Middle Classes', p. 229. Clerks had previously formed the backbone of a unit such as the City Imperial Volunteers in the South African War at the turn of the century (R. Price, *An Imperial War and the British Working Class*, p. 199).
8. *RNSMB:* pp. 9, 36 & 40.
9. Ibid., p. 23.
10. Ibid., p. 5.
11. Surgeon-General Bedford in *Minutes of Evidence Taken Before the Select Committee on the Military Service (Review of Exemptions) Act, 1917* (hereafter referred to as 'Shortt Committee'), Parliamentary Papers, 1917–18, III, 327, Appendix 1, q. 1125. On the systems of medical examination, and the politics that propelled them, see: J. M. Winter *The Great War*; idem, 'Military Fitness and Civilian Health'; and K. Grieves, *The Politics of Manpower*. See also W. G. Macpherson ed., *History Of The Great War Based On Official Documents* –

Medical Services, General History, vol. I, pp. 118–37 'The Medical Examination of Recruits'.

12. See D. Gill and G. Dallas, *The Unknown Army,* p. 28; Niall Ferguson, *The Pity of War,* p. 102; J. M. Winter, *The Great War,* p. 29; R. J. Q. Adams and Philip Poirier, *The Conscription Controversy,* pp. 28–30.

13. The Census for 1901 reveals that George and Julia Gomm were living at 94 North End Road, Fulham, with their two sons and a female servant, employed as a domestic nurse (PRO: RG 13/63). The details of Richard's fatal illness are given in the entry of death at the General Register Office.

14. LMA: ST.P. BG.146.007, Reception of Male Insane Patients into St Pancras Workhouse (1913–14); ST. P.BG.150.009, Daily Journal, Male Insane Wards, St Pancras Workhouse (1913–14); and LCC. PH. MENT.4.19, Register of Hanwell Asylum (1913–17).

15. LMA: LCC.MIN.1093, Minutes of Hanwell Asylum Sub-Committee (1913).

16. LMA: LCC.MIN.1094, ibid. (1914).

17. Shortt Committee, q. 1125; *RNSMB* p. 4. On the politics of 'fitness' see J. M. Winter, *The Great War,* chapter 2.

18. See Roy Porter, *The Greatest Benefit to Mankind,* pp. 674–75.

19. On norms of manliness in this period see: Joanna Bourke, *Dismembering the Male*; Adrian Caesar, *Taking it Like a Man: Suffering, Sexuality and the War Poets*; Bruce Haley, *The Healthy Body and Victorian Culture*; George Mosse, 'Shell-shock as social disease'; and Elaine Showalter, *The Female Malady.*

20. TNA: PRO WO 95/1372, War Diary of 1/22 Battalion, Royal Fusiliers.

21. IWM: Con Shelf, Lawrence Gameson, Papers, pp. 21–22.

22. TNA: PRO MH 106/2221.

23. Richard Slobodin, *Rivers,* pp. 19–25.

24. C. Myers, *Shell Shock in France,* pp. 82, 36; Ben Shephard, *A War of Nerves,* chapter 2.

25. Myers, ibid., p. 97.

26. TNA: PRO MH 106/2221.

27. C. Myers, *Shell Shock in France,* p. 82.

28. Ibid., pp. 88–89.

29. TNA: PRO MH 106/2221.

30. C. Stanford Read, *Military Psychiatry,* p. 45. Read was the commander of D Block during the Great War.

31. Already in his forties on the outbreak of the war, Capt. Frederick Talbot Clindening was well suited to the task of 'policing' inhospitable frontiers, having served as a medical officer with the British Consulate and Imperial Chinese Customs in Kiukiang.

32. Report, p. 28.

33. Under King's Regulations, a soldier deemed to be insane was discharged from the army and transferred directly to his district asylum. See C. Stanford Read, *Military Psychiatry,* p. 41, and *The King's Regulations and Orders for the Army,* paras 404–10 (London, 1912).

34. See Jose Harris, *Private Lives, Public Spirit,* pp. 243–45; Mathew Thomson, *The Problem of Mental Deficiency.*

35. Entry of birth, General Register Office. I first stumbled upon Albert Norris in a Pauper Examination Book for Lunatics from Wandsworth Union Infirmary where he had been taken following his discharge from the army. I have pieced together his narrative from the following sources: service records of his multifaceted military career at TNA: PRO WO 364/2716/2280–2310; records of his numerous encounters with the Poor Law authorities at LMA: Wa.BG.124.30, Wa.BG.124.34 (Lunatic Reception Orders) and Wa.BG.114.33, Wa.Ba.BG.114.36 (Pauper Lunatic Examination Books); LMA: Wa.BG.119.5, Wandsworth Union Register of Lunatics in Asylums 1911; LCC.PH. MENT.4. 24, Long Grove Asylum Register 1916–25; LCC.MIN.1180–1181, Minute Books for Long Grove; and records of the Mental After Care Association at WL. The yield of any one of these sources may be very limited but together they comprise the shards out of which an incomplete but still accessible narrative can be constructed.

36. Long Grove Asylum was erected on the 1040-acre Horton Manor Estate in Epsom, Surrey, which had been purchased by the London County Council in 1896, eventually providing the site for a number of asylums, including Horton, the Manor, and finally West Park, which came to be known as the 'Epsom cluster', together accommodating more than 7500 mental patients. Though by no means lavish in design, in keeping with their location the Epsom asylums were more suburban in character than the traditional Victorian pauper lunatic asylum, dispersed villa buildings forming part of the accommodation and adding a patina of civility to what was still a degrading institutional environment (Jeremy Taylor, *Hospital and Asylum Architecture*, pp. 152–53).

37. LMA: LCC. MIN.1179, Minutes of Long Grove Sub-Committee of LCC Asylums Committee, September 1915–August 1916.

38. Ibid. The Mental After Care Association was founded in 1879 as the *After Care Association for Poor and Friendless Female Convalescents on Leaving Asylums for the Insane*, widening its scope towards the turn of the century (R. Hunter and I. Macalpine *Psychiatry for the Poor*, p. 67).

39. WL: Records of the Mental After Care Association, SA/MAC, G2/3 Case Agenda Books July 1915–April 1919.

40. J. C. Woolan, 'Hotel London', in George Sims ed. *Living London*, Vol II (London, 1902), pp. 237–38. By the end of the war the lights had been extinguished at De Keyser's royal establishment.

41. Niall Ferguson, *The Pity of War* pp. 102–4; see also R. J. Q. Adams and Philip Poirier, *The Conscription Controversy*.

42. Obituary, *British Medical Journal* (1941) 1, 948.

43. WL: Records of the Mental After Care Association, SA/MAC, B1/29, Annual Report (1916).

PART I THE WAR MENTAL HOSPITAL
   1. IWM: 96/19/1, Capt. H. J. C. Leland, letters.

Chapter 1: The New Lunacy Protest
   1. Nigel Nicolson ed. *The Letters Of Virginia Woolf*, pp. 95, 102.
   2. Hermione Lee, *Virginia Woolf*, pp. 187–88.
   3. Hermione Lee is more even-handed in her treatment of Maurice Craig, but he has received a drubbing at the hands of some literary critics, castigated by Stephen Trombley for his 'reductive view of humanity' and for 'enforcing conformity' in his dealings with Virginia Woolf in which 'doctor and patient were hopelessly at odds' ('*All that Summer She was Mad*': *Virginia Woolf and her Doctors*, pp. 183–208); and by Adrian Caesar for his reponsibility for the pre-war 'stuffing' of Rupert Brooke and the pursuit of 'extremely conservative "moral" and political interventions' in the name of medicine (*Taking it Like a Man*, p. 229). Indubitably Craig was a man of his period, and seen through today's spectacles his sensibility is inevitably flawed, but I shall argue that he was a more interesting and rounded figure, his 'moral' and political interventions more varied and nuanced, than these critics have allowed.
   4. In this section I have drawn largely on David Cannadine, *Class in Britain*; Jose Harris, *Private Lives, Public Spirit*; Patrick Joyce, *Visions of the People*; L. H. Lees, *The Solidarities of Strangers*; and R. McKibbin, *The Ideologies of Class*. See also Eric Hobsbawm, *The Age of Empire*, pp. 53–54; R. Price, *An Imperial War and the British Working Class*, pp. 7–8, 206–207; F. M. L. Thompson, *The Rise of Respectable Society*; and on the 'middle', Geoffrey Crossick, 'Metaphors of the middle'.
   5. Quoted in David Cannadine, *Class in Britain*, p. 121.
   6. Ibid.
   7. Ibid., p. 118.
   8. L. H. Lees, *The Solidarities of Strangers*, pp. 240–42, 295–96.
   9. T. H. Marshall, *Citizenship and Social Class*, p. 24.
   10. Ibid.; L. H. Lees, *The Solidarities of Strangers*, p. 299.

11. Quoted in L. H. Lees, *The Solidarities of Strangers*, p. 326. On the reforms of 1906–14 see also David Powell, *The Edwardian Crisis*, pp. 20–38.

12. Quoted in David Cannadine, *Class in Britain*, p. 107.

13. Mark Harrison has examined the penetration of the new culture of citizenship, and emerging notions of 'entitlement', into military medicine and the consciousness of soldiers and their families. By the end of the nineteenth century, he writes, 'servicemen were beginning to demand health care as a right, and to regard it as a kind of "social wage" earned in the service of their country. They appealed not only to the paternalistic and humanitarian inclinations of certain sections of the community but also to modern concepts of citizenship and justice' ('Medicine and the Management of Modern Warfare: an Introduction', pp. 3–4).

14. J. M. Winter, *The Great War*, pp. 30–31.

15. Niall Ferguson, *The Pity of War*, pp. 20–23, 28; Jose Harris *Private Lives, Public Spirit*, p. 6.

16. Ferguson, ibid., pp. 102–4.

17. George Orwell, 'England Your England', p. 68.

18. John Bourne, 'The British working man in arms', p. 340. J. G. Fuller argues in a similar vein that the wartime volunteer and the conscript alike 'enlisted with no very high conception of the military life'. They remained 'individualists', 'civilians in uniform', for whom 'military life was simply an evil to be borne, and with the coming of the Armistice British troops could not be rid of it fast enough' (*Troop Morale and Popular Culture*, p. 33).

19. *Report of the War Office Commission of Enquiry into 'Shell-Shock'* (London, 1922), p. 6.

20. John Pickstone, 'Production, Community and Consumption'.

21. Jose Harris, *Private Lives, Public Spirit*, p. 60.

22. TNA: PRO MH 58/90, George Newman, 'Memorandum on Lunacy Reform' (1922). George Newman was at this time Chief Medical Officer to the newly created Ministry of Health. For a convincing demonstration that the system of public mental health care was inextricably enmeshed in the institutional and moral landscape of the Poor Law, see Peter Bartlett, 'The Asylum and the Poor Law: The Productive Alliance'; and idem, *The Poor Law of Lunacy*.

23. Maurice Craig, *Psychological Medicine* (1912 edition), pp. 462–63.

24. The following notices are taken from the *Medical Directory* (London, 1917).

25. Commissioners in Lunacy, *9th Annual Report*, 1855, p. 35, quoted in Andrew Scull, *The Most Solitary of Afflictions*, p. 354.

26. Leonard Smith, 'The County Asylum in the Mixed Economy of Care'.

27. William Parry-Jones, *The Trade in Lunacy*, pp. 22–23; John Crammer, *Asylum History*, p. 180.

28. Joseph Melling, 'Accommodating Madness', p. 13.

29. T. Knowles Stansfield, 'The Villa or Colony System for the Care and Treatment of Mental Diseases', *Journal of Mental Science* (1914), 60, pp. 30–37.

30. Diana Gittins describes the privileges enjoyed by middle and lower-middle class private patients at Severalls Mental Hospital between 1913 and 1918 (*Madness in its Place*, p. 20).

31. J. Bucknill, *The Care of the Insane and their Legal Control*, (London, 1880), pp. 3–4, quoted in Andrew Scull, *The Most Solitary of Afflictions*, p. 373.

32. 'The condition of insanity was legally defined in ways which constrained the pauper lunatic as the inverse of the positive citizen. This implied complete exclusion from rational choice and participation in civil society' (Joseph Melling, 'Accommodating Madness', p. 15). To grasp just how complete it was, take a typical entry for the County Lunatic Asylum at Whittingham, Lancs, in the census of 1901. 'Name: PB. Relation to Head of Family/Position in the Institution: Lunatic. Employment Status: Inmate. Infirmity: Insanity' (TNA: PRO RG 13/3961). The period leading up to the Great War saw the gradual transformation of the lunatic asylum inmate into a mental patient under the care of a physician. As Melling remarks, however, this was scarcely a benign step towards modernity, since the fledgling mental patient was hamstrung by social and political ideologies of social efficiency, class degeneration and racial purity. On moral condemnation, see also Philip Bean, *Compulsory*

Admissions, p. 40, and on the political context of the Lunacy Act 1890 see Clive Unsworth, *The Politics of Mental Health Legislation*, pp. 80–111.

33. TNA: PRO FO 383/11/1204.

34. Peter McCandless, 'Liberty and Lunacy: The Victorians and Wrongful Confinement', pp. 339–43.

35. As Mark Harrison has argued, the Boer War had already signalled a sea change in the relationship between the state and public opinion. Turn-of-the-century revelations about the appalling conditions in field hospitals in South Africa during the Boer War had threatened to undermine public morale, and the provision of adequate medical arrangements was now integral to the maintenance of public support for military adventures ('Militarism and Medical Reform 1901–14', unpublished paper). Public opinion was to prove 'at least as significant in the development of military medicine as the drive for administrative rationality' (idem, 'Medicine and the Management of Modern Warfare', p. 4).

36. Roy Porter, *Mind Forg'd Manacles*, p. 270.

37. Thomas W. Salmon, 'The Care and Treatment of Mental Diseases'. In 1904 Dr Paul Jacoby, physician-in-charge of the Provincial Asylum of Orel in Russia, drew upon the reports of Russian medical officers of large numbers of acute psychoses during the wars with Turkey in 1877–78, and against China in 1900, to warn of the conditions predisposing to madness in modern warfare. He advised the 'immediate treatment of insane soldiers in separate tents under special care' who would then have a 'good chance of recovery' ('Madness in Armies in the Field', *British Medical Journal* [1904], 2, pp. 30–31, quoted in Edgar Jones and Simon Wessely, 'The Origins of Military Psychiatry Before the First World War', p. 105). Needless to say, the British authorities paid no heed to this wise counsel. The army authorities had for long been leery of becoming implicated in the care of mad soldiers, especially if they were at all likely to become chronic cases. 'It is not conducive to the interests of the Public Service', the War Office advised Lord Shaftesbury in 1857, 'to have a special Asylum for the permanent care and maintenance of Military Lunatics'. After the Military Lunatic Asylum at Fort Clarence, Chatham, was abandoned in 1844 it was disclosed that some of the officer inmates had been there as long as 20 years. More fitting was the introduction, as in Austrian Military Hospitals, of 'a Mad Ward where soldiers when mad are kept, *until* declared incurable, when they are discharged and placed in ordinary civil lunatic asylums' (TNA: PRO WO 43/764).

38. *The King's Regulations and Orders for the Army*, paras 404–10 (London, 1912).

39. Of the 552 servicemen admitted to D Block between August and December 1914, as many as 383 were home force cases (C. Stanford Read, *Military Psychiatry*, chart following p. 50). Read does not disclose exactly how many of these admissions were dispatched direct to asylums, but concedes that in the early months of the war the military medical authorities maintained their normal practice (p. 41).

40. Lynn H. Lees, *The Solidarities of Strangers*, p. 308. In the pre-war decades observers such as Tredgold had conjured up the spectre of a proliferating population of social misfits such as 'the epileptic, the insane and mentally unstable, the criminal, the chronic pauper and unemployable classes' and the imagery of a degenerate underclass was widely shared (J. M. Winter, 'Arms and Society', p. 199). By no means were they eradicated, but during the war such pejorative images were nudged into the sidelines by more inclusive appeals and judgments. Acknowledging the widespread support from all over the country for the proposal for a minimum pension for disabled servicemen, the Labour MP George Barnes wryly observed that 'it is a somewhat arresting reflection that this improvement in public opinion has come about only when we have ceased to draw our soldiers from the poorest and least articulate section of the community and begun to draw them from the homes of the better to do' (*Parl.Deb.*, 18 November 1914, vol. LXVIII, col. 459).

41. *Parl.Deb.*, 19 May 1915, vol. LXXI, col. 2330.

42. *Parl.Deb.*, 6 Feb 1915, vol. LXX, col. 515.

43. *Parl.Deb.*, 10 June 1915, vol. LXXII, col. 369.

44. *Parl.Deb.*, 6 Feb 1915, vol. LXX, col. 515.

45. *Parl.Deb.*, 14 March 1916, vol. LXXX, col. 1916. The Workmen's Compensation Act (1897) was a standard reference point for class politics and the achievements of organised labour. See P. W. J. Bartrip, *Workmen's Compensation in Twentieth Century Britain.*

46. Lord Knutsford recounts in his memoirs that as early as August 1914 the president of the Psycho-Medical Society had written to the War Office proposing an organization of hospitals for treatment of cases of nerve exhaustion and traumatic neurasthenia (*In Black and White*, pp. 268–71). By 1917 there were five Knutsford Hospitals. The wider social and medical context of the innovative 'special hospitals' (for orthopaedic cases, head and facial injuries, cardiac disorders, tuberculosis etc) that were hastened into existence during the Great War is examined in Roger Cooter, *Surgery and Society in Peace and War.*

47. *The Morning Post*, 9 January 1915.

48. *Report of the Committee Appointed by the President of the Local Government Board upon the Provision of Employment for Sailors and Soldiers Disabled in the War* [Cd 7915] (London, 1915).

49. W. A. Turner, 'Arrangements for the care of cases of nervous and mental shock'.

50. Ibid. Ironically, Moss Side had been designed as a dedicated institution for a 'special needs' group of a rather different kind. To meet the requirements of the Mental Deficiency Act (1913) it had been intended to accommodate 'moral imbeciles', though it was never used as such. Not a few of these putative 'imbeciles', far from being segregated in institutions, were now enlisted as citizen soldiers.

51. *History of the Asylum War Hospitals in England and Wales*, [Cmd.899] (London, 1920).

52. C. Stanford Read, *Military Psychiatry*, p. 42. For a list of military mental hospitals (and of military medical facilities generally) see also an excellent website, www.1914-1918.net

53. *Parl.Deb.*, 19 May 1915, vol. LXXI, col. 2330.

54. C. Stanford Read, *Military Psychiatry*, p. 41, emphasis added.

Chapter 2: 'D Ward (imbecile)'

1. Philip Hoare, *Spike Island*, p. 218.

2. When the commissioners of the Board of Control visited in April 1914 they found 33 patients in residence. Since the previous June, 110 soldiers had been admitted and 94 discharged (*First Annual Report of The Board of Control For The Year 1914*, London 1916).

3. In *Spike Island* Philip Hoare has written a fine history of the Royal Victoria Military Hospital, but he conflates D Block with the Neurological Section and fails to cite the memoir by Major C. Stanford Read, the wartime commander of D Block, *Military Psychiatry*, which gives a clear exposition of the role and operation of the unit. Moreover, Hoare puzzles conspiratorially (p. 283) over the 'lost' Netley records. But they are not lost at all. D Block was merely a clearing station, so the records travelled with the soldier patients, along with the bundle of records that had accompanied them from field hospitals overseas, to their next posting in the war hospital system. Many of them are to be found in the Public Record Office among the records of Napsbury and other war hospitals, and I have come across examples of them in archives right across England.

4. Philip Hoare, *Spike Island*, p. 254. In the Great War the common practice was to segregate mentally disturbed officers and other ranks in separate institutions, but in point of fact the military authorities had long been adept at managing the relations between the ranks and classes within a single institution. In the mid-nineteenth century the Royal Military Lunatic Asylum at Great Yarmouth (subsequently taken over by the Admiralty) accommodated privates in dormitories and officers in single rooms, and the asylum had been designed 'to form a complete separation between the Officers and the Soldiers and prevent the possibility of their seeing or mixing with each other'. It turns out, however, that the separation of the ranks was only intended to last as long as the officer was in an acute state, lest in his madness he became forgetful of his rank and station. Once convalescent, normal hierarchical relations could be resumed, and indeed it was proposed by the Lunacy Commissioners that some of the soldier inmates might be 'beneficially occupied in attending on, or assisting as servants

to, the officers' (TNA: PRO MH 51/42). On the Royal Military Lunatic Asylum see also William Parry-Jones, *The Trade in Lunacy*, p. 68.

5. This and the following examples in this chapter are drawn from TNA: PRO war hospitals records series MH 106/2102 and MH 106/2212–2238 (classified alphabetically).

6. Liddle Collection, Leeds University Archive, 'Footnote to Medical History', typescript by Dr Harold William Hills, n.d. (General Aspects/Shell Shock/Item 13). By Stanford Read's own admission, mechanical restraint was 'freely used' at D Block to control violent patients, 'a canvas suit with blind sleeves which could be tied together if necessary' (*Military Psychiatry*, p. 167).

7. These lessons are detailed in J. M. Winter, 'Arms and Society: The Demographic Context'. 'It is . . . not an exaggeration', writes Winter, 'to suggest that in large parts of working-class Britain, though not among the middle class, there were before 1914 conditions of poverty and ill health which today we associate with countries of the Third World' (p. 195). Roger Cooter ('Malingering in Modernity') pertinently emphasizes the psychologization of malingering in the First World War. The escape route from 'discipline' to 'medicine' was scarcely a benign one, since the suspicions around malingering quickly returned in the shape of the attitude the patient held (or failed to) towards his condition. Even where 'badness' was transformed into 'sickness', 'sickness' still had to reckon with its 'bad' double. The alternative to malingering was not infrequently a category invested with significant moral opprobrium (with perhaps the implication that the putative patient was so useless that he lacked even the talent to malinger).

8. S. Freud, 'Memorandum on the Electrical Treatment of War Neurotics'.

Chapter 3: The Napsbury Cast

1. LMA: H50. A. 01. 23, County of Middlesex Asylums Committee, Minutes of Napsbury Asylum Standing Sub-Committee of Visitors.

2. Ibid.

3. LMA: H50. A. 01. 24.

4. On the history of war hospitals see W. G. Macpherson ed., *History Of The Great War Based On Official Documents – Medical Services, General History*, vol. I, pp. 78–88. The unexpected emotion provoked by the evacuation of asylums was widely acknowledged by contemporaries. 'The sorrow exhibited by many of the patients on being obliged to leave institutions which in some instances had been their homes for years, and the regret shown by members of the staffs in parting with them, were pathetic' (*History of the Asylum War Hospitals in England and Wales*, [Cmd.899] London, 1920, p. 7). For a contemporary account by an asylum superintendent involved in an evacuation see D. G. Thomson, 'A Descriptive Record of the Conversion of a County Asylum into a War Hospital'. Napsbury was just a small nugget in a vast expansion of army medical provision. At the commencement of the war the regular RAMC had 1026 officers, 3168 NCOs and men, and 7000 beds in military hospitals in the UK. By the Armistice it had more than 13,000 officers, 130,000 NCOs and men, 360,000 hospital beds in the UK and 637,746 beds in various theatres of war (TNA: PRO WO 222/223).

5. DRO: HZ.2.5. 6, Papers, Private & Service Patients (1917–19).

6. *History of the Asylum War Hospitals in England and Wales*, [Cmd.899] (London, 1920), p. 31.

7. LMA: H50.A. 01.25.

8. LMA: H50.A. 01.24.

9. TNA: PRO MH 106/1532 Admission & Discharge Book, County of Middlesex War Hospital, Napsbury. All the Napsbury case histories that follow in this and the next chapter are drawn from the TNA: PRO series MH 106/2212–2238 (classified alphabetically).

10. For a dispassionate account of military executions in the Great War see Cathryn Corns and John Hughes-Wilson, *Blindfold and Alone*.

11. Slavoj Žižek, *The Sublime Object of Ideology*, p. 113.

12. Ibid.

13. Some of these recruits had perhaps failed to internalize the lesson extolled by Stanford Read on adaptation to military discipline: 'The curtailment of liberty both in thought and action is for a time hard to bear. This individualism in the normal newly joined recruit soon gives way as he becomes more and more a machine, and the goal idea [sic] of all to work hard, obey, and become efficient soldiers at an early date fills the mind' (*Military Psychiatry*, p. 5). On 'mental defectives' and the army see Mathew Thomson, 'Status, Manpower and Mental Fitness: Mental Deficiency in the First World War'.

14. James Joyce, *Ulysses*, p. 5.

15. On the history of syphilis and GPI see Claude Quétel, *History of Syphilis*. On the shifting moral climate around venereal disease in the British Army during the Great War see Mark Harrison, 'The British Army and the Problem of Venereal Disease'.

16. The Wassermann Test was a diagnostic test for syphilis named after August Van Wassermann, a German bacteriologist.

17. Jonathan Shay, *Achilles in Vietnam*, p. 36.

18. David Cannadine, 'War and Death, Grief and Mourning', p. 195.

19. Ibid., p. 208.

20. Donn Welton, 'Biblical Bodies'.

21. Servicemen at the front on both sides were subjected to a barrage of propaganda about sexual morality and behaviour and the dire consequences that would befall them if they did not exercise the virtues of self-control. See Lutz D. H. Sauerteig, 'Sex, Medicine and Morality during the First World War'.

22. Julia Kristeva, *Black Sun*, p. 189.

23. Ibid., p. 223.

24. Ibid., p. 34.

25. Jonathan Shay, *Achilles in Vietnam*, pp. 36–37.

26. IWM: Con Shelf, Hiram Sturdy, 'Illustrated Account of his Service on the Western Front with the Royal Regiment of Artillery', p. 132.

27. Rudyard Kipling tells the story of an ex-serviceman who went mad after the war because he had witnessed a few years earlier a ghostly encounter in the trenches. Jay Winter perceptively proposes that Kipling was drawing on wartime legends involving communications with the dead (*Sites of Memory, Sites of Mourning*, p. 73).

28. Paul Fussell proposes that 'prolonged threats to the integrity of the body heighten physical self-consciousness and self-love' (*The Great War and Modern Memory*, p. 271). Wanking warriors there may have been in abundance, but they already had their counterparts in civilian life in the alleged masturbatory profligacy of lunatic asylums. Admonitions from the military authorities about 'enslaving habits' were to a large extent a reflection of a more general period preoccupation (Lutz D. H. Sauerteig, 'Sex, Medicine and Morality during the First World War', p. 172). On the eve of the Great War the scourge of masturbation had already driven some psychiatric crusaders to plot drastic remedies, the medical superintendent of Banstead Asylum in London proposing to sterilise inveterate masturbators by tying the excretory ducts of the testicles, thus making the glands useless, an experiment that had been tried with some success in Switzerland. Though the plan was quickly scotched by the Lunacy Commissioners, several of the London County Council medical superintendents were enthusiastic, extolling it as a 'heroic' measure which might 'tend to diminish the habit of masturbation which is fearfully prevalent amongst patients in asylums' [LMA: H11. HLL. A14. 3.11, Hanwell Asylum Letter Book 1907–12, Letter from LCC Asylums Officer, 11 February 1910, 'The Sterilisation Of Insane Masturbators'; LMA: LCC. MIN. 576, Asylums Committee Minutes, March 1909–July 1910, interleaved report 12 April 1910].

'O Lord, that little limping devil', Leopold Bloom reproached himself, 'with careful hand' recomposing 'his wet shirt'. 'Begins to feel cold and clammy. Aftereffect not pleasant. Still you have to get rid of it someway' (James Joyce, *Ulysses*, p. 482). So you may, but it was rather easier to indulge your peccadillo undisturbed if you were from the officer class. There is an obvious class basis to the asylum polemics on masturbation, carried over into the military treatment environments to some degree, a function of the almost entire lack of privacy available to mental patients in public asylums, and to ordinary soldiers in military hospitals, with the result that every twitch of the body was visible to the supervisory stare. In the privacy of their single rooms, mental patients in private asylums, and officers in dedicated institutions such as the Lord Knutsford Hospitals, knew no such scruples. A habitual masturbator from the officer class might be treated by a form of psychoanalysis. William G was admitted to Barnwood House, a private mental hospital near Gloucester, in 1920 exhibiting 'utter lack of control of himself, even admitting this himself as regards self-abuse'. On 18 May: 'psycho-analysis was tried on this patient today by the word associa-tion method'. To the word 'hand', 'stimulus no 87 in the series', the 'patient made no reply and showed a good deal of emotional disturbance'. On being pressed 'he said the word always made him think of his degraded habits'. The following day, however, the hospital resorted to a more traditional remedy for idle hands for the patient was now much 'more cheerful' having 'played a good game of cricket' [GRO: Records of Barnwood House Hospital (D3725), Box 133, Vol. K, Male Casebook]. The literature on masturbation and its ills is surveyed by Leslie Hall, 'Forbidden by God, Despised by Men'. See most recently, Thomas Laqueur, *Solitary Sex: A Cultural History of Masturbation*; and Jean Stengers and Anne Van Neck, *Masturbation: The History of a Great Terror*. The belief that the masturbatory vice was a causal agent in insanity is examined in Edward Hare 'Masturbatory insanity: the history of an idea'.

29. TNA: PRO WO 71/ 416.
30. TNA: PRO WO 71/ 492.
31. TNA: PRO WO 71/ 486.
32. TNA: PRO WO 71/ 487.

Chapter 4: 'Greetings From Napsbury'

1. Arthur Kleinman, *Writing at the Margin*, p. 249, discussing Allan Young's *The Harmony of Illusions*.
2. Eric Leed, *No Man's Land*, pp. 163–64; see also Elaine Showalter, *The Female Malady*, p. 174.
3. W. H. R. Rivers, *Instinct and the Unconscious*, pp. 123, 208, 213. See also Allan Young, *The Harmony of Illusions*, pp. 63–67. 'I don't know that there is "a kind of person who breaks down"', Pat Barker makes Dr Rivers say in the first volume of her justly acclaimed trilogy on the psychological and cultural upheaval of the Great War (*Regeneration*, pp. 105–6). But the historical Rivers's convictions ran the other way and Pat Barker has infused the fictional Rivers in the moral imagination of her own gender and generation.
4. From the preface by W. H. R. Rivers to John MacCurdy, *War Neuroses*, pp. vii–viii. MacCurdy pulls no punches in setting up his moral stall: 'When once the patient sees that his disinclination to return to the front is essentially a selfish desire to avoid his responsibil-ity as a citizen, he is in a position to decide quite consciously whether he wishes to be a slacker or to assume his share of the country's burden. If he has the right stuff in him, he becomes ashamed of his symptoms and begins to control them quite speedily' (p. 85).
5. W. H. R. Rivers, *Instinct and the Unconscious*, pp. 128–29.
6. Allan Young, *The Harmony of Illusions*, p. 66. See also idem, 'W. H. R. Rivers and the War Neuroses'.
7. F. W. Mott, *War Neuroses and Shell-Shock*, pp. 107–8; Woods Hutchinson, *The Doctor in War*, p. 117.
8. Janet Oppenheim, 'Shattered Nerves', p. 106.
9. John MacCurdy, *War Neuroses*, p. 28.
10. Here, for example, is Kurt Singer, director of a neuropsychiatric clinic in Berlin, and a wartime psychiatrist with broader sympathies than most, reflecting on how his wards came to be emptied in November 1918: 'Above all, the Revolution brought the class which com-prised the main contingent of neurotics, that is, the working proletariat, with one stroke into

a position in which neurotic complexes, as the expression of protest of inferiors, the oppressed, and the subordinate were ruled out. . . . The feelings of insecurity and inferiority at the basis of neuroses were removed through the fiction of a higher self-esteem among soldiers. The psyche no longer needed to escape its plight through illness, once it was proclaimed that even the least significant soldier and worker carried the baton in his knapsack, so to speak' ('Das Kriegsende und die Neurosenfrage', *Neurologisches Zentralblatt* [1919] 38, p. 331, quoted in Paul Lerner *Hysterical Men*, p. 212).

11. Arthur Kleinman, *Writing at the Margin*, p. 249. Siegried Sassoon makes an astute observation on the privileged treatment accorded officers who manifested signs of stress after a long tour in the trenches: 'If an officer crumpled up, Kinjack [the commanding officer] sent him home as useless, with a confidential report. Several such officers were usually drifting about at the Depot, and most of them ended up with safe jobs in England. But if a man became a dud in the ranks, he just remained where he was until he was killed or wounded. Delicate discrimination about private soldiers wasn't possible' ('Memoirs of an Infantry Officer', p. 310).

12. Siegried Sassoon, 'Memoirs of an Infantry Officer', p. 312. There is a trench map of Fricourt showing the Old Kent Road, Maple Redoubt and the like among Sassoon's papers in the British Library at BL Add. MS 62550C, f.43. No less defiant was James Joyce's creative achievement in writing *Ulysses* between 1914 and 1921, a war novel *par excellence* that is permeated by the war without once mentioning it. As Tom Stoppard playfully jests in *Travesties* about Joyce's 'war service':

'What did you do in the Great War, Mr Joyce?'
'I wrote *Ulysses*. What did you do?'

(quoted in introduction by Declan Kiberd to the Penguin edition of *Ulysses*, p. ix). Joyce's sensibility was considered 'deficient', insane even, by some of his contemporaries (Edna O'Brien, *James Joyce*, p. 125).

13. Harold Bloom, *Shakespeare*, p. 734.

14. Shakespeare, *Henry IV, Part Two*, III, ii. See Harold Bloom, *Shakespeare*, pp. 306–14.

15. W. A. Turner reports that 10 to 15 per cent of cases at Napsbury War Hospital were discharged to light duty; for Maghull Military Hospital, where 'a form of psychoanalysis' was being 'used with benefit in selected cases', the corresponding figure was 40 per cent ('Arrangements for the Care of Cases of Nervous and Mental Shock', p. 1074). However, Turner was writing in the spring of 1916; later in the war, when the more 'treatable' cases were increasingly dealt with at centres in the field, the return to duty rate at Napsbury was appreciably less than this. From a strictly military standpoint such a lower recovery rate was, of course, abysmal. By contrast, at Shepherd's Bush Military Hospital, Britain's premier orthopaedic hospital, as many as 1000 of the first 1300 men who underwent rehabilitation at the hospital were returned to military action (Jeffrey Reznick, 'Work-Therapy and the Disabled British Soldier in Great Britain in the First World War', p. 200; Roger Cooter, *Surgery and Society*, p. 118).

16. Ian Hacking is very good on these interactive cycles of reaction and counter-reaction, see esp. 'Madness: Biological or Constructed', in *The Social Construction of What?*, pp. 100–24.

17. Neurasthenia has tended to be regarded as a preserve of the educated and superior. See Roy Porter, *Madness: A Brief History*, pp. 152, 201. At Napsbury and other centres during the First World War, on what was perhaps its last collective outing before it joined other diagnostic categories in the lumber room of psychiatric history, it was modestly democratized. For a wide-ranging discussion see Marijke Gijswijt-Hofstra and Roy Porter eds, *Cultures of Neurasthenia*.

18. The circumstances of the Great War appear to have elicited from Dr Hubert Norman, born in 1881, a breadth of human sympathy from which he subsequently retreated. He later became medical superintendent of Camberwell House, a private mental hospital in south London, publishing a rather undistinguished textbook on mental disorders in the late 1920s,

and various antiquarian articles on psychiatric history. His wartime case histories exhibit more sensitivity and spark than anything he wrote subsequently. (Obituary, *British Medical Journal* [1948], pp. 710–71).

Overall, however, the exclusively male medical and nursing staff at Napsbury were cold fish, leaving no trace of their feelings about their charges, and there are no diaries or recollections of the nursing of these soldier mental patients to rival, say, Vera Brittain's entries about Sapper Smith in her war diary (*Chronicle of Youth*, pp. 239, 241, 252). All the same, within the War Mental Hospital universe in Britain there was at least one institution with a predominantly female nursing culture. At the Welsh Metropolitan War Hospital (formerly the Cardiff City Asylum), with provision for 416 mental cases and around 500 orthopaedic beds, a reluctant War Office was persuaded by a tenacious and progressive medical superintendent (now the commanding officer), Dr Edwin Goodall, to permit him to utilize his trained female nurses in the care of psychiatric casualties and to place the nursing staff for the entire war hospital in the charge of a matron (herself a certificated mental nurse). Throughout the war, female nurses served in all the psychiatric wards, with extra pay for those on the more secure wards. There were a few resignations who gave as their reasons for leaving 'did not like the shell shocks', 'could not stand the strain of the shell shock cases' etc, but overall such was the success of these innovations that they were maintained and extended after the war. (Personal communication from Sarah Brady on her Ph.D thesis in progress, 'Nursing in Cardiff during the First World War: A study of the interaction of women, war and medicine in a provincial city', University of Wales, Lampeter).

19. Dr Hawley Harvey Crippen was an American doctor, resident in London, who had murdered his wife, dissecting the body and disposing of her remains, after falling in love with his secretary Ethel de Neve. The fugitive pair were eventually caught and Crippen was executed at Pentonville Prison in 1910.

20. On the history and reputation of Maghull see Ben Shephard ' "The Early Treatment of Mental Disorders": R. G. Rows and Maghull 1914–1918'.

21. A serviceman recalled the disastrous battle at Loos: 'Shellshock was not recognised at that time yet the effects on the onlooker were terrible. . . . We were told that iron discipline would control a man's nerves under any circumstances. I do not know whether this is true, but when I got blown up in the air in this sector, had it not been for some gunner who dragged me into shelter on the canal bank, I would have gone berserk'. (IWM: 87/8/1, R. M. Luther, 'The Poppies are Blood Red', p. 12b).

22. Letter 348, 4 September 1918, to J. W. Haines in R. K. R. Thornton ed., *Ivor Gurney: Collected Letters*, p. 449.

23. There were 72 deaths. *History of the Asylum War Hospitals in England and Wales*, [Cmd.899] London, 1920, p. 45.

24. These advantages were obvious to contemporaries. Reporting on the treatment of shell shock cases in hospitals in the Western Command from 1914–18, Lt Col. E. W. White described: 'The patient has not been under the stigma of certification. No hospital has been devoted solely to mental cases. The benefit to the patient was obvious. He enjoyed to a very large extent the same freedom as the purely medical and surgical patients and a good proportion went out on parole daily. This parole was seldom abused. . . . The patients of the two divisions met at the associated entertainments and the service camaraderie was maintained' (*Daily News*, 12 February 1920, 'Treatment of Shell-Shocked. War Office Methods Explained'). While Ivor Gurney was an inmate 'an officer-friend turned up here and took me to London where we had a little music and chocolate together and lemonade at St Albans' (letter 346, 27 August 1918, in R. K. R. Thornton ed., *Ivor Gurney: Collected Letters*, p. 445). Even so, Gurney had to negotiate tactfully over his pass arrangements.

Coda: Albert Goes To War Again

1. James Joyce, *Ulysses*, p. 223.
2. The sources for this chapter are as in the Prologue, n. 35.

3. A lunatic might be discharged from an asylum either 'recovered' or 'relieved'. 'Relieved' meant not significantly improved but with the implication that the acute symptoms had at least abated. Under the 1890 Lunacy Act it was in the gift of the asylum authorities to determine whether a pauper lunatic whose condition was merely 'relieved' merited discharge, and the relatives had no authority in the matter. However, during the war, asylum committees were mostly highly responsive to the entreaties of relatives, such as George Gomm senior, to care for their soldier kin at home.

PART II JUSTICE FOR THE WAR PSYCHOTIC
1. James Joyce, *Ulysses*, p. 432.

Chapter 5: 'Insane Through Fighting For Their Country'
1. James Joyce, *Ulysses*, p. 556.
2. BL: Sir Matthew Nathan Papers, MS Nathan 485, 5 April 1917.
3. W. A. Turner, 'Arrangements for the care of cases of nervous and mental shock', p. 1074.
4. *Parl. Deb.*, 20 July 1916, vol. LXXXIV, col. 1213.
5. *Parl. Deb.*, 21 August 1916, vol. LXXXV, col. 2279.
6. *Parl. Deb.*, 10 June 1915, vol. LXXII. col. 368; 14 June 1915, vol. LXXII. col. 493.
7. Thomas Salmon, 'The Care and Treatment of Mental Diseases and War Neurosis ("Shell Shock") in the British Army'.
8. TNA: PRO PIN 15/869.
9. *Parl.Deb.*, 21 August 1916, vol. LXXXV, col. 2279; 8 August 1916, vol. LXXXV, col. 1005.
10. James Joyce, *Ulysses*, p. 280.
11. Quoted in Helen Bolderson, *Social Security, Disability and Rehabilitation*, p. 14.
12. Geoffrey L. Hudson, unpublished paper, symposium on 'War, Medicine and the State', Wellcome Institute for the History of Medicine, 4 February 2000; idem, 'Disabled Veterans and the State in Early Modern England'.
13. Quoted in A. Parry and A. E. Codrington, *War Pensions: Past and Present*, p. 12.
14. Ibid., p. 11.
15. Quoted in Helen Bolderson, *Social Security, Disability and Rehabilitation*, p. 15.
16. *Comrades Journal*, June 1919, vol. 1, no. 8, p. 3.
17. Charles Booth, *Life and Labour, First Series, Vol. I: Poverty*, p. 229. The charitable institutions for the orphaned children of soldiers and sailors were equally plagued by scandal. Intended to be a memorial for all time of the generosity of the British people, by the early 1860s the Royal Victoria Patriotic Asylum 'had become a sort of Dotheboys Hall. The children were employed in scrubbing the floors and cleaning the windows so that they did not get much schooling. One poor girl had been burned to death in solitary confinement. Some of the elder pupils were in a state of chronic hysteria through attending revival meetings, and by order of the Secretary had been sent to London to be cured by mesmerism' (A. Parry and A. E. Codrington, *War Pensions: Past and Present*, p. 33).
18. Llewellyn J. Llewellyn and A. Bassett Jones, *Pensions and the Principles of their Evaluation*, p. 23.
19. TNA: PRO PIN 15/1393, 'The History of the Ministry of Pensions' (November 1917).
20. TNA: PRO WO 32/11209, Memorandum 26 February 1916.
21. Beatrice Webb, *The Diary of Beatrice Webb, Vol. III, 1905–24*, p. 275.
22. SRO: CC7/2/1–4 War Pensions Committee, 'Circular no. 9, Local Committees', 27 July 1916.
23. TNA: PRO PIN 15/866, Cyril Jackson to B. Cubitt, War Office, 30 June 1916.
24. On the role and fortunes of the Board of Control, see Mathew Thomson, *The Problem of Mental Deficiency*, pp. 77–110.
25. TNA: PRO PIN 15/866, B. Cubitt, War Office, to Cyril Jackson, 3 July 1916. There was continuing uncertainty over the fate of insane soldiers. In August 1917 the Ministry of Pensions turned to Col. Aldren Turner of the War Office for enlightenment but he, too, strained ('as far as I can make out') at the crepuscular gloom (PIN 15/870).

26. TNA: PRO PIN 15/866, Minutes of Meeting 19 July 1916.
27. Now obsolete, alienist was a contemporary term, with roots in the eighteenth century, for the asylum-based psychiatrist, one who treats 'mental alienation' (Edward Shorter, *A History of Psychiatry*, p. 17). As psychiatry raised its sights beyond the asylum, so the term slipped out of usage.
28. TNA: PRO PIN 15/866, Minutes of Meeting 19 July 1916. See also PRO MH 51/692, Board of Control memorandum, 12 July 1916.
29. TNA: PRO MH 51/692; PIN 15/866, Circular Letter from the Board of Control to the Visiting Committees of County and Borough Lunatic Asylums.
30. TNA: PRO MH 51/692, Memorandum of meeting between Dr H. Bond, Board of Control, and Sir Alfred Keogh, 4 August 191.
31. TNA: PRO PIN 15/866.
32. TNA: PRO PIN 15/869.
33. TNA: PRO T 114/2; T 136/1.
34. TNA: PRO PIN 15/867; PIN 15/869.
35. TNA: PRO PIN 15/862.
36. TNA: PRO: PIN 15/866.
37. The Derby scheme was introduced by Lord Derby, Director-General of Recruiting under Lord Kitchener as Minister of War, in October 1915 in a vain attempt to stave off the inevitability of conscription. In a kind of 'compulsory voluntarism', all eligible males were asked to 'attest' their willingness to serve if called upon, with the promise that married men would be called last (R. J. Q. Adams and P. P. Poirier, *The Conscription Controversy*, pp. 120–21).
38. TNA: PRO MH 51/694. Albert York: 'Admitted to Hospital with very swollen thumb.... Mental condition dull.... No knowledge of his whereabouts. Could not give his Christian name. Found to be practising masturbation. Condition probably due to masturbation'. Opinion of medical board: 'Neither caused nor aggravated by military service. ?Aggravated by misconduct. Total incapacity'. And on another case: 'Never Abroad. Bad character. 2 Drunks'.
39. TNA: PRO PIN 15/1105.
40. TNA: PRO PIN 15/54.
41. TNA: PRO PIN 15/54, Letter from Sir John Collie to A. Hore, Ministry of Pensions.
42. *Parl.Deb.*, 6 March 1917, vol. XCI. cols 255–56. Barnes repeated the calumny in his memoirs a few years later: 'Many were freaks, some were lunatics who had joined up in a lucid moment, some were bone lazy . . . the flotsam of our modern life' (*From Workshop to War Cabinet*, London [1924], p. 146).
43. Quoted in Helen Bolderson, *Social Security, Disability and Rehabilitation*, p. 23. See J. M. Hogge and T. H. Garside, *War Pensions and Allowances*, for a hard-hitting statement of the obligations of the state.
44. BL: Sir Matthew Nathan Papers, MS Nathan 483, 16 December 1916.
45. Helen Bolderson, *Social Security, Disability and Rehabilitation*, p. 23.
46. Joanna Bourke, *Dismembering the Male*, p. 62.
47. TNA: PRO MH 51/692.
48. For wider discussions of Great War pensions policy and its consequences see especially: Helen Bettinson, *"Lost Souls in the House of Restoration"?: British Ex-Servicemen and War Disability Pensions 1914–30* (unpublished Ph.D thesis, University of East Anglia, 2002); Helen Bolderson, *Social Security, Disability and Rehabilitation*; Joanna Bourke, *Dismembering the Male*; Deborah Cohen, *The War Come Home*; and Andrew Latcham, *Journey's End: Ex-Servicemen & The State During And After The Great War* (unpublished D.Phil thesis, University of Oxford, 1997).

Chapter 6: Justice for the Citizen Soldier
1. Sir Norman Moore was President of the Royal College of Physicians and a member of the first war pensions appeal tribunal established in 1917 to adjudicate on disputed entitlement claims. Not until 1919 were appeal tribunals established entirely independent of the

Ministry of Pensions. Even so, Sir Norman delivers a fine sense (sitting by the fireside with the claimant) of the sympathy that some tribunal members at least felt for the mentally traumatized, even those whose period of service had been brief. Of another claimant he writes: 'His service made him mad and so led to his being put into an asylum . . . he seemed damaged by the war and was given compensation' (26 February 1918) [*War Journals of Sir Norman Moore*, Private Collection, TNA: National Register of Archives, ref. 29440 Moore]. I am grateful to Dr Helen Bettinson for bringing this source to my attention.

2. *RNSMB*, p. 8.

3. Ibid., p. 23.

4. *Minutes of Evidence Taken Before the Select Committee on the Military Service (Review of Exemptions) Act, 1917*, Parliamentary Papers, 1917–18, III, 327, Appendix 1, q. 1208.

5. John MacCurdy, *War Neuroses*, p. 129.

6. Samuel Hynes, *The Soldier's Tale*, pp. 64–66.

7. LMA: St.BG.Wh.108.17–19, Correspondence Whitechapel Union (1916).

8. LMA: Wa.BG.124.40, Reception Orders Wandsworth Union (1922).

9. WL: Royal Army Medical Corps Muniment Collection, RAMC 446/18, ' "Shell Shock": Extract from proceedings of a Court of Enquiry into failure of a party of 11th Border Regt., 97th Inf. Bde. 32nd Division, to carry out an attack, as ordered, on 10 July, 1916'. Emphasis in the original.

10. On the 'militarization' of social relations in Britain – 'liberal militarism' as it has been termed – see: Roger Cooter, 'War and modern medicine'; Roger Cooter and Steve Sturdy, 'Of War, Medicine and Modernity'; David Edgerton, 'Liberal militarism and the British State'; Mark Harrison, 'Medicine and the Management of Modern Warfare'; and Ann Summers, 'Militarism in Britain before the Great War'.

11. D. Kaufmann, 'Science as Cultural Practice: Psychiatry in the First World War', p. 142.

12. 'Mr E. M. Forster has described how in 1917 he read "Prufrock" and others of Eliot's early poems, and how it heartened him at such a time to get hold of poems that were "innocent of public-spiritedness": "They sang of private disgust and diffidence, and of people who seemed genuine because they were unattractive or weak. . . ." ' (George Orwell, *Inside the Whale*, p. 574).

13. Jose Harris, *Private Lives, Public Spirit*, pp. 6, 13, 16.

14. Montagu Lomax, *The Experiences of an Asylum Doctor*, pp. 17, 197–199; on Lomax see T. W. Harding, ' "Not Worth Powder and Shot" '.

15. Samuel Hynes, *The Soldier's Tale*, pp. 31–32.

16. Montagu Lomax, *The Experiences of an Asylum Doctor*, p. 198. For Daddy's incarnation as Hilary Fairfield, a no less feminized service lunatic, in Clemence Dane's play, *A Bill of Divorcement* (1921), see Chapter 19, n. 5, below.

17. TNA: PRO PIN 15/867; MH 51/692, 'Service Patients', Misc. Correspondence (1916–22).

18. TNA: PRO PIN 15/1393 'History of the Ministry of Pensions' (November 1917).

19. Ibid. See also Joanna Bourke, *Dismembering the Male*, pp. 65–67. In the view of the Treasury the terms of the 1917 Royal Warrant 'regarded as a whole' were of 'unexampled liberality'. The flat rate for a full pension was raised from 25/- to 27/6d. per week. A bonus of 20 per cent was added in November 1918 bringing it to 33/- and in 1919 it was raised to 40/- (Helen Bolderson, *Social Security, Disability and Rehabilitation*, pp. 26, 28). The percentages for injuries to the testicles were added later (TNA: PRO T 136/1, letter to Ministry of Pensions, 25 October 1917).

20. For officers a privileged system of wound pensions still existed, condemned as 'sentimental' by the Disability Pensions Committee which demanded that the 'system of compensation for wounds' be brought 'into accord with prevailing medical opinion' (PRO: WO 32/11222, *Final Report of the Disability Pensions Committee*, 1921). The principle of equality between wounds and diseases had already been asserted (though in equal measure resisted) as early as 1902, and even the Treasury had commented adversely on the class distinction that underpinned what it deemed 'anomalous' wound pension arrangements (TNA: PRO WO 32/11400; see also WO 163/7).

21. TNA: PRO PIN 15/1393 'History of the Ministry of Pensions' (November 1917); PIN 15/102 'Memorandum for Judge Parry' (1917).
22. John Turner, *British Politics and the Great War*, pp. 191, 193, 197; John Stevenson, *British Society 1914–45*, pp. 75, 77, 87.
23. Samuel Hynes, *A War Imagined*, pp. 153, 132–33.
24. Quoted in Ben Shephard, *A War of Nerves*, p. 56.
25. Beatrice Webb, *The Diary of Beatrice Webb, Vol. III, 1905–24*, pp. 223, 252, 274–75.
26. Gertrude Himmelfarb, *Poverty and Compassion*, p. 376.
27. *Minutes of Evidence Taken Before the Select Committee on the Military Service (Review of Exemptions) Act, 1917*, Parliamentary Papers, 1917–18, III, 327, Appendix 1, q. 1170.
28. Ibid., q. 1189.
29. On emerging concepts of justice and the new culture of citizenship that had been developing since the late nineteenth century see Jose Harris, *Private Lives, Public Spirit*, pp. 6, 10, 16; Mark Harrison, 'Medicine and the Management of Modern Warfare', pp. 3–4; and idem, 'Sex and the Citizen Soldier', p. 227; and Lynn Hollen Lees, *The Solidarities of Strangers*, p. 295. See also Christopher Lawrence and Anna-K. Mayer eds, *Regenerating England*.
30. This was just the position taken by J. M. Hogge and T. H. Garside on the obligations of the state towards the serving soldier: 'It is the fact of service, no matter the character of such service, which creates the obligation' (*War Pensions and Allowances*, p. 22).
31. TNA: PRO PIN 15/862; MH 51/694.
32. TNA: PRO MH 51/694.
33. TNA: PRO PIN 15/862; MH 51/694.
34. BL: The papers of Sir Matthew Nathan, MS Nathan 486.
35. W. G. Macpherson et al., *History Of The Great War Based On Official Documents – Diseases of the War*, vol. II, p. 9; Ben Shephard, *A War of Nerves*, p. 28.
36. Quoted in Lynn Hollen Lees, *The Solidarities of Strangers*, p. 241.
37. Jose Harris, *Private Lives, Public Spirit*, p. 16.
38. TNA: PRO PIN 15/102 'Memorandum for Judge Parry' (1917).
39. This was a moment in an emerging politics in West European states since the late nineteenth century involving the redefinition of justice in terms of needs and rights, and the moderation of disparities of income and class by equality of status, that was the beginning of the welfare state. These developments have been ably analyzed in a comparative perspective by Peter Baldwin in *The Politics of Social Solidarity*. The faltering fortunes of the mentally ill in Britain in the twentieth century among these solidaristic hopes and promises are discussed in Peter Barham and Marian Barnes, 'The Citizen Mental Patient'.
40. TNA: PRO MH 51/694.
41. TNA: PRO PIN 15/693. Cyril Jackson expressed himself reluctant to write to the wife of a claimant, not least because 'the cause of the disease is not one that you would usually discuss with a wife'.
42. TNA: PRO MH 51/694. On this issue Sir John Collie was on the side of the progressives, declaring that: 'No medical man of any experience either of venereal disease in the working classes, or those serving in HM forces, can deny that every case of General Paralysis of the Insane in a discharged soldier has directly been aggravated by the conditions of service, independent of shell shock or traumatism of any kind' (PRO PIN 15/368, letter, 2 May 1917). Ironically, the other ranks rather than officers were the main beneficiaries of this change of outlook. Acknowledging 'the virtual disappearance in the later stages of the war of any social distinction between officers and men', the Treasury was still insistent in 1921 that traditional standards should be maintained and that cases of venereal disease and its sequelae among officers should be classed as 'misconduct': 'The officer, whatever his moral standards or social class, is selected from among other men for certain specific duties ... among [them] that of setting an example to his men of devotion to duty and exemplary conduct generally' (PRO PIN 15/368).
43. TNA: PRO MH 51/694. 42. Much though Sir Matthew Nathan, the Permanent Secretary,

looked askance at Craig's liberal views, within the current political climate he quickly made himself indispensable. 'I saw Dr Maurice Craig . . . on the subject of his offering to assist the Department in its difficulties with regard to lunatics' (PRO PIN 15/879, memorandum of interview, 9 September 1917).

44. TNA: PRO PIN 15/862; MH 51/694.
45. Jose Harris, *Private Lives, Public Spirit*, pp. 2–3; see also Arthur Marwick, *War and Social Change in the Twentieth Century*, pp. 80–81.
46. See Arthur Kleinman, *The Illness Narratives*. As Helen Bolderson points out, though the maximum flat rate for war disability pension remained at 40/- per week after 1919, it 'continued to compare favourably with national insurance sickness and disablement benefits and with workmen's compensation, and rose in value in relation to wages' (*Social Security, Disability and Rehabilitation*, p. 28).
47. TNA: PRO PIN 15/1541, 9 February 1918.
48. TNA: PRO PIN 15/1399. Nathan had had both a military and an administrative career, having served in the Nile expedition 1886, Lushai expedition 1889, as a colonel in the Durban Light Infantry, governor successively of the Gold Coast, Hong Kong and Natal, and latterly as Under-Secretary in Ireland where, along with other members of the executive, he had been censured and sent home for failing to warn the government of the 1916 uprising. There was nothing in his background or career that disposed him to sympathy with the psychiatric casualties of the war and he met the *bouleversements* of traditional moral codes with unconcealed distaste. A bachelor, he retired to bed early, consuming the entire oeuvre of Jane Austen in the later months of 1917, and in January embarking on Mrs Gaskell's *Cranford* for the third time in two years (BL: The papers of Sir Matthew Nathan, diary).
49. Ibid.
50. TNA: PRO PIN 15/1400; PIN 15/810.
51. TNA: PRO PIN 15/807.
52. Ibid.
53. TNA: PRO PIN 15/808.
54. TNA: PRO PIN 15/810.
55. George Mosse, 'Shell-shock as Social Disease', p. 104.
56. TNA: PRO PIN 15/810.
57. Ibid.

Coda: Albert Gets a War Psychosis Pension
1. The sources for this chapter are as in Prologue, n. 35.
2. Of the 160,545 men examined by the National Service Medical Boards in the London Region between January and October 1918, as many as 60,031 (37.4%) were placed in Grade III and 17,869 (11.1%) in Grade IV (those who were considered 'totally and permanently unfit for any form of Military Service'). Of those examined, 3066 were identified as having diseases of the nervous system (a quarter were rejected and the rest placed in Grade III) and 656 as suffering from insanity (three-quarters rejected, the rest in Grade III) [RNSMB, p. 25].
3. On the politics of 'fitness' see J. M. Winter, 'Military Fitness and Civilian Health in Britain during the First World War'.
4. On the increased mortality among the inmates of lunatic asylums during the Great War, see John Crammer, 'Extraordinary Deaths of Asylum Inpatients during the 1914–18 War'.
5. John Pickstone, 'Production, Community and Consumption'.

PART III 'REVOLTING' PSYCHOLOGY
1. *British Medical Journal* (1917), I, 64.

Chapter 7: How the Weak Progress
1. Emil Kraepelin, 'Psychiatric Observations on Contemporary Issues', pp. 258–59, 261–62. On Kraepelin, see Eric J Engstrom and Matthias M Weber, 'Emil Kraepelin (1856–1926)'.

2. See Paul Lerner, *Hysterical Men*, pp. 193–222.
3. Karl Bonhoeffer, quoted in Paul Lerner, *Hysterical Men*, p. 194.
4. Emil Kraepelin, 'Psychiatric Observations on Contemporary Issues', pp. 263–64.
5. 'Cutting nature at the joints' is Edward Shorter's translation of 'die Erreichung möglichster Naturwahrheit' (*A History of Psychiatry*, p. 355, n.16).
6. Johnstone, T. 'The case for dementia praecox'; Peter Barham, *Schizophrenia and Human Value*, pp. 37–42.
7. Andrew Scull, *The Most Solitary of Afflictions*, p. 324.
8. Quoted in Andrew Scull, *The Most Solitary of Afflictions*, pp. 324–25.
9. See Volker Roelcke, 'Biologizing Social Facts', pp. 388–98; idem, 'Electrified Nerves, Degenerated Bodies', pp. 185–91. On the rise of a 'racial' psychiatry see Paul Weindling, *Health, Race and German Politics*. Kraepelin's evolving preoccupations with states of psychological weakness and psychic degeneracy processes are discussed in Robert Barrett, *The Psychiatric Team and the Social Definition of Schizophrenia*, pp. 206–10.
10. Henry Maudsley, *The Physiology and Pathology of the Mind* (London, 1867, p. 202); quoted in Daniel Pick, *Faces of Degeneration*, p. 208.
11. Emil Kraepelin, 'Psychiatric Observations on Contemporary Issues', p. 262.
12. See W. Schivelbusch, *The Railway Journey*.
13. Ralph Harrington, 'The Railway Accident: Trains, Trauma and Technological Crises in Nineteenth Century Britain', p. 53.
14. Greg A. Eghigian, 'The German Welfare State as a Discourse of Trauma', p. 110; Paul Lerner, 'From Traumatic Neurosis to Male Hysteria', pp. 149–54.
15. Andrew Scull, *The Most Solitary of Afflictions*, p. 316.
16. Mathew Thomson, *The Problem of Mental Deficiency*; Peter Barham, 'Mental Deficiency and the Democratic Subject'.
17. Daniel Pick, *War Machine*, p. 254.
18. Woods Hutchinson, *The Doctor in War*, pp. 109, 112, 115, 117.
19. See the illuminating discussions of Britain, France, Germany, Italy and the USA in Mark Micale and Paul Lerner eds, *Traumatic Pasts*. See also Ben Shephard, *A War of Nerves*, pp. 97–108.
20. Paul Lerner, *Hysterical Men*, pp. 18–23; idem, 'Rationalizing the Therapeutic Arsenal', p. 125.
21. On Hermann Simon see Michael Burleigh, *Death and Deliverance*, pp. 30–33.
22. Paul Lerner, *Hysterical Men*; idem, 'Rationalizing the Therapeutic Arsenal'; idem, 'From Traumatic Neurosis to Male Hysteria'.
23. Michael Burleigh, *Death and Deliverance*, p. 11.
24. Quoted in Michael Burleigh, *Death and Deliverance*, pp. 11–12.
25. Emil Kraepelin, 'Psychiatric Observations on Contemporary Issues', p. 268.
26. John Crammer, 'Extraordinary Deaths of Asylum Inpatients during the 1914–18 War'.
27. See Mark Micale, 'The Psychiatric Body', p. 331; see also Martin Stone, 'Shellshock and the Psychologists'.
28. Doris Kaufmann, 'Science as Cultural Practice: Psychiatry in the First World War and Weimar Germany', p. 138.
29. See John Macnicol, *The Politics of Retirement in Britain 1878–1948*, and David Powell, *The Edwardian Crisis: Britain 1901–14*.
30. On the increasingly psychological world inhabited by a diverse constituency of Britons after 1900, see Mathew Thomson, 'Psychology and the "Consciousness of Modernity" in Early Twentieth-century Britain'.
31. Niall Ferguson, *The Pity of War*, pp. 28–29.
32. Michael Ignatieff, *The Warrior's Honor*, p. 114.
33. John Keegan, *The First World War*, p. 456.
34. IWM: Con Shelf, Lawrence Gameson, Papers, pp. 52–53.
35. After the war, 'congestion' was democratized: 'nobody *now* thinks it bearable to sleep eleven

in a room' (George Orwell, *The Road to Wigan Pier*, p. 59). A rich and historically informed reflection on 'need' is Michael Ignatieff, *The Needs of Strangers*.

36. Letter, dated 19 January 1917, quoted in Samuel Hynes, *A War Imagined*, p. 161.

37. On the shop floor of mainstream psychiatry old habits and prejudices died hard, but in progressive circles in this period too, after Freud's argument for the universality of infant masturbation started to acquire currency, what to the previous generation had been an aberration, or a sign of degeneration, was now reconfigured as a developmental stage we all pass through (Thomas Laqueur, *Solitary Sex*, p. 394).

Chapter 8: Psychosis and Life

1. D. W. Winnicott, 'Leucotomy' (1949) in *Psycho-Analytic Explorations*, p. 547.

2. Quoted in Gillian Beer, 'Forging the Missing Link: Interdisciplinary Stories', in her *Open Fields*, p. 127.

3. G. E. Smith and T. H. Pear, *Shell-shock and Its Lessons*, pp. 1–3. For a recent and splendidly Proustian odyssey through the emotional landscape of human lives see Martha Nussbaum, *Upheavals of Thought: The Intelligence of Emotions*.

4. Robert Armstrong-Jones, 'The psychopathy of the barbed wire', *Nature*, September 1917, vol. 100, pp. 1–3.

5. G. E. Smith and T. H. Pear, *Shell-shock and Its Lessons*, p. 82.

6. Ibid., p. 110.

7. On 'natural' and other kinds see Ian Hacking, 'Madness: Biological or Constructed?', in his *The Social Construction of What?*

8. Henri Ellenberger, *The Discovery of the Unconscious*, pp. 286–88. Eugen Bleuler's approach to psychosis was later invigorated by his son Manfred who succeeded him as director of the Burghölzli. On father and son, see Peter Barham, 'Manfred Bleuler and the Understanding of Psychosis'. On psychosis see G. E. Berrios, 'Historical aspects of psychoses: 19thC issues'.

9. Gerald Grob, *The Mad Among Us*, p. 143.

10. Ibid., p. 148; Henri Ellenberger, *The Discovery of the Unconscious*, p. 817.

11. G. E. Smith and T. H. Pear, *Shell-shock and Its Lessons*, p. 29.

12. Ibid., pp. 89–90.

13. See Paul Lerner, *Hysterical Men*, pp. 230–32.

14. G. E. Smith and T. H. Pear, *Shell-shock and Its Lessons*, pp. 87–88.

15. See Millais Culpin, 'An Autobiography'; and obituary of Millais Culpin (1974–1952) in *British Medical Journal* (1952), pp. 727–28. See also Millais Culpin, 'Clinical Psychology and Some Forgotten Episodes'.

16. Millais Culpin, 'An Autobiography'.

17. The classic account of the leap from one paradigm to another, as into an incommensurable world, is Thomas Kuhn, *The Structure of Scientific Revolutions*.

18. Millais Culpin, 'An Autobiography'.

19. Ibid.

20. Millais Culpin, *The Nervous Patient*, p. 15.

21. Trench foot was a serious cause of disability in the early part of the war especially, responsible for some 20,000 casualties in the British Army by the end of 1914. Throughout the war almost 75,000 men, suffering from trench foot or frostbite, were admitted to hospitals in France (Ilana Bet-El, *Conscripts*, pp. 94–95). Improvements in trench conditions and in hygiene sharply reduced the production of cases.

22. Millais Culpin, *Medicine: And the Man*, pp. 4–5, 7, 28.

23. Ibid., p. 16.

24. Ibid., pp. 18, 19.

25. Millais Culpin, *The Nervous Patient*, pp. 9–10.

26. C. Stanford Read, 'The Major Psychoses in General Practice', pp. 233–36, 248–49. Psychosis was a hot topic in this period. See also John Rickman, 'A Survey: The Development of the Psychoanalytical Theory of the Psychoses' (1926–7).

27. Henry Maudsley, *The Pathology of Mind* (London, 1895) quoted in Maurice Craig, *Psychological Medicine*, p. 23.
28. Maurice Craig and Thomas Beaton, *Psychological Medicine*, p. 69.
29. Royal Commission on Lunacy & Mental Disorder, Minutes of Evidence, Part 1, q. 9394 (London, 1926); see also Maurice Craig, *Nerve Exhaustion*, p. 107.
30. J. R. Lord, *The Clinical Study of Mental Disorders* (London, 1926, p. 33).
31. Hubert Norman, *Mental Disorders* (London, 1928, pp. 232–33).
32. John Bowlby, *Personality and Mental Illness*, p. 187 (emphasis in the original).
33. Ibid., pp. 127–28. Aubrey Lewis inveighs against an outmoded psychiatry in which 'conjectures about "degeneration" and "the neuropathic taint" ' take the place of 'critical study' (p. 86).Contributing to a collection sponsored by the Eugenics Society, the object of which was 'to supply to the general practitioner the means of dealing with requests for a eugenic prognosis' (p.v), Lewis appeals for humility in the physician and debunks the assumption (shared by authorities such as Frederick Mott) that 'there was one, almost mystical "neuropathic taint", "morbid hereditary predisposition" . . . which might manifest itself in any sort of mental disorder or defect' ('The Inheritance of Mental Disorders', p. 114).
34. James Joyce, *Ulysses*, pp. 613–14. The report of Dr Malachi Mulligan, sex specialist, by contrast, tells that Bloom is 'bisexually abnormal', 'born out of bedlock', 'prematurely bald from self-abuse', and has 'recently escaped from Dr Eustace's private asylum for demented gentlemen' (ibid., p. 613).
35. Letter, 15 November 1919, in F. Robert Rodman ed., *Selected Letters of D. W. Winnicott*, p. 1.
36. D. W. Winnicott, 'Prefrontal Leucotomy' (1956) in *Psycho-Analytic Explorations*, p. 554.
37. D. W. Winnicott, *Human Nature*, p. 10; idem, 'Leucotomy' (1949) in *Psycho-Analytic Explorations*, p. 546. Especially in his concern with the mutations of individuality or individuation, Winnicott both drew from and contributed to a wider movement of, broadly, idealist thought, linking biology with social commentary, in which C. S. Sherrington and Julian Huxley were key players between the wars. See most recently Roger Smith, 'Biology and values in interwar Britain'. Smith's summary of part of Sherrington's argument could apply equally to Winnicott: 'Evolution is marked by the rise of individuality in the face of the potentially disruptive forces' (p. 221).
38. Alison Light, *Forever England*, pp. 72–73. Joyce's endorsement of Leopold Bloom's feminized manliness is admiring but in equal measure skittish. 'O, I so want to be a mother', he has Bloom say (*Ulysses*, p. 614). Bloom, remarks George Orwell, 'is a rather exceptionally sensitive specimen of the man in the street' (*Collected Essays, Journalism & Letters*, vol 1, p. 152). On Joyce, the 'new womanly man', and the gender preoccupations of his period see the introduction to the Penguin edition of *Ulysses* by Declan Kiberd, pp. xlix–lxiv.
39. D. W. Winnicott, *Human Nature*, p. 2; idem, *Clinical Notes on Disorders of Childhood*, p. 4. See also Brett Kahr, *D. W. Winnicott: A Biographical Portrait*.
40. Idem, *Human Nature*, p. 19.
41. Idem, *Clinical Notes on Disorders of Childhood*, pp. 87–88.
42. Idem, *Human Nature*, p. 150.
43. Ibid., p. 117.
44. Ibid., p. 158.
45. Ibid., pp. 117–18.
46. Reported in the *British Medical Journal* (1936), II, p. 94.
47. Ironically, Emil Kraepelin's father, Karl, was an opera singer and music teacher who after falling on hard times and taking to drink had become a travelling story-teller, with some success. At the time of his death he had for many years been spurned by his son. Kraepelin's famous system of *Zahlkarten*, or counting-cards, on which he assigned patients he was following to a number of predetermined categories was a methodological device nicely calculated to repulse story-telling urges in his patients and to stifle the remembrance of his father. See Eric J. Engstrom and Matthias M. Weber, 'Emil Kraepelin (1856–1926)'; and Volker Roelcke, 'Biologizing Social Facts'.

48. D. W. Winnicott, *Human Nature*, pp. 10, 80, 86, 158. Radical ideas surfaced in other psychiatric cultures in these tumultuous times. Russian psychiatrist and artist Girsh Segalin, writing in the 1920s, believed that the division between normal and abnormal should be abandoned. The distinction, he argued, should lie not between illness and health but between productive and unproductive illness. In the clinic at the University of the Urals in Ekaterina where he was based he painted a gigantic tableau, using patients as models, titled 'Madhouse or Victims of the War'. Alas, it was lost during the next war (Irina Sirotkina, *Diagnosing Literary Genius*, pp. 164–67).
49. Richard Rorty, *Truth and Moral Progress*, p. 11.

PART IV HOMECOMINGS
  1. William Blake, from the Preface, 'And did those feet in ancient time', to *Milton* (written and illustrated 1804–1810).

Chapter 9: Family Fortunes
  1. GA: G4 (89), G61 (164–65), G61 (169–70), letters of Dorothy Gurney. For Ivor Gurney's own letters from this period see R. K. Thornton ed., *Ivor Gurney: Collected Letters*.
  2. TNA: PRO MH 106/2212.
  3. TNA: PRO MH 106/2213.
  4. TNA: PRO WO 363/C 1977.
  5. LMA: Wa.BG.124.37.
  6. Ibid.
  7. LMA: B.BG.542.63, Bermondsey Union, Reception Orders (1918–19).
  8. LMA: Wa.BG.124.35, Wandsworth Union, Reception Orders, 1917; Wa.BG.114.36, Pauper Examination Book For Lunatics, 1917.
  9. LMA: Wa.BG.124.35, Wandsworth Union, Reception Orders, 1917; Wa.BG.114.37, Pauper Examination Book For Lunatics, 1917–18.
  10. LMA: Wa.BG.113.33 and 39.
  11. TNA: PRO PIN 15/904, 25 October 1918. Nor did the hardships of families abate between the wars: 'the problems of the chronically sick and the families which lost their male wage-earner had changed little since the years before the Great War. Prolonged illness in a working-class family, especially a large family, usually meant a bitter struggle against poverty' (John Stevenson, *British Society 1914–45*, p. 136). In September 1930 Richard W, a Service Patient at Whittingham Asylum since the war, was the recipient of a grim letter from a former neighbour: 'I am very sorry to tell you that your wife Ellen is dead, the operation has finished her. She died on Thursday morning at 5.50, and we haven't a penny to bury her with. So if you can do anything to help will you kindly let us know as soon as possible'. 'This man's wife Ellen is dead and liable to be buried as a pauper', the medical superintendent anxiously notified the pensions office, 'can you telegraph me authority to expend out of any accumulated balance you have in his a/c for her funeral' [LRO: Records of Whittingham Hospital, HRW 12/115].
  12. Nelson case, no. 4.
  13. LMA: B.BG.558.3, Bermondsey Union, Relieving Officer's Notebook; TNA: PRO PIN 15/904; LMA: Be.BG.266.21, Letters from Bethnal Green Union to Ministry of Health.
  14. A wife's sympathy was not necessarily unconditional, even when there might have been a financial interest. Mary Land was forced to flee the family home with her newborn baby because of her husband Albert's cruelty. Albert was classified as a Service Patient when he was admitted to Long Grove Asylum but, tellingly, in the account Mary gave to William Haggis, Relieving Officer, there was no mention of Alfred's war service as having any bearing on the case. Instead, Haggis received from Mary an unadorned narrative of marital abuse (LMA: Wa.BG.114.51).
  15. TNA: PRO MH 106/2215.
  16. TNA: PRO MH 106/2225. Spelling and punctuation as in original.
  17. LMA: Wa.BG.114.49; Wa.BG.124.41.

18. LMA: Hh.BG.75.2, Hammersmith Union, Register of Cases in Institutions.
19. LMA: F.BG.57, Minutes of Fulham Board of Guardians.
20. LMA: LCC.PH.MENT.4.24, Long Grove Asylum Register (1916–25).
21. Dr T. Knowles Stansfield, letter, *The Times*, 19 September 1919.

Chapter 10: Officialdom and the Pensioner
1. TNA: PRO MH 51/692.
2. LRO: CC/HBM/4, Minutes of Lancashire Asylums Board (1913–19).
3. TNA: PRO MH 51/692. There are countless examples that testify to the mental strains of war on non-combatants. Mary Jones was sent to Long Grove Asylum in June 1917 in an excited state alleged to have been caused by 'worry about son in army', singing hymns day and night, alternating with bawdy songs; Lilian Donovan was sent to Hanwell in the same month after 'worrying about father in the army', weeping and wailing, 'imagining she is falling down and is to be beaten'; and Russian-born Max G was removed to Colney Hatch in a profound state of melancholy, unable to sleep for six weeks after receiving a letter announcing the death of his father, the climax of a train of bereavements and deprivations, two brothers already killed in the war, his mother losing her sight, and his sisters starving. When Sophia Dowding, widow of Berty Augustus Dowding, who was killed in the Battle of Neuve Chapelle in March 1915, was taken to Long Grove in January 1916, her sister declared herself very much surprised and deeply grieved: 'the only way I can account for it is that my sister never got over the loss of her husband, no doubt it preyed on her mind'. No doubt it did, but it may also have preyed on Sophia's mind that her sister, though living in a neighbouring district, had not seen her for four years and so could scarcely have been much support to her in her bereavement [LMA: Wa.BG.114.32; Wa.BG.124.35; H12.CH.B.15.5; Wa.BG.114.32]
4. LRO: CC. HBM. 4, Minutes of Lancashire Asylums Board (1913–19).
5. TNA: PRO MH 51/692.
6. LMA: LCC. MIN. 693, Minutes of Asylums General Purposes Committee (1914–17).
7. TNA: PRO PIN 15/870.
8. Ibid. Joanna Bourke (*Dismembering the Male*, p. 69) claims that overseas service was a requirement for entitlement to a war disability pension but, as the example of Henshall Gater shows, this holds only for the early part of the war.
9. LMA: H11.HLL.A14.3.12.1, Records of Hanwell Asylum, Letter Book (1915–27). Such ceremonial largesse was shortlived and in 1920 provision was drastically reduced. Quite apart from the expense, the authorities had become concerned about the adverse effects on recruitment of the continuing spectacle of military funerals. 'It is neither possible nor desirable', opined a War Office spokesman, 'for the Regular Army to continue to provide military funerals and military honours for all ex-soldiers. The Army's prime function is to train as a Striking Force for the Crown and not to provide a gigantic "Undertaking" Corporation for the population of the United Kingdom' [TNA: PRO WO 32/4849, Military Funerals For Ex-Soldiers: Revision Of Policy 1920–23].
10. LMA: Hanwell Asylum, Letter Book, ibid. In August 1918 the medical superintendent of Long Grove had already taken issue with inequities in recent austerity measures imposed by the Board of Control, remonstrating over a 'grossly unjust' distribution of jam and cheese to 'staff and private and Service patients instead of those people who by their work required it', i.e. the worker patients on whom the asylum economy depended (LMA: LCC. MIN. 1181).
11. TNA: PRO PIN 15/875; PIN 15/876.
12. On the Treasury and interwar social policy see Deborah Cohen, *The War Come Home*, p. 28; Jose Harris, 'Society and the State in Twentieth-Century Britain', pp. 76–80; and Mathew Thomson, *The Problem of Mental Deficiency*, pp. 77–78, 85–86.
13. TNA: PRO PIN 15/907.
14. Ibid; PIN 67/53.
15. TNA: PRO T 114/2; T 136/1; PIN 15/872. Incurable insanity did not provide grounds for divorce in Britain until 1937 (see p. 342).

16. TNA: PRO PIN 67/53.
17. TNA: PRO PIN 67/55.
18. TNA: PRO PIN 15/872.
19. DRO: HZ/2/5/6, Papers: Private & Service Patients (1917–19).
20. Service lunatics also had advocates among feminist groups. Miss Gilbertson of the *National League of Rights for Soldiers' and Sailors' Wives and Relatives* informed the Whitechapel Union in October 1918 that she was 'desired by Miss Pankhurst to write to you on behalf of Mrs Hannon, 5 Hamilton Rd, Bethnal Gn, mother of Pte Frances Hannon, 123475, RAMC Labour Coy, now an inmate of Claybury Asylum', regarding his pension claim (LMA: St.BG.Wh.108.27). Miss Pankhurst was Sylvia Pankhurst, suffragette, communist, and committed pacifist, who engaged in philanthropic work in the East End of London during the war. The hon. secretary of the League was Mrs George Lansbury. See Barbara Winslow, *Sylvia Pankhurst*, pp. 94–95.
21. TNA: PRO PIN 67/52.
22. TNA: PRO PIN 15/867.
23. Ibid.
24. Asked by the Medical Research Committee in January 1920 to submit a list of all military patients treated in Hanwell Lunatic Asylum from beginning of the war to the present, the medical superintendent replied that 'we have had some hundreds of these military patients'. However, 'of the many whose cases are not considered by the Ministry of Pensions to be Service Patients' he is unable to verify the information he holds since 'obviously one cannot rely on the statements of a lunatic' [LMA: H11.HLL.A14.3.12.1, Records of Hanwell Asylum, Letter Book (1915–27)]. Though there was inevitably dispute over the size of the unrecognized population, the reality of its existence was incontrovertible. The Ministry of Pensions acknowledged in 1925 and again in 1937 that there were 'many pensioners and ex-service men in mental institutions whose mental condition is not a liability of the Ministry at the present time' [TNA: PIN 67/72; PIN 67/73, letter, Adair Hore to the Board of Control, 23 July 1937]. It was claimed by the Ex-Services Welfare Society in 1938 that there was a population of around 10,000 unrecognized ex-servicemen in mental hospitals in Britain. Their methodology was a little suspect, however, for they had invited medical superintendents to submit the numbers of ex-service patients in their institutions who would like to receive a gift of cigarettes at Christmas, a sure-fire basis on which to achieve an inflated estimate [TNA: PRO PIN 15/3144, letter from Admiral Sir Reginald Tyrwhitt to Minister of Pensions, 4 April 1938; see also ESWS: Minutes of Executive Committee, 6 May 1937].
25. TNA: PRO PIN 15/873; PIN 67/72.
26. TNA: PRO WO 364/2716/2293–2296.
27. Nelson, case no 6. Spelling as in original.
28. TNA: PRO PIN 26/21156.
29. TNA: PRO PIN 26/17095.
30. TNA: PRO PIN 26/20827.
31. TNA: PRO PIN 26/16721.
32. TNA: PRO WO 95/4291.
33. The following account of George Collins is drawn from TNA: PRO PIN 26/16763.
34. TNA: PRO PIN 15/883.
35. TNA: PRO PIN 26/16799. Emphasis in orginal.
36. The position of the Irish veteran of the Great War was scarcely an enviable one. In 1921 the Ministry of Pensions reported on the grievous difficulties in placing neurasthenic ex-servicemen in Ireland in employment 'owing to the present hostile attitude which is directed collectively and individually against men who served in the late War. . . . It seems very questionable, even if the country becomes settled again, whether the ex-soldier will not be regarded still as an outcast and an undesirable by his fellow men' (TNA: PRO PIN 15/899). Efforts by the Ministry of Pensions to introduce the Service Patient scheme in Ireland had met with official indifference, not assisted by a mistake in the drafting of the arrangements in which insane Irish ex-servicemen had been classified as criminal lunatics (TNA: PRO PIN

15/898). After the war the Irish government set its own rules for the repatriation of ex-servicemen, much to the consternation of British officials. The Secretary to the Colonial Office ruefully remarked in 1924: 'our power of removing lunatics and paupers to Ireland [which was always one-sided, as Ireland had no corresponding power to remove lunatics and paupers to Great Britain – a fact which was always resented] has disappeared . . . as a result of the setting up of the Free State' (PRO: T 161/223, 'Disposal of Service Criminal Lunatics who are Natives of the Irish Free State'). See also Myles Dungan, *'They Shall Not Grow Old': Irish Soldiers and the Great War.*

37. TNA: PRO PIN 26/16783. But the pensions authorities had their revenge. When Michael Cunningham died in May 1939, they rejected an application from his son for assistance with funeral expenses, maintaining that the illness from which he died was unconnected with his war service.

38. TNA: PRO PIN 26/17111.

Chapter 11: 'A Very Public Madness'

1. Lynn Hollen Lees, *The Solidarities of Strangers*, pp. 295–96.

2. On the development of medical services under the Poor Law in the late nineteenth and early twentieth centuries see especially Lynn H. Lees, *The Solidarities of Strangers*, pp. 275–81; on the Poor Law and its institutions, M. A. Crowther, *The Workhouse System: 1834–1929*; and on mental health care within the Poor Law system, Peter Bartlett, *The Poor Law of Lunacy.* Despite the medicalizing trend, the mental ward still occupied a somewhat equivocal role in the Poor Law universe. In some localities (as in Fulham and Wandsworth) it had been integrated into the infirmary before, or immediately after, the Great War, but in Westminster it was still solidly entrenched in the workhouse.

3. LMA: St. BG. Wh. 108. 27, Correspondence Files, Whitechapel Union, memorandum issued by the Metropolitan Sub-Committee of the Association of Poor Law Unions (1918).

4. LMA: Wa. BG. 114. 46.

5. LMA: Wa. BG. 114. 44; Wa.BG.124.38. For a short period the Tooting Military Neurological Hospital was the scene of some brave experiments in the psychological treatment of epilepsy and quasi-epileptoid symptoms, with only limited success. War pensioner Henry Moore was admitted in January 1922 in a dazed condition, muttering, and refusing food: 'On Feb 4 he had series of 7 "fits". For two days afterwards he was dissociated and talkative, imagining that he had killed God or the King or his father, and that he was to be shot in consequence. Feb 13th: 4 "fits" followed by a dazed, dull period but no phantasy. March 1, 15, 23: 3 "fits" each time, with rapid recovery to normal. April 4: 4 "fits" followed by 12 hours very confused. April 11 and 12th: 6 "fits" after which he became very rough requiring restraint. . . . His fits were of an Hysterical Type' (W. E. Bond, MO i/c). At this point Bond was forced to give up on Moore and transfer him to Dr Frank Nixey at the Wandsworth Infirmary ('patient is morose and resentful with a leaning towards truculence') for removal to Cane Hill Asylum [LMA: Wa.BG.124.39]. He later co-authored a book with Ronald Rows venturing a psychological perspective on epilepsy which seems to have been largely forgotten (R. Rows and W. E. Bond, *Epilepsy: A Functional Mental Illness*, London, 1926. See Ben Shephard, ' "The Early Treatment of Mental Disorders": R. G. Rows and Maghull 1914–1918', p. 456).

6. LMA: H11.HLL.A14.3.12.1, Records of Hanwell Asylum, Letter Book (1915–27), letter from the Medical Superintendent of Bexley Asylum on behalf of all the LCC Medical Superintendents, 14 June 1922.

7. LMA: St.BG.Wh.108.28, Correspondence Files, Whitechapel Union.

8. LMA: We. BG. CW. 39. 5, Circular to Boards of Guardians from Local Government Board, December 1917, 'Soldiers & Sailors Disabled by Mental Disorder – Arrangements for Classification & Treatment'.

9. The 'mental' wards formed part of what had been built in the 1850s as the St George's Union Workhouse, or the Little Chelsea Workhouse as it was also known. 'Little Chelsea' was,

however, an ironic misnomer, for on census night in 1901 it boasted 1623 inmates (TNA: PRO RG 13/76). In 1913 St George's Union merged with the neighbouring Westminister & Strand Union to form the City of Westminster Union, and the workhouse was renamed the Fulham Road Workhouse. Though an Infirmary had been established adjacent to the Workhouse as early as 1878, and renamed St Stephen's Hospital in 1924, the mental wards continued to form part of the original workhouse establishment, now restyled the Westmininster Institution, through into the 1930s.

10. 'Alleged lunatics' were invariably searched on admission and could be charged for the services they received if they were found to have money on them. The Master reported that when Florence Chaplin was admitted on 18 October 1916 she had £4.4.10 in her possession and when she was discharged on 3 November 'I handed to her £2.17.4, retaining the balance of £1.17.6 for doctor's fee and maintenance'. Ex-servicemen were generally exempted from charges. Edgar Warner, a discharged soldier, had 9/- on him when he was admitted to the observation ward on 16 April 1919. 'I returned this to him when discharged on April 26th'. George White 'admitted to the Observation Ward on July 2nd had 14/- on him. As he was a discharged soldier and suffered from epileptic seizures, therefore not being able to do much work, I handed him the money, without deduction, on his discharge on July 4th' (LMA: We.BG.CW.27.4, Minutes of the Institution Committee, Fulham Road Workhouse).

11. Under the chairmanship of John Coutts, members of the workhouse committee frequently visited the establishment: 'We have this day visited the Male Observation Ward. There are some bad cases here and both padded rooms are occupied' (LMA: We.BG.CW.27.3, Gerard Wallop and A. G. Hartley, 16 May 1917); 'Visited institution this day. Old Men's Infirm Ward, Observation Ward, Bakehouse, Kitchen, Stores etc. Meat very good. I tasted the Rolled Oats which was being used as porridge, very good. In the Observation Ward there is an Indian doctor . . . this is his second visit here' (Ibid., W. Smith, 25 June 1917).

12. Unless otherwise indicated, the remainder of this account is draw from the Medical Officer's Casebooks on Apparent Lunatics for the Fulham Road Workhouse, LMA: We. BG. CW. 59. 4–9, Male Record Books (1917–23).

13. James Joyce, *Ulysses*, p. 444.

14. Jacob Bronowski, *The Man Without a Mask*, p. 14; see also Marion Milner, *The Suppressed Madness of Sane Men*, p. 296. For another historical moment in which 'madmen' felt emboldened to present their credentials at court see Christopher Hill, *The World Turned Upside Down*, pp. 277–84.

15. In June 1919 there were fears for the King's safety amidst alarms about the 'abnormal state of mind' of aggrieved ex-servicemen insisting upon making their representations to His Majesty in person (Helen Bolderson, *Social Security, Disability and Rehabilitaton*, p. 40). In the early modern period, trespassers upon royal property, and those who used imprudent or passionate language about the monarch, 'speaking daingerous words', frequently wound up in Bethlem Hospital (Joseph Andrews et al., *The History of Bethlem*, pp. 351–52, 356–57).

16. Not that all of them were satisfied with the treatment they received. One Samuel Irwin was brought into the observation ward by the police shortly after the Armistice, having been apprehended in the central hall of the House of Commons setting light to the orders of the day. Having renounced his delusions a week later, soon after his discharge he filed a complaint, alleging that 'he had to lay on a bed, the sheets of which were stained with human filth, and the blankets were fairly caked with it', and that he had been served stinking herrings at dinner. The Master denied the first charge, insisting that 'every fresh patient that comes in has fresh sheets and blankets on his bed' but was more circumspect about the fish (LMA: We.BG.CW.27.4). Irwin typified a less deferential attitude towards authority, invigorated by the Great War, with expectations of customer satisfaction.

17. Frequently there was close liaison with relatives but sometimes there was a breakdown in communication. At an inquest in July 1917 into the death of an inmate by suicide following his discharge from the observation ward, it was alleged that: 'no notice of the impending discharge was given to the relatives . . . the discharge was made after so short a detention (6 days) . . . and founded upon evidence furnished by the lunatic himself without

any enquiry from those he lived with'. In his defence, Dr Sandiland maintained that during the time the patient was in the workhouse not one single fact emerged to indicate insanity, and that the relatives had neither visited the patient nor offered any information (LMA: We.BG.CW.27.3).

18. LMA: We.BG.CW.54.1, Attendants' Report on Male Patients in the Observation Ward.

Chapter 12: Demobbed to the Asylum

1. TNA: PRO MH 51/692.
2. Ibid.
3. Ibid.; PIN 15/866.
4. See Joany Hichberger, 'Old Soldiers'.
5. TNA: PRO PIN 15/873.
6. LMA: LCC.MIN.584, Minutes of Asylums & Mental Deficiency Committee.
7. TNA: PRO MH 58/1, 'Anatomy Acts: Ex-Service Patients who die in Institutions while receiving treatment at the expense of the Ministry of Pensions'. The administration of the Anatomy Acts now fell to the newly-established Ministry of Health: 'The Ministry of Pensions are again pressing for steps to be taken to ensure that the body of a pensioner will not be handed over for anatomical purposes. Presumably only a general circular will satisfy them' (MH 58/4, 28 July 1923). And that is what they got – to all county and borough asylums and local authorities. On the history of the Anatomy Acts and the terrors they provoked see Ruth Richardson, *Death, Dissection and the Destitute*.
8. LMA: LCC.MIN.610, Asylums & Mental Deficiency Committee: Presented Papers, Circular from Board of Control September 1921 (emphasis added). For a deceased pauper mourning rites were not considered at all necessary and were frequently prohibited by the parish authorities. The pauper corpse 'rotted in anonymity', just as pauper lunatics were rotting prematurely in lunatic asylums (Julie-Marie Strange, 'Only a pauper whom nobody owns', p. 148). 'Stripped of all mourning paraphernalia the pauper coffin bore little indication of the individual personality of the corpse or those who mourned it' (ibid.). The Ministry of Pensions was, of course, obliged to make concessions to lunatic war pensioners, and to the sensibilities of their relatives, in their dying as much as in their living, and to provide a measure of support for 'respectful' and 'respectable' burials. They could not have done otherwise, for by the time of the Great War aversion to a pauper burial was felt ever more keenly. In their niggardly gestures, however, the Pensions authorities frequently gave the impression that officialdom had *already* buried these lunatic miscreants in common graves, 'paupers' pits', unrecognizable as graves because there were no commemorative markers, and were reluctantly being forced to disinter them and attach names and signs to them.
9. DRO: Records of Digby Mental Hospital (4034A), HZ.2.5.7, Papers: Private & Service Patients. It was frequently alleged that the uniform size of pauper coffins meant that larger corpses were 'indecently' crammed in them (Julie-Marie Strange, op.cit.).
10. The notion of 'asylumdom' I take from Andrew Scull, 'Rethinking the History of Asylumdom'.
11. DRO: Records of Digby Mental Hospital (4034A), HZ. 2.5.7, Papers: Private & Service Patients.
12. Ibid.
13. *Parl.Deb.*, 10 February 1922, vol. CXLVIII, c. 552.
14. SFRO: Records of St Audry's Hospital (ID 407), B1/13B, Male Admissions, 1914–18; B1/14, Male Admissions, 1918–20; B5/1, Medical Register (Male) 1916–20; B7/6, Register of Discharges and Transfers 1916–21.
15. LMA: H12.CH.B.15.5, Records of Colney Hatch Asylum, Case Book: Male Patients Discharged in 1923. On Jewish participation in the Great War see Eugene Black, *The Social Politics of Anglo-Jewry 1880–1920*, pp. 356–88; on Jewish immigrants in London see Roy Porter, *A Social History of London*, pp. 301–02, and J. White, *Rothschild Buildings: Life in an East End Tenement Block 1887–1920*. Colney Hatch invariably had a sizeable community of Jewish patients, employed a Jewish cook and, sporadically, an interpreter, and in 1925 arranged for the construction of a Jewish mortuary. See now also Carole Anne Reeves,

'Insanity and Nervous Diseases amongst Jewish Immigrants to the East End of London, 1880–1920', unpublished Ph.D thesis, University of London (2001), pp. 253–66, 320–21.

16. LMA: H12.CH.B.15.3, Case Book: Male Patients Discharged 1919–20. Misgivings many of them undoubtedly had, but there were staunch patriots among these ranks, especially perhaps among the displaced, anxious to bond with their adoptive homeland. Thus Francisco E, a Service Patient in Colney Hatch Asylum, 'is intensely pro-British in his dress even to the extent of having a union jack sewn on his vest. He buys maps of London and makes a study so he says of London, calculating distances etc'. His diagnosis? 'Confusional insanity'! [LMA: H12.CH.B.15.10].

17. Ibid.

18. LMA: H12.CH.B.15.4, Case Book: Male Patients Discharged 1921–22.

19. There were other members of ethnic minorities who, even though they might have made their home in England for a considerable period, now found themselves, under the circumstances of war when the line between friends and foes was being drawn more tightly, on the wrong side of it, their private lives made the object of official scrutiny. Julius Koenig had for some years been living in furnished rooms at Putney, and for a time had led a very active associative life as a member of the Automobile Club, the Royal Motor Boat Club and the junior Athenaeum, though recently he had become rather reclusive, having quarrelled with friends and relatives, believing that everyone was tampering with his food and drink. In July 1915 he was branded an Austrian enemy alien and removed to Colney Hatch, Asylum, his belongings bundled into two leather bags and a tin trunk by the relieving officer and his landlady. So now the hapless Mr Koenig could justifiably feel tampered with! [LMA: Wa.BG.114.31]. Still, by no means would he have found himself alone at Colney Hatch, for over the next year or so he was joined by Austrians, Germans and others with an alien whiff about them to the official nose, who had been corralled in camps such as Knockoloe on the Isle of Man and had now broken down under the strain of confinement and severance from their families. These included: Josef Pass, tailor; August Gertoner, waiter; Nikolas Kolodzig, waiter; Lathan Pinker, Jew and egg chandler; Celeste Segna, stonemason; Peter Buch, baker; Sulivan Mohamed, seaman (religion: 'Mehomedan' [sic]); Hans Anderson, fireman; and Wadi Bracks, ship's fireman. Of course, this was in any case mostly a marginal and transient crowd, but we should not for that reason assume that the impact of war was any less emotionally and materially disruptive either for the individual or his kin [LMA: St P.BG.146.10]. For a list of aliens detained in lunatic asylums within the Metropolitan Police District see: TNA: PRO HO 45/11522/287235.

20. LMA: H12.CH.B.15.4, Case Book: Male Patients Discharged 1921–22.

Coda: A Disappointed Homecoming

1. Letter 321, 22 March 1918, to Marion Scott in R. K. R. Thornton ed., *Ivor Gurney: Collected Letters*, p. 416.

2. Letter 184, 1 April 1917, to Marion Scott, ibid., p. 238.

3. Letter 310, February 1918, to F. W. Harvey, ibid. p. 399; letter 225, 21 September 1917, to Marion Scott, ibid., p. 328.

4. Letter 184, 1 April 1917, to Marion Scott, ibid., p. 238; letter 177, 23 March 1917, to Marion Scott, ibid., p. 231.

5. Letter 52, October 1915, to Herbert Howells, ibid., p. 52.

6. Letter 106, 5 July 1916, to Marion Scott, ibid., p. 115. Emphasis in original.

7. Letter 231, 8 August 1917, to Marion Scott, ibid., p. 297.

8. Letter 119, 24 August 1916, to Marion Scott, ibid., p. 138.

9. Letter 323, 28 March 1918, to Marion Scott, ibid., p. 418.

10. Letter 459, 9 December 1922, to Marion Scott, ibid., p. 550; letter 450, November 1922, to Dr Harper, ibid., p. 544.

11. Letter 452, November 1922, to Marion Scott, ibid., pp. 545–46. 'Electrical delusion' is period psychiatric idiom for a patient's conviction that his thoughts and feelings were being tampered with or controlled by electrical influences.

12. On the failure to grasp the nettle of resettlement see Helen Bolderson, *Social Security, Disability and Rehabilitation*, pp. 38–47; Joanna Bourke, *Dismembering the Male*; Deborah Cohen, *The War Come Home*; and Seth Koven, 'Remembering and Dismemberment: Crippled Children, Wounded Soldiers and the Great War in Britain'. On the erosion of the hopes that had been invested in work therapy in the aftermath of the war, see Jeffrey Reznick, 'Work-Therapy and the Disabled British Soldier in Great Britain in the First World War'.

13. F. Scott Fitzgerald, *The Great Gatsby*, pp. xlviii–xlix.

14. 'To the Prussians of England', Ivor Gurney, *Selected Poems*, p. 7.

15. Letter 351, 11 September 1918, to J. W. Haines, op. cit., p. 455.

16. 'First Time In', Ivor Gurney, *Rewards of Wonder*, p. 98.

17. Unpublished poem, 'After War', GA: G 53 (53).

18. 'Strange Hells', Ivor Gurney, *Rewards of Wonder*, pp. 81–82.

19. George Walter, 'Introduction', Ivor Gurney, *Rewards of Wonder*, p. 15.

20. 'Strange Service', Ivor Gurney, *Severn & Somme* and *War's Embers*, p. 26.

21. R. K. R. Thornton and George Walter in Ivor Gurney, *Best Poems* and *The Book of Five Makings*, p. 14.

22. According to his service records Ivor Gurney was in fact awarded a weekly pension of 8/3d. from 5 October 1918 to be reviewed in 52 weeks (TNA: PRO WO 363/G 1495/0179). At this time the full pension rate was 27/6d. which would have given him a 30% pension. His award was very likely raised to 12/- in line with the increase in the flat rate to 33/- in November 1918.

23. GA: G55(1–7), letter to the Metropolitan Police Force from City of London Mental Hospital, Dartford, n.d. Emphasis added. Reproduced in full in Michael Hurd, *The Ordeal of Ivor Gurney*, pp. 1–3. The full pension of 25/- to which Gurney refers was the basic pension rate before it was raised in 1917.

24. 'First Time In', Ivor Gurney, *Rewards of Wonder*, pp. 97–98.

25. GA: G85 (50), letter to J. W. Haines from City of London Mental Hospital, Dartford, March 1925.

PART V HARD TIMES
1. George Orwell, *The Road to Wigan Pier*, pp. 43–44.

Chapter 13: 'Any Man In Any Street'

1. 'The brain worn soldier', *Manchester Dispatch*, 25 August 1917; TNA: PRO PIN 15/862. In protesting the conditions to which they were subjected, Service Patients found advocates among organized labour, though their advocacy was frequently less than convincing. In August 1920 a delegation led by Ben Tillett MP, representing the interests of the 268 ex-servicemen in Prestwich Asylum, near Manchester (the same asylum that was in the following year to be the object of Montagu Lomax's exposé), made serious allegations to the Ministry of Pensions as to 'general conditons, diet, neglect and harsh treatment of patients, lack of surgical and medical attention, and wrongful detention'. When the commissioners of the Board of Control visited the asylum to investigate, from only 11 patients did they 'receive any complaint which was not at once obviously the outcome of insanity' and of these 'several proved on being probed . . . to be the result of delusions and hallucinations'. Moreover, not a few of those who ventured discontents were 'men with bad histories'. As to the rump, 'no complaint or expression of discontent of any kind was received, indeed many of them spoke in very favourable terms of their treatment' (*Seventh Annual Report of the Board of Control for the Year 1920*, 'Special Inquiry into the Conditions and Treatment of Service Patients in Prestwich Asylum', pp. 15–17). When Ben Tillett and his delegates were invited to meet the commissioners at the asylum, Tillett pleaded other engagements and the rest failed to attend. One may reasonably surmise from this that organized labour was no less intimidated by the Board of Control, and so-called experts in insanity, than were the asylum inmates themselves. Delegations from ex-servicemen's associations were also sometimes cajoled by medical superintendents into adopting a more deferential tone and accepting that reality was after all pretty much as the doctor told it.

2. *Parl. Deb.*, 10 February 1922, vol. CXLVIII, c. 552.
3. 'The present arrangement in England gives rise to so much dissatisfaction that the question of separate asylums is again under consideration' (TNA: PRO PIN 15/ 898, 11 June 1919).
4. *Report of Departmental Committee of Inquiry into the Machinery of Administration of the Ministry of Pensions*, 1921.
5. Ward Muir, *Observations of an Orderly: Some Glimpses of Life and Work in an English War Hospital* (London, 1917, p. 108).
6. *Parl. Deb.*, 26 October 1921, vol. CXLVII, cc. 1001–1002; 20 July 1922, vol. CLVI, cc. 2250–2251. Major George Tryon held office as Minister of Pensions over a remarkably long period, in the Conservative administrations of 1922–January 1924, and November 1924–1929, and again in the National Government 1931–1935. Captain Charles E. Loseby was MP (National Democratic Party) for Bradford East in the Coalition Government from 1918 to 1922 when he lost to the Labour Party as a National Liberal Candidate. He was extremely vocal on behalf of a number of ex-servicemen's causes, and was closely involved with the Ex-Services Welfare Society in promoting treatment alternatives for ex-servicemen in asylums (see chapter 16). He was clearly personally sympathetic towards people with fringe or deviant experiences who were marginalized or treated with suspicion by the state, for he was a spiritualist and as a practising barrister defended the medium Helen Duncan against the Whitehall security establishment when she was tried under the 1735 Witchcraft Act in the next war (TNA: PRO DPP 2/1234). In November 1921 he convened a meeting at the House of Commons, addressed by Montagu Lomax, to discuss the position of ex-servicemen in lunatic asylums. 'Asylum administration in this country came in for serious and sensational criticism at a meeting . . . to protest against ex-servicemen suffering from brain trouble being sent to such institutions. . . . Dr Lomax, formerly an asylum doctor, said some remarkable things. . . . "What will be the lot of the ex-soldier who is condemned to pass the greater part of his life in an asylum of this kind? What chance has he of recovery? He is sent to what is often a living death under a system which is rotten to the core"' (States of Guernsey Island Archives: Loseby Collection, cuttings file, *Western Mail*, 10 November 1921).
7. TNA: PRO T 172/1121, Memoranda Concerning the National Federation of Discharged and Demobilised Soldiers & Sailors (1920); 'Ex-service Men Mentally Affected', *Lancet*, 10 December 1921.
8. Dr T. Knowles Stansfield, letter, *The Times*, 19 September 1919 (TNA: PRO PIN 15/871).
9. TNA: PRO PIN 15/871. By 1918, wrote George Orwell, 'everyone under forty was in a bad temper with his elders, and the mood of anti-militarism which followed naturally upon the fighting was extended into a general revolt against orthodox and authority' (*The Road to Wigan Pier*, p. 129).
10. Roy Porter, 'The history of Bethlem/ histories of Bethlem', unpublished paper presented at conference on 'Insanity, Institutions and Society', University of Exeter, April 1997. On the politics of committals to Bethlem ('large numbers of patients were sent by the War Office'), see Jonathan Andrews et al., *The History of Bethlem*, pp. 349–53, 356–58. In 1919, after the interlude of the war, with public opinion now deflected from the army, the military medical authorities speedily resumed normal business, once more discharging regular soldiers showing signs of insanity direct to public asylums after the briefest of sojourns in a military treatment facility.
11. See, especially, Ted Bogacz, 'War Neurosis and Cultural Change in England 1914–22: the Work of the War Office Committee of Enquiry into "Shell-Shock"'.
12. BL: Lord Southborough Papers, Box 4, transcript of speech in the House of Lords, 28 April 1920.
13. *Report of the War Office Commission of Enquiry into 'Shell-Shock'* (hereafter *Report*), p. 188.
14. BL: Lord Southborough Papers, Box 4, typescript of articles published in *The Times*, 2–5 September 1922.
15. *Report*, p. 5.

16. D. K. Henderson, 'War Psychoses: An Analysis of 202 Cases of Mental Disorder Occurring in Home Troops', pp. 187–88.
17. *Report*, p. 6.
18. Ibid., p. 58.
19. Ibid., p. 112. Ted Bogacz also remarks on the arrogance of the Committee: '. . . they were extremely class conscious as is evident in their patronizing tone when discussing the "lower orders" and other ranks.' ('War Neurosis and Cultural Change in England 1914–22', p. 237).
20. Quoted ibid.
21. Ibid., p. 21.
22. Woods Hutchinson, *The Doctor in War*, p. 117; Lord Moran, *The Anatomy of Courage*, p. 26.
23. Arthur Kleinman, *Writing at the Margin*, p. 249.
24. *Report of the Inter-Allied Conference on the After-Care of Disabled Men* (London, Ministry of Pensions, 1918, pp. 118–20).
25. Mathew Thomson, 'Status, Manpower and Mental Fitness', p. 154.
26. Maurice Craig, *Nerve Exhaustion*, p. 108.
27. *RNSMB*: pp. 18–20.
28. LRO: Records of Whittingham Hospital, HRW 12/115, Reception Orders 1909–20.
29. GRO: Records of Horton Road Hospital, HO 22/83/2/ 100–101, Certificate of Medical Superintendent of an Asylum. On the history of the association between sunstroke and mental disorder, see Jonathan Andrews, 'Letting Madness Range: Travel and Mental Disorder', pp. 47–53.
30. DRO: Records of Digby Mental Hospital (4034A), HZ/2/5/6, Papers: Private & Service Patients (1917–19).
31. GRO: Records of Horton Road Hospital, HO 22/70/72, Male Casebook (1918–21).
32. DRO: Records of Digby Mental Hospital (4034A), HZ/2/5/7, Papers: Private & Service Patients (1917–19).
33. George Orwell, 'England Your England', in: *Inside the Whale and Other Essays*, p. 89.
34. Andrew Saint, *London Suburbs*, p. 78.
35. Charles Booth, *Life And Labour of The People in London, Vol. II Streets and Population Classified* (Macmillan: 1892).
36. Roy Porter, *London: A Social History*, pp. 304–5.
37. The Summary Reception Order was the formal instrument in the 1890 Lunacy Act under which pauper lunatics were most commonly admitted to asylums. The Wandsworth Infirmary was constructed adjacent to the St John's Hill Workhouse in 1870. After the Wandsworth Board of Guardians created a new workhouse on another site in the borough in the 1880s, all the buildings on the St John's Hill site were integrated into the Infirmary. By contrast with Westminster, for example, the observation ward always belonged to the Infirmary establishment.
38. William Robinson, 'The Future of Service Patients in Mental Hospitals'.
39. They are all drawn from Pauper Lunatic Examination books and Receptions Orders for the Wandsworth Union, LMA series Wa.BG.114. 37 et seq. and Wa.BG.124.36 et seq.
39. Lord Moran, *The Anatomy of Courage*, pp. 13, 20, 22.

Chapter 14: Lunatic Officers
1. Siegfried Sassoon, *Diaries 1915–18*, p. 183.
2. TNA: PRO PIN 15/901.
3. M. Petter, ' "Temporary Gentlemen" in the Aftermath of the Great War: Rank, Status and the Ex-Officer Problem'. Government revenues from income taxes increased almost fourfold in 1920 from pre-war rates.
4. There is a list at TNA: PRO PIN 15/2023, 'Schedule of Ex-Officers Admitted to County and Borough Asylums' (1922), comprising 4 captains, 1 skipper (RNR) and 17 lieutenants.
5. LMA: Wa.BG. 114.49; Wa.BG.124.41.
6. TNA: PRO PIN 15/901; PIN 15/900.

7. TNA: PRO PIN 15/900–902.
8. PRO: PIN 15/902.
9. Ibid.
10. PRO: 15/901.
11. Barnwood had more than its share of shattered Blimps. 'Always regarded as rather stupid', Major F joined the Army in 1900 and went to India, spending his time riding, hunting and playing polo, returning a few years before the War 'to take up his duties as Squire of his Parish'. When war broke out he rejoined his regiment but after being sent to hospital for a 'nervous breakdown' found that his regiment no longer required him and started drinking very heavily. He continued drinking from then on, showing an increasing mental deterioration. When 'he defaecated through the night onto his bedroom carpet', his wife was ordered to remove him as 'a person unfit for retention as a Voluntary Boarder'. By contrast, Colonel T, another retired army officer who had taken to drink, consuming 'a bottle of whiskey and a bottle of port besides numerous casual drinks every day', showed more insight into his depression, making every effort to get well, after five weeks returning home by day to work in his garden [GRO: Records of Barnwood House Hospital (D3725), Box 108, Vols A & C, Voluntary Boarders' Registers].
12. The *Daily Mail* of Monday 24 May 1915 carried a large advertisement on the front page for the 'Superb Picture Record of the Year', a 'glorious record of the brave deeds that are building up and cementing the British Empire in a bond of blood-brotherhood', a 'concise and thrilling history of the . . . glowing stories of the great episodes of the War'. Inside was a rather less heroic tale of 'blood-brotherhood': 'The most appalling catastrophe in British railway history occurred on Saturday May 22nd, near Gretna, 8 miles north of Carlisle. Three trains collided, one a troop train from Edinburgh carrying 500 men of the 7th Royal Scots'. Said a soldier returning home on leave from Flanders: 'The scene that followed was far worse than anything I saw in the trenches'.
13. TNA: PRO PIN 26/21745; WO 374/32013; WO 95/4321, War Diary of 7th Battalion Royal Scots.
14. TNA: PRO PIN 26/21400; WO 374/14735.
15. Interview with Mr Frederick Forder, formerly Principal Nursing Officer, Old Manor Hospital, 21 July 1999. Needless to say, there were limits to the forbearance of the authorities. Lieutenant Montague A regularly pestered the War Office from the Old Manor with entreaties to be given a grant as a secret service agent. 'He is known to us as a shell-shocked officer suffering from delusions . . . he has for some time been a patient in a mental home . . . we suggest that his letter might, as on previous occasions, remain unanswered' (4 October 1938, on behalf of Colonel, M15). In the early 1950s, shortly after he had attacked Dr Taylor by rugby tackle, throwing him to the ground, he became the beneficiary of a pre-frontal leucotomy operation, a fashionable procedure at the time, with little or no result, for he remained 'deluded, garrulous, rambling and disconnected' [TNA: PRO WO 374/368; WRO: Records of Old Manor Hospital (J7), 190/90].
16. Maurice Craig, *Psychological Medicine*, p. 436.
17. TNA: PRO PIN 26/21156. Waltraud Ernst has also shown how in British India in the first half of the nineteenth century the consequences of becoming insane were far less drastic for an officer than they were for a common soldier (*Mad Tales from the Raj*, pp. 119–20).
18. GA: G4 (98, 118–19), letters, September 1922.
19. Ibid., G4 (10, 168), letters, November–December 1922.
20. Ibid., G61 (337, 226), letters, August 1927 and 1929 (n.d.).
21. When the Board of Control visited in 1931 there were 19 Service Patients in the hospital. Though the commissioners were impressed by the docility of the inmate community ('there was very little noise and we saw no signs of disturbance'), something was clearly amiss, for they recommended 'physical exercises as a means to the return of co-operation among patients. We believe that daily classes in drill would prove of real advantage to many patients'. The record does not reveal whether Ivor Gurney and his fellows became beneficiaries of this

counsel [Corporation of London Record Office, records of Dartford Mental Hospital, Medical Superintendent's Office, 1928–46].

22. *Annual Report of the Ex Services Welfare Society* (1927). Even before 1930 the ex-service residents of the Bow Arrow Villa at Dartford were voluntary boarders.

23. See, eg, GA: Box 4 (68), letter from Marion Scott to Dr Robinson, 28 January 1937.

24. GA: G61 (102).

25. Though the Ministry frequently imposed curbs on the capacity of Service Patients in asylums to accumulate savings, funeral expenses were rarely denied.

26. 'Before the war', remarks George Orwell, 'you were either a gentleman or not a gentleman, and if you were a gentleman you struggled to behave as such, whatever your income might be'. Even after the war there was a substantial constituency of 'shabby gentility' intent upon maintaining appearances, embracing 'most clergymen and schoolmasters . . . a sprinking of soldiers and sailors and a fair number of professional men and artists' (*The Road to Wigan Pier*, pp. 114–16).

Chapter 15: 'Hardening'

1. George Orwell, *The Collected Essays, Journalism and Letters: Volume 2*, p. 271.

2. LMA: So.BG.72.234.

3. TNA: PRO T 161/1054; T 161/228.

4. TNA: PRO PIN 15/594.

5. TNA: PRO T 161/1054; PIN 15/2027.

6. TNA: PRO: PIN 15/863. For a brief season the Ministry had succumbed to continental influences, for implicit here is a view of dementia praecox more in accord with the theories of Adolf Meyer and Eugen Bleuler (see chapter 8).

7. TNA: PRO T 161/228.

8. TNA: PRO T 161/228; PIN 15/2512; MH 51/696. A number of medical superintendents complained that the curtailment of the grant was a crass economy, calculated to cause discontent and deterioration in patients, but the Treasury was resolute: 'the great danger is not simply our having to find the extra 2/6d a week for these cases but the fact that this concession would lead to our giving allowances to the relatives on the very high pensioner scale. I think that we should therefore sit tight on the 2/6d question' (T161/228/S23312, 19 May 1924).

9. TNA: PRO PIN 26/20783. On 'moral imbecility' see Mathew Thomson, *The Problem of Mental Deficiency*, pp. 244–45.

10. TNA: PRO PIN 15/3161. Articles appeared in the popular press deriding the 'gratuitous unkindness' of the Ministry of Pensions in notifying an ex-soldier that he was suffering from 'confusional insanity' or some such condition ('A Lunatic at Large. Brutal methods of Pensions Ministry', *John Bull*, 3 September 1922).

11. Edward Shorter, *A History of Psychiatry*, p. 119.

12. Frederick Mott, *The Lancet*, 26 January 1918, p. 127.

13. *Royal Commission on Lunacy & Mental Disorder, Minutes of Evidence, Part 2* (London, 1926), q.16,935.

14. Sir Frederick Mott, speech at Queen's University Belfast, *Journal of Mental Science* (1924) vol. 70, p. 694.

15. William Robinson, 'The Future of Service Patients in Mental Hospitals'.

16. LMA: LCC.MIN.608, Asylums and Mental Deficiency Committee, Presented Papers 1920.

17. *John Bull*, 19 October 1918.

18. SFRO: Records of St Audry's Hospital, ID 507/A2/16, Dr James Whitwell in Annual Report, 1921.

19. Beatrice Webb, *Our Partnership*, (London, 1948, p. 431), quoted in G. Himmelfarb, *Poverty and Compassion*, p. 377. See also G. R. Searle, *The Quest For National Efficiency*, pp. 241–42.

20. Quoted in G. Himmelfarb, op. cit., pp. 366–67.
21. TNA: PRO PIN 15/57.
22. Ibid. Born in 1878, Hebb became D.G.M.S. in 1933. In 1937 he was appointed Hon. Physician to the King but it is not known whether he was given the opportunity to practise his 'hardening' techniques on poor stuttering George.
23. Ibid.
24. Ibid. On 'treatment and training colonies' for ex-servicemen who had contracted tuberculosis on active service during the Great War, see Linda Bryder, *Below the Magic Mountain*, pp. 157–66.
25. TNA: PRO: PIN 15/880.
26. TNA: PRO PIN 15/58.
27. Ibid. On facial disfigurement, see Andrew Bamji, 'Facial Surgery: The Patient's Experience'.
28. TNA: PRO PIN 15/56.
29. TNA: PRO PIN 15/58.
30. TNA: PRO PIN 15/58.
31. TNA: PRO PIN 15/2401, from notes on 'the constitutional factor' circulated in 1928.
32. TNA: PRO PIN 15/878; PIN 15/880.
33. By comparison with war psychotics only a very small proportion of war neurosis cases were awarded pensions on an assessment of 50% and above. It would obviously be grossly misleading to treat these disparities as a reliable index of the degree of suffering and disablement that was actually involved.

War Disability Pensions for Neurasthenia (1929 figures)

70–100%	2,878	4.9%
40–60%	6,843	11.7%
30% or less	48,681	83.4%
TOTAL	58,402	

[source: T. J. Mitchell and G. Smith, *Medical Services: Casualties and Medical Statistics of the Great War*, p. 349]. The official statistics for psychiatric disabilities should in any case be treated with some caution, and are almost certainly an underestimate of the real extent of psychological suffering, since the collection of data was frequently haphazard and inconsistent (Edgar Jones and Simon Wessely, 'Psychiatric Battle Casualties: An Intra- and Inter-war Comparison', p. 242). There were also other conditions which fell into this controverted zone, such as cases of epilepsy caused by trauma or concussion due to military service. Pointing out that many service epileptics were only assessed at 20 to 30% because their fits were relatively infrequent, a clinician questioned whether there had been adequate appreciation of their suffering since 'a man who has more than one fit in four weeks is just as handicapped in terms of holding a job as a man who has several fits a week'. Classify them as cases of Jacksonian Epilepsy, the same clinician proposed, the real McCoy in the epilepsy universe, and the injustice would be remedied, for they would then be eligible for 100% disability pensions. However, while admitting that 'the unemployability of epileptics was a matter of great difficulty', the Ministry studiously refused to extricate them from a limbo in which their hardships received only partial, and faltering, official recognition (TNA: PRO PIN 15/56).
34. WYAS: Records of Storthes Hall Hospital (C. 416), 1/285, Sub-Committe Minutes, 1922–24.
35. It was first mooted by the Minister of Pensions in February 1923: 'We, the Ministry, are going to start as an experiment separate arrangements for the treatment of selected certified cases of a hopeful type. . . . We shall begin tentatively with one or two small establishments' (*Parl. Deb.*, 20 Feb 1923, vol. CLXVII c. 986).
36. David Cannadine, *Class in Britain*, p. 128.
37. Ross McKibbin, *Class and Cultures: England 1918–51*, pp. 527, 529, 533.
38. Ross McKibbin, *The Ideologies of Class*, pp. 273, 284; David Cannadine, *Class in Britain*, p. 135.

39. DRO: Records of Digby Mental Hospital (4034A), HZ/2/5/8, Papers: Private & Service Patients. 'The notion that the working class have been absurdly pampered, hopelessly demoralised by doles, old-age pensions, free education, etc., is still widely held', wrote George Orwell (*The Road to Wigan Pier*, p. 124).

40. *Royal Commission on Lunacy & Mental Disorder, Minutes of Evidence, Part 2* (London,1926), q.16,935.

41. LMA: H12. CH. B.15.6, Records of Colney Hatch Asylum, Case Book: Male Patients Discharged in 1924.

42. The examples that follow are drawn from WYAS, Records of Storthes Hall Hospital (C.416): 5/157, 159–63 case sheets for Service Patients; 5/387 Daily Report Book; 5/832 Register of Discharges and Transfer of Service Patients (1924–31).

43. DRO, Records of Digby Mental Hospital (4034A), HZ. 2. 5. 7, Papers: Private & Service Patients.

44. F. W. Mott, *War Neuroses and Shell-Shock*, p. 88. As late as 1930 even the Director General of Medical Services at the Ministry, just returned from a tour of his fiefdom, was led to remark on the undue dependence of his medical superintendents on military role models and disciplinary practices, as though they had never demobilized, such as issuing 'routine' orders and posting them on the public notice boards, along with the names of malefactors to whom penalties had been applied (TNA: PRO PIN 15/2664).

45. Of the 417 admissions over the period 1924–31, just 7 were discharged 'recovered' and 108 'relieved', which included all those who made their own decisions over how they were going to lead their lives, as well as those who were either sent home or to other Ministry of Pensions rehabilitation establishments, accounting for roughly 30 per cent of the total. It is, perhaps, instructive to compare Storthes Hall with Red Star, the experimental hospital for trauma or shell shock patients, veterans of the First World War and of the Russian Civil War, that was established near Yalta in the Crimea in 1923 by a group of pioneering military psychiatrists. The clientele were not hard to come by, since in the Soviet Union there were an estimated 1.5 million veterans from the First World War alone who were too ill to work or even to resume family life. The bleak social and economic climate was, however, scarcely propitious for such an experiment and the inmates received little sympathy from the wider populace. Therapeutic hopes soon evaporated and in less than four years the venture was closed (Catherine Merridale, *Night of Stone*, pp. 148, 150–52).

Chapter 16: The Service Patients Between The Wars

1. James Joyce, *Ulysses*, pp. 83–85.

2. TNA: PRO MH 95/3, Board of Control: Whittingham Mental Hospital (1920–28).

3. *Royal Commission on Lunacy & Mental Disorder, Minutes of Evidence, Part 2* (London, 1926), qq. 14,250–14,251; 14,258–14,259.

4. LMA: H11.HLL.A7.7.1, Records of Hanwell Asylum, Medical Superintendent's Reports, 1923–5.

5. TNA: PRO PIN 15/2006. This is, of course, a very British pre-occupation. At the moment when he was widely perceived to be no longer king of his castle, the former prime minister John Major was famously imaged by the cartoonist Steve Bell wearing his underpants over his trousers.

6. WRO: Records of Old Manor Hospital (J7), 171/6, Admissions and Discharges (1920–42).

7. William Parry-Jones, *The Trade in Lunacy*, p. 43.

8. WRO: Records of Old Manor Hospital (J7), 190/83–84, Case Books, Male Patients (1923–52).

9. Ibid.: 190/77, Case Book, Male Patients (1913–35).

10. Ibid.

11. Ibid.: 190/89, Case Book, Male Patients (1954–60).

12. Interview with Mr Michael Bourke, 21 July 1999; interview with Mr Michael Heffernan, 15 June 1999.

13. Gertrude Smith, *The Old Manor Hospital* (Salisbury, ?1978, p. 66).

14. Of course, this was exactly in the spirit of the recommendations of the Lunacy Commissioners to the Royal Military Lunatic Asylum at Great Yarmouth in the mid-nineteenth century, see chapter 2, n. 4.

15. This paragraph draws upon an interview with Mr Frederick Forder, formerly Principal Nursing Officer, Old Manor Hospital, 21 July 1999.

16. Letter, *Morning Post*, 16 August 1917; TNA: PRO PIN 15/870.

17. Obituary of Sir Frederick Milner (1849–1931), *The Times*, 9 June 1931. Thus an editorial in the *Comrades' Journal*: 'read also the words of Sir Frederick Milner, known and revered throughout the length and breadth of the country for his unflaggingly persistent championship of disabled men, acknowledged even by Mr J. M. Hogge, M. P. to be the pioneer of all pension reforms in the war' (November 1918, p. 5).

18. TNA: PRO PIN 15/2499, Armistice Appeal, November 1922, and letter from Sir Frederick Milner to Sir John Butcher, 'Lest We Forget', 20 September 1923. For several decades, however, this was a society that dared not fully speak its name. Though the letterhead carried banners referring to the 'severer forms of neurasthenia and mental breakdown' or the 'war psychoses and neuroses', it was not until 1958 that 'mental' was admitted into the title and it became the Ex-Services Mental Welfare Society. On the work of the Society, see Roy Brook, *The Stress of Combat, The Combat of Stress*. In the early 1920s there was quite a lot of interaction with the British Legion which at this stage also was hotly adversarial. A resolution from the Paddington Branch of the Legion deplored the 'action of Parliament in allowing men who through their War Service have become mentally deranged being placed in Poor Law institutions and being treated as paupers and further demands that the Ministry of Pensions takes immediate steps to provide suitable accommodation for these heroes' (ESWS: Minutes, 29 August 1923). The most militant member of the executive committee of the Society was also an official representative of the metropolitan area of the Legion (ibid., 18 July 1923). Such militancy was shortlived, however, for the following year representatives of the Legion were induced publicly 'to express their satisfaction at the work done by the Ministry of Pensions in connection with mental disabilities' and to dissociate themselves from the recent sentiments of the Ex-Services Welfare Society (PRO: PIN 15/2499). At local levels, however, the British Legion continued to be active in assisting mentally disabled servicemen and their families.

19. TNA: PRO PIN 15/2499, 27 Sept 1923.

20. TNA: PRO PIN 15/2500. See also Ministry of Pensions position statement, 'The Ex-Services Welfare Society and their Appeal on Behalf of Mentally Broken Ex-Servicemen' (1924) [PIN 15/2499]. Though the state became more interventionist during and after the Great War, it also forged new alliances with the voluntary sector. Such intransigent rejection of charitable endeavour was by no means typical and was less an early intimation of welfare state collectivism than of a defensive posture in an area in which the state was very unsure of itself. On the evolving relationship between the state and the charitable sector see Geoffrey Finlayson *Citizen, State and Social Welfare in Britain*.

21. TNA: PRO PIN 15/749, Shorthand Notes of an Interview with the Ex-Services Welfare Society, 12 June 1926. Present: Lt Col. the Hon. G. F. Stanley, Sir Lisle Webb, Mr Ralph Millbourn (Chairman of Executive Committee), Dr E. Mapother (Hon Medical Consultant) and Mr E. Howard (General Secretary). That the Ministry thought it necessary to produce a verbatim record of the entire proceedings is sufficient indication of the light in which it viewed the Society. Though relations remained fractious for some time, in the early 1930s they became more co-operative.

22. *The Times*, 19 September 1924, 'Ex-Service Home at Beckenham'.

23. TNA: PRO PIN 15/2502.

24. To the chagrin of the Ministry the opening ceremony had attracted medical luminaries such as Sir Thomas Horder whose name was embossed on the Society's letterhead as a Vice-President throughout the interwar years. Sir Thomas explained the purpose of the Home and 'as a medical man' told supporters 'how very much he recognized that they were moving in the

right direction' (*The Times*, 23 October 1924, 'Ex-Service Home at Beckenham. Opening Ceremony'). On the equivocal politics and meanings of medical holism with its concern for the 'whole person', and for person-centred approaches, as a counter to medical and techno-logical reductionism, see Christopher Lawrence and George Weisz eds, *Greater than the Parts: Holism in Biomedicine*, esp. Christopher Lawrence, 'Still Incommunicable: Clinical Holists and Medical Knowledge in Interwar Britain' on Thomas Horder and his context.

25. The allegation that 21 ex-service nurses were in lunatic asylums was not strictly accurate for they were accorded the same privileges as officers and treated in private or registered hospi-tals. A few examples of these cases are in the PIN 26 series of individual war disability pension files in the Public Record Office.

26. TNA: PRO PIN 15/2498. Still in 1928 this elegiac tone was maintained: 'The slain of the great tragedy have passed out of the turmoil and the bewilderment. But what of those who fought and still live – but with clouded minds and shattered nerves – the 6000 in Asylums and the 30,000 Nervous Wrecks?'. The Society's appeals resonated with those (though by no means exclusively with those) who subscribed to the myth of the futile war analysed by Samuel Hynes in *A War Imagined*, chapter 21. A convert to the myth was Sir Philip Gibbs, the former war journalist, and for many years a Vice-President of the Society, who extolled the work of the Society in 'Wounded Souls. A Plea for Nerve-Strained Victims of the War' (*Overseas*, January 1927, pp. 39–42), to which the Ministry of Pensions took exception (PRO: PIN 2502).

27. TNA: PRO PIN 15/2499, letter from Professor George Robertson to the General Secretary, Ex Services Welfare Society, 12 July 1924.

28. TNA: PRO PIN 15/2499.

29. TNA: PRO PIN 15/2500; WO 363/L278. The authority of the asylum doctor in this period consisted largely in the unerring confidence with which he pronounced on the psychic demise of the mental patient. This was, of course, perfectly in the spirit of Emil Kraepelin's morbid outlook on mental illness (discussed in chapter 7). Of course, sometimes he was proved wrong with embarrassing consequences (see chapter 19, n. 4).

30. Peter Campbell, 'The History of the User Movement in the United Kingdom', p. 218. As to the Ministry of Pensions, it occupies a rather doleful place in the cultural imagination, impo-tent and dreary. Indicatively, the cuckolded husband in Graham Greene's novella, *The End of the Affair*, was a high-ranking civil servant at the Ministry. My thanks to Helen Bettin-son for pointing this out to me.

31. ESWS: Annual Reports. It was reported in June 1925 that a letter from Dr Mapother had been received stating that he was willing to examine the patients of the Society for £1.11.6 per consultation, this to take place in Harley St, and to support any claim for pensions, but his name was not to be used in the propaganda of the Society. The innovative role of the Society in the development of psychiatric rehabilitation in Britain has been rather underplayed, though it is acknowledged by Douglas Bennett, 'The Historical Development of Rehabilitation Services', p. 17. The Society was not alone in advocating alternatives to the asylum in this period. For an alternate tack, see Louise Westwood, 'A Quiet Revolution in Brighton'.

32. TNA: PRO PIN 67/48, letter from the Accountant General, October 1947.

33. TNA: PRO PIN 67/70.

34. TNA: PRO PIN 15/2006.

35. TNA: PRO PIN 15/2005.

36. TNA: PRO PIN 15/3161.

37. *21st Annual Report of the Ministry of Pensions*, 1937–8. The King concluded his message with the 'earnest hope that your sufferings may speedily be alleviated by the treatment you are now receiving'. It cannot have been lost on the Ministry that this sentiment would have provoked ribald laughter among the Service Patients in mental hospitals right across the land. Famously, David Wilkie's painting of 'Chelsea Pensioners Receiving the London Gazette Extraordinary of Thursday, June 22nd 1815, Announcing the Battle of Waterloo', exhibited at the Royal Academy in 1822 to enormous acclaim, proclaimed the inclusion of the veter-

ans of war in a national narrative, and in the catalogue Wilkie provided a brief entry for each pensioner detailing his military career. In actuality, however, this was an idealized vision of patriotic harmony, for only a minority of veterans were well cared for by the state, the majority were thrown into beggary, many of them radicalized or criminalized by their disillusionment (Nicholas Tromans, *David Wilkie*, pp. 89–91; Joany Hichberger, 'Old Soldiers', pp. 52–55).

38. ESWS: Minutes, 6 May 1937, re letter received from Sir Adair Hore, Ministry of Pensions.

39. TNA: PRO PIN 67/52. Though the Ministry was reluctant to admit it to enquirers, potentially quite a tidy sum might have been standing to the credit of a single Service Patient who had been in a mental hospital for some years. An inmate of Menston Mental Hospital in West Yorkshire, in 1927 Private Clifford Bartle was receiving a war disability pension of 40/- weekly. After the deduction of maintenance charges, and an allowance of 5/- for his aged father, there was a weekly balance of 4/10d. accumulating in his favour (PIN 67/54).

40. The medical superintendent of Devon County Mental Hospital at Exminster enquired in July 1924 if a Service Patient could build up credits against the future purchase of a musical instrument or a gramophone as a 'personal comfort'. But in the conception that the Ministry held of what a service lunatic in a public asylum merited for his 'comforts', there was no place for such 'superior' enjoyments (TNA: PRO PIN 15/3159; PIN 67/47). In certain respects the situation of war pensioners in mental institutions was a continuation of the indignities and injustices they had endured on active service with the army, for here also the soldier was maintained by the state, and army pay (roughly 3/6d. per week for the private soldier after an allowance had been sent home to the family) was really only pocket money (and deemed inadequate as that) rather than a proper wage for a job done. As Ilan Bet-El explains, there was a widespread feeling of rights denied among rank-and-file soldiers in the Great War who thought of themselves as workers in uniform with the job description of fighting (*Conscripts*, pp. 139–40).

41. T. H. Marshall, *Citizenship and Social Class*, p. 36.

42. TNA: PRO PIN 67/70.

43. TNA: PRO PIN 67/73.

44. TNA: PRO PIN 67/69.

45. TNA: PRO PIN 67/60.

46. TNA: PRO PIN 67/61. Already on the eve of the Armistice the question had been earnestly posed of how to 'convince the disabled man that he is the property of the government' (Major Robert Mitchell, Ministry of Pensions, *Report of the Inter-Allied Conference on the After-care of Disabled Men*, London, Ministry of Pensions, 1918, p. 73).

47. TNA: PRO PIN 67/70.

48. Ibid.

49. Having joined the NHS, the Old Manor became part of the Knowle Group of Hospitals and one quickly has the impression that the surviving Service Patients rather stood in the way of the spirit of militant modernization that was then abroad. 'The general planning', the Annual Report for 1954 intoned, 'is handicapped by the nature of the existing patient population', for recent and recovering cases must be catered for 'in a hospital already populated with chronic private and ex-private patients, many of whom belong to the upper age groups'.

50. TNA: PRO PIN 15/2401.

51. Ibid.

52. TNA: PRO WO 32/2949.

53. TNA: PRO PIN 15/2401.

54. TNA: PRO PIN 15/2399; PIN 15/2401. On the deliberations of the Horder Committee see also Ben Shephard, *A War of Nerves*, pp. 166–68; and idem, ' "Pitiless Psychology": The Role of Prevention in British Military Psychiatry in the Second World War'.

55. TNA: PRO PIN 15/2401. Citing the total number of around 13,000 pensions for war psychosis which had been awarded by 31 March 1929, it was contended that the war had not

increased the general incidence of insanity [ibid.] But this was a spurious basis on which to mount such a claim, for the figure of 13,000 comprised not the whole assembly of mentally disordered ex-servicemen of the Great War, but precisely those ex-servicemen whose conditions had been agreed by the Ministry after extensive examinations to have been caused or aggravated by their war service. By the Ministry's own admission there was a considerable population of ex-servicemen in mental hospitals for whom liability had not been accepted, and even if the estimate of around 10,000 advanced by the Ex-Services Welfare Society was somewhat exaggerated, it was certainly sizeable (see chapter 10 n. 23). Now that at this late date the Ministry was intent upon demolishing the carefully erected fence that separated these two groups, it follows that it is this total population which would have to be taken into account.

56. Hubert Bond, 'Obituary of T. E. Knowles Stansfield', *Journal of Mental Science* (1939), 85, pp. 1131–39.

57. ESWS: Minutes, 7 September 1939. Despite all this tough talk, once hostilities started concessions were soon made, and more war pensions for psychiatric disabilities were awarded during the Second World War than some have supposed (Edgar Jones et al., 'War Pensions [1900–1945]: Changing Models of Psychological Understanding', p. 377). Ironically, such was the inconsistency in the official position that in December 1940 it was decided to re-introduce the Service Patient scheme for 'New War Lunatics', as they were known, the Ministry of Pensions extolling its virtues to the Treasury (TNA: PRO PIN 15/2511). By contrast with the Great War, however, the authorities maintained a firm control over the terrain of war psychosis and, far from being a barnstorming gathering of military malcontents of one kind and another, Service Patients from the 'New War' formed a very select club.

58. TNA: PRO PIN 15/2987.

Coda: Connie and Alex

1. DRO: Records of Digby Mental Hospital (4034A), UH.4.4., Service Patients (1917–40).
2. LRO: Records of Whittingham Hospital, HRW 3/3–4, Medical Superintendent's Reports.
3. WRO: Records of Old Manor Hospital (J7), 190/83, Case Book, Male Patients (1923–52); 195/1, bundles of letters (1922–50).

PART VI MAD ACTIVISTS OF THE GREAT WAR

1. Peter Campbell, 'The History of the User Movement in the United Kingdom', pp. 219–20. For two decades and more until it closed, Campbell was an intermittent inmate of Napsbury Psychiatric Hospital, and he has written a fine poem placing himself and his fellows in the line of 'the battered boys from Flanders' who descended upon Napsbury between 1915 and 1919:

> Their names are scratched within the linen store.
> The clothes you cadge are still the clothes they wore.
> ('Night and Morning', in: John Rety ed., *In the Company of Poets*).

Chapter 17: Independent Lives

1. Ross McKibbin, *Classes and Cultures*, p. 529.
2. On citizenship between the wars see Abigail Beach, 'Potential for Participation: Health Centres and the Idea of Citizenship c. 1920–1940'; Mark Harrison, 'Sex and the Citizen Soldier: Health, Morals and Discipline in the British Army during the Second World War'; and Mathew Thomson, 'Constituting Citizenship: Mental Deficiency, Mental Health and Human Rights in Inter-War Britain'.
3. John Pickstone, 'Production, Community and Consumption: the Political Economy of Twentieth Century Medicine'.
4. TNA: PRO PIN 15/; Llewellyn J. Llewellyn and A. Bassett Jones, *Pensions and the Principles of their Evaluation*, p. 47. On the rhetoric of work therapy, and its failure to deliver on its promise in the aftermath of the war, see Jeffrey Reznick, 'Work-Therapy and the Disabled British Soldier in Great Britain in the First World War'.

5. J. R. Lord, *Mental Hospitals and the Public: The Need for Closer Co-Operation*, pp. 2, 24.
6. Jose Harris, *Private Lives, Public Spirit*, p. 13.
7. Alison Light, *Forever England*, p. 8. Joanna Bourke also remarks on domesticity as an ideal (*Dismembering the Male*, p. 23). As David Cannadine instances, the icon of 'homeliness' in this period was premier Stanley Baldwin's pipe (*In Churchill's Shadow*, pp. 166–67).
8. 'The Government Actuary's enquiry shows that the mortality of 1914–18 War Pensioners in the eight years 1954–61 was about 16 per cent higher than that of the general male population of comparable age in Great Britain' (TNA: PRO PIN 67/99).
9. See chapter 6, n. 45.
10. On the deeply ambiguous politics of 'community care' across the twentieth century see especially Mathew Thomson, *The Problem of Mental Deficiency*, pp. 149–79, and also Peter Barham, 'From the Asylum to the Community: the Mental Patient in Postwar Britain'.
11. Nelson, case no 1.
12. Nelson, case no 2.
13. Nelson, case no 12.
14. TNA: PRO PIN 26/16799.
15. TNA: PRO PIN 26/16791.
16. TNA: PRO PIN 26/16982.
17. Nelson, case no. 16.

Chapter 18: War Psychosis Pentathlons
1. 'Survey of War Pensions from 1916' in: *Nineteenth Annual Report of the Ministry of Pensions* (London, 1937).
2. DRO: Records of Digby Mental Hospital (4034A), HZ/ 2/ 5/ 8, Papers: Private & Service Patients.
3. *Royal Commission on Lunacy & Mental Disorder, Minutes of Evidence, Part 2* (London, 1926), q. 12,547.
4. TNA: PRO PIN 26/16880.
5. Of course, these are still very much the concerns of mental health system survivors today. See the Mental Health Testimony Archive, a video-based oral history of mental health care from the point of view of those who have experienced it, covering the years 1925–85 but with a primary emphasis on the post-war period, in the National Sound Archive at the British Library (C905). Some of the links between the generations are considered in Peter Barham, 'The English Mental Patient in the Twentieth Century: Continuity and Discontinuity', unpublished paper, Ango-Dutch-German Workshop on Social Psychiatry and Ambulant Care in the 20th Century, July 2002, Wellcome Trust Centre for the History of Medicine at University College London.
6. TNA: PRO PIN 26/16763.
7. TNA: PRO PIN 26/20827. In actuality as a recreation cycling cut across classes, both the middle and working classes taking it up enthusiastically in the interwar period, with 1.5 million cycles sold annually (Ross McKibbin, *Classes and Cultures*, p. 379).
8. TNA: PRO T 161/1019.
9. Nelson, case no 7. Though complaints about the thickness of mental hospital bread were becoming quite common, asylum authorities generally observed that patients were partial to the thick slice. 'The bread given the patients for tea seemed to be very thickly cut', observed a delegation of Guardians who visited Long Grove in 1920, 'and considering it is served to old and young of all classes alike we suggest that attention be drawn to this matter'. As far as the medical superintendent was concerned, however, the patients were all of one class. That was just how the patients liked it, he rejoined (LMA: LCC.MIN.1183).

Chapter 19: Caring: Familes and Doctors
1. James Joyce, *Ulysses*, p. 486.
2. Nelson, case no. 15. On processes of mourning, and coping with loss, after the Great War, see Jay Winter, *Sites of Memory, Sites of Mourning*, esp. chapter 2, 'Communities in Mourning'.

3. Nelson, case no. 3.

4. Samuel Hynes, *A War Imagined*, p. 375.

5. If the insanities of the Great War brought a new urgency to the debate about untenable marriages, they also punctured complacent assumptions about 'incurable insanity'. The hope, or alternately the fear, that the dead might after all awaken was a period preoccupation, and by no means peculiar to the Ministry of Pensions. These issues are cleverly enacted in the tensions and conflicts of three generations of women around an ex-serviceman who has been an asylum inmate since the war ('shell-shock') in Clemence Dane's play, *A Bill of Divorcement*, which opened to critical acclaim in 1921. Presciently set in a utopic future in the 1930s in which the recommendations of the Royal Commission have been enacted, the action turns on Margaret Fairfield's decision finally to divorce her husband, Hilary, and remarry. She is encouraged to overcome her scruples by her progressive daughter Sydney: 'If father had been dead fifteen years, would you say "I hope I'm doing right?" And he *is* dead. His mind is dead. You know you've done all you can'; and by the family doctor preaching the virtues of expedience: '... call it common sense. If a man can't live his normal life, it's as if he were dead'. Just a week before the nuptials, however, Hilary escapes from the asylum and returns home, not recovered exactly, but by no means mad. 'Ah, we cry after the dead', snorts Miss Fairfax, the elderly aunt 'but I've always wondered what their welcome back would be'. The asylum doctor, the hapless Rogers ('inexplicable ... all precautions taken'), is berated for having deceived the family ('the doctors said incurable'), his authority in tatters. In the event the new marriage goes ahead and Sydney contracts to look after her nerve-stricken father. This is not exactly a triumph for Sydney's liberal values, for now she embraces her aunt's wisdom: '... we're nervy all of us, we're nervy. Your poor father would have been no worse than the rest of us if it hadn't been for the war'. Sydney, the creature of the New Ways ('I'm not nineteenth century'), is thrown back on herself: 'Insanity! A thing you can hand on! And I told Kit [her fiancé] that it was shell–shock!'. With their gender-indeterminate names, Sydney and Hilary are interchangeable and it falls to the family doctor to spell out the eugenic moral: 'Why, face it man! One of you must suffer. Which is it to be? The useful or the useless? The whole or the maimed? The healthy woman with her life before her or the man whose children ought never to have been born?' Daddy narrowly escapes a fate as a career lunatic only to face a reckoning with his biological destiny as an incubus on the social body. The idea of 'incurable insanity' has not so much been disposed of as rebranded more in tune with the times [See also discussion in Samuel Hynes, *A War Imagined*, pp. 375–78].

6. Liddle Collection, Leeds University Archive, letter from Margaret C to Peter Liddle, 20 September 1994 [General Aspects/Shell Shock/Item 12].

7. This section is based on interviews with John, Maurice and Roy H, and an e-mail exchange with George H, in February and March 1998. I gratefully acknowledge their kindness in sharing with me their memories of their father.

8. GRO: Records of Horton Road Hospital (HO22), 64/2, Medical Register (1919–31).

9. The official position was that claims had to be made within 'seven years of discharge or within seven years after 31 August 1921', the official date for the termination of the war, whichever date was earlier (TNA: PRO PIN 67/48).

10. TNA: PRO PIN 26/16813.

11. On the spiritualist revival see Jay Winter, *Sites of Memory, Sites of Mourning*, pp. 54–77.

12. Nelson, case no. 5.

13. LRO: Records of Whittingham Hospital, HRW 12/115, Reception Orders.

14. Until after the Second World War, panel (state insurance) patients were not given a chair when they saw the doctor and had to stand throughout the consultation (Julian Hart, 'Going to the Doctor', p. 552).

15. Julian Hart observes: 'It is hard for later generations to appreciate the hostility of almost all British GPs in the first two-thirds of this century to any psychiatric diagnoses other than the gross institutionalized end-stage psychoses they had seen as students' ('Going to the Doctor', p. 553).

16. Nelson, case no 17.

17. Manfred Bleuler, *The Schizophrenic Disorders*, p. 417; see also, Peter Barham, *Schizophrenia and Human Value*, p. 44.
18. Nelson, case no 19.
19. Nelson, case no 20.

Chapter 20: Futures
1. On the genre of the case history, see Jonathan Andrews, 'Case Notes, Case Histories and the Patient's Experience of Insanity'.
2. Letter, *The Times*, 2 February 1921.
3. DRO: Records of Digby Mental Hospital (4034A), HZ/ 2/ 5/ 8, Papers: Private & Service Patients.
4. Nelson, case no 4.
5. Nelson, case no 6.
6. On the history and politics of asylum closures, see Peter Barham, *Closing the Asylum*.

Coda: The Captain's Valedictory Letter
1. The records of Captain Haws are at TNA: PRO PIN 26/ 21745.
2. Elaine Showalter, 'Hysteria, Feminism and Gender', p. 335.

Afterword: Remembering the Forgotten Lunatics
1. James Joyce, *Ulysses*, p. 219.
2. James Joyce, *Ulysses*, p. 353.
3. LMA: H12. CH. A. 8. 2.
4. Stanley Hauerwas, *Suffering Presence*, p. 26.
5. See Michael Ignatieff, *The Needs of Strangers*; Lynn Hollen Lees, *The Solidarities of Strangers*.
6. Mathew Thomson, *The Problem of Mental Deficiency*, pp. 52–53. In the event, a compromise was reached whereby current residents of asylums or prisons were excluded but reinstated once they were released.
7. As Alasdair MacIntyre remarks, 'it is only in the context of human relationships that acknowledging the pains and griefs and hopes and expectations of others makes sense. Hence our knowledge of others – or our lack of it – depends on what the form of our moral relationships are' (quoted in Peter Barham, *Schizophrenia and Human Value*, p. 50).
8. For his services in connection with soldiers suffering from shell shock and mental disability, Maurice Craig (1866–1935) was awarded a CBE in 1919 and a knighthood in 1921. Right up to his death, he was a leading light in the National Council for Mental Hygiene, one of the constituent organizations to merge into the National Association for Mental Health in 1942, which he had helped to found in 1922, becoming chairman in 1928. According to his obituarist, Craig used to say that 'having worked for many years within walls of a mental hospital, he was devoting the rest of his life to keeping people from becoming candidates for those institutions . . . he felt increasingly that the preventive aspect of mental disorder was the main one' (*The Lancet* [1935], 1, 119–20).
9. See Mark Micale and Paul Lerner eds, *Traumatic Pasts*; Ian Hacking, *Rewriting the Soul*; and Allan Young, *The Harmony of Illusions*.
10. Quoted in Arthur Marwick, *War and Social Change in the Twentieth Century*, p. 82.
11. Reading Tom Main's account of the famous Northfield experiment, and how the idea of the therapeutic community burst upon him ('one evening I suddenly realized the *whole* community, all staff as well as all patients, needed to be viewed as a troubled larger system which needed treatment'), we appreciate that this is the kind of insight that might have reached out to the 'mad saluters' of Storthes Hall, the Old Manor and elsewhere, many of whom were palpably reflecting the unacknowledged troubles of a larger system ('The Concept of the Therapeutic Community', p. 136).
12. Arthur Marwick, *War and Social Change in the Twentieth Century*, p. 92.
13. Millais Culpin, *Medicine: And the Man*, p. 54. The ex-servicemen I have been discussing

are drawn almost entirely from the 5.7 million men who passed through the British Army during the Great War, including wartime enlistments of 4.9 million, representing 22.11 per cent of the male population of the United Kingdom. These figures do not include enlistments from the dominions and colonies in the forces of the empire, a total of 2,881,786, nor the participation of American forces (Ian Beckett, 'The Nation in Arms 1914–18', p. 13). On Australian psychiatric casualties see A. G. Butler, *The Australian Army Medical Services in the War of 1914–18*, vol. III, chapter XVI, 'The War-Damaged Soldier'. On the fortunes of Anzac veterans after the war, see Alistair Thomson, *Anzac Memories: Living with the Legend*, and Stephen Garton, *The Cost of War: Australians Return*. On Canada, see Desmond Morton and Glenn Wright, *Winning the Second Battle*; and on American veterans, Caroline Cox, 'Invisible Wounds: The American Legion, Shell-Shocked Veterans, and American Society, 1919–24'. In India the hospitality of British war pension arrangements was extended only to British servicemen and to officers in the Indian Army. On the administration of imperial war pensions in India see TNA: PRO PIN 15/ 737–742. It is apparent that quite a number of Indian ordinary rankers who had served the imperial cause were admitted to asylums. For the provinces of Madras, Bombay, Bengal, United Provinces, Punjab, Burma, Bibar and Orissa, Central Provinces and Berar, and Assam, there were less than 20 service admissions per annum immediately before the Great War, but between 1914 and 1920 there were 915 in all, 346 in 1918, the majority probably in the Punjab (*Parliamentary Papers*, Accounts & Papers, 13, Statistical Tables 1924–5, Vol XVIII, table 195). Though some Indian other rankers were awarded disability pensions by the Indian government, the fate of this group is unknown.

14. Kirby Farrell, *Post-Traumatic Culture*, pp. 2, 21.
15. See also Allan Young (*The Harmony of Illusions*, p. 212) on patient satisfaction with the diagnosis of post-traumatic stress disorder (PTSD).
16. TNA: PRO WO 364/ 380.
17. 'In truth, post-combat syndromes are inevitably the result of an interaction between predisposing, pre-enlistment factors and the experience of military service. As a result, the emphasis put on either variable becomes yet another barometer of attitudes to psychological injury – a hostile climate stressing pre-service constitution and a sympathetic one stressing the traumatic exposure' (Edgar Jones et al., 'War Pensions (1900–1945): Changing Models of Psychological Understanding', p. 377). The ineluctable ambiguity that I accent here is, perhaps, in the spirit of Ian Hacking's argument about 'an indeterminacy in the past' ('Indeterminacy in the past').
18. Writes Allan Young: 'the traumatic memory is a man-made object. It originates in the scientific and clinical discourses of the nineteenth century; before that time, there is unhappiness, despair and disturbing recollections, but no traumatic memory in the sense that we know it today' (*The Harmony of Illusions*, p. 141). Ian Hacking, 'Indeterminacy in the past', casts a sceptical eye on the claims and counter-claims in the debate about whether historical actors, such as the soldiers executed for desertion in the Great War, can be said to have been suffering from PTSD. The dynamic relations between symptoms, diagnostic labels and culture in the reporting and interpretation of post-combat syndromes are explored in a recent study: Edgar Jones and Simon Wessely, 'Psychiatric Battle Casualties: an Intra- and Interwar Comparison'; and Edgar Jones et al., 'Post-combat Syndromes from the Boer War to the Gulf War'.
19. Robert M. Young, 'The House of Trauma' (2001), unpublished paper, Centre for Psychotherapeutic Studies, University of Sheffield, accessible at: www.human-nature.com
20. See Ilana Bet-El, *Conscripts: Lost Legions of the Great War*, pp. 179–209. Seth Koven draws attention to the 'dialectic between remembering and forgetting, presence and absence, in the language of war', describing how after the Great War the 'British state and society constructed institutions and discourses' that permitted people 'simultaneously to remember and forget, depending on political circumstances' different classes of victims ('Remembering and Dismemberment: Crippled Children, Wounded Soldiers and the Great War in Britain', p. 1169). But why is it good to remember lost groups or communities such as the forgotten lunatics?

The memorializing of the dead and the creation of a community of memory, argues Avishai Margalit in *The Ethics of Memory*, helps to underwrite the solidarities to which we aspire in our current projects.

21. Reporting on the remaining 62 Service Patients in Long Grove Mental Hospital in November 1946, the medical inspector for the Ministry of Pensions wrote: 'The remainder of our patients from the Great War are, as we must expect, becoming more and more enfeebled and deteriorated. Nearly half of them are now returned as unemployable, while half of their number now receive neither visits nor letters from relations' (LMA: LCC.MIN.1196).

22. See, eg, Niall Ferguson, *The Pity of War*, p. 437.

23. Quoted in Charles Doherty, 'The War Art of C. R. W. Nevinson', p. 56; and Jonathan Black, 'A Curious, Cold Intensity: C. R. W. Nevinson as a War Artist', pp. 34–35.

24. Quoted in Jonathan Black, op. cit., p. 34.

25. From a letter to Major Lee but never sent, quoted in Charles Doherty, op. cit., p. 58.

26. From a later newspaper interview, quoted in Jonathan Black, op. cit., p. 35.

27. James Joyce, *Ulysses*, p. 201.

28. Writing about the historiography of the Irish Famine, Colm Tóibín remarks: 'What interests me here is the resonance of the names, all common in Ireland now. John Healy's two daughters, or Mary Connell, found dead by a rick of turf: the names are enough to allow you to imagine them, to think you may have known them. Pondering the names makes you wonder about the whole enterprise of historical writing itself, how little it tells us, how brittle are the analyses of administrative systems in the face of what we can imagine for ourselves just by seeing a name with a fact beside it' (*The Irish Famine*, p. 14).

Bibliography

Adams, R. J. Q. and Poirier, Philip *The Conscription Controversy in Great Britain 1900–18* (London, 1987)

Andrews, Jonathan 'Case Notes, Case Histories and the Patient's Experience of Insanity at Gartnavel Royal Asylum, Glasgow, in the Nineteenth Century', *Social History of Medicine* (1998), 11, 2, pp. 255–81

────── 'Letting Madness Range: Travel and Mental Disorder c. 1700–1900' in: Richard Wrigley and George Revill eds, *Pathologies of Travel* (Amsterdam, 2000)

Andrews, Jonathan; Briggs, Asa; Porter, Roy; Tucker, Penny; and Waddington, Keir *The History of Bethlem* (London, 1997)

Baldwin, Peter *The Politics of Social Solidarity: Class Bases of the European Welfare State 1875–1975* (Cambridge, 1990)

Bamji, Andrew 'Facial Surgery: The Patient's Experience', in: Cecil, H. and Liddle, Peter eds, *Facing Armageddon: The First World War Experienced* (London, 1996)

Barham, Peter *Schizophrenia and Human Value: Chronic Schizophrenia, Science and Society* (London, 1995, 2nd edition)

────── *Closing the Asylum: The Mental Patient in Modern Society* (Harmondsworth, 1997, second edition)

────── 'Manfred Bleuler and the Understanding of Psychosis' in: Ellwood, J. ed., *Psychosis: Understanding and Treatment* (London, 1995)

────── 'From the Asylum to the Community: the Mental Patient in Postwar Britain' in: Gijswijt-Hofstra, Marijke and Porter, Roy eds, *Cultures of Psychiatry and Mental Healthcare in Postwar Britain and the Netherlands* (Amsterdam, 1998)

────── 'Mental Deficiency and the Democratic Subject', *History of the Human Sciences* (1999), 12, pp. 111–14

────── and Barnes, Marian 'The Citizen Mental Patient' in: Eastman, Nigel and Peay, Jill eds, *Law without Enforcement: Integrating Mental Health and Justice* (Oxford, 1999)

Barker, Pat *Regeneration* (London, 1995)

Barrett, Robert *The Psychiatric Team and the Social Definition of Schizophrenia: An Anthropological Study of Person and Illness* (Cambridge, 1996)

Bartlett, Peter *The Poor Law of Lunacy: The Administration of Pauper Lunatics in Mid-Nineteenth Century Britain* (Leicester, 1999)

────── 'The Asylum, the Workhouse, and the Voice of the Insane Poor in 19th Century England', *Internat. Journal of Law and Psychiatry* (1998), 21, pp. 421–32

────── 'The Asylum and the Poor Law: The Productive Alliance' in: Melling, J. and Forsythe, B. eds, *Insanity, Institutions and Society, 1800–1914* (London, 1999)

Bartrip, P. W. J. *Workmen's Compensation in Twentieth Century Britain* (Aldershot, 1987)

Beach, Abigail 'Potential for Participation: Health Centres and the Idea of Citizenship c. 1920–1940' in: Lawrence, C. and Mayer, Anna-K. eds, *Regenerating England: Science, Medicine and Culture in Inter-War Britain* (Amsterdam, 2000)

Bean, Philip *Compulsory Admissions to Mental Hospitals* (Chichester, 1980)

Beckett, Ian F. W. *The First World War: The Essential Guide to Sources in the UK National Archives* (Public Record Office, 2002)

—— 'The Nation in Arms, 1914–18' in: Beckett, I. and Simpson, K. eds, *A Nation in Arms: A Social Study of the British Army in the First World War* (Manchester, 1985)

Beer, Gillian *Open Fields: Science in Cultural Encounter* (Oxford, 1996)

Bennett, Douglas 'The Historical Development of Rehabilitation Services' in: Fraser N. Watts and Douglas Bennett eds, *Theory and Practice of Psychiatric Rehabilitation* (Chichester, 1983)

Berrios, G. E. 'Historical aspects of psychoses: 19thC issues', *British Medical Bulletin* (1987), 43, pp. 484–98

Bet-El, Ilana *Conscripts: Lost Legions of the Great War* (Stroud, Glouc., 1999)

Black, Eugene C. *The Social Politics of Anglo-Jewry 1880–1920* (Oxford, 1988)

Black, Jonathan 'A Curious, Cold Intensity: C. R. W. Nevinson as a War Artist' in: *C. R. W. Nevinson: The Twentieth Century* (London, 2000)

Bleuler, Manfred *The Schizophrenic Disorders: Long-Term Patient and Family Studies* (New Haven, 1978)

Bloom, Harold *Shakespeare: The Invention of the Human* (London, 1999)

Bogacz, T. 'War Neurosis and Cultural Change in England 1914–22: the Work of the War Office Committee of Enquiry into "Shell-Shock"', *Journal of Contemporary History* (1989), 24, pp. 227–56

Bolderson, Helen *Social Security, Disability and Rehabilitation: Conflicts in the Development of Social Policy* (London, 1991)

Booth, Charles *Life and Labour of the People in London, First Series, Vol. I: Poverty* (London, 1891)

Booth, Charles *Life And Labour of The People in London, Vol. II: Streets and Population Classified* (London, 1892)

Bourke, Joanna *Dismembering the Male: Men's Bodies, Britain and the Great War* (London, 1996)

Bourne, John 'The British working man in arms' in: Cecil, Hugh and Liddle, Peter H. eds, *Facing Armageddon* (London, 1996)

Bowlby, John *Personality and Mental Illness* (London, 1940)

Bradley, Harriet 'The Seduction of the Archive: Voices Lost and Found', *History of the Human Sciences* (1999), 12, 2, pp. 107–22

Brittain, Vera *Chronicle of Youth: Great War Diary 1913–1917*, ed. Bishop, Alan (London, 1981)

Brodersen, Momme *Walter Benjamin: A Biography* (London, 1996)

Bronowski, Jacob *The Man Without a Mask* (London, 1947)

Brook, Roy *The Stress of Combat, The Combat of Stress* (Brighton, 1999)

Brown, Peter *Poverty and Leadership in the Later Roman Empire* (Hanover, New Hampshire, 2001)

Bryder, Linda *Below the Magic Mountain: A Social History of Tuberculosis in Twentieth-Century Britain* (Oxford, 1988)

Burleigh, Michael *Death and Deliverance: 'Euthanasia' in Germany 1900–1945* (Cambridge, 1994)

Butler, A. G. 'Moral and Mental Disorders in the War of 1914–18' in: *The Australian Army Medical Services in the War of 1914–18*, Vol. III (Canberra, 1943)

Caesar, Adrian *Taking it Like a Man: Suffering, Sexuality and the War Poets* (Manchester 1993)

Campbell, Peter 'The History of the User Movement in the United Kingdom' in: Heller, Tom; Reynolds, Jill; Gomm, Roger; Muston, Rosemary and Pattison, Stephen eds, *Mental Health Matters* (London, 1996)

—— 'The service user/survivor movement' in: Newnes, Craig; Holmes, Guy and Dunn, Calizie eds, *This is Madness: A Critical Look at Psychiatry and the Future of Mental Health Services* (Ross-on-Wye, 1999)

Cannadine, David *In Churchill's Shadow: Confronting the Past in Modern Britain* (London, 2002)

Cecil, Hugh and Liddle, Peter H. eds, *Facing Armageddon* (London, 1996)

—— *Class in Britain* (New Haven, 1998)

———— 'War and Death, Grief and Mourning' in: Whaley, Joachim ed., *Mirrors of Mortality: Studies in the Social History of Death* (London, 1981)

Cobb, Richard *Reactions to the French Revolution* (Oxford, 1972)

Cohen, Deborah *The War Come Home: Disabled Veterans in Britain and Germany, 1914–39* (Berkeley, Calif., 2001)

Cooter, Roger *Surgery and Society in Peace and War: Orthopaedics and the Organization of Modern Medicine, 1880–1948* (London, 1993)

———— 'War and Modern Medicine' in: Bynum, W. F. and Porter, R. eds, *Encyclopaedia of Modern Medicine* (London, 1993)

———— 'Malingering in Modernity: Psychological Scripts and Adversarial Encounters during the First World War', in: Cooter, R., Harrison, M., and Sturdy, S. eds, *War, Medicine and Modernity* (Stroud, Glouc., 1999)

———— and Sturdy, S. 'Of War, Medicine and Modernity: An Introduction' in: Cooter, R., Harrison, M., and Sturdy, S. eds, *War, Medicine and Modernity* (Stroud, Glouc., 1999)

Corns, Cathryn and Hughes-Wilson, John *Blindfold and Alone: British Military Executions in the Great War* (London, 2001)

Cox, Caroline 'Invisible Wounds: The American Legion, Shell-Shocked Veterans, and American Society, 1919–24' in: Micale, Mark and Lerner, Paul eds, *Traumatic Pasts: History, Psychiatry and Trauma in the Modern Age, 1870–1930* (Cambridge, 2001)

Craig, Maurice *Psychological Medicine: A Manual on Mental Diseases for Practitioners and Students* (London, 1912, second edition)

———— *Nerve Exhaustion* (London, 1922)

———— and Beaton, Thomas *Psychological Medicine: A Manual on Mental Diseases for Practitioners and Students* (London, 1926, fourth edition)

Crammer, John *Asylum History* (London, 1990)

———— 'Extraordinary Deaths of Asylum Inpatients during the 1914–18 War', *Medical History* (1992), 36, pp. 430–41

Crossick, Geoffrey *The Lower Middle Class in Britain 1870–1914* (London, 1976)

———— 'Metaphors of the middle: the discovery of the petite bourgeoisie 1880–1914', *Transactions of the Royal Historical Society* (1994), 6, pp. 251–79

Crowther, M. A. *The Workhouse System: 1834–1929* (London, 1981)

Culpin, Millais *The Nervous Patient* (London, 1924)

———— *Medicine: And the Man* (London, 1927)

———— 'An Autobiography', *Occupational Psychology* (1949), 23, pp. 1–13

Dane, Clemence *A Bill of Divorcement* (London, 1921)

Doherty, Charles 'The War Art of C. R. W. Nevinson' in: *Imperial War Museum Review No. 8* (London, 1993)

Dungan, Myles *'They Shall Not Grow Old': Irish Soldiers and the Great War* (Dublin, 1997)

Dworkin, Ronald *Sovereign Virtue* (Cambridge, Mass., 2000)

Edgerton, David 'Liberal militarism and the British State' *New Left Review* (1991), 185, pp. 138–69

Eghigian, Greg A. 'The German Welfare State as a Discourse of Trauma' in: Micale, Mark and Lerner, Paul eds, *Traumatic Pasts: History, Psychiatry and Trauma in the Modern Age, 1870–1930* (Cambridge, 2001)

Ellenberger, Henri F. *The Discovery of the Unconscious: The History and Evolution of Dynamic Psychiatry* (New York, 1970)

Engstrom, Eric J. and Weber, Matthias M. 'Emil Kraepelin (1856–1926)' in: Freeman, H. ed., *A Century of Psychiatry* (London, 1999)

Ernst, Waltraud *Mad Tales from the Raj: The European Insane in British India 1800–1858* (London, 1991)

Farrell, Kirby *Post-traumatic Culture: Injury and Interpretation in the Nineties* (Baltimore, 1998)

Ferguson, Niall *The Pity of War* (London, 1998)

Finlayson, Geoffrey *Citizen, State and Social Welfare in Britain 1830–1990* (Oxford, 1994)

Fitzgerald, F. Scott *The Great Gatsby*, with an introduction by Tony Tanner (Harmondsworth, 1990)

Freud, Sigmund 'Memorandum on the Electrical Treatment of War Neurotics' (1920, published 1955) in: *The Standard Edition of the Complete Psychological Works of Sigmund Freud*, Vol. XVII (London)

Fuller, J. G. *Troop Morale and Popular Culture in the British and Dominion Armies, 1914–18* (Oxford, 1990)

Fussell, Paul *The Great War and Modern Memory* (Oxford, 1975)

Garton, Stephen. *The Cost of War: Australians Return* (Oxford, 1996)

Gerber, David ed., *Disabled Veterans in History* (Michigan, 2000)

Gill, D. and Dallas, G. *The Unknown Army* (London, 1985)

Gijswijt-Hofstra, Marijke and Porter, Roy eds, *Cultures of Neurasthenia from Beard to the First World War* (Amsterdam, 2001)

Gilman, S., King, H., Porter, R., Rousseau, G. S., and Showalter, E. *Hysteria Beyond Freud* (Berkeley, LA, 1993)

Gittins, Diana *Madness in its Place: Narratives of Severalls Hospital, 1913–1997* (London, 1998)

Gregory, Adrian *The Silence of Memory* (Oxford, 1994)

Grieves, K. *The Politics of Manpower* (London, 1988)

Grob, Gerald N. *The Mad Among Us: A History of the Care of America's Mentally Ill* (Cambridge, Mass., 1994)

Gurney, Ivor *Best Poems* and *The Book of Five Makings*, edited by Thornton, R. K. R. and Walter, George (Manchester, 1995)

—— *Selected Poems*, edited by Walter, George (London, 1996)

—— *Rewards of Wonder: Poems of Cotswold, France, London*, edited by Walter, George (Manchester, 2000)

—— *Severn and Somme* and *War's Embers*, edited by Thornton, R. K. R. (Manchester, 1987)

Hacking, Ian *Rewriting the Soul* (Princeton, 1995)

—— *The Social Construction of What?* (Cambridge, Mass. 1999)

—— 'Indeterminacy in the past: on the recent discussion of chapter 17 of *Rewriting the Soul*', *History of the Human Sciences* (2003), 16, pp. 117–24

Haley, Bruce *The Healthy Body and Victorian Culture* (Cambridge, Mass., 1978)

Hall, Leslie 'Forbidden by God, Despised by Men: Masturbation, Medical Warnings, Moral Panic and Manhood in Great Britain, 1850–1950', *Journal of the History of Sexuality* (1992), 2, pp. 365–87

—— '"War always brings it on": War, STDs, the Military, and the Civilian Population in Britain 1850–1950', in: Cooter, Roger; Harrison, Mark and Sturdy, Steve eds, *Medicine and Modern Warfare* (Amsterdam, 1999)

Harding, T. W. '"Not Worth Powder and Shot": A Reappraisal of Montagu Lomax's Contribution to Mental Health Reform', *British Journal of Psychiatry* (1990), 156, pp. 180–87

Hare, Edward 'Masturbatory insanity: the history of an idea', *Journal of Mental Science* (1962), 108, pp. 1–25

Harrington, Ralph 'The Railway Accident: Trains, Trauma and Technological Crises in Nineteenth Century Britain', in: Micale, Mark and Lerner, Paul eds, *Traumatic Pasts: History, Psychiatry and Trauma in the Modern Age, 1870–1930* (Cambridge, 2001)

Harris, Jose *Private Lives, Public Spirit: Britain 1870–1914* (Oxford, 1993)

—— 'Society and the state in Twentieth Century Britain', in: Thomson, F. M. L. ed., *Cambridge Social History of Britain, 1750–1950*, Vol. III (Cambridge, 1990).

Harrison, Mark 'The British Army and the Problem of Venereal Disease in France and Egypt during the First World War', *Medical History* (1995), 39, pp. 133–58

—— 'Medicine and the Management of Modern Warfare: an Introduction', in: Cooter, R., Harrison, M., and Sturdy, S. eds, *Medicine and Modern Warfare* (Amsterdam, 1999)

—— 'Sex and the Citizen Soldier: Health, Morals and Discipline in the British Army during the Second World War' in Cooter, R., Harrison, M. and Sturdy, S. eds, *Medicine and Modern Warfare* (Amsterdam, 1999)

Hart, Julian Tudor 'Going to the Doctor' in: Cooter, R. and Pickstone, J. eds, *Medicine in the Twentieth Century* (Amsterdam, 2000)

Hauerwas, Stanley *Suffering Presence* (Notre Dame, Indiana, 1986)

Henderson, D. K. 'War Psychoses: An Analysis of 202 Cases of Mental Disorder Occurring in Home Troops', *Journal of Mental Science* (1918), 64, pp. 165–89

Hichberger, Joany 'Old Soldiers' in: Samuel, R. ed., *Patriotism: The Making and Unmaking of British National Identity*, Vol. III (London, 1989)

Hill, Christopher *The World Turned Upside Down* (London, 1972)

Himmelfarb, Gertrude *Poverty and Compassion: The Moral Imagination of the Late Victorians* (New York, 1991)

Hoare, Philip *Spike Island: The Memory of a Military Hospital* (London, 2001)

Hobsbawm, Eric *The Age of Empire 1875–1914* (London, 1987)

Hogge, J. M. and Garside, T. H. *War Pensions and Allowances* (London, 1918)

Hudson, Geoffrey L. 'Disabled Veterans and the State in Early Modern England', in: Gerber, D. ed., *Disabled Veterans in History* (Michigan, 2000)

Hughes, Clive 'The New Armies' in: Beckett, I. and Simpson, K. eds, *A Nation in Arms: A Social Study of the British Army in the First World War* (Manchester, 1985)

Hunter, R. and Macalpine, I. *Psychiatry for the Poor* (London, 1974)

Hurd, Michael *The Ordeal of Michael Gurney* (Oxford, 1984)

Hutchinson, Woods *The Doctor in War* (London, 1919)

Hynes, Samuel *The Soldier's Tale: Bearing Witness to Modern War* (London, 1998)

—— *A War Imagined: The First World War and English Culture* (London, 1990)

Ignatieff, Michael *The Needs of Strangers* (London, 1984)

—— *The Warrior's Honor: Ethnic War and the Modern Conscience* (London, 1998)

Johnstone, T. 'The case for dementia praecox', *Journal of Mental Science* (1909), 55, pp. 64–691

Jones, Edgar and Wessely, Simon 'Psychiatric Battle Casualties: an Intra- and Interwar Comparison', *British Journal of Psychiatry* (2001), 178, pp. 242–47

—— 'The Origins of Military Psychiatry Before the First World War', *War & Society* (2001), 19, pp. 91–108

Jones, Edgar; Palmer, Ian; and Wessely, Simon 'War Pensions (1900–1945): Changing Models of Psychological Understanding', *British Journal of Psychiatry* (2002), 180, pp. 374–79

Jones, Edgar et al., 'Post-combat Syndromes from the Boer War to the Gulf War: a cluster analysis of their nature and attribution', *British Medical Journal* (2002), 324, pp. 1–7

Joyce, James *Ulysses* (London, 1992, edited by Kiberd, Declan, first published 1922)

Joyce, Patrick *Visions of the People: Industrial England and the Question of Class 1848–1914* (Cambridge, 1991)

Kahr, Brett *D.W. Winnicott: A Biographical Portrait* (London, 1996)

Kaufmann, D. 'Science as Cultural Practice: Psychiatry in the First World War and Weimar Germany', *Journal of Contemporary History* (1999), 34, pp. 125–44

Keegan, John *The First World War* (London, 1998)

King, Alex *Memorials of the Great War in Britain* (Oxford, 1998)

Kleinman, Arthur *The Illness Narratives* (New York, 1988)

—— *Writing at the Margin: Discourse Between Anthropology and Medicine* (Berkeley, Calif., 1995)

Knutsford, Viscount Sydney Holland *In Black and White* (London, 1926)

Koven, Seth 'Remembering and Dismemberment: Crippled Children, Wounded Soldiers and the Great War in Britain', *American Historical Review* (1994), XCIX, pp. 1167–202

Kraepelin, Emil 'Psychiatric Observations on Contemporary Issues', trans. and intro. by Eric J. Engstrom, *History of Psychiatry* (1992), 3, pp. 253–69 [first published in 1919]

Kristeva, Julia *Black Sun: Depression and Melancholia* (New York, 1989)

Kuhn, Thomas *The Structure of Scientific Revolutions* (Chicago, 1962)

Laqueur, Thomas 'Memory and Naming in the Great War' in: Gillis, J. R. ed., *Commemorations: the Politics of National Identity* (Princeton, 1994)

———— *Solitary Sex: A Cultural History of Masturbation* (New York, 2003)

Lawrence, Christopher and Weisz, George eds, *Greater than the Parts: Holism in Biomedicine 1920–50* (Oxford, 1998)

Lawrence, Christopher and Mayer, Anna-K. *Regenerating England: Science, Medicine and Culture in Inter-War Britain* (Amsterdam, 2000)

Lawrence, Jon 'Material Pressures on the Middle Classes' in: Jay Winter and Jean-Louis Robert eds, *Capital Cities at War* (Cambridge, 1997)

Lee, Hermione *Virginia Woolf* (London, 1996)

Leed, Eric *No Man's Land* (Cambridge, 1979)

Lees, Lynn Hollen *The Solidarities of Strangers: The English Poor Laws and the People, 1700–1948* (Cambridge, 1998)

Leese, Peter *Shell Shock: Traumatic Neurosis and the British Soldiers of the First World War* (London, 2002)

Lerner, Paul *Hysterical Men* (New York, 2003)

———— 'Rationalizing the Therapeutic Arsenal: German Neuropsychiatry in World War I' in: Berg, M. and Cocks, G. eds, *Medicine and Modernity: Public Health and Medical Care in Nineteenth and Twentieth-Century Germany* (Cambridge, 1996)

———— 'From Traumatic Neurosis to Male Hysteria: The Decline and Fall of Hermann Oppenheim, 1889–1919' in: Micale, Mark and Lerner, Paul eds, *Traumatic Pasts: History, Psychiatry and Trauma in the Modern Age, 1870–1930* (Cambridge, 2001)

Lewis, Aubrey 'The Inheritance of Mental Disorders' in: Blacker, C. P. ed., *The Chances of Morbid Inheritance* (London, 1934)

Light, Alison *Forever England: Femininity, Literature and Conservatism between the Wars* (London, 1991)

Llewellyn, Llewellyn, J. and Bassett Jones, A. *Pensions and the Principles of their Evaluation* (London, 1919)

Lomax, Montagu *The Experiences of an Asylum Doctor* (London, 1921)

Lord, J. R. *Mental Hospitals and the Public: The Need for Closer Co-Operation* (London, 1927)

MacCurdy, John T. *War Neuroses* (Cambridge, 1918)

Macdonald, Lyn *The Roses of No Man's Land* (London, 1980)

Macnicol, John *The Politics of Retirement in Britain 1878–1948* (Cambridge, 1998)

Macpherson, W. G. ed., *History Of The Great War Based On Official Documents: Medical Services, General History*, Vol. I (London, 1921)

Macpherson, W. G, Herringham, W. P., Elliott, T. R., and Balfour, A. eds, *History Of The Great War Based On Official Documents: Diseases of the War*, Vol. II (London, 1923)

Main, Tom 'The Concept of the Therapeutic Community: Variations and Vicissitudes' in: *The Ailment and other Psychoanalytic Essays* (London, 1989)

Margalit, Avishai *The Ethics of Memory* (New York, 2002)

Marshall, T. H. *Citizenship and Social Class* (Cambridge, 1950)

Marwick, Arthur *War and Social Change in the Twentieth Century* (London, 1974)

———— *The Deluge: British Society and the First World War* (2nd edition, London, 1991)

McCandless, Peter 'Liberty and Lunacy: The Victorians and Wrongful Confinement' in: Andrew Scull ed., *Madhouses, Mad-Doctors and Madmen* (London, 1981)

McKibbin, Ross *The Ideologies of Class: Social Relations in Britain, 1880–1950* (Oxford, 1990)

———— *Classes and Cultures: England 1918–51* (Oxford, 1998)

Melling, Joseph 'Accommodating Madness: New Research in the Social History of Insanity and Institutions' in: Melling, J. and Forsythe, B. eds, *Insanity, Institutions and Society, 1800–1914* (London, 1999)

———— and Forsythe, B. eds, *Insanity, Institutions and Society, 1800–1914* (London, 1999)

Micale, Mark 'The Psychiatric Body' in Cooter, R. and Pickstone, J. eds, *Medicine in the Twentieth Century* (Amsterdam, 2000)

——— and Lerner, Paul eds, *Traumatic Pasts: History, Psychiatry and Trauma in the Modern Age, 1870–1930* (Cambridge, 2001)

Milner, Marion *The Suppressed Madness of Sane Men* (London, 1987)

Mitchell, T. J. and Smith, G. *History of the Great War Based on Official Documents. Medical Services: Casualties and Medical Statistics of the Great War* (London, 1931)

Moran, Lord *The Anatomy of Courage* (London, 1945)

Morton, Desmond and Wright, Glenn *Winning the Second Battle: Canadian Veterans and the Return to Civil Life* (Toronto, 1987)

Mosse, George 'Shell-shock as social disease', *Journal of Contemporary History* (2000), 35, pp. 101–8

Mott, F. W. *War Neuroses and Shell-Shock* (London, 1919)

Myers, C. S. *Shell Shock in France, 1914–1918* (Cambridge, 1940)

Nicolson, Nigel ed. *The Question Of Things Happening: The Letters Of Virginia Woolf*, Vol. II, 1912–22 (London, 1976)

Nussbaum, Martha C. *Upheavals of Thought: The Intelligence of Emotions* (Cambridge, 2001)

O'Brien, Edna *James Joyce* (London, 1999)

Oppenheim, Janet *'Shattered Nerves': Doctors, Patients and Depression in Victorian England* (Oxford, 1991)

Orwell, George *Inside the Whale and Other Essays* (Harmondsworth, 1962)

——— *The Road to Wigan Pier* (London, 1962, first published 1937)

——— *The Collected Essays, Journalism and Letters: Volume 2* (London, 1968)

Parry, A. and Codrington, A. E. *War Pensions: Past and Present* (London, 1918)

Parry-Jones, William Ll. *The Trade in Lunacy* (London, 1972)

Peacock, A. T. and Wiseman, J. *The Growth of Public Expenditure in the United Kingdom* (London, 1967)

Petter, M. '"Temporary Gentlemen" in the Aftermath of the Great War: Rank, Status and the Ex-Officer Problem', *Historical Journal* (1994), 37

Pick, Daniel *Faces of Degeneration* (Cambridge, 1989)

——— *War Machine: The Rationalisation of Slaughter in the Modern Age* (London, 1993)

Pickstone, John 'Production, Community and Consumption: The Political Economy of Twentieth-Century Medicine' in: Cooter, R. and Pickstone, J. eds, *Medicine in the Twentieth Century* (Amsterdam, 2000)

Porter, Roy *Mind Forg'd Manacles* (London, 1987)

——— *London: A Social History* (London, 1994)

——— *The Greatest Benefit to Mankind* (London, 1997)

Powell, David *The Edwardian Crisis: Britain 1901–14* (London, 1996)

Price, R. *An Imperial War and the British Working Class: Attitudes and Reactions to the Boer War 1899–1902* (London, 1972)

Quétel, Claude *History of Syphilis* (Oxford, 1990)

Read, C. Stanford *Military Psychiatry in Peace and War* (London, 1920)

Rety, John ed., *In the Company of Poets* (London, 2003)

Richardson, Ruth *Death, Dissection and the Destitute* (Harmondsworth, 1989)

Rickman, John 'A Survey: The Development of the Psychoanalytical Theory of the Psychoses', in: *Selected Contributions to Psychoanalysis* (London, 2003)

Rivers, W. H. R. *Instinct and the Unconscious: A Contribution to a Biological Theory of the Psycho-Neuroses* (Cambridge, 1920)

Robinson, William 'The Future of Service Patients in Mental Hospitals', *Journal of Mental Science* (1921), 67, pp. 40–48

Rodman, Robert F. *The Spontaneous Gesture: Selected Letters of D. W. Winnicott* (London, 1999)

Roelcke, Volker 'Biologizing Social Facts: An Early 20th Century Debate on Kraepelin's Concepts of Culture, Neurasthenia and Degeneration', *Culture, Medicine and Psychiatry* (1997), 21, pp. 383–404

——— 'Electrified Nerves, Degenerated Bodies: Medical Discourses on Neurasthenia in Germany, circa 1880–1914' in: Gijswijt-Hofstra, Marijke and Porter, Roy eds, *Cultures of Neurasthenia from Beard to the First World War* (Amsterdam, 2001)

Rorty, Richard *Truth and Moral Progress: Philosophical Papers* (Cambridge, 1998)

Rose, Jonathan *The Intellectual Life of the British Working Classes* (New Haven, 2001)

Saint, Andrew *London Suburbs* (London, 1999)

Salmon, Thomas W. 'The Care and Treatment of Mental Diseases and War Neurosis ("Shell Shock") in the British Army', *Mental Hygiene* (1917), 1, pp. 509–47

Sassoon, Siegfried 'Memoirs of an Infantry Officer', in *The Complete Memoirs of George Sherston* (London, 1937)

—— *Diaries 1915–18*, Hart-Davies, Rupert ed. (London, 1983)

Sauerteig, Lutz D. H. 'Sex, Medicine and Morality during the First World War' in: Cooter, R., Harrison, M., and Sturdy, S. eds, *War, Medicine and Modernity* (Stroud, Glouc., 1999)

Sayce, Liz *From Psychiatric Patient to Citizen* (London, 2000)

Schivelbusch, W. *The Railway Journey* (Oxford, 1986)

Scott, W. J. *The Politics Of Readjustment: Vietnam Veterans Since The War* (New York, 1993)

Scull, Andrew *The Most Solitary of Afflictions: Madness and Society in Britain 1700–1900* (New Haven, 1993)

—— 'Rethinking the History of Asylumdom', in: Melling, J. and Forysthe, B. eds, *Insanity, Institutions and Society, 1800–1914* (London, 1999)

Searle, G. R. *The Quest For National Efficiency* (Oxford, 1971)

Shay, Jonathan *Achilles in Vietnam: Combat Trauma and the Undoing of Character* (New York, 1994)

Shephard, Ben *A War of Nerves: Soldiers and Psychiatrists, 1914–1994* (London, 2000)

—— ' "The Early Treatment of Mental Disorders": R.G. Rows and Maghull 1914–1918' in: Freeman, H. and Berrios, G. E. eds, *150 Years of British Psychiatry, Volume II: The Aftermath* (London, 1996)

—— ' "Pitiless Psychology": The Role of Prevention in British Military Psychiatry in the Second World War', *History of Psychiatry* (1999), 10, pp. 491–524

—— 'Shell-Shock', in: Freeman, H. ed., *A Century of Psychiatry* (London, 1999)

Shorter, Edward *A History of Psychiatry* (New York, 1997)

Showalter, Elaine *The Female Malady* (London, 1985)

—— 'Hysteria, Feminism and Gender' in: Gilman, S., King, H., Porter, R., Rousseau, G. S., and Showalter, E. *Hysteria Beyond Freud* (Berkely, LA, 1993)

Sirotkina, Irina *Diagnosing Literary Genius: A Cultural History of Psychiatry in Russia 1880–1930* (Baltimore, 2002)

Slobodin, Richard *Rivers* (Stroud, Glouc., 1997)

Smith, G. E. and Pear, T. H. *Shell-shock and Its Lessons* (Manchester, 1917)

Smith, Leonard 'The County Asylum in the Mixed Economy of Care, 1808–1845' in: Melling, J. and Forsythe, B. eds, *Insanity, Institutions and Society, 1800–1914* (London, 1999)

Smith, Roger 'Biology and Values in Interwar Britain: C. S. Sherrington, Julian Huxley and the Vision of Progress', *Past and Present* (2003), 178, pp. 210–43

Stengers, Jean and Van Neck, Anne *Masturbation: The History of a Great Terror* (New York, 2001)

Stevenson, John *British Society 1914–45* (Harmondsworth, 1984)

Stone, Martin 'Shellshock and the Psychologists' in: Bynum, W.F., Porter, R. and Shepherd, M. eds, *The Anatomy of Madness*, Vol. II (London, 1985)

Strange, Julie-Marie 'Only a Pauper Whom Nobody Knows: Reassessing the Pauper Grave', *Past & Present* (2003), 178, pp. 148–75

Summers, Anne 'Militarism in Britain before the Great War', *History Workshop Journal* (1976), 2, pp. 104–23

Taithe, Bernard *Defeated Flesh: Medicine, Welfare and Warfare in the Making of Modern France* (Manchester University Press, 1999)

—— 'The Red Cross Flag in the Franco-Prussian War: Civilians, Humanitarians and War in the "Modern Age" ' in: Cooter, R., Harrison, M., and Sturdy, S. eds, *War, Medicine and Modernity* (Stroud, Glouc., 1999)

Taylor, Jeremy *Hospital and Asylum Architecture in England 1840–1914* (London, 1991)

Thompson, F. M. L. *The Rise of Respectable Society* (London, 1989)

Thomson, Alistair *Anzac Memories: Living with the Legend* (Oxford, 1994)

Thomson, D. G. 'A Descriptive Record of the Conversion of a County Asylum into a War Hospital for Sick and Wounded Soldiers in 1915', *Journal of Mental Science* (1916), 62, pp. 109–35

Thomson, Mathew *The Problem of Mental Deficiency* (Oxford, 1998)

—— 'Status, Manpower and Mental Fitness: Mental Deficiency in the First World War' in: Cooter, R., Harrison, M., and Sturdy, S. eds, *War, Medicine and Modernity* (Stroud, Glouc., 1999)

—— 'Constituting Citizenship: Mental Deficiency, Mental Health and Human Rights in Inter-War Britain' in: Lawrence, C. and Mayer, Anna-K. eds, *Regenerating England: Science, Medicine and Culture in Inter-War Britain* (Amsterdam, 2000)

—— 'Psychology and the "Consciousness of Modernity" in Early Twentieth-century Britain' in: Daunton, M. and Rieger, B. eds, *Meanings of Modernity: Britain from the Late-Victorian Era to World War II* (Oxford, 2001)

Thornton, R. K. R. ed., *Ivor Gurney: Collected Letters* (Northumberland, 1991)

Titmuss, Richard *Essays on 'The Welfare State'* (2nd edn, London, 1963)

Toíbín, Colm *The Irish Famine* (London, 1999)

Tromans, Nicholas *David Wilkie* (London, 2002)

Trombley, Stephen *'All that Summer She was Mad': Virginia Woolf and her Doctors* (London, 1981)

Turner, John *British Politics and the Great War* (New Haven, 1992)

Turner, W. A. 'Arrangements for the Care of Cases of Nervous and Mental Shock Coming from Overseas', *The Lancet* (1916), I, pp. 1073–75

Unsworth, Clive *The Politics of Mental Health Legislation* (Oxford, 1987)

Webb, Beatrice *The Diary of Beatrice Webb, Vol. III, 1905–24*, MacKenzie, Norman and Jeanne eds (London, 1984)

Weindling, Paul *Health, Race and German Politics Between National Unification and Nazism, 1870–1945* (Cambridge, 1989)

Welton, Donn 'Biblical Bodies' in: Welton, Donn ed., *Body and Flesh: A Philosophical Reader* (Oxford, 1998)

Westwood, Louise 'A Quiet Revolution in Brighton: Dr. Helen Boyle's Pioneering Approach to Mental Health Care, 1899–1939' *Social History of Medicine* (2001), 14, pp. 439–57

White, J. *Rothschild Buildings: Life in an East End Tenement Block 1887–1920* (London, 1980)

Winnicott, D. W. *Clinical Notes on Disorders of Childhood* (London, 1931)

—— *Human Nature* (London, 1988)

—— *Psycho-Analytic Explorations*, Winnicott, C., Shepherd, P. and Davis, M. eds, (London, 1989)

Winslow, Barbara *Sylvia Pankhurst: Sexual Politics and Political Activism* (London, 1996)

Winter J. M. *Socialism and the Challenge of War* (London, 1974)

—— *The Great War and the British People* (London, 1985)

—— *Sites of Memory, Sites of Mourning* (Cambridge, 1995)

Winter, J. M. 'Military Fitness and Civilian Health in Britain during the First World War', *Journal of Contemporary History* (1980), 15, pp. 211–44

—— 'Arms and Society: The Demographic Context', in: Beckett, I. and Simpson, K. eds, *A Nation in Arms: A Social Study of the British Army in the First World War* (Manchester, 1985)

Young, Allan *The Harmony of Illusions: Inventing Post-Traumatic Stress Disorder* (Princeton, New Jersey, 1995)

—— 'W. H. R. Rivers and the War Neuroses', *Journal for Hist. Behav. Sci.* (1999), 35, pp. 359–78

Žižek, Slavoj *The Sublime Object of Ideology* (London, 1989)

Acknowledgements

I am hugely indebted to a diverse network of colleagues, friends, and others encountered along the way, but for whose advice, expertise and, as often as not, fellowship this project would never have come to fruition. Bill Bynum and Roy Porter encouraged me in this inquiry from the moment it was hatched. I acknowledge the support of the Wellcome Trust in contributing towards the costs. Needless to say, it had never been my intention to make Roy Porter the dedicatee of this book. In one of the last conversations I had with him before his untimely death, he urged me to finish it for the typically Porterly reason that he was eager to read it. Naturally, I hope that he would have found some pleasure in the result. Among historians, Mark Harrison, Michael Neve and Mathew Thomson all read the manuscript and gave me the benefit of their critical counsel. Michael Neve coaxed me gently into making some changes that in retrospect were quite pivotal in making the argument more intelligible. Peter Campbell, Vyvyan Kinross and David Miller kindly undertook to appraise the text for its accessibility and I am most grateful to them. I am thankful also for the helpful comments of two anonymous readers for Yale University Press.

Mark Harrison and Mathew Thomson have from the outset been generous in sharing ideas and unpublished papers with me and my entire feeling for the subject of this book has been much influenced by my encounters with their work. Vyvyan Kinross's keenly solicitous inquiries as to the welfare of Capt. Haws spurred me to get the book completed and give the Captain his due. Helen Bettinson has generously given me leads from her own research that I would never have found on my own. The conversations and lunches I have enjoyed with her helped to make the unpromising subject of war pensions surprisingly palatable. Edgar Jones assisted my passage into the War Pensions Archive at Nelson, Lancashire, gave me valuable support and comradeship on site, and has kept me informed on his own research. I had the good fortune to meet Paul Lerner when he was at the Wellcome Institute (as it then was) in London, and I have enjoyed a stimulating dialogue with him for some years now, stemming from his own research into psychiatry and war in Germany. Ben Shephard knows far more about military psychiatry than I could ever hope to and he has been a constant source of information and good-humoured advice that has certainly saved me from some blunders.

I have also benefited greatly from the opportunities that have been given me to present this work as it has progressed at the universities of Essex, Oxford, Sheffield, and Warwick, at the Wellcome Trust Centre for the History of Medicine at University College London, and at the Historial de la Grande Guerre, Peronne-Somme. At different stages along the way numerous individuals have responded to my inquiries, given me advice or information, pointed me in a direction, or simply nudged me along the road with their curiosity and enthusiasm for the subject. I wish to thank particularly: Jonathan Andrews, Peter Barber, Joanna Bourke, Sarah Brady, Harriet Bradley, Clive Carrier, Cecil Connington, Roger Cooter, Colin Crawford, Stan Eden, Michael Fishwick, Eilidh Garrett, Paul Griffiths, Lesley Hall, Brian Harding, Tim Harding, Bernard Harris, Rhodri Hayward, Geoffrey Hudson, Maurice Hudson, Christopher Lawrence, Esther Leslie, Peter Liddle, Hilary Marland, Roger Maxwell, Elaine Murphy, Braham Myers, D. M. Ogier, Ian Palmer, Rob Perks, Julian Pooley, Denise Poynter, Jenny Robb, Julia Shephard, Derek Shiel, Roger Smith, Nafsika Thalassis, Paul Thompson, Trevor Turner, Keir Waddington, Simon Wessely, Paul Whittle, Jay Winter, and Robert M. Young.

For the opportunity to hear from those who still remembered the Service Patients at the Old Manor Hospital, Salisbury, I thank: Ian Brennan, Gina Percy, Michael Bourke, Frederick Forder, Michael Heffernan, and David Nobbs. A number of psychiatrists who were already frequenting the wards of mental hospitals when Service Patients were still in residence generously shared their recollections with me: the late Douglas Bennett, David H. Clark, John Crammer, Hugh Freeman, the late Denis Leigh, and Henry Rollin. Tony Boden kindly glossed for me Ivor Gurney's signature on the mount of the portrait of him in uniform. Patrick Loobey and Nigel Roberts produced just the illustrations that had eluded me. For permission to quote from sources for which they hold the copyright I thank the following: Carcanet Press for the published poems and letters of Ivor Gurney; the Trustees of the Ivor Gurney Trust for unpublished poems and letters in the Gurney Archive at Gloucester Central Library; and Ann Moore for the war journals of Sir Norman Moore.

For permission to consult the records of hospitals and institutions of which they are the legal heirs, and for their readiness to help with my inquiry, I wish to thank the following authorities: Barnwood House Trust for Barnwood House Hospital; Camden and Islington Health Authority for Friern Hospital; Department of Social Security for the First World War pension records in the War Pensions Archive; East Suffolk Local Health Services NHS Trust for St. Audry's and St Clement's Hospitals; Exeter and District Community Health

Service NHS Trust for Digby and Exminster Hospitals; Guild Community Health Care NHS Trust for Whittingham Hospital; Huddersfield Health Care Services NHS Trust for Storthes Hall Hospital; Kingston and District Community NHS Trust for Long Grove Hospital; Lancaster Priority Services NHS Trust for Lancaster Moor Hospital; Leeds Community and Mental Health Services NHS Trust for High Royds Hospital; Salisbury Health Care NHS Trust for Old Manor Hospital; Severn NHS Trust for Horton Road Hospital; and Surrey Oaklands NHS Trust for Netherne Hospital.

For access to material in their archives I am grateful to: Archives and Manuscripts, Wellcome Trust Library for the History and Understanding of Medicine; Bodleian Library, University of Oxford; British Red Cross; Department of Documents, Imperial War Museum; Corporation of London Record Office; Devon County Record Office; Ex-Services Mental Welfare Society; Gloucestershire County Record Office; Hertfordshire Archives and Local Studies; Ivor Gurney Archive, Gloucester Central Library; Lancashire County Record Office; Liddle Collection, Leeds University Archive; London Metropolitan Archives; 'Not Forgotten' Association; Public Record Office; States of Guernsey Island Archives Service; Suffolk County Record Office; Surrey History Centre; West Yorkshire Archive Service; and Wiltshire County Record Office. A number of county archivists went out of their way to assist me in securing the permissions I required to consult their records, making phone calls and fielding questions from the relevant authorities on my behalf. My thanks for the kindness shown me by the staff at all the institutions I have mentioned and also at: British Library; London Library; National Register of Archives; and University of London Library.

I am much indebted to Chris Fagg as copy editor and Emily Lees as picture researcher. Adam Freudenheim's enthusiasm and critical acumen as editor has been invaluable. David Miller, my agent, has been a doughty champion of this book from an early stage. My wife, Jennie Metaxa, has lived with this project from the very beginning, and contributed to it in innumerable ways, though it must be admitted that she will not be entirely sorry to see this lost legion finally troop out of our lives. It need hardly be said that I alone am responsible for what I have written in this study. It makes no claim to be exhaustive, and the recruiting office will still be pleased to hear from those with memories or records to enlist in the honourable company already on active service in these pages (e-mail: FLGW2004@yahoo.co.uk).

Index

Note: A plate is indicated in bold, an illustration in the text by italics.

ignored by the War Office
'Shell-Shock' Commission
234–35
Ivor Gurney not classified as 265
lived through revolution in health
care 357–59
as lunatic Chelsea Pensioners
211–13
many could be decertified, the
Ministry of Pensions admits
276
numbers of 373, 375–76
opinions of asylum authorities as to
181–85
personalized underclothing for
288–89
proposal to attire them in military
uniforms 211–13
provision for compared to other
disabled groups 187–88
provisions for deemed inadquate
185–86
rebelling against the Ministry of
Pensions 303
in Second World War 416n.67
Service Patient John Peters loses his
drawers 213–14
viewed with ambivalence by the
authorities 214, 300, 302
see also medical superintendents;
Old Manor Hospital, Salisbury;
Pensions, Ministry of; Storthes
Hall Mental Hospital
Shakespeare, William 79
Shay, Jonathan 68, 71
shell shock
bigamous marriage attributed to
242
case of at Armentières 83–85
cases in asylums 237–41, 291–92,
343, 346
cases in Poor Law mental wards
202–05, 209–10, 237
claims rejected by the Ministry of
Pensions 195–96
co-option of label by relatives
176, 238

criticism of physical explanations of
154, 157
as dedicated diagnosis and
treatment system for officers 4,
238
emotional origins of 151–55
establishment tries to regain control
of 233–34
as expression of patient power
84–85, 238
'funk' or shell shock? x, 17–18, 47
historiography of 233–34
and insanity 151–52, 195,
237–38, 345, 348, 356, 418n.4
as ironic commentary on traditional
heroism 212
Ivor Gurney and 167, 226, 263
as metaphor for unmanly behaviour
132
military authorities question
legitimacy of 17–19, 50–51,
63–64, 83, 85
as 'minor psychoses' 157
as 'nervous unfitness' 143
origins of term 6
policy over influenced by public
opinion 5
as rallying point for a mental
health counter-culture 83
as screen for cowardice and
inadequacy 236, 283
as self-diagnosis 60, 86–87, 237,
353
still suffering from in the 1960s
352–54
War Office Commission of Enquiry
into 233–37
Shell Shock and Its Lessons (G. E.
Smith and T. Pear) 150–55
shell-shocked
as half-men 237
as psychopaths 245
Shoolbreds Department Store 12, 14,
20, 380n.4
Simon, Hermann 144
Smith, G. Elliot 150–51, 154, 155,
161, 234

Index Number of admissions. Transfers are not to be numbered consecutively with the admissions, but should be numbered in red ink as a separate series.	Regiment, Battalion, Corps, or other Unit	Squadron, Battery, or Company	Regl: No.	Rank	Surname	Christian Name	Age	Service
T 10844	Lab. Coy.	150	117175	Pte.	Brown	Harry	30	1 $\frac{1}{12}$
" 10845	3 Ray. Fusrs	-	705	"	Thomas	H. J.	26	3 $\frac{0}{12}$
" 10846	4 Res. Glosters	-	241281	"	Gurney	Ivor	27	2 $\frac{9}{12}$
" 10847	R.G.A.	153 Siege	73404	Gr.	Roe	WR	41	1 $\frac{1}{12}$
" 10848	27 Nthln Fus	"C"	24473	Pte.	Scott	J.W.	23	3 $\frac{0}{12}$
43.	ASC. mT	5. Div.	M2/31236	"	Rolfe	Harry	34	2 $\frac{6}{12}$
" 10849	3. Coldstreams		21655	"	Yates	C.H.	21	2
" 10850	6. Dorsets	R.	17449	"	Harvey	J	39	2 $\frac{5}{12}$
" 10851	R.G.A. 55	A.A.	198261	Gr.	Stygall	Edgar	32	1 $\frac{6}{12}$
10852	A.O.C.	2 Sub	019244	L/c	Etheridge	E.	26	2 $\frac{7}{12}$
" 10852	2/4 Yor Lancs	"C"	34	L/c	Austwick	John. W	31	3 $\frac{7}{12}$
" 10853	6. Dorsets	"C"	14384	Pte.	Adsett	William D	34	3 $\frac{2}{12}$
" 10854	1/4 Cheshires	"B"	202504	"	Allen	John. A	41	3 $\frac{9}{12}$
" 10855	1/4 Cheshires	"C"	293163	"	Bancroft	John	24	2 $\frac{6}{12}$
" 10856	2.L.N Lancs	"C"	8820	"	Boxer	Harold	30	11 $\frac{2}{12}$
" 10857	12/13 N. Fus.	"C"	39545	"	Bickers	George	19	1 $\frac{2}{12}$
" 10858	2/4 S.L.9.	"B"	202218	"	Bryer	Robert. H	33	2 $\frac{4}{12}$
" 10859	7. Cheshires	HQ.	290036	"	Bracegirdle	Hugh	36	3 $\frac{7}{12}$
" 10860	1/6 B. Watch.	"D"	17591	L/c	Buick	William	34	3 $\frac{4}{12}$
" 10861	1/5 A&S. Hdrs	"D"	S/20702	Pte	Blair	J.	44	3 $\frac{7}{12}$
" 10862	2.L.N Lancs	"B"	8919	L/c	Brown	W.	29	11 $\frac{1}{12}$
" 10863	1/5 Devons	"A"	203565	Pte	Brooking	Harold	20	1 $\frac{5}{12}$
" 10864	13 R. Scots	"C"	18137	Sgt	Chittleburgh	William	41	3 $\frac{5}{12}$
" 10865	R.F.A.	51. Div.	645145	Dr	Cunningham	Alec	26	3 $\frac{4}{12}$
" 10866	6. Blk. Watch.	"B"	291690	Pte	Chisholm	David	28	2 $\frac{3}{12}$
" 10867	4 Cheshires	"I"	201644	L/c	Calwood	Archur	21	3 $\frac{8}{12}$
" 10868	2.L.N Lancs	"C"	8409	L/c	Callan	Archur	30	12 $\frac{10}{12}$
" 10869	5.K.O.Y.L.I.	"A"	24494	Pte	Coburn	George	21	2 $\frac{7}{12}$
" 10870	1/5 A&S Hdrs	"C"	200588	"	Chandler	C.	24	3 $\frac{10}{12}$
" 10871	1. Herefords	"D"	235132	Cpl.	Carless	Percy	22	6 $\frac{4}{12}$
" 10872	1/5 K.O.S.B.	"C"	242654	L/c	Cook	Fred	29	3
" 10873	8.W. Yorks	"A"	61623	Rfm	Cooper	Thomas H	19	1 $\frac{1}{12}$
" 10874	1/4 Cheshires	"C"	202432	Pte	Crompton	Henry. J.	24	4 $\frac{5}{12}$
" 10875	1/1 Herefords	"P"	35642	"	Casely	George	22	3 $\frac{4}{12}$